The Sport Studies Reader

What is the social significance of sport?

How can we study sport as a social phenomenon?

Sport is a central feature of society, and has been studied by social scientists for many years. *The Sport Studies Reader* provides a comprehensive resource for students and teachers, leading the reader through theory and research in Sport Studies, taking in classic as well as contemporary essays from international authors in the field.

The Sport Studies Reader is divided into nine themed sections covering key sociological, historical, cultural and research methodological writings, each introduced by Alan Tomlinson and contextualised within the overall development of sport studies for the reader. Each section contains:

- introduction to theme and discussion of context
- study and seminar questions for each theme
- recommended further reading.

WITHDRAWN

Bringing together the work of some of the most influential authors in the field, *The Sport Studies Reader* represents an essential foundation for approaching the study of sport and its role in society.

Alan Tomlinson is Professor of Sport and Leisure Studies and Head of Research at the Chelsea School, Brighton University, UK.

The Sport Studies

Reader

Edited and introduced by

Alan Tomlinson

LONDON AND NEW YORK

First published 2007
by Routledge
2 Park Square, Milton Park, Abingdon, Oxon OX14 4RN

Simultaneously published in the USA and Canada
by Routledge
270 Madison Ave, New York, NY 10016

Routledge is an imprint of the Taylor & Francis Group, an informa business

© 2007 Editorial material and selection, Alan Tomlinson; individual chapters,
the respective contributors

Typeset in Perpetua and Bell Gothic by
Florence Production Ltd, Stoodleigh, Devon
Printed and bound in Great Britain by
The Cromwell Press, Trowbridge, Wiltshire

British Library Cataloguing in Publication Data
A catalogue record for this book is available from the British Library

Library of Congress Cataloging in Publication Data
The sport studies reader/edited and introduced by Alan Tomlinson.
            p. cm.
        Includes bibliographical references and index.
    1. Sports – Sociological aspects – Textbooks.   I. Tomlinson, Alan.
    GV706.5.S7384 2006
    306.4'83 – dc22   2006023337

ISBN10: 0–419–26020–X (hbk)
ISBN10: 0–419–26030–7 (pbk)

ISBN13: 978–0–419–26020–2 (hbk)
ISBN13: 978–0–419–26030–l (pbk)

Contents

SECTION FOUR
Media

SECTION EIGHT
Subcultures

Preface

I am grateful to colleagues and students over the years at the University of Brighton's Chelsea School (Sport and Leisure Cultures), for support and stimulation. This Reader was first conceived and commissioned several years before completion of the project and I would like to thank successive editors and editorial staff at Routledge for continuing to support and keep faith in the project: Sally Wride, Liz Mann, Edwina Welham, Simon Whitmore, Samantha Grant and Kate Manson. I am especially grateful to the last two for driving me to completion of this project with professional and practical forms of support.

My daughters, Alys, Rowan, Jo, and Sinead have seen this book on the web pages of the publisher for some years now, and will be amused to see it materialize as a real product. My wife Bernie has great motivational skills as well as the priceless quality of unflappability – and I am sure that she will be pleased to see this particular project finished.

Alan Tomlinson
Brighton, East Sussex
Campillergues, Languedoc
June 2006

Acknowledgements

The publishers would like to thank the following for their permission to reprint their material:

Avery, Gillian. (1991) 'The Best Type of Girl', *The Best Type of Girl: A History of Girls' Independent Schools,* London: André Deutsch, pp. 266–76.

Bailey, Peter. (1978) 'Rational Recreation and the New Athleticism', *Leisure and Class in Victorian England: Rational Recreation and the Contest for Control, 1830–1885,* London: Routledge & Kegan Paul, pp. 124–9 and pp. 145–6. Reproduced by permission of Taylor & Francis Books, UK.

Barnett, Steven. (1990) 'Potting the Gold – The Sponsorship Game', *Games and Sets: The Changing Face of Sport on Television,* London, British Film Institute, pp. 171–89.

Baudrillard, Jean. (1998) 'The Drama of Leisure or the Impossibility of Wasting One's Time', *The Consumer Society: Myths and Structures,* English translation, London: Sage Publications, pp. 149–58.

Beal, Becky. (1995) 'Disqualifying the Official: An Exploration of Social Resistance Through the Subculture of Skateboarding', *Sociology of Sport Journal*, 12 (3), Leeds: Human Kinetics Publishers, pp. 252–67.

Blain, Neil, Boyle, Raymond and O'Donnell, Hugh. (1993) 'Sport, Delivery Systems and National Culture', *Sport and National Identity in the European Media,* Leicester: Leicester University Press (a division of Pinter Publishers), pp. 18–36.

Bourdieu, Pierre. (1978) 'Sport and Social Class', *Social Science Information*, 17 (6), London: Sage, pp. 819–40.

Bourdieu, Pierre. (1984) 'The Universes of Stylistic Possibles', trans. Richard Nice, *Distinction: A Social Critique of the Judgement of Taste,* London: Routledge & Kegan Paul, pp. 208–25. Reproduced by permission of Taylor & Francis Books, UK.

Brohm, Jean-Marie. (1978) 'Theses Towards a Political Sociology of Sport', *Sport: A Prison of Measured Time*, London: Ink Links, pp. 45–52. First published as *Critiques du Sport* © Christian Bourgois Editeur, 1976.

Carrington, Ben. (1998) 'Sport, Masculinity and Black Cultural Resistance', *Journal of Sport and Social Issues*, 22 (3), London: Sage Publications, pp. 275–98.

Cashmore, Ernest. (1982) 'Black Sportsmen', *Black Sportsmen*, London: Routledge & Kegan Paul. Reproduced by permission of Taylor & Francis Books, UK.

Caudwell, Jayne. (1998) 'Sex and Politics: Sites of Resistance in Women's Football', in Cara Aitchison and Fiona Jordan (eds), *Gender, Space and Identity: Leisure, Culture and Commerce*, Brighton: Leisure Studies Association.

Clarke, Gill. (1995) 'Outlaws in Sport and Education? Exploring the Sporting and Education Experiences of Lesbian Physical Education Teachers', in Lesley Lawrence, Elizabeth Murdoch and Stan Parker (eds), *Professional and Development Issues in Leisure, Sport and Education*, Brighton: Leisure Studies Association, pp. 45–58.

Corrigan, Paul. (1979) 'What Do Kids Get Out of Football?', *Schooling the Smash Street Kids*, Basingstoke: Macmillan Education, pp. 111–17.

Cunningham, Hugh. (1980) 'Class and Leisure in Mid-Victorian England', *Leisure in the Industrial Revolution, c.1780–c.1880*, London: Croom Helm, pp. 110–39. © Croom Helm. Reproduced by permission of Taylor & Francis Books, UK.

Davies, Andrew. (1992) 'Men: Poverty, Unemployment and the Family', *Leisure, Gender and Poverty: Working-Class Culture in Salford and Manchester, 1900–1939*, Bucks: Open University Press, pp. 30–54. © Andrew Davies 1992.

Debord, Guy. (1994) 'The Commodity as Spectacle', *The Society of the Spectacle*, trans. Donald Nicholson-Smith, © 1994, New York: Zone Books, pp. 25–34.

Deem, Rosemary. (1986) 'Women and Sport', *All Work and No Play? A Study of Women and Leisure*, Maidenhead: Open University Press.

Donnelly, Peter. (1981) 'Toward a Definition of Sport Subcultures', in Marie Hart and Susan Birrell (eds), *Sport in the Sociocultural Process*, 3rd edn, Iowa: Wm C. Brown Company Publishers, pp. 565–88.

Dunning, Eric. (1999) 'Sport, Gender and Civilization', *Sport Matters: Sociological Studies of Sport, Violence and Civilization*, London: Routledge, pp. 219–55. Reproduced by permission of Taylor & Francis Books, UK.

Dunning, Eric, Murphy, Patrick and Williams, John. (1981) 'Ordered Segmentation and Hooligan Violence', in Alan Tomlinson (ed.), *The Sociological Study of Sport: Configurational and Interpretive Studies*, Brighton: Leisure Studies Association/British Sociological Association, LSA Publication No. 18, pp. 36–52.

Elias, Norbert and Dunning, Eric. (1986) 'The Quest for Excitement in Leisure', *Quest for Excitement: Sport and Leisure in the Civilizing Process,* Oxford: Blackwell, pp. 63–90. © Norbert Elias and Eric Dunning 1986. See also forthcoming edition of *Quest for Excitement: Sport and Leisure in the Civilizing Process*, 2007 as vol. 7 of *The Collected Works of Norbert Elias*, published by University College Dublin Press (UCD), Dublin.

Fleming, Scott. (1994) 'Sport and South Asian Youth: The Perils of "False Universalism" and Stereotyping', *Leisure Studies*, 13, London: E & FN Spon, pp. 159–77. http://www.tandf.co.uk/journals.

Fleming, Scott and Tomlinson, Alan. (1996) 'Racism and Xenophobia in English Football', in Udo Merkel and Walter Tokarski (eds), *Racism and Xenophobia in European Football*, Aachen: Meyer & Meyer Verlag, pp. 79–100.

Frankenburg, Ronald. (1957) 'Football and Politics in a North Wales Community (Pentrediwaith)', *Village on the Border: A Social Study of Religion, Politics and Football in a North Wales Community*, London: Cohen & West.

Gruneau, Richard. (1983) 'Problems of Agency and Freedom in Play, Games, and Sport', *Class, Sports, and Social Development*, Massachussetts: The University of Massachusetts Press.

Gruneau, Richard and Whitson, David. (1993) 'Hockey and the New Politics of Accumulation', *Hockey Night in Canada: Sport, Identities, and Cultural Politics*, Toronto: Garamond Press.

Guttmann, Allen. (2004) 'Rules of the Game', *Sports: The First Five Millenia*, Massachussetts: University of Massachusetts Press.

Hall, M. Ann. (1995) 'Feminist Activism in Sport: A Comparative Study of Women's Sport Advocacy Organizations', in Alan Tomlinson (ed.), *Gender, Sport and Leisure: Continuities and Challenges*, Aachen: Meyer & Meyer Verlag, pp. 217–50. First published in 1995 by CSRC, Chelsea School Research Centre.

Hargreaves, Jennifer. (1994) 'Theories of Sport: The Neglect of Gender', *Sporting Females: Critical Issues in the History and Sociology of Women's Sports*, London: Routledge. © 1994 Jennifer Hargreaves. Reproduced by permission of Taylor & Francis Books, UK.

Hargreaves, Jennifer. (2000) 'Men and Women and the Gay Games', *Heroines of Sport: The Politics of Difference and Identity*, London: Routledge, pp. 166–73. Reproduced by permission of Taylor & Francis Books, UK.

Hargreaves, John. (1986) 'The Autonomy of Sport', *Sport, Power and Culture: A Social and Historical Analysis of Popular Sports in Britain*, Cambridge: Polity Press, in association with Basil Blackwell, Oxford, pp. 1–15.

Hargreaves, John. (1986) 'Class Divisions', *Sport, Power and Culture: A Social and Historical Analysis of Popular Sports in Britain*, Cambridge: Polity Press, in association with Basil Blackwell, Oxford, pp. 75–86.

Hargreaves, John. (1986) 'Constructing Media Sport', *Sport, Power and Culture: A Social and Historical Analysis of Popular Sports in Britain*, Cambridge: Polity Press, in association with Basil Blackwell, Oxford, pp. 138–60.

Hoberman, John. (1993) 'Sportive Nationalism', *The Changing Politics of Sport*, Lincoln Allison (ed.), Manchester: Manchester University Press, pp. 15–36.

Hoch, Paul. (1972) 'Owning and Selling the Spectacle', *Rip Off the Big Game: The Exploitation of Sports by the Power Elite*, New York: Doubleday & Company, pp. 127–46. Used by permission of Doubleday, a division of Random House.

Holt, Richard. (1989) 'Survival and Adaptation', *Sport and the British: A Modern History*, Oxford: Oxford University Press, pp. 57–73.

Holt, Richard and Mason, Tony. (2000) 'Sensationalism and the Popular Press', *Sport in Britain 1945–2000*, Oxford: Blackwell Publishers, pp. 114–19.

Houlihan, Barrie. (1990) 'The Politics of Sports Policy in Britain: The Example of Drug Abuse', *Leisure Studies*, (9) 1, London: E & F N Spon, pp. 55–69. http://www.tandf.co.uk/journals.

Huizinga, Johan. (1949) 'The Play-Element in Contemporary Civilization', *Homo Ludens: A Study of the Play Element in Modern Culture*, London: Routledge & Kegan Paul, pp. 221–31. Reproduced by permission of Taylor & Francis Books, UK.

Itzkowitz, David C. (1977) 'Myth and Ideal', *Peculiar Privilege: A Social History of English Foxhunting 1753–1885*, Sussex: The Harvester Press, pp. 17–29, 176–7, 202–5.

Jackson, Brian. (1968) 'On the Bowling Green', *Working Class Community: Some General Notions Raised by a Series of Studies in Northern England*, London: Routledge & Kegan Paul, pp. 99–110. Reproduced by permission of Taylor & Francis Books, UK.

James, C.L.R. (1963) 'The Proof of the Pudding', *Beyond a Boundary*, London: Stanley Paul & Co., an imprint of the Hutchinson Publishing Group, pp. 217–43. © 1963 Executor to the Estate of CLR James. Reprinted by permission of The Random House Group.

James, C.L.R. (1963) 'The Light and the Dark', *Beyond a Boundary*, London: Stanley Paul & Co., an imprint of the Hutchinson Publishing Group. © 1963 Executor to the Estate of CLR James. Reprinted by permission of The Random House Group.

Klein, Alan M. (1993) 'Pumping Irony: Crisis and Contradiction in Bodybuilding', *Little Big Men: Bodybuilding Subculture and Gender Construction*, New York: State University of New York Press, pp. 137–58.

Lasch, Christopher. (1979) 'The Degradation of Sport', *The Culture of Narcissism: American Life in an Age of Diminishing Expectations*, New York: W.W. Norton & Company, © 1991 by Christopher Lasch. Used by permission of W.W. Norton & Company.

Long, Jonathan, Carrington, Ben and Spracklen, Karl. (1997) '"Asians Cannot Wear Turbans in the Scrum": Explorations of Racist Discourse within Professional Rugby League', *Leisure Studies*, 16 (4), London: E & FN Spon, pp. 250–9. http://www.tandf.co.uk/journals.

Lowenthal, Leo. (1961) 'The Triumph of Mass Idols', *Literature, Popular Culture, and Society*, New Jersey: Prentice-Hall, pp. 114–36.

Maguire, Jennifer Smith. (2002) 'Body Lessons: Fitness Publishing and the Cultural Production of the Fitness Consumer', *International Review for the Sociology of Sport*, 37 (3/4), London: Sage Publications, pp. 449–64. © International Sociology of Sport Association and Sage Publications.

Malcolmson, Robert W. (1973) 'Social Change', *Popular Recreations in English Society 1700–1850*, Cambridge: Cambridge University Press, pp. 158–71. Reproduced with permission of the author and publisher.

Mandell, Richard D. (1972) 'Sportsmanship and Nazi Olympism', *The Nazi Olympics*, London: Souvenir Press, pp. 65–94. Reprinted by the University of Illinois Press, 1987. © 1987 by Richard D. Mandell. Used with permission of the author and the University of Illinois Press.

Mangan, J.A. (1981) 'Athleticism', *Athleticism in the Victorian and Edwardian Public School: The Emergence and Consolidation of an Educational Ideology*, Cambridge: Cambridge University Press, pp. 1–10.

Manning, Frank. (1973) 'Black Clubs in Bermuda', *Black Clubs in Bermuda: Ethnography of a Play World*, New York: Cornell University Press, pp. 29–30, 36–38, 60–61. Used by permission of the publisher, Cornell University Press.

Marsh, Peter, Rosser, Elisabeth and Harré, Rom. (1978) 'Life on the Terraces', *The Rules of Disorder*, London: Routledge & Kegan Paul, pp. 59–82. Reproduced by permission of Taylor & Francis Books, UK.

Mason, Tony. (1980) 'Amateurs and Professionals', *Association Football and English Society 1863–1915*, Sussex: The Harvester Press, pp. 69–81. © Tony Mason.

Mason, Tony. (1988) 'The Traditional Sporting Press in Britain', *Sport in Britain*, London: Faber & Faber, pp. 46–50.

Middleton, Audrey. (1986) 'Marking Boundaries: Men's Space and Women's Space in a Yorkshire Village', in Philip Lowe, Tony Bradley and Susan Wright (eds), *Deprivation and Welfare in Rural Areas*, Norwich: Geo Books.

Miller, Toby, Lawrence, Geoffrey, McKay, Jim and Rowe, David. (2001) 'Global Sport Media', *Globalization and Sport: Playing the World*, London: Sage Publications, pp. 60–94.

Prendergast, Shirley. (1978) 'Stoolball – The Pursuit of Vertigo?', *Women's Studies International Quarterly*, 1, Oxford: Pergamon Press (Elsevier).

Rigauer, Bero. (1981) 'Top-Level Sports and "Achievement"', *Sport and Work*, trans. Allen Guttmann, © New York: Columbia University Press, pp. 14–27. Originally *Sport und Arbeit* © 1969, 1979 Bero Rigauer. Reprinted with permission of the publisher.

Roche, Maurice. (1993) 'Sport and Community: Rhetoric and Reality in the Development of British Sport Policy', in J.C. Binfield and John Stevenson (eds), *Sport, Culture and Politics,* Sheffield: Sheffield Academic Press, pp. 72–112.

Schiller, Herbert I. (1989) 'The Transnationalization of Corporate Expression', *Culture, Inc.: The Corporate Takeover of Public Expression*, Oxford: Oxford University Press, pp. 111–34.

Scraton, Sheila. (1987) '"Boys Muscle In Where Angels Fear to Tread" – Girls' Sub-Cultures and Physical Activities', in John Horne, David Jary and Alan Tomlinson (eds), *Sport, Leisure and Social Relations*, London: Routledge & Kegan Paul; reissued in 1993 by The Sociological Review, pp. 160–86. © The Editorial Board of The Sociological Review 1987, 1993.

Sugden, John. (1987) 'The Exploitation of Disadvantage: The Occupational Sub-Culture of the Boxer', in John Horne, David Jary and Alan Tomlinson (eds), *Sport, Leisure and Social Relations*, London: Routledge & Kegan Paul, reissued in 1993 by The Sociological Review, pp. 187–207. © The Editorial Board of The Sociological Review 1987, 1993.

Sugden, John and Bairner, Alan. (1992) '"Ma, there's a helicopter on the pitch!" Sport, Leisure and the State in Northern Ireland', *Sociology of Sport Journal*, (9) 2, Leeds: Human Kinetics Publishers, pp. 154–66.

Talbot, Margaret. (1995) 'The Politics of Sport and Physical Education', in Scott Fleming, Margaret Talbot and Alan Tomlinson (eds), *Policy and Politics in Sport, Physical Education and Leisure*, Brighton: Leisure Studies Association, pp. 3–26.

Veblen, Thorstein. (1899) 'Modern Survivals of Prowess', *The Theory of the Leisure Class: An Economic Study of Institutions*, Basingstoke: Macmillan, pp. 164–82.

Wacquant, Loïc (1995) 'Pugs at Work: Bodily Capital and Bodily Labour Among Professional Boxers', *Body & Society*, 1 (1), London: Sage Publications, pp. 65–93.

Werbner, Pnina. (1996) 'Fun Spaces: On Identity and Social Empowerment among British Pakistanis', *Theory, Culture & Society: Explorations in Critical Social Science*, 13(4), London: Sage Publications for the TCS Centre, Faculty of Humanities, Nottingham Trent University, pp. 53–79.

Whannel, Garry. (1992) 'Narrative: The Case of Coe and Ovett', *Fields in Vision: Television Sport and Cultural Transformation*, London: Routledge, pp. 140–7. Reproduced by permission of Taylor & Francis Books, UK.

Wheaton, Belinda and Tomlinson, Alan. (1998) 'The Changing Gender Order in Sport? The Case of Windsurfing Subcultures', *Journal of Sport and Social Issues*, 22 (3), London: Sage Publications, pp. 252–74.

Wilson, John. (1988) 'Leisure and Nationalism', *Politics and Leisure*, London: Unwin Hyman, pp. 149–73.

The publishers have made every effort to contact authors and copyright holders of works reprinted in *The Sport Studies Reader*. This has not been possible in every case, however, and we would welcome correspondence from individuals or companies we have been unable to trace.

The Reader and sport studies: a general introduction

■ Alan Tomlinson

T HIS READER – a collection of edited Readings in the traditional pedagogic genre – is designed to make more accessible some of the classic sources and themes that have established sport studies as a sphere of serious academic work, integrated with a selection of more contemporary pieces informing debate and study in the field. When the United Kingdom's first degree programmes in sport science and sport studies were established in the late 1970s and the early 1980s, there was a dearth of source materials available for emergent general syllabi and specialist areas of study. Yet for those institutions introducing these innovative programmes, things were not too bad: student class numbers were low, quality control was assumed rather than policed, seminar sessions might consist of perhaps a dozen students, there was plenty of scope for personal tutorials, and – in the case of the Chelsea School at least – a discipline-based syllabus could be delivered over the full three years of the undergraduate programme. In the early models of the sociocultural study of sport at Brighton, I could take a term on history, a term on theory, a term on policy and participation in the first year; and in the second year look in more detail at selected aspects such as the media or subcultures before, in the final year, offering some specialist work fitted to the needs and interests of the students. All of that was possible with annual intakes of twenty-four students. It was frustrating that there were few useful teaching texts available, apart from some North American-based readers and polemics. But with close and sustained contact with the students, in the climate of an excitingly emergent discipline, combined with access to studies and monographs that had recognized the importance of sport and leisure as important historical or social scientific topics, quality could be achieved in an evolving, incremental fashion.

A quarter of a century on, it is a very different picture. Sport studies has been extremely successful and has forged its own space and profile in the university marketplace.

Few programmes take a mere two dozen students per intake. Lecturers are also expected to be researchers, and contribute to the sports-related subject panel of the United Kingdom's Research Assessment Exercise (RAE), and so in turn to the status and credibility of the subject area in the wider academic community. From autumn 2006, in a move that has stunned university colleagues in neighbouring European countries such as France and Germany, undergraduates will have to pay £3,000 per annum tuition fees; and in many universities, these students will also have less contact with their teachers than at any time in the history of the sector. This is no time, therefore, to give students relatively indiscriminately long lists of books for recommended purchase. I know of too many cases where such lists have distorted the budgets of keen students, who have found that the so-called vital text gets just a passing mention, as well-intentioned but misguided tutors fuel their first years with the latest research that has been undertaken for reasons other than teaching: the first-year lecture course is not a performance space for experimenting with RAE material. The course-based Reader, then, has never looked more useful and necessary.

That is the context in which this Reader has been produced. It is for novice students undertaking degree-level studies in sport studies and related areas such as leisure studies. It is even more important, in an age of information retrieval and the 'google option', to provide access to enduring sources – ones that have stood the test of time and scholarly scrutiny. How can we teach history when websites provide uncritical and little justified timelines at the touch of a keyboard or the click of a mouse? One way is to read some proper historical scholarship and consider the question of periodization. The Reader's opening section covers theoretical debates on and conceptual approaches to understanding sport; but the second section comprises Readings on eighteenth-, nineteenth- and twentieth-century sport activities and institutions. These histories are a reminder that ideas are necessary, but are little more than speculation without evidence. The third section, 'Politics', offers ways of thinking about the effect of political institutions upon sport, at the levels of local culture, national policy and international relations. Some public sector policy debates are also included in this section, to show how sport's profile has been raised in the political sphere. The fourth section, 'Media', looks at different media institutions, at the values that are perpetuated by the written and the broadcast media, and at particular media forms that have been concerned with sport and an increasing emphasis in consumer culture upon the body. The fifth, sixth and seventh sections cover 'Class, community and cultural reproduction', 'Race and ethnic identities' and 'Gender and sexualities'. Class, race and gender have long been recognized as primary sources of social divisions in society, but can also be seen more positively as crucial influences upon forms of personal and cultural identity. In integrated social scientific research the experienced researcher will look at these aspects in an interrelated fashion, and the organization of the Reader may be seen as somewhat traditional. But debates concerning class and inequality, race and ethnicity, and gender and patriarchy are hardly marginal, and have obvious relevance to any understanding of the genesis and nature of contemporary sports. I am strongly of the view that students entering the field of sport studies need to know about the particularities of class, race and gender that have shaped sport and leisure cultures in the modern period. The final two sections – 'Subcultures', and 'Consumption and spectacle' – express my own view of what marks out sports as particularly significant aspects of social and cultural life. Sports, as sources of identity-formation and meaning-making, have lent themselves to subcultural formations; and as the commercial and international scale of sport has expanded dramatically, its consumerist profile and its potential for spectacular staging have become increasingly prominent. After the nine sections, I present an outline of further conceptual themes (globalization, identity, space and the body), and comment on how sport studies researchers do – and should – go about their research. Although much of the content of the Reader might best be described as sociological, this final commentary is a plea for the interdisciplinary potential of the field, and for students entering the field to engage with methodological questions concerning how the best research is done.

Other editors would, of course, choose different selections, and I have not included sections on some important areas. There could well have been a section on geographies and also one on economics. Certainly, important geographical and economic themes are covered in the Readings. These include the nature of public space, and the political economy of elite sports, covered by anthropologists and sociologists.

In recommendations for further reading, I have suggested some more specialized sources for the themes and approaches covered. Any editorial choice will be idiosyncratic, though hopefully not eccentric: two further, personal factors have influenced my decisions. One is that students have found *Understanding Sport. An Introduction to the Sociological and Cultural Analysis of Sport* (co-authored by John Horn, Garry Whannel and myself, London, E & FN Spon, 1998) suited to their introductory studies, being a textbook pitched at the level of analysis and evaluation of the scholarly evidence, rather than the topic of the day. It is useful, therefore, to make available some of the conceptual and empirical materials and sources that were reported in that text, and a number of the Readings in this volume have been chosen to offer greater access to some of those sources. In teaching terms, this Reader can certainly be seen as a partner to *Understanding Sport*. The second factor is that although I have almost all of the seventy-two sources on my personal library shelf, it has become increasingly clear that many of these sources are far from accessible, and hence not as widely read as they deserve to be. Some university libraries – including the splendid library at the University of Brighton's Eastbourne site – have even withdrawn some of these classic titles from their shelves. The selection of the seventy-two Readings is based upon my belief that a maturing field must be aware of its pedigree, and its students guided to some of the pioneering work in and formative contributions to the field.

There is now a burgeoning literature in sport and leisure studies, so why a Reader such as this? The answer is that, as far as my own thirty years of teaching are concerned, these are sources that have worked: as stated earlier, that have endured. The Reader is not designed as a state-of-the-art review of the nine specialist topic areas: students can produce these themselves in specialist projects and final-year work. The book is based upon a set of pedagogical and scholarly beliefs: that theoretical and conceptual debate should be open-minded; that good scholarship does not date; that empirical studies based upon strong and convincing evidence are essential. Sport is not the same thing in 2007 that it was 250 years ago. So where did it come from? What was it that shaped the most prominent contemporary forms? This Reader cannot answer all such questions for all sports. But in bringing together sources that cover a range of sports in various historical, social and cultural contexts, it shows how respected scholars have generated some of those answers. A Reader is a halfway house between the textbook overview and the specialist character of the research journal or monograph. Studying these selected excerpts should stimulate the student to go to the full source, the related classic research monograph, or the latest relevant research journal publication; and allow the student to appreciate how sport studies knowledge is generated, how evidence is located, evaluated and reported. Read closely and critically, the selections cannot fail to generate key questions concerning the social context of sport, its cultural distinctiveness in particular settings, and its persisting – many would argue increasing – significance in our contemporary societies. I offer my own version of these key questions in the introduction to each section, but I do not prescribe a list of questions after each Reading or each section. Rather, after the sectional introductions to the Readings, I provide pithy follow-up commentaries on the theme, with some suggestions as to more specialist and/or recent sources and research to which the keen student might turn.

Professor Alan Tomlinson
Sport and Leisure Cultures
Chelsea School (Eastbourne)
University of Brighton
Brighton, June 2006

Conceptualizing and theorizing sport

INTRODUCTION

WHAT IS THE MEANING AND SIGNIFICANCE of sport, and its varied forms, in relatively modern, contemporary societies? In answer to this fundamental question, some theorists have proposed distinctive readings of sport, so fuelling debate on the influences that have made sport what it is, the relation of sport to culture more generally, and the type of sport that has come to prominence in modern society. The first eight Readings introduce concepts and theories that have been influential in the development of the field.

The **Johan Huizinga** Reading is from the Dutch cultural historian's classic study of the play element in culture. Huizinga's specialist area of study was the Middle Ages but he also studied comparative cases, such as (the United States of) America. His emphasis on play, and its expression in a variety of cultural forms, is a reminder that the study of such areas is not a separate endeavour, cut off from broader social and cultural analysis: rather, the study of the ludic, or play, element in culture should be undertaken in an integrated fashion. While reading Huizinga, ask yourself what he means when he refers to an 'eternal play element', and do you agree that 'basic forms of sportive competition . . . are constant through the ages'?

French social scientist **Jean-Marie Brohm's** approach to sport is avowedly critical, drawing upon particular approaches in the critical tradition associated with nineteenth-century philosopher and social scientist Karl Marx, whose major project was the critical analysis of capitalist society. Brohm adopts the version of Marxist thought most closely identified with the French theorist Louis Althusser, for whom many forms of culture were little more than the tools used by powerful (usually economically privileged) groups in controlling less powerful groups. Sport, for Brohm, is therefore something that serves the interests of the current system: an activity through which (along with other institutions such as education and the media) the masses are controlled by the ruling elite: in Althusser's words, sport is an *ideological state apparatus* (ISA), and sometimes *a repressive state apparatus* (RSA). Reading Brohm, make a checklist of his criticisms of sport, and consider what dimensions of the sporting experience he may be overlooking or ignoring.

Bero Rigauer is a German sociologist who studied under the German critical theorist Theodor Adorno: the latter once wrote: 'Modern sports belong to the realm of unfreedom, no matter where they are organized' (*Prisms*, London, Neville Spearman, 1967: 81). Rigauer is interested in the characteristics that sport appears to share with work, and those features of work that oppress the majority of the population in modern industrial societies. He finds in the achievement principle of modern Western societies a set of defining characteristics that shape the work that most people do, and the top-level sports that those societies promote and support. When reading Rigauer on these areas, look back at Huizinga — was Huizinga writing about an element that Rigauer had no grasp of? Also, see what points the Brohm and the Rigauer conceptualizations have in common, in terms of people's experiences of sport, as both players and spectators.

Allen Guttmann, a humanities scholar and sports historian in the United States — and heralded by Stanford scholar Hans Ulrich Gumbrecht (*In Praise of Athletic Beauty*, Belknap, Harvard University Press, Cambridge, MA, 2006: 258) as 'simply the master of all sports historians' — has written numerous studies of sport and its diffusion across the world, in different societies and in distinctive forms such as the Olympic Games. The Reading included here is from his ambitiously titled *Sport — The First Five Millennia*; in this Reading you are offered a working definition of sport, and a reaffirmation of Guttmann's list of characteristics of modern sports, first published in his seminal *From Ritual to Record: The Meaning of Modern Sports* (New York, Columbia University Press, 1977). Pick your favourite top-level sport (to use Rigauer's term), and see if these seven characteristics help you see more deeply into the character of that sport.

Norbert Elias and his protégé and collaborator **Eric Dunning** have been the pioneers of the development of figurational sociology (Elias, in a series of hugely influential studies; Dunning, in innovative and ground-breaking applications of this approach in the analysis of sport). Central to their approach has been the notion of the civilizing process, and the proposition that forms of sport and leisure (which offer possibilities of excitement) change 'in the course of a civilizing process'. Look, in this Reading, at the significance that is claimed for what Elias and Dunning term *mimetic* activities, and apply this term to examples of sport and games with which you are most familiar.

Richard Gruneau is a Canadian scholar of sport and the communications media, and his analyses of sport draw upon the sociological theorizing of Anthony Giddens, and the work of cultural historians and cultural theorists such as Raymond Williams. In these excerpts from the opening chapter of his book, Gruneau looks to bring together what we might call the subjective aspects of sport with the more external influences that affect all human beings and the sports that they do. He does this by reviewing different theories and conceptual approaches, including those of Huizinga, Guttmann and Brohm. While reading Gruneau, hold in mind therefore your own responses to those three theorists.

John Hargreaves is a British sociologist whose work on sport, power and culture has been widely influential. His seminal study from which these excerpts are taken is a synthesis of historical and contemporary sources and studies. He recognizes the centrality of the concept of power to the critical understanding of sport, and finds in the popular sports of the working classes a form of resistance to dominant cultures: this approach identifies sports as forms of struggle, over which meanings are disputed or contested. Consider what influences curtail what Hargreaves calls the 'autonomy of sport'.

Jennifer Hargreaves is a British sociologist and cultural studies specialist whose work on women's experience of sport and physical education has been at the forefront of feminist work in sport studies, and has included a critique of sport studies itself as favouring men. She provides here a critique of male-dominated approaches in sports history and sociology, and argues that women's experiences of sport must be much less marginalized in 'academic discourse'. In developing her work Hargreaves has employed the ideas of Italian thinker Antonio Gramsci: what are the main features of his concept of hegemony, as Hargreaves uses them in her approach to understanding the experience of sporting females (in a patriarchal world)?

COMMENTARY AND FURTHER READING

These selections have illustrated just some of the approaches that have been adopted in seeking to illuminate and understand the place of sport in society, and Western industrialized, late modern societies in particular. There exist more theoretical perspectives than have been included here, but I have chosen particularly influential and comprehensive approaches rather than providing an encyclopaedic listing of all possible conceptual approaches and theoretical perspectives.

Some of the Readings and the positions adopted by their authors will, in all likelihood, have appeared to be irreconcilable; and this raises the fundamental but challenging question of epistemology, the issue of the nature of knowledge and the theory of knowledge. Readers with multi-disciplinary backgrounds crossing the natural sciences, the social sciences and the humanities will have noticed that theoretical debate does not take place in the same way in the social sciences as it does in, say, experimental or laboratory sciences. Interpretation rather than explanation is the goal of much work in social-science-led sport studies. And this kind of work can also be bound up with issues of ontology, theories of being and existence. To follow up such questions, students can consult Grant Jarvie and Joseph Maguire's *Sport and Leisure in Social Thought* (London and New York, Routledge, 1994), and, on general approaches in social science as well as the questions of epistemology and ontology, Grant Jarvie's *Sport, Culture and Society: An Introduction* (London and New York, Routledge, 2006: 19–31). To see how various theorists' work has been discussed in terms of their application to the study of sport, go to Richard Giulianotti's *Sport and Modern Social Theorists* (Basingstoke, Palgrave Macmillan, 2004). This edited collection includes essays on some of the major thinkers mentioned in this section – such as Karl Marx, Antonio Gramsci, Norbert Elias, Theodor Adorno and Anthony Giddens. Jennifer Hargreaves also reflects in that volume on the 'manifestly muddled, complex' (p. 202) and contradictory nature of sport feminism. Other writers covered in the Giulianotti book, whose work appears in later sections of this Reader, are C.L.R. James, Jean Baudrillard and Pierre Bourdieu. On the relevance of the concept of power, see John Sugden and Alan Tomlinson's opening chapter in their edited book *Power Games: A Critical Sociology of Sport* (London and New York, Routledge, 2002).

Whatever follow-up reading you do, remember that concepts are the building blocks of theory, and that theory needs to be developed on the basis of evidence. By all means draw upon your own experiences as you begin to try out the applicability of concepts and theories, but to develop adequate ways of theorizing you will need to consistently consider the balance between empirical material (the examples that you draw upon, the data that you generate – in short the evidence available) and your conceptual and theoretical formulations.

And do not be overly concerned about definitive definitions of sport. In *The Leisure Industries* (Basingstoke, Palgrave Macmillan, 2004: 81) Ken Roberts writes that it is 'a sociological cop-out' to 'say that something is a sport if people (the ordinary members of society) regard it as such'. Roberts considers it 'unsatisfactory to sidestep the definitional problem in this way', and claims that 'sport' should have four characteristics: separateness from the rest of life, in its rules, place and time; skill, improvable by practice and preparation; energy, requiring stamina and exertion; and competitiveness, geared to winning. It is fun to have the usual discussions about snooker, darts, chess, ballroom dancing and cheerleading: but despite Roberts's argument, it remains important and interesting to raise appropriate theoretical questions about the genesis, character and social significance of forms and practices recognized as sport in a particular time and place. If you choose to use this Reader sequentially, the conceptual and theoretical Readings give you an entrée into ways of thinking about sport: these can be available in your interpretive toolkit as you explore Histories, in the following section, and consider in some detail issues concerning the genesis of modern sports in Britain.

Johan Huizinga

THE PLAY-ELEMENT IN CONTEMPORARY CIVILIZATION

[. . .]

THE QUESTION TO WHICH we address ourselves is this: To what extent does the civilization we live in still develop in play-forms? How far does the play-spirit dominate the lives of those who share that civilization? The nineteenth century, we observed, had lost many of the play-elements so characteristic of former ages. Has this leeway been made up or has it increased?

It might seem at first sight that certain phenomena in modern social life have more than compensated for the loss of play-forms. Sport and athletics, as social functions, have steadily increased in scope and conquered ever fresh fields both nationally and internationally.

Contests in skill, strength, and perseverance have, as we have shown, always occupied an important place in every culture either in connexion with ritual or simply for fun and festivity. Feudal society was only really interested in the tournament; the rest was just popular recreation and nothing more. Now the tournament, with its highly dramatic staging and aristocratic embellishments, can hardly be called a sport. It fulfilled one of the functions of the theatre. Only a numerically small upper class took active part in it. This one-sidedness of medieval sporting life was due in large measure to the influence of the Church. The Christian ideal left but little room for the organized practice of sport and the cultivation of bodily exercise, except in so far as the latter contributed to gentle education. Similarly, the Renaissance affords fairly numerous examples of body-training cultivated for the sake of perfection, but only on the part of individuals, never groups or classes. If anything, the emphasis laid by the Humanists on learning and erudition tended to perpetuate the old under-estimation of the body, likewise the moral zeal and severe intellectuality of the Reformation and Counter-Reformation. The recognition of games and bodily exercises as important cultural values was withheld right up to the end of the eighteenth century.

The basic forms of sportive competition are, of course, constant through the ages. In some the trial of strength and speed is the whole essence of the contest, as in running and skating matches, chariot and horse races, weight-lifting, swimming, diving, marksmanship, etc.[1] Though human beings have indulged in such activities since the dawn of time, these only take on the character of organized games to a very slight degree. Yet nobody, bearing in mind the agonistic principle which animates them, would hesitate to call them games in the sense of play — which, as we have seen, can be very serious indeed. There are, however, other forms of contest which develop of their own accord into 'sports'. These are the ball-games.

What we are concerned with here is the transition from occasional amusement to the system of organized clubs and matches. Dutch pictures of the seventeenth century show us burghers and peasants intent upon their game of *kolf*; but, so far as I know, nothing is heard of games being organized in clubs or played as matches. It is obvious that a fixed organization of this kind will most readily occur when two groups play against one another. The great ball-games in particular require the existence of permanent teams, and herein lies the starting-point of modern sport. The process arises quite spontaneously in the meeting of village against village, school against school, one part of a town against the rest, etc. That the process started in nineteenth-century England is understandable up to a point, though how far the specifically Anglo-Saxon bent of mind can be deemed an efficient cause is less certain. But it cannot be doubted that the structure of English life had much to do with it. Local self-government encouraged the spirit of association and solidarity. The absence of obligatory military training favoured the occasion for, and the need of physical exercise. The peculiar form of education tended to work in the same direction, and finally the geography of the country and the nature of the terrain, on the whole flat and, in the ubiquitous commons, offering the most perfect playing-fields that could be desired, were of the greatest importance. Thus England became the cradle and focus of modern sporting life.

Ever since the last quarter of the nineteenth century, games in the guise of sport,[2] have been taken more seriously. The rules have become increasingly strict and elaborate. Records are established at a higher, or faster, or longer level than was ever conceivable before. Everybody knows the delightful prints from the first half of the nineteenth century, showing the cricketers in top-hats. This speaks for itself.

Now, with the increasing systematization and regimentation of sport, something of the pure play-quality is inevitably lost. We see this very clearly in the official distinction between amateurs and professionals (or 'gentlemen and players' as used pointedly to be said). It means that the play-group marks out those for whom play is no longer play, ranking them inferior to the true players in standing but superior in capacity. The spirit of the professional is no longer the true play-spirit; it is lacking in spontaneity and carelessness.[3] This affects the amateur too, who begins to suffer from an inferiority complex. Between them they push sport further and further away from the play-sphere proper until it becomes a thing *sui generis*: neither play nor earnest. In modern social life sport occupies a place alongside and apart from the cultural process. The great competitions in archaic cultures had always formed part of the sacred festivals and were indispensable as health- and happiness-bringing activities. This ritual tie has now been completely severed; sport has become profane, 'unholy' in every way and has no organic connexion whatever with the structure of society, least of all when prescribed by the government. The ability of modern social techniques to stage mass demonstrations with the maximum of outward show in the field of athletics does not alter the fact that neither the Olympiads nor the organized sports of American Universities nor the loudly trumpeted international contests have, in the smallest degree, raised sport to the level of a culture-creating activity. However important it may be for the players or spectators, it remains sterile. The old play-factor has undergone almost complete atrophy.

This view will probably run counter to the popular feeling of today, according to which sport is the apotheosis of the play-element in our civilization. Nevertheless popular feeling is wrong. By way of emphasizing the fatal shift towards over-seriousness we would point out that it has also infected the non-athletic games where calculation is everything, such as chess and some card-games. [. . .]

The attempt to assess the play-content in the confusion of modern life is bound to lead us to contradictory conclusions. In the case of sport we have an activity nominally known as play but raised to such a pitch of technical organization and scientific thoroughness that the real play-spirit is threatened with extinction. Over against this tendency to over-seriousness, however, there are other phenomena pointing in the opposite direction. Certain activities whose whole *raison d'être* lies in the field of material interest, and which had nothing of play about them in their initial stages, develop what we can only call play-forms as a secondary characteristic. Sport and athletics showed us play stiffening into seriousness but still being felt as play; now we come to serious business degenerating into play but still being called serious. The two phenomena are linked by the strong agonistic habit which still holds universal sway, though in other forms than before.

The impetus given to this agonistic principle which seems to be carrying the world back in the direction of play derives, in the main, from external factors independent of culture proper – in a word, communications, which have made intercourse of every sort so extraordinarily easy for mankind as a whole. Technology, publicity, and propaganda everywhere promote the competitive spirit and afford means of satisfying it on an unprecedented scale. Commercial competition does not, of course, belong to the im-memorial sacred play-forms. It only appears when trade begins to create fields of activity within which each must try to surpass and outwit his neighbour. Commercial rivalry soon makes limiting rules imperative, namely the trading customs. It remained primitive in essence until quite late, only becoming really intensive with the advent of modern communications, propaganda, and statistics. Naturally a certain play-element had entered into business competition at an early stage. Statistics stimulated it with an idea that had originally arisen in sporting life, the idea, namely, of trading records. A record, as the word shows, was once simply a memorandum, a note which the innkeeper scrawled on the walls of his inn to say that such and such a rider or traveller had been the first to arrive after covering so and so many miles. The statistics of trade and production could not fail to introduce a sporting element into economic life. In consequence, there is now a sporting side to almost every triumph of commerce or technology: the highest turnover, the biggest tonnage, the fastest crossing, the greatest altitude, etc. Here a purely ludic element has, for once, got the better of utilitarian considerations, since the experts inform us that smaller units – less monstrous steamers and aircraft, etc. – are more efficient in the long run. Business becomes play. This process goes so far that some of the great business concerns deliberately instil the play-spirit into their workers so as to step up production. The trend is now reversed: play becomes business. A captain of industry, on whom the Rotterdam Academy of Commerce had conferred an honorary degree, spoke as follows:

> Ever since I first entered the business it has been a race between the technicians and the sales department. One tried to produce so much that the sales department would never be able to sell it, while the other tried to sell so much that the technicians would never be able to keep pace. This race has always continued: sometimes one is ahead, sometimes the other. Neither my brother nor myself has regarded the business as a task, but always as a game, the spirit of which it has been our constant endeavour to implant into the younger staff.

These words must, of course, be taken with a grain of salt. Nevertheless there are numerous instances of big concerns forming their own Sports Societies and even engaging workers with a view not so much to their professional capacities as to their fitness for the football eleven. Once more the wheel turns. [. . .]

. . . [L]et us be on our guard against two misunderstandings from the start. Firstly, certain play-forms may be used consciously or unconsciously to cover up some social or political design. In this case we are not dealing with the eternal play-element that has been the theme of this book, but with false play. Secondly, and quite independently of this, it is always possible to come upon phenomena which, to a superficial eye, have all the appearance of play and might be taken for permanent play-tendencies, but are, in point of fact, nothing of the sort. Modern social life is being dominated to an ever-increasing extent by a quality that has something in common with play and yields the illusion of a strongly developed play-factor.

Notes

1   A happy variation of the natatorial contest is found in *Beowulf*, where the aim is to hold your opponent under water until he is drowned.

2   It is probably significant that we no longer speak of 'games' but of 'sport'. Our author may not have been sufficiently familiar with the development of 'sport' in the last ten or twenty years, here and in America, to stress the all-important point that sport has become a business, or, to put it bluntly, a commercial racket [Trans.].

3   Note G.K. Chesterton's dictum: If a thing is worth doing it is worth doing badly! [Trans.]

Jean-Marie Brohm

THESES TOWARDS A POLITICAL SOCIOLOGY OF SPORT*

1 Sport and imperialism

(a) *The origins of modern sport*

MODERN SPORT, organised into national and international sports federations, is an imperialist phenomenon, in the marxist sense of the term. Sport developed in this form essentially from 1880–1900 onwards, in other words, at the beginning of the age of imperialism, analysed by Lenin.

The first modern Olympic games were held in Athens in 1896 and then in Paris in 1900, while the first major sports competitions such as the Tour de France or the FA Cup were organised at around the same time. Sport was directly linked to the interests of imperialist capital. The early Olympic games, in Paris, Saint-Louis and London, were organised in conjunction with Universal Exhibitions or Trade Fairs.

(b) *The organisation of sport*

From the start, the international organisation of sport was tied to imperialist international organisations. Sport served as both a supportive institution and as an ideological cover. Following both the 1914–18 and the 1939–45 World Wars, the organisation of international sport benefited from imperialist attempts to control the world. Since then, international sport has been inextricably linked to super-national organisations, in particular the UN and UNESCO. Today, the Olympic Movement and the IOC (International Olympic Committee) are closely tied to the UN and more specifically to US Imperialism. Brundage, the President, is American [This article was written in 1971 – Ed.] Within the framework of peaceful coexistence, the International Olympic Movement fully reflects the interests of imperialism. The cosmopolitan, 'pacifist' ideology expressed in the Olympic ideal is in reality none other than the hypocritical ideology of imperialism, which 'leads to war, as surely as the storm clouds lead to the storm'.

The set-up of world sport is not just held together by its own ideology of 'peace between peoples' and by its own organisation. For imperialist sport is closely dependent on imperialist institutions and treaties such as NATO, SEATO etc. There are very close links between civilian and military sport. For instance, Western military sport is tied directly to NATO and constitutes a spearhead of North Atlantic imperialism. The international organisation of sport constitutes a 'World Government of Sport', responsible for:

- organising international competitions,
- dealing with relations between national federations,
- laying down rules for different sports and supervising their application, settling disputes, deciding sanctions etc.,
- recognising world records,
- developing an ideological Charter for 'universal sport'.

(c) *Sport and peaceful coexistence*

As an international reality, sport is a very *precise reflection of the relation of forces between imperialism and the bureaucratic state-bourgeoisie of the 'socialist' countries* (or to use Trotskyist terminology, the Stalinist bureaucracy).

In 1921, at the Third Congress of the Communist International, a 'Red Sports International' was set up, with the aim of organising working-class sportsmen and women against the bourgeoisie. For a whole period, the USSR refused to establish sporting relations with the imperialist countries. But following the Stalinisation of the USSR and the adoption of the counter-revolutionary policy of 'socialism in one country' and 'peaceful coexistence', the USSR established sporting relations with more and more countries, particularly following the end of the Second World War.

In 1952, one year before Stalin's death, the USSR took part in the Helsinki games, thereby coming into the Olympic Movement. Since that time, world sport and the Olympic games have been regarded by both the imperialist states and by the Stalinist, bureaucratic states as an important element of peaceful coexistence. The Olympic sports ideology is a hypocritical ideology which seeks to hide the reality of the class struggle behind so-called 'brotherhood between the peoples'. The reality behind the 'peace' of the sports field or the 'truce' of the Games is that sport is a grim analogue of the permanent state of war under imperialism, as can be seen by looking at the recent Olympics.

Thus the Olympic games in Melbourne in 1956 were unable to conceal the fact that the French and British imperialists were in the course of intervening in favour of the Zionist imperialists of the state of Israel with their Suez adventure. At the same time, tanks sent by the Russian Stalinist bureaucracy were bloodily crushing the revolution of the workers' councils in Hungary.

Then in 1968, all the imperialist countries sent their Olympic teams to Mexico, shortly after the Diaz Ordaz government had had student demonstrators shot down. Earlier that year, the Stalinist bureaucracy had betrayed the great general strike of May and June in France, while American imperialism was bombing, burning and killing in

Vietnam. Meanwhile, the troops of the Red Army and the Warsaw Pact were invading Czechoslovakia to put down the Czech intellectuals and workers and smash the popular mobilisation of the Prague Spring.

On a world scale, sport has always been linked to the twists and turns of the international class struggle. And sport itself, notably the Olympic Movement, is an important ideological element in this struggle.

2   Bourgeois sport and the capitalist state

(a)   *All the structures of present-day sport tie it to bourgeois, capitalist society*

Sport is dependent on the development of the productive forces of bourgeois society. Technical progress in sport closely follows the technological and scientific development of capitalism. Bourgeois sport is a class institution, totally integrated into the framework of capitalist production relations and class relations. Like other class institutions, such as the university, the army etc.

And finally, as a phenomenon of the superstructure, sport is linked to all the other superstructural levels of capitalist society. The organisational unity of sport is ensured by the repressive grip of the bourgeois state. Moreover, sport as an ideology, transmitted on a huge scale by the mass media, is part and parcel of ruling bourgeois ideology.

(b)   *Sport and the state*

From the start, the development of sport has been tied to that of the state. Like all other class institutions and structures, sport is mediated through the state which locks in all the structures of society as a whole. When the process of establishing bourgeois nation-states has been set in train by bourgeois revolutions such as the French Revolution of 1789, *sport has tended to participate in the process of development of these states.*

Most major national liberation movements which have fought for the establishment of nation-states have consciously made use of physical activities and mass sport *as a means of creating a national identity.*

First Example: Jahn[1] and anti-Napoleonic, German nationalism – the establishment of a German nationalist movement, leading to the national unification of Germany under Prussian rule.

Second Example: Mao Tse-Tung, whose early work, 'A Study of Physical Education', was to help to strengthen Chinese youth physically and mentally in the struggle against Western Imperialism and local, feudal reaction.[2] Physical education was thus a factor in the process of the bourgeois democratic revolution.

Third Example: Today all colonial and semi-colonial countries which achieve independence *structure the population by means of mass, state-run sport*, as an integral part of the establishment of their nation-state.

In situations where the state dominates all political existence, as under fascist or military/police régimes, or under the dictatorship of a Stalinist, bureaucratic state-bourgeoisie, sport is simply a structural part of the state repressive apparatus, particularly the army.

In this type of state, mass sport is merely a para-state institution for regimenting youth, which operates along with other reception organisations such as state-controlled youth movements, Scouts, the army etc. This was the set-up, for example, in Hitler's Germany, Stalinist Russia or in France under the Vichy régime. In this case the basic political functions of sport are:

—   to control youth activities,
—   ideological regimentation,
—   pre-military training on nationalist lines: preparation for the 'defence of the fatherland'.

In the period of the death-agony of imperialism, bourgeois states tend increasingly to become strong, police-states, like for example the De Gaulle/Pompidou régime. In this case too, sport shares the general aims of the bourgeois state, in the widest sense of the term: sport becomes *State Sport*:

—   sports structures, federations, clubs etc., are closely tied into the state apparatus;
—   the state itself promotes state sport through a state doctrine: an official approach to sport which is enforced by the creation of a special administrative structure: the Ministry of Youth and Sport;
—   top ranking sportsmen and women are state athletes with the job of promoting the state's official propaganda;
—   the state imposes competitive sport in schools as the compulsory mode of physical education.

(c) *Sport and the capitalist organisation of production*

Sport as an activity characteristic of bourgeois industrial society, is an exact reflection of capitalist categories. And as Marx explained,[3] economic categories reflect the structures and principles of organisation of the capitalist mode of production. The vertical, hierarchical structure of sport models the social structure of bureaucratic capitalism, with its system of competitive selection, promotion, hierarchy and social advancement. The driving forces in sport – performance, competitiveness, records – are directly carried over from the driving forces of capitalism: productivity, the search for profit, rivalry and competitiveness.

Sport as a technology of the body structurally reproduces capitalist repressive techniques: the division of labour, ultra-specialisation, repetition, training, the abstraction of space and time, stereotyped movements, the parcelling up of the body, measurement, stop-watch timing, Taylorism, Stakhanovism. . . .

Sport treats the human organism as a machine, in the same way as the worker becomes a mere appendage of the machine in the capitalist system.[4] Sport as an ideology reproduces and strengthens the ideology of alienated labour: work, continuous effort, struggle, the cult of transcending one's own limitations, the cult of suffering, the cult of self-denial, self-sacrifice etc. Sport is a morality of effort which conditions people for the oppressive work of the factory.

(d) *Sport and state monopoly capitalism*

(i) Sport as an activity involving the circulation of money and capital is thus totally tied up in the financial and economic network of monopoly capitalism. Professional sport with its show-business, its betting and its financial speculation, is just the most glaring aspect of this process.

(ii) Trusts, banking groups and monopolies use major international competitions to reinforce their domination, as for example, in the skiing events at the Grenoble Winter Olympics. Moreover major national and international competitions require huge mobilisations of capital and economic resources: thus the choice of site for the Olympic Games is the object of fierce competition between multi-national firms.

(iii) Sport also develops its own industries on a broad, capitalist basis, through the manufacture of equipment and the promotion of sporting goods. Financial trusts, such as Rothschild, were quick to develop and profit from the sports and leisure industry, Winter Sports and the 'Club Méditerranée'.

(e) *Sport and capitalist showbusiness*

Spectator sport is a commodity sold along normal capitalist lines. Sportsmen and women themselves are commodities, bought and sold according to the law of supply and demand, viz. the famous 'transfers' of professional footballers.

As soon as spectator sport becomes caught up in the capitalist web, the door is inevitably open to every kind of 'abuse' and 'fiddle': shamateurism, the star-system and the hunt for high fees.

As a form of mass entertainment, sport is a process whereby the population is reduced to an ideological mass. Sport is a means of regimentation and de-humanisation – see, for example, the role of football in Brazil, Britain or Spain, or of cycling in Italy and France, or of baseball in the USA etc. Spectator sports are a mass political safety-valve, a system of social diversion and an element in pre-military conditioning. Moreover, it is worth noting that most major competitions are controlled, if not actually run, by the police and the army, as was the case at the Mexico and Grenoble Games. In other words sport, as one of the factors for maintaining law and order, is usually controlled by the forces of law and order.

The ceremonies at major sports competitions are just like big military parades or pre-fascist rallies, with their 'traditional' or military music, the flag rituals, rhythmic marches, national anthems and medal ceremonies. The best examples of this kind of ceremonial are provided by the Hitlerite Games of 1936 in Berlin and the Mexico Games, controlled by the same *Granaderos* who had taken part in the repression of the student movement.

(f) *Sport and the ruling ideology*

Sport is a concentrated form, an officially promoted microcosm, of all the ideological prejudices of bureaucratic, bourgeois society:

—   the cult of the champion and the star-system;
—   the cult of promotion, social advancement and the hierarchy;
—   the myth of transcending one's own limitations through effort;
—   character building;
—   sexual repression – the healthy life etc.;
—   the brotherhood of man – everyone united on the sportsfield;
—   nationalism and chauvinism.

3   Institutional repression

- Sport is a social process for the continuous repression of childhood drives. As a socialising institution, sport channels the sexual drives of the adolescent in a repressive direction, through sublimation, unconscious repression and diversion.
- As Freud showed, sport replaces libidinal pleasure with the masochistic pleasure obtained from movement. As sports trainers are constantly stressing: 'It's when it hurts that it's doing you good!'
- Sport is a process whereby codified, stereotyped 'bodily techniques' are imprinted with the aim of producing automatic, adaptive reflexes.
- Sport is the repressive cultural codification of movements.
- Sport helps to shape the super-ego of the adolescent: external repression is internalised through the mediation of the trainer, the representative of bourgeois values and the bourgeois social order.
- *Sport is alienating. It will disappear in a universal communist society.*

Jean-Marie Brohm, April 1971

Notes

*This is an expanded version of an article which first appeared in *Le Chrono Enrayé* No. 8 (May–June 1972).

1   On this question see: J. Ulmann, *De la Gymnastique aux Sports Modernes*, PUF, Paris, 1965, pp. 277 on.
2   One can find some extract and a commentary of this text in S.R. Schram, *The Political Thought of Mao Tse-Tung*, Penguin Books, London, 1969, pp. 152–60.
3   'Just as in general when examining any historical or social science, so also in the case of the development of economic categories is it always necessary to remember that the subject, in this context contemporary bourgeois society, is presupposed both in reality and in the mind, and that therefore categories express forms of existence – and sometimes merely separate aspects – of this particular society, the subject; (. . .) This has to be remembered because it provides important criteria for the arrangement of the material.'

Karl Marx, *Introduction to a Critique of Political Economy*, in *The German Ideology*, part I, Lawrence & Wishart, London, 1970, p. 146.

4   'Owing to the extensive use of machinery and to division of labour, the work of the proletarians has lost all individual character, and, consequently, all charm for the workman. He becomes an appendage of the machine, and it is only the most simple, most monotonous. and most easily acquired knack, that is required of him.' K. Marx and F. Engels, *Manifesto of the Communist Party*, in K. Marx/F. Engels, *Collected Works*, Vol. 6, Lawrence & Wishart, London, 1975, pp. 490–1.

Bero Rigauer

TOP-LEVEL SPORTS AND 'ACHIEVEMENT'

Top-level sports

TODAY'S FANS REACT with polemics, rage, and even hate when an idolized athlete or team fails to live up to their expectations.[1] The founder of the modern Olympic Games, Pierre De Coubertin, helped bring about this state of affairs when he impressed upon sports the motto *citius, altius, fortius* (faster, higher, stronger). The motto corresponds to "belief in progress and, in the emphasis on achievement, to the principles of industrial society."[2] One simply cannot "do" sports "mildly" and "in moderation," for "in the 'freedom to go all out' is hidden an alluring force," the quest for records. Coubertin sought to justify this force with references to "the power of emulation."[3] Achievement was put forth as a typical characteristic of sport. Achievement "is the most striking essential element in sports . . . : the striving for achievement, for the highest achievement, for records." The desire to set records is remarkable because the athlete voluntarily undertakes fantastic physical efforts that are normally avoided at all costs."[4] Whether one can really speak of "voluntarily" accepted physical effort is quite problematical; the individual who resolves to participate in top-level sports has already subordinated himself to a high degree to the reigning system of values and conventions of behavior. To do top-level sports means to be forced to achieve—in order to fulfill society's expectations of achievement.[5] [. . .]

. . . [T]he concept of achievement has taken on ideological functions in the realm of sports. The next step is to illustrate the sociological and ideological connections between sports and work by describing certain achievement-oriented forms of behavior and consciousness. In doing so, we shall concentrate on top-level sports, by which we mean a complex of social behavior which is directed toward the best possible individual and team athletic achievements. Top-level sports may include both amateurs and professionals. The concept of "social labor" as we use it here refers to individual or collective action, regardless of economic gain, which is directed at maximum achievement. In the products of work, the individual seeks to realize characteristic socially transmitted ideas. A parallel between the products of work and sports can easily be discerned: in both cases, the shaping of individual products appears as the highest goal.

Doing sports and working are both based on human achievement. In sociological terms, "achievement" involves material and nonmaterial values of human behavior which are expressed in factors of optimal qualities or quantities. With respect to achievement, there is a correlation between the orientation of the individual and the expectation of his environment. Unless an athletic achievement meets social expectations, it will not be accepted as such. Similarly, the norms of economic life must be followed if achievements are to be acknowledged as such.

The data of achievement are established, replaced, and administered by the ruling groups of society. They are dissociated quickly from their initiators and, as impersonal institutionalized values, exert a social coercion upon all of us. The objective form of this coercion is the ideology of achievement.

"Achievement"

A dominant model for behavior in the behavioral system of work and top-level sports

In the realm of top-level sport as in that of social labor, the achievement principle dominates. The success of human actions is now measured by the reaching or surpassing of set norms of achievement. Individuals, groups, and institutions are ranked according to their success or failure to achieve. Those who do not strive to fulfill the acknowledged norms of achievement are discredited; they cannot claim high social prestige. The ability to achieve and success in achieving function as the highest social values. It seems almost self-evident that one of the imperatives of modern physical education calls for the best possible individual achievement for any given "psychophysical potential." The relationship of this imperative to the economically defined conception of work is obvious. Thus, the systematic "increase in physical and spiritual stimulus in order to reach the optimal functioning capacity of the organism" is the real goal of athletic training. The connection with the world of work is unambiguous when one of the fundamentals of physical education is that improvements in achievement are possible only "through the planning of the work."[1] Similar formulations appeared long ago in the writings of the efficiency expert F.W. Taylor. Taylor argued that the individual found his greatest "prosperity" in striving for occupational achievement. In other words, "the development of individual capacity to its completest fulfillment enables each individual to attain vocational perfection."[2] Interestingly enough, Taylor uses team sports to exemplify his thesis: every player must seek "to mobilize all his strength to help his team to victory"; if he fails to do this, he "will be scorned by all."[3]

Implicit in both top-level sports and social labor is the demand that we continually raise the level of our achievement. This demand manifests itself in the establishing of goals which are continuously corrected upwardly. The norms of achievement have only provisional validity. "In modern sports' characteristic striving for higher levels of achievement, for records of speed, and for the many-sided development of movement-skills, we can see mirrored the development of modern industrial technology, with all its concomitant demands," namely the demand of the productive sector for particular movement-skills which the worker must provide.[4] Decisive is the optimal occupational achievement, which accounts in turn for optimal production. And this kind of achievement has been adopted from the behavioral model of top-level sports. Peak production and the concept of the record, no matter in what form, no matter in which field of behavior, are typical characteristics of a productivity-oriented, industrial, marketplace society where the most capable competitor receives the best exchange values for his products.

Today, records are no longer set accidentally and without preparation. "In our time, a world record is normally the result of teamwork by scientists, doctors, coaches, masseurs, and sometimes pacers as well as the athletes themselves."[5] Despite this teamwork, scientifically prepared attempts to set records are almost always stymied by human unpredictability, by indecision, and by sudden lapses in ability. A record cannot be wholly planned and predicted. Similar phenomena are observable within the world of work, where individual achievement is increasingly dependent upon collective achievement. While the founders of the great industrial enterprises of the nineteenth and early twentieth centuries were able to rely on their own judgment in assessing the economic situation, today we have specialists concerned with planning, study of the market, analysis of the state of competition. And these specialists often work in teams, taking the place of the omni-competent activists of earlier times. They create specialized bodies of knowledge, which are the precondition for a general increase in achievement levels. In sports, the 10,000-meter runner is trained and handled by a specialist or even by a staff of specialists. Available data are gathered and analyzed as part of the training program. The top-level athlete has himself become a specialist. [. . .]

Top-level sports and social labor have, in their common fixation on occupational or on work-like models of behavior, developed into open systems. Individual achievement, not inherited symbols of status, functions as the criterion for social mobility. This theorem still possesses undiminished validity, for material factors continue to condition changes in social status. To a limited degree we can observe a cause-effect relationship between achievement and social mobility in both spheres: i.e. in work as well as in athletic contests, a successful performance results in social mobility. The achieving employee of a bureaucratic apparatus can rise to a better paying classification just as the achieving athlete can move up to a better team. Both gain social prestige through such a change in position. Simultaneously, however, diminishing capacity and performance carries with it the danger of social and material downward mobility or even the danger of exclusion from the competition. Top-level sports and social labor internalize the achievement principle and make it a central category in their repertory of goals. They realize the achievement principle within a rationalized system of behavior demanding a high degree of conformity.

Notes

Top-level sports

1   Psychoanalytic theory offers an explanation for this: the emotional attachment of an individual to an idealized object is transformed into hatred at the moment of disillusionment.

2 G. Lüschen, "Der Leistungssport in seiner Abhängigkeit vom soziokulturellen System," *Zentralblatt für Arbeitswissenschaft*, 19 (1962): 187.

3 H. Lenk, *Werte—Ziele—Wirklichkeit der modernen Olympischen Spiele* (Schorndorf, 1964), p. 84.

4 C. Diem, *Wesen und Lehre des Sports und der Leibeserziehung* (Berlin, 1960), pp. 13–14.

5 Sport psychologists have tried to define athletic achievement as a psychological experience—the individual experiences situations of special quality during the achieving. These psychologists ignore the social determinants of the situation.

"Achievement"

1 K. Deschka, *Trainingslehre und Organisationslehre des Sports* (Vienna & Munich, 1961), pp. 6–7.

2 F.W. Taylor, *Die Grundsätze wissenschaftlicher Betriebsführung* (Munich & Berlin, 1913), p. 7.

3 Ibid., p. 11.

4 A. Wohl, "Die gesellschaftlich-historischen Grundlagen der bürgerlichen Sports," *Wissenschaftliche Zeitschriften der DHfK*, 6 (1964): 5–93, p. 52.

5 W. Umminger, *Helden—Götter—Übermenschen. Eine Kulturgeschichte menschlicher Höchstleistungen* (Düsseldorf & Vienna, 1962), p. 367.

Allen Guttmann

RULES OF THE GAME

SPORTS ARE A HUMAN UNIVERSAL, appearing in every culture, past and present. But every culture has its own definitions of *sport*. Quibbles about these definitions are tedious, but a lack of clarity can muddle one's research. You can't study sports if you aren't clear about what you want to study, which is why mixed-bag studies are confused by the inclusion of board games, card games, dancing, cycling to work, window-shopping, and sunbathing. England's General Household Survey, for example, classifies housewives as sports participants if they walk to the bakery and the greengrocer's shop.[1] This does not seem reasonable. My working definition of *sports* sites them within a paradigm that is quite specific about sport's relationship to *play*, *games*, and *contests*.

People work because they have to; they play because they want to. The pleasures of *play* are intrinsic rather than extrinsic to the activity. In a word, play is autotelic (from *auto*, "its own," and *telos*, "goal, end, or purpose"). In theory, play "evokes an activity without constraint but also without consequences for the real world."[2] (In practice, of course, there may be all sorts of consequences.) This activity can be divided into two types—spontaneous play and rule-bound or regulated play.

Spontaneous play is impulsive, voluntary, and uncoerced. Examples abound. A boy sees a flat stone, picks it up, and sends it skipping across the still waters of a pond. A Nobel laureate delivering an acceptance speech amuses herself and the audience with an impromptu pun. Neither action is premeditated, and both are at least relatively free of cultural constraint. They provide us with an ecstatic sense of pure possibility.

The second type of play has rules and regulations to determine which actions are acceptable and which are not. These rules transform spontaneous play into *games*, which can, accordingly, be defined as rule-bound or regulated play. Leapfrog, chess, "playing house," and basketball are all games, some with rather simple rules, others governed by lengthy sets of regulations. Do the constraining rules and regulations contradict my assertion that play is autotelic? Not really. Not if we willingly surrender spontaneity for the sake of playful order. We continue to remain outside the domain of material necessity and we don't expect our games to feed or clothe or shelter us. We freely obey the rules we impose upon ourselves because they—the rules—are what constitute the game.

Of my four examples, chess and basketball are obviously different from leapfrog and "playing house." The first pair of games involves competition, the second does not. One can win a game of chess or basketball, but it makes no sense to ask who has won at leapfrog or "playing house." In other words, chess and basketball are *contests*. Anthropologists who ignore this competitive-noncompetitive distinction have come, wrongly, to the conclusion that some cultures have no games.[3]

A final distinction separates contests into two categories: those that require physical prowess, i.e., *sports*, and those that do not. Football and shuffleboard are handy examples of the first category, while Scrabble and poker will do to exemplify the second. The sports that have most excited the passions of participants and spectators have required much more physical prowess than a friendly game of shuffleboard. For good reason, sports heroes commonly demonstrate uncommon strength, speed, stamina, agility, dexterity, and endurance. It must be understood, however, that physical prowess is a necessary but not a sufficient characteristic of sports. The simplest sports require *some*— but not very much—intellectual effort. "Stay in your lane" should suffice as the last-minute instruction to a slow-witted sprinter. Other sports, like baseball, call for a considerable amount of mental alertness.

To summarize: sports can be defined as *autotelic physical contests*. On the basis of this definition, I have more than once proposed a simple inverted-tree diagram.

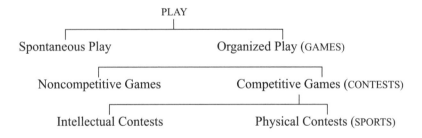

Despite the clarity of the definition, all sorts of questions arise. Some are easily answered. Is mountain climbing a sport? It is if one understands the activity as a strenuous contest between the climber and the mountain or as a competition among climbers eager to be the first to accomplish a difficult ascent. Are jogging and working out in a fitness studio sports? Here, too, it depends on whether or not the activity is done competitively. Automobile races present a different problem. Are the drivers in the *Le Mans Grand Prix* and the Indianapolis 500 really *athletes*? They are if one believes that physical skill and endurance are required to survive the grueling competition. What should one say about competitions in domestic activities such as weaving, sewing, and cornhusking? Although the amount of physical effort they require is not great, they fit my definition as clearly as do workplace competitions in logrolling, plowing, and calf-roping. The first group is seldom mentioned in histories of sports because men have almost always decided which physical contests are socially and culturally important and which are not. I am ready to welcome a history of sports that pays as much attention to women's contests—of all sorts—as it does to men's contests, but the source materials for this kind of radically revisionist history are not yet, and may never be, available.[4]

There is one question that threatens to upset my neatly arranged definitional applecart. Spontaneous play is autotelic, but reluctant children compelled by their parents or teachers to compete in a game of soccer are not really engaged in play for its own sake. Neither are the superstars of professional sports if their only motivation is a monthly million-dollar paycheck. "Radical autotelism" is an untenable position.[5] In the real world, as a practical matter, motives are usually mixed and often quite impossible to fathom. In the real world, people become involved in sports for all sorts of extrinsic reasons—for prestige, economic gain, course credit, improved cardiovascular fitness, stress reduction—as well as for the intrinsic pleasures of a physical contest. The psychological tests used to determine the motivations of today's athletes are blunt instruments, and they are obviously no help at all when we speculate about the motives of Roman gladiators or Heian-period Japanese archers. Unless we have evidence to the contrary, it is reasonable to give the players the benefit of a doubt and to assume that they really are motivated by at least a measure of intrinsic satisfaction, by the pleasure of finding, discovering, knowing, realizing, actualizing, and developing the self.[6] Michael Jordan, returning from retirement, did not *need* his paycheck. I believe him when he says that he loves basketball.

A number of theorists—mostly European—have analyzed sports to say what they *signify*, what they *mean*. Some have gone for essences. For Bernard Jeu, all sports were "a meditation on death and violence." For Michel Bouet, skiing suggested "the idea of spatial penetration." The ephemeral trail left upon the snow by the skier is "a mystification of the temporal by the spatial." The snow itself is "an embodiment of silence." I am fascinated by speculations like these, but—in the last analysis—I agree with anthropologists like Ommo Grupe who conclude that a sport means whatever the participants, embedded in their cultures, say it means. In the last analysis, the attribution of significance is what Gunter Gebauer termed "an essentially arbitrary process." The influential Dutch psychologist F.J.J. Buytendijk asserted that kicking games are *essentially* masculine while throwing games are *essentially* feminine. This tells us something about the state of Dutch culture in 1952. It tells us nothing about soccer and baseball, then or now.[7]

Although my initial paradigm of play–games–contests–sports is unhistorical, in that it purports to define these concepts and their relationships one to another wherever and whenever they occur, what follows this introductory chapter is a cultural *history* of sports that attempts to relate sports to *some* of their political, economic, social, religious, and cultural contexts. My emphasis is on the forms and functions of a number of exemplary sports as they have appeared at different times and places. To play with a bit of ancient insight: *Tempora mutantur, mutantur ludi in illis* (Times change and sports are changed with them). A refusal to recognize this mutability of form and function lies behind the dogmatic assertions—"sports = capitalist exploitation = patriarchal domination"—that appear, much too often, in journals devoted to the study of sports.[8]

Although "grand narratives" are definitely out of fashion among those who believe that we live in "postmodernity," much of what follows consists of narration explicitly or implicitly organized within a comprehensive historical framework derived, in part, from Max Weber and from Norbert Elias. Basic to this framework are three convictions:

(1) The formal–structural characteristics of modern sports are strikingly different from those of premodern sports. (2) Premodern sports have tended either to acquire the formal-structural characteristics of modern sports or to survive on the margins of the mainstream as what Raymond Williams called "residual culture." (3) The evolution from premodern to modern sports is an instance of what Elias called—somewhat tendentiously— "the civilizing process," in the course of which the members of a society internalize values that reduce the level of expressive (but not instrumental) interpersonal violence.

Modern (as opposed to premodern) sports can be defined by a set of seven interrelated formal-structural characteristics.[9] Preliminary discussion of them can be condensed, somewhat cryptically, into seven short paragraphs.

Secularism. Modern sports are not related to the transcendent realm of the sacred. Sports in premodern societies frequently occurred as an aspect of religious observance. The Olympic Games, for example, were sacred to Zeus, and Japanese *shinji-zumô* was performed at temple and shrine festivals.

Equality. Modern sports require, at least in theory, that everyone—including the elderly and the handicapped—be admitted to the game on the basis of his or her athletic ability. In addition, the rules must be the same for all contestants. Premodern sports frequently excluded people on the basis of social class, religion, ethnicity, or gender, and the rules for premodern sports often varied with variations in social status.

Specialization. Many modern team sports (rugby, soccer, and American football) have evolved from earlier, less differentiated games and many (baseball, cricket) have a gamut of specialized roles and playing positions. At the elite level, individual athletes rely on an ancillary team of supportive specialists. The Dutch Olympic swimmer Inge de Bruijn, for instance, arrived in Sydney with two coaches, two masseuses, two physiologists, a nutritionist, a sports psychologist, and a personal trainer.[10]

Bureaucratization. Local, regional, national, and international bureaucracies now administer every level of modern sports from Little League Baseball to the World Cup Final. Lacking this kind of administrative structure, premodern sports usually took place under the aegis of local political or religious authorities.

Rationalization. Modern sports are a prime example of what Max Weber called *Zweckrationalität* (instrumental rationality). Sports contests take place in built-to-purpose facilities where scientifically trained athletes compete with standardized equipment on the basis of constantly revised rules and regulations that are looked upon as means to an end. Rationalization leads also to abstraction, to what Georges Vigarello calls *déréalisation*.[11] The equestrian vaulter's whinnying, restlessly moving mount becomes the gymnast's quietly immobile "horse," and the backyard hurdler's leafy hedges are replaced by the track athlete's lightly constructed portable rectangles. In every way, premodern sports exhibited a much lower level of instrumental rationality.

Quantification. In modern sports, as in almost every aspect of our daily lives, we live in a world of numbers. At their panhellenic athletic festivals, the ancient Greeks measured neither the times runners ran nor the distances throwers threw (and they had no standardized units for temporal or spatial measurement in the unlikely event that they were concerned about the numbers).

Obsession with records. The unsurpassed quantified achievement, which is what we mean by a sports record, is a constant challenge to all who hope to surpass it.[12] André Obey, a French athlete and man of letters, wrote lyrically of his hope that his daughter would "one day recite the litany, not of battles but of records, more beautiful than the labors of Hercules."[13] Without the prerequisite of a quantified achievement, premodern athletes were unable to set—and were perhaps unable even to imagine—sports records.

For each of these generalizations about the stark contrast between the present and the past, there are exceptions. For example, the achievements of ancient Roman charioteers and seventeenth-century Japanese archers were quantified. There were, in other words, anticipations of modernity in sports as in other institutions. Isolated examples, however, do not constitute a system. In considering the contrast between premodern and modern sports, one must bear in mind that the characteristics of modernity are not a random collection of arbitrary attributes. They fit together like the pieces of a puzzle.

Unfortunately, modernization theories have fallen into unwarranted disfavor. The paradigm of modernization can be misinterpreted to imply that the observed changes occurred as part of some uniform and inevitable process that must of necessity and by some preordained schedule transform each and every aspect of each and every society in precisely the same way—which is nonsense. The paradigm of modernization can also be misused as a facile instrument of ethnocentric ethical judgment—as if modern ways were somehow a *moral* as well as a technological advance beyond traditional folkways. Although nineteenth-century observers may have felt optimism about the future, their children and grandchildren have experienced the adverse effects as well as the benefits of modernization. Toxic wastes and the threat of thermonuclear catastrophe are as much a part of modernity as are laser surgery and electronic telecommunications.

If the disavowal of assumptions about the alleged inevitability, ubiquity, and desirability of modernization seems like an inadequate response to criticism, one may reasonably ask if there is a better way, in the domain of sports, to understand the contrast between a medieval game of folk-football and the globally televised spectacle of soccer football's World Cup Final? In the last analysis, the *usefulness* of the modernization paradigm is the best argument for its continued use.

Notes

1   Chris Gratton and Peter Taylor, *Economics of Sport and Recreation* (London: Spon, 2000), p. 69.
2   Roger Caillois, *Les Jeux et les hommes* (Paris: Gallimard, 1958), p. 7.
3   John M. Roberts, Malcolm J. Arth, and Robert R. Bush, "Games in Culture," *American Anthropologist*, 61:4 (August 1959): 597–605.
4   David Belden, *L'Alpinisme* (Paris: L'Harmattan, 1994); Linda J. Borish, "'A Fair, Without the Fair, Is No Fair at All,'" *Journal of Sport History*, 24:2 (Summer 1997): 155–76. The main focus of my own history of women's sports is on sports that are played by both men and women; see *Women's Sports* (New York: Columbia University Press, 1991).
5   Bernard Suits, *The Grasshopper* (Toronto: University of Toronto Press, 1978), p. 146.
6   These are among the motives named by athletes studied in Michel Bouet's unsurpassed study, *Les Motivations des sportifs* (Paris: Éditions universitaires, 1969).
7   Bernard Jeu, "Toute-puissance et immortalité . . .," *Ethno-Psychologie*, 27:1 (March 1972): 20; see also his *Le Sport, la mort, la violence* (Paris: Éditions universitaires, 1972); Michel Bouet, *Signification du sport* (Paris: Éditions universitaires, 1968), pp. 211, 214; Ommo Grupe, *Vom Sinn des Sports* (Schorndorf: Karl Hofmann, 2000); Gunter Gebauer,

"Wettkampf als Gegenwelt," in *Aktuelle Probleme der Sportphilosophie*, ed. Hans Lenk (Schorndorf: Karl Hofmann, 1983), p. 345; F.J.J. Buytendijk, *Das Fußballspiel* (1952; Würzburg: Werkbund-Verlag, n.d.), pp. 19–20. In response to Buytendijk, see Hannelore Ratzeburg, "Fußball ist Frauensport," in *Frauen Bewegung Sport* (Hamburg: VSA, 1986), pp. 85–94.

8   I refer to "exemplary sports" because histories are different from encyclopedias. Readers curious about *midwam*, *milakia*, and the many other sports that I have not mentioned can consult the English translation of the *World Sports Encyclopedia*, edited by Wojciech Liponski (St. Paul, Minn.: MBI, 2003), which includes entries for more than three thousand sports.

9   Allen Guttmann, *From Ritual to Record* (New York: Columbia University Press, 1978), pp. 15–55.

10   Rick Reilly, "Unsynchronized Swimming," *Sports Illustrated*, 93 (October 18, 2000): 34.

11   Max Weber, *Wirtschaft und Gesellschaft*, 2 vols (1920); Cologne: Kiepenheuer & Witsch, 1964); Georges Vigarello, *Une Histoire culturelle du sport* (Paris: Robert Laffont, 1988).

12   Richard D. Mandell, "The Invention of the Sports Record," *Stadion*, 2:2 (1976): 250–64.

13   André Obey, *L'Orgue du stade* (Paris: Gallimard, 1924), p. 35.

Norbert Elias and Eric Dunning

THE QUEST FOR EXCITEMENT
IN LEISURE

[. . .]

AS FAR AS ONE CAN SEE, leisure activities as a social area for loosening non-leisure restraints are to be found in societies at all stages of development. The Dionysian festivals of the ancient Greeks – the religious excitement or 'enthusiasm', as Aristotle called it – and the carnivals of medieval Christian communities are examples. In former days, many types of religious activities had functions analogous to those which leisure activities have today – many leisure activities of our own time, particularly those of the 'mimetic' class have functions akin to those which some types of religious activities had in former days. But while pressures and restraints as well as special leisure areas for relieving and loosening them appear to exist in all known societies, their character and the whole balance between them changes in the course of a civilizing process. In the course of such a process, restraints upon the behaviour of people become all-embracing. They become more even, fluctuate less between extremes, and become internalized as a personal armour of more or less automatically operating self-control. However, close analysis of the long-term civilizing process indicates that social developments in this direction produce counter-moves towards a balancing loosening of social and personal restraints. One can observe balancing counter-moves of this kind in some areas of contemporary life, among them in the field of leisure. New developments in music and the theatre and new forms of singing and dancing are examples. Perhaps the more active spectator participation in sports events which is observable even in countries which are traditionally rather reserved such as Britain is another. They represent a moderate break through the ordinary cover of restraints and, particularly among the young, an enlargement of the scope and the depth of open excitement.

   In contemporary societies of this type, as one can observe, it is no longer a framework of religious activities and beliefs which provides scope for a balancing relaxation of restraints.

But whatever their character, the compensatory excitement and emotionality which assert themselves in some of the leisure activities in these societies – in connection with specific changes in their structure and particularly in the distribution of power between different age-groups – are themselves tempered by civilizing restraints. At the same time, the greater public tolerance with regard to the display of overt excitement in recent times shows only in a more pronounced and direct manner the general function of leisure activities, particularly that of the specific class we have mentioned. As a precise sociological term for this class is lacking, we have called it the 'mimetic' class. Most, though not all, leisure activities belong to it, from sports to music and drama, from murder films to Westerns, from hunting and fishing to racing and painting, from gambling and chess to swinging and rocking, and many others. Here, as elsewhere, the quest for excitement, for the Aristotelian 'enthusiasm', in our leisure activities is complementary to the control and restraint of overt emotionality in our ordinary life. One cannot understand the one without the other. [Here is a preliminary classifying scheme which we have called 'the sparetime spectrum'.] [. . .]

Sparetime activities: preliminary classification[1]

1   *Private work and family management*   To this class belong the many household activities including the provision of a home itself. All major and minor purchases, all the various personal financial transactions, all planning for the future belong here. So does the management of one's children, the whole family strategy including family disputes and many related tasks. All these activities require special aptitudes which have to be learned. This sphere as a whole tends to take up more time as the standard of living rises. As a field of research, apart from such problems as those of household expenditure, the field of private work and family management is still largely unexplored. Many of the activities connected with it are hard work. Much of it has to be done whether one likes it or not. After a time, it tends to become routinized in each family to a greater or lesser extent. One can hardly call it leisure.

2   *Rest*   To this class of activities belong sitting and smoking or knitting, daydreaming, pottering about the house, doing nothing in particular and, above all, sleeping. One may call this class of activities leisure, but it is clearly distinct from a host of other leisure activities mentioned later as representative of the mimetic class such as sport and theatre.

3   *Catering for biological needs*   To leave no room for misunderstanding: all the biological needs for which we have to cater, in our spare time as elsewhere, are socially patterned – eating and drinking as well as defecating, love-making as well as sleeping. These needs recur: one tries to satisfy them. They rise; they demand fulfilment. The fulfilment is pleasurable. They are stilled and abate, only to rise again later when the rhythm is repeated. Eating, drinking and love-making irradiate into other classes, directly or indirectly, particularly the class of sociability. They can all be – and they usually are – routinized up to a point but they can be and could also be in fact de-routinized from time to time in a more deliberate manner than is often the case. At the same time, they all have this in common with the mimetic class: they can provide heightened enjoyment provided one is able to cater for them in a non-routine manner, such as eating out for a change.

4   *Sociability*   This, too, is non-work though it may involve considerable effort. It ranges from highly formal to highly informal sociability with many intermediary grades. To this class belong activities which are still work-related such as visiting colleagues or superiors, going for an outing with the firm, as well as others which are not work-related such as going to a pub, to a club, to a restaurant or a party, gossiping with neighbours, being with other people without doing much else, as an end in itself. The types of sociability as a form of spending one's spare time, as far as one can see, differ greatly in different strata of society. Like classes 1 and 2, this class of spare-time activities still remains largely unexplored.

5   *The class of mimetic or play activities*[2]   Many enquiries into and discussions about leisure activities are focused on activities of this type. The others are often taken for granted. This enquiry, too, is mainly concerned with this class, for although a growing number of investigations are devoted to it, the distinguishing characteristics of this type of activities do not, in any of them, stand out very clearly for our understanding. Much attention has been devoted to single aspects or to single problems, relatively little to the basic structure, to the common characteristics of this class of activities. The activities themselves show great diversity. To this class belong such leisure activities as going to the theatre or a concert, to the races or the cinema, hunting, fishing, bridge, mountaineering, gambling, dancing and watching television. Activities in this class are spare time activities which have the character of leisure whether one takes part in them as actor or spectator, as long as one does not take part in them as a specialized occupation from which one earns a living; in such a case, they cease to be leisure activities and become a form of work, entailing all the obligations and restraints characteristic of work in societies of our type – even if the activities as such are felt to be highly enjoyable. [. . .]

The specific functions of sport, theatre, racing, parties and all the other activities and events usually associated with the term 'leisure', especially of all mimetic activities and events, have to be assessed in relation to [the] ubiquity and steadiness of excitement control [demanded in 'modern' societies]. This is the polarity with which we are concerned here. In the form of leisure events, particularly those of the mimetic class, our society provides for the need to experience the upsurge of strong emotions in public – for a type of excitement which does not disturb and endanger the relative orderliness of social life as the serious type of excitement is liable to do. [. . .]

We came across this problem first in connection with the study of football. At a later stage, one will have to consider the differences among types of mimetic events which we rank as higher and lower in the hierarchic order attributed to them. But in order to arrive at a stage of enquiry where that may be possible, it is first necessary to determine with greater precision the characteristics which mimetic events of all kinds have in common. One can perhaps see the problem better if one adds an example from the field of sport to those which have already been given. People may speak of the pleasurable excitement for which they look in all these pastimes in different terms. Young people may say after a performance by the Beatles that they 'got a kick' out of it. Older and more sedate people may say after a play they liked, 'I was greatly moved'. Football fans may tell you that they were 'thrilled'. But although there are differences which have to be explored, a strong element of pleasurable excitement and, as a necessary ingredient of the pleasure, a degree of anxiety and fear, is always present whether it is the tension-excitement derived from going to the races, especially when one has a little flutter on the side, or the much quieter but more profound excitement one may derive from listening to Beethoven's Ninth Symphony when the choir, singing Schiller's 'An die Freude', works up to its tremendous climax.

There are great variations in the way in which the pleasurable excitement, the enjoyable stirring of the emotions provided by leisure activities, can express itself, and, until we have studied in greater detail the connections between the structure of the leisure activities and that of the emotional resonance they find in actors or spectators, it would be premature to put forward even tentative explanations for the varieties of enjoyment provided.

The study of football, we found, with all its limitations, lends itself rather well, and perhaps better than many others, to a clarification of at least some of the basic problems which one encounters in the mimetic field. Here one can study very closely the rather complex correspondence between the dynamics of the mimetic event itself and the psychological dynamics of the spectators. [. . .]

It may not be easy to find a clear consensus with regard to the characteristics of plays or symphonies which provide a high and low degree of audience satisfaction, although the difficulties may not be insuperable even in the case of concerts in spite of the greater complexity of the problems. With regard to sport-games such as football, the task is simple. If one follows the game regularly one can learn to see, at least in broad outline, what kind of game figuration provides the optimum enjoyment: it is a prolonged battle on the football field between teams which are well matched in skill and strength. It is a game which a large crowd of spectators follows with mounting excitement, produced not only by the battle itself but also by the skill displayed by the players. It is a game which sways to and fro, in which the teams are so evenly matched that first one, then the other scores and the determination of each to score the decisive goal grows as time runs out. The tension of the play communicates itself visibly to the spectators. Their tension, their mounting excitement in turn communicates itself back to the players and so on until tension reaches a point where it can just be borne and contained without getting out of hand. If, in this manner, the excitement approaches a climax, and if then suddenly one's own team scores the decisive goal so that the excitement resolves itself in the happiness of triumph and jubilation, that is a great game which one will remember and about which one will talk for a long time – a really enjoyable game.

There are many shades and degrees of enjoyment and fulfilment which the *cognoscenti* can find in such a leisure activity. Not all, by any means, provide optimum fulfilment. A very exciting game may be lost by one's own side. In that case people as a rule will still carry home the after-taste of their pleasurable excitement, but this enjoyment will not be quite as unmixed as it is in the first case. Or a very good game might end in a draw. At this point, one already begins to enter an area of controversy. The consensus – very high in the cases we have mentioned – is likely to diminish until one reaches the other end of the scale where one finds again a high degree of consensus. In football, as in all other mimetic events, there are undoubted flops. For an enquiry into leisure satisfactions, it is no less relevant to study the distinguishing characteristics of flops than it is to study those which provide optimum fulfilment. Unsatisfactory games are for instance those where one side is so superior to the other that the tension is lacking; you know beforehand more or less who is going to win. There is hardly any surprise in the air and without surprise, no excitement. People do not get much pleasure out of such a game. One could give other examples, but the essentials have been mentioned.

It would not be difficult, then, to map the mimetic events of a particular type along a scale. One of its poles can be represented by leisure events which provide optimum enjoyment, the other by those which, with a high degree of consensus, are considered a flop. The majority of events, evidently, would lie between the two poles, but a good deal of information can be gained from an analysis of the two extremes. It could serve, and it has in fact served us to some extent, as a pilot study for the preparation of studies on a larger scale. Enquiry into the structure of events providing maximum and minimum satisfaction by itself contributed a great deal to the understanding of the correspondence between the social dynamics of a particular type of leisure event such as football and the personal dynamics leading to greater or lesser enjoyment on the part of individual participants. Although we are apt to classify the latter as psychological and the former as sociological, they are in fact wholly inseparable, for the greater or lesser enjoyment of those who participate in a particular type of leisure event, as actors or spectators, is the *raison d'être* for the existence of these events. It provides the criterion for the distinctive structure of leisure events, for distinguishing those which are successful and those which are a flop. Again, one can well imagine the development of leisure events which, on their part, open and educate their public to greater perceptiveness and enrichment. Academic divisions thus need not prevent the recognition of the intimate relationship between what may otherwise be separated in the form of physiological, psychological and sociological problems.

It would not be too difficult to design types of enquiries with regard to football and other sports which would make it possible to attack the same problem from the individual and the social levels at the same time, provided one is ready to use a unified theoretical framework. What has been said points in that direction. It would be quite possible, for instance, at least at the physiological level, by measuring changes in the pulse rate, heartbeat and breathing of spectators during a football game, to determine the most elementary aspects of the rising and falling waves of excitement among them. It would be equally possible, particularly if one were to use films, to determine the rising and falling waves in the tension-balance of a game. One could try to find out whether and in what ways the physiological aspects of spectator enjoyment and excitement differ in the presence of games at the optimum from those at the opposite end of the scale. Nor would it be difficult to design survey enquiries in order to enlarge our understanding of these correspondences between the social dynamics of games and the individual and crowd dynamics of spectators.

These examples indicate one of the ways in which empirical enquiries in the relatively controllable field of sport could serve as models for enquiries into other mimetic leisure activities from dog-racing to tragedy, from pushpin to poetry. By and large, we are still at a stage where ideas as to what *people* should do with their leisure time are apt to take precedence over studies of what they do in fact. Hence the former are not always based on a firm knowledge of the nature and the structure of existing leisure activities as they actually are.

Notes

1   This is the preliminary draft from which, after a number of experimental probes, the more precise and comprehensive typology of the 'spare-time spectrum' emerged. [See chapter 2 of the volume from which this edited extract is taken.]

2   The term 'play' can be employed in a variety of senses, and the looseness with which it is often used opens up the way for specific difficulties and misunderstandings. Although we have tried to indicate clearly the sense in which we use the term, it seemed useful to have at one's disposal a more specialized term for the class of spare-time activities to which we refer [as this fifth class of activities]. The choice of the term 'mimetic' will become clearer in the course of our essay.

Richard Gruneau

PROBLEMS OF AGENCY AND FREEDOM IN PLAY, GAMES, AND SPORT

As so often, the two dominant tendencies of bourgeois cultural studies—the sociology of the reduced but explicit "society" and the aesthetics of the excluded social remade as a specialized "art"—support and ratify each other in a significant division of labour. . . . It is this division, now ratified by confident disciplines, which a sociology of culture has to overcome and supercede [*sic*], insisting on what is always a whole and connected social material process.

—Raymond Williams, 1977

AT THE RISK OF considerable simplification, one can say that two related problems seem to have defined much of the core of sociological theory. The first might simply be called "the problem of human agency." Its expression can be found in the attempt to reconcile the tensions between voluntarism and determinism, freedom and constraint, and subject and object in social life and history. Stated more simply, the problem of agency involves an attempt to understand the degree to which human agents, whether individual or collective, are constrained to think and act in the ways they do.[1] The second problem might be labeled "the problem of class inequality and structural change." The essence of this problem lies in the attempt to identify and explain the rise and decline of specific socioeconomic structures and the cultural formations associated with them. Guided by these concerns, writers in sociology's classical tradition sought consciously to specify those social conditions that achieved a certain balance between freedom and domination, expression and repression at different moments in history, and to analyze the individual and collective actions that created these conditions.

I believe that to adequately understand the role of sport in social development, we must view sport in the context of the problems of human agency, class inequality, and structural change. [. . .]

The paradoxes of play, games, and sports

At some point play touches all of us. We play for fun, for fantasy, for excitement. In some cases our play seems spontaneous and freely innovative. In other cases it is more regulated and orderly. Yet, no matter what form it takes, there is a sense in which play often appears to transcend the practical affairs of everyday life. In play we seem to be absorbed in a reality that has its own limits of time and space, its own purposes and special emphases. Play allows us to be totally frivolous about important things in our work-centered lives or to be completely serious about things that are trivial. In either case, because we so deeply enjoy such apparent freedom, we are prone to celebrate play's expressive qualities and creative autonomy.

There is, of course, a great deal more to human play than apparent freedom of expression, peak experiences, or transcendental fantasy. While play certainly has its aura of unreality—its sense of abstract form—the nature and meaning of this form are greatly influenced by different social structural relations and cultural formations. When people organize their play in order to play with or against others, they create rules whose expressed purpose is to define standards for playing that are binding on all the players and that insulate the activity from the society-at-large. These rules are not spontaneous individual creations, rather they are cultural products that stem from the collective social experiences of the participants. Thus, while one of the purposes of rules is to separate play from reality, the very act of rule construction has the effect of embedding play deeply in the prevailing logic of social relations and thereby of diminishing its autonomy. For this reason, the study of play is haunted by a fundamental paradox. Play gives the impression of being an *independent and spontaneous* aspect of human action or agency and at the same time a *dependent* and *regulated* aspect of it.

The significance of this paradox becomes more evident if we consider the institutionalized character of so much of what passes for play in modern life. Games and sports, for example, by their very nature as highly structured, institutionally defined social practices, are frequently so overregulated and instrumental that they often seem only nominally related to play in its simplest expressive form. We tend to say that games and sports are "played," but the rules, customs, styles, and purposes of many of these activities seem almost completely determined by the social and cultural environments that frame them. In some cases, most notably high-level international "amateur" or commercial sports, it is often argued that little is left of play's freedom and creatively expressive character.

This relationship between the spontaneous and independent versus the regulated and dependent aspects of play, and those activities that are ostensibly "played" (e.g., games and sports), has attracted the attention of many writers and has always confused them. The confusions have been of two sorts. First, the range of human activities that can be classified as "playful" is extremely broad. Involved are activities as diverse as kicking a stray can in the street, singing in the shower, daydreaming, children's games, community recreation, and highly organized competitive sports. The definitional line between "play" and "sport" in these examples seems determined by the ways in which social structural and cultural forces have stylized play of certain types in an institutional fashion (i.e., a way of playing becomes the way of playing), but it is always difficult to know exactly where this line occurs.[2] One may find moments of play in big-time sports, but is it possible to argue that such sports in themselves are inherently playful?

The second set of confusions is even more complex. For all the generality of the themes discussed in the social analysis of play, games, or sports, many writers often appear to be writing about another subject altogether—a subject embedded in the seemingly paradoxical relationships between the autonomous and determined character of play, games, and sports, but not evident in the terms of discourse commonly used in the analysis of these activities. The real subject in question here is the relationship of play, games, and sports to the broader problems of human agency and freedom in social and individual life.

Consider, for example, some of the questions scholars have raised (not always consciously) in their assessments of the social significance of play, games, and sports. Is play an assertive, expressive act that involves an attempt to expand one's personal powers and exercise a form of creative control over an immediate environment? Or is it nothing more than simple fantasy, an escape from reality? If a free form of individual play is a dramatic culture-creating force, as so many writers seem to assert, does its organization into social or collective forms introduce such constraints that play loses its free culture-creating capacities and thereby becomes nothing more than a mirror of limiting social conditions? To what extent and under what circumstances can sport be seen as a negation of play or, conversely, as an example of play's "essential" character extended into the broader spheres of institutional life in society? Can it be said that play, games, and sports have any "essential" qualities at all? These questions are all ways of asking when and in what ways human beings exercise their powers as conscious, knowledgeable, historical actors both in and through play, games, and sports. Most of the questions also suggest concern about the nature of the social conditions under which specific actions might occur, about the kinds of limits these conditions set upon agency, and about whether these limits curtail freedom or provide the circumstances for its effective exercise.

Now on the last issue in particular, there has been a great debate among students of sport over the degree to which voluntary human actions and the free, playful expression of human powers are evident in the individual and collective experiences provided by games and sports. Much of the writing on sport dramatically proclaims that games and sports are notable forums for the voluntary expression of freedom, creative mastery, enjoyment, self-awareness, and human development. However, there are many writers who have been extremely critical of such assumptions. For example, in some theories it is suggested that sport is "determined" by social and cultural forces in a way that insures [sic] its separation from human freedom and human creative capacities. In other theories it is suggested that sport is cut off from human freedom only under certain circumstances. And, in still other theories, it is suggested that sport offers only nominal or illusory freedom at the expense of the development of people's powers to act politically in an unjust world that requires transformation. [. . .]

Conclusion: play, games, and sports as structure and agency

In this chapter I have attempted to identify a series of fundamental paradoxes about the seemingly autonomous and independent character of play, games, and sports and their dependent and regulated character. Most significant among these paradoxes are the roles played by the constitutive boundaries which are created in and out of human experience for the expressed purpose of separating play, games, and sporting activities from necessity and from social reality. These boundaries—seen variously as rules, traditions, beliefs, and organizational structures—have been interpreted by some writers as necessary for the effective exercise of freedom in and through play, games, and sports, and they have been seen by others as somehow inimical to the exercise of such freedom.

The writers I have discussed have all incorporated elements of these paradoxical features of play, games, and sports into their various analytic projects. Although their perceptions often differ on substantive issues, I have argued that Huizinga . . . and Guttmann . . . lapse into forms of idealist abstraction as ways of explaining the nature and significance of sport and its role in social development. As a result [both] have tended either to ignore or underplay the significance of material history as a part of the constituting processes of the intentions of players, and of the rules, traditions, beliefs, and organizations which define play, games, and sporting activities at different historical moments. Jean-Marie Brohm, on the other hand, goes too far in reducing games and sports (as distinct from spontaneous play) to simple reflections of materialist categories. Brohm's analyses are also frequently functionalist. Thus, as in the case of all functionalist analyses—whether Marxist or Liberal—the constitutive features of cultural production as a whole social and material process are downgraded and recast in the form of a systemic teleology: games and sports become features of the abstract needs or "requiremerits" of a reified functioning structure. [3]

In contradistinction to these views, the position I have been attempting to sketch out emphasizes that play, games, and sports ought to be seen as constitutive social practices whose meanings, metaphoric qualities, and regulatory structures are indissolubly connected to the making and remaking of ourselves as agents (individual and collective) in society. To put the matter another way, rather than view any feature of play, games, and sports as some sort of transhistorical essence, need, or transcendent metaphysical form, or rather than see them as activities simply reducible to a "separate" material reality, I am opting for a view where play, games, and sports are all regarded as irreducibly constitutive of our social being. They are, in differing ways, all forms of social practice. As a result, even their "essential" or formal qualities cannot be conceived of independently of the organizing principles, expectations, conflicts, and disappointments that define lived social experience at any given historical moment.

My position on the relationship of freedom to play, games, and sports is built on the above assumption. Simply stated, I would adopt Steven Lukes's view that human agents (viewed individually or collectively) consist historically in a set of expanding and contracting abilities and are always faced with expanding and contracting opportunities. [4] Together, these expansions and contractions constitute varying forms of "structured possibilities" which specify "the powers of agents, varying between agents and over time for any given agent." Given this, I would insist that if we are to avoid the simplistic view that spontaneous play is always an expression of freedom, and that "structured" games and sports are always constraining; or, conversely, the view that *all* games and sports are simply organized expressions of play and thereby guarantee "positive freedom"; then we will have to be more sensitive to the dialectical relationships between socially structured possibilities and human agency. In other words, we must struggle to avoid one-sided considerations of players as voluntary agents acting in the absence of constraining structures and of structures which do not allow for the creative and transformative capacities of players.

Obviously this struggle will require that we be quite specific about the nature of the limits and possibilities that can be associated with play, games, and sports as "structured" forms of human activity.[5] I think it crucial to recognize as a general principle that any given structure may have the capacity to both open up and close off different possibilities and choices. In the case of games and sports, for example, the rules, traditions, and organizations which define them may be both enabling and constraining. But how do we decide on the conditions which variously influence these options for different agents or groups of agents? The answer is a historical one, and requires that we situate our study of play, games, and sports in the context of understanding the historical struggle over the control of rules and resources in social life, and the ways in which this struggle relates to structured limits and possibilities.

Notes

1   See Steven Lukes, "Power and Structure," in *Essays in Social Theory*, p. 3.

2   I am not going to take the space here to conduct a detailed analysis of the literature devoted to clarifying formal definitions of play, games, and sports. I will only say that, although widespread variations exist in this literature on certain issues, there nonetheless appears to be an underlying consensus on the "formal" characteristics of each of these activities. Following Huizinga, play is usually seen to be a generic activity that is expressive, nonutilitarian, meaningful, and pursued for its own sake. Play can be seen to be spontaneous and unorganized or it can be more rule-bound, structured, and regulated. In the case of the latter, as Guttmann points out in *From Ritual to Record* (chap. 1), it is common to suggest that all forms of such organized play can be called games. There are, of course, great variations of game forms. Besides ranging in their degrees of organization and instrumentality, Roger Caillois (*Man, Play and Games*) has noted that games also emphasize characteristic elements such as mimicry, chance, vertigo, and competition. But it is the agon, the contest, that most writers in the West have been drawn to. Game-contests which involve a demonstration of physical exertion or skill have received special attention. The modern institutionalized versions of these game-contests provide the foundation for today's sports. As I suggest in the main body of this chapter, however, there is considerable debate about the degrees of overlap between play, games, and sports, especially over the degree to which sport can be *generically* related to play. I would argue strongly that much of this debate, focused as it is at the level of abstract classification, misses the point. For, ultimately, if the meanings and significations of play, games, and sports are historically and socially constituted, then wrangling over abstract definitions will only offer the broadest of ideal-typical insights at the expense of a more adequate understanding of the activities as contested and varying processes and practices. Play, games, and sports are not abstract "things" to be concretely defined; rather they are complex processes and relationships that can never be adequately encapsulated into rigid definitional schemes or formula. However, for some of the better attempts to work out such schemes and formulas see Alan Ingham and John Loy, "The Social System of Sport: A Humanistic Perspective," *Quest* 19 (1973); John Loy, "The Cultural System of Sport," *Quest* 29 (1978); Allen Guttmann, *From Ritual to Record* (chap. 1); and Alan Ingham, *American Sport in Transition: The Maturation of Industrial Capitalism and Its Impact on Sport*.

3   For a recent and detailed history of functionalism as a theoretical frame of reference in sociology see Giddens, "Functionalism: Après la lutte," in *Studies in Social and Political Theory*.

4   Lukes, "Power and Structure," p. 29.
5   I think it necessary to say an additional word here about the term "structure." "Structure" generally refers to two related conditions in social scientific research. Conventionally, it refers to a set of habitual or institutionalized social practices (relationships) that take on a systemic existence independent of any one individual's action (e.g., the social structure). It has also been used to refer to "deeper," more abstract relations which guide and shape human practices—relations expressed, for example, in the constitutive logic of language or in a particular measure of human production (e.g, the wage/labor or surplus value relation). As a general rule I am skeptical of completely "structuralist" explanations, especially those which separate abstract forces from human agency. Yet, I would argue strongly that in acknowledging the actions of agents, one must be careful not to lose sight of "determinations" not readily apparent in the experiences of individuals. Although particular arrangements of agents and particular sets of "rules" in social life are not completely "determining," they nonetheless define the nature of the limits within which agents act and the possibilities that are generally available to them. A recognition of these arrangements and rules, and an analysis of their structuring and restructuring through the actions of agents, is the core of any study of social development.

References

Caillois, R. *Man, Play and Games.* New York: The Free Press, 1961.

Giddens, A. *Studies in Social and Political Theory.* New York: Basic Books, 1977.

Guttmann, A. *From Ritual to Record: The Nature of Modern Sports.* New York: Columbia University Press, 1978.

Huizinga, J. *Homo Ludens.* Boston: Beacon Press, 1955.

Ingham, A.G. "American Sport in Transition: The Maturation of Industrial Capitalism and Its Impact on Sport." Ph.D. dissertation, University of Massachusetts, 1978.

Ingham, A.G. and Loy, J.W. "The Social System of Sport: A Humanistic Perspective." *Quest* 19, 1973.

Loy, J.W. "The Cultural System of Sport." *Quest* 29, 1978.

Lukes, S. *Essays in Social Theory.* New York: Columbia University Press, 1977.

Williams, R. *Marxism and Literature.* Oxford: Oxford University Press, 1977.

John Hargreaves

THE AUTONOMY OF SPORT

THE EXTENT TO WHICH a given cultural formation is enabled to feed the
power network also depends crucially, on its own particular character, that is on
those autonomous features which distinguish it from others as a specific type of cultural
formation. The realm of sport encompasses a bewildering diversity of radically different
kinds of activity, which defies a watertight definition – from the local hunt, and pub
darts match, village cricket, intercollegiate rowing and little-league football, to professionalized mass entertainments like the Football League, the Wimbledon Tennis Championships,
heavyweight boxing and horse-racing. Some of this activity plainly has little if any connection
with power. Despite the complexity, in our view sufficient distinguishing characteristics
can be identified which enable us to analyse how, in specific conditions, the sport–power
relation may be constituted.

First, sports to one or other degree embody an irreducible element of play. Play is
a type of activity having no extrinsic purpose or end, and as such it is a form of activity
which enjoys a universal appeal.[1] Sports play is not always unalloyed by other motives
or considerations – financial gain, prestige, etc. – and in specific instances (politicized
and professional sport for example) play may be by no means the most important element.
But the ludic impulse is, nevertheless, always present to some degree at least, existing
in tension with disciplined, organized aspects of sporting activity. Secondly, sports play
tends to be highly formalized: in many cases it is governed by very elaborate codes or
statutes. Sports play in this sense is far from being spontaneous: it is by convention rule-
oriented, and to have no rules would be a contradiction in terms. Whether the rules
are, in fact, being followed, is therefore an ever-present issue in the conduct of sports,
and in this sense we could say that not only are sports rule-oriented – they can be rule-
obsessed. Rule-structured play, like play in general, 'suspends reality', but in this case
through the acceptance of formal codes ordering the use of space, time and general
behaviour. In choosing to structure their activity thus, both participants and onlookers

are indulging in a form of 'play-acting', and in this respect the activity can be said to be 'unserious' or set aside from normal life. Play-acting is also involved in sporting activity when 'display' before an audience is one of the objectives. In addition, many sports were associated historically with the great festivals and to varying extents are still conducted in a spirit of festivity, a spirit which, by 'turning the world upside down', suspends while simultaneously challenging reality.[2]

Thirdly, sports involve some element of contest between participants. The rules which structure sporting contests, however, unlike those that structure competition and conflict in the real world, deliberately set out to equalize conditions of participation, that is, they are intended to be neutral, so that no one party to the contest has an advantage over the other(s). Since a contest within neutral rules makes the outcome inherently uncertain and in principle unpredictable, the very point of the activity is negated when either the rules are biased in favour of one or other party, or when the contestants are matched unevenly, for then the outcome does indeed become predictable. The uncertainty of the contest's outcome and the attendant tension it creates lends a unique excitement to sports, compared with other activities involving play, and it is probably one of the main reasons why sports become so often the subject of intense interest and emotion. Paradoxically, the deep commitment which sports often arouse [sic] also makes them deadly serious affairs as well as unserious ones.

Three other attributes of sporting activity which have received much less attention are crucial in any consideration of the sport–power relation. The play-acting, contest, and uncertainty elements ensure that sports are an intrinsically dramatic means of expression, and an audience in addition transforms them into a form of theatre.[3] We argue that sports fall within the province of 'the popular', and in so far as they take on the attribute of a dramatic performance they can be said to constitute a form of popular theatre, arguably the most popular contemporary form of theatre. Also, sports often seem to involve their participants, the audience and commentators, in much the same way as a theatrical performance: participants are enabled to put on a show and in a way, play a part; onlookers can identify with contestants; and both players and audience can project their thoughts and feelings. Sports can thus constitute regular public occasions for discourse on some of the basic themes of social life – success and failure, good and bad behaviour, ambition and achievement, discipline and effort and so on.

Secondly, strongly associated with the dramatic element, sporting activity is frequently characterized by ritual practices. Ritual activity is rule-governed behaviour of a symbolic character which draws the attention of its participants to objects of thought and feeling which are held to be of special significance. These may be multiple and occur at different levels of meaning. Ritual symbols 'condense many referents uniting them in a single cognitive and affective field. Each has a "fan" or spectrum of referents which tend to be interlinked by what is usually a simple mode of association, its very simplicity enabling it to interconnect a wide variety of signification'.[4] Ritual symbols may very powerfully denote, and connote as well, what is important to participants. Plainly, the ritual of official state occasions and that surrounding the major state institutions in Britain – the Coronation, the State Opening of Parliament, Remembrance Sunday, the ceremonial of the law courts, and so on – constitutes a powerful collective representation of the social and political order, focusing people's attention on the national symbols in a manner designed to invoke their loyalty, that is, it helps to define as authoritative certain preferred ways of seeing power and society. But we contend that much activity of a ritualized nature is effective in performing the same function precisely because it is not normally defined as 'political', and in our view, in specific conditions, many aspects of sports come into the category of 'political ritual'.[5]

Sports are extremely rich in symbolization and undoubtedly possess the capacity to represent social relationships in a particularly striking, preferred way. Notably, this is accomplished through the elaborate pageantry and ceremonial, even at the local level, with which organized sports surround themselves – the parades, opening and closing ceremonies, victory ceremonies, the special accoutrement worn by contestants and officials embellished well beyond technical necessity, the sacred connotations of sports settings, etc. We argue that not only the great national sports events, like the Football Association Cup Final, take on the character of a political ritual, when the Queen, the Prime Minister and other figures of state are in prominent attendance, the national anthem is sung, military bands march and play, 'Abide with Me' is sung and so on, but also that, for example, school sport and local community sport can function to symbolize or encode preferred views of the social order and thus legitimize power relations.

This should become clearer when we consider a further absolutely central characteristic of sports. Although the degree of physical input varies from sport to sport, the primary focus of attention in sport as a whole is the body and its attributes – its strength, skill, endurance, speed, grace, style, shape and general appearance are tested and/or put on display. This need not imply that the mind is not involved: judgement, motivation and aesthetic awareness are integral to physical performance; but it is the body that constitutes the most striking symbol as well as the material core of sporting activity. The primacy accorded to the mind in Western civilization has ensured that social analysis has been largely confined to the mechanisms for the transmission of values, norms, attitudes, emotions, ideologies, or whatever; and consequently the body has been almost entirely eliminated from social-science discourse.[6] Yet control over the appearance, treatment and functioning of the body is an important aspect of social order in all societies, and the elaboration and refinement of such forms of control has been critical in the emergence and development of modern societies.[7] Bodily appearance, posture, movement, gesture, facial expression, eye contact, adornment, smell – these elements constitute a message system or language structuring social action.[8] The body is, then, an emblem of society, and the ritual practices governing its usage symbolize and uphold fundamental social relationships and bind individuals to the social order.[9] Changes in body ritual and general body usage indicate fundamental changes in social relationships and interference with them has serious implications for social and cultural reproduction. The more the social situation exerts pressure on individuals the more the social demand for conformity tends to be expressed by demands for physical control. The greater the conceptual distancing between social and physical bodies, the more threatening is the loss of control over the body and body processes to the social order. Just as the child in becoming a native speaker learns the requirements of society, so the child learning the body code also learns the social requirements. In so far as body appearance and usage are integral to the conduct of sports, these considerations point to the ways in which sports as ritual practices may function to symbolize and uphold the social order and thus feed the power network.

We argue not only that the body symbolizes power relations, but furthermore, that power is literally incorporated or invested in the body, most obviously perhaps through such practices as gymnastic exercises, muscle-building, nudism, practices glorifying the body beautiful, and insistent, meticulous work on the bodies of children, hospital patients, keep-fit enthusiasts and sports participants. Such work reproduces the social body: it exemplifies the materiality of power and culture in the sense that social relations are the outcome of material operations on the bodies of individuals carried out with the aid of a vast economy and technology of control. The body is not the object of consensus – it is the site of social struggles, indeed, we can say there is a battle for control of the body.[10] In holding that sports constitute one of the main arenas where that struggle ensues, we take the view that the restrictive, relatively ponderous forms of control perceived as a prerequisite for the efficient functioning of industrial capitalism in the nineteenth and earlier twentieth century are no longer needed, and that sports are increasingly implicated in a new, currently emergent form of control.[11] Under the impact of consumer culture especially, the restrictive deployment of sexuality for example, is attenuated and sexuality is now deployed more through techniques of eroticization. Instead of repression we have control by stimulation. The body is clearly an object of crucial importance in consumer culture and its supply industries; and sports, together with fashion, eating and drinking outside the home, cooking, dieting, keep-fit therapy, other physically active leisure, advertising imagery, and a battery of aids to sexual attractiveness, are deployed in a constantly elaborating programme whose objective is the production of the new 'normalized' individual.

To thematize sport as an object of struggle, control and resistance, that is as an arena for the play of power relations, is of course ultimately to thematize its achievements with respect to human freedom and implicitly to raise the question of the transformational potential of sport in this regard. Societies like Britain and others to which organized sport spread from these shores, would be, in a genuine sense, unquestionably different places in its absence.[12] Whether they would be better places without sports depends on one's value standpoint. We do not attempt to address this important, vexacious question although plainly our study is value-oriented in its choice of problem to investigate. We consider the achievements of sport instead, with specific reference to the effects on the power position of subordinate groups and, in particular, its effect on the trajectory of the British working class. Broadly speaking, we consider sports somewhat of a mixed blessing from this point of view. Logically, we do consider it to be part of the analyst's task to identify those points at which involvement in sport contains a potential for going beyond the present power balance. In our conclusion we tentatively suggest a number of ways sport–power relations may generate a potential for evening-up somewhat the present unequal power balance in Britain. Whether one wishes to recommend them as points to which pressure should be applied, and develop strategies for doing so, is a matter of one's political commitment. For what it is worth, it seems to us that Britain would be a better place if such a change were to come about.

Notes

1   J. Huizinga, *Homo Ludens* (Paladin, London, 1970). See also R. Caillois, *Man, Play and Games* (Free Press, New York, 1961); R. Sennett, *The Fall of Public Man* (Cambridge University Press, Cambridge, 1977).

2   C. Hill, *The World Turned Upside Down* (Penguin, London, 1975); P. Burke, *Popular Culture in Early Modern Europe* (Temple Smith, London, 1978).

3   G. Stone, 'American Sports, Play, and Display', in E. Dunning (ed.), *The Sociology of Sport* (Cass, London, 1971).

4   V.W. Turner, 'Symbols in Ndembu Ritual', in D. Emmett and A. McIntyre (eds), *Sociological Theory and Philosophical Analysis* (Macmillan, London, 1970).

5   S. Lukes, 'Political Ritual and Social Integration', *Sociology*, 9 (2), (1975).

6   Foucault is the outstanding exception. See also B. Turner, *The Body and Society* (Basil Blackwell, Oxford, 1984).

7   N. Elias, *The Civilizing Process* (Basil Blackwell, Oxford, 1982), Vol. 1.

8   J. Benthall and T. Polhemus (eds), *The Body as a Means of Expression* (Allen Lane, London, 1975).

9   M. Douglas, *Natural Symbols* (Penguin, Harmondsworth, 1973).

10   P. Bourdieu, 'Sport and Social Class', *Social Science Information* (17 June 1978) notes this, but does not give it the analytical importance that Foucault does.

11   Z. Bauman, 'Industrialization, Consumerism, and Power', *Theory, Culture, and Society*, 1 (2), (1983). Bauman does not refer to sport, as such, in this connection.

12   See R. Gruneau, *Class, Sports and Social Development* (University of Massachusetts Press, Amherst, 1983) for an insightful analysis of Canadian sport in this respect.

Jennifer Hargreaves

THEORIES OF SPORTS
The neglect of gender

[. . .]

A COMMON CHARACTERISTIC of the various sports sociology perspectives is the marginalization of women's experiences and relationships of gender. In this respect, the history of sports sociology reflects the long history of male domination of modern sports and dominant ideas about sexual difference. Sports history and sociology reflect the male dominance of academic discourse.

It has been particularly difficult to transcend traditional assumptions that differences between the sexes are biological rather than cultural, and that feminine- and masculine-appropriate sports and male sporting superiority are in the 'natural' order of things. The notion that human behaviour is parallel in many ways to that of other primates underpins the argument that differing cultural behaviour between men and women is rooted in biology:

> we behave culturally because it is in our nature to behave culturally, because natural selection has produced an animal that has to behave culturally, that has to invent rules, make myths, speak languages, and form men's clubs, in the same way that the hamadryas baboon has to form harems, adopt infants, and bite its wives on the neck.
>
> (Tiger and Fox 1971: 20)

Although this extreme version of biological determinism is not prevalent in sports sociology, nevertheless biological determinism is influential in the general discourse of sports academia. For example, Desmond Morris's (1981) explanations of human aggression in sports as instinctive male behaviour are popular and influential; in the elite field of cultural analysis, the argument that sports are the 'natural' domains of men because of the innately different biological and psychological natures of men and women, has been given legitimacy (Carroll 1986); and the ideology of sexual difference is validated in the sports sciences (Hargreaves 1982: 2). To explain the cultural at the level of the biological encourages the exaggeration and approval of analyses based on distinctions between men and women, and masks the complex relationship between the biological and the cultural. As Paul Willis (1982: 119) points out, 'to know, more exactly, why it is that women can muster only 90% of a man's strength cannot help us to comprehend, explain, or change the massive feeling in our society that a woman has no business flexing her muscles anyway'.

Although sociologists of sport and leisure have provided a critique of biological determinism, at the same time they are implicated in the reproduction of ideas about sexual difference through the content and organization of their own work. There have been three main approaches: first, to disregard women by using the term 'sports' unproblematically, ignoring that what is really being examined is *male* sports from which generalizations are made about the experiences of all humans, and to refer to 'society' as if it is a single community in respect of men and women (Dunning 1971; Parker 1976). The second approach, which has been a reaction to the influence of feminism, is to devote some space to female sports and discussions of gender (usually a separate chapter or section) in an essentially male-oriented account (Coakley 1990; Elias and Dunning 1986; John Hargreaves 1986; Jarvie 1991). There is a tendency in both these approaches to fail to distinguish between sex and gender and implicitly to incorporate male-defined definitions and values. This book is characterized by the third, specifically feminist and minority perspective, which is a sociology exclusively of female sports (Boutilier and San Giovanni 1983; Lenskyj 1986). The last approach, unlike the other two, does not construct the female as 'the Other', but rather attempts to subvert dominant gender relations in sports sociology. However, because the whole of the history of modern sports has been based on gender divisions, even radical accounts of women's sports tend to focus on perceived *differences* between men and women, rather than on the less obvious *relations* of power between them. In general, therefore, sports sociology texts do not give equal treatment to male and female sports or integrate gender relations thoroughly into their analyses. [. . .]

In an attempt to explain theoretically the complexities of the relationship between freedom and constraint in sports, theorists have turned to the work of Antonio Gramsci (1971; see also Anderson 1976), and specifically to the concept of 'hegemony'. Hegemony has been used to explain continuities *and* discontinuities in sports: the ways in which dominant meanings and interests which are inherited from past traditions engender opposition and have to be defended, while new meanings and different interests are constantly being worked out and struggled for (see Chapters 1 and 2 in Hargreaves 1982; Clarke and Critcher 1985; Gruneau 1983, 1988; John Hargreaves 1986). Hegemonic configurations of power are understood to be part of a continual process of change which incorporates negotiation and accommodation, a 'lived system of meanings and values – constitutive and constituting' (Williams 1977: 110).

Hegemony describes a form of control which is *persuasive*, rather than coercive. It is understood to be the result of people's positive reactions to values and beliefs, which, in specific social and historical situations, support established social relations and structures of power. This is very different from straightforward indoctrination. Hegemony resists the idea that people are passive recipients of culture and keeps intact what is arguably the inherent *humanism* of Marxism. Hegemony embodies a sense of culture as a way of life imbued with systems of meanings and values which are *actively* created by individuals and groups in different social settings, such as families, schools, the media, leisure contexts and sports. Culture is not assumed to be the 'whole of society', it is analytically distinct from political and economic processes, but, together with them, makes up the totality of social relations. Economic and cultural forces are assigned mutually constitutive roles, rather than the former having a determining effect upon the latter. The concept of hegemony proposes a dialectical relationship between individuals and society, accounting for ways in which individuals are both determined and determining, and it allows for cultural experiences such as sports to be understood as *both* exploitative *and* worthwhile (Gramsci 1971; Anderson 1976; Williams 1977).

Hegemony operates essentially as a result of the subtle effects of ideology – a material effect which is confirmed by the mundane realities of people's lives, through which it becomes 'commonsense' (Larrain 1979). Because sports are vastly popular, and can be compelling and enjoyable, they are important vehicles for the transmission of ideology. But hegemony is never total: although the specific task of ideology is to legitimize dominant power relations and produce cultural continuity, dominant ideas are not the only ones – there is always the potential for oppositional ideas to subvert dominant ones and lead to cultural change. Dominant and subordinate groups are not necessarily, therefore, unambiguously winners or losers.

Ideology is rooted in human 'praxis' – an essentially social activity in which ideas and meanings cannot be separated from action. New ideas about sports cannot *change* them, they can only, possibly, *lead* to change; to become real they have to be put into practice, and hence the key to change is the way people produce their lives in common. Ideas and meanings evolve, show continuity and undergo change, not because of their internal content, but because people interrelate with one another in particular social contexts. Sports are thus conceived as constitutive processes – parts of life that are structured by society and history, but also the result of actions and changing relationships. In this formulation, consciousness is not passive, but incomplete, inconsistent and transitory. Hegemony theorists do not view sports as 'all-or-nothing' phenomena, as determinist interpretations imply, but as areas of life which contain contradictions. In this formulation, it is argued that there is neither total incorporation into existing sports structures, nor absolute rejection of them.

Applying the concept of hegemony to the histories of sports enables them to be understood as a series of struggles for power between dominant and subordinate groups – the result of conflicting interests over unequal sports resources in specific social contexts. However, antagonistic class relations have provided the focus for such accounts, and although reference has been made to the relationship between class and gender, and even to the way that class and gender divisions are constructed *together*, there have been no attempts to explore this relationship rigorously or to look at the specific complexities of male hegemony (Clarke and Critcher 1985; Gruneau 1983, 1988; John Hargreaves 1986). Because of the relative silence on women's sports and gender divisions, there is an implication that class is the root cause of women's as well as men's oppression in sports, and that problems of gender are secondary. This is the position also of orthodox and structuralist Marxists and it has serious theoretical limitations because it does not deal with the complexities of the relationship between, as well as the relative independence of, capitalist relations and patriarchal relations.

However, it is possible to apply the concept of hegemony specifically to male leadership and domination of sports (J.A. Hargreaves 1986). Male interests predominate in most sports, and in many of them male hegemony has been more complete and more resistant to change than in other areas of culture. Nevertheless, male hegemony in sports has never been static and absolute, but is a constantly shifting process which incorporates both reactionary *and* liberating features of gender relations. The concept of male hegemony recognizes the advantages experienced by men, in general, in relation to women, but recognizes also the inability of men to gain total control. Some men and some women support, accommodate, or collude in existing patterns of discrimination in sports that are specific to capitalism and to male domination while other men and women oppose them and struggle for change. Male hegemony is not a simple male vs female opposition, which is how it is often presented, but complex and changing.

Hegemony theory may provide a better framework for understanding how, in sports, as in other cultural activities, gender relations are part of a complex process specific to capitalist social relations. The complexities and contradictions of women's sports embody specific economic and political arrangements which intersect with such factors as class, age and ethnicity, as well as gender relations. The crux of feminist criticisms of all varieties of Marxism is that sexual categories are not intrinsic to Marxist concepts, but have only been appended to them. This was true of all sports sociology until the 1980s, when specifically feminist versions emerged. . . .

References

Anderson, P. (1976–7), 'The Antinomies of Antonio Gramsci', in *New Left Review*, No. 100.

Boutilier, M. and San Govanni, L. (1983), *The Sporting Woman*, Champaign, Ill.: Human Kinetics.

Carroll, J. (1986), 'Sport, Virtue and Grace', in *Theory, Culture and Society*, Vol. 3, No. 1: 91–9.

Clarke, J. and Critcher, C. (1985), *The Devil Makes Work: Leisure in Capitalist Britain*, London: Macmillan.

Coakley, J. (1990), *Sport in Society*, 4th edn, St Louis: Times Mirror.

Dunning, E. (ed.) (1971), *The Sociology of Sport*, London: Frank Cass.

Elias, N. and Dunning E. (1986), *Quest for Excitement: Sport and Leisure in the Civilizing Process*, Oxford: Basil Blackwell.

Gramsci, A. (1971), *Selections from the Prison Notebooks*, Q. Hoare and P. Nowell Smith (eds), London: Lawrence & Wishart.

Gruneau, R. (1983), *Class, Sport[s] and Social Development*, Amherst, Mass, University of Massachusetts Press.

Gruneau, R. (1988), *Popular Cultures and Political Practices*, Toronto: Garamond Press.

Hargreaves, J.A. (ed.) (1982), *Sport, Culture and Ideology*, London: Routledge & Kegan Paul.

Hargreaves, J.A. (1986), 'Where's the Virtue? Where's the Grace? A Discussion of the Social Production of Gender Relations in and through Sport', in *Theory, Culture and Society*, Vol. 3, No. 1: 109–23.

Hargreaves, John (1986), *Sport, Power and Culture*, Cambridge: Polity Press.

Jarvie, G. (ed.) (1991), *Sport, Racism and Ethnicity*, London: Falmer Press.

Larrain, J. (1979), *The Concept of Ideology*, London: Hutchinson.

Lenskyj, H. (1986), *Out of Bounds: Women, Sport and Sexuality*, Toronto: Women's Press.

Morris, D. (1981), *The Soccer Tribe*, London: Cape.

Parker, S. (1976), *The Sociology of Leisure*, London: Allen & Unwin.

Tiger, L. and Fox, R. (1971), *The Imperial Animal*, New York: Holt, Rinehart & Winston.

Williams, R. (1977), *Marxism and Literature*, Oxford: Oxford University Press.

Willis, P. (1982), 'Women in Sport in Ideology', in J.A. Hargreaves (ed.), *Sport, Culture and Ideology*, London: Routledge & Kegan Paul.

SECTION TWO

Histories

INTRODUCTION

THERE IS WIDESPREAD RECOGNITION that the most prominent forms
of top-level or elite sport have become increasingly international, and that sport can
therefore be seen as an indicator of globalization. The indisputably important theme of
globalization is covered in the Afterword to this Reader. In an introductory phase of
study, though, it remains essential to understand the forces that have shaped the present
in which we are interested. If sport is about tradition and memory, and different sports
draw upon different sources of tradition and memory, an historical understanding is not
a mere option: for an adequate grounding in sport studies, it is essential to have some
grasp of the primary historical forces and influences. The Readings in this section straddle
three centuries, and are chosen with a focus upon the social and cultural history of sport
in Britain.

Modern sports did not spring from nowhere. They were creations of the forces and
trends of their time. And it can be argued that they displaced well-established activities
(or practices). The first Reading is from **Robert W. Malcolmson**'s major study of popular
recreations in English society from, 1700 to 1850: it identifies the forces of social change
in the late 1700s and the early 1800s that led to the demise of more traditional popular
recreations. He talks of a 'new, more militant morality' that took hold among the influential
social groups and identifies which these groups were, and what their motives were in
opposing traditional forms of sport and play. Malcolmson's study is social history at its
most rigorous and impressive too. Look at where his evidence comes from. Obviously,
historians must work with documents. What kind of documents does Malcolmson draw
upon? Malcolmson himself divides his primary sources into five categories: books, sermons,

essays, pamphlets and tracts of the historical time, relevant to popular recreations; local studies from the past; literary sources such as autobiographies, memoirs, journals, diaries and poetry; parliamentary papers; and newspapers and periodicals. His secondary sources include theses, essays and articles, and books. Drawing on such an extensive range of materials, what is the balance, in this kind of historical writing, between evidence and analysis, narrative and argument?

Effective forces may have been mobilized against traditional sports and pastimes, but 'old ways of playing', as British historian **Richard Holt** writes, have in certain circumstances persisted. The Reading on 'survival and adaptation' looks at cock-fighting, bull-fighting and dog-fighting, and the ways in which these sorts of activities resisted reform movements. Most importantly, he shows what kinds of communities were most conducive to the survival of popular traditions, and portrays the nature of the wider culture in which such traditions could survive. These examples include the regional sport of 'knur and spell', and illustrate vividly the central theme of Holt's ground-breaking and comprehensive study, the analysis of the dynamics of continuity and change in Britain's sport history.

One of the most enduring legacies of Britain's sport history has been the model of team games established in the public schools in the nineteenth century, and the third and fourth Readings are concerned with the values that these practices represented. **J.A. Mangan**'s pioneering work provides the first of these Readings, from the opening section of his study of athleticism as it was established in the public schools of the nineteenth and early twentieth centuries. He sees athleticism as an educational ideology, and that ideology as an influence in spheres – such as professional adult life and war – far beyond the school classroom or playing field. The founder of the modern Olympic Games, Baron Pierre de Coubertin, was an admirer of the athleticist ideology, and its adoption by the ancient universities of England, Oxford and Cambridge, as well as the US Ivy-league universities such as Harvard and Yale. Think how the model of sport established in these schools for elite British males changed and evolved in different settings and future historical periods. What, then, was on offer for the schoolgirls of Britain's privileged classes? **Gillian Avery**'s history of girls' independent schools shows that the schoolteachers in the girls' schools included physical education zealots and converts to the cause of physical activity as training for life. When reading the accounts gathered by Avery, note what forms of activity these initiatives took. And how would you best summarize the shift in the significance of games that took place at the turn of the nineteenth and twentieth centuries? Look carefully at how Avery has based her study upon the analysis of memoirs, reports, and institutional documents and records.

While the educated and privileged classes in Britain were inculcated into the spirit of team games and athleticist pursuits, much effort was expended to extend the benefits of sport and exercise in other areas. Concern was expressed in Victorian Britain about the effects of new industrial and urban developments, and the 'new athleticism', as **Peter Bailey** calls it in the fifth Reading in this section, was seen as a means of producing a healthier populace (to make a better army), or even of uniting different social groups. Rational recreation – forms of sport and leisure that could be seen as improving or reforming – was something that was seen as good for all social classes. Bailey shows what influences underlay this spread of athleticism: as you read his work, think how in more recent times moralizers and governments may have come up with the same rationale for sport and forms of exercise.

Reformers and apologists for the new forms of physical education, team games and exercise, the rational recreationists, talked a language of social harmony, a project that in reality was an attempt to bring together social groups and classes. **Hugh Cunningham**, in the sixth Reading, examines the social impacts of these attempts. Cricket is a primary focus in this Reading, and the 'process of appropriation' the main conceptual emphasis. Who was appropriating what in this example, and for what reasons? When he considers other sport and leisure institutions – working-men's clubs and football, for instance – he concludes that ideologies imposed from above did not necessarily have the desired effects: in football, working-class players and teams might accept sponsorship and patronage from the middle classes, but without submitting to their 'control and values' (p. 128 of Cunningham original). Also, the middle classes went their own way, aping the aristocracy, appropriating popular forms for themselves, and inventing new class-specific sport and leisure forms. So what is Cunningham's overall conclusion about the use of sport and leisure to bring people together in Victorian England?

In the penultimate Reading of the section the focus is upon professional football. Athleticism generated a code of playing sport that celebrated the notion of fair play, its associated values and the ethos of the amateur. The tensions between amateur and professional were to dominate the development of British sport for much of the subsequent century. Here, English social historian **Tony Mason** provides a revealing account of the ways in which these tensions framed the early development of football in England. Note the Football Association's compromise at its special general meeting in 1885. If it had not made such a compromise, perhaps the United Kingdom might today have had one national footballing side for the single nation-state – discuss.

The final Reading in the section draws from vivid oral historical testimony on working-class culture in inter-war Salford and Manchester (in north-west England). English historian **Andrew Davies** documents the male-dominated sport and leisure practices of the working-class men of those communities. The importance of the pub – remember, this was noted by Malcolmson at the end of the first Reading in this section – is strongly emphasized, as is the significance of local sports. Not everyone could afford to watch professional football; nor, in periods of unemployment and acute poverty, frequent the pub. Do Davies's oral historical testimonies describe an homogeneous working-class culture of sport?

COMMENTARY AND FURTHER READING

Taken together, these Readings provided cameos of sport's place in English society at different points in the general history of the development of sport. It is clear that sport has multiple histories, not one simple, timeline-able history. The historical task is to periodize the development of particular sports, to identify and trace the impact of the most influential initiatives, to understand the motivations of those who established, played and watched the evolving sports. It is not adequate to offer some children's encyclopaedic style of historical account, or what I have called a Book of Genesis approach to sport history (*The Game's Up: Essays in the Cultural Analysis of Sport, Leisure and Popular Culture*, Aldershot, Ashgate, 1999: 34–5). In such approaches, the story of sport is related as a self-generating history, with little sense of sport's cultural distinctiveness and social significance. These Readings have been selected to avoid such a restricted approach, and some obvious themes come to the fore in the selection: the male-dominated nature of sports (in both pre-industrial and more recent historical contexts), the influence of team games and the British model of sport in its athleticist ideology and amateur code, the emergence of professional and more commercialized forms of sport, the local nature of some sports, the contribution of sport to class culture or the experience of community, and the processes of appropriation and contestation in the making of modern sport.

One way of following up these Readings is to pick a case study of your own, choosing one particular sport, and consider how these themes relate to the social history of that sport. An outstanding model for this is available in Tony Mason's *Sport in Britain: A Social History* (Cambridge, Cambridge University Press, 1989), in which Mason and eight other scholars have written historical accounts of ten of the most popular sports of the day (according to evidence about playing and watching evidence): angling, athletics, boxing, cricket, football, golf, horse-racing, lawn tennis, rowing, and rugby union. Mason reminds us that sport's 'changes and continuities cannot be understood without some awareness of the wider world' (p. 10). Look at the cases in Mason's book, and consider what further changes might have occurred in the contemporary history of the sport during the 1990s and the early 2000s. For post-Second World War accounts of the social place of sport, see too Richard Holt and Tony Mason's *Sport in Britain 1945–2000* (Oxford, Blackwell, 2000), and Martin Polley, *Moving the Goalposts: A History of Sport and Society since 1945* (London and New York, Routledge, 1998).

On the history of women's sports, consult Jennifer Hargreaves, *Sporting Females: Critical Issues in the History and Sociology of Women's Sports* (London and New York, Routledge, 1994). Hargreaves goes into rigorous and marvellous detail on the persistent marginalization of women in the story of the development of modern sport, and shows the extensive influence of social class upon the limited options available to women.

The importance of sport in the context of local culture is covered in Alan Tomlinson's *Sport and Leisure Cultures* (Minnesota, MN, University of Minneapolis Press, 2005): in Chapters Eight and Nine, the contributions of cricket and 'knur and spell' to community and class-cultural identity are explored. See also Jeffrey Hill and Jack Williams (eds), *Sport and Identity in the North of England* (Keele, Keele University Press, 1996): an excellent collection of studies exploring issues of local identity.

Historical approaches are covered in Eric G. Dunning, Joseph A. Maguire and Robert E. Pearton's edited collection *The Sports Process: A Comparative and Developmental Approach* (Champaign, IL, Human Kinetics, 1993), which includes an analysis by Allen Guttmann of the cultural diffusion of sports, and a discussion by Joseph Maguire of the global sport development represented by the arrival of American football in Britain. More historical analyses are provided in the collection *Sport Histories: Figurational Studies of the Development of Modern Sports* (London and New York, Routledge, 2004), edited by Eric Dunning, Dominic Malcolm and Ivan Waddington.

Why study history? This is not a question confined to sport studies, and the US sociologist C. Wright Mills dedicated a chapter to a discussion of 'the uses of history' in his 1959 book *The Sociological Imagination* (Harmondsworth, Penguin, 1970). For him, 'every well-considered social study . . . requires a historical scope of conception and a full use of historical materials' (pp. 161–2). We know that the present is a product of the past. Only with an informed historical sensitivity can we identify key shifts and discontinuities, processes of social and cultural change, which have taken sports in one direction rather than another.

The study of the history of sport has flourished in the last three decades in the United Kingdom, and in selecting case studies and topics, students entering the field would be well advised to avoid self-promotional websites riddled with uncorroborated claims, and instead work through the relevant articles in specialist journals such as *The International Journal of the History of Sport* and *Sport in History*. Both journals dedicate certain issues to particular themes, and in August 2006 *Sport in History* (Vol. 26, No. 2) examined the nature and impact of Roger Bannister's first four-minute mile achieved in May 1954. This is another way of studying sport as a kind of cultural history: take a single sporting moment or achievement, and ask where it came from, what it has meant and how it has impacted on the future. In doing this, though, never ignore the 'wider world' which Tony Mason, and all the contributions in this section of the Reader, recognize as the key to undertaking a meaningful study of the social history of sport.

Robert W. Malcolmson

SOCIAL CHANGE

[. . .]

W E [HAVE] EMPHASIZED the remarkably conservative sentiments, the paternalistic norms and patterns of behaviour, which are evident in the culture of the first half of the eighteenth century. Many gentlemen, with their respect for antiquity, were favourably disposed to tradition, to ritual and ceremony (especially when the ceremony reinforced their own authority), to robust and manly sports, to festive indulgences (as long as they were not too disorderly or expensive), to old, time-honoured customs; and they were little inclined to meddle with the people's affairs on the grounds of religion or morality. Old-fashioned paternalism included a large dose of tolerance – tolerance, of course, within certain well understood limits – and as J.H. Plumb has recently reminded us, 'Patriarchalism remained a powerful feature in English social attitudes' after the Restoration.[1] A defence of the Book of Sports, published in 1708, was just one expression of this hardy strain of Tory traditionalism, vehemently anti-puritan in temper:

> from that time [the death of Charles I] to this, we have been loaded with the pretended Statutes of Reformation; Laws, which if they were to be strictly executed, a Man must not be allow'd to drink a Pot of Ale, or take a Walk in the Fields, or play at Cudgels, or go to the Morrice Dancers, or any such innocent things on the Sabbath Day. But, Thanks be to God, the Awe of these things, which by the Policy of our Puritanical Invaders, was impressed on the Minds of Our People, begins to wear off again; and were we but once rid of some of our pretended Zealots for good Manners, whose Pretences have still made too much Impression, even in our Days; We might have some Hopes that those Days of Liberty might be restor'd . . .[2]

The puritan outlook, however, was by no means banished. Restoration and eighteenth-century dissent helped to keep alive at least some of the old belief, including its antagonism towards 'idle customs'. 'Lord ever keep me in good and sober Company,' wrote a Lancashire nonconformist in his diary for 26 May 1738, 'and ever give Grace and Strength to watch and guard against mad Frolicks, foolish Sports, unseasonable and dishonourable Diversions, and wicked and sinful Irregularities' (he had been to the races that afternoon).[3] By the middle of the eighteenth century Methodism was helping to reinvigorate this tradition of 'ethical rigorism'.[4] We have also stressed the strength and prevalence of those sentiments which favoured a rigorous labour discipline, and those were probably of even greater significance than the tradition of religious austerity (though the two outlooks were often closely related). Many of the commentators on social and economic issues, and others as well, were keenly opposed to the habits of popular leisure; their concern for economic growth allowed slight sympathy for activities not obviously productive. To them what was of doubtful economic value could only be deplored, and theirs was a view which was acquiring appreciating support.

These, in fact, were the two dominant types of social outlook, and both traditions were vigorously alive around the beginning of the eighteenth century; they offered competing standards for assessing social behaviour and they represented opposing models of the desirable society – the one essentially backward-looking, the other energetically 'progressive'. The century after the Restoration can be seen as a period of transition in a specific sense: during these years the two principal traditions existed side by side as the crucial ingredients in a cultural admixture, and it was not until the second half of the eighteenth century that the victory of one tradition, and the disintegration of the other, can be clearly discerned. It is important to appreciate the resilience of the conservative tradition, especially the habit of paternalism, and to recognize its continuing hold on social attitudes, for there is a danger that its prevalence and power may be underestimated: historians are sometimes inclined to pronounce the death of decaying traditions long before their actual expiry. [. . .]

In agricultural regions the impact of 'reform' was relatively slight. The late seventeenth-early eighteenth-century movement for the reformation of manners, for example, seems to have been concentrated in London and the larger provincial towns; in the countryside it enjoyed only fleeting and usually hesitant support, if any at all.[5] 'Country clergymen, in particular – clergymen interested in the cause of reformation like James Smith of Cambridgeshire or Samuel Wesley of Lincolnshire – felt that reforming societies, although they might serve the cause in cities, were difficult to organize in the country and relatively ineffective.'[6] There are few indications that much was being done in rural areas to curtail Sunday sports,[7] and numerous pieces of evidence suggest that Sunday recreations continued to be practised, and occasionally even condoned. In 1752 the parish of Owston, Lincolnshire, reported 'The parishioners not very regular, especially the young people as to keeping the Lord's day free from sports and diversions.'[8] It was reputed that Thomas Robinson, rector of Ousby, Cumberland, in the early eighteenth century, was accustomed, 'after Sunday afternoon prayers, to accompany the leading men of his parish to the adjoining ale-house, where each man spent a penny, and only a penny: that done, he set the younger sort to play at foot-ball, (of which he was a great promoter) and other rustic diversions'.[9] A contributor to Hone's *Every-Day Book* recalled that 'When a boy, football was commonly played on a Sunday morning, before church time, in a village in the west of England, and the church-piece was the ground chosen for it.'[10] Many country gentlemen were still sympathetically disposed to established customs and were not inclined to judge them overly nicely on 'moral' grounds; they were concerned to preserve their reputations according to traditional standards, and for the most part they were willing to accede to the conventional expectations concerning the customs of their localities and their own social responsibilities. [. . .]

By the end of the eighteenth century the opposition to traditional recreation had clearly gained the upper hand. Refinement had triumphed over rusticity: the violence (or semi-violence), the 'vulgarity' and 'coarseness' of many customary sports were no longer so readily accepted; indeed, it was only after the middle of the century that most gentlemen came to regard them as brutal, gross, and uncivilized, 'The country affords almost as strong instances of cruelty, as [the] town,' declared a moralist in 1765, 'for wrestling, singlestick, or even foot-ball, are never considered as diversions by the common people, but as attended with danger, mischief, or blood-shed.'[11] The spirit of Addison, Steele, and their followers was gradually absorbed by the high culture, and popular and genteel tastes became increasingly dissociated from each other. 'Rude jollity and merriment of country feasts and fairs much less frequent now, than formerly', noted an observer in the early nineteenth century of the villages in the Lincolnshire wolds: 'The refinement of manners, and a greater separation between the different ranks of masters and servants, together with the extending influences of sectarian preachers have repressed much of this old hospitality.'[12] Upper and lower class standards for evaluating social behaviour came to have little in common (considerably less, certainly, than they had had around 1700), and the customs which the people continued to honour were increasingly regarded from above as primitive, disorderly, sometimes immoral, and usually at odds with the basic standards of social propriety. In 1777 John Brand was able to speak of 'the present fashionable Contempt of old Customs'.[13]

The disposition towards traditionalism was gradually weakened by the growing concern for 'improvement', a value which had many faces: refinement of manners, 'rational' tastes, the cultivation of moral sensibilities, restraints imposed on some forms of personal indulgence, the streamlining of certain social and economic practices in the interest of greater efficiency. The gentry, clergy, and large farmers became less and less inclined to conform to many of the older expectations concerning the conduct of their relations with the common people. In the third quarter of the eighteenth century, for instance, the rector of Chinnor, Oxfordshire, dispensed with the custom of entertaining his parishioners at the rectory on Easter Monday, though he continued to support the feast at a public house.[14] The paternalistic norms, especially those of tolerance and obligation, were losing force, and there was a waning interest in the kinds of patronage and ceremonial commitments which had previously been widely accepted. [. . .]

. . . [T]here were still a number of gentlemen who, for a variety of reasons, continued to support the traditional practices and very much regretted their demise. Recreations continued to be regarded by some gentlemen as useful social tranquillizers: they encouraged cheerfulness, mollified the people's discontents, diverted their attention from political concerns, and sometimes served as occasions of harmless tension-release They were thought to contribute to the stability of the existing social order; they helped to dampen down conflict and to reinforce sentiments of social well-being. This, for instance, was one of the arguments which William Windham advanced against the early efforts to outlaw bull-baiting.[15] Robert Slaney declared that without recreation, the common people would 'become gloomy, morose, and dissatisfied, and would be ready on every opportunity to break into riot and rebellion'. 'In order that the poorer classes should be happy and contented,' he argued, it is not enough that they have adequate wages, and are thereby insured against poverty and sickness in old age. Privation of suffering is not enjoyment: that they may be cheerful at labour, they should have the reasonable hope of relaxation from toil before them, and look to a holiday occasionally for amusement. This is of the utmost consequence, not merely to the poor, but to the security of the great. The main title by which the few who are rich hold possession is, that the many who are not be contented and amused.[16]

Some of the defenders of traditional sports stressed the encouragement they gave to manly discipline and to martial qualities. Sport, it was argued, was the training ground for courage, perseverance, physical vigour, and group loyalty. This was a view which had often been expressed. Athletic sports, thought one writer, 'are an excellent preparation for the military exercises, and render men fit to become defenders of the country'.[17] William Windham claimed of the common people that 'it is not unfair to attribute to their manly amusements much of that valour which is so conspicuous in their martial achievements by sea and land. Courage and humanity seem to grow out of their wholesome exercises'.[18] Similarly, a correspondent who approved of the Derby Shrovetide football match remarked that 'I did not see a blow given, nor hear an oath uttered, and could not help anticipating what the power and spirit of these men would be who strove so hard for such an object, whenever their energy should be called forth in their country's service.'[19]

With the full development of a capitalist society, and the consequent aggravation of class hostilities, men of conservative leanings were inclined to entertain a longing for a social order of patriarchal harmony, the sort of order which some of them associated with community recreations. [. . .]

But these had become very much minority concerns well before the mid-nineteenth century. With the exception of some traditional squires, nostalgic Tories, gentlemen of pleasure, and of course many of the common people themselves, the decline of 'rude diversions' and of 'vulgar games' was generally applauded. It was reported in 1848, for example, that 'the silly pagan custom, happily sinking into desuetude, of men's parading the streets dressed in colored rags and white external petticoats, was practised at Louth by half a dozen money-hunters on Monday last (Plough Monday)',[20] and this was the kind of 'progressive' view which was most often heard and most widely supported, at least among the people who counted – people of the middle class, evangelicals, the moulders of public opinion, and (increasingly) members of the landowning class. For the most part popular diversions were no longer sanctioned, and all sorts of customary practice were being subjected to close examination. 'Ancient customs are very well in their way . . . but some are indeed more honoured in the breach than in the observance', as one source mildly put it.[21] 'I know of nothing more detracting to the respectability of our town,' wrote an inhabitant of Derby, 'than the beastly and disgusting exhibition, absurdly called the "Foot-ball play" . . . This relic of barbarism, for it deserves not a better name, is wholly inconsistent with the intelligence and the spirit of improvement which now characterize the people of Derby.'[22] This was a typical outlook, only expressed here with particular vigour. 'Seen at hand,' confessed William Howitt, 'there is a vulgarity in most popular customs that offends invariably our present tastes.'[23]

Around the end of the eighteenth century an aggressive moral earnestness re-emerged in public life, sweeping aside much of the complacency which remained and galvanizing men for the task of moral reform. 'Is it not a palpable truth,' asked Henry Zouch in

1786, 'that a spirit of unbounded licentiousness is gone forth, and every where pervades the land?'[24] 'Moral' considerations rose to the forefront in public debate, imposing increasingly rigorous criteria for the assessment of every form of social behaviour. Moral values were more vigorously injected into play activities, and it came to be assumed (as one historian has said) that 'if recreation was permissible at all, it must be "rational" and must prepare mind and body for work, instead of being an end in itself.'[25] 'Rational amusement' became a Victorian cliché, an expression of approval only for those pleasures which were patently moral and improving in intent. The new, more militant morality came to be widely accepted and powerfully promoted, and its most zealous advocates were energetic and persevering in the cause of reform. One such activist was Denys Rolle, Esq., of Devon, whose obituary in 1797 pointed out that

> as a magistrate, he was remarkably attentive to the morals of the people within his district, and successively laboured, though with great and long opposition, in suppressing village-alehouses, cock-fighting, and bull-baiting. Torrington, near which his seat stands, was a place much disgraced with these worse than savage diversions, and Mr Rolle took extraordinary pains to correct the evil. For this evil he not only exerted his authority, as a magistrate, with great zeal and impartiality, but circulated large impressions of a pamphlet, written by himself, against such cruel amusements. In 1789 he printed an address to the nobility and gentry, circulated privately, calling for their concurrence in the great object which he had in view, of parochial reformation.[26]

A closer regulation of popular behaviour, an improvement in the common people's tastes and morals, a reform of their habitual vices, the instilling in them of discipline and orderliness: these were some of the principal objectives of the movement for the reformation of manners which arose in the later 1780s and matured during the following half century. By the early years of Victoria's reign there must have been few localities which were not experiencing the efforts of parson or squire, employer or chapel, philanthropic lady or temperance reformer, Bible society or charitable foundation, to civilize the labouring people and to enlighten them as to their real interests. A memorandum of a Sunday School teacher in Fulletby, Lincolnshire, in 1846 is just one illustration of a movement which had penetrated virtually all corners of the land, though not always without opposition; before the Sunday school was established (around 1826), he said,

> the sabbath day in our village was awfully desecrated. The young men and youths, and some of the married men too, usually spent the chief part of the day in playing games of chance, football, nurspell, etc. by which the rising generation were allured to sabbath-breaking; and were brought under the demoralizing influence of wicked pursuits, and evil company.
>
> Under the counteracting influence of the Sunday School a change for the better soon began to manifest itself; and though there was still much sabbath-breaking and immorality among our youth, to lament over, gambling on the Sabbath day was almost abolished until the present year, when it has been revived by the farm servants in the village; a set of raw, thoughtless, youths who have never had the moral training of a Sunday School.
>
> The revival of these pastimes on the Sabbath has already had its influence upon our Sunday School; and has given me considerable pain, and not a little

trouble. Sometimes a few of the elder boys will come in late – hurried – and confused, and on inquiring the cause I have ascertained that a game at football was being played somewhere in the parish, and thus some have been tempted to impinge upon the hours allotted to school, and others who ought to be present to play truant. The evil is further manifested by their inattention; their thoughts are so full of play that for the rest of the time it is difficult to engage their attention, or to prevent them from whispering to each other; and on leaving school they have eagerly ran off to the forbidden pastime, and I have only mourned to see the seed I have been attempting to sow fall by the way side, to be trodden underfoot, or devoured by the fowls of the air.[27]

'A mighty revolution has taken place in the sports and pastimes of the common people', wrote William Howitt at the beginning of Victoria's reign.[28] During the previous century the character of popular leisure had been very substantially overhauled, and most of these remarkable changes had occurred, or at least been significantly accelerated, since about the 1780s. The recreational culture of the Cornish miners, for example, was very noticeably eroded during the late eighteenth and early nineteenth centuries.[29] Virtually all contemporaries were in agreement concerning the basic facts of this trend, even when their assessments differed sharply. 'The few remnants of our old Sports and Pastimes are rapidly disappearing,' observed an Oxfordshire parson, 'and this is, in my opinion, a change much to be lamented.'[30] Football was said by a writer in 1823 to be 'an exercise which has dwindled down to nothing, compared to the estimation in which it was formerly held'.[31] 'In my own recollection,' said Howitt, 'the appearance of morris-dancers, guisers, plough-bullocks, and Christmas carollers, has become more and more rare, and to find them we must go into the retired hamlets of Staffordshire, and the dales of Yorkshire and Lancashire.'[32]

The decline of popular recreation, it is clear, was intimately associated with the gradual breakdown of what we now call 'traditional society'. With the rise of a market economy, and the accompanying development of new normative standards and material conditions for the conduct of social relations, the foundations of many traditional practices were relentlessly swept away, leaving a vacuum which would be only gradually reoccupied, and then of necessity by novel or radically revamped forms of diversion. Traditional recreation was rooted in a social system which was predominantly agrarian, strongly parochial in its orientations, marked by a deep sense of corporate identity; it could not be comfortably absorbed into a society which was urban-centred, governed by contractual relations, biased towards individualism, increasingly moulding its culture in a manner appropriate to the requirements of industrial production. In the new world of congested cities, factory discipline, and free enterprise, recreational life had to be reconstructed – shaped to accord with the novel conditions of non-agrarian, capitalistic society – and the reconstruction was only gradually accomplished over a period of several generations. One indication of the very limited supply of alternative (and attractive) forms of diversion during much of the nineteenth century is the overwhelming importance of the public house as a recreational centre for the common people. 'In England,' thought Joseph Kay, 'it may be said that the poor, have now no relaxation, but the alehouse or the gin palace.'[33] Although this was an exaggeration, it was an understandable one. 'At present,' remarked Robert Slaney in 1833, 'the poor workman in the large manufacturing town, was actually forced into the public house, there being no other place for him to amuse himself in.'[34] And by this time conditions in the countryside were often not much different.

In the short run, then, in this period of exceptionally acute social change, the dislocation of recreational life was keenly felt and only marginally alleviated. The low point of this particular process of social depression was roughly coincident with the second quarter of the nineteenth century: much of the traditional culture had disintegrated, and the new possibilities were only beginning to emerge. The reshaping of popular leisure was largely a phenomenon of the period after 1850.

Notes

1   J.H. Plumb, 'Plantation Power', *New York Review of Books*, xiv, No. 4 (26 February 1970), 16.

2   *A Briefe Defence of the several Declarations of King James the First, and King Charles the First, Concerning Lawful Recreations on Sundays* (n.p., 1708), p. 24.

3   *The Diary of Richard Kay, 1716–1751, of Baldingstone near Bury: A Lancashire Doctor*, ed. W. Brockbank and F. Kenworthy (Publications of the Chetham Society, 3rd series, xvi, 1968). p. 23.

4   John A. Newton, *Methodism and the Puritans* (Friends of Dr Williams's Library, Eighteenth Lecture, 1964), pp. 16–17.

5   Dudley W.R. Bahlman, *The Moral Revolution of 1688* (New Haven, Conn., 1957), *passim*; Reginald Lennard (ed.), *Englishmen at Rest and Play: Some Phases of English Leisure 1558–1714* (Oxford, 1931), p. 179.

6   Bahlman, *Moral Revolution*, pp. 97–8.

7   See, for instance, W.B. Whitaker, *The Eighteenth-Century English Sunday: A Study of Sunday Observance from 1677 to 1837* (London, 1940), pp. 33–4.

8   Joan Varley, 'An Archdiaconal Visitation of Stow, 1752', *Reports and Papers of the Lincolnshire Architectural and Archaeological Society*, New Series, III (1948), 160; cf. H.A. Lloyd Jukes (ed.), *Articles of Enquiry Addressed to the Clergy of the Diocese of Oxford at the Primary Visitation of Dr Thomas Secker, 1738* (Oxfordshire Record Society, XXXVIII, 1957), pp. 25, 46, 143, and 150.

9   William Hutchinson, *The History of the County of Cumberland*, 2 vols. (Carlisle, 1794), volume 1, 224n.

10 William Hone, *The Every-Day Book*, 2 vols (London, 1825–7), volume II, col. 374. For other evidence concerning the customary character of Sunday recreation, see W. Litt, *Wrestliana; or, An Historical Account of Ancient and Modern Wrestling* (Whitehaven, 1823), pp. 51–2; *Gentleman's Magazine*, LXXXIX (1819), part I, 110, and XCII (1822), part I, 223; and *Wesleyan Methodist Magazine*, 3rd series, v (1826), 73–4. As late as the early 1830s it was being claimed by one clergyman that some magistrates, 'on the strength of the "Book of Sports", refuse to interfere with games, except such as are unlawful, on the Sunday'. ('Report from the Select Committee on the Observance of the Sabbath Day', *Parliamentary Papers*, 1831–2, VII, p. 430, evidence of J.W. Cunningham, vicar of Harrow, Middlesex.)

11 *Village Memoirs: In a Series of Letters Between a Clergyman and his Family in the Country, and his Son in Town* (London, 1765), p. 76. I am indebted to Mr J.D. Walsh for this reference.

12 Society of Antiquaries, Edward James Willson Collection (Lincoln), XIII, p. 62.

13 John Brand, *Observations on Popular Antiquities* (Newcastle upon Tyne, 1777). Revised edn by Henry Ellis, 2 vols (London, 1813), p. 333.

14 *V.C.H. Oxfordshire*, VIII (1964), 75.

15 'The habits long established among the people,' he argued in 1802, 'were the best fitted to resist the schemes of innovation; and it was among the labouring and illiterate

part of the people that Jacobinical doctrines had made the smallest progress . . . Out of the whole number of the disaffected, he questioned if a single bull-baiter could be found, or if a single sportsman had distinguished himself in the Corresponding Society . . . The efficient part of the community for labour ought to be encouraged in their exertions, rather by furnishing them with occasional amusements, than by depriving them of one . . . for, if to poverty were to be added a privation of amusements, he knew nothing that could operate more strongly to goad the mind into desperation, and to prepare the poor for that dangerous enthusiasm which was analogous to Jacobinism.' (*Parliamentary History*, XXXVI, pp. 833–4 and 839, debate of 24 May 1802.)

16 Robert A. Slaney, *Essay on the Beneficial Direction of Rural Expenditure* (London, 1824), pp. 130 and 195–6; cf. pp. 124–8. See also Lord John Manners, *A Plea for National Holy-Days* (London, 1843), p. 19.

17 John A. Lawrence, *A Philosophical and Practical Treatise on Horses, and on the Moral Duties of Man Towards the Brute Creation*, 2 vols (London, 1796–8), volume II, 9. Cf. John Godfrey, *A Treatise upon the Useful Science of Defence, Connecting the Small and Back-Sword, and Shewing the Affinity between Them* (London, 1747), dedication; and A. Jones, *The Art of Playing at Skittles: or, the Laws of Nine-Pins Displayed* (London, 1773), pp. 9–11.

18 *Parliamentary History*, XXXV, p. 206, debate of 18 April 1800. Cf. Pierce Egan, *Pierce Egan's Book of Sports and Mirror of Life* (London, 1832), p. 11, col. 2, and p. 170, col. 1; and J.C. Reid, *Bucks and Bruisers: Pierce Egan and Regency England* (London, 1971), pp. 12–13, 20, and 134–5.

19 *Derby Mercury*, 9 February 1815.

20 *Stamford Mercury*, 14 January 1848.

21 *Stamford Mercury*, 15 January 1864.

22 *Derby and Chesterfield Reporter*, 9 February 1844.

23 William Howitt, *The Rural Life of England*, 2 vols (London, 1838), volume II, 151.

24 Henry Zouch, *Hints Respecting the Public Police* (London, 1786), p. 16.

25 'Work and Leisure in Industrial Society: Conference Report', *Past & Present*, No. 30 (April 1965), 101, comment of B.H. Harrison. For a general statement concerning some of the aspects and implications of 'rational amusement', see the comments of Baptist W. Noel in 'Minutes of the Committee of Council on Education', *Parliamentary Papers*, 1841, XX, p. 172.

26 *Gentleman's Magazine*, LXVII (1797), part II, 1, 125. See also the interesting account of genteel doubts about the staging of a popular drama in the *Monthly Magazine*, VI (1798), 9–10; and E.P. Thompson, *Education and Experience* (Leeds U.P., Fifth Mansbridge Memorial Lecture, 1968), pp. 9–14, which includes a lengthy extract from this source.

27 Lincolnshire R.O., 'Fulletby Sunday School, The Teacher's Diary 1846', Winn. 1/2, pp. 2–3.

28 William Howitt, *The Rural Life of England*, 2nd edn (London, 1840, 1 vol.), p. 515.

29 John Graham Rule, *The Labouring Miner in Cornwall c.1740-1870: A Study in Social History*, Unpublished Ph.D thesis, University of Warwick, 1971, pp. 76–80.

30 J.A. Giles, *History of Witney* (London, 1852), p. 57; cf. Joseph Kay, *The Social Condition and Education of the People in England and Europe* (2 vols.; London, 1850), I, 231.

31 Litt, *Wrestliana*, p. 51; cf. Frederick Gale, *Modern English Sports: Their Use and their Abuse* (London, 1885), p. 49.

32 Howitt, *Rural Life* (1840), p. 422.

33 Kay, *Social Condition*, I, 231.

34 *Parliamentary Debates*, 3rd series, XV, p. 1,054, debate of 21 February 1833.

Richard Holt

SURVIVAL AND ADAPTATION

THE DEGREE TO WHICH a wide range of old-established sports continued to be practised into the late nineteenth century and beyond has tended to be overlooked. This is hardly surprising in the light of the enormous impact of organized team-games in the last quarter of the century. Until recently sports history has tended to be written by middle-class amateurs, who did not consider traditional pursuits to be 'sport' in their own amateur sense. The impression of decay was reinforced by the 'pessimistic' school of social history, which saw the Industrial Revolution as a cultural catastrophe, destroying old ways of playing through the imposition of grim industrial rhythms, urban dislocation, and middle-class interference. Hence the idea that there was a 'leisure vacuum', a hiatus between 'the good old days' and the emergence of new standardized and commercial forms of sport, has taken hold. However, cultural change is far more complex than this. Deeply held attitudes and habits do not die out overnight. During the second half of the nineteenth century and even into this century a wide range of old-established sports continued to be popular. To get a better understanding of the tension between change and continuity in sport we have to look at the limitations of the reform movement, even amongst employers, and at the relatively slow decline of the fighting and gambling traditions of roughs and young rakes who made up the 'Fancy'. And this confines continuity to urban Britain. Not surprisingly in certain well-defined rural areas the vigour of old sports was almost undiminished.

Although cock-fighting and bull-baiting had been prohibited and officials of the RSPCA endeavoured to enforce the ban, there is no doubt that cruel animal sports persisted. Alan Metcalfe has shown how cock-fighting was carried on in the mining communities of south Northumberland into the 1870s. Four men were prosecuted in Liverpool for cock-fighting in 1871 and in 1875 police broke up a cock-fight at the Aintree racecourse. The *Day's Doings* of 1871 reported a visit to a three-row cockpit with sixty or so spectators in a northern industrial town at which there were merchants and labourers present.

The magazine was especially shocked by the presence of a small girl sitting happily on her father's knee. A few members of the nobility continued to take an interest in the sport. The Marquis of Hastings was prosecuted for organizing a cock-fight at his ancestral home of Donnington Hall in 1863. As late as 1895 *Cocking and Its Votaries* was privately published in handsome binding and with coloured plates making 'it quite plain that not a few wealthy Englishmen still follow up this sport—stealthily but with much zeal'. In the Lake District the holding of cock-fights in farms was an open secret up until the Second World War. It was still going on in the 1950s when a social anthropologist noted that cockfighting was 'handed down within the family, deriving a high value from its mode of transmission'. 'Its appeal,' he added, 'is undoubtedly strengthened by the fact that it is done surreptitiously in defiance of laws to which the community has never given its assent.' 'Game-cock fights,' recalled Bill Lightfoot of Wigton between the wars, 'we used to go to a lot of them. We used to have them at Islekirk, at Redhall.' On one occasion, while calling in at a pub, 'a bit of a row struck up over these cocks . . . so they went in that stable there and clipped two out, and there was an old body called Mrs Watson in the Sun there, and they just pushed all the chairs and they had a fight in the kitchen. Forty-four or forty-five years ago. I liked a cock-fight.' This was in the 1970s, but he added 'there's a fair bit of it goes on still. I'll tell you who has a full set of spurs'.[1]

Obviously it is very difficult to assess the extent to which such activities survived in the cities. A careful study of Leicester suggests that from the 1870s the power of the licensing authorities made it too dangerous for publicans to permit their premises to be used for cock-fights. However, dog-fights certainly continued especially in their traditional stronghold in the Black Country. In the 1850s 'dogs were still bred for fighting; but to avoid the police, contests were held secretly at night'. Dog-fighting was specifically banned under an act of 1911 but an authoritative source on the sporting traditions of the area interviewed by the BBC in 1985 claimed that matching Staffordshire bull-terriers was widely and more or less openly done until the 1930s. Men would bring their dogs to certain well-known pubs and agree to match them, and at least one prominent nobleman was involved. That this tradition lingers on was made abundantly clear in the successful prosecution of seven men for organizing and filming such a fight in July 1985. It took several years of undercover work to penetrate this secretive and violent subculture. There was a strong suspicion on the part of the investigators that they had only revealed the tip of an iceberg. Dog-fights, alleged the RSPCA, were held in the emptied swimming-pool of a large house in the stockbroker belt, where tell-tale blood and hair could be quickly hosed away. Badgers too are still baited occasionally. Bill Lightfoot, the Cumbrian cock-fighter, also admitted a fondness for badger-baiting between the wars. 'On Sundays Mott and me went for badgers . . . [around] an old pipe there at Aikbank, once got four badgers out of it. Fletcher Gale was with us that day. Terriers would bait them then we would club them.' Although there is no doubt that such formerly widespread activities are now the province of a very small minority, it is highly probable that the enthusiasm for such contests has always outstripped the ability of the police and the animal protection lobby to prevent them from taking place more often than might be imagined. A covert tradition of cruel sports survived in the countryside, the full extent of which is still unknown.[2] [. . .]

The persistence of popular traditions is most evident in the enclosed world of the mining communities. In the pit villages of South Northumberland there were bowling matches, quoits, rabbit-coursing, dog-racing, pigeon-flying. Here cock-fighting was carried on after the legal ban, and there were seven prosecutions in 1850 alone. However, mine-owners and the Northumbrian gentry generally left the miners alone to get on with their sports, their drinking, and the gaming that went with it. The pub was the focus of this mining culture and publicans were their makeshift sponsors. The English alehouse survived the Industrial Revolution and continued to adapt to the recreational needs of its regulars. Pubs often ran bowling matches which involved covering an agreed distance in the fewest throws of a heavy iron ball. These were very popular. Each pit had its own champion and there were informally acknowledged champions for the whole coalfield. Whatever the sport, miners tended to play only with miners and even then rarely with miners from other coalfields. Despite the spread of the railways and the speed of communication miners remained happily locked into a fiercely masculine and introverted sociability based on pit pubs like the Astley Arms at Seton Delaval, which in 1879 had a bowling-track, a quoit-alley, and seating for 700. Even in Newcastle itself there was clear evidence of the continuity of country sports into the 1880s in the suburbs of Byker and Elswick among the shipyard and heavy industrial workers. The inner city pubs no longer ran workers' sports, but no fewer than twenty-five pubs outside the old city walls organized bowling, coursing, quoits, and other similar activities at the end of the New Year holiday in 1885. Much of this carried on into the Edwardian and inter-war years alongside the new world of professional football, which drew the miners into Newcastle and Sunderland on Saturday afternoons. Alan Metcalfe, who has opened up this submerged tradition for us, maintains that the exploits and anecdotes of the great bowlers were still remembered and personally recounted to him in the working-men's clubs of the pit villages in the 1970s.[3] [. . .]

The tension between the forces of continuity and the 'otherness' of what we call 'modern' sport is the central theme of this book. So links between old and new ways of playing will occur and recur. Cricket and horse-racing, for instance, derived part of their appeal from the sense of the pastoral they evoked. Similarly hunting and shooting were steeped in affection or nostalgia for the countryside, the glory of 'getting away from it all', getting out of town and into the carefully preserved woods and well-tended fields that comprised the 'natural' world. Working men, who bred pigeons or greyhounds, were obscurely celebrating another aspect of traditional country sports. Such themes are woven into the wider argument of what is to come. . . . [E]xamples of explicit survival . . . were not ancient sports that were enjoyed as self-conscious folkloric displays like the 'traditional' football match at Jedburgh or Ashbourne, but sports that were part of a customary life that was still vital and popular. For a few old games survived even in economically advanced areas, though obviously they were more important and tenacious in remoter places like the Highlands of Scotland and the west of Ireland.

Knur-and-spell is perhaps one of the most remarkable examples of survival. The name comes from *knorr*, a Teutonic term meaning a knot of wood; 'spell' probably derives from the Old Norse *spill*, meaning a game; and Norsemen apparently played a game called *nurspel*. Strutt attests to its popularity in the north of England. The game involved a player hitting the 'knur', a small ball rather like a large marble, with a special bat. In Lancashire the ball was suspended from a gallows-like contraption, while in Yorkshire it was flipped into the air from a spring-loaded trap. In each case the object was the same: to hit the object as far as possible. Contests of twenty-five or so 'wallops' or 'rises' were held between two players or 'laikers', who would often wager on the outcome. The sport always attracted spectators. In 1826 on Woodhouse Moor in Yorkshire a match for 40 guineas was held over forty rises and large crowds continued to flock to the moors around Sheffield, Barnsley, Colne, and Rotherham. There were all kinds of little tricks to help drive the spell distances of 200 yards or more but the essence of the thing was simple enough—'tha clouts it as far down t'meader as tha can, 'cause foithest wins, tha' sees. And if it come to a moutch [dispute], then tha' measures from t' pin wi' a squeer chain.' New and old sports sometimes happily coexisted—a point that can all too easily be overlooked by those who wish to set up a rigid and precise distinction between traditional and modern forms. Jerry Dawson, who was born in 1888 near Burnley, combined playing football as goalkeeper for Burnley from 1906 to 1929, winning a cup-winner's medal and an England cap, with being a champion at knur-and-spell. At this time the game had a significant regional following which continued into the 1930s. Champions like Billy Baxter, who became 'world champion' at Colne in 1937, was a kind of folk-hero in many a northern household along with others like the Machin brothers, Willie Lamb, Joe Edon, Tom Ellis, and Arthur Cooper. As late as 1970 a crowd of 3,000 gathered on Easter Tuesday on the moors at the Spring Rock Inn near Elland in Yorkshire to see the annual championship. The sport had survived and even acquired a little modest sponsorship.[4] [. . .]

Let us conclude by taking a look at the games people played in a mid-Victorian county town before the arrival of Association football. Lancaster was at the heart of an agricultural community with a relatively large professional and commercial élite. Careful recent work has revealed an archery club composed of gentry, clergymen, surgeons, and merchants, and a rowing club which was similarly exclusive requiring the wearing of special dress and the holding of dinners. These clubs were for the small town élite and maintained their social pre-eminence by a black-ball system. In 1841 a cricket club was formed by eight middle-class men, some of whom were already in the archery and rowing fraternity. Sixty-eight of the seventy-one members of the cricket club have been identified, all drawn from non-manual occupations as one might expect of members of a club who often played on a Tuesday, had their own insignia and wore straw hats. Skilled workers formed the majority of a new club set up in 1859. This group, along with shopkeepers, seems to have been active in the world of bowls, which tended to be organized at greens owned by innkeepers in accordance with the long-standing association of sport and drink. Significantly these private clubs, mostly for the better-off and the very skilled, were of recent origin and minority interest. Up to the 1870s popular sports were still being organized around a seasonal calendar of wrestling, racing, rowing matches, quoits, and athletics as well as such festive staples as the 'gurning' or grimacing contests. Closeness to the Lake District where there was a long history of wrestling made this event especially popular and local champions included a joiner, a tin worker, and a wheelwright. Lancaster nicely encapsulates the delicate balance between old and new ways of playing, between private clubs and popular traditions in the middle years of the nineteenth century.[5]

Notes

1   Metcalfe, 'Organised Sport', p. 475; Rees, Development of Physical Recreation in Liverpool', MA thesis (Liverpool Univ., 1968), p. 175; for *Cocking and its Votaries*, see

Strutt, *Sports and Pastimes*, p. 226; W.M. Williams, *Gosforth: The Sociology of an English Village* (1956), p. 134; M. Bragg, *Speak for England* (1976), p. 394.

2   J. Crump, 'Amusements of the People', Ph.D. thesis (Warwick Univ., 1985), p. 325; *Guardian*, 1 Aug. 1985, p. 17; Gash, *Aristocracy and People*, p. 345; Bragg, *Speak for England*, p. 394.

3   P. Clark, *The English Alehouse* (1983); Metcalfe, 'Organised Sport'; also A. Metcalfe, 'Sport in Nineteenth Century England. An Interpretation', presented at the Second World Symposium on the History of Sport and Physical Education, note 10, and personal communication.

4   *Oxford Companion*, pp. 510–13.

5   M. Speake, 'The Social Anatomy of Participation in Sport in Lancaster in Early Victorian England', [ed. Arlott] in *Proc. XI HISPA International Congress*, ed. J.A. Mangan (1987), pp. 91–100.

References

Arlott, J. (ed.), *Oxford Companion to Sports and Games* (Oxford, 1976).

Bragg, M., *Speak for England* (London, 1976).

Clark, P., *The English Alehouse: A Social History 1200–1830* (London, 1983).

Crump, J., 'The Amusements of the People: The Provision of Recreation in Leicester, 1850–1914', Ph.D. thesis (Warwick University, 1985).

Gash, N., *Aristocracy and People: Britain 1815–1865* (London, 1979).

Metcalfe, A., 'Organised Sport in the Mining Communities of South Northumberland, 1880–1889', *Victorian Studies*, **25**, Summer 1982.

Rees, R., 'The Development of Physical Receation in Liverpool during the Nineteenth Century', MA thesis (Liverpool, 1968).

Speake, M., 'The Social Anatomy of Participation in Sport in Lancaster in Early Victorian England', in *Proceedings of the XI HISPA International Congress*, ed. J.A. Mangan (Glasgow, 1987).

Strutt, J., *The Sports and Pastimes of the People of England* (1903 edn), reissued with a preface by N. and R. McWhirter (London, 1969).

Williams, W.M., *Gosforth: The Sociology of an English Village* (London, 1956).

J.A. Mangan

ATHLETICISM

Prologue

FIVE YEARS AFTER THE GREAT WAR an aggressive pamphlet entitled *The Public Schools and Athleticism* appeared. It was a condemnation of the excessive interest in games in the schools by an obscure schoolmaster, J.H. Simpson.[1] It struck an unpleasantly discordant note amid applause which had begun some sixty years earlier and which, in an atmosphere of post-war nostalgia, had risen to a crescendo.

Simpson was more than a critic. He sought understanding as well as reformation. He asserted that games were an ostentatious and pervasive feature of the public school system, and argued that the study of this 'athleticism' was crucial to a comprehension of the system as a whole. Despite this observation there has been no close scrutiny of athleticism in the public schools.[2] This is a regrettable omission. The ideology strongly influenced the schools between 1860 and 1940; its widespread adoption had extensive educational and social repercussions. No history of the British public school and no record of British educational ideologies can be complete without a consideration of this controversial movement. [. . .]

There has never emerged an exact and universally acceptable definition of a public school.[3] This is not for want of trying. A wide variety of writers have struggled with the problem.[4] The definition adopted in this book is Vivian Ogilvie's since it combines clarity, comprehensiveness and qualification, and would meet with widespread understanding and acceptance. Ogilvie assures us that the principal characteristics of a public school are: it is for the well-to-do, expensive, predominantly boarding, independent of the state, but neither privately owned nor profit making. He points out, however, that there are illustrious public schools which fall out of line in one or other particular: these constitute exceptions within the general rule. The rule (in its full-blown form) 'is an independent, non-local, predominantly boarding school for the upper and middle classes'.[5]

The public schools so defined are diverse in origin, history and type. At least six important nineteenth-century groupings may be discerned. The most famous group was the 'Great Public Schools', the subject of a royal commission set up in 1861, the Public Schools Commission or Clarendon Commission (after the chairman, Lord Clarendon).[6] The schools investigated were Eton, Harrow, Rugby, Winchester, Shrewsbury, Charterhouse, Westminster, St Paul's and Merchant Taylors.[7]

Throughout the nineteenth century, the period of the great expansion of public school education, other groupings emerged or were consolidated. The most amorphous was the large group of Denominational Schools: Roman Catholic, such as Stonyhurst (1793), Ampleforth (1802), Ratcliffe (1847) and Beaumont (1861); Quaker, such as Sidcot (1808) and Bootham (1823); Methodist, such as Kingswood (1848), Leys (1875) and Ashville (1877); and other Protestant Nonconformist, such as Mill Hill (1808), Caterham (1811) and Bishop's Stortford (1868). All were formed to provide an alternative education to that provided by the schools of the Established Church following the reform of the Penal Laws in the late eighteenth century.

A further grouping was the Proprietary Schools. These were financed initially by shareholders who purchased the right, in consequence, to nominate pupils. Cheltenham was the first: 'There were 650 shares, each share entitling the holder to nominate one pupil (usually, of course, held by the parent). If the proprietors should fail to nominate pupils, then the governors could do so.'[8] Other schools of this type include Marlborough (1843), Rossall (1844), Malvern (1865) and Dover College (1871).

Edward Thring became headmaster of Uppingham Grammar School in 1853. He transformed this small, unprepossessing local grammar school into an expensive national boarding school for the upper classes. A similar process of transformation occurred at several other institutions, including Sherborne, Tonbridge, Repton, Giggleswick, St Bees and Sedbergh. These schools became known on this account as 'Elevated Grammar Schools'.

A little before Thring in Rutland raised Uppingham to the ranks of a school for the wealthy, Nathaniel Woodard in Sussex had embarked on a more ambitious project: a network of Anglican middle-class schools throughout England. Originally only one, Lancing College (1848), was intended as a school for the better-off, but ultimately this was to be the fate of them all. By the time of his death in 1891 there were six Woodard boys' public schools: Lancing (1848), Hurstpierpoint (1849), Ardingly (1858), Denstone (1868), King's College, Taunton (1880) and Ellesmere (1884).

Finally, there were a number of schools financed and owned by a single individual, usually the headmaster: the Private Venture Schools. One such school was Loretto, a small boarding school outside Edinburgh, founded in 1827 by the Rev. Dr Langhorne, an English curate of the Scottish Episcopal Church. In 1862 Loretto was purchased by Hely Hutchinson Almond who modelled it on the lines of an English public school. By the end of the century it had become a small but famous public school in his hands. Other schools of this type include Merchiston (1833), Radley (1847), Bradfield (1850), Bloxham (1860), Monkton Coombe (1868), Wrekin (1879), Wycliffe (1882) and Abbotsholme (1889). [. . .]

Ideologies,[9] it has been argued, are essentially the outcome of man's need for imposing intellectual order on the world.[10] Whatever their purpose a plethora of definitions exists.

At the crudest level an ideology may be defined as a set of principles held by individuals or groups. At a more subtle level it may be regarded as a set of principles which determines action by providing a means of distinguishing between acceptable and unacceptable ideas. Even more expansively it is the whole complex of ideas and feelings linking the members of a group together with the means whereby these are established;[11] it embraces not only what is believed but the means of ensuring belief. There are further definitions to be considered. Some have regarded ideologies as forms of deceit, as pseudo-principles, obscuring the real reasons for action.[12] Others have considered that ideologies are simply value-judgements disguised as statements of fact to give them credibility.[13]

These several definitions are all useful conceptual tools with which to explore athleticism as an ideology in the public schools.[14] One purpose of this study is to demonstrate that it embraced a complex of ideas and feelings deliberately and carefully created through ritual and symbol; that it was, on occasion, a form of 'pseudo-reasoning', a deliberate rationalisation for ambitions such as status and power; and that it constituted value-judgements masquerading as facts to reinforce commitment. There is no one simple meaning of ideology in the context of public school athleticism. The term is a conceptual alembic. To reinforce this critical point by employing a different metaphor: the meanings resemble the layers of an onion, one hides within another. . .

The concept of athleticism, of course, may also be variously interpreted.[15] The *Shorter Oxford Dictionary* defines it in neutral and unsubtle terms as 'the practice of, and devotion to, athletic exercises'. In contrast, two scholars, in the similarity of their interpretation, form a small, but sharp comminatory chorus with a large modern audience. In their view athleticism was a malign fashion. The most distinguished historian of the English public school saw athleticism in crude pathological terms: 'the late Victorian schools nurtured vices of their own. Probably the most important was the worship of the athlete with its attendant deification of success, and the mere physical virtue of courage';[16] and the most recent historian of British physical education has been no less harsh in his judgement: 'By athleticism is meant the exaltation and disproportionate regard for games which often resulted in the denigration of academic work and in anti-intellectualism.'[17]

Edward Lyttelton, an observer of the ideology in action in the nineteenth century, took a more balanced view.[18] Athleticism had dangers: particularly distraction from intellectual pursuits. It also possessed advantages: the stimulation of health and happiness and good moral training. Lyttelton readily admitted athleticism was 'a training shackled by many an antiquated abuse and sadly marred by countless stupidities',[19] but he felt it played a valuable part in the education of the higher classes.

Cyril Norwood, early in the twentieth century, attempted to distinguish between 'over-athleticism' – the attachment of wrong values to games, and athleticism – 'part of the ideal of the English [educational] tradition'.[20] He saw the latter as the attempt to implant certain ideals of character and conduct through the games field: 'a game is to be played for the game's sake . . . no unfair advantage of any sort can ever be taken, [yet] . . . within the rules no mercy is to be expected, or accepted or shown by either side; the lesson to be learnt by each individual is the subordination of self in order that he may render his best service as the member of a team in which he relies upon all the rest; and all the rest rely upon him: . . . finally, never on any occasion must he show the white feather.' Norwood concluded: 'If games can be played in this spirit, they are a magnificent preparation for life.'[21]

Today it is fashionable and to a degree wise, to look askance at such a naive and frequently abused faith in the educational virtues of the playing fields as demonstrated by Norwood and his ilk; but at the same time it is as well to remember that we are reacting, possibly predictably, with extremism to extremism. It is perhaps salutary to recall that English education has embraced the belief in the efficacy of sport *inter alia* for character building since Tudor times.[22]

Lyttelton and Norwood remind us of a period truth. Athleticism was all its critics claim of it; yet it was more. The clichés of modern conventional judgement must be resisted, the validity of contemporary generalisations must be challenged. They owe much to fashion, less to impartiality. If athleticism often degenerated into the self-absorption of Caliban, it frequently aimed to effect the selflessness of Ariel. Apparently it was *sometimes* successful. According to Philip Mason, for example, the games-trained officers from the public schools won an engaging fidelity from the Indian soldier, for their selfless leadership. Mason borrowed a description from the philosopher George Santayana to depict this imperial elite at its best: 'Never since the heroic days of Greece has the world had such a sweet, just, boyish master'. The reason, it appears, lay in a simple diet. 'Hardy as Spartans and disciplined as Romans' these masters carried the qualities they had learned on the games field into their military careers and led with boyishness, decision and courage.[23]

Reality is occasionally attractive. By virtue of its obscenity, the 'athleticism' described by T.C. Worsley in *Flannelled Fool* does not have to be the entire truth for all public schools and public school boys. Mason may have access to an equally valid reality. And Ray, the decent games player in *Tell England*, might have had just as much substance in the flesh as Cayley, the brutal athlete in *The Harrovians*.[24] In a passage totally contradictory of his later outspoken attack on public school games cited above [see note 16], even E.C. Mack discovered virtue in their imperial consequences. He argued that the training largely acquired on the games field was the basis of courage and group loyalty that created 'responsible, honourable boys, willing to give their lives unquestioningly to the preservation and expansion of Empire',[25] and considered that if world conditions had remained as they were in 1870, there was much of substance in the argument that public schools were worthy institutions, admirably serving the interests of the upper classes. The empire and the public school boy's contribution to it lasted beyond 1870. Mason's valedictory embraced the Indian army of the twentieth century.

The purpose of this brief defence of athleticism is not to gloss over deficiencies but to strike unaccustomed balance; it is an attempt to break a lance in the interests of accuracy. The public schools' considerable concern with games was not wholly vicious. It had nobility; it did reflect 'love of the open air, of sport and pluck and fair play'.[26] To borrow (and slightly adapt) Robert Nisbet's striking phrase, athleticism was 'a neologism born of moral passion'[27] as well as a Simpsonian term of justifiable disparagement. Physical exercise was taken, considerably and compulsorily, in the sincere belief of many, however romantic, misplaced or myopic, that it was a highly effective means of inculcating valuable instrumental and impressive educational goals: physical and moral courage, loyalty and cooperation, the capacity to act fairly and take defeat well, the ability to both command and obey. These were the famous ingredients of character training which the public schools considered their pride and their prerogative.[28]

The extract below supplies a period flavour of the once widespread educational certainty surrounding games in the public school system:

> Many a lad who leaves an English public school disgracefully ignorant of the rudiments of useful knowledge, who can speak no language but his own, and writes that imperfectly, to whom the noble literature of his country and the stirring history of his forefathers are almost a sealed book, and who has devoted a great part of his time and nearly all his thoughts to athletic sports, yet brings away with him something beyond all price, a manly straightforward character, a scorn of lying and meanness, habits of obedience and command, and fearless courage. Thus equipped, he goes out into the world, and bears a man's part in subduing the earth, ruling its wild folk, and building up the Empire; doing many things so well that it seems a thousand pities that he was not trained to do them better, and to face the problems of race, creed and government in distant corners of the Empire with a more instructed mind. This type of citizen, however, with all his defects, has done yeoman's service to the Empire; and for much that is best in him our public schools may fairly take credit.[29]

The situation is clear from this and similar pronouncements. For many in the Victorian and Edwardian public schools, games became 'the wheel round which the moral values turned'.[30] It was a genuinely and extensively held belief that they inspired virtue; they developed manliness; they formed character. At the same time there were certainly casuists who used moral argument as a cover for simple pleasure. There were also opportunists, especially housemasters, who saw the value of games in terms of control and publicity.

The truth of the matter is that the ideology involved virtuousness, indulgence and expedience; it embraced idealism, casuistry and opportunism. It was, in fact, a complex manifestation. . . .

Notes

[All dated publications were published in London, unless otherwise stated.]

1   Simpson (1883–1959) was subsequently to achieve some small measure of distinction in English education. After experience as an assistant master at Gresham's and Rugby, and as a junior inspector at the Board of Education, he had become the first headmaster of Rendcombe College, Cirencester, in 1920. He remained there twelve years. From 1932 to 1944 he was principal of the College of St Mark and St John, Chelsea. He wrote several books dealing with his liberal educational ideas and experiences: *An Adventure in Schooling* (1917), *Howson of Holt* (1925), *Sane Schooling* (1936), *Schoolmaster's Harvest* (1954) and of course *Public Schools and Athleticism* (1923).

2   It has been considered, but only briefly and in very general terms, in histories of the public school system, histories of education and histories of physical education.

3   J. Wakeford, *The Cloistered Elite* (1969), p. 9.

4   For example, Alicia Percival, *Very Superior Men* (1973), pp. 3–10; J. Graves, *Policy and Progress in Secondary Education 1902–1942* (1943), pp. 178–9; Ian Weinberg, *The English Public Schools: the sociology of an elite education* (New York, 1967), pp. ix–xiii; Guy Kendall, *A Headmaster Reflects* (1937), p. 22; G. Kalton, *The Public Schools: a factual*

survey (1966), pp. 4ff; *The Public Schools and the General Education System* (the Fleming Report, 1944), appendix A, pp. 106ff.

5   Vivian Ogilvie, *The English Public School* (1957), p. 8.

6   Its task may be understood from the full title of the published findings: *Report of Her Majesty's Commissioner Appointed to Enquire into the Reserves and Management of Certain Colleges and Schools, and the Studies Pursued therein; with an Appendix and Evidence* (1864).

7   The last two of these schools were day schools. This study of athleticism is confined to public boarding schools – space forbids a wider sample. An interesting discussion of the evolution of games in two public day schools (Dulwich and Manchester Grammar School) is to be found in John Mallea, 'The Boys' Endowed Grammar Schools in Victorian England: the educational use of sport' (unpublished Ph.D. thesis, Columbia University, 1971). *The Report of the Bryce Commission on Education* (1895) referred to the seven boarding schools of the Clarendon Report as the 'Great Public Schools'.

8   Brian Gardner, *The Public Schools* (1973), p. 164.

9   The term 'ideology' was coined by the French philosopher Destult de Tracy, at the end of the eighteenth century. For an outline of its creation see Daniel Bell, *The End of Ideology* (New York, 1961), pp. 394–5.

10 For a discussion of the emergence of ideologies in social groups see 'Ideology' in David L. Sills (ed.), *International Encyclopedia of the Social Sciences* (New York, 1968), pp. 66ff.

11 For a discussion of this wider definition, and for a subtle and seminal consideration of the term 'ideology', see J.M. Burns, 'Political ideology' in N. MacKenzie (ed.), *A Guide to the Social Sciences* (1966), pp. 205–23.

12 The view of Marx and Engels discussed in K. Fletcher, *The Making of Sociology* (1971), p. 406.

13 Gustave Bergmann, 'Ideology' in May Brodbeck (ed.), *Readings in the Philosophy of the Social Sciences* (1968), p. 127.

14 Notice has been taken of the advice of Asa Briggs, namely that history students should seek the assistance of specialists in the social sciences when the insights are relevant. See Asa Briggs, 'History and society' in MacKenzie (ed.) *Guide to the Social Sciences*, pp. 39–40.

15 While widely used as a descriptive and analytical term it is not always defined. In particular, P.C. Mcintosh in his *Physical Education in England since 1800* (2nd edn, 1968), devotes three chapters to it but fails to provide a definition!

16 E.C. Mack, *Public Schools and British Opinion Since 1860* (New York, 1941), p. 126.

17 W.D. Smith, *Stretching Their Bodies* (Newton Abbott, 1975), p. 18. Circular causality, in fact, existed. It is more appropriate to recognise that middle-class anti-intellectualism and contempt for the classical curriculum prevailing in the schools were major *causes* of athleticism as well as consequences. For a discussion of this point, see chapter 5 below.

18 Edward Lyttelton, 'Athletics in public schools', *Nineteenth Century*, Vol. VII, No. 35 (Jan. 1880), pp. 43ff. Lyttelton (1855–1942) was typical of the later nineteenth-century genre of public school headmasters: 'schoolmaster, Divine and cricketer' (*DNB*, 1941–50). He was educated at Eton and Trinity Hall, Cambridge. From 1882 to 1890 he was an assistant master at Eton. After serving as headmaster of Haileybury (1890–1905), he returned to Eton as headmaster (1905–16). In his youth he was a famous cricketer, captain of Eton eleven (1874) and captain of Cambridge (1878). His Cambridge eleven defeated the Australians in 1874, and he was the only man in England to score a century against them. But with regard to athleticism he wore no rose-tinted spectacles. He took an objective view of it in his writings: *Schoolboys and Schoolwork* (1909) and *Memories and Hopes* (1925).

19 Lyttelton, 'Athletics', p. 57.

20   Cyril Norwood, *The English Tradition of Education* (1929), p. 143. Norwood (1875–1956) represented the new public school headmaster of the twentieth century: layman, academic and games player. In 1901 he abandoned his civil service post at the Admiralty and became an assistant master at Leeds Grammar School. He subsequently became one of the most distinguished educationalists of the first half of the twentieth century. In 1906 he became headmaster of Bristol Grammar School, revived its fortunes and became known as 'its second founder'. Despite a lack of experience of public boarding schools he became headmaster of Marlborough in 1916. Ten years later on the urging of the Archbishop of Canterbury he took up the headmastership of Harrow with a mandate 'to raise the standard of work and discipline' (*DNB*, 1957–60). Norwood was a staunch supporter of the English public school, and a forceful advocate of team games. He wrote a number of books on education in which a discriminating admiration of the English public school is apparent. See in particular *The Higher Education of Boys in England* (1909) (written in conjunction with A.H. Hope) and *English Tradition of Education*.

21   *English Tradition of Education*.

22   Dennis Brailsford, *Sport and Society* (1969), p. 25.

23   Philip Mason, *A Matter of Honour: an account of the Indian Army; its officers and men* (1974), p. 391. The sentiment recalls E.W. Hornung's poem about his son, an Old Etonian, entitled 'Last Post' in his *Notes of a Camp Follower on the Western Front* (1919), p. 2:

> Still finding war of games the cream
> And his platoon a priceless team
> Still running it by sportsman's rule
> Just as he ran his house at school.

24   Ernest Raymond's *Tell England: a study in a generation*, first published in 1922, was a novel of the public school boy at war; its heroes such as Ray, were decent, uncomplicated games-playing men and boys. Arnold Lunn's *The Harrovians*, first published in 1913, was a deliberate attack on the philistine 'aristocracy of muscle' at Harrow before the Great War. Cayley was a callous but courageous member of this aristocracy.

25   E.C. Mack, *Public Schools and British Opinion 1780–1860: an examination of the relationship between contemporary ideas and the evolution of an English institution* (1938), p. 108.

26   D.M. Stuart, *The Boy Through the Ages* (1926), p. 281.

27   R.A. Nisbet, *The Sociological Tradition* (paperback edn, 1970), p. 23.

28   This is clear from many sources including headmasters, assistant masters, ex-pupils and mere admirers. For restrained examples see S.A. Pears (assistant master at Harrow 1847–54, and subsequently headmaster of Repton 1854–74), *Sermons at School: short sermons preached at Repton School Chapel* (1870), p. 10; J.E.C. Welldon (headmaster of Harrow 1884–95), *Recollections and Reflections* (1915), p. 138; Cyril Norwood (headmaster of Marlborough 1916–25 subsequently Harrow 1926–34), 'The boys boarding schools' in J. Dover Wilson (ed.), *The Schools of England: a study in renaissance* (1928), p. 16; Stephen Foot (bursar and assistant master at Eastbourne College 1920–34), 'Public schools' in *Nineteenth Century*, vol. XCIX, no. 587 (Feb. 1926), p. 1961; Archibald Douglas Fox (Harrow pupil 1892–7), *Public School Life: Harrow* (1911), p. 58; Sir Ernest Barker (ed.), *The Character of England* (Oxford, 1947), pp. 447–8. For particularly committed examples see Oxonian–Harrovian, letter to *The Times*, 30 Sept. 1889, p. 3; Eustace Miles, 'Games which the nation needs', *Humane Review* (1901), pp. 211–22; E.B.H. Jones, 'The moral aspect of athletics', *Journal of Education*, June 1900, pp. 352–4.

29   T.L. Papillon (1841–1926), quoted in Bernard Darwin, *The English Public School* (1931), p. 21.

30   T.C. Worsley, *Barbarians and Philistines* (1940), p. 107.

Gillian Avery

THE BEST TYPE OF GIRL

Physical education

'THE OLDER VIEW OF PHYSICAL CULTURE for girls had been concerned with grace and posture rather than with health and activity,' recalled one school chronicler. 'Walking and perhaps riding were the only actual exercise, and apart from that the girl was trained, as it were, more like a plant than an animal, by fastening her to various sorts of rigid framework.'[1] Girls were made to lie on backboards, had their chins held up by iron collars, their backs pulled back by steel hands. Mary Martha Sherwood (1775–1851), author of *The History of the Fairchild Family*, one of the most famous evangelical children's classics, in childhood was made by her father to translate fifty lines of Virgil every day, standing in stocks to straighten her back, with an iron collar round her neck.[2] As has been said, the only exercise taken by the old-fashioned seminary was walking in crocodile (a term which seems to have first been used about 1870). When the Mount abolished their crocodiles in 1900 one girl, at least, felt nostalgic: 'I rather liked walking in a crocodile, it felt friendly and rather important.' But it was held to be a nuisance to passers-by in York, though for a time it was thought to be enough if the girls went into single file when they met pedestrians. 'We then practised in the garden, the seniors, armed with coal pans and other impediments, meeting the croc at various corners.'[3] A few schools had callisthenics classes, but Mr Fearon, appointed by the Taunton commissioners to report on the metropolitan area, found that of a hundred private schools for girls, sixty provided no form of exercise other than 'walking abroad, croquet and dancing', and thirty-two provided only a form of callisthenics, which was often unpopular with parents as it was an expensive extra.[4] He attributed much female ill-health to lack of exercise, and stressed in his report that proprietors of schools 'ought to provide their pupils with games which shall be sufficiently difficult to thoroughly divert their minds'.[5]

Two of the headmistresses who gave evidence to the Commission were themselves aware of the importance of exercise. Miss Buss told the commissioners that at North London Collegiate callisthenics was compulsory for everyone, four days a week, and the younger children were encouraged to take exercise in the playground.[6] Miss Beale said that at Cheltenham they had 'a room specially fitted with swings etc. It is to be wished that croquet could be abolished, it gives no proper exercise, induces colds, and places the body in a crooked posture; besides, as it does not fatigue, girls are able to go on for five or six hours and induced to be idle'.[7] A few headmistresses like Alice Ottley feared that games might rub off the delicate bloom of femininity. She detested women's cricket, for instance, which she allowed only the little girls of her school to play.

In the absence of trained female instructors, schools often had to import army sergeants to drill the girls. 'We had a sergeant from the Barracks who came to teach us drill,' a founder member of Norwich High School recalled. 'His voice was terrific, and one day the Headmistress came in and said "My good man, will you please modulate your voice?" at which he took a deep breath and shouted louder.'[8] [. . .]

But by this time [the early twentieth century] Swedish drill, taught by experts, was fashionable. It reached the smarter schools via the elementary schools. (The latter were obliged by the terms of the 1870 Education Act to provide two hours of physical education for boys, and were in effect the pioneers of PE as a universal subject.) The method was brought over to England by Madame Sofia Helena Bergman (she married Dr Per Österburg in 1886 and was subsequently known as Bergman-Österburg), who had studied at the Royal Central Gymnastics Institute in Stockholm the Ling methods of exercising each part of the body in turn, taking care not to develop one part at a different rate from the others. In 1881 the London Schools Board appointed her Superintendent of Physical Education in Girls' and Infants' Schools, and the following year she organized a drill display in which hundreds of London schoolchildren took part, watched by a large and distinguished audience including the Prince and Princess of Wales.

In 1885 she opened a gymnasium (which later became the Dartford College of Physical Training) to train teachers. But though the girls played team games, Madame Bergman Österburg never grasped their rules, and if she did attend a match was apt to be unclear whether the players were supposed to hit or kick the ball. She felt passionately that her mission was to improve the lot of women:

> I try to train my girls to help to raise their own sex, and so to accelerate the progress of their race . . . If [women] studied the laws of health and lived free, untrammelled lives, with plenty of physical exercise, they would not be the sickly, careworn beings so many of them are at present.[9]

[. . .] Though Edward Thring had installed a gymnasium and a swimming pool at Uppingham in the 1850s, for girls the former was not by any means usual. Kent College's, purpose-built in 1886, must have been one of the earliest. The headmistress of the Lady Eleanor Holles School, then at Hackney (Julia Maria Ruddle, 1878–95), is supposed to have begged the governors not to build a gymnasium because such exercise was unladylike. As late as 1923 Mother Clare of Brentwood Ursuline Convent was reporting with grim satisfaction that inspectors were beginning to show 'disapproval of much that takes place in the drill lessons'. She picked out somersaults, cart-wheels, leap-frog and tunnel-ball as particularly undesirable. A Catholic inspector had remarked that she could not understand superiors of convents allowing such activities. Simple Swedish exercises were quite enough, with pupils being taught how to walk and dance gracefully.[10] Dancing, of course, had been a feature of the old-style seminary, but this was a social accomplishment rather than an outlet for exercise, and dance as part of physical education did not appear until the latter became more sophisticated. Some schools in the early part of this century took up English country dancing – it features in many of Elsie J. Oxenham's books[11] – and Greek dancing and eurhythmics were fashionable in the 1920s and 30s. Ardent disciples claimed much for both. In Greek dancing

> Not only are the physical powers developed; the sight of the unhastening movements of the dance gives rest to eyes tired with the unrhythmic kaleidoscope of modern life, the sound of great choric odes or divine melodies brings peace to ears weary with the harsh noises of machinery; the contemplation of the arts of the ancient world soothes the spirit and sets it free from the confining walls of cities, to roam in the great spaces of nature and of the human soul.[12]

Eurhythmics, the system of combined muscular and musical instruction developed by Emile Jaques-Dalcroze . . ., is intended to make feeling for rhythm a physical experience. It teaches the interpretation of music through movement, and at one time at schools like Moira House was a way of life in itself. Greek dancing had been started for a few of the older girls at Mary Datchelor School in 1927, and the 'green tunics and elegant hairbands' inspired such envy that it was introduced for all, 'and now girls disport themselves as nymphs and butterflies and seagulls and heaven knows what else'.[13] Both of these were supplanted in later years by the Laban free dance system. Rudolf Laban, who had escaped from Nazi Germany in 1938 and settled in England, evolved a whole philosophy of movement as a means of human expression. His free dance was a useful antidote to the constricting formality of the classical ballet taught at independent schools from the 1920s onwards, which only the advanced who had fully mastered the technique could use for self-expression.

But dance tended to belong to the smaller, more idiosyncratic school. In the public schools it was games that mattered. It is both sad and salutary to remember that what was to become such tyranny started off as fun. Writing in the Francis Holland, Clarence Gate, magazine in 1892 the hockey captain earnestly invited her readers to try the game, adding 'All who have played it declare it to be one of the most exciting and exhilarating games they know. It is as thrilling as football without the strong element of danger . . . Hockey is not in the least dangerous; with the exception of a few trifling bruises, no one is likely to get hurt.' Her girlish enthusiasm, and the notion that you played games because they were fun, is a far cry from the hectoring severity of the school's lacrosse captain writing in the magazine forty years later.

> One or two girls, shirking the drudgery, have given up the game altogether. Let them clearly understand that this is not showing a sporting spirit. In future all slackers will be turned out of the Club, so that its members may be looked upon as earnest, hardworking players – who play, play up, and play the game.

At first games were spontaneous, initiated by the girls themselves (though the girls of the Royal School in the 1880s got no further than buying a football and learning to blow it up). The Misses Lawrence and later Miss Dove at Wycombe Abbey incorporated games into the curriculum from the start, but this was unusual. Even at St Leonards it was optional and unorganized in the early days. There was merely a games club with a rule that 'any members failing to play at least once a week for three weeks, without proper excuse, will be fined the sum of 2d'. The club lapsed, and an elected school captain was made responsible for seeing that everybody played at least once a week; there were many who never did more than that. 'Goals' and rounders were played in the winter; cricket and tennis in the summer. 'Goals' was able to accommodate any number of players. The weapon was a cross between a heavy walking stick and a shepherd's crook, and the only copy of the rules was in the captain's pocket and open to the widest interpretation.

Bedford High School in the late 1880s and the 1890s played the same sort of game.

> The goal posts were two sticks at one end and the large chestnut tree and the privet hedge. We had practically no rules, except that we always changed places after a goal was scored; if the ball went out, whoever reached it first threw it in, and we played with the stick in either hand as we liked, and with the front or the back of it. With the arrival of Miss Lea we began to learn that there were rules, though we must have been extraordinarily difficult to teach, as I remember how keen we were on our own peculiar game.[14]

Similarly the upper sixth at Worcester rebelled against being pulled up in their rushings to and fro. They indicated that they had never played games like that, and if they were going to be ordered about so much the game might as well be called a lesson. At Blackheath High School an 1880s pupil said there appeared to be no limitation on numbers at their games of hockey; it seemed as if the whole of the upper school took to the field at once. There were no rules, except a vague one about offside. 'Goals were generally scored from a confused mêlée, in which the ball was pushed over the line by sheer weight of numbers . . . I do not know when I have enjoyed any game more.'[15] [. . .]

Brighton and Hove High School in 1886 was playing football in the same carefree spirit, but with a greater degree of organization. Their playground was a mass of stones and gravel which quickly wore out leather, and the game was often interrupted by the ball bursting –'Our balls get done for very much more easily than they otherwise would,' said the school magazine. But the writer reckoned that their game had improved, though she had criticisms:

> A few of the smaller members of the Club have a great tendency to hop over the ball, instead of kicking it; whilst others are terribly afraid of it and think only of getting out of the way of kicks; others make gallant dashes at the ball, but, on second thoughts, think they had better leave it to their opponents.[16]

But by 1900 the carefree abandon had gone out of team games (except at small schools like Prior's Field, where 'we could not very well play hockey with only six girls, so we purchased a football, and all of us . . . used to have the most exciting times with it'.) The City of Cardiff High School magazine gave hints on the clothes that should be worn ('Hard hats and hat pins are dangerous, but a cap may be used. The shins may be protected by shin-guards or gaiters'), and pointed out that it was a 'sanitary necessity, often neglected by women', to take a 'warm (not hot) bath' afterwards.

> In conclusion, it may be remembered that one of the chief defects in present girls' play is a certain slackness; they are not quick enough in 'bullying', or in taking their places at a 'throw-in', or in getting on to the ball from a corner-hit, or in following up their own hits. Further, in playing matches, they have not sufficient knowledge of the game to divine the weak places in the game of their opponents . . . They should also learn to stop the ball otherwise than with the skirt.

And twenty years after those gloriously ad hoc games at Blackheath, the school had settled down to the ritual of matches, 'We appeared at morning school in our black skirts and "wasp" blouses, with the yellow ties that were the "colours" . . . our hair was plaited with a tightness that was more utilitarian than beautiful, and tied with yellow ribbon. At Prayers we sang "Fight the Good Fight" with great feeling.'[17] St Swithun's in 1896 at their first outside match, against Queen Anne's, Caversham, had been suitably daunted by the professionalism of their rivals (who had won). The team who 'were all dressed in scarlet and looked to us very burly and experienced' had declined suet pudding at lunch time, and according to St Swithun's tradition, were discovered afterwards 'lying on the floor resting in preparation'.[18] But in this year The Laurels won its first away match.

> I only know the feelings of those who stayed at home – we waited in almost breathless anxiety till the telegram came. And how we cheered the victors back to the Laurels, and what a welcome we gave them, as we ushered them in with the well-known strains of 'See the conquering heroes come'.[19]

The stage is now set for the grim earnestness with which games were taken at the larger girls' schools in the early twentieth century. [. . .]

The Sacred Heart nuns had always put great stress on the importance of innocent recreation, and at Roehampton they were playing cricket and tennis in the 1870s. The game of cache-cache, peculiar to them alone and remembered with ecstasy by all 'old children', was held to have peculiarly beneficial effects on the character. 'Few school games are as fine a training in endurance, self-control, discretion and chivalrous honour,' claimed a member of the order.[20] You had to restrain your excitement when twenty or thirty of you were lying in a haystack or some outbuilding, or up in the rafters, while enemy spies crept round nearby. You had to control the urge afterwards to boast about the superb new hiding place, and you never, never looked, when the game was over, to see where the other side was coming from.

Cache-cache seems to have been universally loved, which was more than can be said for most team games. [. . .]

Individual schools had their own traditions. Wroxall Abbey played rugby football from time to time, the rumour being that when the school was in Rugby it played on the Rugby School fields. And at Runton Hill an epic game called 'valley ball' used to be played, invented by the headmistress, Miss Vernon Harcourt.

The entire school would turn out, and stand shoulder to shoulder in two lines, like a crocodile . . . The object of the game was for one house to touch down the ball in the opposing house's camp on the top of the opposite hillside, having crossed the valley . . . Miss Vernon Harcourt would hurl the ball into the air and the game would be on. The game raged down and up the steepest valley that JVH could find in the Roman Camp. One might run with the ball, but when tackled one had to pass, but backwards, as in Rugby football. I used to spend most of the game face downwards in the bracken, all breath knocked from my body, while the two teams, North and South, tramped heavily by on my shoulder blades. But I was fairly well off. Frances sprained an ankle. Viola had long scratches down her face. Even JVH, bounding high in the air, tooting on her whistle, occasionally hurt herself. I imagine that for the rest of the girls of Runton Hill, valley netball has a great nostalgic significance, like the Eton Wall Game.[21]

Notes

1   Janet Whitcut: *Edgbaston High School: 1876–1976*. 1976, p. 49.
2   Sophia Kelly (ed.): *Life of Mrs Sherwood*. London: Darton, 1857, p. 51.
3   H. Winifred Sturge and Theodora Clark: *The Mount School, York, 1785 to 1814, 1831 to 1931*. London: Dent, 1931, p. 40.
4   *Schools Inquiry Commission Report*, vol. I, pp. 548–9.
5   Ibid., vol. VII, appendix XII, p. 587.
6   Ibid., vol. V, p. 265.
7   Ibid., vol. V, p. 740.
8   Prunella R. Bodington (ed.): *Norwich High School 1875–1950*, p. 40.
9   Jonathan May: *Madame Bergman-Österburg*. London: Harrap, 1969, p. 52.
10 John Berchmans Dockery OFM: *They That Build: the life of Mother Clare of Brentwood*. London: Burns & Oates, 1963, p. 138.
11 See Mary Cadogan and Patricia Craig: *You're a Brick, Angela*. London: Gollancz, 1976, pp. 162 et seq.
12 Ruby Ginner: *The Revived Greek Dance*. London: Methuen, 1933, p. 20.
13 *The Story of the Mary Datchelor School, 1887–1957*. London: Hodder & Stoughton, 1957.
14 K.M. Westaway (ed.): *A History of Bedford High School*. 1932, p. 49.
15 Mary C. Malim and Henrietta C. Escreet (eds): *The Book of the Blackheath High School*. 1927, p. 108.
16 M.G. Mills: *Brighton and Hove High School 1876–1952*. 1953, p. 39.
17 Malim and Escreet (eds), op. cit., p. 115.
18 Priscilla Bain: *St Swithun's: a century history*. Chichester: Phillimore, 1984, p. 9.
19 Barbara Bourke (ed.): *The Laurels 1872–1972 Wroxall Abbey*, p. 15.
20 Mary Catherine Goulter: *Schoolday Memories*. London: Burns & Oates, 1922.
21 Nancy Spain: *A Funny Thing Happened on the Way*. London: Hutchinson, 1964, p. 31.

Peter Bailey

RATIONAL RECREATION AND
THE NEW ATHLETICISM

O NE OF THE MORE REMARKABLE FEATURES of the expanding
world of mid-Victorian leisure was the innovation of organised and codified athletic
sports – a broad category of activities which comprised primarily the athletics of track
and field events, as the term is understood today, together with a reconstructed version
of football, and the previously reformed game of cricket. In the 1860s public school men
began to carry their enthusiasm for the reformed canon of athletic sports through into
adult life, and by the Jubilee year of 1887 Gladstone was pointing to the popularity of
these sports as a measure of the nation's improved taste in recreation. 'For the schoolboy
and the man alike', he observed, 'athletics are becoming an ordinary incident of life.'[1]
Thereafter the practice spread still more widely and moved one reputable historian of
the period to contend that 'the suburban middle class made organised games rank among
England's leading contributions to world culture.'[2] In today's world sport is recognised
as a powerful instrument for commanding social conformity, with a unique role to play
in counteracting divisive forces such as class and race.[3] How did it commend itself to
the Victorians, and what part did it play in the prescriptions of rational recreation?

I

There were those contemporaries who were persistently hostile to the growing cult
of organised games, but they need not detain us long; the intellectual strengths of
their case could do little to check the tide of popular enthusiasm. John Ruskin, Matthew
Arnold and Wilkie Collins were among those who attacked the worship of athletics as
boorish and dehumanising. In 1869 Collins enjoyed considerable literary success with his
novel 'Man and Wife' in which the central figure, Geoffrey Delamayn, is an athlete
whose life is brutalised by his sport. In the preface Collins makes it quite clear that

Delamayn represents a new type, 'the rough in broadcloth', who constitutes a serious menace to society.[4] Recalling this indictment some twenty years later, Montague Shearman, barrister, athlete and author of discerning and respected handbooks on sport, commented that the English public had admired the story but refused to swallow its message; to Shearman it was by then self-evident that 'the athletic movement has benefited the people at large.'[5]

For the most part the new-style athleticism won a good press and recommended itself as an eminently rational, even spiritual, recreation. In mid-Victorian England, in particular, the preoccupation with the maintenance of national military preparedness led to a new respect for physical education. In the 1830s and 1840s reformers had talked of the Health of Towns; the capitalised imperative in following decades became the Health of the Nation. The shift is significant. The previous concern had been that the disease and misery of the new manufacturing towns would demoralise the working classes, make them easy prey for the political agitator, and lead them to subversion and revolt. After 1848 the fear of the governing classes was of assault from without, more than from within. In 1850, contemplating the welter of self-congratulation at England's escape from the fires of the continental revolutions, John Stores Smith, a Manchester businessman, declared England 'the forlorn hope of European life'. Smith was impressed less by the fact of her survival than by the extent of her vulnerability which, in the light of his study of other once-great nations, suggested the danger of immediate decline. This theme gained currency. In 1852, in the course of reviewing the activities and publications of the growing number of vegetarian and homeopathic societies, the 'Westminster Review' – while enjoying itself a little at the expense of the 'potato gospel' – pointed out 'how unfailing an accompaniment of the decline of empires is the depreciation of the national habit of body'. A proper concern for the nation's health, continued the journal, came 'just in time for that great contest with European tyranny during the remainder of the century, which is apparently to be the part of England and America'.[6] The Crimean War, the invasion scare of 1859 and the dramatic rise of Prussia increased alarm at the imminence of such a contest, and gave new emphasis to the traditional utility of sport in preserving the fitness of the nation's physical stock. Thus the Volunteers played their games in the service of England's security.[7]

The call for effective exercise was addressed to town dwellers of all classes, for the debilities of city life seemed to threaten rich as well as poor. Of the former, Leslie Stephen noted in 1870:

> The class which does not live by manual labour, and which at the same time
> has very little opportunity for hunting and fishing, has increased in an enormous
> ratio, and is still increasing. We are living more and more in towns and
> treading closer upon each other's heels.

Though he was apprehensive at the dangers that the popularity of athletic sports posed to intellectual life at the universities, Stephen allowed that they met the need for physical recreation ('some good stupid amusement') for the urban middle classes. Some traditional prescriptions were in any case now simply impractical – as John Morley pointed out, 'the persistence of doctors in urging horse exercise is, to the majority, absurd.'[8] Among this majority were the clerks and shopmen, whose work, according to 'The Times', demanded only the slightest of physiques: 'Civilisation wants light men – they don't want six feet to vault over counters and run up steps at a draper's shop.' At the time of the Crimean War the paper warned that the nation could not rely upon such insubstantial material to win future Inkermans, unless nimbleness was reinforced with muscle and stamina. Thirty years later, in a survey of modern English sport, Frederick Gale concluded that only organised games had saved the 'counter skippers' from effeminacy.[9] The working classes were never in danger of effeminacy, but city life blighted their health to an extent which alarmed doctors and disappointed recruiting sergeants. William Hardwicke, medical officer for health in Paddington in the 1860s, urged the case for state promotion of games and gymnastic exercises to halt this degeneration, and Lord Brabazon, chairman of the Gardens and Playgrounds Association, moved the same case twenty years later on the evidence that nearly half the recruits seeking enlistment in the services were rejected for physical incapacity.[10]

Physical recreation received further endorsement from major contemporary figures. We have seen in a previous chapter how Charles Kingsley imparted a spiritual gloss to sport and bodily exercise. His emphasis upon their necessary practice as a duty to one's country became more insistent after his conversion to Darwinism (an ideology whose popularity increased the general concern over national health). Another Darwinian, Herbert Spencer, maintained that 'the contests of commerce are in part determined by the bodily endurance of the producers.'[11]

Under the influence of such teachings sport became a medium for training the young to meet with the diverse challenges of a naturally harsh and competitive world. 'Games,' declared the physician to Rugby School, 'produce a just ambition to excel in every phase of the battle of life.'[12] The language of games became the language of adventure and the highest endeavour, designed to sustain the young under fire, whether from fast bowlers or insurgent tribesmen. A Scottish divine expressed his delight at a youthful game of cricket in the following terms:[13]

> How I love to mark the quick, watchful glance of the eye as the ball comes speeding on which will decide for 'our Club' the honour of the day, and to mark on the faces of those who go out, the look which was on that of François I as he wrote to his mother after the battle of Pavia, 'Tout est perdu hormis l'honneur.'

In Newbolt's popular poem 'Vitai Lampada', it is the voice of a schoolboy that rallies the ranks during some desperate desert action: 'Play up! Play up! and play the game!'

The public school was the principal laboratory in which the young were exposed to sport as a test for greater things to come, and it was here that the games ethos was refined. Men like Dr Arnold at Rugby had promoted organised games to instil discipline and self-government in schoolboys who, in the unreformed public schools of the early nineteenth century, had often sought their recreation in organised riot.[14] The full returns on this practice stood out clearly by the 1880s when Edward Lyttelton considered the merits of public school athletics:[15]

> Firstly by being forced to put the welfare of the common cause before selfish interests, to obey implicitly the word of command, and act in concert with the heterogeneous elements of the company he belongs in; and secondly, should it so turn out, a boy is disciplined by being raised to a post of command,

where he feels the gravity of responsible office and the difficulty of making prompt decisions and securing a willing obedience.

Personal courage tempered by the team spirit, and a respect for authority under the governance of fair play – these were the key values in the new rationale of sport, and also served as important social controls off the field. Devotees of sport internalised its values: N.L. Jackson, a prominent and influential athlete of the 1880s and 1890s, decorated his memoirs with an ample definition of sportsmanship, to which he attributed lessons in self-control, compassion and honesty, maintaining in conclusion that 'it unconsciously directs every action of your life'. 'Athleticism,' asserted Charles Box, cricket writer and popular philosopher, 'is no unimportant bulwark of the constitution . . . [it] has no sympathy with Nihilism, Communism, nor any other "ism" that points to national disorder.' Contemporaries felt too that the values of the games field could be fed back into business life to correct the unrelieved materialism and excessive appetite for speculation that seemed to have superseded what were represented as the essentially moral endeavours of the pioneer heroes of nineteenth-century capitalism.[16]

Sport could be effective in indoctrinating hoi polloi as well as public schoolmen. A testimony on this count comes from H.B. Philpott, an early historian of the London School Board:[17]

> It is as true for the children of mechanics and labourers, as for the children of merchants and professional men, that manly sports, played as they should be played, tend to develop unselfish pluck, determination, self-control and public spirit. Observe a group of Board School cricketers after they have undergone a period of friendly supervision . . . No one quarrels with the placing of the field. . . . the young captain does not bawl 'butter fingers' or 'silly fathead' whenever a catch is missed . . . the batsman bowled for a duck neither shouts that 'it ain't fair' nor punches the umpire . . . No, they have learned to 'play the game'. And the change is not a matter of cricket only; in becoming better cricketers they have become better boys.

Philpott also remarked on the 'moral salvation' effected by football, but it is significant that he should pay most attention to the social therapies of cricket, for it was this game which was constantly made to serve as a metaphor for the ideal society. Although there was a thorough-going commercial sector in cricket, the general banishment of gambling from the game recommended it as a reformed sport. It carried with it long-standing associations of a bucolic, pre-industrial society; it was in fact a perfect vehicle for the myths of Merrie England. Cricket, wrote one representative commentator in the course of a political reform tract of the late 1850s, afforded 'a happy and compendious illustration of English characteristics and English social institutions. . . . the truly English republican element of a mixture of classes with the right man in the right place, is nowhere better exemplified than in the cricket field.'[18] The game was applauded as a civilising influence in the new towns, not least because it was credited with disciplining the spectator as well as the participant. Recording progress in Yorkshire, John Lawson observed that 'it is not uncommon now [1887] for the people of Pudsey to be seen applauding their opponents by clapping hands' (the reactions of sixty years previous had been somewhat more curmudgeonly).[19]

Thus the new model athletic sports boasted some impeccable credentials: they provided a regimen which brought physical fitness to the individual, toughening him against the debilities of city life and maintaining his readiness for armed service; they also provided an education in self-discipline and team work which acted as a moral police over the individual's life at large; adapted to the new circumstances of modern society they yet retained sentimental historical associations of social harmony and the fraternity of all classes in sport. At the very least they were recommended as an antidote for what, by all accounts, seems to have been the common complaint of Victorian town dwellers – indigestion. [. . .]

Much of the practice of sport in England remained segregated along class lines. The new athleticism had provided sport with credentials which gave unprecedented emphasis to its capacity for imparting the highest moral and social values. Despite these recommendations, there had been no extensive move to propagate the new games codes among the masses. The middle-class enthusiasts of the new athleticism mostly discouraged working-class participation, in order to prevent contamination from the corrupt practices attributed to popular sport, and to reserve the new games as a medium for defining class status. In the much vaunted 'republic of sport', only cricket received special dispensation as the one game whose mystique resisted popular corruption and kept the base mechanics in their place; otherwise, the working classes were to be left the basic commons of military drill and callisthenics. Despite the antipathies of its self-appointed governors, the working classes took up the new athleticism with avidity. The process of diffusion needs further research and explanation, but it seems clear that reformers played a more limited role than has previously been suggested. There was a strong appetite for sport among English workingmen and, while they took readily to the new models, they showed in the case of football a determination to adapt them to the circumstances and needs of their own culture.

Notes

1   W.E. Gladstone, Locksley Hall and the Jubilee, 'Nineteenth Century', xxi (1887), pp. 1–18.

2   R.C.K. Ensor, 'England, 1870–1914' (1936), p. 164. Salvador de Madariaga's epigram is at once less congratulatory and ominously more specific: 'One Englishman, a fool; two Englishmen, a football match; three Englishmen, the British Empire.' Quoted in J.L. and B.Hammond, 'The Growth of Common Enjoyment' (Oxford, 1933), p. 9.

3   E.g. G. Magnane, 'Sociologie du sport' (1947), p. 43: 'Sport is the chief pole of attraction toward approved activities: licit, consciously social and, in the broadest sense of the term, docile.' Quoted in E. Weber, Gymnastics and sports in fin de siécle France: opium of the classes?, 'American Historical Review', lxxvi (1971), p. 91. See also 'Sport and the Community: Report of the Wolfenden Committee on Sport for the Central Council of Physical Recreation' (1960), p. 6: 'Sportsmanship . . . in its deeper (and usually inarticulate) significance . . . still provides something like the foundations of an ethical standard . . . in hard practice it is no bad elementary guide to decent living together in society.' For a practical discussion of this contemporary orthodoxy, see E. Dunning, ed., 'Sport: Readings from a Sociological Perspective' (Toronto, 1972), pp. 233–78.

4   W. Collins, 'Man and Wife', 3 vols (1870), i, pp. viii–xi; B. Haley, Sports and the Victorian world, 'Western Humanities Review', xxii (1968), pp. 115–25.

5   M. Shearman, 'Athletics and Football' (1889), p. 241. This is one of the Badminton series of handbooks which provides a useful introduction to Victorian sport. Contemporary material is too diffuse to admit of a meaningful select bibliography here. The first-fruits of modern scholarly research are noted below.

6   J.S. Smith, 'Social Aspects' (1850), pp. 1, 43; Physical puritanism, 'Westminster Review', i, new series (1852), pp. 405–42.

7   Physical strength, 'SR', 10 December 1859; J. Hulley's address to the Athletic Society of Great Britain, 'Athletic Review and Journal of Physical Education', 2 July 1867.

8   L. Stephen, Athletic sports and university studies, 'Fraser's Magazine', ii, new series (1870), pp. 691–704; J. Morley, 'Studies in Conduct' (1867), pp. 256–65.

9   'The Times', 5 August 1858, and a debate by correspondence during the Crimean War, recalled by L. Blanc, 'Letters on England', 4 vols (1866–7), i, pp. 32–5; F. Gale, 'Modern English Sports: Their Use and Abuse' (1885), p. 60.

10 W. Hardwicke, Recreation for the working classes?, 'Trans. NAPSS' (1867), pp. 471–7, 552–7; Lord Brabazon, The decay of bodily strength in towns, 'Nineteenth Century', xxi (1887), pp. 673–6 and his 'Social Arrows' (1886). Lord Elcho had tried, unsuccessfully, to pass a bill through the Commons in 1862 to organise a national programme of gymnastic training. The big railway companies instituted physical tests for job applicants in the mid-1870s and reported a large number of rejects.

11 C. Kingsley, 'Health and Education' (1874), pp. 2–17; H. Spencer, 'Education, Intellectual, Moral and Physical' (1861), pp. 146, 173. For Darwinism in medical terms, see H.W. Acland, 'National Health: Health, Work and Play' (1871); for popular Darwinism, G.J. Romanes, Recreation, 'Nineteenth Century', vi (1879), pp. 401–24.

12 C. Dukes, 'Health at School' (third edn, 1894), p. 284.

13 J. Kay, 'The Church and Popular Recreations' (Edinburgh, 1883), p. 10.

14 W.H.G. Armytage, Thomas Arnold's views on physical education, 'Journal of Physical Education', xlvii (1955), pp. 27–44; Dunning, Development of modern football, op. cit., pp. 133–51.

15 E. Lyttelton, Athletics in public school, 'Nineteenth Century', vii (1880), pp. 43–57. Educators also recommended games as a counter to 'unnatural lusts' prevalent in public schools. See (Thomas Markby), Athletics, 'Contemporary Review', iii (1866), pp. 374–91; 'The Science of Life: A Pamphlet addressed to All Members of the Universities of Oxford and Cambridge and to All Who Are, or Who Will Be Teachers, Clergymen, or Fathers' (1877).

16 N.L. Jackson, 'Sporting Days and Sporting Ways' (1932), pp. 9–10; C. Box, 'Musings for Athletes' (1888), p. 167. See also T. Cook, 'Character and Sportsmanship' (1927); Dunning, loc. cit.

17 H.B. Philpott, 'London at School: the Story of the School Board' (1904), p. 127. I owe this reference to Raphael Samuel.

18 G.J. Cayley, 'The Working Classes: Their Interest in Reform' (1858). Cricket had in fact been criticised in its early years for mixing inferiors and superiors, see J. Strutt, 'The Sports and Pastimes of the People of England' (Methuen reprint edn, 1903), p. 102. For its mythical qualities, see, e.g., T. Sparks (C. Dickens), 'Sunday Under Three Heads' (1836), pp. 39–44.

19 J. Lawson, 'Letters to the Young on the Progress in Pudsey' (Stanninglen, 1887), p. 63. The claims made for cricket were many and remarkable, but one in particular I find irresistible; it comes from Thomas Hughes, reporting a letter from an officer in

the engineers before Sebastopol: 'The round shot which were ever coming at him were very much like cricket balls from a moderately swift bowler; he could judge them quite as accurately, and by just turning round when the gun which bore on him was fired, and marking the first pitch of the shot, he could tell whether to move or not, and so got on with his work very comfortably.' Physical education, 'Working Men's College Magazine', May 1859.

Hugh Cunningham

CLASS AND LEISURE IN MID-VICTORIAN ENGLAND

[. . .]

HISTORICALLY AT MID-CENTURY the hope that the classes might be brought together in leisure had two distinct roots. On the one hand were those who had opposed the attack on popular leisure in the later eighteenth and early nineteenth centuries, arguing instead for a paternalist patronage of the people's customs and sports. These, they claimed, brought the classes together, prevented effeminacy and promoted patriotism. The attack on popular leisure seemed to them motivated by class interest. The Cruelty to Animals Bill of 1809, said Windham, was 'A Bill for harrassing and oppressing certain Classes among the lower Orders of His Majesty's Subjects'.[1] And this kind of argument appealed not only to Tory traditionalists but also to middle-class people with a social conscience and radical disposition. On the other hand there was rational recreation which was a first if hardly explicit admission on the side of reformers that there was something to Windham's accusations. The remedy they proposed of course was quite different. They advocated not the preservation of the past but the creation of new institutions and activities. Within these, they argued the respectable of all classes could meet in harmony. [. . .]

. . . [T]he process of appropriation . . . is most clearly evident in the history of cricket. In the early nineteenth century cricket was morally suspect. We can see why if we look at Miss Mitford's famous description of a country cricket match in the 1820s. She carefully distinguishes the type of cricket she is writing about from others:

> I doubt if there be any scene in the world more animating or delightful than a cricket-match – I do not mean a set match at Lord's Ground for money, hard money, between a certain number of gentlemen and players, as they are called – people who make a trade of that noble sport, and degrade it into an

affair of bettings, and hedgings, and cheatings, it may be, like boxing or horse-racing; nor do I mean a pretty *fête* in a gentleman's park, where one club of cricketing dandies encounter another such club, and where they show off in graceful costume to a gay marquee of admiring belles . . . No! The cricket that I mean is a real solid old-fashioned match between neighbouring parishes, where each attacks the other for honour and a supper, glory and half-a-crown a man. If there be any gentlemen amongst them, it is well – if not, it is so much the better.

Cricket, like so many other sports, was 'noble', but liable to be degraded. And even in this idealised village cricket match the morally sensitive would note that money is passing hands, and that for lack of gentry patronage, it was the publicans who organised the game. In less idealised form, and at much the same period, cricket at Pudsey was unknown

except as played mostly in the lanes or small openings in the village – with a tub leg for a bat, made smaller at one end for a handle, a wall cape, or some large stone, set on end for a stump (called a 'hob'), and a pot taw or some hard substance covered with listing and sometimes sewed on the top with twine or band. They were all one-ball overs if double cricket was played; no umpires, and often those who cheated the hardest won.[2]

It was from these suspect origins, much more than from the gentry-sponsored games of the south, that cricket emerged as a popular spectator sport in the first half of the century. In 1824 there were 17,000 spectators at a match in Sheffield, and in 1835 20,000 working-class men, women and children watched the Nottingham versus Sussex match. These and other less notable games were reported in that journal of the Fancy, *Bell's Life in London*, and there was only pardonable exaggeration in its editor's claim in 1844:

I attribute the Extension of the Game of Cricket very much to the Paper of which I am the Editor. Having been the Editor Twenty Years, I can recollect when the Game of Cricket was not so popular as it is at the present Moment; but the Moment the Cricketers found themselves the Object of Attention almost every Village had its Cricket Green. The Record of their Prowess in Print created a Desire still more to extend their Exertions and their Fame. Cricket has become almost universal . . .[3]

Indeed, but under auspices which must make the respectable shudder. And probably more important than the journals of the Fancy was something equally worrisome, the role of the professional. As Mandle has written, 'In England, cricket, hitherto a game for gentry and their servants or a knock-about recreation for self-employed Midland weavers, entered national life through the itinerant efforts of William Clarke's All-England Eleven from 1846 on.' Clarke was a Nottingham man, a bricklayer by trade, a fine bowler, and an astute manager; he paid each of his men £4 a match, and took the balance of takings for himself. He soon had rivals. In 1852 John Wisden formed the breakaway 'United England Eleven', in 1858 Sherman and Chadband organised a 'New All England

Eleven', in 1862 Fred Caesar was responsible for 'Another New All England Eleven' and in 1865 for the United South of England Eleven. These were touring professional teams, and as Altham and Swanston acknowledge, 'were truly missionaries of cricket, winning to knowledge and appreciation of the game whole districts where hitherto it had been primitive and undeveloped'. In 1859 there occurred the first overseas tour, all professional, to America and Canada, and in 1861 the first, again all professional, to Australia. In the light of these developments there can be no dissent from the conclusion of C.L.R. James that in the development of cricket 'The class of the population that seems to have contributed least was the class destined to appropriate the game and convert it into a national institution. This was the solid Victorian middle class.'[4]

The process of appropriation owed something to a change in the rules in 1864, legalising over-arm bowling, but much more to the achievements of one man, W.G. Grace. In the early 1860s county cricket, the key to upper- and middle-class control, was in a most rudimentary state. It was only in that decade that the county cricket clubs of Hampshire, Lancashire, Middlesex and Yorkshire came into being. Grace, entering the first-class scene in 1864, was an immediate and spectacular success. His achievement, helped by the legalisation of overarm bowling, was to reverse the trend whereby the professionals dominated the game, and he did it by outplaying them; of 40 matches between the Gentlemen and the Players between 1865 and 1881 the Gentlemen won 27 and lost only 5. Through these victories the amateurs could reassert their control over the game, and reduce the professionals to a subordinate position. As James writes, 'It is not possible that cricket would have reached and held the position it did among the upper classes if the Gentlemen, that is to say the products of the public schools and the universities, had been as consistently and cruelly beaten as they had been by the professionals before W.G. began.'[5]

By the late 1860s the Eton versus Harrow match had become an important part of the London season. By 1870 the counties were ranked according to performance, and in the course of that decade the last book-makers were removed from Lord's. The MCC after a period in the doldrums began to revive. Upper- and middle-class control was being asserted, and on the basis of it the moral qualities of cricket could safely be preached. Christians now exalted in their prowess at the game, rather than denied it. And in Pudsey those primitive beginnings were but a dim memory from the past; in the 1880s Joseph Lawson could write that cricket

> has had a most wonderful influence for good on the young men of Pudsey — not only on the players, but on the spectators as well. By cricket, players are taught patience, endurance, precision and courage. They are taught self-respect and gentlemanly conduct in bowing to the decision of the umpires, and derive physical benefit as well. The discipline taught by the game of cricket is great and invaluable . . .

With such a comment, we may safely say, the process of appropriation was complete.[6]
[. . .]

There can be little doubt that the desire for exclusivity was the most important reason for the failure of the hope that class conciliation might be achieved in leisure. Quite simply the Industrial Revolution had created what Trollope in 1868 described as 'the largest and wealthiest leisure class that any country, ancient or modern, ever boasted'. As a class which gained at least part of its identity from its possession of leisure, the spending of that leisure in exclusive and status-enhancing settings was of paramount importance. . . . [T]he class showed considerable ingenuity in securing for itself the desired exclusivity. In the seaside resorts, for example, it appropriated to itself fashionable seasons within the year as well as whole areas of towns. In all this it behaved no differently from the leisure class of early modern times; indeed it was this very behaviour that confirmed that it was indeed a class.[7]

For centuries it had been traditional in European society to see an occasional recreational release for the populace as necessary in the interests of social control. In the mid-nineteenth century in Britain, the emphasis was different; it was not to maintain the social order by allowing the people a modicum of those 'violent delights' which Jerrold thought typical of Londoners as late as 1870.[8] It was, in consciousness of the growth of class feeling in the first half of the century, to halt and reverse the process; not to abandon authority, nor allow it on occasion to be mocked, but to reassert its legitimacy by the class-conciliatory nature of the leisure that was offered. Some middle-class Victorians strove earnestly, through co-operative workshops and the like, to reform the experience of work. Many more, accepting as given the nature and permanence of capitalism, strove to mitigate the hardships it entailed for the working class by organising their leisure for them, and doing it in such a way as to emphasise, they hoped, the spirit of community not of class.

Their efforts were doomed to failure. Community can hardly be created when the wish for it comes almost exclusively from one side of the class barrier. It is even less likely to do so when some of the promoters of the ideal are concerned solely to assimilate, not to give and take. In the class conciliation projects of the mid-Victorian years, the concern to establish authority was as evident as the desire for reconciliation. The building of community through leisure also bore the marks of wishful thinking, of escapism, of retreat to an ideal, patriarchal, gentry-dominated society. For respectable liberal middle-class Victorians to whom revolution was anathema, and the cash nexus of capitalism socially and morally distasteful, the reform of leisure, and at the same time an emphasis on its importance, offered the best hope of a socially harmonious civilisation.

The debates on leisure in the mid-Victorian years, then, have a different tone from those of earlier decades. The aim set by the middle class for itself was more ambitious and positive. It reflected the deep concern about class division, and in seeing the solution to it in leisure, it both inflated the importance of leisure and helped in the process of delimiting it. Leisure had imposed upon it perhaps the supreme task confronting the ruling Victorian middle class, that of improving class relations, and there could be no greater testimony to its new stature The task imposed upon it, however, was too great. If anything in the third quarter of the century and beyond, leisure became more rather than less confined by class boundaries as new class-specific entertainment flourished. And leisure itself proved to be something which could not simply be utilised to serve the immediate purposes of a hegemonic middle class.

Notes

1   W. Windham, *Speeches in Parliament*, 3 vols. (London, 1812), Vol. 3, p. 315.

2   M.R. Mitford, *Our Village*, 5 volumes, 1824–32, p. 169; J. Lawson, *Letters to the Young on Progress in Pudsey During the Last Sixty Years*, Stanninglen, 1887, reprinted Caliban Books, Firle, 1979, pp. 62–3.

3   J. Ford, *Cricket, a Social History 1700–1835* (Newton Abbot, 1972), p. 123; W. Howitt, *The Rural Life of England*, Vol. II, 1838 (reprinted 1 Vol., Shannon 1971), pp. 273–8; S.C. of the House of Lords to inquire into the Laws respecting Gaming, PP 1844 (604), Vol. VI, q. 234.

4   W.F. Mandle, 'Games People Played: Cricket and Football in England and Victoria in the Late Nineteenth Century', *Historical Studies*, Vol. 15 (1973), p. 511, and 'The Professional Cricketer in England in the Nineteenth Century', *Labour History*, no. 23 (1972), p. 2; H.S. Altham and E.W. Swanston, *A History of Cricket*, 4th edn (London, 1948), p. 88; C.L.R. James, *Beyond a Boundary* (London, 1976), p. 159.

5   R. Bowen, *Cricket* (London, 1970), pp. 106–19; James, *Beyond a Boundary*, pp. 157–84.

6   P.C. McIntosh, *Physical Education in England since 1800*, revised and enlarged edn (London, 1968), p. 55; Bowen, *Cricket*, pp. 113–14; P. Scott, 'Cricket and the Religious World in the Victorian Period', *Church Quarterly*, Vol. III (1970), pp. 134–44; Lawson, *Progress in Pudsey*, p. 63.

7   A. Trollope (ed.), *British Sports and Pastimes* (London, 1868), p. 18; J. Walton, 'Residential Amenity, Respectable Morality and the Rise of the Entertainment Industry: The Case of Blackpool 1860–1914', *Literature and History*, No. 1 (1975), pp. 62–78.

8   G. Doré and B. Jerrold, *London, A Pilgrimage*, 1872, reprinted New York, 1970, pp. 161–2.

Tony Mason

AMATEURS AND
PROFESSIONALS

[. . .]

ORGANISED FOOTBALL, based on a widespread acceptance of a more or less uniform code of laws, expanded quite quickly through the 1870s, with areas of particularly rapid growth being located in Greater London, Birmingham and Staffordshire, Lancashire, the West Riding of Yorkshire and the Eastern Midlands. When London clubs met clubs from the regions, which they were doing more often as the 1870s drew to a close, they usually won. Members of all social classes played although the majority of players were increasingly working men. But in and around London both the Football Association and the leading clubs were dominated by either leisured gentlemen or by professionally or commercially employed products of the public and grammar schools. Most of these men almost certainly subscribed to some variant of the healthy mind in the healthy body syndrome. Play was good for you but it was also done for fun. Indeed, that was why it was good for you. It was not to be confused with work which was also good for you. Playing for money was something gentlemen did not do.

It is difficult to be exact about when football players were first paid for playing. As early as 1876 Peter Andrews and James J. Lang had left Scotland to play for the Heeley club in Sheffield, but although they were often said to have been the first professionals no satisfactory evidence has ever been uncovered.[1] [. . .]

The first stage of the problem of professionalism in association football manifested itself in the crisis surrounding importation. Importation was the playing of men brought into the town, district or team from outside. The borrowing of players from other clubs for important matches, particularly knock-out cup-ties, began to grow with the increase in number of those competitions at the end of the 1870s.[2] Some particularly sought-after players might appear for several different clubs in the same cup competition during one season.[3] Such activities were considered by many leading football officials to be outside the spirit of the game, particularly when the imported 'professors' came from north of the border. Local clubs, it was argued, should consist of local players.

> I understood when I gave my mite towards purchasing the handsome cup (the Lancashire Football Association's trophy) that it was for Lancashire lads, and they alone. If the richer clubs can afford to pay professionals, let them do so, but when they compete for our grand trophy, let the true Lancashire lads have equal chance of winning it.[4]

Importation undoubtedly caused ill feeling and some clubs apparently went to a good deal of trouble to seek it out and expose it. According to a letter to the magazine *Football*, in early 1883, Nottingham Forest had several placards put up in the streets of Sheffield offering a reward of £20 to any person who would bring them evidence to establish that three players who had recently appeared for Sheffield Wednesday in a cup-tie against Forest had not been members of the Wednesday club until just before the game.[5] [. . .]

But as we noted above importation was really the first stage of the struggle over professionalism and local football associations responded to the problem in different ways in accordance with their interpretation of their own local situation. In Lancashire, for example, which by the 1880s clearly had more than just a few imported players, not to mention actual paid men, the football association tried to ban imported players from cup-ties in 1882, but the clubs threw out the recommendation of the committee.[6] Most people at the meeting said they did not like importation but that fairness could not be neglected when considering how to deal with it. As the Bolton Wanderers representative said 'the Scotch players in their team had put them in a position that they would not otherwise have attained . . . in the football world'.[7] The compromise reached at the A.G.M. in May 1882 was to insist on two years of continued residence before players born outside the county could play in cup-ties. Nor would players be allowed to play for more than one club in the various cup competitions in the same season.[8] The Sheffield F.A. went somewhat further in 1883 when they decided to require any footballer, who was objected to on the grounds of professionalism, to prove to the satisfaction of the committee that he had not received more than travelling and hotel expenses. They also insisted on the one club per player per season rule for all cup-ties.[9] The Birmingham F.A. refused to believe the problem existed much locally but threatened to deal firmly with any local players accepting inducements from outside.[10]

But it was professionalism, rather than importation, that was the subject of a good deal of public and, one suspects, private discussion in the game from about 1883 onwards, with Lancashire being the focus of most of the comment. Looking forward to the new season of 1883–4, the *Athletic News* indicated the changes which it thought had taken place over the preceding three or four years. Football, which was played and enjoyed almost free of expense, 'has developed into a vast business institution. A club now needs as much managing as a big shop, whilst there are many concerns which do not enjoy the turnover of which some of our leading clubs can boast.' The paper went on to note that Bolton Wanderers had expended £1,082 in the previous season and their balance in hand was only £11. With most matches played at home, where had the money gone? The answer was clear enough: into the players' pockets.[11]

What was wrong with that? The opponents of professionalism replied with two major arguments. First, to accept professionalism would mean accepting that what up until then had been a voluntary leisure activity run by the participants for the participants would in future become a business. It would then be run like any other business and that would mean maximising profits by playing to win, if not at all costs, then with not too much attention to sporting scruples. Second, in such a situation, the larger, wealthier clubs, by paying the most money, would secure the best players and the smaller clubs, with relatively meagre financial resources, would have to do the best they could. Many would not survive in the best company. The effect of this would be to damage irreparably the old structure of the game based, as it was, on essentially local rivalries. In addition to these two major arguments there was a subsidiary one: that the football professional stood by himself because in nearly all other cases

> the professional is looked upon as a teacher of the game or sport by means of which he gains a livelihood, while at football the paid man is simply one who is called upon to give as good a display of his powers as he can, in order that the club which engages him may make its matches as attractive as possible, and so draw together large attendances. When he can't do this, he is replaced by others, hence the concentration on winning by fair means or foul.[12]

Those in favour of making the professional a legal part of the structure of association football were divided, although not necessarily equally, into two groups by virtue of the reasons with which they defended their views. The first group felt that the whole issue was inflated and the remedy very simple. As the *Sporting Life* succinctly put it,

> there can be no possible objection to the recognised payment of men who cannot afford to pay for amusement, and we can see no reason why the principle which exists in almost every sport should be considered detrimental to football. The sooner the Football Association opens its eyes to the fact that the recognition of professionalism is a certainty in time, the better it will be for the consolidation of the game.[13]

The second, and perhaps more influential, group agreed that professionalism existed and that although stamping it out might still be possible it would also be very difficult. [. . .]

The timing of the final, if somewhat protracted, discussions at the Football Association was determined by the disqualification of Preston North End from the F.A. Cup in January 1884 and the subsequent threat on the part of the thirty-six prominent northern clubs to leave the Association and form their own British Football Association in the autumn of the same year.[14] . . . The [F.A.'s] committee's proposals in favour of legalisation were accepted at a special general meeting on 20 July 1885.[15]

No player was to be termed an amateur who received any remuneration or consideration above his necessary hotel or travelling expenses. Eligibility for cup matches would depend on birth or residence for the past two years within six miles of the ground or headquarters of the club for whom the professional wished to turn out. Professionals were not to sit on any F.A. committees, nor to represent their own or any other club at any meeting of the Football Association. Professionals would not be allowed to play for more than one club in any one season without the special permission of the F.A. committee. Infringements of the rules would be punished by suspensions.

Was it simple class prejudice which underlay the opposition to professionals? There were undoubtedly many who shared the view of W.H. Jope, a leading member of the Birmingham Football Association, that 'it was degrading for respectable men to play with professionals'. The *Sporting Mirror* alleged that there had been no such thing as amateur-professional distinctions in the middle of the nineteenth century. 'A crack performer, whether at athletics or anything else, if desirous of earning laurels in the arena, had to contend with anyone who would throw down the gauntlet.' It was only when gentlemen 'found that they were unable to hold their own in leading events that exception was taken to leading performers on account of their social status and a clique established'.[16] C.W. Alcock, on the other hand, told the meeting of the Football Association in February 1884 that 'he had sounded the greater number of amateurs, and he found very few of them objected to play with professionals, but they did object to play with them as amateurs'.[17] Moreover, we have already noted the important role which young professional men and businessmen in general, and ex-public school and university men in particular, had played in introducing association rules to their districts and recruiting working men for the teams.

We do not have a detailed socio-occupational breakdown of the delegates to those meetings of the Football Association in 1884–5 nor do we know in any detail who voted for what. We would expect most representatives of Lancashire clubs, irrespective of whether they were solicitors or manufacturers, to want to preserve a system which had enabled their teams to improve their game. Similarly it would not surprise us to find the bastions of southern amateurism in the opposite camp. London against the provinces or North v. South differences may be important here. Pre-existing rivalry had been sharpened by the north's successes in the F.A. Cup since Blackburn Rovers had been the first northern club to reach the final in 1882. Olympic won the next year and Rovers in 1884 and 1885.[18] [. . .]

. . . The conflict surrounding the amateur-professional issue in football went simmering on throughout our period, shot through as it was with North-South rivalries and punctuated by accusations of class prejudice. The selection of teams to represent England in matches against the other home countries was a particular area in which ill-feeling was generated. They were chosen, of course, by a committee of the Football Association and prior to the end of the 1870s, were usually composed of London-based amateur players. The first professional to play in the major fixture, England against Scotland, did so in 1886. The Scots, who as we saw earlier, had not recognised professionalism, objected and although their objection was rejected, the player in question was made to wear a different shirt from the rest of the eleven.[19] In the same year the *Athletic News* complained that the F.A. 'did their level best to make the pros look like pros' in the Gentlemen v. Players match. 'Dark blue jerseys savour more of the collier than anything else, and the Gentlemen were clad in spotless white shirts. The difference was marked as doubtless it was intended to be.' In spite of their increasing lack of success against professionals, amateurs continued to find it relatively easy to get into England teams right up to 1900.[20] And an amateur would always be appointed captain. In 1894–5, for example, the Professionals played the Amateurs in an international trial at Nottingham and won 9–0. Consequently only one amateur was chosen for the England side but he was appointed captain.[21] When this phenomenon had first occurred, in 1892, it had raised ticklish questions of protocol. How should the amateur who was to lead the professionals on the field, relate to them off it? N.L. Jackson wrote in *Pastime*, the magazine which he edited, that 'paid football players are supposed to be inferior in manners and breeding to the average run of cricket professionals; and it might be supposed that the solitary amateur in the English team, who, as captain, was called upon to associate to some extent with his men, would have found his position more or less irksome. As it happened, however, these particular professionals turned out to be men of easy and gentlemanly demeanour, and they found their captain a very sociable companion.'[22] The *Athletic News* by this time rarely allowed a slur to be cast on the professional game save by itself. Least of all would the paper stand idly by and see the professional patronised by one of the high priests of southern amateurism. Its reply, the truth of which does not appear to have been contested, throws interesting light on the relationship between amateur and professional at the highest level of the game.

> We have very little doubt that well behaved English pros would have 'found their captain a very sociable companion' had their captain given them a chance, but it hardly seems the right thing to our unsophisticated mind for a captain of an international team not to recognize his men on a long railway journey, not to speak to them in any way, to travel in a separate compartment, to dine away from them at the hotel, to leave them severely alone until driving off to the match, and generally to behave as if he were a superior sort of being. . . . Sport levels all classes. It is a rare good text, Mr. Jackson.[23]

Jackson, sound fellow, was unrepentant and in his autobiography published in 1932 he claimed that class prejudice or snobbishness were irrelevant to the issue. For example, amateurs and professionals preferred to dine separately and for two good reasons, namely that the professionals liked to dine earlier in order to be able to attend a music-hall or theatre and that they 'all felt a little constrained when with the amateurs, thinking that they could not talk among themselves so freely as they might wish'.[24] Moreover, he had returned to the attack in 1900 when arguing that amateurs should not be compelled to mix with pros if they desired to play for England but should be at liberty to choose. Servants did not dine with their masters in the dining room, nor did they come and go through the front door and professional footballers were paid servants. 'The amateurs, if they are *bona fide*, must be at some expense to play the game, and as such are as much the masters of the game as *bona fide* amateurs are at cricket.'[25]

Masters and servants. In a sense that goes to the root of what Alcock and those who supported him were aiming at when they proposed in 1884–5 that professionalism should be legalised. [. . .]

Notes

1   See A. Gibson and W. Pickford, *Association Football and the Men Who Made It* (1906), Vol. I, p. 59, 'Tityrus', *The Rise of the Leaguers from 1863–1897: A History of the Football League* (Manchester, 1897), pp. 105–6; and an article by C.E. Hughes in *C.B. Fry's Magazine* Vol. III, 13 April 1905, p. 41. Wednesday brought Lang down from Scotland to play in a Sheffield cup match in 1878. *Sheffield Independent* 28 January 1878. On Lang see R.A. Sparling and *The Romance of The Wednesday* (Sheffield, 1926) pp. 35–6.

2   The first F.A. Cup competition was in 1871–2; both the Sheffield and Birmingham F.A.'s had knock-out competitions from 1876–7, Stafforshire's senior Cup was first competed for in 1877–8, Blackburn's began in 1878–9, as did that of Berks and Bucks, and Lancashire's in 1879–80.

3   *Athletic News* 14 January 1880, *Sheffield Daily Telegraph* 27 February 1883.

4   'Fair Play' in *Athletic News* 25 January 1882. See also 8 February 1882.

5   *Football* 24 January 1883. The letter writer was contemplating putting up a similar sum for proof that the Forest officer who authorised the reward offer was of sound mind at the time.

6   See Minutes of the Lancashire Football Association 25 January, 6 February 1882.

7   *Blackburn Standard* 11 February 1882.

8   Minutes Lancashire Football Association A.G.M. 27 May 1882. The Lancashire F.A. also ruled that 'a man actually undertaking an engagement for his livelihood out of the county, and thereby residing beyond its limits for any protracted period shall not be eligible'. *Athletic News* 8 February, 31 May 1882. Blackburn Olympic were disqualified from taking any further part in the Lancashire Cup competition of 1882–3 for importing a player from Sheffield. *Preston Herald* 4 November 1882. Players today who have appeared for one club in the F.A. or Football League Cups may not appear for another in the same season.

9   *Sheffield Daily Telegraph* 27 February 1883. *Athletic News* 26 December 1883.

10   *Athletic News* 24 October, 14 November 1883.

11   Ibid. 1 August 1883.

12   *The Field* 27 June 1891. Cricket professionals were nearly always bowlers (although many of them could bat as well). In many club and county sides it was their job to bowl to the gentlemen, who were nearly always batsmen, thus providing them with practice. For further comparisons between the football and cricket professional see below chapter four.

13   *Sporting Life* 15 September 1884.

14   For a list of the clubs see Appendix I [p. 102]. Upton Park, a team of London amateur players, objected to North End on the grounds that their eleven had included professionals although they did not return the money received as their share of a large attendance at the match at Preston which was drawn 1–1. The charge of professionalism against North End was not proven but the club was found guilty of importing men from other towns and finding them what were thought to be excessively well paid jobs in order that they might play football for Preston. See *Athletic News* 23 January 30, 5 November 1884, *Blackburn Standard* 2 February 1884. The *Preston Herald* claimed that North End's players were 'following their respective employments' in the latter part of the 1883–4 season. *Preston Herald* 9 April 1884.

15   *Athletic News* 7 July 1885. As late as May 1885 the Committee of the Birmingham and District F.A. had voted 13–5 against legalising professionalism. Birmingham and District FA. Committee Minister 7 May 1885.

16   *Sporting Mirror* Vol. II August 1881–January 1882, p. 165.

17   *Preston Herald* 1 March 1884. There was also the notion that it was more manly to become a professional than to remain a paid amateur. *Athletic News* 9 October 1899.

18   That football in the South had lost prestige in the eyes of Northerners is indicated by a satirical headline in the *Athletic News* of 14 November 1883 over a report of a match between the Old Etonians and Hendon: 'The Bitter Cry of Outcast London'!

19   C. Francis, *A History of the Blackburn Rovers Football Club 1875–1925* (Blackburn, 1925), p. 198, A. Gibson and W. Pickford, vol. IV, op. cit. pp. 108–12. It was J.H. Forrest's first 'cap'. See below chapter four, p. 12, *Athletic News* 21 December 1886.

20   The Corinthians did win many matches against professional sides but they were themselves a representative eleven made up of the best amateur players of the day, mostly ex-public school and university footballers based in London and district. However, there were exceptional years. See chapter seven below. In 1892, for example, only one amateur played for England against Scotland.

21   E. Needham, *Association Football* (1900), p. 75. The first professional to captain England was Robert Crompton in 1900.

22   *Pastime* 6 April 1892. Jackson went on to say that 'the only members of the English Party who manifested any constraint were certain officials, who seemed to be painfully conscious of their inferiority in social qualities. It is a pity that the present commercial organization of football should bring such men to the front.'

23   *Athletic News* 11 April 1892. The idea that 'sport levels all classes' will be returned to in chapter eight below. In county cricket, of course, this was the golden age of the amateur player. He not only enjoyed separate changing facilities from the professionals and the title of Mr but he also entered the field of play by a separate gate.

24   N.L. Jackson, *Sporting Days and Sporting Ways* (1932), pp. 175–6.

25   *Athletic News* 15 January 1900.

Appendix I

List of clubs represented at a meeting to discuss the formation of a British Football Association 1884

Accrington	Hurst
Accrington Grasshoppers	Kersley
Astley Bridge	Little Hulton
Barnes Rovers	Loneclough
Bell's Temperance	Manchester and District
Bolton Wanderers	Nelson
Bolton Association	Newton Heath
Bolton and District Charity Cup	Padiham
Association	Park Road (Blackburn)
Bradshaw	Preston North End
Burnley	Peel Bank Rovers (Accrington)
Burnley Ramblers	Preston Swifts
Burnley Trinity	Rawtenstall
Burnley Union Star	Rossendale
Burnley Wanderers	Sunderland
Clitheroe	Turton
Darcy Lever	Walmersley
Great Lever	Walsall Swifts
Halliwell	Wigan

This total of 36 clubs plus the Bolton and District Charity Cup Association contained at least eight major clubs. Moreover, the possibility that other clubs would join could not be ruled out.

Source: Athletic News 5 November 1884.

Andrew Davies

MEN
Poverty, unemployment and the family

LEISURE WAS CENTRAL to the formation of masculine identities in working-class neighbourhoods. Drinking, gambling and sport, three of the cornerstones of 'traditional' working-class culture, were all heavily male-dominated, and men were identified by their hobbies or by the pubs where they drank as 'regulars', as well as by their occupations and political or religious allegiances. Pub life was especially important to men's networks, as relations between neighbours, kin and workmates could be maintained through a night's drinking. Moreover, men used pubs to carve out a terrain which was exclusively male. By convention, women were barred from the vault, usually, the biggest room in any pub, which effectively formed a masculine republic.[1] [. . .]

The impact of poverty upon leisure is frequently discussed in working-class autobiographies. Richard Heaton was born in the Hope Street district of Salford . . . in 1901. At a number of points in his autobiography, *Salford my home town*, Heaton comments on the fragile balance between the management of poverty and the pursuit of leisure which he observed during his childhood and youth. His father, a carter, suffered a spell of unemployment prior to the First World War, so the family depended for a while on public assistance. His father was a skilful darts player:

> The landlord of the local pub put up prizes on Saturday nights — legs of mutton, beef or rabbits — and for a copper anybody could compete for them. The highest scorer with three darts was the winner and more than one prize was brought home to Boundary Street. That would mean a feast of a meal for our Sunday dinner, with some for tea and leftovers on Monday. For the rest of the week there was very little, except for the threepenny's of meat from Markendale's [abattoir shop] each day.
>   I remember my father bringing home one Friday night a china clock set. It consisted of a clock and two vases, all carved in lovely patterns. They were

put on the mantelpiece and I saw my mother eyeing them lovingly. I knew she would have liked to have kept them and my father told her they were hers. She kept them for a day or two, but eventually they went the same way as the other things. She said we had to eat, so that was that. My father was the captain of the local pub team, so you can see why the Sunday dinners came home so regularly.[2]

The clock, like the medals his father won, went from the publican to the pawnbroker. Landlords recognized the domestic tensions that drink could arouse, and responded by offering material rewards which men could use in turn to justify their 'right' to leisure. Significantly, these competitions, staged in the vault of the pub from which women were barred, were held for prizes designed to appeal to women as household managers. [. . .]

. . . [D]rinking was only one of a series of leisure activities which were regulated by poverty. For example, although betting was commonplace in working-class districts, a visit to the racecourse in Salford was beyond the means of many local residents. Mr Perry described the racecourse in Ordsall at the turn of the century:

> . . . there used to be a plot of land over the race course on Trafford Road . . . and people who couldn't afford to go into the race used to stand there and watch the races. They used to call that 'skinner's hill'. And the lads used to go round selling pencils to them, to mark their race cards.[3]

Oral evidence confirms that football was a major focus of interest, but perhaps surprisingly, when the sport is recalled, it is often without reference to Manchester United or City. Mr Johnstone described Harpurhey in North Manchester in the inter-war years:

> *Did many people go to watch football?*
> I don't recollect anybody in my acquaintance going to watch first-class football, but an awful lot of people watched the local clubs. There was one well-known club called Miles Platting Swifts, and another one, called Manchester North End. But there was a lot more interest in local sports.

His father was a keen footballer who had played briefly as an amateur for Crewe Alexandra: 'He never went to the City, or Manchester [United]. Quite honestly I don't think a lot of people could afford it, even in those days it was a shilling, or one and six to get in.'[4]

Documentary sources confirm that many people were unable to afford to go to professional matches,[5] so despite the growth of football as a mass spectator sport, watching United or City was never a universal pastime. A survey of Manchester council estates in 1937 found that on the estates on the outskirts of the city, particularly the Wythenshawe estate over 6 miles from the centre, many men were unable to afford the extra transport costs incurred in attending Manchester United or City matches. Although the corporation estates housed some of the better-paid manual workers in the city, the higher municipal rents and the cost of journeys to work meant that men who moved to the estates had to accept lower disposable incomes in return for a cleaner environment.[6] Although as Hobsbawm suggested, professional football was central to the national pattern of working-class culture by 1900, the sport still excluded women and many men despite its capacity to draw massive crowds.[7]

In contrast to the emphasis upon professional football among social historians, retrospective accounts show that the sport retained a local base, and suggest that neighbourhood rather than civic loyalties were aroused. Matches between teams drawn from Salford pubs were played on patches of waste ground in the poorest areas of the city, with communal wagers of 6d. or 1s. per player at stake, and these contests aroused passions as strong as any professional encounter. Mr Lomas described contests between pub teams in the Adelphi:

> They used to play football on the [Adelphi] croft for a shilling a man, which was quite a good sum of money. And they used to play different pubs. The Adelphi pub would play the Rob Roy or the Olive Branch.
> *Would anybody watch those games?*
> Oh yes, it was quite a Sunday afternoon entertainment. The teams had followers, gangs, and chaps that went in the pub that didn't play football. They'd come down, twenty or thirty strong . . . And they'd all be round the croft and they used to shout the team on. They'd nothing else to do.
> *Did they wear a kit in those pub games?*
> No kit, no studs, they just turned out in the ordinary day clothes.
> *What would they have on their feet?*
> Ordinary boots or shoes.[8]

At this level, football was informally organized, and provided a free spectacle. [. . .]

Retrospective evidence confirms that in Salford as in London, men's networks, which often hinged upon pub culture, were severely disrupted by unemployment. Men without work were thus denied access to the principal arena of masculine leisure, and in areas where pubs did operate as channels of labour market information, this further circumscribed an unemployed man's chances of finding work.

Professional sport, another of the staple elements of 'traditional' working-class culture, was similarly undermined by unemployment. During the inter-war period, there was some recognition of the impact of trade slumps upon attendances at football and rugby league matches: at Old Trafford, Manchester United's ground, and at the Willows, Salford's rugby league ground in Weaste, prices for those out of work were reduced, to enable more unemployed men to attend.[9] However, the willingness by the clubs to cut their prices indicates that they were aware that unemployment had an adverse effect upon crowds. In Liverpool, the Pilgrim Trust found that during the 1930s:

> On a Saturday afternoon, when an important League match is on, the unemployed men in Liverpool turn out and gather along the streets where the crowds go up by foot, tram, bus or motor car to watch it. To watch a match is in itself a second-hand experience and the unemployed man . . . has to make do with this substitute for it.[10]

Unemployment also led to a serious decline in sports such as pigeon fancying, which required a consistent commitment of resources. Mass Observation's survey of Bolton showed that the sport was in decline by the late 1930s. Colliers, who in Bolton as in

Salford were among the keenest fanciers, told observers that short time and unemployment in the local mining industry had undermined the basis of the sport. Too many men without work were unable to enter birds for races.[11] [. . .]

Walter Greenwood reflected upon the social impact of unemployment at length in both *Love on the dole* and *There was a time*, and there is a striking convergence between the two works. The autobiography repeats detailed points made in *Love on the dole*, as though Greenwood sought to confirm that his fictional portrayal was based upon the reality of life in Hanky Park during the 1920s. For example, the exclusion from leisure suffered by the central characters in the novel matches the experiences of his own acquaintances, as depicted in *There was a time*.[12]

In his autobiography, Greenwood claimed that even young men, usually among the most privileged working-class consumers, were severely affected by the loss of work:

> Segregation asserted itself in subtle ways. Those who were out of work tended to avoid their luckier counterparts and the embarrassment was mutual. Pay day brought a constrained uneasiness. 'Where are we going tonight?' The customary question of a week-end among friends was avoided if, standing by in the group, were any whose pockets were known to be empty. For those who had a job, the sight of friends to whom all doors of entertainment and conviviality were closed could bring sharp, apprehensive shivers, aware as they were that this fate could be anybody's in these uncertain times.[13]

This echoes the findings of the *New survey of London life and labour*, which reported that older unemployed men avoided pubs through the same fear of mutual embarrassment. Clearly, the collective masculine world of pub vaults and football terraces could be only partially reproduced during periods of high unemployment. [. . .]

The 'traditional' working-class leisure activities – the pub, sport, gambling, cinema and the seaside holiday – were all regulated by financial constraints, and the denial of leisure was an important element of the burden of poverty. Yet within this framework, participation in leisure hinged upon competing notions of masculinity: some men saw themselves primarily as breadwinners, and chose to lead family-orientated lifestyles; others identified with the masculine spheres of pub vaults and sport, and placed their own desires before the needs of their families. Men with comparable incomes thus had widely different leisure patterns.

Notes

1   See V. Hey, *Patriarchy and pub culture* (London, 1986).
2   R. Heaton, *Salford my home town* (Swinton 1982), p. 7.
3   M.S.T.C. (Manchester Studies Tape Collection, Manchester Metropolitan University) 491/2. The 'Manchester' racecourse was situated in Ordsall until 1905, when the races moved to Kersal, an outlying Salford district.
4   Interview with Mr P.J.
5   J. Hilton (ed.), *Why I go in for the pools* (London, 1936); see also T. Mason, *Association football and English society 1863–1915* (Brighton, 1980), pp. 148, 154–8.
6   The higher cost of living on municipal estates was discussed by F. Thompson, 'A survey of the development of facilities for recreation and leisure occupation on new housing estates, with special reference to Manchester', unpublished thesis for the Diploma in Social Study, University of Manchester, 1937, p. 65.

MEN: POVERTY, UNEMPLOYMENT AND THE FAMILY

7   See E. Hobsbawm, *Worlds of labour: Further studies in the history of Labour* (London, 1984), Chs 10 and 11.

8   Interview with Mr L.L.

9   Interviews with Mr C.P. and Mr R.P.

10   Cited in T. Mason, op. cit., note 42, p. 148.

11   Mass Observation, *The pub and the people* (London, 1987 edn), n. 7, pp. 284–91.

12   See A. Davies, 'Leisure and poverty in Salford and Manchester, 1900–1939', unpublished Ph.D. thesis, University of Cambridge (1989), p. 60.

13   W. Greenwood, *There was a time* (London, 1967), n. 58, p. 223.

SECTION THREE

Politics

INTRODUCTION

THE OLD ADAGE THAT SPORT AND POLITICS must not mix has long been superseded. Sport is important not least because it has political significance. It is used by governments, contributes to expressions of national and regional identity and politics, and can be used as a form of cultural politics in challenging injustices in the world. Sports institutions themselves are widely political in the ways in which they operate. The Readings in Section Three show how, to adapt an early feminist slogan, the personal is the political, as well as how nations and governments have used or sought to use sport, in examples ranging from the staging of high-profile international events to the arguments that have raged over the nature of the physical education curriculum in England.

Trinidadian **C.L.R. James**, radical-Marxist literary and cultural critic, cricketing fanatic and West Indian nationalist, was one of the earliest writers and campaigners in the Caribbean to see the connection between sport and politics. His work *Beyond a Boundary* is recognized as a contemporary literary, political and cultural classic, showing the serious political role of sport in a society. He calls cricket 'first and foremost a dramatic spectacle', belonging with 'theatre, ballet, opera and the dance' (p. 192 of his book), but also recognizes the inherently political character of such cultural activities and institutions. This Reading is about how James led a campaign to appoint the first black captain of the West Indies. It makes the case with eloquence and conviction for sport as a sphere of cultural politics, a potential vehicle for social change and progress. But this, James demonstrates, cannot happen without personal commitment and vision.

International sporting exchanges and competitions date from the later 1800s, and political regimes soon saw the potential political and propagandistic use of high-profile sporting occasions, contests and events. The first modern Olympic Games in Greece (in the summer of 1896) was seen by the Greek monarchy as a means of bolstering its fragile hold on power; the first football World Cup was staged (and won) by Uruguay in 1930 in Monte Video, Uruguay, as a celebration of the centenary of the Uruguayan constitution. In the build-up to the 1936 Berlin Olympics, Nazi Germany could see the vast potential of the Games for presenting its supremacist ideology to the world. In the second Reading, **Richard D. Mandell,** US cultural historian, provides an account of international responses to an Olympics taken on by the Nazi Party when it came to power in 1933. Which nations – or more precisely, their politicians and sport administrators – were sympathetic to the Nazi regime, and what most impressed them about the preparations? In answering these questions, consider how sport could be argued for as separate from politics, and at the very same time be used for ruthlessly political purposes.

John Hoberman, US languages and cultures scholar, has brought a distinctive critical intelligence to bear on international sport, concentrating on the analysis of ideological systems, forms of nationalism and the worldwide culture of drug use in high-performance sport. In this third Reading, his influential concept of sportive nationalism is outlined with reference to a range of societies – covering the former Soviet Union, Canada, Switzerland and Norway. For Hoberman, sportive nationalism is the 'ambition to see a nation's athletes excel in the international arena'; and it 'may be promoted by a political elite or it may be felt by many citizens without the promptings of national leaders' (see p. 16 of Lincoln Allison (ed.), *The Changing Politics of Sport* (Manchester University Press, 1993). It is obvious what a political regime such as Fidel Castro's Cuba has sought to achieve through sport; but less obvious is what Western industrial democracies seek to gain from sportive nationalism. Hoberman shows both the excesses and the positive sides of sportive nationalism. While reading about the examples used, also think of other examples of sportive nationalism from a context with which you are familiar.

Few societies have offered such opportunities for the study of the politics of sport as Northern Ireland. It has been part of the United Kingdom of Great Britain and Northern Ireland since 1921, but in parts of its sporting culture, and under the wing of the Gaelic Athletic Association, it has also been part of the united sporting culture of the whole island of Ireland. **John Sugden** and **Alan Bairner** have studied this extraordinary and sometimes tragic case extensively. In this fourth Reading, and with perhaps the most arresting title of any of the Readings in this book, they look at the explicit political uses that the state can seek to make of sport and leisure. What are these contrasting uses, and what forces in Northern Ireland might work against the goals of the state?

Cricketing tours took place within the British Empire in the later years of the nineteenth century. After a low-profile and modest start in 1896, the Olympic Games established itself in the international calendar. International football matches escalated after the formation of the Fédération Internationale de Football Association (FIFA) in 1904. What attracted nations to these apparently pointless contests? **John Wilson** takes a broad-brush approach in the fifth Reading, taking as a starting point the increasing recognition by nation-states of the importance of leisure and sport 'in affirmations of identity and unity' during the half-century before the First World War. He covers some complicated and revealing cases on the use of sport for nationalist purposes – disputes over Chinese nationhood, boycotts of South Africa, German rehabilitation after both world wars. How internationally widespread, though, is this nationalist exploitation of sport? Look at Wilson's final points as you ponder this question.

Closer to home for UK readers, the sixth Reading focuses upon the background to sport politics and the development of sport policy in Britain. **Maurice Roche** looks at the sports authorities as a kind of political community, and also, alongside this, what he calls 'the national community of British society as a whole'. Look at his eye-catching answers to these questions, especially his assessment that 'the policy community has been little short of a disorganized shambles'. Roche published this analysis in 1993, and added a postscript on the new government Department of National Heritage, re-branded by the Labour government of 1997 as the Department for Culture, Media and Sport. After reading Roche's analysis, explore whether there is a more coherent policy community one-and-a-half decades further on. Does the stunning victory of the London 2012 campaign in Singapore on 6 July 2005 offer evidence of a more effective community?

Roche's analysis is the first of three Readings concerned with the politics of policy and policy-making. Inevitably, in looking closely at particular cases, the nature of institutional political power is a central concern. Academic and activist **Margaret Talbot** counteracts some of the claims to political neutrality that have been made for the world of sport and physical education, and shows how political capital can be made out of physical education by interested parties which, hypocritically, leave the institutions responsible for delivering the curriculum under-resourced and ineffectual. National governing bodies of sport, too, Talbot contends, become caught in this trap. It would be a revealing exercise to evaluate governmental claims that sport and school sport have been revitalized since 1995. Is 'appreciation and understanding of context' by policy-makers any more advanced than when Talbot was providing her critical overview?

The sixth and seventh Readings in this section highlight problems concerning the making, implementation and co-ordination of sport policy. If diverse bodies represent competing interests, will it be possible for any coherent policy at all to emerge in a democratic society that is so supportive of the rights of varied institutions to speak for their own interests? The final Reading in this section is from the work of English political scientist **Barrie Houlihan**. He outlines established approaches to analysing the policy-making community, and offers the case of drug abuse as evidence of the lack of any identifiable policy-making community in Britain. Published in 1990, he outlined clearly at that time what was needed in order to establish one. Does Britain now have one, or has it got any closer to having one?

COMMENTARY AND FURTHER READING

As the Readings have illustrated, the case for the political significance and currency of sport has been well made. Sport is political in personal, cultural and institutional ways; sport politics are expressed at local, regional, national, international and supranational levels. A general overview confirming these levels of the political in sport is provided by Barrie Houlihan in 'Politics and Sport' (Jay Coakley and Eric Dunning (eds), *Handbook of Sports Studies*, London, Sage, 2000: 213–27). There, Houlihan discusses politics and sport by focusing upon the role of the state and politics in sport looking at questions such as commercialization, sponsorship and inequality. For Houlihan's fuller analysis of sport policy and its processes, networks and communities – with comparative examples including Canada, Australia and the US, as well as the UK – see his *Sport, Policy and Politics: A Comparative Analysis* (London and New York, Routledge, 1997). In a later article he has reaffirmed that the wish of sport administrators and politicians to 'keep politics out of sport' has long been abandoned, and proposes an advocacy coalition framework ('acf') for the analysis of policy, recognizing the power of policy-brokers and the different sets of interests that make up a dominant policy paradigm – see 'Public Sector Sport Policy: Developing a Framework for Analysis' (*International Review for the Sociology of Sport*, Vol. 40. No. 2, 2005: pp. 163–85).

Lincoln Allison has also contributed to the *Handbook of Sport Studies* (London, Sage, 2000). His overview of 'Sport and Nationalism' (pp. 344–5) covers national identity, nationalism and national responses to global trends and developments. He talks of the 'immense added meaning that a sense of shared national identity gives to watching a team and (sometimes) an individual perform' (p. 345). This captures the collective potential of sport to express aspects of a nation; or tensions within and across the definition of the national, as in the case of Scottish football fans buying Argentinian shirts in 2002 or Trinidad and Tobago shirts in 2006, when those nations encountered England in the football World Cup. For comparative accounts of some of the complexities of these expressions of the national, in cases ranging across North American and Western European societies, see Alan Bairner, *Sport, Nationalism and Globalization: European and North American Perspectives* (Albany, State University of New York Press, 2001).

On selected aspects of the politics of sport, see too Lincoln Allison's edited collection *The Global Politics of Sport: The Role of Global Institutions in Sport* (London and New York, Routledge, 2005). This includes coverage of the governance of world football on the international level, and of the cultural politics of sporting heroism. Critical political analysis is necessary for cultural and policy interventions. When the great political forces of the time are identified, it is always worth remembering that political forces are the sum of the actions of human actors and peopled institutions. Toby Miller and George Yudicé conclude an overview of the history of cultural policy with the observation that 'getting to know cultural policy and intervening in it is an important part of participating in culture. Resistance goes nowhere unless it takes hold institutionally' (*Cultural Policy*, London, Sage, 2002: 34). Intervening in these ways is a way of engaging with – and indeed potentially changing – the 'public mind'. A prerequisite to such a form of engagement is an understanding of the scope and scale of the political, and the Readings in this section have been chosen in order to lay the foundations of such a prerequisite.

C.L.R. James

THE PROOF OF THE PUDDING

ONCE IN A BLUE MOON, i.e. once in a lifetime, a writer is handed on a plate a gift from heaven. I was handed mine in 1958. I had just completed a draft of this book up to the end of the previous chapter when I returned to the West Indies in April 1958, after twenty-six years of absence. I intended to stay three months, I stayed four years. I became the editor of a political paper, the *Nation*, official organ of the People's National Movement of Trinidad, and the secretary of the West Indian Federal Labour Party. Both these parties governed, the one Trinidad, the other the Federation of the West Indies. These were temporary assignments, as I made clear from the start.

Immediately I was immersed up to the eyes in 'The Case for West Indian Self-Government'; and a little later, in the most furious cricket campaign I have ever known, to break the discrimination of sixty years and have a black man, in this case Frank Worrell, appointed captain of a West Indies team. I saw the beginning, the middle, but I am not at all sure that I have seen the end of violent intervention of a West Indian crowd into the actual play of a Test match. The intimate connection between cricket and West Indian social and political life was established so that all except the wilfully perverse could see. It seemed as if I were just taking up again what I had occupied myself with in the months before I left in 1932, except that what was then idea and aspiration was now out in the open and public property.

On January 30th, 1960, there crowded into the Queen's Park Oval at Port of Spain over 30,000 people, this out of a total population of some 800,000. They had come to see a cricket match and I for one loved them for it. They have been slandered, vilified and at best grievously misunderstood. I can't say that I understand them, I wouldn't make such a claim, but at least I have always paid attention to them and their reactions to politics as well as to cricket. I have something to say on their behalf.

Particularly that day they had come to sun themselves in West Indies batting, 22 for none on the previous evening. Alas, the West Indies batsmen collapsed and were 98 for eight! At that stage Singh was given run out. The crowd exploded in anger, bottles began to fly; soon they flew so thickly that the game could not be continued. The Governor; the Premier, Dr. Eric Williams; Learie Constantine, apologized to M.C.C. in England and to the M.C.C. team. The majority placed the blame on a few hooligans. Some few hinted at political tensions. Others talked vaguely about betting. There is not a little truth here and a little truth there which can all add up to something. There is not a glimmer of truth in all this. And if anything annoyed the Trinidad public it was to be lectured about the umpire being the sole judge. They continue to say that they know this and in fact on innumerable occasions have shown that they do.

First, to get out of the way what was not the cause of the explosion. In Melbourne in 1903 there took place a demonstration famous in cricket history. Its cause has never been in doubt. Australia had begun their second innings against England 292 behind. Trumper and Hill made a stand for the fourth wicket and by brilliant and courageous batting were putting Australia back in the game. Playing such cricket as from all accounts no one on the ground had ever seen before, not even from him, Trumper hit Braund for three fours in an over and forced the last ball past mid-off. The batsmen ran three, took another for a bad throw and tried for a fifth. Hill was given run out and both pavilion members and the crowd around the ropes protested so violently and so long that the protests re-echo in the pages of the history books to this day.

There is no problem here. The Australians had been losing, they had seen a chance of winning and winning by play grand and gallant. Hill as a popular idol was second only to Trumper. Hill went back to the wicket to continue batting, which showed that he thought he was in. This was enough to unloose the pent-up emotions.

Nothing of the kind has ever taken place in the West Indies.

When the bottle-throwing in Trinidad began the score was 98 for eight, nearly 300 behind. Not a soul on the ground believed that Ramadhin could make twenty. They would have cheered Singh as a hero if he had made ten. The fate of the match was not at stake. [. . .]

What then caused the 1960 and other outbursts? It was the conviction that here, as usual, local anti-nationalist people were doing their best to help the Englishmen defeat and disgrace the local players. That is the temper which caused these explosions and as long as that temper remains it will find a way to express itself. This particular political attitude is not declining. It is increasing, and will increase until a new social and political regime is firmly established and is accepted by all.

The history of this in the West Indies is as old as the West Indies itself. No imperialist expatriates can rule an alien population alone. The British therefore incorporated the local whites into their ranks. Later, as the pressure from the people grew, the light-skinned were given privileges. Universal suffrage and the nationalist passions and gains of the last fifteen years have driven many of the former privileged classes to side openly with the British, with Americans, with all or any who for one reason or another find themselves in conflict with or hostile to the nationalist movement. There is the seat of disturbance. It is particularly true of Trinidad. Against Britain as such there is surprisingly little hostility. And despite the passions aroused over the desire for the return of Chaguaramas,[1] where there is an American naval base, and recurrent spasms of anger at racial persecution in the United States, America and Americans are not unpopular.

But those suspected of anti-nationalism are usually rich whites and their retainers. Local politicians, editors, officials, policemen, selectors, umpires, are under scrutiny whenever they have to act on behalf of or on the side of what the people consider a nationalist cause. People feel that in the past some have served the foreigners against the local people and that many of them are still doing it. The nearer the people get to independence, the greater is the suspicion that the enemies of independence and nationalism are scheming against them. You will find this conflict running through every aspect of life in Trinidad, where political development has been late and is all the more explosive. This type of suspicion is embedded deep in the minds of the majority of the people. [. . .]

It is an historical commonplace that social explosions take place when most of the fundamental causes of dissatisfaction have been removed and only a few remain. This is the result of a feeling of power. In West Indies cricket today selection is honest and straightforward and sometimes brilliant. Anyone, whatever his colour, can become captain of an island team. That is all the more reason why it is the captaincy of the West Indies side on which attention centres.

Clyde Walcott cannot by any stretch of fact or imagination be called a cricket Bolshevik, a term applied to Worrell in the past. Yet Clyde in his *Island Cricketers* had made several pointed references. [. . .]

I was editor of a newspaper. I was primed for action and made up my mind to clean up this captaincy mess once and for all. When the M.C.C. tour drew near I gave notice in the *Nation* that I proposed to wage an all-out campaign for Worrell to replace Alexander as captain. My argument was simply this: there was not the slightest shadow of justification for Alexander to be captain of a side in which Frank Worrell was playing.

Worrell had been offered the captaincy after the 1957 season in England, but owing to his studies at Manchester University he had had to refuse. That offer didn't matter very much to some of us who were watching. Worrell as captain at home or in India was bad enough, but that could be swallowed by the manipulators. What was at stake was the captaincy in Australia and still more in England. Their whole point was to continue to send to populations of white people, black or brown men under a white captain. The more brilliantly the black men played, the more it would emphasize to millions of English people: 'Yes, they are fine players, but, funny, isn't it, they cannot be responsible for themselves—they must always have a white man to lead them.'

The populace in the West Indies are not fools. They knew what was going on and, if not altogether sure of all the implications, they were quite sure that these, whatever they might be, were directed against them. I was told of an expatriate who arrived in Trinidad to take up an important post which the people thought should be filled by a local candidate. Such a storm arose that the expatriate had to be sent away. In 1959 British Guiana was thrown into turmoil and strikes over a similar issue and the Governor had to retreat. In cricket these sentiments are at their most acute because everyone can see and can judge.

What do they know of cricket who only cricket know? West Indians crowding to Tests bring with them the whole past history and future hopes of the islands. English people, for example, have a conception of themselves breathed from birth. Drake and mighty Nelson, Shakespeare, Waterloo, the Charge of the Light Brigade, the few who did so much for so many, the success of parliamentary democracy, those and such as those constitute a national tradition. Underdeveloped countries have to go back centuries to rebuild one. We of the West Indies have none at all, none that we know of. To such people the three W's, Ram and Val wrecking English batting, help to fill a huge gap in their consciousness and in their needs. In one of the sheds on the Port of Spain wharf is a painted sign: 365 Garfield Sobers. If the old Maple–Shannon–Queen's Park type of rivalry was now insignificant, a nationalist jealousy had taken its place.

All this was as clear to me as day. I tried to warn the authorities that there was danger in the air. Many of them, I am sure of this, were unable even to understand what I was saying. [. . .]

The theory of a few hooligans is not only dangerous but without sense. I know of no instance where a few hooligans have disrupted a major public function, unless they knew or sensed that public opinion was either on their side or at least neutral. I have made systematic enquiries both at the time and since and a secret poll would to this day show a majority for the view: 'Wrong, yes, but the people had to do something.' A recurrent defiance was the following: 'The bottles should have been thrown into the pavilion.' Not a word was ever said against the English players.

Who doubts the validity of the above has to reckon with what now followed. I had been waiting to get a sight of Alexander as captain and before the Test was over I launched an attack against his captaincy: Alexander must go. I based it on Worrell's superior experience and status and Alexander's errors of judgment. I refused to make it a question of race, though I made it clear that if the rejection of Worrell was continued I would reluctantly have to raise the racial issue. To have raised it would have switched the discussion away from cricket and involved all sorts of other issues. The anti-nationalists, with their usual brazenness, would have countered with 'Race introduced into sport'. And in any case everybody in the West Indies understood what I was leaving out even better than what I was actually writing.

The effect was beyond all expectation. The *Nation* was an official organ and a highly political paper. (Some even queried whether such a paper should express an opinion on cricket captaincy at all.) They were wrong. This was politics and very serious politics. The 'Alexander Must Go' issue was sold out by the day following publication. People who had read or heard of the article rushed around looking for copies to buy. The man in the street expressed deep feelings. 'Thank God for the *Nation*.' 'Someone to speak for us at last.' He was not speaking about the explosion. The *Nation* had been as uncompromising as any in condemning it. [. . .]

It was hard on Alexander. He was not a good captain and in any case he was keeping wicket, which is no place for a captain. But it was hard on me also. Alexander is a fine soccer player, he kept wicket magnificently, he is a good defensive bat and is a hard fighter. I put my scruples aside and I think that for the first, and I hope the last, time in reporting cricket I was not fair. But I was determined to rub in the faces of everybody that Frank Worrell, the last of the three W's, was being discriminated against. Charles Bray of the *Daily Herald*, no mean campaigner himself, told me that he wondered how I was able to keep it up. I would have been able to keep it up for fifty weeks, for there was fifty years' knowledge of discrimination behind it and corresponding anger. When I confessed I was angry, even sympathizers balked at this. According to the code, anger should not intrude into cricket. I understood them well, I had been as foolish in my time. According to the colonial version of the code, you were to show yourself a 'true sport' by not making a fuss about the most barefaced discrimination because it wasn't cricket. [. . .]

. . . [C]onsidered opinion is that the campaign for Worrell was the most popular and the most effective of all the *Nation* campaigns. The people simply saw it as a part of the whole movement. There might be arguments, and considerations to be taken into account in regard to the other issues—this one they understood and accepted completely. All art, science, philosophy, are modes of apprehending the world, history and society. As one of these, cricket in the West Indies at least could hold its own. A professor of political science publicly bewailed that a man of my known political interests should believe that cricket had ethical and social values. I had no wish to answer. I was just sorry for the guy. [. . .]

The secretary of the West Indian Football Association is my brother Eric. He had managed two teams to England, had brought one to the West Indies and was bringing another. He had been the secretary of the Government committee in charge of the projected stadium. About the cricket controversies he was noncommittal, but everyone knew that the Football Associations which he was responsible for were run on strictly democratic lines, all clubs and all classes represented, and were supported by the entire community. The football organization interested me enormously, owing to the perfect integration of all elements in the community. That it is so is no accident, and nationalist politics are not confined to speeches and laws. My brother has made it that way and kept it that way, though he will recoil with horror at the mere thought of being called a politician. [. . .]

So there we are, all tangled up together, the old barriers breaking down and the new ones not yet established, a time of transition, always and inescapably turbulent. In the inevitable integration into a national community, one of the most urgent needs, sport, and particularly cricket, has played and will play a great role. There is no one in the West Indies who will not subscribe to the aphorism: what do they know of cricket who only cricket know? But what is most strange is that what I have written here and in the early chapters on Maple–Shannon–Queen's Park [see Reading 41] has been known to everyone in the West Indies for the last fifty years. Yet it had been allowed to fester under the surface, a source of corruption and hypocrisy. From now on that is over.

Notes

1   That agitation is for the time being deadened—C.L.R.J.

Richard D. Mandell

SPORTSMANSHIP AND NAZI OLYMPISM

[. . .]

I N SEVERAL NATIONS that were traditional supporters of the modern Olympic Games, Nazism and indeed a certain enthusiastic, though slovenly, kind of Nietzschean, anti-philosophical, political philosophy became chic. Here and there one heard pragmatical praise for Adolf Hitler. After all, crazy as his program might have sounded in the 1920's, it was working in the 1930's. So, in spite of the fact that, in their preparations for their Olympics as well as in other aspects of life, the National Socialists were violating established rules of domestic and international behavior, protests from outside Germany were unusual.

In Great Britain, traditionally a refuge for political persecutees and the place where such German-Jewish athletes as Daniel Prenn and Alex Natan fled shortly after the revolution of 1933, totalitarian projects as antidotes to the inactivity of the traditional politicians were having a vogue.[1] In his newspaper articles Winston Churchill praised Benito Mussolini and Adolf Hitler as preferable to the specter of Communism—then considered the likely ideological haven of the desperate masses of unemployed. Walter MacLennon (also Baron Citrine, a Trades Union official and consulting member of the Government) wrote a pamphlet, "Under the Heel of Hitler: The Dictatorship over Sport in Nazi Germany."[2] MacLennon's trumpeting for a campaign of formal protests against the Nazification of German sport made little impression on the English. The British Olympic Committee, itself composed principally of the titled aristocrats whose moral assistance Baron Pierre de Coubertin had always preferred, was frightened by the prospects of a Red revolution and was inclined to reject any political calls to action by an avowed leftist. The British Olympic Committee devoted itself to the task of locating funds for a large team for 1936. [. . .]

Still, the only really enthusiastic greetings of the preparations for the 1936 Games came from Japan and Italy . . .

Japan had long since embarked on a national sports program the results of which were demonstrated at Los Angeles in 1932. Japanese eagerness to make a mark at Berlin was intense, since the nation was in the control of military adventurers who viewed sport as a paramilitary activity. Like Hitler and his lieutenants, the Japanese leaders were keen to use the sporting fields as stages for advancing the prestige of the nation. The Japanese were also determined to demonstrate sporting sophistication in order to obtain the Olympiad for Tokyo in 1940. Mussolini's Fascists also favored a patriotically oriented sports program and saw in National Socialist Germany a sort of sister regime. Italian preparations for the eleventh modern Olympiad were costly and characteristically enthusiastic.

The American reaction to the *Gleichschaltung* or forced coordination of German sport was quite another matter. The Americans actually produced a serious and frightening (for the Nazis at least) protest movement. [. . .]

At a meeting in the United States of the Amateur Athletic Union (A.A.U.) on November 21, 1933, the delegates, with but one exception, voted for a boycott of the 1936 Games unless the position of Germany vis-à-vis her Jewish athletes be "changed in fact as well as in theory." Gustavus T. Kirby of the American Olympic Committee had proposed the resolution and was vigorously supported by Avery Brundage, then president of the American Olympic Committee. [. . .]

. . . [W]ell-publicized suggestions appeared here and there that the United States ought to boycott the Nazi Olympics. Nervously and with a fanfare of international publicity, the German Olympic Committee finally announced in June 1934 that twenty-one Jewish athletes had been nominated for the German training camps. Understandably suspicious, the American Olympic Committee dispatched Brundage himself to Germany to make an on-the-spot investigation.

Upon his return, Brundage revealed himself to be one more important personage dazzled by the order, relative prosperity, and joy that most travelers observed in Germany in those years. On the basis of his interviews with Jewish leaders (who, one hostile journalist noted, were always met in cafés and were always chaperoned by Nazi officials) Brundage concluded that the Germans were observing the letter and the spirit of Olympism. And on the basis of his recommendations the American Olympic Committee voted to participate in the XIth Olympiad. [. . .]

The lavish production at Los Angeles had been for some 1,500 athletes. Berlin was preparing for 3,500. After the Germans, the Americans had the largest team. Despite the continuing economic slump and the uncertainty of international politics (or, on the other hand, perhaps as psychological antidotes to them) other nations also sent large teams. Like the citizens of the ancient Greek city-states, all the world's patriots were eager to grasp at the prestige to be gathered by their Olympic victors. The Germans had overconscientiously prepared welcomes to impress, even overwhelm their visitors. For example, when their own misscheduling forced the French team to appear at the Olympic Village at 1:30 A.M. they were still greeted by corridors of Hitler youths holding torches high and playing waltzes.[3]

The man most responsible for all these preparations was Dr. Carl Diem. He was born in Würzburg on June 24, 1882. As a teenager in the 1890's he was a middle- and long-distance runner at a time when track events as practiced among the Anglo-Saxons were almost unknown among his countrymen who were quite devoted to gymnastics. Diem founded his first sporting club, Macromannia, in Berlin when he was seventeen.

He was a burly, short man and a perfect miracle of channeled energy. After 1900 his special track event was competition army field pack marching. He led the German expeditions to the Athens Games of 1906 and to the Olympics of 1912 in Stockholm, 1928 in Amsterdam, and 1932 in Los Angeles. For twenty years after 1913, Dr. Diem was the secretary of the German government's Commission for Sport and Recreation (*Generalsekretär des Deutschen Reichanschusses für Leibesübungen*) and during this time he founded and built the principal German school for recreation teachers, *Die deutsche Hochschule für Leibesübungen*, in Cologne. Diem traveled a lot and knew many languages. The Turkish government consulted him regularly concerning its recreation programs. He designed athletic architecture and athletic festivals in Germany. All the while Diem was engaged in his promotional work he was producing a stream of scholarly and theoretical writings of the highest quality. Only a fanatically uncritical admirer of Pierre de Coubertin would dispute the claim that Carl Diem is the greatest sports historian and most profound theorist of sport education of this century [the twentieth century]. He was expertly knowledgeable about the ball games of the pre-Columbian Indians, field hockey in ancient Egypt, Mongolian polo, and the starting lines for the sprinters in ancient Greek stadiums.[4]

Like most prominent bureaucrats in the amateur athletics movement, Diem was an almost slavish admirer of Coubertin. [. . .]

Diem also introduced some technological innovations into the projected sports meeting. Since the new stadium would hold more than 100,000 people, there was an urgent need for a strong loudspeaker that would not produce interior echoes. The German electrical industry complied, improving the loudspeaker devised for the Nuremberg rallies. [. . .]

A new showplace in Berlin and a sort of tour de force that combined German hospitality with German method was the Olympic Village in Berlin. In 1932 the Californians had provided isolated, simple housing for the athletes who had come to America to compete. Diem established a new standard. The army engineers were in charge of erecting the German Olympic Village. Its builder and organizer, Captain Wolfgang Fuerstner, had been in charge of the Wehrmacht's sporting program. Like so many other functionaries who at this time directed programs intended to impress the foreigners, Fuerstner was given almost a free hand relative to the financial and other resources he could draw on. The village itself was situated in a birch forest and near some small lakes beyond the western suburbs of Berlin. Besides the meeting halls and commons, there were 160 houses of brick, stone, and concrete. A house held 24 to 26 men in double rooms each of which had a wash basin, a shower, and a toilet. Two stewards speaking the athletes' language were quartered in every house. Just before the athletes arrived the whole area had been landscaped and the peaceful lake provided with coveys of snow-white ducks. All this was intended to obliterate the signs of rapid construction.

Like the participants in the Nuremberg rallies, each of the thousands of athletes, coaches, and officials at the village had long before been given a series of colored slips that plainly cited the house, room, and bed he was to occupy. He also had color-coded books of meal tickets indicating for him and for the staff of the village the food he would get and details of his special care. The athletes were told of the precise kinds of transportation they would use from the village to the sites of the various events. The British official report afterward recalled the terrific melee on the first morning of the Games when 3,000 men tried all at once to board the buses for the *Reichssportfeld*, the central athletic complex. There would have been no confusion "provided the competitors carried out the instructions issued by the German authorities with regard to departure."[5]

The international camaraderie that the Nazis were eager to demonstrate to the photographers and journalists who were directed to the Olympic Village was, in fact, achieved. Planning, painstaking care, and the alert sensitivity of the domestic staffs had, among the male athletes at least, made for an atmosphere of easy sociability. Shotputters met to compare notes of technique; weight lifters publicly flexed. Tourists gathered to observe the seriousness, strenuousness, and amazing agility of the Japanese swimmers as they limbered up. No one publicly objected to the incessant noise making and ebullient horseplay of the Italian soccer players. In the evening athletes from all over the world gathered in the common rooms for reading, card games, or to watch movies of events that had taken place that day. The gymnasts were especially grateful for the daily films that permitted them to see what the judges had seen shortly before. Fuerstner [the German Army's athletic program director] had provided barbers, medical care, and even dentists. The Ministry of Propaganda offered for free distribution a picture of a Chinese athlete suffering some complicated dental work that would have been terribly dear at home. Tasteful bulletin boards had indexes of masseurs including special ones for the cyclists. The Americans had American mattresses; the Swiss and Austrians had their familiar feather comforters; the Japanese had mats on the floor. Around the quiet, idyllic lake at the village was a tree-shaded jogging track. On the lake, for the use of the Finns, was a faultless, torrid sauna the benefits of which they eagerly extended to others.

The care and feeding of the almost four thousand men from fifty nations at the Olympic Village was entrusted to the stewards' department of the North German Lloyd combine whose network of passenger ship lines covered the whole world. There was no common menu. Each national cuisine was reproduced for the guests of new Germany. [. . .]

. . . [T]he housing for the male athletes in Berlin was devised not only for their benefit, but for purposes of putting the new regime in a good light. The women who competed were much less observed and much less comfortable. The forty-nine American female athletes and officials were taken to the women's dormitory, Friedrich Friesen Hans, a utilitarian dormitory near the *Reichssportfeld* that was surrounded by a high, wrought-iron fence. Once there, the women of all nations were isolated and put under the strict supervision of the Baroness von Wangenheim, a humorless Prussian with tiny eyes and great jowls below which she wore a thin string of very fine pearls. For some time there was no heat in the rooms and the food was inadequate both as regards quality and quantity.[6] The Baroness was unresponsive to frequent requests for improvement in living conditions. [. . .]

There is a strange postscript to add about the devoted administrator who oversaw the planning and construction of the Olympic Village. As was mentioned earlier, Captain Fuerstner was director of the German army's athletic program. It happened that he was also one of the few non-Aryan "blind spots" that the Wehrmacht was permitted by the Nazis. A few weeks before the foreign athletes arrived, Fuerstner was suddenly and inexplicably replaced at the Olympic Village by a certain Lieutenant Colonel Werner von und zu Gilsa. Then he was dismissed from the army—a personal calamity the loyal officer had never considered possible because of the frequent testimonials he had received for his good work. Though he, like the *Mischling* Dr. Theodor Lewald, was grossly demoted to being a piece of smiling window dressing, Fuerstner publicly voiced no displeasure and continued to serve nominally as second in command at the village until after the Games were over. Then, after a banquet honoring von und zu Gilsa for his services to the Reich in making the 1936 Olympics a success, Fuerstner killed himself with a single shot when he returned to his army barracks. The German press was at once instructed to explain that the officer had died after an automobile accident, but the truth leaked to foreign journalists. This unforeseen vignette required some sort of cover-up and retribution. General Werner von Blomberg, the Minister of Defense, arranged for a well-publicized funeral with full military honors.[7] For some weeks afterward the walls of the deserted Olympic Village were a favorite place for the Nazi zealots to scrawl obscene slogans against "the Jew Fuerstner" and against the Jews in general.

High-ranking Nazis were, of course, keenly aware that Germany was being watched by travelers for corroborating incidents of racial atrocities. There was, in fact, a confrontation between Hitler and Count Baillet-Latour, the Belgian *grand seigneur* who was president of the International Olympic Committee and who, publicly at least, made strong pronouncements that the Nazis were keeping their promises not to offend the sensibilities of their foreign guests. While motoring to Garmisch-Partenkirchen to open the winter Games, Baillet-Latour was astonished to see many vicious anti-Semitic posters along the German highways. As soon as he arrived at Garmisch he demanded and obtained an immediate audience with the Führer and through Paul Schmidt, the interpreter, they argued. Such ornaments were impossible preludes for a festival for all races and nations, shouted the great aristocrat. Hitler declared he could not alter "a question of the highest importance within Germany . . . for a small point of Olympic protocol." Baillet-Latour asserted that it was "a question of the most elementary courtesy," assumed an air of intransigency and threatened a cancellation of the winter and summer Games.

> Though stymied a bit at first, Hitler began to talk glibly, exciting himself more and more while staring at a corner of the ceiling. Soon he seemed oblivious to the presence of his companion and it was almost as though he was in a sort of trance. Schmidt ceased translating and waited for "the crisis" to pass—being familiar with this kind of scene.

Then the chancellor fell silent for several tense minutes. The Belgian was silent too. Suddenly Hitler blurted, "You will be satisfied; the orders shall be given," and brusquely ended the interview by leaving the room. When Baillet-Latour returned to Brussels by car, he saw no signs. The offensive placards were taken from the roads until the Games were over.[8]

Notes

1   See Colin Cross, *The Fascists in Britain* (London, Barrie and Rockcliff, 1962).

2   London, Trades Union Congress General Council, 1936, 31 pp.

3   Comité Olympique français, *La Participation française aux jeux de la XIième Olympiade* (Paris, 1936), p. 26.

4   The reader can consult the notes on Diem's scholarly work in Chapter 9 [of the original publication].

5   British Olympic Association. *The Official Report of the XIth Olympiad Berlin 1936* (London, British Olympic Association, 1937), p. 31.
6   *American Olympic Committee*, 1936, p. 72.
7   *The New York Times*, August 21, 23, 1936.
8   André G. Poplimont, "Berlin 1936," *Bulletin du Comité international olympique*, No. 56 (October 15, 1956), pp. 19–20.

John Hoberman

SPORTIVE NATIONALISM

S PORTIVE NATIONALISM IS NOT a single generic phenomenon; on the contrary, it is a complicated socio-political response to challenges and events, both sportive and non-sportive, that must be understood in terms of the varying national contexts in which it appears. Sportive nationalism is poorly understood for two basic reasons. First, we still do not understand the symbolic potency of the athlete for modern societies, a symbolic role that always survives changes in official ideology. Why do these people achieve such popularity in a wide variety of societies? Which psychological processes make it possible for black athletes to 'represent' predominantly white societies? How is athletic prowess converted into other kinds of prowess in our minds? Do any of these processes vary in quality or intensity from one society to another? These questions address sportive nationalism as a mass psychological phenomenon. What is more, they tend to suggest that the feelings that are involved in sportive nationalism are too diffuse and intangible to be understood.

While these feelings may, indeed, be finally indefinable, we can also study sportive nationalism as the more tangible behaviour of empowered individuals and institutions. In this sense, sportive nationalism exists, not as an inchoate mass emotional condition, but as the product of specific choices and decisions made by identifiable political actors.

This political process has taken different forms in different political cultures. In the Soviet Union, the official promotion of competitive sport began during the 1930s, in conjunction with feverish industrialisation and the Stalinist cult of the Stakhanovite superworker who broke records like an athlete. This rehabilitation of sport was, of course, achieved under the aegis of an official ideology.[1] In the United States, the Amateur Sports Act passed by Congress in 1978 aimed at promoting American success in international sports competitions but offered no accompanying ideological strictures.[2] Smaller states have practised an even more intense sportive nationalism as a deliberate and carefully managed policy. The former East German state created an unparalleled high-performance sports establishment for the purpose of winning international stature and domestic political credibility for the Communist regime.[3] It is now known that East German authorities mobilised over a thousand scientists, physicians and trainers in its programme to develop successful athletes by means of anabolic steroids.[4] Canada presents a similar, if less extreme, example of a small state administered by a government with specific political needs – national unity above all – that could be addressed (if not solved) through a self-assertive sports policy that included 'direct, forceful involvement in the development of elite athletes'.[5] *A Proposed Sports Policy for Canadians*, a document presented to the Canadian Amateur Sports Federation in 1970, clearly emphasised the development of elite athletes.[6] Indeed, for years after its triumph at the 1978 Edmonton Commonwealth Games, Canada was frequently referred to as 'the East Germany of the Commonwealth', a sobriquet that inevitably reappeared during the Ben Johnson scandal of 1988.[7]

For the Canadian government of Prime Minister Brian Mulroney the Ben Johnson affair was deadly serious political business – a public relations disaster that threatened to dismantle an official policy that linked Canadian state identity quite explicitly to international success in high-performance sport.[8] Here, as in East Germany, steroids became nothing less than a national security issue. Consequently, the Dubin Commission of Inquiry, appointed by the federal government itself to investigate doping in Canadian sport, was in large measure an exercise in political damage control – a wholly unintended consequence of sportive nationalism and the drugs it requires to be successful in the steroid age.[9]

There are many examples of sportive nationalism and its improbably extreme effects on otherwise sober people. We are all familiar with the extravagant fantasies of national grandeur that have often taken the form of athletic ambition. During the 1986 World Cup soccer matches in Mexico City, for example, the Argentine footballer Diego Maradona described as 'crazy' those Argentine legislators who had demanded a boycott of the game against England out of residual bitterness over the Falklands Islands war. The Argentine players even went so far as to present gifts to the members of the British team on the field.[10]

Is there, one might ask, a connection between such fantasies of national grandeur and sociopolitical instability? It is tempting to assume that the hysterical element one detects in the national football mania of Argentina or Brazil is related in some way to their precarious political structures, to hyperinflation, or crushing foreign debts, and to the military-sponsored terror of their recent pasts. The frequent association of sportive nationalism and domestic political tensions might even reflect a societal need for occasional cathartic outbursts to relieve feelings of anger and frustration. We might thus assume that politically stable and prosperous societies are likely to be immune to the aggressive mass psychology of sportive nationalism.

But that is not necessarily the case. In fact, exaggerated, even sinister, outbreaks of sportive nationalism can occur in societies that are both stable and wealthy. A case in point is the wave of chauvinism that swept over Switzerland in February 1987 after its skiers achieved a staggering series of victories at the world championships – a surge of popular emotion that included an ugly streak of xenophobic scorn for the foreign athletes who could not match the native champions. The writer Peter Bichsel commented: 'I am unleashed. This has nothing to do with sport, but rather with Switzerland. We are anything but a peaceful people.'

But not all Swiss saw this episode of national delirium in the same way. Adolf Ogi, president of the agrarian-conservative Swiss People's Party and himself a former manager of the Swiss Skiing Federation, offered the following explanation: 'Erika and Pirmin, but also Maria Walliser, come close to an ideal image of the youthful Swiss: modest, as we all are to some extent, and successful, as we would all like to be.' At the same time, as Ogi pointed out himself, these idealised figures are something more than quiet bucolic youths who have done well in the wider world. 'In business and in politics,' he says, 'there are only a few people who, in critical situations, are capable of responding in two short minutes to the command "On your marks, get set!" and make the most fateful kinds of decisions.' In short, for this observer the high-performance athlete symbolized nothing less than national survival in the unforgiving environment of international economic competition. Muscular strength and co-ordination fuse with economic strength and co-ordination into a metaphorical relationship, so that each of these twin dynamisms implies the other.

Does this metaphor play a role in the real world? Many newspaper and magazine advertisements that equate corporate and athletic achievement suggest that it does. The recent triumphalist response of the Norwegian prime minister to the gold medals won by her country's skiers at the 1992 Albertville Winter Olympic Games is a particularly suggestive case study of this metaphorical sportive nationalism. Indeed, her painstaking attempts to convince her countrymen that Olympic victories could actually be translated into success in the larger World Capitalist Games illustrate the underlying pathos of all small-country sportive nationalism . . .

This theory does not account, however, for the timing of the Swiss incident. Indeed, constant demands on the Swiss economy would, according to this model, produce constant eruptions of nationalist feeling. According to the Swiss journalist Jürg Bürgi, this episode had its roots in Swiss dissatisfaction with the modern world and the plagues it has visited upon the once-sheltered society that has not known war for five hundred years. Environmental disasters and the endless stream of refugees seeking safety and employment in Switzerland had poisoned the national mood to the bursting point. Given this national state of mind, sportive nationalism could assume its classic function of hurling a combination of megalomania and resentment against the outside world.[11]

All of the anecdotal evidence considered up to this point links sportive nationalism to political pathology. But we might also speculate that sportive nationalism plays a 'normal' symbolic role for smaller nations that have few opportunities to assert themselves against much larger states. If this is the case, then the more civilised forms of sportive nationalism may have to be recognised as an inherent right of the 'minor' nations that participate in international sport.

The idea that some national communities actually have a psychological need to assert themselves through sportive achievement is intriguing. The ideal test case would be a small and culturally homogenous national community, economically productive and politically stable, displaying no unusual need for the emotional compensations of sporting success in the international arena.

Let us use Norway as a good approximation to the ideal test case. In 1985, after a considerable amount of public discussion regarding government financing of sport, the parliamentary leader of the conservative (Høyre) party, Jo Benkow, stated that sport should not be a special priority for state funding and that social welfare measures were more important. What is more, he was prepared to defend this position even if it cost him political support.

This call for restraints on state funding for sport is especially interesting because it came from a conservative politician. For reasons I do not have time to analyse in this context, conservatives will generally support sportive nationalism – indeed, virtually all nationalist initiatives – more often and with greater fervour than centrists or leftists. And yet an independent Christian (and, therefore, conservative) newspaper that supported Benkow's position noted that 'a number of ardent souls on the right' should heed his message on sport funding.[12]

Jo Benkow's provocative moderation in the area of sport confirms the broad political consensus behind Norway's traditional welfare policies. But it would be misleading to suggest that Norwegian society is immune to concerns about its competitiveness in high-performance sport. English and Norwegian soccer fans, for example, are likely to remember the famous outburst in 1981 by a Norwegian television commentator, Bjœrge Lillelien. Following Norway's 2–1 upset victory over the English team, Lillelien seemed to go berserk, screaming 'William Shakespeare, Francis Drake, Winston Churchill . . . we've beaten you all!'[13] This most un-Norwegian display of naked chauvinist passion confirmed that sportive nationalism could breach even the famous self-containment of the Scandinavians.

In fact, Norwegian sportive nationalism is usually tempered by a sober practicality, irrespective of whether it is responding to victory or defeat. In February 1988, for example, Norway's Olympic athletes returned from the Calgary Winter Olympic Games after a dismal performance. Never before had a Norwegian team come home without a gold medal. The significance of this failure was discussed in an editorial that appeared in the conservative Oslo newspaper *Aftenposten*. The purpose of this editorial was not to lament a dark day in the history of Norwegian sport, but rather to determine whether sporting success is of authentic value to the national community. One conclusion was that, although gold medals do not rank with economic performance and educational achievement as foundations of national security, they have played a role in building national self-respect. What is more, Norwegian anxieties about doing conspicuously well in the winter sports is rooted in a long tradition that teaches virtually all children to ski and skate because these practical skills are a way of life. This commentary concludes by noting that a limited, focused programme to develop high-performance athletes in certain traditional disciplines answers an authentic psychological need of the nation; and that the mass media should reduce the indiscriminate pressure exerted on many athletes to perform at the highest level.[14]

Four years later this situation had utterly reversed itself. The 1992 Albertville Winter Games witnessed the greatest Norwegian Olympic performance in history – nine gold, six silver and five bronze medals. Even before the Games, Prime Minister Gro Harlem Brundtland had welcomed in the New Year by declaring that 'Excellence is typically Norwegian' citing the achievements of successful (women) handball players, skiers and the Oslo Philharmonic.[15] Now she immediately seized the opportunity to address the topic of high performance on the editorial page of Norway's largest and most respectable newspaper. Gold-medal victories, she declared, had provided a windfall of positive publicity for Norway, and only two years before the opening of the 1994 Winter Olympic Games in Lillehammer. Norwegian athletes had done valuable service as 'ambassadors of Norwegian initiative', reinforcing self-confidence at home while convincing potential customers abroad that Norwegian companies, like Norwegian athletes, had to be taken seriously. The finely tuned co-operative effort and 'team spirit' of the Norwegian Olympic team, the prime minister wrote, must be emulated by the economic sector. 'In the years ahead, we must do a better job of asserting ourselves internationally in arenas other than sports and culture,' she warned. She went on to imply that athletes and business people were really playing the same game, whether inside or outside the stadium: 'Large sectors of our export industry have been competing hard in both the European Cup and the World Cup' – an effective metaphorical strategem for a sports-minded body politic with the prospect of European Community membership on its mind. Indeed, with impressive political legerdemain, Prime Minister Brundtland managed to deliver this blunt warning about international economic competitiveness without once mentioning her hard-driving campaign to persuade Norwegians that they should enter the EC – an economic major league naturally feared by people accustomed to a less Darwinian existence and the creature comforts of deeply rooted local economies.[16] Nor was this an 'ideological' issue of left and right. The only 'ideology' (or *Weltanschauung*) left standing in this debate was the competitive ethos itself.

In short, Norwegian responses to national Olympic performance in both 1988 and 1992 included some impressively sober assessments by leading politicians. Here was sportive nationalism at its calculating best, first looking inward for the historical foundations of national character (Benkow), then looking outward to the markets that could ensure national survival (Brundtland). The Norwegian experience shows that it is simply irresponsible to approach sportive nationalism as though it were a kind of mass psychosis beyond our understanding. On the contrary, it is sport's legendary effects in the political world that have prompted us to overestimate the irrational factor. 'We must invest in sport because it contributes to the identification of the citizen with the state,' a West German sports official stated after the 1988 Seoul Olympiad.[17] While the ultimate basis of this identification may well be 'irrational', planning to create it is not.

Notes

1   John Hoberman, *Sport and Political Ideology*, University of Texas Press, 1984, pp. 193–4.
2   Roy A. Clumpner, 'Pragmatic coercion; the role of government in sport in the United States', in Gerald Redmond, ed., *Sport and Politics* [The 1984 Olympic Scientific Congress Proceedings, Vol. 71, Human Kinetics, 1986, 7.]
3   See, for example, Hoberman, *Sport and Political Ideology*, pp. 201–18.
4   See, for example, Steven Dickman, 'East Germany; science in the disservice of the state', *Science*, 254, 4 October 1991, 26–7
5   Donald Macintosh and C.E.S. Franks, 'Canadian government involvement in sport: Some consequences and issues', in Redmond, ed., *Sport and Politics*, p. 21.
6   G.A. Olafson and C. Lloyd Brown-John, 'Canadian international sport policy: a public policy analysis,' in Redmond, ed., *Sport and Politics*, p. 71.
7   I am indebted to Bruce Kidd for explaining to me the origins of this phrase.
8   For an elegant analysis of the Canadian government's predicament during the Johnson affair see John J. MacAloon, 'Steroids and the state: Dubin melodrama and the accomplishment of innocence', *Public Culture*, 2, spring 1990, 41–64.
9   The authors of the Dubin report note that 'since the mid-1970s [government support of sport] has increasingly been channeled towards the narrow objectives of winning medals in international competition'. See *Commission of Inquiry into the Use of Drugs and Banned Practices Intended to Increase Athletic Performance*, Canadian Government Publishing Centre, 1990, p. 43.

10 'Rowdyism mars Argentine win,' *Boston Globe*, 23 June 1986.

11 Jürg Bürgi, 'Sie spinnen, diese Schweizer', *Der Spiegel*, 23 February 1987.

12 'Hoyre og idrettspengene', *Ukens nytt* [Oslo], 20 April 1985.

13 This quotation is not a verbatim, but rather a more or less accurate, version of Lillelien's outburst.

14 'Et norsk nederlag', *Ukens nytt*, 3 March 1988.

15 Gro: 'Det er typisk norsk avære god', *Ukens nytt*, 7 January 1992, 8.

16 Gro Harlem Brundtland, 'Vi kan hvis vi vil', *Aftenposten*, 22 February 1992, 2. Not long after making this pitch on competitiveness to the Norwegian nation, Prime Minister Brundtland provoked a domestic political storm by suggesting that Norway's gold medals at the Albertville Games were due to the policies of her own Labour Party (Arbeiderpartiet). At least two gold-medal winners, the skiers Vegard Ulvang and Finn Chr. Jagge, objected to this use of Olympic athletes for political purposes. See 'Storm rundt Gro etter uttalelser om OL-gull', *Ukens nytt*, 3 March 1992, 5.

17 This statement was made by Professor Klaus Heinemann, Professor of Sociology at the University of Hamburg and chairman of the Scientific Council of the German Sports Association (DSB). See 'Industrie läßt sich nicht von Effekten leiten', *Süddeutsche Zeitung*, 11 October 1988.

John Sugden and Alan Bairner

'MA, THERE'S A HELICOPTER ON THE PITCH!'

Sport, leisure, and the state in Northern Ireland

[. . .]

IN NORTHERN IRELAND . . . where there is a serious problem of order, . . . it is difficult to ignore the proximity of sport to politics when during a Gaelic football match a heavily armed helicopter hovers deafeningly just about the heads of the players before disappearing into the confines of a corrugated-iron fortress built by the British Army on the adjoining field, an area of land which was, before the "Troubles," part of the playing area—or when a number of expensive new municipal sport and leisure facilities are constructed, at taxpayers' expense, alongside military and police stockades in the most troubled areas of Belfast.

At one level, the presence of the military and armed police in or around sporting events simply illustrates the need for increased security at any popular gathering place in this deeply divided community. However, such shows of force are also indicative of a marginally submerged struggle through which the Northern Ireland state attempts to increase its control of civil society through the penetration and manipulation of sport in the Province. Likewise, the expansion of Belfast's leisure services has been explained in terms of matching resources to community need. However, it too reveals another level at which the state seeks to influence popular behavior by gaining access to the leisure time of ordinary citizens. [. . .]

The failure of devolved, provincial government to deal adequately with the current Troubles led in 1972 to the imposition of a form of direct rule from Westminster. Under the terms of this arrangement, major policy decisions over matters of security, economic development, social services, and the like are orchestrated by the British government and implementation is supervised by a secretary of state for Northern Ireland, his ministers, and the administrative bureaucracy of the Northern Ireland office. In addition, district councils have been stripped of many traditional duties in areas such as housing, education, and town planning and instead are left with responsibility for the relatively uncontroversial matters such as technical services, parks, and leisure services. Even in these areas, important questions of policy and capital finance are dealt with by ministers responsible to the secretary of state for Northern Ireland.

However, while ultimate control lies in London, the process through which political authority is exercised in the Province becomes diffuse and subject to regional redirection as central government policy is translated into practice by locally based civil servants, members of the security forces, and district councillors. The manner through which the state influences sport and leisure in Northern Ireland is a good illustration of this process of diffusion and redirection whereby consequences do not always follow intentions. [. . .]

. . . [W]ithin approximately 10 years Belfast went from being one of the UK's most underprovided cities to becoming one of the most well-endowed in western Europe. The development of 14 leisure centers in Belfast far exceeds Sports Council recommendations for a city of no more thin 400,000 people. [. . .]

The extensiveness of the provision of leisure facilities and opportunities in Belfast is not open to question. It is the original rationale for provision, its day-to-day operation, and its impact on the social and political make-up of the community that raise controversial questions of statecraft. From the perspective of those responsible for running the city's leisure services, such provision is justified as a response to the recreative needs of civil society, particularly in areas of social deprivation. [. . .]

There is no public record of the discussions surrounding the decision-making process through which Northern Ireland received and implemented its leisure windfall. However, in 1988 during a televised interview, Dr. Brian Mawhinney, the minister currently responsible for the public funding of sport and leisure in Northern Ireland, admitted that in the past the state had attempted to use leisure as a means of channeling the energies of young people away from direct involvement in political violence.

While carrying out research for "Workers Playtime," a radio documentary on leisure, Huntley (1987) uncovered evidence suggesting that the Troubles were the catalyst for the rapid expansion of Belfast's leisure services and that the political will and material wherewithal for such development originated in Westminster. Huntley interviewed a number of politicians, senior civil servants, and local government officials who had been key players in the establishment of Belfast's leisure services in the 1970s. John Saulters, assistant secretary at the Department of Education until 1983, saw a clear connection between the efforts of the British government to pacify the Province in the 1970s and the extensive leisure center building program for Belfast during the same period. This view is shared by Jim Hull, deputy principal officer at the Department, who makes the "control" factor explicit:

> In the 1970s, money was running out of our ears. The Government saw that it was extremely important to provide facilities in Belfast, because if you got them there at ten in the morning and kept them there until late afternoon, then they weren't dragging up stones and slabs to throw at the police at night.
> (Huntley, 1988, p. 44)

Alan Moneypenny, the director of the Antrim Forum, Northern Ireland's first major leisure center, agrees that the expanded volume of provision in Belfast resulted in part from the city's civil disturbances. In the 1970s Paddy Devlin was a local councillor and an influential member of the Leisure Services Committee, the body that planned the structure of provision in Belfast. While recognizing a genuine community need for increased provision, he believes that it was really to prevent young people from rioting that such an extensive program was financed by the central government:

> We set up 14 not 8 (leisure centers), because the Sports Council in England who drew up the figures hadn't the problems we had—they didn't have the population massacring themselves. In order to stop the rioting it was agreed that 14 would be needed.
>
> (Huntley, 1988, p. 45)

Thus there is evidence that at all levels of the delivery system, central and local government and professional leisure administration, there was an awareness that Belfast's leisure windfall was to some extent caused by the state's desire to harness this aspect of civil society to a broader strategy of social control in Northern Ireland. There is also evidence in support of another aspect of our argument (Sugden & Bairner, 1986): Rather than promoting cross-community integration, the actual pattern of public leisure provision established in the city has reinforced sectarian polarization.

Policy may have been decided at Westminster, but it was enacted through a series of offices and agencies which, toward the planning and building stages of development, came progressively closer to the divisive currents that are indigenous to the Province. Central government, through the Department of Education, provided the bulk of money for the building program and, in consultation with the sports councils (for England and for Northern Ireland) and the local leisure services committees, dictated broadly what the design and contents of Belfast's leisure centers should be. However, it was to be the local taxpayers who would finance the day-to-day running of the centers, and therefore city councillors had a major say in determining local demand and identifying the areas where these facilities would be located.

Research by both Huntley (1987, 1988) and Knox (1987) indicates that the issue of leisure provision was seen by many local councillors as one of "us versus them" (Protestant vs. Catholic; Loyalist vs. Nationalist), and in council chambers the map of provision was clearly influenced by a balance of cross-community claims. [. . .]

This pattern is a reflection of two things: sectarianism and pragmatism. It is sectarian in the sense that it has been influenced by local politicians who have sought to maximize their constituents' interests. In any other UK context this could be applauded as a civic duty, but in Belfast local council constituencies are almost exclusively either Nationalist/Catholic or Loyalist/Protestant. Once in place, leisure centers do become an important community resource, but for one community and not the other, and this adds to sectarian polarization in the city.

At the Department of Education, Jim Hull is critical of the results of central government funding:

> It would have been much better to site the centres on a more widespread basis. A lot of the community centres and some of the leisure centres through- out the Province are being virtually run by paramilitaries, and the decent citizen is just not welcome. If they were situated in more neutral areas of the

city, then people who wanted to use the facilities could have travelled to them, and I think that would have been a much better idea. Now, everybody is just becoming further entrenched in their own wee corners and can't get out.

(Huntley, 1988, p. 50)

[. . .] Paradoxically, by applying a British model of rational recreation to Northern Ireland, the state may have helped to keep the working class divided at the cost of fueling the more potent sectarian divisions that are at the root of serious public disorder in the Province. There is even doubt that leisure centers in opposing communities are a significant deterrent to disruptive behavior. Of one thing we can be certain: The presence of leisure centers in one community or another, whether they be "green" or "orange," does little to deter a return to the streets, albeit by leaner and fitter young men, should the latest episode of the Troubles demand it. This is a further example of how consequences do not necessarily follow intentions when the state seeks to extend its influence into civil society. [. . .]

At a formal political level, and through a variety of paramilitary channels, Northern Ireland's union with Britain continues to be challenged by organizations such as the IRA. However, such formal oppositional positions must have a broad cultural platform, and in this regard the most important counterhegemonic cultural organization in the Province, with the possible exception of the Catholic Church, is the Gaelic Athletic Association (GAA).

There can be no doubting the political heritage of the GAA. It was founded in 1884 by a group of sports enthusiasts who were also Irish nationalists and who saw the revival of traditional Gaelic pastimes as an important adjunct to the wider struggle against British rule. . . . [T]he GAA is explicitly counterhegemonic, as the following extract from the members' handbook illustrates:

> The Association is a National Organisation which has as its basic aim the strengthening of the National Identity in a 32 County Ireland through the preservation and promotion of Gaelic games and pastimes. (1985, p. 1)

In this respect the GAA in Northern Ireland can be construed as an element in the nationalists' struggle to subvert the union. As such it provokes a similar response from the state as any other source of opposition to the prevailing order. In practice, however, the state's relationship with the GAA is complicated, both because of the intricate nature of the political process and because of the ambiguous role that sport plays in social organization and social control in any society. From the perspective of central government, the GAA is a paradox, being at the same time both an important structure for community stability and a potential threat to political security. This accounts for the contradictory treatment the GAA receives at the hands of the state. [. . .]

. . . [W]hile one part of the British state sponsors this organization, in other areas of central government the GAA is viewed with suspicion and its activities are monitored accordingly. However, what begins as suspicion at Westminster when translated into practice in Northern Ireland could easily be interpreted as overtly sectarian harassment. Surveillance of individual GAA members together with their clubs and activities is based on the premise that although they may be meeting for the purposes of sport, by their membership in the GAA they have proclaimed a nationalist political preference. Their sporting involvement is viewed as a covert means of affiliating with those of a similar political persuasion.

Surveillance takes various forms, ranging from random checks on the movements of GAA members to more permanent structures of vigilance such as the construction of police and army barracks on or adjacent to Gaelic playing fields. The best known example is the security forces' installation in Crossmaglen which was constructed on the town's Gaelic playing fields and which inspired the title of this paper. [. . .]

Many Protestants in Northern Ireland regard individual members of the GAA not merely as potential troublemakers but as active representatives of an alien tradition that threatens the Protestant and unionist way of life. Members of the security forces reared in the unionist tradition are likely to be influenced by this view in their routine dealings with those associated with the GAA. It certainly did not go unnoticed in Nationalist (republican) circles when early in 1988 Aiden McAnespie was shot dead by a British soldier when crossing the border on his way to play Gaelic football. Neither did it escape the attention of Loyalists (unionists) when at McAnespie's funeral the usually provocative tricolor flag of the Republic was replaced by a Gaelic football jersey as a drape for his coffin. [. . .]

The state in its many guises in Ireland deals with the GAA in dramatically contradictory fashion. Central government provides financial support which local government does its best to block, and the judiciary penalizes local government for being sectarian. Meanwhile the security forces continue to treat the GAA with something only marginally short of contempt. The GAA, as an element of civil society, is encouraged by the state in its educative capacity to try to achieve the acquiescence of Northern Irish Catholics, but it is also the object of considerable attention on the part of coercive elements of political society that deem its role to be essentially counterhegemonic. Thus it is a mistake to assume that the state is monolithic in its approach to solving problems of order.

Conclusion

The most obvious conclusion to be drawn from this is that sport and leisure as aspects of civil society may only reveal themselves clearly as foci for political/hegemonic struggle during times of protracted civil unrest. Such manifestations may well be the end results of continuous historical processes, but it is only when the cooperation and control of civil society itself is at stake, as in Northern Ireland, that the state is forced to show its hand. However, what the state has learned in its dealings in the Province is that, as part of civil society, neither sport nor leisure can be mobilized automatically in support of the established forces of law and order. As aspects of popular culture, they are as likely to be part of the undercurrents that fuel dissent. As such they are neither easy to penetrate nor manipulate and, to paraphrase Ralph Miliband, once the state targets sport and leisure as battle fronts in the war to establish hegemony, it discovers them to be highly contested territory (1977, pp. 51–54).

This is further complicated by the fact that the contest for civil society in Northern Ireland occurs not just between social classes but also between Catholics and Protestants, various groupings of Nationalists and Loyalists, and the multiple façades of the British state. In terms of sport and leisure, the state in Northern Ireland has at least two faces:

an open and smiling countenance that supports community integration and cross-border cooperation, and, closer to the scene, a scowl that accompanies coercion and force to maintain the status quo.

On the surface a conventional British model of community recreation and "sport for all" is encouraged. In practice, however, this model tends to reinforce rather than ameliorate sectarian divisions. At a local level, through the activities of politically motivated pressure groups, local politicians, and ultimately the security forces, sport and leisure have become part of Northern Ireland's wider cultural and political conflict. Thus, while sport and leisure may not be the Province's most important battle grounds, they are by no means the least significant.

References

Gaelic Athletic Association (1985). *Cumann Luthcheals Gael*. Dublin: Stylest Print.

Huntley, D. (1987, April 5). *Workers Playtime*. BBC Radio Northern Ireland.

Huntley, D. (1988). *Community interest or political pressure: Public leisure provision in Belfast*. Unpublished manuscript, University of Ulster.

Knox, C. (1987). Territorialism, leisure and community centres in Northern Ireland. *Leisure Studies*, **6**, 212–237.

Miliband, R. (1977). *Marxism and politics*. Oxford: Oxford University Press.

Sugden, J. and Bairner, A. (1986). Northern Ireland: The politics of leisure in a divided society. *Leisure Studies*, **5**, 341–352.

John Wilson

LEISURE AND NATIONALISM

THE YEARS BETWEEN 1870 AND 1914 can be regarded as the period when state, nation and society began to converge. Seen from below, the state increasingly defined the largest stage on which the crucial activities determining human lives as subjects and citizens were played out. Political elites became increasingly aware of the importance of 'irrational' elements such as national holidays, ceremonies and festivals in binding the loyalty of people to this new entity and for marking the boundaries between 'us' and 'them'—aliens, foreigners, strangers. As we shall see, all manner of leisure pursuits, and sport in particular, have played an important role in these affirmations of identity and unity.

Regardless of political regime, modern societies now routinely use leisure to make claims for nationhood, to establish the boundaries of their nation-state, to establish an identity for their people, to deny the claims of other peoples for nationhood, to integrate existing conglomerates into national communities and to symbolize and reaffirm hierarchies of power and status among the nations of the world. Modern communications technology makes sporting competitions of national interest immediately available to citizens at home, who are much more likely to identify with the elite athletes representing their country than they would identify with artists, or even politicians. [. . .]

Pastimes can also be used by states to strengthen their hold over the allegiance of the people, to unite and solidify the nation. Popular pastimes can equally well be used by groups seeking to resist this integration. Finally, nationalism plays a role in the internal organization of leisure activities. For example, the international sporting order helps shape how a nation's sporting associations operate and how sport resources are distributed within the country. [. . .]

It is bureaucratized play, or sport, that is used as a weapon in international conflict, not the more amorphous world of leisure.

Achieving nationhood

In a new nation, sports have a dual function in the building of national identity and national competence. Nation-building is ultimately connected with social mobility, which implies people moving physically, but even more mentally, as they broaden their horizons. Social mobilization starts from the center of a social system and spreads outward to the periphery. Sporting activities do likewise. Sports can thus play a role in the mobilization of peripheral countries to new awareness and hence in social development. In the case of nations forged out of many formerly constituent units, the demarcation of the nation-state requires a show of strength and unity. Sporting success in the international arena, which is highly visible and easy to quantify, is ideally suited for this purpose. The use of sport to inculcate political loyalties to the system as a whole, transcending bonds of kinship, language and locale, has been widespread in the Western world and, after the Second World War, in the communist-bloc countries and their non-European satellites.

Even countries that do not use sport to achieve a sense of national unity find it useful when making a claim for international acceptance. Almost literally, the arena in which the credibility of this claim is judged is usually the Olympic Games. The games are available for this purpose because, ironically, the Olympic movement has pursued two contradictory goals. The Olympic Charter declares the nonpolitical purpose of the Olympic movement. Supporters of the Olympic movement have attempted repeatedly to preserve Olympism by diminishing nationalism within amateur sports. They have constantly sought to restrict the use of national flags and anthems and the use of official 'points' tables.

On the other hand, the revival of the Olympic Games had strong nationalist motives, a series of early reforms paved the way for subsequent nationalist manipulations of the games, and most modern participants have blatant nationalist motives. Pierre de Coubertin himself saw the Olympics as helping restore the vigor of French youth and building loyalty to and pride in France. The 1896 Olympic Games in Athens were primarily used as a tool for achieving national unity by a Greek dynasty under domestic pressure. In the games of the 1900s, political identification of competitors soon led to national teams, a tendency encouraged by Coubertin's insistence on a parade of athletes by nation at the beginning of the games and the raising of the flag and playing of anthems during the victory ceremonies. Olympic rules actually allowed medal tables between 1896 and 1914. The 'First New Nation,' the United States, was also the first to advertise itself through its victories in the modern political sport system; as early as 1906 the American press was scoring the Olympics on a national basis (Kanin, 1978, p. 249). Soon thereafter no athlete would be allowed to compete as an individual or appear in Olympic events out of national uniform. The original Olympic Charter calls for the 'support of Government' and gave nations the task of holding elimination trials. The International Olympic Committee (IOC) has persisted in using national Olympic committees as its base, refusing requests for recognition from sports' organizations not affiliated with these national committees; and the committees, in turn, have identified themselves with the nation state in order to establish their claim to legitimacy.

It comes as no surprise, then, that problems of national identity arose almost immediately after the revival of the Olympic Games and have continued to plague the movement as nations and would-be nations use this forum to stake a claim to legitimacy on the world political stage. The Finns protested at having to compete under the Russian flag in 1908 and 1914. Bohemia, one of the founding members of the Olympic movement, was prevented from participating by Austria-Hungary after 1912. In the early 1920s both Morocco and the Philippines wanted to enter the games under their own emblems and flags but, because they were not self-governing, were forced to compete as part of their governing nation's teams. Special dispensation had to be sought from France and the United States to permit these countries to compete as autonomous bodies.

The emergence of the People's Republic of China on to the world stage was also symbolized by its acceptance into the system of international sport competition. The issue was greatly complicated by the continued existence of a rival claim to the title of China, from the government on Formosa. In its first vote on this question, in 1954, the IOC opted to recognize both Chinas.

> In this way they followed the political developments of the day. Their ruling, for all intents and purposes, recognized two separate states: Peking–China and Formosa–China. To that extent they did not sacrifice their rules, for the rules stated that their [sic] could be only one committee per country. By recognizing two committees they recognized two countries.
>
> (Espy, 1979, p. 45)

Despite its claim to be the one true China, the PRC seems to have accepted this ruling and prepared in earnest for the 1956 Melbourne Olympics, only to withdraw at the last minute because of Nationalist China's participation. In 1958 the PRC severed all connections with the IOC. It did not immediately return when, in 1959, the IOC removed Nationalist China from its rolls as a body representing all of China. The Nationalist Chinese competed as 'Taiwan' for the first time in the 1960 Rome games. By the 1960s the PRC was more concerned with the threat of the USSR to its security than the threat of the West and used sport to underscore differences within the communist camp itself. It organized a military sport meet in 1964 which involved thirteen communist states but gave pride of place to Albania, Romania, Mongolia, North Korea and North Vietnam— all acolytes of China and hostile to the Soviets (Kanin, 1978, p. 269).

Sport is used to make gestures of international hostility and rejection which, if other means were used, might be too provocative or disruptive of alliances. The sport boycott of South Africa is a case in point, where countries which cannot agree on commercial sanctions can unite to withdraw sporting relations. Conversely, sport can be used to give a sense of 'normalcy' when international tensions are high. Between the two world wars, English soccer touring teams, along with many other sporting organizations, traveled abroad and played along guidelines laid down by the Foreign Office. The Football Association was given firm instructions concerning which countries they should visit and which they should avoid, although in public the government presented a totally different face, and spokesmen openly denounced the idea of political interference in sport (Walvin, 1975, p. 126). These visits helped reinforce the normalcy of the fascist regimes in Germany and Italy.

In the 1958–66 period of the cold war Soviet-American track and field meets were one of the few arenas in which members of the two countries met. They survived the U-2 incident, the second Berlin crisis, the Cuban missile crisis and the abrupt changes in both superpower regimes in 1963–4. The athletic meets became a victim of the American escalation of the air war in Vietnam when the Soviets refused to attend the scheduled Los Angeles track meet in 1966. Sporting ties have not been sufficient to repair relations between Cuba and the United States. Even though sport exchanges between the United States and Cuba have received a fair amount of publicity, they have not served to break new political ground for the two countries.

Countries can use international sport to resume a place on the stage after a period of being an international pariah. Germany's return to international respectability after the First World War was signaled in 1928 with its readmission to the Olympic movement. The Federal Republic of Germany was readmitted to the Olympic movement in 1951 only after its national committee had 'publicly apologised for World War II and the German atrocities' (Espy, 1979, p. 29).

The Soviets were admitted to the Olympic movement in 1952, but on terms negotiated by the Soviets that would clearly indicate their difference from the Western nations that had dominated international sports between the wars. For example, they demanded Russian be made an official language of the Olympic movement and that Soviet officials be guaranteed a seat on the executive committee of the IOC. The culmination of the Soviets' efforts to achieve respectability in the international sporting arena was their hosting of the 1980 Olympic Games, which gave them a chance to show off not only on the athletic field but also in technology and social organization.

Sport was an important tool in the guided restoration a of Japan after 1945. 'Olympic veteran McArthur ordered baseball competition renewed and arranged for the participation of Japanese swimmers in American meets' (Kanin, 1981, p. 83). Sport was one of several ways the United States government tried to make sure that American values took hold at all levels of Japanese society. A measure of the extent of the incorporation of Japan's sport into the international order was the country's hosting of the Olympic Games in 1964. By then the games had become truly pan-national events, part of the global village and only loosely attached to the people of the hosting nation. 'The 1964 Olympic Games were a typically Western event, barely touched by elements of Japan's own cultural heritage' (Kanin, 1981, p. 84).

Long before then, the hosting of the Olympic Games had become perhaps the most dramatic means for a country to stake its claim to be at the center of the world stage. The Japanese were not concerned about the 'unJapanese' character of their games because their interest was in gaining acceptance as a legitimate trading partner, a modern nation, at the core of the world's economy. Mexico's hosting of the 1968 Olympics in Mexico had a similar purpose. The Mexicans deliberately sought to overcome their status as a Third World, debtor nation by agreeing to host an expensive event. Hosting the games would signal their parity with and independence of the United States. They also sought, in the cultural events surrounding the games, to revive the spirit of revolutionary independence that had founded the nation. Mexico's hosting of the 1986 FIFA World Cup amidst a mounting debt crisis had a similar aim.

There can be no doubt, then, that sport is a popular tool for the assertion of nationhood. But we should not exaggerate its importance on the world scene. Highly bureaucratized competitive sports are a creature of the Western capitalist world, and their role has not been so salient in the birth and development of the many new nations that have emerged with the collapse of colonialism. In both Africa and South-East Asia, elite athletes have been trained to act as ambassadors for their countries, and regional confederations (e.g. the All-Africa Games, GANEFO) have been formed to provide an arena for non-Western ideas about sport. But sport has been placed on the back burner when it comes to allocating resources for national development, physical culture being secondary to providing shelter, clothing and nourishment. African countries have viewed sport in a 'lethargic manner' (Uwechue, 1978, p. 546), while those in South-East Asia have fine programs for sport 'on paper—and little else' (Uwechue, 1978, p. 538). Sport *can* be a tool of national integration, but the human and material resources needed to make it perform this task are usually unavailable or otherwise committed in newly emerging nations outside the West. [. . .]

Sport, national integration and disintegration

Nation-building demands not only the delineation of national boundaries but the integration and unification of the new state into a cohesive unit. Nationalism thus also has an inward-looking aspect as the new nation seeks to homogenize its population. Immigration is restricted to those who 'fit,' new immigrants are subjected to socialization into citizenship values, domestic culture is standardized and a distinctive national character molded.

Sports and leisure in general have been extensively used in this aspect of the nationalization process. In the United States, for example, baseball was said to be 'only second to the public schools as a teacher of American mores to the second generation' (Riess, 1980, p. 25). Only games and pastimes that affirmed the new national character were promoted, while 'alien' pastimes were frowned upon. Sports which emerged as mass spectator events in the United States during the final quarter of the nineteenth century did not appear haphazardly: 'the sorting process was aimed at finding games that recalled the basic traditions that had formed "Anglo-Saxon" personality and character' (Mrozek, 1983, p. 166). In the nationalization process, ancient games, or 'imports,' are taken over and adapted to better fit the national character. 'Qualities that were supposedly American were imputed to football and baseball, which, in turn, were presumed to generate those values in the players' (Mrozek, 1983, p. 160). Each sport had created for it a myth of national origins, located in a specific time and place.

The Americanization of games was taken very seriously, although motives were often as pecuniary as they were patriotic. The drive to Americanize baseball was led by Albert Spaulding, an early professional star who later owned the Chicago Cubs and ran a sporting goods company that came close to monopolizing the market. He managed to create such an interest in the origins of baseball that a blue-ribbon committee of seven prominent citizens, including two United States Senators, was set up to decide once and for all where the game had begun. The committee concluded in 1907, on the flimsiest of evidence, that baseball had indeed originated in America in 1839 when Abner Doubleday supposedly laid out the first baseball diamond in Cooperstown, a site which has since become a 'shrine' of baseball fans. In 1939 the US Post Office placed its imprimatur upon this history by issuing a commemorative stamp to mark the centennial anniversary of the birth of 'America's game' (Riess, 1980, p. 16).

Political elites were quick to associate themselves with the rise of sports. Senator Henry Cabot Lodge, scion of two distinguished New England families, together with Theodore Roosevelt and Elihu Root, then Secretary of War, linked sport to a general program for renewing their society and reordering world affairs. Roosevelt, although an indifferent athlete, made much of his interest in sport and encouraged the armed services to use sport as part of their training programs to improve fitness, agility, strength and aggression (Mrozek, 1983, p. 47). Roosevelt was of the opinion that 'Sport did not imitate other experiences that yielded values which society favored; it actually produced them by means that occasionally resembled activities other than athletics' (Mrozck, 1983, p. 32). Here we see that same coupling and merging of military training and national defense as we see in the 'physical culture' programs of communist countries. [. . .]

Nation-states seek to suppress leisure activities with a strong regional identity, while regions, especially those in which nationalist movements are active, will seek to preserve, revive and affirm regionally distinctive leisure activities. Soccer competitions between Scotland and England exemplify the attitudes of many Scottish people to England. They are regarded as David-and-Goliath affairs, soccer being one of the few remaining institutions which maintain for the Scots a feeling of rivalry with England. Rugby was, and remains, an aspect of the national identity of Wales. During the resurgence of Welsh nationalism in the postwar period, rugby became 'more emphatically a national passion than ever' (Morgan, 1981, p. 348). During the formation of the Irish independence movement, Gaelic football was revived, and popularized.

In France bullfighting is most popular in the southwest (e.g. Provence): 'the question of the *corrida* became involved in the revival of Provençal nationalism' (Holt, 1981, p. 120). The national government has chosen not to move forcefully against this highly controversial sport, despite pressure in Paris from interest groups, because of the intense hostility to this in the southwest, whose residents brand animal rights and humane society activists as 'deracinated metropolitan intellectuals.' 'The supporters of bullfighting argued their case in terms of the legitimate autonomy of regional traditions in an over-centralized state. The challenge to the *corrida* was interpreted as yet another affront to the identity and integrity of the Midi' (Holt, 1981, p. 120). There is, however, a paradox in the strong identification of French bullfighting with a specific region. Bullfights are very popular with tourists, and there is no doubt this sport is also designed in large part to extract tourist money. However, converting the sport into a tourist spectacle threatens a total loss of authentic regional identity for this activity.

References

Espy, R. (1979), *The Politics of the Olympic Games* (Berkeley: University of California Press).

Holt, R. (1981), *Sport and Society in Modern France* (Hamden, Conn.: Archon Books).

Kanin, D. (1978), 'Superpower sport in cold war and detente,' in B. Lowe (ed.), *Sport and International Relations* (Champaign, Ill.: Stipes), pp. 249–62.

Kanin, D. (1981), *A Political History of the Olympic Games* (Boulder, Colo.: Westview Press).

Morgan, K. (1981), *Rebirth of a Nation: Wales 1880–1980* (Oxford University Press).

Mrozek, D. (1983), *Sport and American Mentality, 1880–1910* (Knoxville, University of Tennessee Press).

Riess, S. (1980), *Touching Base: Professional Baseball and American Culture in the Progressive Era* (Westport, Conn.: Greenwood Press).

Uwechue, R. (1978), 'Nation building and sport in Africa,' in B. Lowe (ed.), *Sport and International Relations* (Champaign, Ill.: Stipes), pp. 538–50.

Walvin, J. (1975), *The People's Game: A Social History of British Football* (London: Allen Lane).

Maurice Roche

SPORT AND COMMUNITY
Rhetoric and reality in the development
of British sport policy

[. . .]

T HE NOTION THAT SPORT IS NOT just a community but is also in
important respects a market, an economy, has received some recognition in recent
years by sport policy makers (Sports Council 1987). However, what has perhaps been
less well recognized is the degree to which markets and purely economic relationships
can undermine the things that we normally associate with community—habit, tradition,
shared memories and sentiments, a moral order and so on. There is an argument to
consider which suggests that the growth of market relationships provides an incentive
for the growth of voluntary association and of community in this sense. But the inherent
privatism and divisiveness of markets, their fostering of private corporate power and
their disdain for democratic values and the role of government all militate against our
most basic and enduring experiences of community. In sport the growth of commercialism
has clearly had profound consequences in the last ten to fifteen years. Some of these
consequences may have been beneficial for the sport world, but many others—including
much of the media's influence on major sporting events such as the Olympics, and the
pressures and incentives for elite sportspeople to cheat by using drugs—have had a
seriously corrosive effect at least on the elite community of sport.[1] This economic dimension
of our modern social order is the necessary background for my discussion of the national
and sport policy communities. However, my explicit references to it will be brief, and
I will return to it again briefly in my concluding remarks.

This chapter is organized into two main parts. These discuss two main themes: the
idea that there are major gaps between rhetoric and reality concerning the relationship
between sport and community, first, in the 'sport policy community' and, secondly, in
the 'national community' addressed by the 'Sport for All' policy and by the related
policies pursued in Britain particularly since the 1970s. However, since it is necessary

to consider how best to analyse sport's social functions and effects, we must first turn briefly to a consideration of the analytic and sociological perspectives needed for a proper understanding of modern sport and sport policy.

Sport's functions: perspectives on sport's role in modern society

The phrase 'Sport and the Community' as used in policy debates and documents (or variants such as 'in' or 'for' the community) bring together two concepts which look clear enough at first sight but which turn out on closer inspection to be slippery and to have a diversity of possible meanings. To grasp adequately these slippery concepts of 'sport' and 'community', their roles in sport policy and the gap between sport policy rhetoric and social reality, it is necessary to adopt a sociological perspective. In the past the most useful perspectives in this field have tended to be those which use a *functionalist* framework, but I will adopt a more pragmatic and in some ways *post-functionalist* approach. A perspective is necessary which recognizes the functionalist characteristics of sport in modern society and attempts to take full account of its conflictive and disorganized characteristics (. . . Offe 1985; Lash and Urry 1987).

When considering sport's social role we need to recognize its 'dysfunctions' as well as its 'functions', and also the extent to which it reflects and is affected by the disintegrative and disorganized characteristics of its social context. Sport has long considered itself to be a socially integrative moral force. In this morally idealistic form it has been culturally pervasive among British sport enthusiasts (McIntosh 1968, 1979), particularly the middle-class, upper-middle-class and aristocratic supporters of sport in the British 'establishment' (Dunning and Sheard 1979; Whannel 1983; Hargreaves 1986). But sport has another face. It is in many ways a socially divisive force (Allison 1986), and one which promotes a form of culture which is not only narrow and specialist but also morally narcissistic and escapist (Lasch 1980: ch. 5). Sport, of its very nature (and, crucially, within the institutions of the sport world itself), is divisive and differentiating rather than integrative and unifying in relation to both its own and the wider community. Sport thrives on differences, divisions and conflict in the communities in which it is organized and which it affects. Sport divides winners from losers, activist sports from 'passive' sports, elite players from ordinary participants. Further, it has always been organized in ways which reflect and reproduce the main social divisions of modern society: divisions of class, gender, age, ethnicity and handicap. Finally there is the very notion that there is such a single and unitary thing as sport at all. There are certainly sports, multitudes of them, and there may be some provisional agreement on what it is that most of them share, namely rule-governed competition usually involving bodily movement of some kind and often involving special equipment and locations. But the sheer diversity of activities, of parts of the body and of forms of equipment and locations are astounding. The point here is that in addition to sport in general being a relatively specialized form of leisure or work, a specialized sector of modern culture, each individual sport is in itself highly specialized and has little in common with any other sport. (An analogous point has been made about 'games' and 'language games' by the philosopher Wittgenstein [1963 para. 23 and 24].)

This means that the 'house of sport', while presided over by several multi-sport institutions and agencies is, nonetheless, organized by a host of specialist governing bodies which have little in common with each other. This fragmented situation is only marginally relieved by the fact that at the elite level many sports are periodically brought together at large multi-sport events such as the Olympic Games, and in multi-sport forums and other such contexts as those provided by media coverage of sport. But because of the specialized and exclusive nature of its constituent parts, sport is always capable of fragmentation and atomization.

Assuming that sport can be said to form a community at all, this community must be seen to be a very distinctive and vulnerable one. It is unlike many of the other models and images of community operating in the surrounding society, such as those of national citizenship, family, ethnicity, locale, age, class and gender. Sport offers forms of membership and participation in collective action and experience which may be temporarily strong but which are transient and ultimately weaker and more vulnerable than those on offer in the rest of modern culture, economy and politics. Yet sport policy has often tended to take it for granted that sport has something to give to the national community, and indeed that it has more to give than to receive. The general thrust of my discussion in this paper is that it would be better for sport and the community if sport policy were to develop a clearer sense of sport's limits, not to mention its vulnerabilities and its need to maintain its own community. This suggests that we should be sensitive to the tendencies in contemporary society towards internal over-complexity, as well as towards external dependencies and vulnerability to external (particularly economic) forces. We should of course look for indicators and effects of functional processes—ideological coherence, system production and so on—in the world of British sport. But we should be equally prepared to find evidence of the post-functional phenomena of endemic system-disorganization and impotent policy-making in the world of sport. (For a discussion of these phenomena in the world of tourism see Roche 1992, 1993.) With these perspectives and issues in mind we turn to the British sport policy community.

The sport policy community

Before exploring the effort to use sport to heal the social divisions and inequities of Britain's national community, we need to consider its sport policy community. My line of argument will be that there is much truth in the ironic maxim, 'Physician, before you try to heal others first heal yourself.' That is to say, the effort to produce positive national community benefits by means of sport has been undertaken by one of the most divided, confused and conflictive policy communities in British politics. Interestingly, the sport policy community is not greatly divided along party lines, although the ten years of Thatcherism in the 1980s undoubtedly introduced a party-ideological element. Equally interesting is the fact that it is one of the few British political community conflicts publicly to involve members of the aristocracy and royal family, for such people generally assume a background role in modern British politics. The general problem is that the legitimacy, credibility and effectiveness of using sport to heal national social divisions is continually undermined by the endemic internal divisiveness of the sport policy community itself. Perhaps the community would indeed be best advised to heal itself first.

It is perhaps appropriate to use sporting metaphors to describe the British sport policy community. I will outline the main 'players' in the policy 'game' and then turn to some of the main events in the course of play since the 1970s, but particularly in the 1980s. Practical and theoretical functionalists would no doubt like to view the game as a *team* game played for (or, depending on the level of one's cynicism, against) the best interest of the British public and involving co-operation between the players. However, the policy game in reality has been more like a series of contests and competitions between the players, very often with the public as bemused onlookers. I shall return to this point presently.

To set the scene it is helpful to distinguish between 'power' and 'authority' in the sport and sport policy worlds. I am mainly concerned with authorities who have some sort of acknowledged and 'official' responsibility to speak and to act on behalf of a number of sports, usually at a national level. The issue of power is separate one. While sport authorities have some power, most financial power lies outside their hands in the control of various other agencies and sectors. There is, therefore, underlying all of the policy pronouncements of sport authorities, a basic gulf between the rhetoric of authority and the power to act, to control and to produce outcomes. It is beyond the scope of this essay to give a full account of the structures of *both* power and authority in sport and my focus will be confined to the structures of authority. Nonetheless it is important that this context of power and the gulf between authority and power should be borne in mind in what follows. In addition there is the relationship between sport and the civil and criminal law. It is worth noting that the rules of sport and sporting authority exist within the context of the civil and criminal law. The existence of the law has all too often been ignored within sport because of sport's presumed capacity to be self-governing. But it is now increasingly being turned to the control of violence, fraud and discrimination within sport which the traditions of self-government have failed to control.

British sport is a mosaic composed of a few large-scale and powerful mass spectator sports and a multitude of smaller-scale sports of varying levels of power and prestige. The multitude of smaller sports are mainly organized for the benefit of the participants. Some, such as rowing and athletics, have a long tradition and high prestige and can attract significant commercial sponsorship. However, even in the recent burgeoning of commercial interest in sports, most of them operate with relatively little financial resource. Authority to make and uphold the rules of particular sports (within the law) lies with the host of particular sport governing bodies. It thus lies in voluntary associations of citizens in civil society, and is in no sense a direct function of the state. Britain has a long-established tradition of such sporting self-government. These are brought together in various multi-sport authorities, and we will come to these in a moment.

In the British sport and sport policy world, power and prestige do not necessarily imply authority. A few sports (specifically mass spectator sports like football, tennis, golf, cricket and motor racing), together with their governing bodies, their major clubs, and their media and commercial backers, have considerable power or de facto influence on the relationship between sport and the national community. But, as distinct and unrelated sports, they have little or no collective presence in official sport policy-making, and little authority commensurate with their power.

There are other 'players' in the general power game around sport. First, there are the mass media, particularly the press. These provide sport as an entertainment spectacle and contribute to public debate on sport policy issues. Secondly, in elite spectator sport, there are organizations of participants, such as the Professional Footballers'

Association (PFA), and organizations of spectators and supporters, such as the Football Supporters' Association (FSA), both of which can exercise some limited influence (when and if consulted) on policy formation in areas of concern to them. Finally, there are the various arms of parliament, as distinct from government. During the 1970s and 1980s parliament has made its view on sport policy known on a number of significant occasions: for example in 1973 in the Lords Select Committee on Sport and Recreation (Cobham Report), in 1975 in the debate on the White Paper on Sport and Recreation, in 1985–86 in the Commons Environment Committee Report on Sports Administration (Rossi Report) and in more recent debates on the Football Spectators Bill.

Sport policy 'players': the authorities

The authority to generate, influence and otherwise make policy relating to many sports or sport as a whole is distributed between six main sorts of organization. Of the six main 'players' in the policy game three are governmental, two are sporting and one is of an intermediate 'quango' status between the worlds of government and sport. The two sporting organizations each have a multi-sport remit and high prestige, but they have relatively little financial resource commensurate with this, and they remain self-governing and not governmental organizations. They are the British Olympic Association (BOA, founded 1905) and the Central Council for Physical Recreation (CCPR, founded 1935). The first, and most visible, of the three governmental agencies is the sports minister (or, now, heritage secretary) and his or her support staff in the Ministry of the Environment (established in 1964). In addition two other governmental agencies should be noted which in fact dispose of far greater resources for sport and physical recreation than the minister, but which are usually less visible and less recognized as playing a part in sport. One is the Department of Education and Science, operating through and in collaboration with Local Education Authorities. The DES defines and delivers the physical education curriculum to the nation's youth and finances the massive investment in staff and facility resources (sports halls, school playing fields) necessary to do this. The other category of governmental organization relevant to sport policy is that of local authority recreation departments, which collectively dispose of the vast bulk of public sector funding for sports-relevant facilities (leisure centres, sports halls, swimming pools, playing fields) in Britain. Finally, there is the most visible agency involved in the determination of national sport policy, the Sports Council. This was founded in 1964 as an advisory body and it was given the right to public finance and executive powers under a Royal Charter in 1972. Like the other great cultural policy quangos of the 1960s and 1970s (for example the Arts Council, the Countryside Commission, the Press Council, the Schools Council), the Sports Council was supposed to be independent and answerable to the fixed terms of its charter, rather than to the changing policies of governments. It was intended to operate at arm's length from the state rather than simply as an arm of the state.

Evidently there is considerable scope in the policy context outlined here for governmental versions of what elements of sport policy for the community ought to be obstructed, detoured around, or otherwise rendered ineffective. Besides the minister there are five distinct and often competing 'players' in the policy authority game, plus the powers at large in the main mass spectator and media sports. As noted earlier, these sports have little presence in multisport organisations like the CCPR and BOA, but nonetheless they appear to have, particularly in the case of football, great de facto powers to influence popular images of and attitudes to sport at national and local community levels. The potential that these divisions of power and authority create for disorganizing rather than organizing sport policy and sport as a political community is considerable. But it is worth emphasizing the following point: the Sports Council may be seen by the public as responsible for the concept of 'Sport for All' and for a policy aimed at bringing the benefits of sport (such as they are) to the community, but its real powers to finance and deliver such a policy are extremely limited in comparison to some of the other players in the policy game and other de facto powers in the sport world. And, of course, its powers are ultimately limited by the degree of interest in and toleration of sport that the community is prepared to show.

Authority may or may not follow money, but power certainly does. In this context it is worth bearing in mind the financial power, measured in financial terms, of different organizations and sectors in the sport policy game. In 1985 the Sports Council received approximately £32 million from the government to spend in accordance with its various policies, particularly 'Sport for All', also for the support of high-performance and elite sport. We should note, first, that this figure was matched by an equivalent amount spent by the minister for sport and recreation through Urban Programme Grants for community-orientated sports activities. However, by contrast, these figures for direct central government spending in support of explicit sport policy were dwarfed by the massive levels of spending on sport by three other sectors: the local authorities, the voluntary sector and the commercial sector. In 1985 English local authorities between them spent approximately £800 million, the voluntary sector spent approximately £1.5 billion, while consumer spending on sport and sport-related goods and services, and thus income to retailers and producers, to the media and to professional sports (setting aside gambling: £1.2 billion) was approximately £2 billion (Sports Council 1988a: 57). It is arguable that the real power to determine sport policy follows spending power and lies in these sectors rather than in the hands of the Sports Council and the minister. [. . .]

Toward a conclusion

I have reviewed British sport policy from the point of view of the notion and ideal of 'community'. I have considered two main aspects and meanings of 'community', namely the political community of sport policy-making 'authorities' and the national community of British society as a whole, and I have come to two main conclusions about these two sport communities. First, the policy community has been little short of a disorganized shambles. Besides the personalities, traditions and organizations involved this may also reveal the influence of waves of long-term structural changes in British society. The late Victorian compromise between the aristocracy and industrial middle class produced as one of its cultural effects the culture of sport—the games, the governing institutions and the 'amateur' ideology of modern sport (see Dunning and Sheard 1979; Cunningham 1980). The mid-20th century creation of the welfare state added a very different layer of ideology, of politicization and professionalism, to this picture (Roche and Smart 1984). Finally, the global and post-industrial resurgence of capitalism and consumerism in the late 20th century has added another very different layer of ideology and economic interests into the mix. With traditions, professions, organizations and personalities representing at least these three structural waves all currently involved in the struggle for power and authority in sport policy, it is not at all surprising that policy is disorganized. My main conclusion here is that there is a deep and demoralizing gulf between the concept of a national sport policy (which implies an assumption of, and certainly aspires to, coherence and unity) and the realities in the sport policy community.

Secondly, a number of points need to be made about the national community as the target for sport policy. Notwithstanding 'Sport for All' policy, the majority of people in Britain (leaving aside their forcible exposure to physical education in school) have not been much affected by or interested in participating in sport. Even their interest in spectating sport does not look substantial compared with their interests in such other leisure pursuits as entertainment, tourism and media consumption. It is hard to make a case that sport policy has had any serious influence here, as indicated by the long-term persistence of the 'Wolfenden gap' and other indicators of the supposed 'participation problem'. [. . .]

Finally, what popular interest there is in sport is divided and reflects the social divisions of society along lines of class, gender, ethnicity, age and handicap. A stronger view would be that, besides reflecting social inequalities and divisions, sport (and unwittingly 'Sport for All' policy) has tended to produce and even to heighten them. This is surely one of the underlying stories to be read in recent Sports Council documents, particularly its major strategy review in 1987, *Sport and the Community: Into the 90s*. These three points lead to my second main conclusion, that there are major gaps between British sport policy rhetoric and the historical and social realities surrounding the low rates of participation in sport and physical recreation by the British people. [. . .]

Postscript

This chapter has followed the story of British sport policy to 1990. The creation in 1992 of what was effectively a British Ministry of Culture—the Department of National Heritage—brought sport, media, tourism and arts policy and funding under the same umbrella and gave cultural representation at Cabinet level. It remains to be seen whether this reorganization will provide a sufficient basis for solving the problems confronting British sport policy. Readers who wish to pursue these issues should turn to two recent studies: Barrie Houlihan's thorough analysis of sport policy before the establishment of the Department of National Heritage (Houlihan 1991) and Simson and Jenning's account of power, money and drugs in the modern Olympics (1992). Simson and Jennings, with Maurice Roche (1993), concentrate on the international commercialization and politicization of sport and its great events and the implications for the growing problems facing sport culture.

Note

1   Lucking 1982; Tomlinson and Whannel 1984; Donohue and Johnson 1986.

Bibliography

Allison, L. (ed.) 1986 *The Politics of Sport* (Manchester: Manchester University Press).

Cunningham, H. 1980 *Leisure in the Industrial Revolution* (London: Croom Helm).

Donohoe, T. and N. Johnson 1986 *Foul Play: Drug Abuse in Sports* (Oxford: Basil Blackwell).

Dunning, E. and K. Sheard 1979 *Barbarians, Gentlemen and Players: A Sociological Study of the Development of Rugby Football* (London: Martin Robertson).

Hargreaves, Jennifer (ed.), 1982 *Sport, Culture and Ideology* (London: Routledge & Kegan Paul).

Hargreaves, John 1986 *Sport, Power and Culture* (Cambridge: Polity Press).

Houlihan, B. 1991 *The Government and Politics of Sport* (London: Routledge).

Lasch, C. 1980 *The Culture of Narcissism* (London: Abacus).

Lash, S. and J. Urry 1987 *The End of Organised Capitalism* (Cambridge: Polity Press).

Lucking, M. 1982 'Sport and Drugs', in Jennifer Hargreaves 1982.

McIntosh, P. 1968 *Physical Education in England Since 1800* (London: G. Bell & Sons).

McIntosh, P. 1979 *Fair Play: Ethics in Sport and Education* (London: Heinemann).

Offe, C. 1985 *Disorganised Capitalism* (Cambridge: Polity Press).

Roche, M. 1992 'Mega-Events and Micro-Modernisation: On the Sociology of the New Urban Tourism', *British Journal of Sociology*, 43.4, pp. 563–600.

Roche, M. 1993 'Mega-Events and Urban Policy', *Annals of Tourism Research* (forthcoming).

Roche, M. and B. Smart 1984 'Governing Bodies: An Analysis of Rationalisation in British Sport Policy and Administration', n.p.

Simson, V. and A. Jennings 1992 *The Lord of the Rings: Power, Money and Drugs in the Modern Olympics* (London: Simson & Schuster).

Sports Council 1987 *The Economic Impact and Importance of Sport in the UK* (London: Henley Centre/Sports Council).

Sports Council 1988a *Into the 90s: A Strategy for Sport 1988–1993* (London: Sports Council).

Tomlinson, A. and G. Whannel (eds.) 1984 *Five Ring Circus: Money, Power and Politics at the Olympic Games* (London: Pluto Press).

Whannel, G. 1983 *Blowing the Whistle: The Politics of Sport* (London: Pluto Press).

Wittgenstein, L. 1963 *Philosophical Investigations* (Oxford: Basil Blackwell).

Margaret Talbot

THE POLITICS OF SPORT AND PHYSICAL EDUCATION

[. . .]

THE MYTH OF THE APOLITICAL nature of sport and physical education remains, with many of their representatives choosing to ignore or deny political process or influence, even proclaiming the apolitical nature of sport or education as a defining characteristic and a moral code. Yet many of these representatives have themselves played an important part in locating physical education and sport in the political sphere. [. . .]

Sport and education (including physical education) have long claimed political neutrality and denied or ignored the influence of power. Even when the contexts in which they operate have demonstrably become inextricably linked with government policy, there remains disingenuous denial of the role of politics in sport and physical education. This disingenuousness extends further, to become the basis of a dichotomy – the expectation that government finance will be provided for investment and support, while maintaining the assumption that there is no accountability for this funding; that there should be no state interference in the affairs of sport and physical education; and that funding will be allocated or continue merely because sport and physical education are self-evidently "good" for society. Government disingenuousness similarly leads to a dichotomy, for example, where there is expectation that systems will fulfil new roles and duties, or respond to fundamental change, without the additional resources required. The Policy Statement on Sport (Department for National Heritage, 1995) is an example: it provides sport and physical education with leverage, but little real additional currency.

The meanings and uses of the term "politics" can contribute to the understanding of the way prevailing views are maintained or challenged, decisions are made, resources allocated, and structures changed as a result of ideological belief or rhetoric. The title of Harold Lasswell's book, *Politics: Who Gets What, When, How?*, is perhaps the most concise definition, but it does not illuminate the processes which are so crucial to those outcomes.

I am adopting the general position that "politics" can be present in all social interactions and relationships, in accepting the essential definition of politics as the *exercise of power* (Worsley, 1964), a central tenet of both Marxist and feminist theory and praxis (Stanley, 1991). Such a concept of politics broadens the definition beyond what politicians do, to include the *exercise of control, constraint and coercion*; at the same time, it does not deny the possibility of *agency*, the capacity of individuals or groups to influence events.

It is not unusual for members of professions or interest groups to deny that power structures have any influence on their lives, or to assume that their organisational leaders will take care of any political in-fighting on their behalf, or in some cases, will prevent them ever having to hear about tensions or struggles for survival or influence. Such views are not infrequently shared by those leaders themselves, some of whom appear to have particular views of their role in membership organisations. As one senior administrator of a National Governing Body (NGB) responded when asked how he managed the tensions between running the NGB more professionally and the requirement that a membership organisation should provide means for the membership to express their views: "*We're not here to consult our members — we're here to represent them*" (Abrams *et al.*, 1995). [. . .]

Politics is often described as "*the art of the possible*" (usually attributed to R.A. Butler). John Evans and Dawn Penney (1993) have referred to the policy process as "*a relational activity*". What has interested me over the last decade, is the number of examples of apparent failure to understand, or capacity to ignore as irrelevant, each others' social worlds and means of expression, by both government (including Ministers and civil servants) and professional and interest groups. One example is the evident gap between, on the one hand, Ministers' and government rhetoric about "putting school sport back at the heart of school life" (Major, 1995), and on the other, the actual resources and frameworks for sport in most state schools. Ministerial pronouncements are made apparently without the benefit of either knowledge or understanding of existing structures and delivery systems, or of their constraints and limitations. In some cases, Ministers appear unaware of the effects of their own or their government's policies and decisions on the delivery mechanisms on which they now depend for the delivery of new policies. During the construction of the National Curriculum for physical education, representations by the Department of Education and Science (DES) PE Working Group to Robert Atkins, the then Minister of Sport, about the adverse effects of the demise of the physical education advisory service, led him to declare that he would see to it that every local authority *would* have a PE adviser. He was apparently unaware (or chose to ignore) that this demise had been one of the effects of his own government's sustained withdrawal of resources from, and curtailment of power of, local government.

Similarly, protests and resistance by interest groups have frequently revealed their dangerous lack of knowledge of how to engage the interest of Ministers, and lack of understanding of the strength of prevailing ideologies and conceptions. During the BAALPE (British Association of Advisers and Lecturers in Physical Education) conference in July 1995, which coincided with the launch of the Government's Policy Statement on Sport "Raising the Game" (Department for National Heritage, 1995), I watched with some dismay as proponents of dance berated a (sympathetic) senior Department of Education and Employment civil servant on the negative effects the Statement would have on dance, ignoring his admirable attempts to help them to appreciate dance's privileged place in physical education, notwithstanding the powerful influence of Ministerial (including Prime Ministerial) views of elite, male team sport.

It is possible that these dichotomies, the disjunctures between ideology and policy on the one hand, and structure and practice on the other, are the basis for the many anomalies and contradictions which professionals working in physical education and sport have to manage. Both the National Curriculum, including physical education, and the National Governing Bodies of Sport – the voluntary sector of sport – have become contested areas. I intend to use aspects of these contests to illustrate the effectiveness of different groups in the "art of the possible" – and to explore why some dominant ideologies endure, and others change, even when protected and promulgated by people in structural positions of authority and power. [. . .]

A rather different example of power processes is the relationship between the Sports Council and the NGBs of sport. It has been Sports Council policy for several years to encourage the NGBs to increase their efficiency and productivity by rationalising their structures and professionalising their personnel and services: grant-aid leverage and advocacy by Sports Council liaison officers have been the main means of this encouragement. On the face of it, this is a reasonable and overdue change; in some sports, the proliferation of governing bodies for the various disciplines or branches of the sport, or for the four home countries, had led to duplication of effort, wasted resources, and confusion in international communication and competition.

However, there are potential losses in this shift towards increasingly professional organisations representing the interests of the whole sport. Since British sport depends heavily on volunteers, their contributions and needs require consideration and protection. In sports where single sex or single discipline organisations have merged, the interests and voices of women or other less powerful groups have lost visibility and influence (Abrams, Long, Talbot and Welch, 1995). These changes in the National Governing Bodies of Sport are examples of more informal political processes, within a macro political climate driven by government policy and ideology.

The distinguishing characteristics of NGBs of sport have been identified through two major pieces of research undertaken for the Sports Council at Leeds Metropolitan University (Long *et al.*, 1992; Abrams *et al.*, 1995). These characteristics can be summarised as: frequently inadequate staff size for separate strategic and operational management; limited capacity to respond to changes in context; "stakeholding" cultures emanating from the self-investment by voluntary officers, and resulting in inherent conservatism and resistance to change; lack of clear accountability structures and systems; tensions between voluntarism and business demands; poor communication; recurrent financial problems; ambivalence or confusion regarding autonomy and accountability; unwieldy committee and decision making cycles; lack of stability and high turnover of paid staff.

These NGB characteristics are illustrated by the concerns identified in a recent consultative document for British Athletics (Radford, 1995), and provide reasons for resistance to certain aspects of professionalisation: the most prevalent are fear of loss of influence and autonomy, by individuals or groups; and *"suspicion that market forces had replaced sporting and social values as the most important motivation force"* (Radford, 1995: p. 20).

Increasingly, NGBs are having to provide more services with less resources, be more efficient in the way they carry out their business, improve the quality and the quantity of their provision, and update the skill base of the professional and voluntary work force. They are also having to plan more for the long term and strategically, and be more financially aware. This highlights the potential problems for sports organisations, especially in the context of the increased expectations held for non-statutory agencies. [. . .]

In both Canada and Britain, there has been widespread uncritical *acceptance of the dominant strategic planning approach to sports policy*, and limited visibility of any consideration of the potential losses and gains in processes related to strategic planning. Underlying the strategic planning model is the assumption of rationalism and business-related performance evaluation criteria which may be inapplicable or misleading when applied to sports voluntary organisations, and there is little critical examination of the values and assumptions implicit in such an approach. In Canada the intention has been explicitly to rationalise NSO [National Sports Organisation] structures and to improve Canada's international sport performance, with ethical and equity issues, including regional inequities within the Canadian sports system, apparently being seen as secondary and less important:

> Underlying both issues, indeed, is a further question which is not strategic at all, but rather a matter of values and social priorities.
>
> (Whitson and Macintosh, 1989: p. 437)

The characteristic of diversity of interests among sports organisations can be a strength which can be overlooked, particularly when considering rationalisation or other moves towards "efficiency". Whitson and Macintosh (1989) argued that in the new Canadian policy structures, where priorities have been so radically altered and where the coercive power of grant aid has been used by Sport Canada, those people in NSOs who might have disputed the change in values and priorities have effectively been marginalised, and many others have become alienated or have been lost to the sport system. [. . .]

Macintosh and Whitson's (1990) analysis of the effects of macro changes on . . . NSOs in Canada provides useful comparisons with the British context. They outline the ways in which federal government, through Sport Canada, and by separating the funding and ideologies of recreational and representative, competitive sport, has pressured NSOs away from a voluntarist, fiercely autonomous, devolved regional structure and culture, towards becoming more "professional", centralised and government-dependent organisations whose major function is to produce Canadian international competitors. One major cost, according to Macintosh and Whitson (1990), is "the routine subordination of equity concerns to the production of performance" (p. 103). [. . .]

. . . [D]istinctions between the structures and context of Canadian and British sport should provide the Sports Council with cause to consider the wider context for future national policy, despite Ministerial and governmental apparent conviction that centralisation and greater control are desirable and necessary. Despite the amount of literature relating to the influence of power in organisations and relationships between the government and professions, it is striking how little it appears to be used by sports policy makers.

It is also striking how *gender blind* most of this work is. There is, however, a growing body of literature providing critiques from the point of view of gender power relations and engendered structures and reward systems, and their role as barriers and catalysts in organisational change and progress towards gender equity (see for example Davidson and Burke, 1994; Hearn and Parkin, 1983; Itzin and Newman, 1995; Kanter, 1977; Mills and Tancred, 1992; Tancred-Sheriff and Campbell, 1992). These studies raise further questions about the same organisational issues relating to ethnicity, class, age and disability – other power relations which seem to be less visible and to have been less well theorised in this area, especially in relation to organisations in sport and physical education.

In the context of sports organisations, a range of distributional analyses have been completed, which clearly illustrate the inequities in opportunity and position between men and women (Beamish, 1985; Fasting, 1993; Fitness and Amateur Sport, 1982, 1986; Hall, 1987; Macintosh and Beamish. 1987; Talbot, 1988; Talbot, 1990b; White and Brackenridge, 1985). These inequities remain broadly similar in voluntary, governmental or commercial sports organisations, although they appear to be more marked in NGBs.

More recently, there have been more analytical approaches, including focus on the experiences of women in sports organisations, and the processes and practices of resistance and protection which stem from masculine hegemonies and serve to prevent women either obtaining positions or advancing through organisations. (See, for example, Bryson, 1987; Fasting and Sisjord, 1986; Macintosh and Beamish, 1987; Macintosh et al., 1987; Macintosh and Whitson, 1990; Talbot, 1990b; White et al., 1990; Whitson and Macintosh, 1988, 1989.) Some studies have wider significance than to illustrate the effects of gender power relations and examples of entrenchment by reactionary males in NGBs. They also illustrate the pervasiveness and power of inequitable practices and attitudes in NGBs; Sports Council policy is still not influencing these organisations, despite more than a decade of equity policies and strategies. The hostile reactions in the Press and by the public, to Jim McKay's (1992) research on the experiences of Australian women in national sports organisations, also show the deep-seated nature of prejudice (Miranda, 1993; Sydney Morning Herald, 1993). They throw into sharp relief the unquestioned ways in which sports structures and ideologies are not merely defended, but are actually defined and perpetuated by masculine hegemonies and male definitions of sport.

To conclude, these examples of the influence of political processes on physical education and sport confirm the paramount need for understanding of *context*, for researchers, for policy makers and for practitioners. Context includes the dynamics of how decisions are made and the ways key players resist, accommodate, implement or drive change. There are also implications for the education and training of both future sports policy makers and sports scientists: appreciation and understanding of context must be prerequisites in courses of initial training and post-experience professional development.

The shared task for researchers, policy makers and practitioners is not to ignore dominant ideologies, but to put them into perspective and to understand how they are formed, shaped and maintained. The tendency in contemporary research and commentary has been to focus on the pervasiveness of ideologies and social systems, possibly because most academics feel that they are on the outside, looking in. But there are now sufficient links between researchers and people involved in the policy process for that focus to shift, towards understanding the influence of key players, of tracing the effects of individual and group agency and subversion. If some of these key players will share their experiences and their struggles with researchers, both should be in a better position to influence events.

References

Abrams, J., Long, J., Talbot, M. and Welch, M. (1995) *The impact of organisational change on Governing Bodies of Sport*. A research report to the Sports Council. Leeds: Leeds Metropolitan University.

Beamish, R. (1985) 'Sport executives and voluntary associations: A review of the literature and introduction to some theoretical issues', *Sociology of Sport Journal*, Vol. 2, No. 3: pp. 218–232.

Bryson, L. (1987) 'Sport and the maintenance of masculine hegemony', *Women's Studies International Forum*, Vol. 10, No. 4: pp. 349–360.

Davidson, M. and Burke, R.J. (1994) *Women in management: Current research issues*. London: Paul Chapman Publishing.

Department for National Heritage (1995) *Sport: Raising the game*. Government Policy Statement on Sport. London: Department for National Heritage.

Evans, J. and Penney, D. (1993) 'Playing by market rules: Physical education in England and Wales after ERA', in G. McFee and A. Tomlinson (eds) *Education, sport and leisure: Connections and controversies*. Chelsea School Topic Report 3. Eastbourne: University of Brighton, pp. 17–33.

Fasting, K. (1993) *Women and sport. Monitoring progress towards equality: A European Survey*. Oslo: Norwegian Confederation of Sport, Women's Commission.

—— and Sisjord, M.-K. (1986) Gender, verbal behaviour and power in sports organisations', *Scandinavian Journal of Sport Science*, Vol. 8, No. 2: pp. 81–85.

Fitness and Amateur Sport (1982) *Women in sport leadership: Summary of National Survey*. Ottawa: Fitness and Amateur Sport Women's Program.

—— (1986) *Sport Canada Quadrennial Planning and Evaluation Guide 1988–92*. Ottawa: Fitness and Amateur Sport.

Hall, M.A. (1987) 'Women Olympians in the Canadian sport bureaucracy', in T. Slack and C.R. Hinings (eds) *The organization and administration of sport*. London: Sport Dynamics, pp. 101–126.

Hearn, J. and Parkin, P.W. (1983) 'Gender and organizations: A selective review and critique of a neglected area', *Organization Studies*, Vol. 4, No. 3: pp. 219–242.

Itzin, C. and Newman, J. (1995) *Gender, culture and organizational change*. London: Routledge.

Kanter, H.M. (1977) *Men and women of the corporation*. New York: Basic Books.

Long, J., Talbot, M. and Welch, M. (1992) *The effectiveness of Sports Council services to Sports Governing Bodies*. Research report to the Sports Council. Leeds: Leeds Metropolitan University.

Macintosh, D. and Beamish, R. (1987) 'Female advancement in national level sport administration positions', paper presented at ICHPER/CAHPER Conference Vancouver, British Columbia.

——, Beamish, R., Whitson, D., Greenhorn, D. and MacNeill, M. (1987) *Professional staff and policy making in National Sport Organisations*. Research report presented to Social Sciences and Humanities Research Council of Canada. Kingston: Queen's University.

Macintosh, D. and Whitson, D. (1990) *The game planners: Transforming Canada's sport system*. Montreal and Kingston: McGill-Queen's University Press.

McKay, J. (1992) *Why so few? Women executives in Australian sport*. Queensland: Department of Anthropology and Sociology, University of Queensland.

Major, J. (1995) 'Prime Minister's Introduction', in *Raising the game*. Government Policy Statement on Sport. London: Department for National Heritage.

Mills, A.J. and Tancred, P. (eds) (1992) *Gendering organizational analysis*. Newbury Park, California: Sage.

Miranda, C. (1993) 'Report fails to address its principal concern', *The Canberra Times*, 26 February.

Radford, P. (1995) *Athletics 21: Strategic planning for British athletics in the 21st century: A consultation document*. Birmingham: British Athletics.

Stanley, L. (1984) 'How the social science research process discriminates against women', in S. Acker and D. Warren-Piper (eds) *Is higher education fair to women?*. London: Nelson, pp. 189–209.

Sydney Morning Herald (1993) 'Masters', 14 November: p. 16.

Talbot, M. (1988) 'Their own worst enemy? Women and leisure provision', in E. Wimbush and M. Talbot (eds) *Relative freedoms: Women and leisure*. Milton Keynes: Open University Press, pp. 161–176.

——(1990b) 'Women and sports administration: Plus ça change . . .'. Paper presented at General Assembly of International Sports Federations, Monaco.

Tancred-Sherif, P. and Campbell, E.J. (1992) 'Room for women: A case study in the sociology of organizations', in A.J. Mills and P. Tancred (eds) *Gendering organizational analysis*. Newbury Park, California: Sage, pp. 31–45.

White, A., Mayglothling, R. and Carr, C. (1990) *The dedicated few: The social world of women coaches in Britain in the 1980s*. Chichester: West Sussex Institute of Higher Education.

Whitson, D. and Macintosh, D. (1988) The professionalization of Canadian amateur sport: Questions of power and purpose', *Arena Review*, Vol. 12: pp. 81–96.

——(1989) 'Rational planning versus regional interests: The professionalization of Canadian amateur sport', *Canadian Public Policy*, Vol. XV, No. 4: pp. 436–449.

Worsley, P. (1964) 'The distribution of power in industrial societies', in P. Halmos (ed.) *The Development of Industrial Societies, Sociological Review Monograph* No. 8.

Barrie Houlihan

THE POLITICS OF SPORTS POLICY IN BRITAIN
The example of drug abuse

[. . .]

TO ARRIVE AT A SATISFACTORY DEFINITION of a policy community, it is necessary to consider three factors: first, the general characteristics of communities; second, their membership; and third, their issue scope. Following Friend *et al.* (1974), Laffin defines a policy community as 'a relatively small group of participants in the policy process which has emerged to deal with some identifiable class of problems that have or could become the concern of central government' (Laffin, 1986, p. 110). This small group is characterized by its continuity, 'implicit authority structures' (Richardson and Jordan, 1979, p. 94), insularity (Rhodes, 1986), 'consensual style' and 'system of shared implicit authority' (Jordan, 1981, p. 105 and p. 107, respectively) and shared values (Hogwood, 1979; Dunleavy, 1981). Rhodes identifies as a further characteristic a high degree of vertical interdependence; in other words, 'a non-executant role for central departments which are dependent on other organisations for the implementation of policies' (Rhodes, 1986, p. 23).

With regard to membership, Hogwood argues that a 'crucial feature of policy communities is that the community consists, not only of civil servants and ministers, but also of relevant "recognized" interest groups and other governmental bodies, both appointed and elected local authorities' (Hogwood, 1987, p. 18). One aspect of membership on which there is a high degree of agreement is the centrality of professions (Wistow and Rhodes, 1987; Sharpe, 1985). It is argued that professionals constitute a potentially cohesive and influential lobby within a policy community (Laffin, 1986, p. 109).

The third feature of policy communities is the range of issues with which they can legitimately deal. In general, policy communities deal with routine or normal issues for, by their very nature, they function effectively only so long as issues can be satisfactorily resolved using the pool of resources available to the community. However, there will be issues that bypass communities, possibly as a consequence of disinterest or neglect by the community or because the issue has been redefined as the property of another (more powerful) policy community, or where there is a dispute between communities over the 'ownership' of an issue (Hogwood, 1987, pp. 46–54).

Part of the value of using the concept of a policy community to study the process of policy making is that it provides a set of related concepts that enable the researching of 'detailed case studies' and 'the comparative analysis of several policy areas' (Wistow and Rhodes, 1987). It also enables an examination of the pattern of recurring relations between members, the nature, extent and source of value consensus, and the degree to which issues are the property of identifiable groups of actors in the policy process.

There is much in the literature of policy making to suggest that the development of a policy community is a sign of a mature policy area where boundaries are acknowledged and the expertise of the community members is respected. This description would seem more appropriate to policy areas such as housing and education than to sport. Indeed, Wistow and Rhodes describe leisure and recreation as an 'issue network' (Wistow and Rhodes, 1987, p. 8) which is less integrated and has a larger number of participants, with a lower degree of interdependence, stability and continuity than a policy community. Accepting that issue networks and policy communities represent different positions on a continuum of the policy process, some important questions arise. First, there is the question of whether Wistow and Rhodes are accurate in their description. Second, is whether there are any signs of development in the sport policy area which would suggest that the characteristics associated with a policy community are emerging. Third, are there good prospects for the development of a mature policy community for sport? These questions are addressed through the examination of the issue . . . [of] drug abuse by athletes.

Characteristics of the policy area

The policy area of sport is characterized by its lack of a clear statutory base, the large number of government agencies and their specialist nature, the fragmentation of administrative and policy responsibility, and the generally low salience of sport policy to the government of the day.

There is scant reference to recreation or sport in the legislation of the last fifty years, and where it is mentioned it invariably provides for permissive, rather than mandatory, powers. For example, the Countryside Act (1968) permits local authorities to provide recreational facilities in the countryside and the Local Government (Miscellaneous Provisions) Act (1976) permits local authorities to provide 'such recreational facilities as it thinks fit'. Where a duty is imposed it is either vague or peripheral to sport and active recreation (see Travis et al., 1981, pp. 51–6 for a fuller discussion). A statutory framework has a number of potential advantages for a nascent policy community. First, statute can provide a formal allocation of responsibilities to organizations and a formal expression of interrelationships within the community. Second, it can provide an expression of values which helps to foster community identity and cohesion.

The problems for the policy community resulting from the absence of a statutory framework are compounded by administrative fragmentation. Although the Department of the Environment is the leading government department because of its overall responsibility for sport, a number of other departments have a significant involvement. For example, the Home Office is responsible for the law and order aspects of sport, the Department of Education and Science oversees sport in schools, and the Foreign Office coordinates discussions with the European Community, the Council of Europe and other governments on sporting issues. In general, central government provides a considerable amount of finance but is not involved in an executive capacity, preferring to operate through the local authorities and specialist quasi-independent agencies (quangos) exemplified by the Sports Council and the Countryside Commission. Executive responsibility is largely shared between government agencies and local authorities. The latter provide the bulk of public sector leisure facilities and have some important responsibilities for the regulation of private facilities; for example, acting as the licensing authorities under the Safety of Sports Grounds Act (1975).

A further set of actors in the policy community is the governing bodies of sport. As well as being actors in the policy process in their own right, most of the major governing bodies are also members of the Central Council of Physical Recreation which represents their interests to the government, primarily through the Sports Council. Most of the national governing bodies affiliate to international organizations responsible for the development of the sport and the organization of international competition. Finally, there are influential organizations such as the British Olympic Association (BOA) and its international parent body (IOC), and the Commonwealth Games Federation. All three bodies are organizing associations rather than governing bodies but they do make rules for their events, for example on drug use and testing, which participants must accept.

A final, and particularly important, characteristic of the policy area is the degree to which the concerns of those involved in sport are marginal to those of the government and the major political parties (see Benington and White, 1986, p. 78). To a considerable degree this has been the result of a broad consensus that sport is an inappropriate sphere for party political intervention and that it is a marginal arena for the translation of party philosophy into policy proposals. [. . .]

Drug abuse and sport: the development of policy

. . . [T]he actors in the policy community for drug abuse by athletes fall into three main categories; namely, central government departments, government agencies and governing bodies (domestic and international). The Department of the Environment, with its broad responsibility for sport, has a major involvement and liaises closely with the Sports Council in the development of policy towards drug abuse. The major source of complexity arises from the large number of governing bodies involved. Some degree of coherence is provided by the CCPR which co-ordinates the various national governing bodies and acts as a consultative body to the Sports Council. Because of the nature of the drug abuse problem there is heavy involvement by a series of international sporting bodies, most notably the BOA and the IAAF (International Amateur Athletics Federation).

Ben Johnson's positive urine test at the 1988 Olympics and the subsequent enquiry by the Canadian government has focused world attention on a persistent, though frequently neglected, problem in athletics. The first sign that the use of drugs to enhance sporting performance was systematic and regular among athletes rather than exceptional emerged in the 1960s. This realization prompted action both internationally and domestically. In 1962 the IOC passed a resolution against 'doping' followed, a year later, by a definition of doping by the Council of Europe, while in Britain the Sports Council formed a working party to examine drug abuse in sport. Drug tests were first introduced for major international competitions towards the end of the 1960s; the World Cup in 1966, the Olympics in 1968 and the Commonwealth Games in 1970.

While the response by the major sporting organizations seems to have been unequivocal and prompt, there are several aspects of the development of policy on drug abuse which have remained vague or problematic. Among the issues either unresolved or only partially resolved are: the problem of producing an agreed list of prescribed drugs; developing acceptable techniques and procedures for drug testing, and finally, developing a consensus among the governing bodies regarding appropriate punishments.

At first sight the consensus within sport condemning the use of drugs to enhance performance is firm. There are numerous examples of high-minded statements by administrators, politicians and many athletes pointing out the incompatibility between the use of drugs and the ideals on which sport is based (see for example Killanin in IOC, 1976). The early rhetoric regarding drug abuse was based on the moral grounds that it constituted cheating, but more recent statements adopted more pragmatic arguments, particularly related to health, reflecting some of the hesitation and ambiguity apparent within the sporting community.

The Johnson Enquiry and the Coni Report (1988) in Britain suggest that deeply ambivalent attitudes towards the use of drugs in sport exist and that the early consensus in opposition to drug use was more apparent than real. Few sportsmen would publicly support the sensational assertion by American Harold Connolly that 'The overwhelming majority of athletes I know would do anything and take anything, short of killing themselves, to improve athletic performance' (*Sunday Times*, 2.10.88), but there are suggestions that many accept that drug taking is increasingly a part of preparation and training in a wide range of sports. Not only is there a growing acceptance that the extent of drug use has probably been seriously underestimated, but there are also signs that the fundamental objection to the use of drugs, that it is unethical and a form of cheating, is being challenged in professional sport. R.H. Nicholson, deputy director of the Institute of Medical Ethics and life member of the National Rifle Association, suggests that there are no overriding ethical reasons that force one to conclude 'either that drug taking by an individual sportsman is necessarily unethical, or that the governing bodies of sport must have rules to prevent and punish drug taking' (Nicholson, 1987, p. 29).

The ambiguous response from sportsmen and women and the debate over the ethical basis for denying drug use have both affected progress in developing an effective policy on the issue. Although policy statements have been published, progress in agreeing a list of proscribed drugs, testing procedures and sanctions has been much slower. Of the three problems, that of developing a list of proscribed drugs has probably been the easiest to achieve. The recent DOE publication by Moynihan and Coe (1987) provides a comprehensive list of the classes of drugs prohibited. In general, cycling, snooker and shooting apart, there has been little public disagreement over the list of banned drugs. Most governing bodies of sport have adopted the Sports Council's guidelines and incorporated them into their own regulations and codes of conduct. Yet it must be acknowledged that linking the continuation of a Sports Council grant to compliance has encouraged a number of otherwise reluctant governing bodies to toe the line. There has been much greater difficulty in getting agreement on testing procedures and their effective implementation.

Although the Johnson scandal and the accusations against the British Olympic athletes Kerrith Brown and Linford Christie have generated considerable momentum in the campaign to eradicate drug abuse by British athletes, the 1980s have been typified by a considerable lack of standardization in the ways that athletes are selected for testing, the frequency of testing and the circumstances under which tests are administered. As recently as 1986 the All-England Lawn Tennis Club was heavily criticized for its 'relaxed' approach to drug testing. It agreed that tests would be carried out, but after discussion with the men's professional organization, it was agreed that tests would be for drugs of addiction only and that any positive results would not be reported, rather the individual concerned would be required to seek medical advice.

Although the policy community has been given a strong lead by the Minister and the Sports Council, the British Amateur Athletics Board (BAAB) has also been forthright in its support for a rigorous anti-drugs campaign. In 1984 the Sports Council announced that governing bodies were to be required to introduce drug tests. In attempts to implement this policy and to harmonize procedures the Council has not only threatened the withdrawal of grants from governing bodies, but has also invested in the development of scientific methods necessary for effective testing. In the last ten years or so the Council has spent over £500,000 on research and on financing the work of the Drug Control and Teaching Centre at Chelsea College, which the Council is currently bringing under its direct control. In addition, the Council has covered the costs incurred by governing bodies in the administration of tests. However, in 1985, Dickie Jeeps, the Chairman of the Sports Council, reported that

> even with 100% subsidies from the Sports Council to meet the testing costs only twenty-five sports have carried out testing since 1979 and some of those on a very, very limited scale.
>
> (Sports Council, 1986, p. 1)

The limited success of the Council's 1984 initiative is reflected in the recent DOE/ Sports Council paper (Moynihan and Coe, 1987) which acknowledges that too many loopholes exist and that the potential for evasion and manipulation is great. The paper makes a series of recommendations about the need for tighter procedures which would make evasion more difficult.

The culmination of the Council's efforts was the introduction, from April 1988, of random drug testing which included out-of-season testing, involving about 30 of the sports considered to be most prone to drug abuse. This decision was soon endorsed by the IOC and IAAF who both announced in 1989 that they intended to establish 'flying squads' to carry out random out-of-season testing. To a degree, therefore, it is possible to argue that the Sport Council's policy of introducing a rigorous and uniform framework for testing supported by the two major international athletics organizations now exists. Inevitably it remains to be seen how the individual governing bodies implement the policy over the next few years.

In assessing the success of the policy a number of questions need to be considered: First, are governing bodies and individual athletes obliged to take part? Second, how are positive results dealt with? Third, how will the implementation be monitored? On the admission of the Chairman of the Council, there is no legal obligation to participate, either for the individual sportsman or woman, or their governing body. Smith 'anticipated the full cooperation from the governing bodies, and hoped they would penalise individual members' (*The Independent*, 3.11.87). But it is in this area of sanctions that the greatest ambiguity still remains. On the one hand, Coe advocates a 'life ban' for those found guilty of drug abuse, while on the other, Smith talks merely of hoping that governing bodies might refuse to select the guilty for major events. Sir Arthur Gold, Vice-Chairman of the BOA, wants suspension for life while Nigel Cooper, the BAAB's Secretary, wants each case dealt with on its merits. Although the banning of the pole-vaulter, Geof Gutteridge, for life in July 1988 suggests that the hard-liners have won the day, there is still confusion due to the willingness of the IAAF to settle for an 18–24-month suspension for a first offence.

It is confusion like this that fuels the suspicion that when positive results are found, the governing bodies will lack the resolve to take exemplary action. There are, as yet, few reports of the actions of disciplinary committees in dealing with drug abusers and it is therefore unwise to predict how they will react. However, Colin Moynihan has already accused the FA of ignoring positive tests on players. More recently the Sports Council has warned the English Federation of Body Builders to take firmer action against its members found guilty of drug abuse. The Federation has simply warned those found positive and not issued any bans, although it has now been agreed to apply one year bans in order to satisfy the Council. The World Professional Billiards and Snooker Association has, on a number of recent occasions, imposed very light penalties on drug users such as Cliff Thorburn and Bill Werbeniuk.

The key challenge to the Sports Council policy will undoubtedly come from those sports which are popular but not reliant on a Council grant, and where prize money is large and sponsors less concerned with the Council's priorities than with the effect of the sport on sales.

Conclusion

[. . .] [S]ome of the characteristics of a policy community mentioned earlier in the paper are evident. There are signs of both vertical integration and horizontal compartmentalization; there is also a membership which is stable and which involves ministers, government officials and representatives of voluntary and private interests, but there are also significant characteristics missing. Despite the existence of a central group of policy actors, there would appear to be little recognition of their respective roles or an implicit authority structure; more importantly there is, at best, only a shallow value consensus among members. In addition, there is a marked absence of a core of professionals to help give policy development a clear direction. [. . .]

Despite the evidence which suggests the absence of a policy community, there are some signs that one may emerge. Three key preconditions for the successful development of a community are an institutional focus within government, opportunities for routine contact and a degree of value consensus. Regarding the first precondition, while there has been a Minister with responsibility for sport for over twenty years, no Minister, with the exception of Denis Howell who seemed to like the job, has been an impressive figure, or politically influential. Nevertheless, the greater salience of sports issues to government has raised the status of the Minister, if only temporarily, thereby providing a stronger focus for policy development.

Opportunities for routine contact is the second precondition and again these have existed for some time, mainly directed through the Sports Council and the CCPR, and would seem to be well established and extensive, despite periodic outbreaks of bickering between the two organizations. It is the final precondition, a value consensus, which seems to be missing. . . . [T]here seems to be only a superficial agreement about objectives and a marked level of disagreement about the means to achieve them. In particular, there is a problem in reconciling the individualist quality of sporting activity, the autonomy of the governing bodies of sport and the pressure for coordination and control coming from the government and its agent, the Sports Council. Indeed, the best prospect for the emergence of a policy community is as a reaction to persistent government intervention in what are considered to be areas of traditional autonomy for athletes and their governing bodies.

References

Benington, J. and White, J. (1986). The Future Role and Organisation of Local Government, *Functional Study No. 4 Leisure*, INLOGOV, University of Birmingham.

Coni Report (1988) *Drug Abuse Enquiry*, Amateur Athletics Association, London.

Dunleavy, P.J. (1981) Professions and Policy Change: Notes towards a Model of Ideological Corporatism, *Public Administration Bulletin*, No. 36, August. Public Administration Committee London.

Friend, J.K., Power, J.M., Yewlett, C.J.L, (1974) *Public Planning: the Intercorporate Dimension*, Tavistock, London.

Hogwood, B. (1979) Analysing Industrial Policy: a Multi-Perspective Approach, in *Public Administration Bulletin*, No. 29, April, Public Administration Committee, London.

Hogwood, B. (1987) *From Crisis to Complacency*, Oxford University Press, Oxford.

International Olympic Committee (1976). *IOC Medical Controls: Games of the XXI Olympiad*, IOC, Montreal.

Jordan, A.G. (1981) Iron Triangle, Woolly Corporatism and Elastic Nets: Images of the Policy Process, *Journal of Public Policy*, **1**(1), 95–123.

Laffin, M. (1986) Professional Communities and Policy Communities in Central Local Relations, in *New Research in Central Local Relations* (edited by M. Goldsmith), Gower, Aldershot.

Moynihan, C. and Coe, S. (1987) *The Misuse of Drugs in Sport*, Department of the Environment, London.

Nicholson, R.H. (1987) Drugs in Sport, *National Rifle Association Journal*, LXVI (3), 2–4.

Rhodes, R.A.W. (1986) *The National World of Local Government*, Allen & Unwin, London.

Richardson, J.J. and Jordan, A.G. (1979) *Governing Under Pressure*, Martin Robertson, Oxford.

Sharpe, L.J. (1985) Central Coordination and the Policy Network, *Political Studies*, 33, 361–81.

Sports Council (1986) *Drug Abuse in Sport*, Sports Council, London.

Travis, A.S., Veal, A.J., Duesbury, K., White, J. (1981) *The Role of Central Government in Relation to the Provision of Leisure Services in England and Wales*, Research Memorandum No. 86, Centre for Urban and Regional Studies, University of Birmingham.

Wistow, G. and Rhodes, R.A.W. (1987) Policy Networks and the Policy Process: The Case of Care in the Community, paper, PSA Annual Conference, Aberdeen.

Media

INTRODUCTION

THE PRINT MEDIA, closely followed by the broadcast media, have been hugely significant influences upon the making, expansion and reshaping of sport, in particular, of course, high-performance competitive sports as covered by television and associated media. Consider your earliest sporting memory, or your favourite sporting moment. It may have been a winning rally or a saving tackle of your own. But is it not more likely to have been a stroke by a Grand Slam champion, or the challenge of a World Cup defender? And it is equally likely that this might have been relayed to you by the broadcast media, not seen live in the stadium; and that it would have been churned over and celebrated in the print media. It is sport's place in the wider leisure culture, as a focus for spectators and a preoccupation of fans, that guarantees its huge national and worldwide profile. No understanding of sport's cultural profile and social significance is complete without an understanding of the contribution of the media to sport, and sport's contribution in turn to the growth and expansion of those media.

The first Reading in this section is an historical account of the sporting print media in England. **Tony Mason** covers the early years of the sporting press, marked by the launch of the first fully established organ for sports news, *Bell's Life in London*, which was established in 1822 as a general publication, but moved towards a more exclusive concentration on sport. The press was a stimulant for sporting fixtures, advertising events, and brokering betting and gambling, as well as reporting on outcomes of contests. Reading about these early days of the print media, think how, over the ensuing century-and-a-half, the roles of public relations, advertising, sponsorship and reportage were to change as sports and associated sport media developed.

The media do not simply report the event, of course: they are also *part of* the event. The frenzy of the build-up to a high-profile sporting contest includes gossip, opinion, features on personalities involved, reviews and statistical analysis. The follow-up to the event, the post-mortem on the results, can be just as diverse and extended. In the second Reading, **John Hargreaves** concentrates on 'media sport news values' in his examination of the construction of 'media sport'. What does he mean when he talks of media sport 'naturalizing' the social world? What are the main elements that are brought together in constructing media sport?

As professional sports developed and expanded, money was needed to fund facilities, performers and administrators. Some early forms of professional sport could survive on gate-money alone, but it was quickly appreciated that outgoings would exceed income on this simple spectator model; and professional players, seizing opportunities that new levels of celebrity promised, would look at opportunities to make themselves economically secure. Companies and corporations, therefore, saw that expanding sports and their emerging media profile offered opportunities for advertising: the golden triangle, as it has become known, of sport-media-sponsor was to emerge in the second half of the twentieth century as the dominant model for the funding of competitive top-level sport. English media academic and commentator **Steven Barnett** describes in the third Reading the increasing impact of sponsorship on both the funding and the look of sport. Does it matter that a footballer's shirt profiles a financial sponsor more than the club name or crest?

In the introduction to Section Three, C.L.R. James's view of the dramatic element in cricket was quoted. It is obvious but essential to note that one of the most riveting qualities of sport is this dramatic element. In any sport, let alone the drawn-out saga of the five-day cricket match, there is the anticipation of the contest, the tension of the competitive encounter (as long as this is not a mismatch), and the inherent drama in observing, responding to and anticipating the result. Some of this is irrational: note the pandemonium among racegoers as the horses approach the finishing post. But it is genuinely and deeply felt (as well as having financial implications for gamblers): spectators are drawn into the drama of the narrative. Sport draws upon these passions, and media sport constructs events in full awareness of them. English media sport scholar **Garry Whannel** has produced numerous pioneering studies in this area, and the third Reading shows the 'process of narrativization' as it applied to two of Britain's top middle-distance runners in the media coverage of their performances and rivalry at the 1980 Moscow Olympic Games.

Next to the simplicities of the early sporting press, radio coverage and early television coverage (British television offered just three terrestrial viewing channels until the early 1980s), the emergence of satellite and cable channels and, more recently, digital media and the internet has radicalized the media landscape. Media tycoons have seen sport as a vital part of their armoury in creating new markets, whether for cricket in Australia in the 1970s, or football worldwide in the 1990s. Ways of seeing and watching have therefore been transformed. But what is being watched? In the fifth Reading, Scottish media academics **Neil Blain, Raymond Boyle** and **Hugh O'Donnell** compare the sports commentary and discourses of the terrestrial and satellite providers. Some commentators predicted that satellite channels would erode national culture. The authors recognize that their analysis refers to the beginning of 'the age of satellite'. How have delivery systems changed? Have 'individual national identities' remained important?

In the sixth Reading, the social-historical background is returned to. The period following the Second World War forms the background for **Richard Holt** and **Tony Mason**'s discussion of sensationalism in the popular press. Media technologies can change, but media concerns or news values may persist. The Reading shows how the developing area of sport journalism has expanded the limits of what is acceptable as sports reporting. As the print media have expanded their sport coverage, a combination of sensationalism and celebrity feature has emerged. Holt and Mason comment that such changes are not exclusive to the world of sport, and are linked to wider shifts in popular culture. Look at the quote from English footballer Robbie Fowler. Is this interesting? Is this sport journalism?

Of course, sport is in no small part a celebration of the body, and the media profile of sport has embraced the glamorization of the sporting body, while in the wider popular culture the fitness industry has catered for 'Everyman' and 'Everywoman' in their aspirations to combine health, well-being and an appropriately sculpted body image. Sport and physical activity are part of an expanded leisure and consumer culture and industry, and fitness, health and lifestyle magazines are part of that industry. In the penultimate Reading of the section, Canadian sociologist **Jennifer Smith Maguire** reviews the boom in fitness publishing, and provides an analysis of the main themes from a US sample of such publications. Look at your local newsagent's shelves, or the magazine racks in the high-street bookseller's: can you see, in this celebration of the body, a personalization of some relatively new physical/sporting ideal?

The scale of expansion of the sport media has been phenomenal as the print media have sought to retain a niche in the new media age: and broadcasters such as the BBC have been able to compete in the new cybermarkets of instant coverage. In all of this, it is vital to keep asking questions about the 'what' as well as the 'how' of media sport. In the final Reading, though, **Toby Miller**, **Geoffrey Lawrence**, **Jim McKay** and **David Rowe** provide an overview of mediated sports cultures across time and space. They offer a particularly valuable focus upon 'the vast and complex infrastructure that is hidden behind sports tableaux of winners and losers'. Miller and his co-authors identify a global sports complex that comprises more than just some self-contained sphere of sport. They point to 'five simultaneous, uneven, interconnected processes which characterize the present moment in sport: Globalization, Governmentalization, Americanization, Televisualization, and Commodification (GGATaC)' (p. 4 of the original). Studying the sport media we begin to see that sport is at the centre of some of the most important general cultural, political and economic processes of the time.

COMMENTARY AND FURTHER READING

The Readings have been selected to show historical and contemporary trends. They show clearly, with a focus upon the reporting of men's football in Britain, that the sport media have offered a consistent diet to readers and viewers. Jeffrey Hill, in his *Sport, Leisure and Culture in Twentieth-Century Britain* (Basingstoke and New York, Palgrave, 2002: 45–6) identified three ways in which the national popular press has positioned its readers: first, it concentrated on a limited number of popular sports – horse-racing, boxing, cricket and football; second, it covered male interests, all but ignoring women; and third, it was insular or parochial, concerned with British interests. It is a useful task to consider how persistent these emphases have been in the sport media, whatever the technological changes.

As mentioned in the introduction to this section, sport is a source of talk, argument, controversy and the like. Is this one such continuity of emphasis? Raymond Williams commented on the rising profile of sport, from its initial nineteenth-century emergence as part of 'the development of a new urban leisure system': 'The national and international sporting networks form a social dimension of an increasingly significant kind in urban industrial culture' (*Television: Technology and cultural form*, London, Fontana/Collins, 1974: 67, 68). And he also noted that sport generates 'a large sub-culture of sporting gossip which takes a great deal of television time but which was already basically present in newspapers' (ibid.). This is a simple affirmation of the point that the production base of the sport media might change, but the values and content persist.

Much work has been done on content analysis (the rigorous measurement of what the print media have printed) in terms of thematic content, and semiotic analysis (the interpretation of the meaning of images in the media – the process of signification, to cite more technical language). For a collection of research articles on these approaches, and on the production infrastructure of the global media and cultural industry, see the themed issue of the *International Review for the Sociology of Sport* (Vol. 37, Nos 3–4, 2002: Special Issue, Sport in the Media and Cultural Industries). Much evidence is presented here of the continuing male-bias and marginalization – or sexualization – of women athletes in the world media.

Narrative sagas in media sport also produce celebrities and stars. The sport media can build and then destroy the profile and reputation of individual sportspeople. This process is captured, both vividly and schematically, by Garry Whannel in *Media Sport Stars: Masculinities and Moralities* (London and New York, Routledge, 2002). The topic of the heroic in sport is also covered in a fascinating cultural discussion on 'heroism and community' by Fred Inglis: 'there is an argument to be made that . . . a society without heroes is not simply without moral bearings, it is unimaginable' (*The Name of the Game: Sport and Society*, London, Heinemann, 1977: 76). Can you imagine an Australia without Cathy Freeman, a US without Tiger Woods, an England without David Beckham (or their equivalents)? If you can, what would be different about that kind of society? As you read biographies, ghost-written or otherwise, of prominent sportspeople, think too what draws you to them (a Reading in Section Nine, on idols of consumption, is devoted to early US cases of this phenomenon). Andrew Blake argues that most such biographies are no more than hagiography, 'to read once, quickly, and then to forget' (*The Body Language: The Meaning of Modern Sport*, London, Lawrence & Wishart, 1996: 178). Is this overly dismissive? A concentration on individual athletes or sport performers as a case study can also reveal much about a culture – a good example of this is Katherine M. Jamieson's 'Reading Nancy Lopez – Decoding Representations of Race, Class, and Sexuality', the fifth essay in Susan Birrell and Mary G. McDonald (eds), *Reading Sport: Critical Essays on Power and Representation* (Boston, Northeastern University Press, 2000).

The sport media do not, of course, stand still, given the potential gains in capturing national and international audiences and markets. On the implications of digital and related developments for ownership, transmission and mediatization of sport, see Raymond Boyle and Richard Haynes, *Football in the New Media Age* (London and New York, Routledge, 2004). Alternative media forms can be said, in the case of football, to have started with 'fanzines' – see Richard Haynes, *The Football Imagination*: *The Rise of Football Fanzine Culture* (Aldershot, Ashgate/Arena, 1995).

Other valuable general sources include: David Rowe, *Sport, Culture and the Media: The Unruly Trinity* (Buckingham, Open University Press, 1999), with illuminating analyses of sport journalistic practices; Raymond Boyle and Richard Haynes, *PowerPlay: Sport, the Media and Popular Culture* (London, Longman, 2000); and Rod Brookes, *Representing Sport* (London, Arnold, 2002), including discussions on the politics of identity (race and gender) in the media. Raymond Boyle, *Sports Journalism* (London, Sage, 2006) captures the tensions in the trade as the new media challenge old professional practices.

Tony Mason

THE TRADITIONAL SPORTING PRESS IN BRITAIN

THE RELATIONSHIP BETWEEN SPORT and the media has always been an important one. In the middle of the nineteenth century both sport and the transmission of news about it went through a transformation. For newspapers, the steam press, the electric telegraph and the end of state taxes meant that news could be collected, hundreds of thousands of copies could be rapidly and cheaply reproduced and distributed by railway to the most populous parts of the kingdom. Sport began to take on its modern shape once it became a central part of the curriculum of the public schools. It was their products who gave it its rules and staffed its national and many of its local organizations. They and their lower middle-class imitators were sporting evangelists who took their enthusiasms and skills to the people, a people who already had a liking for sporting diversion, though of a relatively rude and coarse kind. It was that liking that had to be brought up to date by playing the same games according to the same rules as their betters. The press was crucial in the process: advertising and publicizing, promoting, even sponsoring and emphasizing a sporting world with its own seasons, festive and holy days.

The first newspaper to mark this growth of sporting news was *Bell's Life in London*. When it began in 1822 it was not a sports-only paper but, as the title suggests, concerned with the goings-on of the capital's rich and fashionable set. But the focus gradually shifted to sporting news though it was still including some non-sporting news in the 1860s. By that time, with a circulation probably in excess of 30,000, it was bringing profits to its owner of an estimated £10,000 a year. The fact that only gentlemen could write for it helped to create a reliable reputation which made it the ideal stakeholder for prize fights and upper-class bets. It appeared on Sundays until the 1860s but late in that decade, in an attempt to match the growth in sport and the increase in public interest, it began to come out on Wednesdays and Saturdays instead. The new schedule could not be sustained in the face of growing competition. *Bell's* monopoly was challenged in 1859 by what became the *Sporting Life*. The new paper concentrated on the turf but also looked at other sports and did it for a penny against *Bell's* fivepence. By 1860 the *Sporting Life* was claiming a circulation of 260,000 and the ability to publish the details of any sporting championship within twelve hours of the event. Certainly it carried more and more varied advertising than *Bell's*. The competition was increased by the emergence of the *Sportsman* in 1865 and, in Manchester, of the *Sporting Chronicle* in 1871. The early 1880s saw Britain possessed of four sporting dailies, *Bell's* having tried to keep up with the competition by emulating it. It could not last and it was *Bell's* who went under, the name being sold to the *Sporting Life*.

By the mid-1880s the British public were supporting three sporting daily newspapers. Moreover all of them had been sporting papers from their inception, noticing very little other news, apart from the stage. They also shared a heavy concentration on horse-racing which by the 1880s was taking place somewhere in Britain on almost every day of the year. But other sports were far from neglected. Finally they all promoted and sponsored sport as *Bell's* had done, holding stakes, and providing judges, referees and trophies, sporting annuals and guides, especially important in the early days of modern sport when all these elements were rare. Finally they were all national, even if one was published in Manchester, and at a penny they were aimed at the masses, rather than the classes which had been *Bell's* main audience.

There was a weekly sporting press too, which late in Victoria's reign was expanding in variety and quality. Not all of these papers had long and profitable lives but two were especially distinguished and successful. The *Field* became the bible of the hunting, shooting and fishing fraternity. Nor did it ignore the turf. Even ball games had their coverage gradually expanded. The *Field* was a very successful family business. Beginning in 1853, it showed a steady decline of profits after 1890, but the £75,000 made in that year on a circulation of 19,000 (but a much greater readership, of course) shows what thirty-two pages of advertisements aimed at gentlemen could achieve and it remained healthy enough.

The *Athletic News*, on the other hand, was equally successful but very different. It was sporting news without the horse-racing and the betting. It had begun in 1875 in Manchester with the aim of bringing the sporting activities of amateurs to the notice of a wider, mainly northern, public. But as football grew in popularity and professional matches began to attract large crowds, the paper moved with the times, concentrating on football and rugby in winter and cricket and athletics in summer, while finding space for most other sports. In 1887–8 it became a penny paper and its concentration on league football boosted its circulation to 180,000 a week from September to April. From 1893 to 1900 its editor, J.J. Bentley, was also President of the Football League which helped to make the paper the voice of the professional game. In barely a decade it had secured a special position in the minds of those sport-conscious clerks and skilled workmen from the Midlands and the North of England who probably made up the bulk of the readership. Other examples of successful weekly sports papers included *Pastime*, 1883–95, based on London and devoted to the propagating of amateur sports, and *Cricket*, 1880–1914, whose editor for a time was Charles Alcock, Secretary of Surrey County Cricket Club, which gave it a semi-establishment point of view.

What appears to have undermined the specialist sporting press was the increasing attention paid to sports news by the morning, evening and Sunday newspapers. Sporting news was one of those items which proprietors thought helped to sell papers and a sign of this was the emergence of the sports page, increasingly pages, almost universally by

1900. In daily papers sport occupied 10 per cent, and sometimes more, of the available space, as it did from the first issue of the halfpenny *Daily Mail* in 1896. Even the *Daily Herald* ran a sports page, although it tried to draw the line at racing tips which would encourage its largely working-class readership to bet. It is true that the more establishment papers treated sport with a shade more circumspection. *The Times* was prepared to honour with its notice what had mysteriously become great national events, like the Derby and the University Boat Race, but it had no sports editor before 1914, employed no tipster and generally looked down its aristocratic nose at sports with large spectator followings like football and what was to become Rugby League – although cricket was another matter.

But not surprisingly, with Sunday following the Saturday afternoon which, by 1880, had generally ousted Saint Monday as the working man's playday, it was the Sunday press which took up sport's dramatic story with enthusiasm. Some Sunday papers were actually set up to specialize in Saturday's results. The *Referee*, for example, was, in 1877, probably the first Sunday newspaper to run a football results column. The *Umpire* from 1884 and the *Sunday Chronicle* from 1886, also set out to exploit the sporting obsessions of a working class that was still hardly buying a daily paper regularly but was dramatically boosting the circulation of the Sundays and projecting their owners into the plutocratic class. The *News of the World* devoted 14 per cent of space to sporting news in 1895 with cricket, football and athletics usually being given more prominence than horse-racing.

A further competitor in what was becoming an increasingly crowded field was the local evening paper. First with the racing results in the week, it could also offer a results service second to none in immediacy via its football specials which appeared early on Saturday nights soon after the matches were finished. *Saturday Night* in Birmingham must have been one of the first in 1882; four pages for a halfpenny and 'everything readable'. It was not long before weekly or evening papers in many parts of the country were bringing out their own results editions, often merely adding a results page to the final issue of the ordinary paper. The first sports-only Saturday special was probably the one produced by Tillotsons of Bolton, the *Football Field and Sports Telegram*, from 1884. Nothing could beat the evening paper in the race to be first with the news, and, more importantly, the winners and the scores. Nor was it only local or national sports news which was featured. Well before 1914, evening papers from Plymouth to Newcastle could include the full scorecard plus a 150-word description of the play in the Australia–England cricket test in Sydney, supplied by the Press Association for ten shillings a day including the cost of the telegrams.

Early sports writers tended to be well-educated gentlemen, their prose distributed in long columns, liberally punctuated by classical allusions and quotations. By the interwar years such writers had all but disappeared save from the very best papers. The popular press went for bigger headlines, eye-catching pictures and a more capricious approach. The writers themselves began to be drawn from the lower middle class and working classes. After the Second World War the competition in Fleet Street prompted a lust for sensations in sport, as in other walks of life. Far from keeping their distance from the sportsman, so that familiarity might not impair judgement, the aim was to get closer, so that the inside stories would be uncovered. No longer need they be about sport itself. Indeed the private lives of the sportsmen and sportswomen increasingly made much better copy. The language of the sports page was progressively characterized by chauvinism, aggression and studied bad taste.

It was the press who first elevated a minority of sportsmen and women into national celebrities, whose names and faces were recognized even by people uninterested in sport; performers whose mere presence on the pitch, at the wicket, on the court or the track would tempt people to the event; the exceptional performer who set the standards of achievement for the majority of more or less ordinary players. Tom Sayers, the mid-Victorian prize fighter was probably the first such star and W.G. Grace undoubtedly the second, becoming the most famous Victorian, ahead even of Gladstone. His image decorated not only newspapers and magazines, but cigarette cards and porcelain. Cricket as the national game has rarely been short of national heroes but none of them, from the Indian Prince Ranjitsinhji to Jack Hobbs and Len Hutton would equal the long lived magnetism of W.G. If he had not died during the First World War there would probably have been a national day of mourning. In the 1930s Fred Perry was probably all that most people knew of tennis, Joe Davis performed the same role for snooker and Henry Cotton for golf. Horse-racing captivated people at both ends of the social spectrum and successful jockeys attracted not only the punters and their money but celebrity status. Steve Donoghue in the 1920s and Gordon Richards from the 1930s to the 1950s were the Lester Piggotts of their time. It is no accident that it was Hobbs, the cricketer, and Richards, the jockey, who were the first sportsmen to be knighted. The people's game was full of heroes, but national celebrity status in that sport had to await radio and TV coverage after 1945, together with an expanding middle-class interest that accompanied it. Billy Meredith played until he was fifty and was perhaps the first star player. But Stanley Matthews was the first to achieve the kind of national recognition reached by the other sportsmen mentioned here. He was also the first footballer to receive a public honour – interestingly only a CBE in 1957. His knighthood came later.

John Hargreaves

CONSTRUCTING MEDIA SPORT

A PERSPECTIVE STRESSING the exogenous structural and cultural constraints on the media can be a useful corrective to attempts to tackle the problem of the media and power purely in terms of a content-analysis of news and current affairs. As Golding and Murdock point out, the determining pressures underlying the construction of what is finally presented to audiences cannot be simply read off the content.[1] But neither, on the other hand, is the character of media sport reducible to the economic and political context and the social background of the personnel. To treat it as such is to neglect what it is about the media themselves as institutions that enables media sport to involve a mass audience so successfully. Like all cultural production, media sport requires elucidation in terms of the specific character of the institutions concerned, the technology that is employed and, above all, the occupational culture of media-sport professionals. It is on this latter aspect we wish to concentrate from now on, in particular, on media-sport news values.

Media professionals claim to be reporting impartially on reality, or merely conveying to the audience 'what actually happened'; but this doctrine of epistemological naturalism will not hold up to an examination of how the media treat sport. Alternatively, it is now a commonplace in media sociology that news is constructed in terms of professionals' values and the routine practices to which they give rise.[2] Sporting events undergo a transformation when they are presented in the media: what appears on the screen and in the press and comes across on radio, is not what the spectator or performer at the event experiences. Media sport does not just present the world as it is, already constructed – it re-presents the world in terms of its own inferential framework and thus creates events with their own features – media events.[3] Sports journalists and editorial staff select from, rank, classify and elaborate the world of sport in terms of a 'stock of knowledge' as to what constitutes sports news. An interpretive framework is thus encoded in the flow of communication to the audience – in the items selected, the language, the visual imagery, the stylistics of the presentation, which constitutes an inducement to the audience to interpret the world reported on in preferred ways. It is as if when readers, listeners and viewers are presented with sport in the media, they are simultaneously issued with a set of instructions or maxims as to how the communication should be read, heard and seen. In order to accomplish this successfully, this inferential framework must be related to the culture of the majority of the audience. The transformation of sport into a media spectacle draws not only on professional values – through the latter it draws on the audience's knowledge, values and expectations, as well as the sports community's.

That media sport intervenes in what it reports on, rather than reporting it as it is, is already clear from the fact that sports have actually been changed to make them more amenable for media coverage. The process of constructing media sport that we are analysing here, however, is of a different order altogether from this aspect.

At the simplest level what is selected for reporting and commentary is often a function of the distribution of information-gathering resources. For economic reasons these tend to be concentrated in areas previously defined by professionals as 'news-worthy', so sports-news gathering tends to be a self-fulfilling prophecy: we receive lots of news about sport in elite nations, and the media professional is constantly surprised by 'upsets' 'shock results', when 'unknowns', notably from Third World countries, defeat the elite. It is perhaps, in many cases, only surprising precisely because of the failure to attend to them earlier.

Media sport operates a preferred view of the social world by naturalizing it.[4] It is because sport is so 'obviously' physical, i.e. concerned with the body, governed by natural laws, which function irrespective of what the observer thinks or feels about them, that it can be claimed to have nothing to do with politics or society and that values can be encoded in reporting on sport. Yet sport is no more or less 'natural' than any other activity in which we indulge collectively – it is socially structured. The main way that sport and social order are naturalized in media sport is through the fiction that sports constitute a separate reality. The separate reality of sport is signified by the routine practice of separating out sport from other news and confining it to a separate sector – the sports section of the newspaper, the sports programme, the sports news. The occasions when sport escapes from its status as separate reality are relatively rare, and they occur when there is an angle present that justifies redefining the item as falling outside this separate reality. In our analysis of a week's popular daily newspapers, out of several hundred sporting stories, on only fourteen occasions did a story involving sport appear outside the confines of the sports section, and in only two out of these was sport the real focus of attention. Half of them were in fact, related to sex, politics and crime, and the rest fell into the 'bizarre' and 'personality' categories. Only one of the fourteen managed to achieve front-page status and predictably this concerned the attempted suicide of a married woman with whom an England international footballer was alleged to be having an affair. In this particular week none of the international-status events managed to reach the front pages, although there were, in fact, three that were theoretically eligible – a world boxing championship fight, the Wightman Cup and the Wales–All Blacks rugby match.

The most usual way sport breaks out to the front page, or becomes a major news item on radio or TV, is when Britain triumphs in an international event. During the Moscow Olympics in 1980, for example, the only time sporting events, as opposed to the boycott, broke through to the front page was when a British performer's fortunes were at stake and when Britain won medals.[5] Otherwise, sport achieves prominence in the main news when it gets pulled into issues over which political forces are mobilized already, such as South Africa and the Moscow Olympics boycott, or football violence and law and order. The institutionalized separation of sport from the rest of 'reality' in the media encodes that notion with which we are all familiar, and which begs the question of the relation between sport and power, namely, that sport has nothing to do with politics. Under the auspices of the 'no politics in sport' rule, media sport as we shall see, can accomplish much ideological work.

The claim to be merely reproducing reality is most tenaciously held and appears to be most persuasive where TV is concerned, which indeed shows the event 'as it is actually happening'. But even here the technology of TV and the preferred practices of the professionals construct sport differently from how the spectator sees it. For example, when football is televised, the positioning of the main camera at the half-way position, on one side of the ground, in the stand, gives a view of the game that is quite different from the view of it from behind the goal.[6] The former approximates more to the perspective of the middle-class spectator, with the cameras taking up an 'impartial' location, giving an equal view of both teams and with the commentator supporting neither team; whereas the latter corresponds to that of the working-class supporter, who has traditionally stood on the terraces in all weathers, behind his team, urging it on in a thoroughly partisan manner. The relatively poor picture quality of TV means the camera can only cover a maximum of an eighth of the pitch in long-shot, if the players are to be at all distinguishable. In face of this technological limitation, English professionals, when compared to others, such as the West Germans, have been found to prefer frequent alternate long-shots with close-ups of individual players, or small groups of players, and it has been calculated that the ratio of time spent on close-ups of this kind to time spent on long-shots, is much greater in British televised football.[7] The viewer's attention tends to be thereby directed away from team strategy, towards the game's more individualistic aspects. The greater proportion of the game that occurs off-camera then has to be filled in for the audience by the commentator, giving him more latitude to interpret the action.[8] What occurs on-camera is also interpreted for the viewer by the commentary ('that was a good goal' etc.) Unlike the spectator at the event the TV viewer's observation is interrupted by 'action replays', which again, typically, close in on the individual performer at what are interpreted as key dramatic, entertaining moments – the tackle and confrontation, the goal, the shot, the save, moments of successful achievement or failure, with individuals' facial expressions and gestures highlighted. More often than not nowadays, the average viewer sees a heavily edited recording of the highlights, a multiple construction of reality, a truncated, action-packed spectacle, injected with pace, which omits the build-ups and the 'dull patches'. The crucial point here is that British TV coverage plainly gives primacy to entertainment when compared with other styles of coverage. The BBC, for example, explicitly acknowledges that action replays are put in for the benefit of the 'mums and daughters' watching, rather than for the connoisseurs, a practice in keeping with TV producers' perceived need to hurry on the pace to keep the audience with the programme.[9] The concurrence of the British press in such practices provides additional evidence of their cultural specificity. West German TV coverage of the World Cup in 1974, which eschewed close-ups for a more 'neutral' coverage, focusing on team play in long-shots, was criticized by columnists like Brian Glanville of The Sunday Times and by Derek Dougan, for its 'lack of professional skills'(!).

Further confirmation that the media do not merely report on events or show them as they actually happen, is provided by the fact that a good deal of work beforehand is put into preparing their audiences for how they should be seen and interpreted, that is, in building up the event. For example, the TV and *Radio Times* and *TV Times Magazine*, with their enormous circulations, built up the 1974 World Cup by nominating several stars beforehand as representatives of their countries' playing styles and national characteristics.[10] The opening sequences of TV sports programmes set the scene immediately prior to the event to be shown. The graphics draw attention to selected aspects and themes, like the Scottish bagpiper symbol at the beginning of ITV's coverage of the 1978 World Cup in Argentina, which signalled the nation's importance *vis-à-vis* others in the competition. The montage of insets, packed with champions in action, at the beginning of BBC TV's 'Grandstand', prepares us for non-stop action and excitement. The use of 'atmospheric' music in the signature tunes (quasi-military, or with an ethnic trace) connotates entertainment, excitement and visits to exotic places.

Impartiality and objectivity is signalled by the practice of analysing performances with the help of accredited experts. Structured access is a fundamental feature of the organization of the media, and the use of the accredited expert in broadcasting is now a time-worn device, which developed originally in BBC news and current affairs programmes as a solution to the problem of establishing objectivity and achieving 'balance' over politically controversial matters.[11] In the press the equivalent of the accredited expert enters through the use of the attributed quotation and the sports-personality-as-writer. Expertise, in signifying objective, factual treatment and knowledgeable opinion, functions to authorize preferred interpretations. Since experts are used as primary definers of reality in the media, who is defined as an expert, which experts are selected from those available, and what kind of questions are put to them by reporters, presenters and anchormen, is crucial in the definition of reality. 'Recognized experts', are selected by professionals, and they are almost invariably former sportsmen or practising performers, or coaches and officials – but these are not necessarily the most expert among those in the field. An additional qualification is that they should be celebrities or stars with entertaining personalities or 'characters' who are good on TV. Little-known or relatively unsuccessful figures, say, a Fourth Division footballer, never appear as experts; it is the elite who are so identified, that is, what is considered relevant is not only what is said, but also who is saying it. A framework of values necessarily underpins the selection and definition of issues in the ensuing analysis, and what the audience is presented with therefore, is a summing up reflecting the values of media professionals and their expert advisers. On this basis performances are assessed and achievement or failure is recorded, praise and blame are allocated, stars are nominated, the level of entertainment rated, whether the rules were adhered to and properly enforced is ascertained and whether nations and representatives conformed to the consensus stereotypes of them. The sports spectacle is thus used, not only to exemplify and judge technical skill, but to prescribe moral values and to comment prescriptively on social relationships.

. . . [T]hose aspects of media sports discourse and routine practice, which are most important in this respect and which articulate on key processes whereby hegemony is achieved . . . [are] order and control, competitive individualism and civil privatism, sex and gender, the primacy of the nation and ethnocentricity tinged with racism. [. . .]

[These five aspects form the basis of the author's analysis in the ensuing sections of his original chapter – editor's note.]

Notes

1   P. Golding and G. Murdock, 'Ideology and the Mass Media: The Question of Determination', in M. Barrett, *et al.* (eds), *Ideology and Cultural Production* (Croom Helm, London, 1979). For analyses stressing political and cultural factors, see: S. Chibnall, *Law and Order News* (Tavistock, London, 1977); M. Tracey, *The Production of Political Television* (Routledge & Kegan Paul, London, 1977); P. Schlesinger, *Putting Reality Together* (Constable, London, 1978). See also P. Elliot, *The Making of a TV Series* (Constable, London, 1972).

2   S. Cohen and J. Young, *The Manufacture of News* (Constable, London, 1973). See, especially, the papers in this volume by Galtung and Ruge, and Hall's discussion of news photos.

3   J. Fiske and J. Hartley, *Reading Television* (Methuen, London, 1978) ch. 10.

4   R. Barthes, *Mythologies* (Jonathan Cape, London, 1972).

5   The front pages of all the national newspapers were analysed over the period 19 July 1980–4 August 1980.

6   E. Buscombe, 'Cultural and Televisual Codes in Two Title Sequences', *BFI Television Monograph No. 4: Football on Television, 1975*.

7   C. Barr, 'Comparing Styles: England v W. Germany', *BFI Television Monograph No. 4*; J. Wyver, 'Pulp on the Pampas: The Game as Light Entertainment', Spoilsports, *Time Out*, 426 (2 June 1978).

8   Barthes, *Mythologies*.

9   Barr, 'Comparing Styles', p. 51.

10   C. McArthur, 'Setting the Scene: *Radio Times* and *TV Times*', *BFI, Television Monograph No. 4*; E. Buscombe and C. McArthur, 'Out of Bounds: The Off-Field Commentators', Spoilsports, *Time Out*, 426 (2 June 1978).

11   Schlesinger, *Putting Reality Together*; Tracey, *The Production of Political Television*.

Steven Barnett

POTTING THE GOLD
The sponsorship game

[. . .]

The competitor's tale

PRECISELY HOW MUCH SPORT EARNS from sponsorship is almost impossible to calculate, since deals are essentially private transactions between individuals, teams or governing bodies and private companies. Most of the major agreements are publicised, and the amounts specified. Many smaller deals, especially at regional or local level, are too insignificant to be reported or notified to the press. When the Howell Report assembled figures for Britain in 1983, it found discrepancies between two sets of figures produced in 1981 – one setting the total at £40 million, the other at £60 million if back-up costs were included. By 1985, the Institute of Sports Sponsorship was estimating expenditure at £140 million per annum. More recently, estimates for 1988 from Sportscan put the total value of sports sponsorship at nearly £200 million, provided by over 2,000 companies. It is generally believed that every sponsorship pound is supported by a pound of PR or advertising, thereby doubling the money made available for the promotion of sport and sporting events. Particularly when set against the money distributed by the Sports Council, sport's income from and dependence on sponsorship is substantial.

In 1981, the Central Council of Physical Recreation (CCPR) was sufficiently concerned about the complex relationship and increasing dependence to initiate an independent inquiry. Its Chairman was Denis Howell, Minister of Sport under the last Labour administration and a former Chairman of the CCPR. This committee published the results of its extensive inquiry, including seventy-three recommendations, at the end of 1983. One of its main concerns was the disposition of both sports governing bodies and competitors towards sponsorship and the increasing inconsistencies in how different sports approached this relationship.

At the forefront of these concerns was the issue of maintaining jurisdiction over the sport, and the point at which there might develop an unhealthy dependence on individual benefactors. 'The Committee finds that while some governing bodies do maintain total control of their sponsorships, others are content to accept financial assistance without supervising the effects of sponsorship upon their sports.' With masterly understatement, but with advice aimed squarely at the more inexperienced authorities who may have lacked understanding of commercial objectives, the report continued: 'We would hope that governing bodies could so arrange their financial affairs that the loss of any one source of income would not lead to the near collapse of the sport in its current form.' Sensible words, which many governing bodies have since acknowledged and acted upon. Unfortunately, as subsequent case studies demonstrated, wise accounting had less to do with the nature or number of sponsors than with the extent or existence of television coverage. Some sponsors, as we shall see, would certainly make a commercial decision to withdraw after a set period – and sometimes at disastrously short notice – regardless of decisions made by television producers. Others, however, would enter into deals on the understanding, either implicit or explicit, that their beneficence would be paraded via recognisable corporate logos on television screens throughout the land. No cameras, no deal. And any number of reserve or potential deals would be unlikely to preserve an event if its survival was dependent entirely on sponsorship.

Amateur boxing's plight was featured in the report as an example of a sport suffering through insufficient attention from broadcasters. The secretary of the Amateur Boxing Association recalled wistfully the nineteen tournaments which used to be televised, reduced now to three programmes a year. Professional boxing still maintains a major presence, but declining television interest in the 45,000 registered amateurs has a depressing impact on income in a sport which, as the ABA secretary said, 'caters mainly for the lower income groups'. Such income could have socially beneficial consequences, 'We have a community role to play as we are a disciplined sport, and yet we provide an opportunity to let youngsters let off steam in a controlled way. We are a boom sport but are not able to attract "boom" money.' With greater television exposure, of course, it would be difficult to keep potential investors out of the ring.

A classic example of how television's desertion can leave sports bodies in dire straits through no fault of their own is canoeing. When the British Canoeing Union (BCU) hosted the 1981 World Championships, Sun Life of Canada agreed to put up £25,000 contingent on television coverage. The BCU could not negotiate a firm contract with the BBC, and Sun Life withdrew leaving 'severe financial embarrassment' in its wake. Only the generosity of other small sponsors, BCU members, and an increased Sports Council grant prevented a large deficit. Under these circumstances, the frustration of governing bodies with broadcasters is understandable even if not entirely justifiable.

Some sports, of course, are in a position to negotiate deals without guaranteed television coverage because of the profile of participants. The Howell Report's example of fencing's twenty-five-year-old deal with Martini and Rossi is entirely due to the more upmarket nature of the sport and its players. Not only is this sort of deal atypical, but it is inevitably worth less to the sponsor than a deal which potentially affords access to many millions of television viewers. While every governing body would accept the wise counsel offered by Howell, none would be prepared to refuse substantial sums of money even when dependent on circumstances and decisions entirely beyond their control. Once television commitments have been made, of course, the problem of finding and replacing sponsors virtually disappears. The Howell Report was full of praise for the sterling efforts of the Amateur Swimming Association in building a portfolio of sponsors at every level of the sport, but had to acknowledge that the ASA'S contract with the BBC 'gives a special bargaining power in the field of sponsorship negotiations'.

Some of the individual competitors interviewed testified to the value of sponsorship money, both in amateur events as the competition became increasingly intense and for professionals who sought an income more in keeping with the requisite investment of time and effort. For anyone who still believes that pure amateurism remains an attainable ideal in the modern sporting world, the Howell Report is required reading. Even before citing the evidence of competitors, it states unequivocally: 'We were left in no doubt that the burden of surviving and succeeding in sport and also in life cannot be treated idealistically as in the past.' Then came the testimony, perhaps the most stirring from ex-Olympic competitor turned professional cyclist, Mick Bennett: 'In my first Olympics in 1972 I had to buy my own jersey and tyres. I lost my job in order to train to represent my country. I paid for my own bike, and only asked for 8p a mile car allowance yet I was refused.' Without any subsidy, his team had to live and train together on the continent. They subsequently won a Commonwealth gold, World Championship silver and two Olympic bronze medals. Top equestrian competitor Lucinda Green echoed the sentiment that total dedication was required by modern competitors, which in turn entailed sacrificing any normal means of earning a living: 'Sport today is all-consuming if you want to reach the top. There is no means of earning a living in a normal way and at the end of, say, ten or fifteen years, competitors can go out of sport without money or a job.'

Having cited evidence, the Howell Report essentially accepted the end of amateurism. 'The demands on competitors, on their pockets and on their time has increased to an extent where they are becoming full-time performers. The slide from pure amateurism to semi- or full professionalism . . . may not be idealistically acceptable but its inevitability was a view often expressed to us.' Once this 'slide from amateurism' has been accepted as a *fait accompli*, competitors' concern that they should be free to exploit every means of self-marketing at their disposal becomes more understandable. Whether sponsorship logos on clothes should be permissible then becomes less of a sports policy issue and more of a broadcasting policy issue. Personal sponsorships are a lucrative source of additional income, whether the money goes into 'trust funds' for amateur athletes or direct to bank accounts for professional cricketers. Competitors want to be free but responsible. According to Steve Ovett, 'The principle of wearing logos is OK but it needs to be responsible. We do not want to be walking billboards.' But cricket's Bob Willis pointed out areas of potential conflict in characteristic style: 'We feel hard done by. I have to whiten out the flashes on my boots, yet, at Wimbledon, people on court are done up like Christmas trees.'

Without clothes advertising, almost entirely a function of the widespread presence of television cameras, there would be less money. With less money, we are told, amateur athletes could not compete at the highest levels. And yet before that first Wimbledon telecast in 1937, amateur athletics seemed to have survived quite happily since the beginning of the century. It is a fascinating but unanswerable question: is it simply a gradual process of evolution that athletes are fitter and races run faster than fifty years ago? And that this evolution happens to coincide with the widespread availability of athletic and sporting spectacles via the broadcast media? Or have the vast sums of money unlocked by those same broadcast media, in particular the money available to individuals via personal endorsements, allowed athletes to devote time to training which their predecessors had to devote to earning a living? It is a sobering, and certainly not implausible, thought that television has been indirectly responsible for creating those very pinnacles of sporting achievement which it then conveys to its armchair spectators.

The sponsor's tale

[. . .] Tangible evidence of the impact of widely televised sponsorship comes from Cornhill's experience with cricket. In 1977, when the insurance company first cemented its relationship with the Test and County Cricket Board, only 2% of the public could spontaneously mention Cornhill when asked to name insurance companies. During 1981, Cornhill assessed its television exposure and emerged with fairly positive evidence: 140 hours of coverage, during one of the most exciting Ashes series in cricket history, provided them with 7,459 banner sightings on screen; 234 verbal mentions on screen; 1,784 references on radio; 659 mentions in the national press, and 2,448 in the provincial press. Not to mention a staggering 21 million calls to British Telecom's score service in 1980. It is therefore understandable that by 1982 their 'spontaneous awareness' score among the general public should have leapt from 2% to 17%. Cornhill's return on their substantial investment was more than the 250 tickets they received per match to oil the wheels of customer liaison. According to Howell, the company itself estimated that 'an increased annual premium income of £10 million could be attributed to the sponsorship'. It is a vivid example of how a little known, and relatively small, financial institution can enhance both reputation and profits through association with both an appropriate sport and a high level of television coverage. [. . .]

. . . [U]nderlying most of the major sponsors' strategic thinking was the importance of television cameras at their events. Some minor event sponsorship was justified by the targeted profile of participants. But sponsors are in no doubt that major deals are dominated by television considerations: 'If it's not on television there's no point to it,' was a characteristic comment. This sponsor, in return for a quarter of a million pounds, had a minimum number of peak-time television hours written into the contract, with a promise of rebates if this was not delivered. Even a minimum audience size was specified. When Canon announced its historic £1 million a year sponsorship of the Football League in May 1983, in the midst of unresolved negotiations between broadcasters and the Football League, it was explicit about the conditions: 'We would have to look at the situation again if there were no television.' Ironically, the sticking point for those negotiations was the contentious issue of shirt advertising, contrary to both IBA and BBC codes of practice but desperately sought by football clubs. Arsenal's astonishing half-million pound deal with the Japanese electronics corporation JVC was, no doubt, equally contingent on successful television negotiations. It was neither the first nor the last time that broadcasters were to find themselves at the centre of a storm, amid accusations of inconsistency and rank hypocrisy.

The broadcaster's tale

As the critical point of this eternal triangle, broadcasters are frequently beleaguered: by sports complaining about lack of airtime, by sponsors complaining about lack of consistency, by internal codes of practice designed to ensure that television does not become a corporate plaything, and by the audience who would ideally like their sport without advertisements or sponsorship banners, and for free. It is a high-wire balancing act from which, inevitably, there are falls.

Broadcasters are well aware of their responsibilities both to sports and to the audience. If they became bloody-minded about levels of exposure to commercial messages, sponsors would start to withdraw, sports would suffer, and ultimately audiences would not have television access to events which they enjoy. Jonathon Martin acknowledges that a realistic attitude to sponsorship from the BBC is important because 'some great events just would not happen any more without sponsors'. Most obviously, there is in television audience terms the consistently most popular sporting event of the year, the Grand National – which would not have survived after the Topham family had Seagram not intervened. BBC television's interest in hockey generated sponsorship interest which in turn helped to fund pre-Olympic matches around the world. By contrast, broadcasters are also aware of the exploitative or 'piggy-back' role of some sponsors. This can occur with events which are not in need of financial assistance to ensure their very survival. They are either popular showpieces which a new sponsor wishes to exploit, or created specifically as commercial vehicles in a bid for more television time. Snooker's massive popularity over the last few years has spawned a plethora of sponsored tournaments which, apart from providing a great deal of cheap television time, does no harm to the annual incomes of those on the professional snooker circuit. In such cases, there is neither a contest of great national importance crying out for a corporate saviour nor a grass roots sports industry able to benefit from an injection of corporate cash.

Television's accommodation of sponsorship needs is not of course entirely dictated by selfless recognition of sport's requirements. Not only would certain audience-pulling events not happen without investment by sponsors seeking television exposure, but their presentation and organisation is likely to benefit from increased resources. The result is a more attractive event and therefore a better television programme. Even more significantly, facilitating income to the sport through television exposure serves to reduce the cash demands that sports will make in return for television rights. Throughout the 1970s, the Football League were content with a joint agreement between the BBC and ITV, because they had only just begun to realise the huge financial potential of sponsorship. The more airtime they could fill, the more sponsorship money they could unlock; better still if football appeared on both networks. ITV's unsuccessful dawn coup for exclusive rights in 1979 served only to inflate rights costs to both channels, but by 1983 more was required. At the end of negotiations in March of that year, Football League club chairmen rejected a £2.6 million per annum deal because the TV companies would not give way on shirt advertising which was bound to provide a substantial additional source of revenue.

At a further meeting in April, both BBC and ITV remained adamant that their rules would not allow for shirt advertising. The Howell Report quotes an LWT spokesman, in what sounds like a rather plaintive plea: 'I am sure, in the end, clubs will feel site advertising revenue is just as important to them as revenue for shirt advertising.' Unfortunately, site advertising had in most cases been thoroughly milked, and anyway could not provide the same lucrative source of funds. The chairman of Tottenham was blunt about the counterbalancing of relaxed sponsorship rules and rights fees: 'I am sure the major clubs would not be looking for an increase in the cash from television if shirt advertising could be agreed. This will provide hundreds of thousands of pounds of extra revenue for clubs.' On 15 July, television surrendered. Shirt advertising would be permitted as long as total coverage did not exceed sixteen square inches and the sponsor's name was no higher than two inches. In return, the networks could screen ten League games, and the League Cup Final, live. And the cost? The same £2.6 million which club chairmen had originally refused.

Once shirt advertising was conceded, there was little left for television to offer in the way of sponsorship. League clubs had taken every advantage of the opportunities available, netting annual sponsorship cash of nearly £20 million. As John Bromley put it: 'They sold the shirt advertising; they sold the ground advertising; they had sponsored the ball; they were getting to the point where there was no more sponsoring possible.' Saturation point meant either accepting little prospect of a real increase in income or looking for other sources of revenue. Right on cue, British Satellite Broadcasting entered the frame to force ITV up to unprecedented heights, and almost overnight the focus of Football League revenue switched from sponsorship to television rights. The American model had come to Britain.

Garry Whannel

NARRATIVE
The case of Coe and Ovett

THE COVERAGE OF THE COE–OVETT 'story' during the Moscow
Olympics of 1980 provides a good case study in the process of narrativisation. Clearly
television did not invent this story, or create its importance within the scheme of things.
It did, however, draw on it heavily as part of its appeal to viewers. In doing so it constantly
foregrounded the events precisely as a story, which can be understood in terms of the
workings of the hermeneutic code (Barthes 1974: 19). The hermeneutic code poses
the initial enigma of a narrative, and gives the text its forward progression towards the
resolution of the enigma. So as not to answer the question too soon, a number of strategies
are adopted. The most relevant here are constant reformulation of the question, the
promise that there will be an answer, and the provision of a partial answer. As opposed
to fiction, in television sport the event itself is clearly not structured by the conventions
of narrative, apart from the basic competitive structure of sport that results in winners
and losers. But in the way television is able to draw upon the inherent hermeneutic of
sport events, to reorganise, to re-present it, it can be said to be narrativising.[1]

Television coverage of the 1980 Moscow Olympics was dominated by the Coe–Ovett
story. It could of course be argued that the prominence given to this story was merely
right, proper and natural. After all, Coe and Ovett are two of the most successful British
athletes ever, they were currently world record holders at their main events, and almost
unprecedentedly joint holders of the 1500m world record. They had virtually never raced
each other and were about to meet in both the 800m and the 1500m in the world's
premier athletics event, the Olympic Games. Is this not a good story by any standards?
To agree that it is an extremely good story does not mean accepting that its dominant
position in the coverage is simply natural. On the contrary, the factors that make it, for
British television, a major story are rooted in cultural assumptions open to analysis.

The high value placed on notions of 'greatest', be it fastest, highest or longest,
ensures a focus upon world record holders. The Olympic Games is supposedly a

competition that determines the best. The strong emphasis placed on British competitors enables audience identification. Sport itself and television coverage of it are both male centred. There is a strong tendency to treat men's events and men's sports more seriously than women's events and women's sports. We see athletics as the premier Olympic sport. This does not mean that it has the same level of prominence in different countries – to the Romanians, for example, gymnastics may appear far more important. Track events are generally given more television prominence than field events. One reason could well be the lack of a tradition of world-class British competitors. But also track events fit the conventions of TV sport more adequately – the competitive aspect is more directly and immediately visible. Finally, British television has always emphasised the middle distance events, often called the 'blue riband' events. This is no doubt influenced by the tradition of good runners and the mystique of Bannister's 4-minute mile, but again it can be suggested that these events fit the needs of television particularly well.

So a middle distance race between two male British world record holders in the Olympic Games is certainly a good story. Indeed, it fits so many of the criteria for prominence that the focus on Coe and Ovett during the second week of the Olympics amounted at times to tunnel vision. Very little time was devoted during the previews to discussing the other runners in the 1500m. In outlining the structure of the Coe/Ovett narrative, I will not distinguish between ITV and BBC, in part because the conventions of television sport are broadly common to both, and in terms of their handling of this narrative the similarities seemed to be more significant than the differences.

1   Posing the question

The Coe and Ovett contest was a major feature of the Olympic coverage right from the opening programmes, in which the central question 'Who will win?' was immediately posed, with an implicit enigma 'which is the greatest?' Coe and Ovett were inscribed from the start as the characters, the contenders; in other words, the question was not who would win the 800m/1500m, but would Coe or Ovett win. Subsidiary questions developed the story, drawing upon contrasts in personal style. The first tangible event was the arrival of each. Coe 'conducts himself impeccably',[2] Ovett was 'greeted like the star he is',[3] the man who has 'done things his way'.[4] The implied good guy/bad guy contrast was invoked. An opposition of experience/youth was introduced, on the basis that, though there was little difference in age, Ovett had had more competition. The heats and semi-finals were comfortably won by Ovett and Coe, and both were regarded as 'going well'.

2   Partial answer

Ovett's victory in the 800m altered the position by giving a partial answer to the question. This called for a reformulation of some of the questions, but also marked a point from which recapitulation of the story could be offered. This happened both within the Olympic highlight programmes and in news bulletins.

3   Periodic organisation (1)

It was a 'golden day for Britain' and a 'triumph for the strong silent man who hates publicity'. The contrast was made between Ovett with 'the gold he wanted so much' and Coe offering 'the briefest of handshakes'. There was talk that the East Europeans tried the only way they knew to stop Ovett (i.e. physically) but 'he's big enough to look after himself' and 'wasn't having any nonsense'. The 'strong silent man had spoken with his feet as he always threatened to do'. Finally we were reminded that this was only a partial answer; 'now we wait for the race of the century part two'.[5]

4   The answer revealed

The 1500m was described as a fantastic run by Coe. After the 'misery of last weekend, now everything is golden again'.[6] Two themes emerged: Coe got 'the revenge he wanted' and Ovett 'takes the defeat well'.[7] A major feature of this resolution was that, while the question 'Who will win?' was resolved, the larger enigma, 'Which is the best?', remained unresolved. This fitted the need for a continuing Coe–Ovett story that could go on providing a point of identification for viewers. Both channels remarked on this: 'the arguments will go on',[8] 'the argument remains, which one is greater'.[9]

5   Periodic organisation (2)

The race was over and the narrative resolved, but not yet completed. The story was in fact re-told in precis form in post-mortem programmes and news bulletins and also in the final highlights programmes. It was of course implicitly a fairy-tale ending. Not only did it produce two gold medals for Britain, not only did the (good guy) hero triumph over adversity, after suffering defeat, crisis of confidence and illness, but the bad guy, magnanimous in defeat, turned out to be a good guy after all. Additionally, in television terms not only was the story a great success in itself, but, in that the final enigma of 'Who is better?' remained unresolved, the continuing story was given a greater impetus for following years.

Rivalry

Reducing the race to a competition between two people presented it as an individual head-to-head contest. Metaphors used to describe this drew upon other models for head-to-head conflict, such as boxing, bullfighting, duelling, war and gladiatorial combat. The race was called a battle, a heavyweight championship, a duel. Winning the 800m was first blood to Ovett. Coe and Ovett were the gladiators, they were at the moment of truth. Coe's victory was revenge. Much was made of the rivalry between the two. ITV put together an edited sequence of preparations for the 800m semi-final with a voice-over suggesting that Coe and Ovett were not on speaking terms and were ignoring each other. Coverage in the media echoed the style of world title boxing coverage. There is some evidence that audiences respond more to commentaries that foreground tension between participants (Bryant *et al*. 1977). The framing of events in terms of head-to-head confrontation – Coe v. Ovett, Decker v. Budd, Fatima Whitbread v. Tessa Sanderson – has been a growing feature of television sport during the 1980s.

Experience v. naivety

After Ovett won the 800m, the contrast of his experience and Coe's naivety was mobilised. Ovett was 'battle hardened', the 'master tactician', the 'man who stamps his authority on a race', 'always in command'. Coe by comparison was said to lack experience and, after the defeat, to lack confidence. He was called tactically naive, his 800m was a tactical disaster, and it was suggested that his preparation may have been inadequate. Within the context of the narrative, the doubts over Coe's experience and confidence constitute problems. Coe, as a character in the narrative, has to overcome these if he is to triumph.

Aggression

The emphasis on such qualities as toughness, commitment, aggression and ability to withstand pressure is a typical feature of the representation of top-level sport. The presence of these qualities in Ovett and possible absence of them in Coe were part of the post-800m reformulation of the story. The subsequent course of the narrative was structured by the need for Coe to acquire these qualities. The first reformulation referred to his lack of aggression and the need for him to become physically involved. The second referred to him gaining in determination, learning aggression and showing signs of aggression. In particular, his brief imitation of a sparring boxer after the 1500m semi-final was taken as a sign of the success of this learning process. The resolution of the narrative provided the proof of the value of this learning process, Coe's victory being taken as a token of his new-found ability to compete.

That the need to learn aggression, or to be aggressive, should be foregrounded in this way conforms to a more general pattern. Study of sport coverage more generally shows that while there is a wide range of qualities invoked – toughness, aggression, commitment, power, courage, ability to withstand pressure, and also balance, poise, judgement, timing, dexterity, speed, accuracy, concentration, flair, imagination – there is a tendency to evaluate more highly the first six of these. In turn these qualities conform closely to conventional constructions of masculinity. There are many factors that have inhibited the progress of women in sport – lack of facilities at school, the hidden curriculum, limited or male-based sport facilities, a lack of leisure in the sense that men have known it.[10] But important, too, is the systematic underpinning of gender difference that the representation of sport provides.

THE BIG SHOWDOWN

The dominance of the Coe–Ovett story provided a perfect overall narrative structure for the Olympic coverage as a whole, offering a way of constantly forging points of identification for the viewer. Moscow offered only a partial answer to the key narrative question, each athlete winning the event that the other was expected to win. In 1981 the two continued to break records whilst avoiding each other. Media coverage and public interest in a confrontation grew in tandem. Athletics amended its rules to allow payment to athletes by means of trust funds, and three races featuring Coe and Ovett were planned for 1982. The event advertised on the *Radio Times* cover of 17 July 1982 was to be the first race of the three. This cover, while not itself a photograph, references and mobilises our familiarity with the codes and conventions of sports photography. It is an attempt to capture for us a photograph that does not exist and so carries with it a promise – the promise of utopia. The cover offers us a golden moment still to come: Coe and Ovett battling it out down the home straight.

It is, I think, an exceptional image, and it is worth briefly highlighting its salient points. It shows two runners in white, whose position, height and apparent weight are very similar. The picture emphasises muscularity. Their eye lines meet in a striking mutual stare. The absences too are striking – no numbers on the vests, no colours denoting sponsors or national affiliation (apart from a residual trace of red and blue in the stripes on the sides of the shorts), no other competitors, no ads, no officials, no trackside equipment, and the crowd a mere blur in the background. The athletes burst out of the frame towards us. The spectacle is perfectly presented for our eye with all extraneous detail erased, as if we had suddenly been blessed with tunnel vision.

The picture mimics photography in many ways: the angle, framing and cropping are all characteristic of athletics photography, as is the way the painting mimics the out-of-focus blue blur of the crowd produced by telephoto lenses. But the *Radio Times* cover is not simply an attempt to capture the realism effect of photography. The rendering of the two runners as physically equal (Coe is in fact shorter and slighter), the elimination of extraneous detail, the almost eroticised stress on muscularity, and the slight hint of caricature, all proclaim the painting. This gives the confrontation a mythic dimension without finally undermining its realness. It promises an ideal moment, and one precisely not available in photographic form.

There is also more than a hint of reference to the Greeks – athletes in white, with connotations of purity and the amateur tradition; but also connotations of gods, Titans, clashes and mythic confrontations. At the time this picture appeared, the British audience was being offered another representation of athletics, also featuring the story of the confrontation between two rivals, both British. The film *Chariots of Fire*, appearing in the wake of the Moscow Olympics, echoed the phenomenon of the Coe–Ovett rivalry by tracing the story of Eric Liddell and Harold Abrahams, who, like Coe and Ovett, both won Olympic gold. The film opens and closes with athletes in pure white, invoking again the pure amateurism of Greek athletics. (This is largely a myth. The Greeks made no firm distinction between amateur and professional, and the Greek Olympians often gained spectacular rewards; Kidd 1984. The term 'amateur' in sport is essentially a product of the attempt of the Victorian bourgeoisie to exclude the working class from their leisure activities.) *Chariots of Fire* eventually turned up on television in 1984 as part of the build-up to the Los Angeles Olympics, and BBC's Los Angeles coverage used the *Chariots of Fire* theme music for its title sequence. There is a complex process of intertextuality at work here, with factual and fictional representations echoing each other.[11]

The *Radio Times* cover was the work of illustrator Mark Thomas, who intended the doomladen navy blue background to produce a stormy setting for the clash of the Titans. Thomas received an unusually elaborate briefing from *Radio Times*. It called for the two to be portrayed in identical fashion, dressed in white, racing for the line, straining for the tape, and bursting out of the frame, with eyes meeting. There should be no sponsors' colours or trademarks, and no national identification. They supplied Thomas with over 100 photographs and slides of the two by way of reference. Only the Moscow 1980 pictures showed the two together.

The showdown offered the utopian fantasy of two great athletes battling it out all the way to the finish, precisely as Roy of the Rovers offers the utopia of heroic football in which our team triumphs against the odds (see Tomlinson 1983). It offered the pleasure of competition. It promised an answer to the long-running Coe–Ovett narrative. At a time when athletics was becoming commercial while still calling itself amateur, it handled the contradiction by invoking virginal white purity. It offered a simple dramatised world – no distractions, no ads, no money, no politics, and an answer to our questions imminent.

Ironically, it was not to be. An injured Coe was forced to withdraw. Taken ill the week before, Ovett ran well below his best. We did indeed see a 'big showdown', with two athletes battling all the way to the tape, but instead of Coe and Ovett it was Dave Moorcroft and Sydney Maree. This precisely demonstrates one central contradiction of television sport. Television constantly attempts to build our expectations and to frame our perceptions, yet ultimately does not control the event itself.

Notes

1   See Pearson (1988) for a similar analysis of television baseball.
2   *Olympics 80*, ITV, 23/7/80.
3   *Olympic Grandstand*, BBC, 22/7/80.
4   *Olympics 80*, ITV, 23/7/80.
5   All quotations in this paragraph are from *ITV News*, 26/7/80.
6   *Olympics 80*, ITV, 1/8/80.
7   *Olympic Grandstand*, BBC, 1/8/80
8   *Olympic Grandstand*, BBC, 1/8/80.
9   *Olympics 80*, ITV, 1/8/80.
10   See Deem (1986), Green, Hebron and Woodward (1987), Griffin *et al*. (1982), K.F. Dyer (1982), J.A. Hargreaves (1985), Pannick (1984), Theberge (1981), Wimbush and Talbot (1989).
11   See Neale (1982), S. Johnston (1985), Tomlinson (1988), and Jarvie (1989b). The BFI Education Department has a study pack and slide set analysing the film.

Bibliography

Barthes, R. (1974) *S/Z*, London: Hill & Wang.
Bryant, J., Comiskey, P. and Zillmann, D. (1977) 'Drama in sports commentary', *Journal of Communication*, Summer, USA.
Deem, R. (1986) *All Work and No Play: The Sociology of Women and Leisure*, Milton Keynes: Open University Press.
Dyer, K.F. (1982) *Catching up the Men*, London: Junction.
Green, E., Hebron, S. and Woodward, D. (1987) *Leisure and Gender*, London: Sports Council.
Griffin, Christine, *et al*. (1982) 'Women and leisure', in J.A. Hargreaves (ed.) *Sport, Culture and Ideology*, London: Routledge & Kegan Paul.
Hargreaves, J.A. (1985) 'Playing like gentlemen while behaving like ladies', *British Journal of Sports History* 2(1), London: Frank Cass.
Jarvie, G. (1989b) 'Chariots of Fire, sporting culture and modern Scotland', *Cencrastus* 38, Edinburgh.

Johnston, S. (1985) 'Charioteers and ploughmen', in M. Auty and N. Roddick (eds) *British Cinema Now*, London: British Film Institute.

Kidd, B. (1984) 'The myth of the ancient games', in A. Tomlinson and G. Whannel (eds) *Five Ring Circus*, London: Pluto.

Neale, S. (1982) 'Chariots of Fire: images of men', *Screen* 23(3/4), London: SEFT.

Pannick, D. (1984) *Sex Discrimination in Sport*, London: Equal Opportunities Commission.

Pearson, Roberta E. (1988) 'Take me out to the ballgame: narrative structure of TV baseball', paper for ITSC Conference, London.

Theberge, N. (1981) 'A critique of critiques: radical and feminist writings on sport', *Social Forces* 60(2), Dec., USA.

Tomlinson, A. (1983) 'Ideologies of physicality, masculinity and femininity: comments on *Roy of the Rovers* and the women's fitness boom', paper presented at International Interdisciplinary Symposium on Gender, Leisure and Cultural Production, Queen's University, Kingston, Ontario, Canada, 30 September–2 October); version published in Alan Tomlinson (ed.) *Gender, Sport and Leisure: Continuities and Challenges*, Aachen: Meyer & Meyer (1997).

—— (1988) 'Situating Chariots of Fire', *British Society of Sports History Bulletin*, No. 8.

Wimbush, Erica and Talbot, Margaret (eds) (1989) *Relative Freedoms*, Milton Keynes: Open University Press.

Neil Blain, Raymond Boyle and Hugh O'Donnell

SPORT, DELIVERY SYSTEMS AND NATIONAL CULTURE

W E WISH TO DRAW into relationship here the discourses, myths and ideologies of sport with those of the culture of national feeling and identity. . . . We intend to examine specifically the interaction between satellite and terrestrial sports broadcasting in this domain. Negrine and Papathanassopoulos have argued that:

> . . . the internationalisation of television is a mosaic made up of many parts: politics, technology, business, diplomacy and industrial policy.
>
> (Negrine and Papathanassopoulos, 1991: 29)

This compound approach is welcome, as is the authors' relative caution in their formulation of what 'internationalisation' is likely to mean in practice. [. . .]

. . . [M]ost sports commentary which we can encounter on terrestrial television will, like most discourse of any kind, support a distinct compound of interests. For example, if the attribution of stability is desirable with regard to British society, then the British football game will become comprehensible through a series of 'givens' which are ahistorical and understood in an essentialist manner, such as the 'flair', 'passion' and 'inconsistency' of the Scottish football game, or the 'grit' of sportsmen from Northern England. (This is as distinct from the sheer talent of Southerners: mythically, Scots and Northerners have qualities like 'flair' and 'grit', as compensations, while the Irish labour incessantly: and the Welsh remain enigmatic). [. . .]

A possible model for the contrast, if there is one, between satellite and terrestrial sporting accounts, is that satellite broadcasting will be formed, as a result of the differences in its mix of interests, in a different mould: it may not, or need not be encumbered with quite the same ideological responsibilities of terrestrial sports broadcasting in those areas where discourse about national culture and identity is most evident. We should qualify this statement by acknowledging (a) that ideology cannot necessarily just, as it were, be left behind with a change in broadcasting organisation and (b) both terrestrial and satellite broadcasters will carry forms of sports programming in which this set of arguments barely applies.

It might even be that satellite sports broadcasting style would consciously try to eschew the sort of reconstitution of the British self and state, and the corresponding construction of various Others, which seems in particular sports programming areas to recur on terrestrial television: not least because of marketing considerations, and not least if it wishes to market cosmopolitanism. And also, as we imply above, in the altered audience conditions whereby it is plain that 'the nation' is not watching the event but rather a small minority of its citizens. [. . .]

Aspects of programming and televisual style on Sky Sports

The most important general tendency to observe in BSkyB's sports coverage is its eclecticism, an eclecticism not only with regard to the provenance of its programmes in production terms, but a partly consequent heterogeneity of styles, modes of address and discursive operation. We say 'partly consequent' because its heterogeneity is also a function of certain aspects of house style. (Incidentally, we would argue that this eclecticism is typical of satellite sports broadcasting in general.) [. . .]

. . . [A]lthough sports such as snooker and darts have, in practice, made huge inroads into sports programming, terrestrial sports output is still understood and reproduced within the national memory as structured upon certain cornerstones, many of which have national significance: Wimbledon, rugby league and rugby union cup and international matches, the Grand National, key football fixtures, and the major international competitions such as football's World Cup and the Olympic Games. [. . .]

. . . [W]e would not wish to suggest that there is no ideological coherence to satellite programming, but if there is a coherence it is the coherence principally of the marketplace rather than that of the stability of the British nation.

We shall begin by looking briefly at the coverage of Italian football, which was carried on BSkyB up until the end of the 1991/2 season, and which is now being shown for at least one season on Channel 4. (Early season Channel 4 coverage of the top Italian league *Serie A* is notably 'Gazzacentric', preoccupied both with Paul [Gascoigne] and his club Lazio at the expense of live coverage of some of the bigger Italian clubs such as Milan and Juventus.) On BSkyB, of note, first, was the fact that there was remarkably little reference at all to the presumed Italianicity of the matches. We have noted, for example, that the Scottish commentator Jock Brown would cover a whole game without any more reference to the nationality of the players than he would make if covering a Motherwell *vs* Dundee United game in Scotland.

In fact the interest was chiefly technical, and further characterised by an open admiration for the Italian game which was unqualified and wholehearted: 'wonderful skill, magnificent skill there from Berti' says Martin Tyler of an Inter Milan match and Trevor Francis adds 'what have we got, two foreigners on the pitch, Matthäus and Julio César, it's an Italian show'. This is not to say that there is never any qualification of any kind based on the strong foreign presence in *Serie A*, but the persistent references, say, to Milan's then Dutch trio or Inter Milan's Germans, which characterises some of the terrestrial output ('Chris Waddle's Marseilles', 'Gary Lineker's Barcelona', 'Jackie Charlton's Ireland', or now 'Gazza's Lazio' and 'David Platt's Juventus') seemed to be missing. (Indeed, it is generally only foreign (i.e. non-Italian) players in *Serie A* whom BSkyB's commentators seemed prone to identifying in national terms: Trevor Francis has Lothar Matthäus putting away a goal 'with an efficiency you can't credit really'.)

A discussion of how the emotional English player Paul Gascoigne may fare in the Italian league was completely free from any impingement from those discourses of British/English national interests which are never wholly absent from terrestrial coverage, suggesting in conclusion that in essence he may as yet lack the experience to co-exist with Italian referees: if anything it was an Italocentric conclusion from an English commentator.

We might say that it was the football that was being sold chiefly as a product, much as we would expect to be sold pasta or, to broaden the European perspective and avoid an uncomfortable comparison, German cars or French perfume. In fact, and in a rather refreshing way, the implication of the manner in which this Italian football programme was marketed, designed and presented is that it was uncomplicatedly evident that Italian football was a superior product. In other words, if a particular ethic dominated here, it was a consumerist one.

The title sequence could not be more different from the Pavarotti-drenched discursive paralysis of the BBC's Italia '90 sequences. There is no signifier anywhere to be found of Italian emotionalism or of any presumed characteristic of Latinity: instead, the suggestion was chiefly of exclusive access to the facts of the Italian game, with a montage of Italian football press reports acting as a visual backing for instances of skill and excitement from a selection of matches. The Italo-literacy suggested by this opening montage as well as by the commentators' very informed comments on events within the Italian football world confirm one's view of this element of BSkyB's coverage as technicist-consumerist, an intelligent connoisseur's selection from the European supermarket, from the delicatessen, as it were.

There could be no greater contrast than between this and Sky Sport's American-produced *Power Hour* of especially histrionic wrestling. The *Power Hour* is not mediated in any way for British audiences and therefore maintains a mode of address entirely suitable for a particular segment of the American audience. As conceded above, this is not without parallel on terrestrial broadcasting although (say) Channel 4's coverage of American Football is mediated for the UK audience. But the *Power Hour* is an extraordinarily American spectacle. Even by wrestling standards, this presentation is inordinately given over to showbiz values: in one bout, a glamorous 'personal assistant' of a rival promoter stalks the ringside while making an 'analysis' of the bout on the laptop computer which she carries with her. The camera and commentary are as interested in her as they are in the match. So the supermarket is a world supermarket and *Serie A* football and American wrestling are two selections.

The eclecticism of programming and the freedom of stylistic borrowing in the trailers and presentation frequently create some rather bizarre conjunctures.

A West Indies *vs* Australia cricket match is publicised by a trailer invoking a large range of clichés about West Indian life (for example heat, passion). A trailer for British rugby league football intercuts shots of the game with shots of a cheetah hunting and bringing down a gazelle, a rhinoceros charging at the camera, and two lionesses fighting: the voice over is particularly strident

Go, go, go for it!! Go for rugby league on The Sports Channel! Every Sunday evening!! Only the fittest survive in the tough, mean, world of British rugby league! The best teams, the biggest clashes . . .

The same ideological/discursive structure is invoked in relation to the selling of Scottish Cup football where Scotland's football is full of 'flair and passion', and where, again, 'survival [is] solely for the fittest'.

What these instances indicate to us is that in no sense is BSkyB consistently eschewing the sorts of deployment of traditional discourses of national or regional character familiar from terrestrial broadcasting. In fact, in this marketing context, BSkyB is reproducing them in especially vigorous form, and outdoing even the Coleman-Motson-Hill conjuncture of BBC football coverage. It's all a question of what is appropriate for the selling of particular products. Italian football is known to be very good, and does not need this kind of marketing. Scottish football is known to need marketing. The overriding principle behind the televising of both, however, is to obtain viewers in economically restricted circumstances, and this project is (relatively) unclouded by other principles.

To complicate matters a little further, much of the actual coverage as distinct from the publicising of these cricket or rugby events does not in fact significantly differ stylistically or discursively from terrestrial TV at all. The tones of Ritchie Benaud, the Australian cricket commentator, are as pervasive in the sky as they are on the BBC's own coverage and that which they import from Australia's Channel 9. The view of the game of cricket or of British rugby league from BSkyB is not in fact radically or even very different from the views of these games available on terrestrial television. So part of BSkyB's discursive mix is a familiar part. (Though as it happens, and as a result of the commentator mix as much as anything, some of the occasionally rather contentious racial innuendos which periodically seep into BBC cricket coverage at lax moments on warm uneventful days do not seem as likely to be reproduced in this context. Echoes of Empire still reverberate around BBC's Test Match coverage: cricket as seen on terrestrial television is an ideology-intensive sport.)[1]

The question of televisual style cannot be explored in any detail in this chapter, but it is worth noting that the forms of eclecticism we have identified have their parallels in, for example, the variable pace of cutting during links and between trailers and programme starts. BSkyB at times uses a fast-cutting style more reminiscent of the staccato continuity of US TV presentation than the carefully punctuated progress of terrestrial TV, but again this is not a uniform factor as it is on US television. Interestingly, while the BBC started using graphics depicting satellites around the time when that sort of technological competition was making itself felt, the BSkyB sets are less hi-tech in appearance than the one currently used, for example, in *Grandstand*, but that should require no explanation. Similarly, the approach to employing presenters and sports pundits has been a mixture of unknown faces and familiar personalities such as Sally Gunnell and Andy Gray.

That BSkyB will not fit into a pattern with regard to discursive formulations on national culture should not, of course, be surprising. That it may share certain of the discursive characteristics of duopoly sports culture is inevitable, in the sense that history and ideology are inescapable, and, furthermore, because there may in certain instances be some similarity of marketing requirements. But that BSkyB should not participate in aspects of the ideological project(s) of duopoly sports broadcasters was likely, given the relative purity of BSkyB's commercial drive, and appears to be confirmed by an examination of its products. [. . .]

. . . [I]f this is the age of satellite, in terms of audience reach it is only beginning. What is chiefly of significance in the examination of current satellite output is not its programming or its styles in themselves.

What is important, first, is that the conception of deregulation and new technology as (either positively or negatively) internationalising in the domain of cultural production is one which requires to be constantly remodified by reference to the limitations of the rupture with the historical and ideological structures of terrestrial broadcasting; and by reference to the irregular and complex effects of the market. Secondly, of significance is the way in which the existence of satellite output and its relatively substantial impact on terrestrial broadcasting in the field of sport forces us to see the latter in a new light. Thirdly, it seems worth predicting that as the post-Maastricht Europe of 1992 attempts (albeit with a degree of increasing uncertainty) to forge closer political and economic links between member states, television sport will continue to operate as an arena in which individual national identities retain important commercial and ideological functions, no matter what the future holds for satellite; and that the concept of a (post)modern satellite-borne sports geography will require further investigation.

Note

1   Murdock (1989) has argued that 'More does not mean different. It means the same ideas and images in a variety of forms and packages . . . You can consume more of what you like (providing you can afford the equipment and the subscriptions) but you are less likely to come across something unfamiliar or challenging'.

Bibliography

Murdock, G. (1989) 'Tearing Down the Wall', *New Statesman and Society*, 25 August 89.
Negrine, R. and Papathanassopoulos, S. (1991) 'The Internationalisation of Television', *European Journal of Communcation*, vol. 6.

Richard Holt and Tony Mason

SENSATIONALISM AND THE POPULAR PRESS

INSIDE STORIES AND BREATHLESS HYPERBOLE were hardly a post-war invention. The inter-war years had seen the mass press take up sport, forcing the closure of the old *Athletic News* and devoting several pages to sport each day. The popular Sundays like the *People* and the *News of the World* had four to six pages of sports reporting. In the summer the quality press had cricket to write about and the *Manchester Guardian* had Neville Cardus, whose career spanned the war and gave a new literary respectability to serious sports writing. The sports pages of the popular daily papers were still largely concerned with news-gathering, though with an increasingly gossipy and speculative twist via football columnists like Alan Hoby 'The Man Who Knows'. However, what he and others like him really knew and what their papers were prepared to print remained quite different things.

The Wolfenden Committee took evidence of the effect of the press on top-level performers in 1958.[1] Denis Compton thought no more than 10 per cent of journalists knew much about the sport they were reporting. Judy Grinham, the Olympic swimmer, said 'she was "knocked for six" when she had a bad report in a newspaper and some swimmers, especially young ones, were absolutely broken hearted'. But now she was a reporter herself 'she saw the journalist's point of view': the editors wanted a story more than constructive criticism and factual reporting. Discussing football, Bill Slater, who had played as an amateur for Blackpool and as a professional in the great Wolves team under Stan Cullis, noted the 'tremendous range of reporting ability' and stressed that 'people had to choose their newspaper according to the type of reporting they wanted'. Slater, who worked as a university lecturer in physical education, 'did not think journalists were particularly cruel to young players' and 'on the whole he felt the press did a good job'. Compton agreed and added that good publicity for a top player meant increased earnings outside the game.

The newspapers were anxious to present a respectable image of the country, covering up sexual scandal as avidly as later generations would expose it. Good behaviour was all-important and sportsmanship had to be seen to extend from the individual to the national level. National pride had to stay within the limits of decent partisanship. Patriotism rather than nationalism was the norm. Consider, for example, England's notorious football defeat at the hands of the United States in 1950. The press was very disappointed but their tone was surprisingly measured by contemporary standards. Imagine what a later generation of journalists would have done to an England team manager who was beaten by 500–1 outsiders. Walter Winterbottom did not have to face the wrath of the *Sun* and managed to stay in the job for another twelve years. Press reaction to the 6–3 defeat at home by Hungary in 1953 was mixed, 'There can be no complaints, we were outplayed . . . by a great Hungarian side,' wrote Charles Buchan in the *News Chronicle*.[2] The press debated whether England had been beaten by a new 'collective' football before deciding that the 'Merry Magyars' had learned the game from an Englishman, and so their victory was also ours.

There were, of course, some complaints. John Barrett 'deplored destructive and sensational writing' about tennis, which he put down to editors 'making mountains out of molehills'.[3] Gordon Pirie thought top athletes were caught between their governing body, which wanted to vet everything, and the press looking for exciting stories. 'A top athlete must be most careful with his words at all times, especially just before or after a race.'[4] It was a case of damned if you do and damned if you don't; if you refused to talk you were surly, if you said too much you were a 'big mouth'. All this has an oddly contemporary feel, although the press was not seen as too much of a problem by most sportsmen and women in the 1950s.

Popular sports coverage changed significantly in the sixties and has moved in a more sensational direction ever since. Coverage reached new heights. By 1980 both the *Sun* and the *Star* gave over 20 per cent of their space to sport with the *Mirror* and the *Express* not far behind with 17.36 per cent and 16.45 per cent respectively.[5] Banner headlines, colour photographs, and coverage of every major game produced a paper where the back pages stretched to the centre and sports stories, especially scandal, often got onto the front page. The tone was increasingly strident and chauvinist. When the *Daily Herald* closed in 1964 to be replaced by the *Sun*, the new tabloid announced it would have 'four rows of teeth' and would settle for nothing less than complete success. Victory at home in the 1966 World Cup fuelled vast expectations and nationalist rhetoric, driving a succession of managers out of the job under a torrent of abuse. Bobby Robson was England manager in the Thatcher years when the tide of popular chauvinism reached its height: 'ON YER BIKE ROBSON'; 'BEAT 'EM OR BEAT IT, BOBBY'; 'SENSELESS! SPINELESS! HOPELESS! or just 'PLONKER'. If England won, the rhetoric instantly went the other way with 'BOBBY'S BEAUTIES' or 'BRING ON THE ARGIES' in a self-conscious reference to the victorious Falklands War which set the tone of the decade.[6]

The *Daily Mirror*, the *Star* and the other tabloids adopted the same style and couldn't resist the chance to rake over the past affairs of 'ROMEO ROBBY'. No wonder Robson, after coming so close to the World Cup final in 1990, decided to leave the England job for a managerial career on the continent. His successor, Graham Taylor, who was thought to be 'good with the press', fared far worse. Dubbed 'Turnip' by the *Sun*, he was mercilessly ridiculed and quickly forced out after England failed to qualify for the World Cup in 1994. Glen Hoddle was a different kind of press victim, sacked for a combination of unconventional beliefs, insensitive comments about disability and, it should be said, increasingly, erratic results. Hoddle's successor, Kevin Keegan, has all the cheerful populism and national enthusiasm the tabloids expect. But they are unlikely to be any more generous should he fail to produce a winning team.

The growing internationalism of sport, especially football, has proved a blessing for sports journalists in search of a story. The papers increasingly picked up the international angle in the 1990s as European players took advantage of the Bosman ruling on the free movement of players. This was perhaps the most striking change in English football as teams like Chelsea and Arsenal fielded some of the best Italian, Dutch or French stars, all of whom had stories to tell about settling in, British football, rumours of return and so forth. This flood of foreign stars had started as a trickle of British players going abroad. Such was the smug insularity of the British that they scarcely thought of buying foreign players, even after the Hungarians and the Brazilians had shown how much better they could play the game. Scotland, in particular, was inward looking, not even recruiting from England and reluctant to recognize the achievements of the 'Anglos' – those Scots, often star players, who went to play in England. Alternately adored and reviled by the press in his native land, Denis Law was 'The King' at Old Trafford. But amongst a 'tartan' press riding the new wave of Scottish nationalism, his gifts were less fully appreciated.[7] From the 1960s England exported some of its best players, usually to Italy and usually not for long. They missed the beer, the English language, even British food. Now the pattern has been reversed with a vengeance with the press riding a ceaseless wave of speculation about new signings.

Famous foreign sportsmen and women seemed to fascinate and dismay the British press in equal measure. Tennis players, in particular, who were only in Britain for a few weeks a year became temporary celebrities as the appetite for drama and sensationalism grew. Maria Bueno and Margaret Smith had been one thing, Billy Jean demanding equal prize money and Martina Navratilova as a lesbian icon were another. In the men's game it was not so much the robotic consistency of Borg which caught the headlines as the arrogant gamesmanship of McEnroe and his refusal to 'play the game'. John McEnroe took up a lot of space in the tabloids and the quality press in the 1980s. 'A brat' he may have been but a brat that made good copy.

The nineties saw a new development in serious sports writing. Sport and culture would no longer be treated as antithetical. Nick Hornby's *Fever Pitch*, a Cambridge graduate's account of his obsession with Arsenal, proved to be one of the books of the decade. There had always been intellectuals who liked sport but now it became commonplace, even fashionable, to say so. There was a steady expansion in the space given to sport in the broadsheet press, more serious discussion and features – and more tabloid-style gossip as well. Women began to break into the male bastion of sports reporting just as girls and women more generally were drawn to 'the new football'. The quality Sunday papers were always on the lookout for a new angle. The *Observer* packed off Booker Prize-winning novelist, literary critic and self-confessed football virgin, A.S. Byatt, to Euro 96. The *Independent* did the same to Germaine Greer, who, 'bathed in testosterone', was much taken with Gazza's inclination to run after a ball 'with the unflagging enthusiasm of a puppy'.[8]

'Gazza' had been of particular interest to intellectuals for some time. His tears in the 1990 World Cup were analysed by the leading social theorist Anthony Giddens whilst the poet, biographer and football fan Ian Hamilton devoted most of an issue of the literary magazine *Granta* to him.[9] Not much of this was likely to have touched Gazza himself whose Geordie philistinism was part of his fascination. Gazza, in fact, took up a great deal of the press in the 1990s from his injuries to his hair cuts, from drinking to domestic violence. *Hello* magazine paid a fortune for the exclusive rights to photograph his wedding reception, which included a picture of the man himself in a gold morning suit toasting the bride from a gleaming urinal. The tabloids were resentful about being excluded, which made their subsequent denunciations of his wife-beating all the more vehement. Their collective indignation was instructive. Sensationalism had its constructive side. Journalists would no longer cover up for sportsmen, who had to take responsibility for their public and private lives. Those like Tony Adams, who succeeded in changing themselves, were the new media heroes: the prodigal sons and reformed sinners. A lesser player's battle with drugs or gambling made better copy than Alan Shearer painting the garden fence.

The new sensationalism, of course, was not confined to sport. It was part of a much wider shift in popular culture, which finally shrugged off the self-improving legacy of the past. The popular Sunday papers had long pandered to the public's fascination with sex and violence like the Victorian 'penny dreadfuls' before them. But from the 1960s the popular dailies went consciously downmarket and their sports coverage went with them. Sports journalism went in two directions: there was an impressive expansion of lively and serious writing about sport, mostly from the 'quality' press, and a headlong rush into scandal in the 'middle market' papers like the *Mail* and *Express* as well as the tabloids. Like the quality press they were no longer able to rely on match reports to sell papers. Sensing the enormous public interest in the people behind the performances, the mass press threw itself into a frenzy of speculation, gossip and sensationalism. Six or eight pages of sport, usually half on football, became the norm and this could expand to fill half the space in the tabloids for big events. A 'good guy' like Gary Lineker could grab the headlines as the nation gathered round to support their striker and his wife when their young son had a serious operation. But it was family break-up rather than family values that the public really wanted – or so the popular press believed. There was nothing like a deserted wife and child pictured alongside her ex-husband frolicking in the surf with a new bikini-clad 'companion' to sell papers.[10]

Sports 'hacks' were a cynical bunch, notably dismissive of anything 'arty' or pretentious, both liberators and destroyers, pushing back the limits of what could and could not be said in public. It was a popular Sunday paper, the *People*, which exposed a gambling and match-fixing scandal in English football in 1965. Of course, there was a vast amount of ordinary reporting, too, especially in the regional and local press. *Match of the Day* only carried the highlights of a few games and even Sky can only cover a fraction of all the football being played. Plenty of fans still like a familiar journalist's account of a game to compare with their own impressions of how the team performed in televised highlights. The sensational and the mundane sit happily side by side. The *News of the World*, the biggest selling newspaper in Britain, cleverly packaged its sports coverage to put big national stories alongside factual regional match reports, often written by former local stars. Jackie Milburn, the hero of post-war Tyneside, wrote a north-east football column for the *News of the World* for twenty years after his retirement. Geordies were less interested in what was said than who was saying it. Press columns, ghosted or not, were a powerful source of myth-making, mixing national stories with local legends.

Current sports coverage ranges from the probing literary article to be found in the weekend sports supplements of the broadsheets – a new feature of good sports writing prompted by the growing middle-class interest in football – to the 'the lad done bad' stories of sex, violence and scandal juxtaposed with ads for sex aids, chat-lines and pornography in the tabloids. The unreconstructed model of aggressive, promiscuous masculinity is alive and well and its most salacious outlet is simply called '*The Daily Sport*'. However, this 'socusoap' with its 'spot the brawl' and unending tales of laddish nights on the town co-exists with a vast amount of serious comment and analysis. The upsurge in new sports magazines, bulging from the shelves, each more glossy than the last, cleverly blends the two angles, appealing to the fan and the man, from complex technical pieces to the picaresque life of a Robbie Fowler who 'fancies any glamorous woman on telly "as long as they've got a fanny and breathe."' Hymns to 'clubbing' and consumption – varieties of Ferrari, BMW or Jaguar are an important part of the story – now play a major part in writing about sport, not so much as a performance, more as a way of life.

Notes

1   Minute of Oral Evidence to the Wolfenden Committee, 12 May 1959.
2   Cited in Stephen K. Kelly, *Back Page Football: A Century of Newspaper Coverage* (Queen Anne, London, 1988), p. 107; we are grateful to Jeff Hill for his insights into England–Hungary in 1953–4.
3   Wolfenden Committee, 12 May 1959.
4   G. Pirie, *Running Wild* (W.H. Allen, London, 1961), p. 10.
5   Cited in J. Hargreaves, *Sport, Power and Culture* (Cambridge, Polity Press, 1986), p. 139.
6   S. Wagg, 'Playing the past: the media and the England football team', in J. Williams and S. Wagg, *British Football and Social Change: Getting into Europe* (Leicester University Press, Leicester, 1991) pp. 230–2.
7   R. Holt, 'King across the border: Dennis Law and Scottish football', in Grant Jarvie and Graham Walker (eds), *Scottish Sport in the Making of the Nation: Ninety Minute Patriots* (Leicester University Press, Leicester, 1994), pp. 62–3.
8   *The Observer*, 30 June 1996; *The Independent*, 28 June 1996.
9   Ian Hamilton, 'Gazza Agonistes', in *Granta* 45 (Penguin, London, 1993).
10 Stuart Cosgrove, *Hampden Babylon: Sex and Scandal in Scottish Football*, is a joyous parody of football and the tabloids, which influenced D. Campbell, P. May and A. Shields, *The Lad Done Bad: Sex, Sleaze and Scandal in English Football* (Penguin, London, 1996).

Jennifer Smith Maguire

BODY LESSONS
Fitness publishing and the cultural production of the fitness consumer

[. . .]

IEXAMINED A SELECTION of health-education-oriented and consumer-oriented US exercise manuals from the late 1970s to late 1990s, comparing successive editions of the same manual and different manuals from both perspectives.[1] In part, I was interested in the differences (or the lack thereof) between texts that are more oriented towards health education (such as the manuals of the American Heart Association, AHA, and the American College of Sports Medicine, ACSM) and those which are more commercial (including the manuals published by lifestyle magazines, such as *Self* and *Men's Health*). Overall, the commonalities far outweighed the differences. [. . .] [The discussion focuses on three themes that] recur over the years across different exercise texts regarding the promotion of particular attitudes towards the body: as a consumer project, as a source of calculable rewards and as a motivational problem.

The boom in fitness publishing

Since the 1968 publication of Kenneth Cooper's *Aerobics*, fitness texts have become consumer products in their own right. *Aerobics* spent 28 weeks on *The New York Times* bestseller list (Justice, 1998) and Cooper followed it with several other bestsellers, including *Aerobics for Women* and *The New Aerobics*, which went through 30 printings during the 1970s. While not the first manual on exercise and its benefits, Cooper's 1968 book marked the start of a wave of fitness publishing (Barbato, 1988) that has continued since (Dahlin, 2001). In an introduction to a later book, Cooper reflected:

When I introduced aerobics as a new concept of exercise, my chief aim was to counteract the problems of lethargy and inactivity which are so widely prevalent in our American population. Therefore, my first book was mainly a motivational book, but also it was an attempt to encourage people to examine more closely the benefits to be gained from regular exercise.

(Cooper, 1970: 5)

The service role of fitness texts is thus made clear: in addition to information about the exercises themselves, the consumer requires education in the benefits of exercise, and in the motivational strategies for adopting fitness as a regular lifestyle activity.

The production of advice about exercise and fitness has increased since the late 1970s. By 1979, when *Self* was launched as the first fitness magazine for women, fashion and women's serials such as *Mademoiselle*, *Vogue* and *McCall's* already had regular fitness and exercise columns. *Shape* joined *Self*, in the women's fitness magazine category in 1981, the same year that Jane Fonda published her *Workout Book*, the ultimate exercise bestseller (Justice, 1998). Fonda's later books and exercise videos also sold in millions – 23 percent of the 15 million exercise videos sold by 1987 were by Fonda (Kagan and Morse, 1988). Other bestsellers in the late 1970s and early 1980s included the running books of James Fixx and George Sheehan, men's workout books by Charles Hix and Arnold Schwarzenegger's biography (Justice, 1998). Popular magazines also targeted men, with *Men's Fitness* and *Men's Health* both launched in 1988.

The rising discretionary incomes and niche marketing of the 1990s created the conditions for the further intensification of the production of lifestyle publishing and periodicals. According to the Magazine Publishers of America, between 1988 and 2000 the number of magazine titles more than doubled, while the number of health and fitness magazines nearly tripled.[2] The four bestselling fitness magazines – *Men's Health*, *Shape*, *Self* and *Fitness* – each has paid circulations of more than a million readers.[3] Hundreds of health and fitness titles enter the publishing market each year. In an article in the publishing trade journal, *Publishers Weekly*, the marketing opportunities of fitness are spelled out for authors and editors:

Consumers have a ferocious appetite for advice telling them what to do, how to act, what to eat and what to shun in order to feel good, spruce up their health and shed uncomely pounds. In fact, the hunger is so great that publishers scramble to sate it with books promising, if not the moon, at least a celestial body and mind.

(Dahlin, 2001: 24)

Overall the amount of press coverage devoted to physical fitness has increased more than sixfold in the US since the mid-1980s.[4]

Understanding the boom in fitness publishing entails identifying the primary fitness consumers. Not surprisingly, consumers of exercise texts – and fitness goods more broadly – are overwhelmingly middle class, with a relatively high proportion of professional and managerial workers. Of the two leading fitness magazines in 2002, approximately 27 percent of *Shape* and 28 percent of *Men's Health* readers were professionals or managers, with average household incomes between approximately $57,500 (for *Shape* readers) and $67,500 (for *Men's Health*).[5] As well, 65 percent of US health club members have household incomes of $50,000 or more. Health club industry research shows that members work more overtime than average (Epaminondas, 2002), suggesting a high proportion of professionals and managers, as these occupations are most likely to work longer work weeks (Jacobs and Gerson, 1998). Furthermore, women outnumber men (nearly two to one in 1988) as the consumers of exercise, health and diet books (Wood, 1988). Although health club membership is relatively even with respect to gender (with women composing 52 percent of all members), the rate of growth of women's memberships surpasses that of men's.[6]

Reflecting particular occupational requirements, attitudes and control over economic, cultural and social forms of capital, different social groups expect different capacities from the body and, consequently, demand different rewards and benefits from the fields in which they operate (Bourdieu, 1984). The growth of the fitness field – and fitness publishing – is inextricable from the tastes and preferences of the groups driving consumption. In particular, there are four areas of 'elective affinity' (Bourdieu, 1984: 241) between the fitness field and its consumers – middle and new middle class men and (especially) women.

First, fitness and fitness education are geared towards the middle class who are disposed to regarding the body as a project to be managed and improved through education and self-improvement as an integral aspect of self-identity and social mobility (Bourdieu, 1984; Crawford 1984; Featherstone, 1982, 1987; Wynne, 1998). This enterprising, investment-oriented attitude towards the body is especially marked for those whose work and social position explicitly depend on bodily appearance and presentation. Since the late 1960s, changes in the labour market have created a new middle class – a large group of people whose work requires performative and appearance management skills. These 'new' professional, managerial, technical, clerical and sales occupations occur within the service-producing sector, and include such individuals as financial brokers, estate agents, public relations and advertising associates, tourism and recreational directors, and other personal and professional service workers (Bourdieu, 1984: 359; Wynne, 1998). The more one's livelihood depends on appearance and personality – on one's 'body-for-others' – the more the individual has at stake in cultivating the body as an enterprise (cf. Bourdieu, 1984; Featherstone, 1987).

Second, the changing social, political and athletic roles of women created a market of consumers for whom physical development was part of a new, empowered lifestyle. In general, women occupy a special position in the post-1960s consumer market in that their large-scale entrance into the labour market – and its higher echelons – marked their emergence as a new breed of consumers. White, middle class women in particular were consuming not as the family provisioners, but as self-directed consumers, investing in themselves because they had the means to do so, and often without competing family obligations, given the postponement of marriage and childbirth. When they did have families, women were often still in the labour market: the percentage of dual-income families has risen steadily over the past 30 years (Jacobs and Gerson, 1998). Since the late 1970s, magazines such as *Self* and *Working Woman* have offered women advice on what to do with their new-found financial, social and political independence. One avenue of personal improvement was physical: buoyed by the feminist discourse of empowerment and legislation such as Title IX, magazines and manuals promoted physical exercise as a way to realize, literally, the goal of empowerment (without necessarily taking on board the complex identity of political activism).

Third, the genre of fitness publishing dovetailed with trends in health care and health promotion at both ends of the spectrum of political power. At the grass-roots level, advocates of demedicalization criticized medical professionals' expanding authority and intervention in everyday life (Fox, 1997; Goldstein, 1992), and called for increasing 'medical self-competence' (Crawford, 1980: 374). In much the same way that the symbolic association between muscles and political empowerment has been marketed to women, fitness has been promoted as a widespread mode of empowerment, through which people – men and women, young, and (especially) old – can take control of their bodies and health. The interest of individuals in (re)claiming control over their health care has also been reinforced at the level of health economics, which have been characterized since the 1970s by a discourse of personal responsibility for risk reduction and the 'duty to be well' (Greco, 1993; see also Crawford, 1979; Ingham,1985; Petersen, 1997). Exercise texts are part of an expanding range of therapeutic and educative devices, such as talk shows and self-help books, that inundate us with advice on how best to care for and improve ourselves.

Finally, the increasing production of fitness advice is linked to the expansion in choices of consumer products and services, which have rapidly multiplied since the early 1970s. For example, in 1972 when Nike began selling sneakers, consumers had few choices for exercise equipment and apparel. In contrast, today's consumer chooses from hundreds of new sneaker models each year, creating a $13.1 billion athletic shoe market in the US (Euromonitor, 2001). As the fitness consumer faces an increasing number of choices within a single product category, he or she increasingly relies on consumer guides, such as product reviews in *Shape* or *Consumer Reports* or the preferences of style leaders such as sports stars and celebrities. The increasing range of consumer choices, then, is accompanied by the production of an array of mutually referential educative and advisory texts that repeatedly remind consumers of their options to purchase.

In summary, two broad social currents coincided to create the necessary conditions for fitness as a lifestyle and leisure industry focused upon the care and improvement of the body . . . the interest of the new middle class and women in self-improvement, empowerment, and health education, and the expanding consumer choices available to them. [. . .]

Consuming bodies

[. . .] Fitness magazines include excerpts from new exercise manuals (sometimes written by their columnists), and profile 'celebrity' personal trainers. Illustrations for exercise articles include 'shot on location' references, thereby promoting both the particular health club setting, and clubs in general as the sites of fitness. Exercise manuals acknowledge the donation of props and space by sporting goods manufacturers and health clubs, akin to the strategies of product placement in Hollywood films. For example, the acknowledgements page of *Self's Better Body Book* (by the publishers of *Self* magazine) reads much like a shopping list:

> Special thanks to: Crunch [health club chain] . . . Weights and Weightbench from the Gym Source, 800-GYM-SOURCE. . . . All the athletic footwear and apparel . . . provided courtesy of LADY FOOT LOCKER. . . . [T]o find

the Lady Foot Locker store nearest you, call 1–800–877–5239. All cosmetics and skincare courtesy of ALMAY. Recommended products. . . . Lipcolor: Stay Smooth Anti-Chap Lipcolor with SPF 25 in Healthy.

(Billings, 1998: 112)

This example of the marketing function of such publishing highlights – in extreme fashion – the ways in which advice about fitness includes the mapping of an entire universe of consumer choices, from 'Healthy' lipbalm to the necessity of the appropriate club and apparel.

Even the AHA, which reassures its readers that fitness does not require a 'personal trainer, fancy gym, or strict diet' (1997: 135), acknowledges the role of consumption:

We'll say it again: All you need to fit in fitness is a comfortable pair of walking shoes. So why spend money on fitness equipment? In a word, *variety*. Variety is not only the spice of life, it's what keeps physical activity *fun*. Boredom, on the other hand, is one of the most common reasons people give for quitting regular exercise.

(American Heart Association, 1997: 96)

The field of fitness is situated within a culture of expectations for fun, immediacy, novelty and variety. Fitness educators, producers and promoters are thus constrained not only by the tastes of consumers, but also by the larger culture of instant gratification. [. . .]

Calculating bodies

[. . .] In the men's workout manual, *Stronger Faster*, for example, health is not only a benefit of exercise, but a quantifiable, predictable profit:

Unlike shortcuts that trim mere seconds or minutes from our crazed schedules, regular exercise . . . actually *adds* quality and years to your life. How much? If a 30-year-old, two-packs-a-day smoker with high cholesterol kicked the smoking habit, changed his diet, and started exercising regularly, he'd add 8 to 10 years to his life . . .

(Kaufman and Kirchheimer, 1997: 24)

[. . .]

Motivating bodies

Much of the content of exercise magazines and manuals addresses the difficult transition, for many participants, from reading about to 'doing' fitness. Managing the body and achieving its calculated rewards faces three basic obstacles. First, the physiological inertia of the body means that change is slow and must be kept up. The body is not only slow to change, but also prone to lose ground through ageing, injury and inactivity. Second, the decline of physical education and increase in sedentary forms of work means that exercise is an increasingly *uncommon* everyday habit; becoming fit requires overcoming the resilience of behavioural patterns of inactivity. Third, exercise involves a lot of work if the participant is to see results, which poses a challenge to an industry that sells fitness as *leisure*. Exercise competes with other (less strenuous and sweaty) leisure activities.

Exercise manuals commonly highlight motivation and persistence as obstacles for fitness consumers. For example, the ACSM warns:

> So now you're motivated to begin a fitness program to improve your fitness, be healthier and live longer. What's the ultimate secret of success? In a word, persistence! . . . Unfortunately, when it comes to lifestyle changes such as exercise, too many people think that it's an all-or-none phenomenon.
> (American College of Sports Medicine, 1998: 13)

A similar warning sets the tone in popular, commercial manuals. For example:

> We don't want you to become a fitness statistic. The fact is, among people who start an exercise program, half quit within eight weeks. *Fitness for Dummies* will give you the knowledge to make sure that *you* stick with fitness for the rest of your life.
> (Schlosberg and Neporent, 1996: 2)

[. . .]

Conclusion

Central to the development and institutionalization of the fitness field has been the cultural production of consumers equipped with an informed awareness of their fitness choices and resources. Fitness texts may thus be viewed as a genre of sensibility manuals and manner guides, which educate individuals in the problems and solutions of social status and consumer lifestyle. The body – its health and appearance – is presented as an enterprise, and lifestyle endorsed as the pattern of investment. Undertaken through vigilant monitoring and continual body work, the success of self-improvement and self-care falls upon the shoulders of the individual.

However, as individuals increasingly bear the responsibility of minimizing their health risks, the quality of population health is deteriorating in significant ways. The seeming paradox in the US of a booming fitness industry and soaring rates of inactivity and obesity is partly resolved when we consider that, by and large, fitness texts provide an education in how to make *lifestyle* decisions more so than *health* decisions. Moreover, these texts represent health and exercise as rational outcomes, presuming that individuals, if provided with sufficient knowledge, will choose to exercise more. However, inactivity and obesity are less the outcomes of rational or irrational actions than they are the 'normal' responses to living in an environment of suburbs and commuting, desk jobs, fast food and television remote controls (cf. Crister, 2001; Farley and Cohen, 2001). Increasing medical self-awareness does little to address the structural conditions that favour inactivity for a significant portion of the population.

Exercise texts supply specific information on physical activity, but also claim to provide the objective, rational solutions to the problems of everyday life: how to choose between the multiplying options of the market; how to optimize your chances of success and happiness, and reduce the risks of failure and disease; how to shape a lifestyle that both conforms and stands out, earning both acceptance and distinction (cf. Rose, 1996). Through the fitness field, our bodies are reflected back to us through the lens of products and services, and consumption is promoted as the primary arena in which we make and remake our bodies. Through consumption we are 'free' to choose, to create and control ourselves – rewards that may be lacking in the world of work. The fitness field, in offering solutions to the concerns of health, empowerment, appearance management and self-improvement, produces the sphere of leisure as a realm of freedom to make the most of oneself, a lesson that is, in many ways, a costly one.

Notes

1   I examined five exercise manuals from the health-education orientation (the American College of Sports Medicine's *ACSM Fitness Book* (1992 and 1998 edns), American Heart Association's *Fitting in Fitness* (1997) and *Fitness Facts* (1989) and its 1992 2nd edn, *The Health Fitness Handbook*); and eight from the more commercially oriented perspective (*The Gold's Gym Weight Training Book* (1978), *Jane Fonda's Workout Book* (1981), *Nautilus Fitness for Women* (1983), *Gym Psych* (1986), *Fitness for Dummies* (1996 and 2000 edns), *Stronger Faster* (from the publishers of *Men's Health* magazine, 1997), and *Self* magazine's 1998 *Self's Better Body Book*).
2   From the Magazine Publishers of America website: http://www.magazine.org.
3   The magazine industry research group, Mediamark Research Inc. (MRI) provides the 2002 circulation data for *Men's Health* (1.69 million), *Shape* (1.68 million), *Self* (1.55 million) and *Fitness* (1.18 million). MRI research information is available on their website at http://www.mriplus.com.
4   The increase in the amount of press coverage is based on a subject search for 'physical fitness' in ProQuest, a content database of magazines and newspapers from the early 1970s. Although imperfect as a measure of press content – particularly given the addition of titles in 1986 – there is a consistent increase in the number of physical fitness 'features'. The number of features rose from 25 in 1980 to 63 (1985), 114 (1986), 331 (1990), 403 (1995), and 717 (2000), a six-fold increase between 1986 and 2000.
5   Readership data from a personal interview with a *Shape* advertising associate, Jan. 2002, and from the *Men's Health* press kit, 2002.
6   Health club industry statistics regarding membership demographics (including income and gender) may be found on the website of the International Health Racquet and Sportsclub Asociation, IHRSA, at http://www.ihrsa.com.

References

American College of Sports Medicine (1992) *ACSM Fitness Book*, Champaign, IL: Human Kinetics.
American College of Sports Medicine (1998) *ACSM Fitness Book*, 2nd edn. Champaign, IL: Human Kinetics.

American Heart Association (1997) *Fitting in Fitness*, New York: Random House.

Barbato, J. (1988) 'Small Waists, Big Sales', *Publishers Weekly* (25 March): 16–24.

Billings, L. (1998) *Self's Better Body Book*, New York: Condé Nast Books.

Bourdieu, P. (1984) *Distinction: A Social Critique of the Judgment of Taste*, Cambridge, MA: Harvard University Press.

Bourdieu, P. and Wacquant, L. (1992) *An Invitation to Reflexive Sociology*, Chicago: University of Chicago Press.

Cooper, K.H. (1970) *The New Aerobics*, New York: Bantam Books.

Crawford, R. (1979) 'Individual Responsibility and Health Politics in the 1970ss', in S. Reverby and D. Rosner (eds) *Health Care in America: Essays in Social History*, Philadelphia: Temple University Press.

Crawford, R. (1980) 'Healthism and the Medicalization of Everyday Life', *International Journal of Health Services* 10: 365–88.

Crawford, R. (1984) 'A Cultural Account of "Health": Control, Release, and the Social Body', in J.B. McKinlay (ed.) *Issues in the Political Economy of Health Care*, New York: Tavistock.

Crister, G. (2001) 'Let Them Eat Fat: The Heavy Truths about American Obesity', *Harper's Magazine* (March): 41–7.

Dahlin, R. (2001) 'Holistic Rules the Day', *Publishers Weekly* (26 Nov.): 24–32.

Epaminondas, G. (2002) 'Find Home, Sweet Home, at the New Haute Gym', *The New York Times* (28 April): IX, 1–2.

Euromonitor (2001) *Sports Equipment in the USA*, Euromonitor Global Market Information Database, retrieved from http://www.euromonitor.com

Farley, T. and Cohen D. (2001) 'Fixing a Fat Nation', *Washington Monthly* (Dec.): 23–9.

Featherstone, M. (1982) 'The Body in Consumer Culture', *Theory, Culture and Society* 2: 18–33.

Featherstone, M. (1987) 'Lifestyle and Consumer Culture', *Theory, Culture and Society* 4: 55–70.

Fox, R.C. (1997) 'The Medicalization and Demedicalization of American Society', in P. Conrad (ed.) *The Sociology of Health and Illness: Critical Perspectives*, 5th edn, New York: St Martin's Press.

Goldstein, M. (1992) *The Health Movement: Promoting Fitness in America*, New York: Twayne.

Greco, M. (1993) 'Psychosomatic Subjects and the "Duty to Be Well": Personal Agency within Medical Rationality', *Economy and Society* 22: 357–72.

Ingham, A.G. (1985) 'From Public Issue to Personal Trouble: Well-Being and the Fiscal Crisis of the State', *Sociology of Sport Journal* 2: 43–55.

Jacobs, J.A. and Gerson, K. (1998) 'Who are the Overworked Americans?', *Review of Social Economy* 56: 442–59.

Justice, K.L. (1998) *Bestseller Index: All Books, Publishers Weekly and the New York Times through 1990*, Jefferson, NC: McFarland & Co.

Kagan, E. and Morse, M. (1988) 'The Body Electronic. Aerobic Exercise on Video: Women's Search for Empowerment and Self-Transformation', *Drama Review* 32(4): 164–80.

Kaufman, B.P. and Kirchheimer, S. (1997) *Stronger Faster: Workday Workouts that Build Maximum Muscle in Minimum Time*, Emmaus, PA: Rodale Press.

Petersen, A. (1997) 'Risk, Governance and the New Public Health', in A. Petersen and R. Bunton (eds) *Foucault, Health and Medicine*, London: Routledge.

Rose, N. (1996) *Inventing our Selves: Psychology, Power, and Personhood*, Cambridge: Cambridge University Press.
Schlosberg, S. and Neporent, L. (1996) *Fitness for Dummies*, Foster City, CA: IDG Books.
Wood, L. (1988) 'Fitness Book Purchasers', *Publishers Weekly* (25 March): 25.
Wynne, D. (1998) *Leisure, Lifestyle and the New Middle Class: A Case Study*, London: Routledge.

Toby Miller, Geoffrey Lawrence, Jim McKay and David Rowe

GLOBAL SPORT MEDIA

Mediated sports cultures

SPORTS REPORTING IN the print and electronic media is deeply reliant on imaging the body. Still photography provides a sense of 'having-been-there' (Barthes, 1977), often through minute attention to the bodies of athletes. Photographic presentations of sporting bodies are largely limited to rigorous motion (during competition) and inertia (for example, at a medal ceremony). The latter image carries most efficiently the idea of the nation. For many spectators, the medal ceremony at major international events like the summer Olympic Games epitomizes national identification and affect. Such rituals are tableaux of bodily dispositions. The athletes, their bodies draped in the colours and insignia of nation and corporation, are led to the ceremony by a functionary. The different heights of the blocks on which they stand spatially signify hierarchy. They bend to receive their medals as in a military service, then turn their gaze to their national flags, also hierarchically arranged, while the national anthem of the winning athlete/team reinforces visual supremacy with aural presence. Apart from flags fluttering in the breeze, the moment is still. At this point, athletes frequently cry – moved perhaps by a sense of individual and, heavily imputed by television and radio commentary, national achievement and responsibility. The stately nature of the ceremony demands that spectators and viewers be serious. It is not unusual for patriotic viewers at home to stand for their national anthem, disciplined, as Foucault (1977) argues, most effectively not by external repression but through externally induced and internally accepted discourses of the social self. If tears well up in their eyes, this discourse of nation has become powerful enough to produce involuntary physiological responses in those subject to it.

National mythologies prosper when internal fissures – class, gender, race, ethnicity, locality, age, sexuality, and so on – are submerged. The risk of displaying differences and divisions to a global audience, rather than asserting the existence of a unified nation, makes the medal ceremony and other less formal aspects of major sporting events subject to strict official control over communication in all its forms — verbal and non-verbal, abstract, and corporeal. Athletes are pressured by national sports committees and media organizations (especially those who have paid for privileged access to them) not to be controversial about issues 'back home' — to preserve the illusion of the united nation for the duration of the event. The IOC, state-licensed and -funded national sports bodies, and the sports market's lucrative sponsorship and endorsement contracts, are decisive in disciplining athletes. The sporting body's marketability is significantly, but not exclusively, influenced by its degree of political quiescence. Race, gender, and sexuality also have a substantial impact on its place in the international cultural economy of sport. We shall examine now the vast and complex infrastructure that is hidden behind these sports tableaux of winners and losers.

Modern sport and the media developed simultaneously and symbiotically, supplying each other with the necessary resources for development: capital, audiences, promotion, and content. The sports media emerged out of a need, first, for the reporting of sports information through the print media and, later, through presentation of sports events via the electronic media (Rowe, 1992a, 1992b; Rowe and Stevenson, 1995). In Britain and Australia, print sports journalism developed from notices about the time and place of forthcoming local sports events, match descriptions, results, and, rather quaintly, the hospitality (usually by 'the ladies') afforded to visiting players (Brown, 1996). As sport became increasingly professional and commodified, it did not disappear from the local print media, but became secondary — even in provincial newspapers — to national and international sport (Rowe, 1999). This progressive detachment of sport and place was first supplemented and then accelerated by radio and television. National public broadcasting organizations like the British Broadcasting Corporation (BBC), the Australian Broadcasting Commission (later renamed a Corporation), and the CBC used such major sporting occasions as the FA Cup Final, the Melbourne Cup horse race, and the Stanley Cup play-offs, to develop outside-broadcast techniques and to engage in state-sanctioned processes of nation-building (Gruneau and Whitson, 1993; Hargreaves, 1986; Haynes, 1999; Whannel, 1992). Once the nation could be reached through the public and commercial sports media (Wilson, 1998), its boundaries could be exceeded as those media carried the nation to distant and dispersed sports events, further building a sense of national identity by encouraging readers, listeners, and viewers to support their national representatives in international sporting competitions.

There has been a dramatic shift in the nature of world television over the past decades. It has been transformed from a comparatively scarce resource to a common one in most parts of the world, moving from a predominantly nation-based and state-run medium towards internationalism and privatization. The global fashion for neoliberalism has: (a) cut down cross-ownership regulations (encouraging capitalists to invest in various media); (b) reduced public-sector budgets (drawing labour, product development, and technological initiative to profit-centred services); (c) opened up terrestrial TV to international capital (undercutting local production); and (d) attacked the idea of public broadcasting as elitist (blurring distinctions between education and entertainment) and inefficient (crowding out investment in the private sector).

Sport has been crucial to these recent developments. As the idea of a universal service that provides broad coverage of news and drama is displaced by all-entertainment networks, sport turns into a cheap source of hours and hours of TV time. At the truly expensive, top end of TV sport, it offers a method of enticing viewers to make the massive monetary and technological shift to digital television (thereby rendering consumers' personal archives obsolete and making them guinea-pigs in the search for economies of scale) by showing favoured sports only on digital systems. France's Canal+ estimates that 40% of its subscribers pay their monthly fees purely to watch soccer (Williams, 1998: M3; Williams 1999: 104). In 1999, the rights to cover European soccer on television cost over US$2 billion as part of this enticement (Croci and Ammirante, 1999: 500).

The IOC (n.d.) proclaims television as 'the engine that has driven the growth of the Olympic movement'. Just as shifts in capitalism are associated with new technology (early nineteenth-century national capitalism and steam, late nineteenth-century imperialism and electricity, twentieth-century multinational capital and electronics: Jameson, 1996: 3) so we might write a history of sport connected to technology – wire reports and the radio describing play across the world from the mid-twentieth century and television spreading cricket, soccer, and the Olympics since the 1960s, communicating ideologies of nationalism and the commodity. At Sydney 2000, not only was the internet popular, but TV placed moving images of Olympic winners from seconds before into commercials. The satellite and digital era promises to erase and rewrite relations of time and space in sport once more. This latter-day profit-making targets audiences defined and developed as part of nation-building by public services.

From the BBC's beginnings in the 1920s, its distinctively public mission has been to unite the nation through live coverage of sport. Quality control in early radio times even included a visually disabled person alongside the commentators who could vouch for the vividness of description (Crook, 1998: 85–86). At the same time, the BBC's payment of £1,500 to telecast the 1948 London Olympics set in train an entirely new relationship between sport and the audiovisual media; a precedent that has grown to consume the resources of its originator ('Sport and Television', 1996). Half a century later, the BBC's 1998 decision to commit vast resources to digitalization caused it to lose the rights to cover English international cricket, leading to Cabinet discussion and public protest. The choice between technological upgrading and a traditional part of the national service was painful. In earlier times, it would not have *been* a choice – both innovation and national service would have been funded from tax revenue.

Sport has long been at the leading edge of TV and technology. When the Communications Satellite Corporation broadcast the 1964 Olympics, a new era began (Kang, 1988) – the very name embracing the technological and the commercial as inseparable technical and social relations. Expansion has continued apace. The number of TV hours watched globally tripled between 1979 and 1991, while more than half the 30 billion people who watched the 1990 men's World Cup did so from Asia, never a football power. The 32 billion viewers of the 1994 event spanned 188 nations, and the 1996 Olympic Games drew 35 billion. The third most significant event is the Commonwealth Games, which draws 500 million viewers. US audiences for NBC's Atlanta Olympics coverage were offered more advertising time than game time, while Hollywood factors in a quadrennial overseas box-office disaster during the weeks when people stay away from the cinema and watch the men's World Cup. And the move into TV time is massive. The NBA is now seen on television in 206 countries across 128 networks and 42 languages, and has its own cable and satellite network ready for digital interactivity – NBA.com TV. Its start-up operation, the Women's National Basketball Association (WNBA), was broadcast in 17 languages across 125 nations in 1999, its third season of existence. In baseball, MLB is seen in 215 countries. The 1999–2000 NFL season was telecast in 24 languages to 182 countries. Fans in Austria, the Netherlands, and Singapore, where no US football games are broadcast on Sundays, were offered webcasts from that season via broad-band. The NHL is also seen around the world, and has websites in France, Finland, Norway, Sweden, Germany, Japan, Slovakia, Russia, the UK, the Czech Republic, and Poland (Herman and McChesney, 1997: 39; Smith, 1997: 114; FIFA, n.d.; Muda, 1998: 223; McAllister, 1997; Pickard, 1997; Wise, 1999; Burton, 1999; 'New Television Deals', 1999; 'International Broadcasters', 1999; 'NFL Full', 1999; Dempsey, 1999a, 1999b; 'Country-by-Country', 1999). By contrast, Australian Rules Football's international circulation is mostly on highlights shows that are given away to networks ('TV Times', 1999).

No wonder that Rupert Murdoch refers to TV sport as News Corporation's 'battering ram' into new markets, while telecommunications corporation TCI calls it 'the universal glue for global content' (quoted in Herman and McChesney, 1997: 75–76). But . . . [n]ational and regional identifications bring into question the 'benefits' of new technology and global capital. Even neoclassical economists have argued against satellite exclusivity, on the ground that 'key sporting events, like the Olympics, the World Cup and the FA Cup . . . generate positive social network externalities' when they are universally available. Folks talk to one another about the shared experience of viewing, which in turn binds them socially, and this 'social capital' may be lost if only a privileged few received transmission of such events (Boardman and Hargreaves-Heap, 1999: 168, 178).

The state has been bombarded by complaints about the takeover of sport by private networks. Citizens regard national sport as a public good (or at least one for which they only pay profit-making entities indirectly). In Germany, for example, it is likely that parts of the next two World Cups of soccer will only be available locally on pay TV, after the European Broadcasting Union, a consortium of public networks, was outbid by Kirch and Sporis in 1996, despite offering US$ 1.8 billion (Hils, 1997; 'Sport and Television', 1996; Boehm, 1998a), When the plan materialized in Germany, there was immediate uproar, with politicians proclaiming free viewing of national-team games as 'a basic right of our citizens' (quoted in Hils, 1997). And when Vittorio Cecchi Gori outbid the Italian public broadcaster RAI for soccer rights in 1996, the Italian state moved in to declare the auction contrary to the public interest, legislating to preclude anyone holding more than 60% of the nation's rights to televise soccer (Tagliabue, 1997: D4; 'Flirtation and Frustration', 1999). Similar legislation was introduced in the UK and France, although cricket authorities persuaded the Blair government that 'their' sport did not belong on the 'A' list in 1998 (Boehm, 1998a; Boyle and Haynes, 2000: 216). But then Telepiu bought exclusive pay rights for the four leading soccer clubs in Italy, forcing audiences to make the digital move and making it harder for competitors to gain custom. When Murdoch announced a second digital platform in Italy for 1999 via partnerships with local football clubs, Mediaset, and Telecom Italia, he was also preparing a US$2.5 billion offer for six years' exclusive coverage of Serie A and B football, countering pay-per-view arrangements between Canal+, its Italian subsidiary Telepiu, and top clubs. Then he purchased a quarter of Kirch, staking out its non-broadcast rights (Williams, 1998: A8; Zecchinelli, 1998; 'Flirtation and Frustration', 1999; Boehm, 1999; Boyle and Haynes, 2000: 210). The criterion of national interest was being circumvented.

The Olympic Charter, which guarantees 'maximum presentation of the Games to the widest possible global audience free-of-charge' (IOC, n.d.) may eventually be interpreted to mean that the Third World will receive analogue signals and the First

World digital. Watching the Olympics on television is meant to be a similar experience for all, as host broadcasters produce the visual text (except for the US, which has its own feed, camera angles, and commentary position). Countries then reterritorialize the text with their own verbal track (Puijk, 1999: 117, 119). Exhaustive studies of the Games as 'a communication phenomenon . . . initially produced in a city, but then "reproduced" in multiple places', suggest that locally modulated coverage constructs very different texts and generates very different responses. Local cultural policy regulated by the state also plays a part, notably the insistence by Arabic countries that women's events not be broadcast and that they hence pay on a pro rata basis (de Moragas Spà et al., 1995: xvi, 22).

Disney/ABC's subsidiary ESPN has been a trendsetter in the televisualization of sport. ESPN International, which began in 1983, telecasts in 21 languages to 182 nations and 155 million households. It has 20 networks across Asia, Australia, and Latin America (the latter has four networks of its own) in addition to syndication deals. A single executive sent to Hong Kong to cover Asia in 1993 is now one of 300 employees based in Singapore at a major production facility (Fry, 1998b: A4; Sandomir, 1999). In 1998, ESPN struck a programming arrangement with the Argentinian military to broadcast in the Antarctic, which had long been a target in order for the company to claim a truly global reach (Fry, 1998a: A1; Fry, 1998b: A4). That reach permits Disney to address a social sector that has conventionally eluded it – middle-class men – and even to penetrate public TV: the PRC's sports network draws half its content from ESPN. The company's slogan is 'Think globally, but customize locally.' That means a degree of local coverage, such as table tennis in East Asia and cricket in India, while Latin American services produce 20% of their programmes (Grove, 1998: A6). But from 1996, ESPN offered 'global buys' to advertisers – the global commodity sign could be attached to the local sports referent (Herman and McChesney, 1997: 83, 63). The network uses Princeton Video Imaging to edit computer-generated visuals advertising goods and services onto real-life stadia, streets, and public space, making it appear as though purely televisual billboards are present at the site of live action (Williams, 1998). As a wonderfully doublespeaking ESPN executive puts it, 'When we say "local" we don't mean that it has to be from that locality, it can be programming from half-way around the world' (quoted in Grove, 1998: A6). Canal+ describes ESPN as 'one of the leading entertainment companies and brands in the "global information society"' (Lescure, 1998). [. . .]

The media–sports–culture complex

Television was the prime motor in the development of post-war sport and its mutating NICL [New International Division of Culture Labour], helping to constitute a sports/media complex (Jhally, 1989) or media–sports–culture complex (Rowe, 1999) of sports organizations, media/marketing organizations, and media personnel (broadcasters and journalists). The future of a sport relates, in large part, to its place within the complex. Dependency of sports organizations upon the media is due to the importance of continued revenue for national or international competitions. The direction of sport incorporation might be viewed as: media exposure → increased revenue → professionalization → more competitive and spectacular play → larger television audiences → further media exposure, and so on. As the media become increasingly important in this cycle, they dictate what they want from the sport (in terms of selling the product to advertisers). Prescribed innovations may be more colourful uniforms, the use of space for advertising on jerseys or the centre of the field, greater flow of play, breaks for advertisements, and other 'improvements' (Maguire, 1993b, 1999; Lawrence and Rowe, 1986; Goldlust, 1987; Cashmore, 1996). Peak sporting organizations find it difficult to resist the changes demanded by sponsors and the media.

This complex places the media at the very heart of sports structures and practices, because without the media's capacity to carry sports signs and myths to large and diverse audiences across the globe, sport would be a relatively minor and increasingly anachronistic folk pursuit. Television coverage, especially in its satellite form, has become the prime unit of currency in the cultural economy of sport. It can be capitalized in many ways – through paying and non-paying viewers, advertisers, sponsors, sports management companies, sports clubs and associations, news organizations, and so on. Most people most of the time encounter sport through the media, no matter how committed they may be as fans, while large sections of potential and intermittently contactable sports audiences are entirely dependent on media coverage for any kind of sports 'fix'. Without significant television coverage, individual sports are widely seen as moribund. The economic infrastructure of professional sport would collapse without the media's material and cultural capital.

This world of televisual sport is intensely competitive, not only between sports but also between sport and other news and entertainment programming. So sport on television is becoming more telegenic – lively, dramatic, digestible, and readable. A tension clearly exists not only between traditional and new telegenic procedures and forms of sport (for example tie-breaks in tennis, shoot-outs in hockey and soccer, and one-day cricket competitions) but also between smaller, traditionally sports-committed television audiences and those which are larger, fickle, and unconstrained by sports 'heritage'.

References

'Country-by-Country Schedule: WORLD' (1999) http://nhl.com/hockeyu/international
'Flirtation and Frustration' (1999) *The Economist* 11 December: 61–63.
'International Broadcasters' (1999) www.majorleaguebaseball.com/u/baseball/mlb-com/int
'New Television Deals Mean More NBA Worldwide' (1999) www.nba.com/ON THE AIR
'NFL Full of Foreign-Born Players' (1999) www.nfl.com/international
'Sport and Television: Swifter, Higher, Stronger, Dearer' (1996) *The Economist* 20 July: 17–19.
'TV Times' (1999) www.afl.com.au

Barthes, R. (1977) *Image–Music–Text.* Trans. S. Heath. London: Fontana.
Boardman, A.E. and S.P. Hargreaves-Heap (1999) 'Network Externalities and Government Restrictions on Satellite Broadcasting of Key Sporting Events.' *Journal of Cultural Economics* 23, no. 3: 167–81.
Boehm, E. (1998a) 'Jocks Itchy Over Costly Cup.' *Variety* 8–14 June: 1, 85.
Boehm, E. (1999) 'Mergers Alter Euro Dynamics.' *Variety* 13–19 December: 68.
Boyle, R. and R. Haynes (1996) *Power Play: Sport, the Media and Popular Culture.* London: Longman.

Brown, P. (1996) 'Gender, Sport and the Media: An Investigation into Coverage of Women's Sport in the *Newcastle Herald and Sydney Morning Herald* 1890–1990'. Unpublished PhD Thesis, University of Newcastle, Australia.

Burton, R. (1999) 'From Hearst to Stem: The Shaping of an Industry over a Century.' *New York Times* 19 December: 11.

Cashmore, E. (1996) *Making Sense of Sport*, 2nd edn. London: Routledge.

Croci, O. and J. Ammirante (1999) 'Soccer in the Age of Globalization.' *Peace Review* 11, No. 4: 499–504.

Crook, T. (1998) *International Radio Journalism: History, Theory and Practice*. London: Routledge.

de Moragas Spà, M., N.K. Rivenburgh, and J.F. Larson (1995) *Television in the Olympics*. London: John Libbey.

Dempsey, J. (1999a) 'WNBA Games Going Global.' *Variety* 14–20 June: 22.

Dempsey, J. (1999b) 'NFL Kicks Off Online in 3 O'seas Markets.' *Variety* 27 September: 6.

FIFA (n.d.) http://www.fifa.com

Foucault, M. (1977) *Discipline and Punish: The Birth of the Prison*. Trans. A. Sheridan. London: Penguin.

Fry, A. (1998a) 'On Top of Their Game: Sports Cabler Casts Net on Four Corners of the Globe and Scores.' *Variety* 19–25 January: A1, A11.

Fry, A. (1998b) 'Savvy Dealmaking Woos Worldly Auds and Coin.' *Variety* 19–25 January: A4, A9.

Goldlust, J. (1987) *Playing for Keeps: Sport, the Media and Society*. Melbourne: Longman.

Grove, C. (1998) 'Tapping into Culture to Find the Right Program.' *Variety* 19–25 January: A6, A16.

Gruneau, R. and D. Whitson (1993) *Hockey Night in Canada: Sport, Identities and Cultural Politics*. Toronto: Garamond Press.

Hargreaves, John (1986) *Sport, Power and Culture*. Cambridge: Polity.

Haynes, R. (1999) 'There's Many a Slip "Twixt the Eye and the Lip": An Exploratory History of Football Broadcasts and Running Commentaries on BBC Radio, 1927–1939.' *International Review for the Sociology of Sport* 34, No. 2: 143–56.

Herman, E.S. and R.W. McChesney (1997) *The Global Media: The New Missionaries of Global Capitalism*. London: Cassell.

Hils, M. (1997) 'Kickup in Germany: Plan to Air Some Soccer Games on PPV Under Fire.' *Variety* 3–9 November: 31.

Jameson, F. (1996) 'Five Theses on Actually Existing Marxism.' *Monthly Review* 47, No. 11: 1–10.

Jhally, S. (1989) 'Cultural Studies and the Sports/Media Complex.' *Media, Sports, and Society*. Ed. L.A Wenner. Newbury Park: Sage. 70–96.

Kang, J-M. (1988) 'Sports, Media and Cultural Dependency.' *Journal of Contemporary Asia* 18, No. 4: 430–43.

Lawrence, G. and D. Rowe (eds) (1986) *Power Play: Essays in the Sociology of Australian Sport*. Sydney: Hale & Iremonger.

Lescure, P. (1998) Letter. *Variety* 19–25 January: A3.

Maguire, J. (1993) 'Globalization, Sport Development, and the Media/Sport Production Process.' *Sport Science Review* 2, No. 1: 29–47.

Maguire, J. (1999) *Global Sport: Identities, Societies, Civilizations*. Cambridge: Polity.

McAllister, M.P. (1997) 'Sponsorship, Globalization, and the Summer Olympics.' Paper delivered to the International Communication Association, Montréal.

Muda, M. (1998) 'The Significance of Commonwealth Games in Malaysia's Foreign Policy.' *The Round Table* 346: 211–26.

Pickard, C. (1997) 'Cup Runneth over Summer's O'Seas B.O.' *Variety* 15–21 December: 9–10.

Puijk, R. (1999) 'Producing Norwegian Culture for Domestic and Foreign Gazes: The Lillehammer Olympic Opening Ceremony.' *Olympic Games as Performance and Public Event: The Case of the XVII Winter Olympic Games in Norway.* Ed. A.M. Klausen. New York: Berghahn. 97–136.

Rowe, D. (1992a) 'Modes of Sports Writing.' *Journalism and Popular Culture.* Ed. P. Dahlgren and C. Sparks. London: Sage. 96–112.

Rowe, D. (1992b) "That Misery of Stringers' Clichés": Sports Writing.' *Cultural Studies* 5, no. 1: 77–90.

Rowe, D. (1999) *Sport, Culture and the Media: The Unruly Trinity.* Buckingham: Open University Press.

Rowe, D. and D. Stevenson (1995) 'Negotiations and Mediations: Journalism, Professional Status and the Making of the Sports Text.' *Media Information Australia* 75: 67–79.

Sandomir, R. (1999) 'When a TV Network is Your Chef.' *New York Times* 8 November: C21.

Smith, P. (1997) *Millennial Dreams: Contemporary Culture and Capital in the North.* London: Verso.

Tagliabue, J. (1997) 'Europe Enters the Big Leagues: Playing Catch-Up to the U.S., Commerce Takes the Field.' *New York Times* 10 September: D1, D4.

Whannel, G. (1992) *Fields in Vision: Television Sport and Cultural Transformation.* London: Routledge.

Williams, M.L. (1998) 'Ad Deals Strike a Cultural Match.' *Variety* 19–25 January: A8.

Williams, M. (1999) 'Soccer Kicky for Congloms.' *Variety* 20–26 September: 1, 104.

Wilson, H. (1998) 'Television's *Tour de Force*: The Nation Watches the Olympic Games.' *Tourism, Leisure, Sport: Critical Perspectives.* Ed. D. Rowe and G. Lawrence. Melbourne: Cambridge University Press. 135–45.

Wise, M. (1999) 'Empty Seats are a Concern for the NBA.' *New York Times* 19 December: 7.

Zecchinelli, C. (1998) 'Murdoch Streams into Italy.' *Variety* 28 December: 1, 12.

Class, community and cultural reproduction

INTRODUCTION

HISTORICAL SELECTIONS INCLUDED in Section Two of this Reader showed the importance of social class in the formation of modern sport cultures. There is much debate about the precise nature of social class in advanced late modern societies. Some argue that the importance of class position and the influences that stem from the social class position into which an individual is born have decreased in an age of increased social mobility. And sport certainly can be a powerful symbol of mobility, based upon market power and earnings, and status that can accrue to the successful sport professional and celebrity. The question of class remains central, though, to any examination of the wider social significance of sport; and it is extremely important to relate these questions too to the changing basis of community, of collectively experienced forms of social and cultural life.

In the first Reading, the US intellectual **Thorstein Veblen** (1857–1929) comments on the place of sports and leisure in the public life of more privileged and powerful social groups in the US in a period when industrialism was emerging. He points to the comparisons that can be made between the leisure class of that society, with its predatory instincts and temperament, and dominant classes of earlier societies in which duelling and fighting were sources of esteem. Sports such as (American) football are comparable, for Veblen, to the wild and untamed pursuits of peoples of a more barbarian temperament. Veblen was an unorthodox academic and his linguistic style draws upon satire and irony, but there was much seriousness to his analysis: especially his connection of sport and the public values expressed in sport to the economic position of what he labelled the leisure class. Think forward a century, when the Henley Regatta, Wimbledon, Cowdray Park polo and Royal Ascot still filled the summer sporting calendar in England, and ask whether sport offers a vehicle for the public expression of the status of a leisure class.

History is not, as these selections demonstrate, a story to be told merely as background. It offers illuminating reminders of what has influenced the present. The second Reading, by US social historian of the English fox hunt **David C. Itzkowitz**, shows how social class aspirations – the desire of upwardly mobile middle classes to acquire still more status – could also affirm the position of the most-established classes. In debates about the morality of hunting in twenty-first-century Britain, as the arguments were mobilized against hunting with hounds, much was made of how fox-hunting held together the disparate elements of a rural community. Look at Itzkowitz's final point, though. What are the consequences, for social class relations, of such cross-class alliances?

Participation figures for sport are an indispensable tool when considering the place of sport in society, though the nature of the survey or study from which such figures stem must always be evaluated closely – and information from the websites of various sport organizations should be questioned when making claims about participation. **John Hargreaves** notes some of these problems in the third Reading in this section, but observes that having these data is better than having no evidence at all. What does his analysis show about the respective participation rates of different occupational groupings? What kind of social and community involvements might middle- and upper-class individuals commit to, that are not so common among working-class people?

The first three Readings have raised comparative, historical and sociological questions. The fourth Reading extracts passages from the work of one of the greatest French sociologists of his time, **Pierre Bourdieu** (1930–2002), and reaffirms the centrality of some of these questions. Bourdieu provides historical and more contemporary examples of the influence of social class upon participation and what he calls 'taste' (his masterpiece study is called *Distinction: A Social Critique of the Judgement of Taste*). Bourdieu has had an immense impact upon the critical sociological study of sport, and in reading these excerpts it is clear that sport has a more than peripheral place in social class relations: '. . . sport, like any other practice, is an object of struggles between the fractions of the dominant class and also between the social classes', he writes in this Reading.

The remaining Readings look at class cultures of sport in relation to community and issues such as inequality, against a background of snapshots in time from the four decades from the 1950s to the 1980s. They have been selected for their illustrative impact, for their focused and qualitative character, and to stimulate cross-temporal as well as cross-cultural comparisons. English anthropologist **Ronald Frankenberg** studied the everyday aspects of village life in a community on the Anglo-Welsh border in the early 1950s. The trademark skills of the anthropologist shine through his book: the attention to descriptive detail; the way in which observations are developed analytically; and the application of appropriate concepts to those observations. Frankenberg shows how the local football club symbolized important aspects of village life, while also confirming hierarchies of class and community status. Frankenberg allows you to undertake studies in close-up, and to see how the large framing influences of a society and its time impact upon the intimate details of ordinary village and community life. Why does the football club lose its capacity as cultural symbol? Again, how does sport connect community and class?

English sociologist and educationalist **Brian Jackson**, a beneficiary of educational opportunities granted by a scholarship to Cambridge University, returned to his native town, Huddersfield, in the northern English county of Yorkshire in the 1960s to explore the nature of class-based community, looking at distinctive working-class activities and institutions. Crown Green bowls is the focus of his attention in this Reading. In describing the activity, locating it in its social and cultural context, he moves towards fundamental questions about the meaning of sport at the recreational and participatory level. Following Jackson's example, any curious investigator could return to his/her community of origin and document aspects of the local everyday cultural and sporting scene, and ask core questions concerning the features of enduring, declining or emerging sport activities.

Sport cultures do not merely reflect wider social values: they express their own values, sometimes in tension with the wider culture (aspects of this will be developed in Readings in Section Eight, 'Subcultures'), but often contributing to ways in which that culture is reproduced. In the penultimate Reading, in research conducted in the 1970s, English sociologist **Paul Corrigan**, in a much reprinted and very accessible book, asks what it is that working-class boys get out of being football fans and players. The ways in which they play can be seen as their own creations, borne out of the choices available to them and the prior experience that they bring to those choices. Tease out the distinctive features of such a working-class youth culture.

The final Reading in the section is by French sociologist-cum-anthropologist and protégé of Pierre Bourdieu, **Loïc Wacquant**, now based in the US. Here the focus is upon the sporting body, the professional preparation of the boxer in the setting of South Chicago in the 1980s. The study was carried out in a black ghetto, and young black men at the heart of Wacquant's analysis saw the potential of using their bodies as a '*form of capital*'. Though boxing holds the promise of an escape from the ghetto, for many of the boxers it was more a means of taking care of their body, and of displaying a powerful body in a dangerous neighbourhood. In what sense, then, can you see a form of cultural reproduction taking place in the urban, black working-class culture of the ring?

COMMENTARY AND FURTHER READING

The Readings in this section have shown that class has continued to be an important influence on sport participation and the character of individual sport cultures. The Readings have shown too that there are important gender dynamics that also influence sport forms, though in many cases and particularly in the cases of selected working-class examples, public sport forms have been dominated by males. To study the culture of sport it is inevitable that there is a need to study the male-dominated forms of a patriarchal class culture. There remains a challenge in sport studies to produce more studies of middle-class and upper-class sports, and also the leisure sports of women in those classes: for example, the pony club, the lawn-tennis club, the golf club and the emergent lifestyle sports (see Readings on skateboarding and windsurfing in Section Eight). It remains a challenge not least because middle- and upper-class cultures are more protective of their environments and less willing to respond to the probing of the researcher.

The fact remains that despite much policy-making in the public sector, initiatives in the commercial marketplace, and lobbying by and for the voluntary sector, sport participation in Britain has remained relatively stagnant over a quarter of a century.

National participation figures are notoriously difficult to unravel in completely reliable ways, but it is clear that there has hardly been a boom in participation despite numerous initiatives and interventions. Sport England's Head of Strategy Research and Planning, Nick Rowe, acknowledged in April 2004 that 'participation rates have remained stubbornly static and inequities in participation between different social groups have continued largely unchanged over the last 30 years or so with perhaps the exception of more women taking part in fitness related activities' (Rowe, 2004: 2–3)*. This persistent pattern in participation in sport leads to the inescapable conclusion that sport, as an activity and a form of committed practice, has contributed to the reproduction of the social order. Citing revealing data on sport participation in Scotland in 2000, Grant Jarvie writes that 'there is good reason for believing that sport and social class have been mutually reinforcing categories in British society for a long time' (*Sport, Culture and Society: An Introduction*, London and New York, Routledge, 2006: 305).

For a general overview of sport and social class, see Alan Tomlinson, 'Social Class and Sport', in George Ritzer's *Blackwell Dictionary of Sociology* (Oxford, Blackwell, forthcoming 2006).

---

* Nick Rowe, 2004, introducing Sport England's *Driving Up Participation: The Challenge for Sport* (academic review papers commissioned by Sport England as contextual analysis to inform the preparation of the Framework for Sport in England), London, Sport England.

Thorstein Veblen

MODERN SURVIVALS
OF PROWESS

T HE LEISURE CLASS lives by the industrial community rather than in it. Its relations to industry are of a pecuniary rather than an industrial kind. Admission to the class is gained by exercise of the pecuniary aptitudes—aptitudes for acquisition rather than for serviceability. There is, therefore, a continued selective sifting of the human material that makes up the leisure class, and this selection proceeds on the ground of fitness for pecuniary pursuits. But the scheme of life of the class is in large part a heritage from the past, and embodies much of the habits and ideals of the earlier barbarian period. This archaic, barbarian scheme of life imposes itself also on the lower orders, with more or less mitigation. In its turn the scheme of life, of conventions, acts selectively and by education to shape the human material, and its action runs chiefly in the direction of conserving traits, habits, and ideals that belong to the early barbarian age,—the age of prowess and predatory life.

The most immediate and unequivocal expression of that archaic human nature which characterises man in the predatory stage is the fighting propensity proper. In cases where the predatory activity is a collective one, this propensity is frequently called the martial spirit, or, latterly, patriotism. It needs no insistence to find assent to the proposition that in the countries of civilised Europe the hereditary leisure class is endowed with this martial spirit in a higher degree than the middle classes. Indeed, the leisure class claims the distinction as a matter of pride, and no doubt with some grounds. War is honourable, and warlike prowess is eminently honorific in the eyes of the generality of men; and this admiration of warlike prowess is itself the best voucher of a predatory temperament in the admirer of war. The enthusiasm for war, and the predatory temper of which it is the index, prevail in the largest measure among the upper classes, especially among the hereditary leisure class. Moreover, the ostensible serious occupation of the upper class is that of government, which, in point of origin and developmental content, is also a predatory occupation. [. . .]

. . . [T]he growth of "college spirit," college athletics, and the like, in the higher institutions of learning [are] . . . manifestations of the predatory temperament [and] are all to be classed under the head of exploit. They are partly simple and unreflected expressions of an attitude of emulative ferocity, partly activities deliberately entered upon with a view to gaining repute for prowess. Sports of all kinds are of the same general character, including prizefights, bull-fights, athletics, shooting, angling, yachting, and games of skill, even where the element of destructive physical efficiency is not an obtrusive feature. Sports shade off from the basis of hostile combat, through skill, to cunning and chicanery, without its being possible to draw a line at any point. The ground of an addiction to sports is an archaic spiritual constitution—the possession of the predatory emulative propensity in a relatively high potency. A strong proclivity to adventuresome exploit and to the infliction of damage is especially pronounced in those employments which are in colloquial usage specifically called sportsmanship.

It is perhaps truer, or at least more evident, as regards sports than as regards the other expressions of predatory emulation already spoken of that the temperament which inclines men to them is essentially a boyish temperament. The addiction to sports, therefore, in a peculiar degree marks an arrested development of the man's moral nature. This peculiar boyishness of temperament in sporting men immediately becomes apparent when attention is directed to the large element of make-believe that is present in all sporting activity. Sports share this character of make-believe with the games and exploits to which children, especially boys, are habitually inclined. Make-believe does not enter in the same proportion into all sports, but it is present in a very appreciable degree in all. It is apparently present in a larger measure in sportsmanship proper and in athletic contests than in set games of skill of a more sedentary character; although this rule may not be found to apply with any great uniformity. It is noticeable, for instance, that even very mild-mannered and matter-of-fact men who go out shooting are apt to carry an excess of arms and accoutrements in order to impress upon their own imagination the seriousness of their undertaking. These huntsmen are also prone to a histrionic, prancing gait and to an elaborate exaggeration of the motions, whether of stealth or of onslaught, involved in their deeds of exploit. Similarly in athletic sports there is almost invariably present a good share of rant and swagger and ostensible mystification—features which mark the histrionic nature of these employments. In all this, of course, the reminder of boyish make-believe is plain enough. The slang of athletics, by the way, is in great part made up of extremely sanguinary locutions borrowed from the terminology of warfare. Except where it is adopted as a necessary means of secret communication, the use of a special slang in any employment is probably to be accepted as evidence that the occupation in question is substantially make-believe.

A further feature in which sports differ from the duel and similar disturbances of the peace is the peculiarity that they admit of other motives being assigned for them besides the impulses of exploit and ferocity. There is probably little if any other motive present in any given case, but the fact that other reasons for indulging in sports are frequently assigned goes to say that other grounds are sometimes present in a subsidiary way. Sportsmen—hunters and anglers—are more or less in the habit of assigning a love of nature, the need of recreation, and the like, as the incentives to their favourite pastime. These motives are no doubt frequently present and make up a part of the attractiveness of the sportsman's life; but these can not be the chief incentives. These ostensible needs could be more readily and fully satisfied without the accompaniment of a systematic effort to take the life of those creatures that make up an essential feature of that "nature" that is beloved by the sportsman. It is, indeed, the most noticeable effect of the sportsman's activity to keep nature in a state of chronic desolation by killing off all living things whose destruction he can compass.

Still, there is ground for the sportsman's claim that under the existing conventionalities his need of recreation and of contact with nature can best be satisfied by the course which he takes. Certain canons of good breeding have been imposed by the prescriptive example of a predatory leisure class in the past and have been somewhat painstakingly conserved by the usage of the latter-day representatives of that class; and these canons will not permit him, without blame, to seek contact with nature on other terms. From being an honourable employment handed down from the predatory culture as the highest form of everyday leisure, sports have come to be the only form of outdoor activity that has the full sanction of decorum. Among the proximate incentives to shooting and angling, then, may be the need of recreation and outdoor life. The remoter cause which imposes the necessity of seeking these objects under the cover of systematic slaughter is a prescription that can not be violated except at the risk of disrepute and consequent lesion to one's self-respect.

The case of other kinds of sport is somewhat similar. Of these, athletic games are the best example. Prescriptive usage with respect to what forms of activity, exercise, and recreation are permissible under the code of reputable living is of course present here also. Those who are addicted to athletic sports, or who admire them, set up the claim that these afford the best available means of recreation and of "physical culture." And prescriptive usage gives countenance to the claim. The canons of reputable living exclude from the scheme of life of the leisure class all activity that can not be classed as conspicuous leisure. And consequently they tend by prescription to exclude it also from the scheme of life of the community generally. At the same time purposeless physical exertion is tedious and distasteful beyond tolerance. As has been noticed in another connection, recourse is in such a case had to some form of activity which shall at least afford a colourable pretence of purpose, even if the object assigned be only a make-believe. Sports satisfy these requirements of substantial futility together with a colourable make-believe of purpose. In addition to this they afford scope for emulation, and are attractive also on that account. [. . .]

Sports—hunting, angling, athletic games, and the like—afford an exercise for dexterity and for the emulative ferocity and astuteness characteristic of predatory life. [. . .]

But those members of respectable society who advocate athletic games commonly justify their attitude on this head to themselves and to their neighbours on the ground that these games serve as an invaluable means of development. They not only improve the contestant's physique, but it is commonly added that they also foster a manly spirit, both in the participants and in the spectators. Football is the particular game which will probably first occur to any one in this community when the question of the serviceability of athletic games is raised, as this form of athletic contest is at present uppermost in the mind of those who plead for or against games as a means of physical or moral salvation. This typical athletic sport may, therefore, serve to illustrate the bearing of athletics upon the development of the contestant's character and physique. It has been said, not inaptly, that the relation of football to physical culture is much the same as that of the bull-fight to agriculture. Serviceability for these lusory institutions requires sedulous training or breeding. The material used, whether brute or human, is subjected to careful selection and discipline, in order to secure and accentuate certain aptitudes and propensities which are characteristic of the ferine state, and which tend to obsolescence under domestication. This does not mean that the result in either case is an all-around and consistent rehabilitation of the ferine or barbarian habit of mind and body. The result is rather a one-sided return to barbarism or to the *feræ natura*—a rehabilitation and accentuation of those ferine traits which make for damage and desolation, without a corresponding development of the traits which would serve the individual's self-preservation and fulness of life in a ferine environment. The culture bestowed in football gives a product of exotic ferocity and cunning. It is a rehabilitation of the early barbarian temperament, together with a suppression of those details of temperament which, as seen from the standpoint of the social and economic exigencies, are the redeeming features of the savage character. [. . .]

In popular apprehension there is much that is admirable in the type of manhood which the life of sport fosters. There is self-reliance and good-fellowship, so termed in the somewhat loose colloquial use of the words. From a different point of view the qualities currently so characterised might be described as truculence and clannishness. The reason for the current approval and admiration of these manly qualities, as well as for their being called manly, is the same as the reason for their usefulness to the individual. The members of the community, and especially that class of the community which sets the pace in canons of taste, are endowed with this range of propensities in sufficient measure to make their absence in others felt as a shortcoming, and to make their possession in an exceptional degree appreciated as an attribute of superior merit. [. . .]

From the evidence already recited it appears that, in sentiment and inclinations, the leisure class is more favourable to a warlike attitude and animus than the industrial classes. Something similar seems to be true as regards sports. But it is chiefly in its indirect effects, through the canons of decorous living, that the institution has its influence on the prevalent sentiment with respect to the sporting life. This indirect effect goes almost unequivocally in the direction of furthering a survival of the predatory temperament and habits; and this is true even with respect to those variants of the sporting life which the higher leisure-class code of proprieties proscribes; as, e.g., prize-fighting, cock-fighting, and other like vulgar expressions of the sporting temper. Whatever the latest authenticated schedule of detail proprieties may say, the accredited canons of decency sanctioned by the institution say without equivocation that emulation and waste are good and their opposites are disreputable. In the crepuscular light of the social nether spaces the details of the code are not apprehended with all the facility that might be desired, and these broad underlying canons of decency are therefore applied somewhat unreflectingly, with little question as to the scope of their competence or the exceptions that have been sanctioned in detail.

Addiction to athletic sports, not only in the way of direct participation, but also in the way of sentiment and moral support, is, in a more or less pronounced degree, a characteristic of the leisure class; and it is a trait which that class shares with the lower-class delinquents, and with such atavistic elements throughout the body of the community as are endowed with a dominant predaceous trend. Few individuals among the populations of Western civilised countries are so far devoid of the predaceous instinct as to find no diversion in contemplating athletic sports and games, but with the common run of individuals among the industrial classes the inclination to sports does not assert itself to the extent of constituting what may fairly be called a sporting habit. With these classes sports are an occasional diversion rather than a serious feature of life. This common body of the people can therefore not be said to cultivate the sporting propensity. Although it is not obsolete in the average of them, or even in any appreciable number of individuals, yet the predilection for sports in the commonplace industrial classes is of the nature of a reminiscence, more or less diverting as an occasional interest, rather than a vital and permanent interest that counts as a dominant factor in shaping the organic complex of habits of thought into which it enters.

David C. Itzkowitz

MYTH AND IDEAL

From its earliest days, foxhunting developed an idealized conception of itself that amounted almost to a mythology. Hunting and non-hunting men alike came to look on hunting as an institution in national and rural life, rather than as a mere sport. This idealized picture was used by hunting people to justify much of what they did, and when the justification was accepted, it passed from the realm of myth to that of reality. People behaved as though the myth were true and so, in effect, it was. The mythology of hunting was a significant factor in its own time. From the point of view of the modern observer, it possesses additional significance because it presents in microcosm many of the attitudes and ideals shared not only by a large segment of the middle and upper classes, but by all classes of country people. That these clearly stated ideals were often contradicted by the actions of hunting people should come as no surprise. But this too is of value, not because we need to be reminded that people often do not live up to their ideals, but because by comparing myth and reality, we are led to a clearer understanding of the meaning of the idealized concepts in the minds of nineteenth-century people.

The idealized view of hunting developed rapidly in the closing years of the eighteenth and the opening years of the nineteenth centuries, that is, at the time when the popularity of the sport was undergoing its first great increase. By around 1820 it was firmly established and was to remain virtually unchanged for the next sixty years, even though the conditions in which it was born had changed. [. . .]

The high moral tone was set early in the nineteenth century by John Hawkes, a friend of Meynell's, who, around 1808, wrote, printed, and distributed to his friends a small pamphlet describing Meynell's hunting techniques. In it he wrote:

> The Field is a most agreeable coffee-house, and there is more real society to be met with there than in any other situation of life. It links all classes together, from the Peer to the Peasant. It is the Englishman's peculiar privilege. It is not to be found in any other part of the globe, but in England's true land of liberty—and may it flourish to the end of time!![1]

Hawkes was among the first to give expression to the ideal that hunting unified all classes. By the 1820s, however, it had begun to appear with increasing frequency, and from that time it remained the foremost argument in the hunting man's arsenal. 'Hunting', wrote a correspondent in the *Sporting Magazine* in 1821,

> is considered by many to be no unimportant advantage to the country in which it is fostered; because it is a social sport—it brings men in various situations of life together, and unites them in the pursuit of the same object.[2]

Hunting people delighted in listing the men in 'humble' positions who loved to hunt. The chimney-sweep who hunted with the Duke of Beaufort in the 1830s was raised to the level of a national celebrity by an article about him in *Bell's Life*,[3] and from then on foxhunters could say, as did the master of the Old Berkshire in 1851, that 'no other country but England knows anything of a sport which allows a chimney-sweep or the lowest man of the community to ride by the side of a duke'.[4] As late as 1886, G.F. Underhill, a leading hunting journalist, could write:

> I even do not hesitate to assert that so long as foxhunting endures, so long will all the classes of English society be safe together: the high from the blights of envy and the spoliation of rapacity, the low from the iron hand of oppression and the insolent spurn of contempt.[5]

The argument, as we can see, remained virtually unchanged in the eighty years between Hawkes and Underhill.

The great attractiveness of this ideal lay in the fact that, though it was simple and straightforward on the surface, it was sufficiently ambiguous to be used to justify a wide range of opinions and practices. It enabled hunting to maintain an image at one and the same time as the most aristocratic and the most egalitarian of English institutions. It enabled what was never more than a small minority of the population to expect that everyone else in the countryside would order his interests so as to foster the amusement of that minority. What is more remarkable is that this expectation was fulfilled.

That the hunting field was open to all no one can deny. This was the result of three factors. The original status of foxes as vermin, which all were encouraged to destroy, meant that they were unprotected by any game law. Even had they been protected, the hounds killed the prey, and so only the owner of the hounds would have had to be qualified to kill game, since the followers were mere spectators. Second, since the hounds killed the fox, there could be no conflict among sportsmen for the prey. Unlike the shooter who was deprived of a bird himself every time one was shot by someone else, it made no difference to the master of hounds whether five or five hundred watched his hounds kill a fox, so long as they did not interfere. It was this lack of possessiveness that endeared foxhunting to so noted a man of the people as William Cobbett, even though he hated shooters and their game laws.[6] Finally, the fact that hunting could only exist if hunting people were allowed to cross the lands of others made it, in the words of one sportsman, 'an amusement of sufferance, and, being so constituted, open to all the world.'[7]

No one, however, could claim that England was a socially egalitarian society in the nineteenth century, and least of all the foxhunters. From the very beginning, the ideal recognized that the social contacts of the hunting field were governed by certain restraints. The very nature of the sport could separate the elements of fraternization and equality. In the course of a hard run all were equal, at least to the extent that differences of riding skill and quality of horses allowed. The dustman was welcome to ride beside the duke, or ahead of him, if he could. But in the course of such a run, fraternization was impossible. Each was too preoccupied with his own riding to be aware of the existence of the other as anything more than a moving obstacle in the field. At the meet of the hounds, on the other hand, when conversation was possible, and when, in fact, there were contacts between members of different classes, these contacts were limited to definite, recognized forms. The sporting farmer or local tradesman, it is true, often exchanged words with members of the local gentry or aristocracy, and these meetings were, in fact, one of the major sources of contact among the various classes, but the relative differences in social station were never forgotten.

The chimney-sweep who hunted with the Duke of Beaufort is an interesting case in point. Though he obviously enjoyed hunting and went well in the run, he seems, at the meet, to have been almost a licensed entertainer. He rode in his chimney-cleaning clothes, carried a chimney brush instead of a whip, and, after being greeted by the duke, saluted him with his brush, leapt up on his saddle, and rode around the crowd on one leg, posing 'like a flying Mercury. . . amid the waving of handkerchiefs, and to the infinite amusement of all present.'[8]

Farmers, of course, occupied a higher social position, but what the hunting man hated above all else, in a member of any class, was pretension. So long as the farmer or tradesman made no pretence to gentility but was content to appear no more than he was, he was welcomed. At the various social events associated with hunting, such as balls, dinners, and races, the social differences were maintained all the more sharply. It was this which led The Times in 1858 to describe the idea of hunting as a bond of society as 'a delusion and snare. It is an excuse for associating with men whom you do not associate with off the field or at the hunting breakfast, and some of whom you could not possibly associate with.'[9] But while The Times was correct as far as it went, it had, in fact, fallen into a snare itself. The hunting ideal had never claimed that hunting was a social leveller or even that one associated freely with all who hunted. The sporting writer 'Scrutator' was quite right to take The Times to task on that point: 'A gentleman may, I suppose, speak to a horse dealer or a coltbreaker in the field, or have a long chat with a neighbouring farmer on agriculture without sitting down at table exchanging visiting cards with either the one or the other.'[10]

The ideal of the hunting field as a meeting place for all classes dates, as we have seen, from the pre-railway age, when, with the exception of the shires and the packs in the immediate vicinity of large towns, the hunting field was made up entirely of local men. Every member of the local community had his known and accepted place in that community, and the unquestioned acceptance of that local social order made social intercourse between members of different classes simple, for no threat to the order could be seen in it.

While hunting people boasted of the openness of the hunting field there is no question that the values the field fostered were conservative and aristocratic, and it was considered to be one of the great benefits of the openness that even the lower classes could be thus embued with gentlemanly ideals. [. . .]

Hunting people never quite resolved the conflict between the image of hunting as a sport of gentlemen and as a sport open to all the people. Sometimes one aspect was stressed, sometimes another. The problem was compounded by the fact that the duality existed. Hunting was open to all, and members of all classes participated, but, on the other hand, the upper classes predominated in all but a few packs. Thus, in 1862, during a dispute over the advantages of hunting versus shooting, *The Field* could, in the same editorial, praise hunting because it amused all classes and yet call it 'essentially the pastime of the country gentlemen of Great Britain'.[11]

That hunting people never tried hard to resolve the dilemma may be interpreted as merely a case of self-serving, but it can also be taken as a sign of a real ambivalence on the part of many. Foxhunting was, in fact, a unique institution, carrying the greatest social *cachet* and looked to by many merely in search of social advancement, and at the same time was an essentially popular sport in many rural districts. Similarly, foxhunting did, in fact, illustrate quite well the possibility of close social contact based on the acceptance of inequality.

Notes*

*Sp. Mag. is *Sporting Magazine: or Monthly Calendar of the Transactions of the Turf, the Chace and Every Other Diversion Interesting to the Man of Pleasure and Enterprise, 1792–1870.*

1   John Hawkes, *The Meynellian Science, or, Fox-Hunting upon System* With Notes upon Fox-Hunting in 1912, a Comparative Study, by The Right Hon. The Earl of Lonsdale, K.G., with some Notes on Present-day Fox-Hunting by Major Algernon Burnaby, D.L., now re-edited by L.H. Irvine (Leicester, 1932), p. 48.
2   *Sp. Mag.*, LVIII (May, 1821), p. 101.
3   *Bell's Life in London and Sporting Chronicle*, 1822–1886, December 18, 1836.
4   Richard Francis Ball and Tresham Gilbey, *The Essex Foxhounds with Notes upon Hunting in Essex*. London, 1896, p. 101.
5   George F. Underhill, *In at the Death. A Tale of Society* (London, 1888), p. vi.
6   William Cobbett, *Rural Rides* (London, 1830), pp. 269–270.
7   'Cecil', in *Sp. Mag.*, CXIII (February, 1849), p. 147.
8   *Bell's Life*, December 18, 1836.
9   *The Times*, September 22, 1858.
10 *Bell's Life*, October 10, 1858.
11 *The Field, or Country Gentleman's Newspaper*, 1853–1895, XX (August 16, 1862), p. 149.

John Hargreaves

CLASS DIVISIONS

THE PROPENSITY TO PARTICIPATE actively in sports varies with social-class membership – the higher the class, the greater the rate of participation (see Table 35.1).

Table 35.1 Class differentiation in sport and recreation

Socio-economic group	% Outdoor		% Indoor		% Watching		% Total pop.
Professional and managerial	52	(15)*	25	(13)	16	(16)	11
Other non-manual	43	(35)	21	(30)	11	(30)	31
Skilled manual	40	(23)	28	(30)	13	(26)	23
Semi- and unskilled manual	27	(21)	14	(19)	9	(23)	29

Note: *The figures in parentheses represent the weight, in percentage terms, of each social-class grouping in the populations participating in each of the three categories of sport.

Source: A.J. Veal, *Sport and Recreation in England and Wales* (Univ. of Birmingham, Centre for Urban Studies, 1979), p. 18, table 4.

Now, measuring class differentials in involvement in sport simply in terms of occupation is unsatisfactory in certain important respects. First, it reduces class to one dimension, the nature of work, whereas classes are constructed politically and culturally as well. The class position of women, for example, is difficult to characterize in terms of occupation since a large proportion of women's work is either tangential to or not encompassed by the labour-market.[1] Most occupational classifications are based in any case upon conventional conceptions of what constitutes men's and women's work and what constitutes skill – conceptions which discriminate against women; and they take no account of the resulting economic differences between men and women, such as the level of income, fringe benefits and qualifications. Even as a measure of men's economic class such categorizations are unsatisfactory, since they take no account of the significance of the relationship between occupation and ownership and control over the means of production.[2] One important consequence is that correspondences between the position of routine non-manual workers – a large proportion of whom are women – and many manual workers are overlooked. We will consider the problematic relation between gender and class further in a moment.

Bearing these drawbacks in mind, when used carefully this kind of data is, nevertheless, better than no data at all. The professional and managerial group is the most involved in sport: in 19 out of 31 activities listed in the GHS [General Household Survey] this group has a greater proportion of its members involved than any other. Other non-manual workers are the second most active group overall, particularly in more individualistic sporting activities like cycling, horse-riding, climbing, tennis, keep fit and yoga. Skilled manual workers are almost equally active overall, and most active in playing and watching football, fishing, ten-pin bowling, billiards, darts, and watching motor sports. Semi- and unskilled workers are easily the least active of all.[3] It should be noted that high rates of participation in the above sense do not necessarily make a group the biggest group in sports overall or in an individual sport, since this depends on the relative size of class groupings in the total population. In fact, other non-manual workers form the biggest group numerically, usually constituting around 30 per cent of participants. Skilled manual workers form the biggest group playing and watching football, fishing, ten-pin bowing, billiards, darts, watching motor sports, field sports, cricket and bowls. Note particularly that skilled workers are the biggest group of participants in the traditionally important major games in Britain – cricket and football.[4] Surveys of the users of local sports centres strongly confirm the pattern of participation shown in national surveys: statistically non-manual workers are over-represented, skilled workers adequately represented, and semi- and unskilled workers grossly underepresented.[5]

Commitment to sport then, in terms of active participation, is higher among non-manual workers as a whole than among manual workers, that is to say in these terms the middle and upper classes are still more involved in sport than the working classes. But put like this the unique level of involvement of the upper working class, in particular of skilled manual workers, is concealed. The significant division is between the latter group and the semi- and unskilled working class. Thus sports continue to mark a cultural boundary among working-class people. In simple numerical terms active participation in sports is dominated by lower non-manual and skilled manual workers, that is, by the lower middle and upper working class. As we know, a significant proportion of lower non-manual workers are working class in terms of their material position and their self-identification, which means the degree of upper-working-class involvement in sports is greater, and consequently, the class as a whole is more sharply divided at the cultural level than appears to be the case at first glance.[6] Since lower-class groups are more involved in gambling and they also rely more on television for their entertainment, it can be assumed that they are relatively more involved in sport through watching and gambling.[7] A BBC survey of the early 1970s for example, found that adults in the lowest social grade spent 45 per cent more time watching TV than adults in higher grades. The mass media take up to two-thirds or more of the total disposable time of this group of heavy users.[8] On these grounds it would seem reasonable to conclude that a greater number and proportion of semi- and unskilled workers are involved in sport than is indicated so far, but in a more passive way than other groups.

Unfortunately, evidence of this kind cannot reveal the concrete pattern of class relations in sport. It is tempting to assume that people with a common cultural interest, whatever their class background, tend to be integrated or pulled together in this respect. Empirical studies of local communities, of working-class culture and of membership of clubs and voluntary associations on the whole, do not bear out this expectation. There is little class mixing between manual and non-manual workers and their families. Working-class people either tend not to join formal organizations, or if they do, they belong to a very limited number of organizations of very much the same type, that is ones with small committees and a large membership, both drawn from the same class, of which the classic example is the working men's club.[9] They are either locked into a relatively dense social network at the local level consisting of family, neighbourhood friends and workmates, which precludes the need for, and reliance on, formally constructed voluntary associations. Or, as seems to be increasingly the pattern as these more traditional arrangements decompose, they are privatized in their non-work lives, having fewer social links outside the immediate family. But in either case the result is segregation of working-class people from other groups.[10]

On the other hand, middle- and upper-class individuals belong to a multiplicity of voluntary associations, and processes of dissociation and social closure largely ensure the class homogeneity of these institutions. On the whole, working-class people tend not to aspire to join anyway, and the middle- and upper-class groupings consciously or unconsciously exclude them. If this is the general pattern of class interaction it should not come as much surprise to learn that the limited sociological evidence available on the conduct of sport at the local level confirms it is no exception in segregating the classes. Some community studies rather unconvincingly suggest that a degree of class mixing takes place in sport, which encourages a shared sense of community. These are mostly studies of more rural-based communities, where traditional patterns of social intercourse and accompanying deferential attitudes are likely to have outlasted those elsewhere.[11] In a more urbanized setting social classes seem not to mix in sporting activity and community sentiment has a different basis. For example, Stacey's early study of Banbury examined the class composition of various types of voluntary associations, including sports organizations – bowls, cricket, football, tennis, cycling, golf, sailing, squash and table tennis – and it shows a fairly clear line of division between classes defined in terms of 'occupational status'. The clubs for squash, rugby, tennis, and bowls were over-whelmingly middle and upper class in social composition, the working-class groupings belonged to a far narrower range of sporting organizations, and where the same game was played by people from different social classes it was organized in separate clubs. Although club committee members as a whole came from higher-status groups, the committees of the different clubs catering for the same sport, but for different social classes, were also different in class composition. Sport, in fact, was a central feature of two separate social networks dividing the upper from the lower groups. It served as an important means of integrating higher-status groups, but was much less important in this respect for the lower. And no one sport represented the unity of the community.[12] The process of social closure through sports is illustrated graphically in Willmott and Young's study of a London suburb, Woodford, in the late 1950s, where they were informed by one of their middle-class respondents:

> Supposing a plasterer or someone like that applied to join . . . we want something a bit higher social standard than that . . . [another informant confided] . . . We welcome anyone who likes a good game. We wouldn't turn a man down for class prejudice, you understand. But we can't let our status down either. He must be able to mix, a good fellow socially. A new member has to be proposed and seconded and no member would introduce a friend he didn't think acceptable. [About other clubs his would not play against] . . . they play well, but socially they are not the same. We gave one of them a game not so long ago – it stood out a mile they were of a different standing. I don't mean to be snobbish, but there it is.[13]

The rather convoluted apologetics here underlines the important demarcating role that sport still played in 'affluent' Britain at the borderline between the middle and working classes. Elaborate procedures of affiliation and the level of subscriptions achieve the effect.

Studies of traditional working-class communities, such as Jackson's account of Huddersfield and Dennis *et al.*'s study of 'Ashton', a coal-mining town in the West Riding of Yorkshire, show how sports reproduced traditional working-class identity and culture in the 1950s and 1960s.[14] Crown-green bowling, Jackson claims, was Huddersfield's most popular sport, engaging as many as 5,000 players in 33 main clubs, centred on local greens, working men's clubs, local Liberal and Conservative associations, and factories and mills. The game is peculiar to, and the property of, the northern working class and serves to knit the class together at the local level. Rugby League football has a similar character and function in Ashton, where, apart from the working men's clubs, the pubs and the cinema, it was the only institution bringing large numbers of people together. The most important social activity, in fact, was supporting the town's team against its rivals among other northern towns. The game's importance at the time and the active nature of support is indicated by the fact that in a town where the male population over the age of eighteen in 1953 was 4,800, attendance at local matches never fell below 3,200 and reached as many as 10,000. In such cases sport reproduces a corporate consciousness among working-class people, the main features of which are a generalized sense of belonging to 'us' against 'them', a pride in manual work and in strength and skill, a desire for active, collective and independent participation in social life and a rigid gender division. But it is doubtful whether such active involvement in, and commitment to, sport at the local level is typical of the class as a whole nowadays, for such communities are either smaller scale and well bounded, or are located in older, declining industrial areas where the sport concerned has a strong regional flavour. Ashton, for example, is neither a typical working-class community, nor even a typical Rugby League town, but a relatively small mining town or industrial village, where most of the team were local miners. In larger-scale, more modern urban settings, although working-class people are involved in sport in ways that largely segregate them from contact with other classes, the contribution that sport makes to a sense of working-class community and class solidarity is likely to be more limited compared with this, and with the contribution sport makes to the cohesion of bourgeois groupings. The reasons for this are highly complex and in order to understand them we must analyse the forces producing internal divisions within the working class, and the non-class forces cutting across working-class solidarity and the way these are reproduced through sporting activity.

Notes

1   A. Dale *et al.*, 'Integrating Women into Class Theory', *Sociology*, 19 (3) (1985).
2   T. Nichols, 'Social Class: Official, Sociological and Marxist', in J. Irvine, I. Miles and J. Evans, *Demystifying Social Statistics* (Pluto Press, London, 1979).
3   A.J. Veal, *Sport and Recreation in England and Wales* (Centre for Urban Studies, University of Birmingham, 1979); B. Rees, *Activists and Non-Activists: Variations in Sports Participation in the UK* (Sports Council, London, 1974); M. Young and P. Willmott, *The Symmetrical Family* (Penguin, Harmondsworth, 1973) p. 215.
4   Veal, *Sport and Recreation in England and Wales*, p. 47.
5   Built Environment Research Group (BERG), *Sport For All In The Inner City* (London, 1978), Sports Council Study 15; *Sport in a Jointly Provided Centre* (London, 1978), Sports Council Study 14; *The Changing Indoor Sports Centre* (London, 1977), Sports Council Study 13; G. Arrowsmith, *Sports Usage and Membership at a Large Urban Leisure Complex: Billingham Forum* (London, 1979), Sports Council Research Working Papers, 17.
6   J.H. Goldthorpe *et al.*, *The Affluent Worker and the Class Structure* (Cambridge University Press, Cambridge, 1969). On the 'Deskilling' thesis see H. Braverman, *Labour and Monopoly Capital* (Monthly Review Press, London, 1974).
7   D. Downes *et al.*, *Gambling, Work, and Leisure* (Routledge & Kegan Paul, London, 1976); *Social Trends*, 9 (1979), table 12.18.
8   Cited in J. Curran and J. Tunstall, 'Mass Media and Leisure', in M.A. Smith *et al.* (eds), *Leisure and Society in Britain* (Allen Lane, London, 1973).
9   S. Hutson, *A Review of the Role of Clubs and Voluntary Associations Based on a Study of Two Areas in Swansea* (Sports Council, London, 1980).
10 Goldthorpe, *The Affluent Worker in the Class Structure*.
11 M. Stacey, 'The Myth of Community Studies', *British Journal of Sociology*, 20 (2), (1969); A.N. Birch, *Small Town Politics* (Oxford University Press, London, 1959); R. Frankenberg, *Village on the Border* (Penguin, Harmondsworth, 1957) and his *Communities in Britain* (Penguin, Harmondworth, 1966); W. Williams, *The Sociology of an English Village: Gosforth* (Routledge & Kegan Paul, London, 1964); R.E. Pahl, *Whose City?* (Longman, London, 1970) pp. 39–42.
12 M. Stacey, *Tradition and Change – A Study of Banbury* (Oxford University Press, London, 1960). See also, M. Stacey *et al.*, *Power, Persistence, and Change – A Second Study of Banbury* (Routledge & Kegan Paul, London, 1975).
13 P. Willmott and M. Young, *Family and Class in a London Suburb* (Routledge & Kegan Paul, London, 1960) p. 97.
14 B. Jackson, *Working Class Community* (Penguin, Harmondsworth 1968) ch. 6; N. Dennis *et al.*, *Coal is Our Life* (Eyre & Spottiswoode, London, 1956).

Pierre Bourdieu

SPORT AND SOCIAL CLASS

I SPEAK NEITHER AS AN HISTORIAN nor as an historian of sport, and so I appear as an amateur among professionals and can only ask you, as the phrase goes, to be 'good sports' . . . But I think that the innocence which comes from not being a specialist can sometimes lead one to ask questions which specialists tend to forget, because they think they have answered them, because they have taken for granted a certain number of presuppositions which are perhaps fundamental to their discipline. The questions I shall raise come from outside; they are the questions of a sociologist who, among the objects he studies, encounters sporting activities and entertainments (*les pratiques et les consommations sportives*) in the form, for example, of the statistical distribution of sports activities by educational level, age, sex, and occupation, and who is led to ask himself questions not only about the relationship between the practices and the variables, but also about the meaning which the practices take on in those relationships.

I think that, without doing too much violence to reality, it is possible to consider the whole range of sporting activities and entertainments offered to social agents – rugby, football, swimming, athletics, tennis, golf, etc. – as a *supply* intended to meet a *social demand*. If such a model is adopted, two sets of questions arise. First, is there an area of production, endowed with its own logic and its own history, in which 'sports products' are generated, i.e. the universe of the sporting activities and entertainments socially realized and acceptable at a given moment in time? Secondly, what are the social conditions of possibility of the appropriation of the various 'sports products' that are thus produced – playing golf or reading *L'Équipe*, cross-country skiing or watching the World Cup on TV? In other words, how is the demand for 'sports products' produced, how do people acquire the 'taste' for sport, and for one sport rather than another, whether as an activity or as a spectacle? The question certainly has to be confronted, unless one chooses to suppose that there exists a natural need, equally widespread at all times, in all places and in all social milieux, not only for the expenditure of muscular energy, but more precisely, for this or that form of exertion. (To take the example most favourable to the 'natural need' thesis, we know that swimming, which most educators would probably point to as the most necessary sporting activity, both on account of its 'life-saving' functions and its physical effects, has at times been ignored or refused – e.g. in medieval Europe – and still has to be imposed by means of national 'campaigns'.) More precisely, according to what principles do agents choose between the different sports activities or entertainments which, at a given moment in time, are offered to them as being possible? [. . .]

. . . [W]e can say that the bodily exercises of the 'élite' are disconnected from the ordinary social occasions with which folk games remained associated (agrarian feasts, for example) and divested of the social (and, *a fortiori*, religious) functions still attached to a number of traditional games (such as the ritual games played in a number of precapitalist societies at certain turning-points in the farming year). The school, the site of *skhole*, leisure, is the place where practices endowed with social functions and integrated into the collective calendar are converted into *bodily exercises*, activities which are an end in themselves, a sort of physical art for art's sake, governed by specific rules, increasingly irreducible to any functional necessity, and inserted into a specific calendar. The school is the site, *par excellence*, of what are called gratuitous exercises, where one acquires a distant, neutralizing disposition towards language and the social world, the very same one which is implied in the bourgeois relation to art, language, and the body: gymnastics makes a use of the body which, like the scholastic use of language, is an end in itself. (This no doubt explains why sporting activity, whose frequency rises very markedly with educational level, declines more slowly with age, as do cultural practices, when educational level is higher. It is known that among the working classes, the abandonment of sport, an activity whose play-like character seems to make it particularly appropriate to adolescence, often coincides with marriage and entry into the serious responsibilities of adulthood.) What is acquired in and through experience of school, a sort of retreat from the world and from real practice, of which the great boarding schools of the 'élite' represent the fully developed form, is the propensity towards activity for no purpose, a fundamental aspect of the ethos of bourgeois 'élites', who always pride themselves on disinterestedness and define themselves by an elective distance – manifested in art and sport – from material interests. 'Fair play' is the way of playing the game characteristic of those who do not get so carried away by the game as to forget that it *is* a game, those who maintain the 'rôle distance', as Goffman puts it, that is implied in all the rôles designated for the future leaders. [. . .]

The theory of amateurism is in fact one dimension of an artistocratic philosophy of sport as a disinterested practice, a finality without an end, analogous to artistic practice, but even more suitable than art (there is always something residually feminine about art: consider the piano and watercolours of genteel young ladies in the same period) for affirming the manly virtues of future leaders: sport is conceived as a training in courage and manliness, 'forming the character' and inculcating the 'will to win' which is the mark of the true leader, but a will to win within the rules. This is 'fair play', conceived as an aristocratic disposition utterly opposed to the plebeian pursuit of victory at all costs. (And then one would have to explore the link between the sporting virtues and the military virtues: remember the glorification of the deeds of old Etonians or Oxonians on the field of battle or in aerial combat.) This aristocratic ethic, devised by aristocrats (the first Olympic committee included innumerable dukes, counts and lords, and all of ancient stock) and guaranteed by aristocrats, all those who constitute the self-perpetuating oligarchy of international and national organizations, is clearly adapted to the requirements of the times, and, as one sees in the works of Baron Pierre de Coubertin, incorporates the most essential assumptions of the bourgeois ethic of private enterprise, baptized 'self-help' (English often serves as a euphemism). This glorification of sport as an essential component in a new type of apprenticeship requiring an entirely new educational institution, which is expressed in Coubertin's writings, particularly *l'Education en Angleterre* and *l'Education anglaise en France*,[1] reappears in the work of Demolins, another of Frédéric Le Play's disciples. Demolins founded the École des Roches and is author of *A quoi tient la supériorité des Anglo-Saxons* and *l'Education nouvelle*, in which he criticizes the Napoleonic barracks-style lycée (a theme which has subsequently become one of the commonplaces of the 'sociology of France' produced at the Paris Institut des Sciences Politiques and Harvard). What is at stake, it seems to me, in this debate (which goes far beyond sport), is a definition of bourgeois education which contrasts with the petty-bourgeois and academic definition: it is 'energy', 'courage', 'willpower', the virtues of leaders (military or indus-trial), and perhaps above all personal initiative, (private) 'enterprise', as opposed to knowledge, erudition, 'scholastic' submissiveness, symbolized in the great lycée-barracks and its disciplines, etc. In short, it would be a mistake to forget that the modern definition of sport that is often associated with the name of Coubertin is an integral part of a 'moral ideal', i.e. an ethos which is that of the dominant fractions of the dominant class and is brought to fruition in the major private schools intended primarily for the sons of the heads of private industry, such as the École des Roches, the paradigmatic realization of this ideal. To value *education* over *instruction*, *character* or *willpower* over *intelligence*, *sport* over *culture*, is to affirm, within the educational universe itself, the existence of a hierarchy irreducible to the strictly scholastic hierarchy which favours the second term in those oppositions. It means, as it were, disqualifying or discrediting the values recognized by other fractions of the dominant class or by other classes (especially the intellectual fractions of the petty-bourgeoisie and the 'sons of schoolteachers', who are serious challengers to the sons of the bourgeoisie on the terrain of purely scholastic competence); it means putting forward other criteria of 'achievement' and other principles for legitimating achievement as alternatives to 'academic achievement'. (In a recent survey of French industrialists,[2] I was able to demonstrate that the opposition between the two conceptions of education corresponds to two routes into managerial positions in large firms, one from the École des Roches or the major Jesuit schools via the Law Faculty or, more recently, the Institut des Sciences Politiques, the Inspection des Finances or the École des Hautes Études Commerciales, the other from a provincial lycée via the École Polytechnique.) Glorification of sport as the training-ground of character, etc., always implies a certain anti-intellectualism. When one remembers that the dominant fractions of the dominant class always tend to conceive their relation to the dominated fraction – 'intellectuals', 'artists', 'professors' – in terms of the opposition between the male and the female, the virile and the effeminate, which is given different contents depending on the period (e.g. nowadays short hair/long hair; 'economico-political' culture/'artistico-literary' culture, etc.), one understands one of the most important implications of the exaltation of sport and especially of 'manly' sports like rugby, and it can be seen that sport, like any other practice, is an object of struggles between the fractions of the dominant class and also between the social classes. [. . .]

It goes without saying that the popularization of sport, down from the élite schools (where its place is now contested by the 'intellectual' pursuits imposed by the demands of intensified social competition) to the mass sporting associations, is necessarily accompanied by a change in the functions which the sportsmen and their organizers assign to this practice, and also by a transformation of the very logic of sporting practices which corresponds to the transformation of the expectations and demands of the public in correlation with the increasing autonomy of the spectacle vis-à-vis past or present practice. The exaltation of 'manliness' and the cult of 'team spirit'[3] that are associated with playing rugby – not to mention the aristocratic ideal of 'fair play' – have a very different meaning and function for bourgeois or aristocratic adolescents in English public schools and for the sons of peasants or shopkeepers in south-west France. This is simply because, for example, a sporting career, which is practically excluded from the field of acceptable trajectories for a child of the bourgeoisie – setting aside tennis or golf – represents one of the few paths of upward mobility open to the children of the dominated classes; the sports market is to the boys' physical capital what the system of beauty prizes and the occupations to which they lead – hostess, etc. – is to the girls' physical capital; and the working-class cult of sportsmen of working-class origin is doubtless explained in part by the fact that these 'success stories' symbolize the only recognized route to wealth and fame. Everything suggests that the 'interests' and values which practitioners from the working and lower-middle classes bring into the conduct of sports are in harmony with the corresponding requirements of *professionalization* (which can, of course, coexist with the appearances of amateurism) and of the rationalization of preparation for and performance of the sporting exercise that are imposed by the pursuit of maximum specific efficiency (measured in 'wins', 'titles', or 'records') combined with the minimization of risks (which we have seen is itself linked to the development of a private or State sports entertainments industry). [. . .]

The most important property of the 'popular sports' is the fact they are tacitly associated with youth, which is spontaneously and implicitly credited with a sort of *provisional licence* expressed, among other ways, in the squandering of an excess of physical (and sexual) energy, and are abandoned very early (usually at the moment of entry into adult life, marked by marriage). By contrast, the 'bourgeois' sports, mainly practised for their functions of physical maintenance and for the social profit they bring, have in common the fact that their age-limit lies far beyond youth and perhaps comes correspondingly later the more prestigious and exclusive they are (e.g. golf). This means that the probability of practising those sports which, because they demand only 'physical' qualities and bodily competences for which the conditions of early apprenticeship seem to be fairly equally distributed, are doubtless equally accessible within the limits of the spare time and, secondarily, the physical energy available, would undoubtedly increase as one goes up the social hierarchy, if the concern for distinction and the absence of ethico-aesthetic affinity or 'taste' for them did not turn away members of the dominant class, in accordance with a logic also observed in other fields (photography, for example).[4]

Thus, most of the team sports – basketball, handball, rugby, football – which are most common among office workers, technicians and shopkeepers, and also no doubt the most typically working-class individual sports, such as boxing or wrestling, combine all the reasons to repel the upper classes. These include the social composition of their public which reinforces the vulgarity implied by their popularization, the values and virtues demanded (strength, endurance, the propensity to violence, the spirit of 'sacrifice', docility and submission to collective discipline, the absolute antithesis of the 'rôle distance' implied in bourgeois rôles, etc.), the exaltation of competition and the contest, etc.

Notes

This article is a translation of a paper given at the International Congress of the History of Sports and Physical Education Association, held in March 1978 at the Institut National des Sports et de l'Education Physique, Paris. The original title was 'Pratiques sportives et pratiques sociales'. The translation is by Richard Nice.

1   Cf. J. Thibault, *Sports et education physique, 1870–1970*, Paris, Vrin, 1973.
2   P. Bourdieu, M. de Saint Martin, 'Le patronat', *Actes de la Recherche en Sciences Sociales* 20/21, 1978, pp. 3–82.
3   Cf. T. Weinberg, *The English public schools*, New York, Atherton Press, 1967, pp. 111–112.
4   Cf. P. Bourdieu *et al.*, *Un art moyen, essai sur les usages sociaux de la photographie*, Paris, Editions de Minuit, 1965.

Ronald Frankenberg

FOOTBALL AND POLITICS IN
A NORTH WALES COMMUNITY
(PENTREDIWAITH)

[. . .]

THE DIVISION BETWEEN THE SOCIAL CLASS represented by magistrates and the class represented by parish councillors . . . is almost, but not quite, congruent with the distinction between 'outsiders' and 'Pentre people'. It is a division which has arisen out of the economic and social life of the village itself. The outsiders, again generally speaking, come in contact with the villagers only as employers or in other positions of authority such as magistrates. But they are known personally to villagers, who treat them with friendliness tinged with respect. Such outsiders contribute to village funds and help the villagers in other ways. In 1953 class antagonism was often overshadowed by personal friendliness. This has not, of course, always been the case, as even a cursory reading of Welsh history demonstrates. Thus a correspondent of *The Times* wrote in 1843:

> It cannot be denied that the people look upon the landlords and gentry and Magistrates, as a *class*, with hatred and suspicion, and if one quarter of the stories are true which I have heard, not without just cause.[1]

Landlords and magistrates 'as a class' are still distrusted and looked upon with suspicion. At the Parish Councils Association meeting which I describe they were attacked as a class. Within Pentrediwaith, however, where their power is now in any case very limited, even the remains of suspicion usually (but not always) gives way to liking based on personal experience. There was a sharper division between the villagers and those who, although they had originated from amongst Pentre people, had prospered economically and were trying to renounce the informal social ties that identified them with the mass of Pentre people.

The class division between parish councillors themselves and participants in the other organs of local government is emphasized in the minds of both the parish councillors and Pentre people in general by the fact that the Parish Council, which represents most closely their interests as wage-earners and as the inhabitants of a particular local area, is almost powerless to change conditions. Pentre people feel that only the Parish Council has a true appreciation of village problems. This feeling is further emphasized by the fact that the Rural District Council and the County Council, which are remote from both a particular locality and the common people, are invested with power which Pentre villagers have often resented even when it was, in fact, operating to their advantage. [. . .]

Many if not all of the social activities which are carried on within Pentrediwaith are imposed upon the village by formal or informal pressures which arise outside the village. This applies with equal force to recreation and to politics. Thus Pentrediwaith chose football as its sport because of the existing framework of Football Associations in the county and the nation. [. . .]

The football club in 1954 finally reached the stage when it was in feud with most of the village women and with so many of the village men that it had no support left. From what villagers told me, I concluded that the male voice choir and the brass band had perished for similar reasons. It seems to me possible that there is a sort of cycle of public activities which rise and fall in this way. [. . .]

Men and women football supporters are organized in separate committees. The one for women, the supporters' club, organizes social events and collects money; the other, the football club, consists of men only, chooses the team and spends what the supporters have collected. [. . .]

Although the parish council acts from time to time for the village as a whole and negotiates on behalf of the village with outside powers, it is not a symbol of village unity and cohesion against the outside world.

During 1953 the village football club provided such a symbol but this was not, of course, its only function in village life. The fact that the outside prestige of the village would be judged by the football club's public appearances did, however, have the effect of giving football a central place in village social activity. In the village details of the internal struggles the football, flower show and fête committees were of paramount importance, trivial though they may seem from outside. [. . .]

Football is only one social activity which brings the village into contact with other villages, but in 1953 it happened to be the most important. [. . .]

Association football is the established sport of this part of North Wales. . . . It is a sport . . . which has a more than specialist appeal. The equipment needed for football is relatively inexpensive and the preparation for a game or a competition is not very arduous. The season is long, from August to May, but leaves the summer free for gardening and holiday activities. Football is very nearly an all-weather game. The Welsh Football Association and the Welsh National League provide a framework in which a village team can take its place. Since this framework exists and other villages have teams it is considered that each important village should be represented in its local League in order to maintain its prestige. The national organization takes (or should take) much of the burden off local organizations since it fixes the length of the season, arranges the fixtures, and lays down the rules. The League provides referees and specifies kick-off times. The village has merely to muster eleven players and some officials and provide a pitch. The rest is provided from above. Finally, association football is above all the British national game. Whatever local and class allegiance there may be to rugby union or rugby league, league and county cricket, or to tennis and still more localized games like marbles, bowls, darts or archery, association football is the one sporting interest and topic of conversation which can cut across all class and regional boundaries.

Pentrediwaith's football club provides participation in this national game for both spectators and players. The spectators keep their eye in for North Wales Coast matches and the Welsh Amateur Cup, for Third Division (North) League matches and cup-ties and for Internationals and the First Division farther afield. To have a village team, especially when composed of local lads, fosters the fanatical partisanship which gives savour even to professional League football in the towns and gives Pentre football an intense importance in the village. The honour of the village and its place in the outside world are at stake in each game and in the day-to-day conduct of the club.

The players enjoy the game, the exercise and the local prestige. They sometimes hope to advance to Oldham or Wrexham in the Third Division or to better North Wales clubs. One or two Pentrediwaith youths in recent years have had trials for Manchester City. It is not forgotten in Pentrediwaith that the fabulous Billy Meredith, Welsh International and player for both Manchester City and United, came from a village in North Wales.

The fact that everyone in the village, almost without exception, is pleased when Pentrediwaith distinguishes itself on the football field does not mean that the village unites, in amity and co-operation, to make the village football team a success. The very intensity of interest that the game arouses leads also to divergencies of opinion. Committees split into overtly and latently hostile groups, often along lines predetermined by family dislikes or by insults incurred in entirely different situations but carried over into the organization of recreation.

The football club

The football committee met once or twice a week to choose the team for the following Saturday and to transact any other business as it arose. The other business often concerned disputes with the League over the non-fulfilment of obligations on both sides. Committee members were expected to travel, at their own expense, on the bus which carried the team to away matches on alternate Saturdays. One of the committee acted as linesman and another as trainer. In addition, members of the committee had to play occasionally as substitutes for players who had failed to turn up. For home games the field had to be marked with lime, the grass cut occasionally and thistles uprooted.

These last three jobs were all arduous and unpleasant. Usually the lime was applied by hand in powdered form. One just filled a bucket with the powder and sprinkled it in handfuls along the lines (or what seemed to be the lines). This job ruined one's clothes, dried one's throat and stung one's hands. It was very expensive in lime and on windy days the marker appeared to have been rolling in flour. Later in the 1953–4 season the club acquired a mechanical marker which employed a lime solution, but the condition of the field reduced its efficiency and made it difficult to use. When there was snow on the ground sawdust was used for marking. Other preparations on the field, which was a pasture during the week, were also arduous and unpleasant. The grass was cut with scythes or even sickles and mole hills had to be flattened. Occasionally turf displaced by pigs had to be replaced. The players had to take their chance of avoiding the cowpats as the committee had no inclination to remove them.

The nets had to be placed in position before home games and the balls inflated and fetched to the pitch. Two committee members had to collect the money at the gate, while another fetched tea from the village at half-time and paid the referee's fee and expenses. After the game the nets had to be taken down again. This was a wet, cold, dirty and awkward job because the nets were tied to the cross-bar with creosoted string and there was no step-ladder. Someone else had to collect the players' dirty clothes and see that they were washed and in good condition for the following week. Finally, according to Football Association rules, the committee is also responsible for the safety of the referee; this is not always a light burden. Thus the committee members had chores to perform as well as decisions to make, and some of them, like marking the field, were both time-consuming and tedious. These jobs were the prerogative of committee members only and the suggestion at committee meetings that others be 'allowed' (sic) to help was at first strongly opposed, although it was eventually adopted.

As the Welsh language served to determine the class composition of the parish council, so the existence of chores limited to some extent the economic class status of members of the football committee. Excluding myself, all those who served as ordinary committee members in seasons 1951–2, 1952–3, and 1953–4 were working men. Even the officers were not far removed. The chairmen during the first two seasons were in fact employers of labour in a very small way, but they worked themselves side by side with their employees. The vice-chairman, the manager of the local Co-operative Stores, helped each week to take the nets down and to collect money at the gate, but he was implicitly excused from the various tasks of preparation of the field. In season 1953–4, the chairman, secretary and treasurer were all white-collar workers, and on several occasions one of them complained to me that cutting grass was not the sort of work he was accustomed to; it made him feel, he said, 'like a bloody navvy'. [. . .]

The committee which carried out all these functions had, as the senior official in its formal structure, a president. He was expected to give a handsome donation to the club but not to preside. In 1952–3 the president was the Welsh-speaking publican of one of the three village pubs. It appears that he did actually preside over informal inquests held in his bar. He gave a £5 donation.[2] In 1953–4 he declined to continue in office, and his place was taken by the English-speaking proprietor of the principal village grocer's shop. He was a newcomer to the village and he did on one occasion preside at a committee meeting but, trained in English public school 'rugger', he apparently did not feel at home and did not come again. He remained a generous supporter of the club.

Next to the president were ten or eleven vice-presidents—local gentry, shopkeepers and publicans who owed their position to their ability and willingness to help financially. Below the vice-presidents was the club committee proper with a chairman, a vice-chairman (representing the Women's Supporters' Club of which, though a man, he was chairman), a secretary, a treasurer and ordinary committee members. Most committee members in season 1953–4 were ex-players for the club. Committee members who still play are not encouraged because of the obvious difficulty of discussing their performances. One man who was very keen on the football club refused an invitation to serve on the committee on the grounds that it would prejudice his chances of being chosen to play for the club. The team captain was an ex-officio committee member but never attended. Only three members of the committee had never played for the club: myself, a Londoner who had come to live in the village and worked in a nearby colliery, and the 'supporters' representative'.

The membership of the football committee was exceptional at the beginning of season 1953–4 in that there were five coalminers serving on it. This was probably the result of disputes in season 1952–3 between the miner secretary and other committee members. It was, however, very characteristic of Pentrediwaith committees (other than those concerned with local government) that their membership did not consist of isolated individuals but of groups united by kinship or other ties. These groups voted, and from time to time resigned, as units. The miners' group in the 1953–4 committee was one example of this; in the previous season an informal drinking-group led by the chairman was another. This latter group resigned as a body at the end of season 1952–3, but when things were going badly in 1953–4 offered to come back as a group. Their offer was accepted, but they changed their minds before the next meeting. When the miner secretary resigned in 1953 he resigned alone, but he continued to discuss the affairs of the club and to exert an influence on them through his informal relations with the miners who remained. One by one during the season they also resigned or just ceased to attend.
[. . .]

At the end of 1951–2 the team stood third, in its League Division. They had up to that time played on a field adjoining the Castell road, between the Council school and the minister's house. This had the disadvantage [to the football club] that it was easy to watch the game from the outside without going into the field at all. In this way villagers could avoid both the entrance payment and getting their feet wet. The danger to the club's revenues arising from this situation was partly met by having a collection among the non-paying spectators, and the response to this expedient was improved by having a policeman to make the collection in his helmet. The new committee, with Charley as secretary, moved from this field to a more remote pitch a little way outside the village and surrounded by other fields. On this new site only paying spectators could see.

This move had its disadvantages. At the old field watching football on Saturday was often a casual affair. People on their way to and from the village had to pass the field. Sometimes they stopped for a moment to watch, became interested and stayed. The general uproar during an exciting game could be heard from all parts of the village and attracted people to the ground. This gave rise to an amusing incident during one particularly hard-fought game with a team regarded as a traditional rival. On this Saturday afternoon a villager going off to shoot rabbits was on his way up the hill leading to the church when he heard a particularly loud roar from the football ground. He returned to the village to see what was going on, became more interested in watching the game than in continuing his shoot and remained. The referee made decisions which the visitors did not approve of and they later complained to the Welsh F.A. At the inquiry which followed the visitors' officials insisted that not only had the Pentrediwaith crowd been aggressive and threatening but that one of them had even brought a shotgun to intimidate the referee.

At the field used in 1953 to come and watch the game was always a deliberate act. No one passed the field or visited it except for the specific purpose of watching football. Some villagers felt, I believe with reason, that by moving in this way outside the village physically, the football club was also isolating itself to some extent from the social life of the village. Only real enthusiasts would follow a losing team in such circumstances. In my opinion, it is highly probable that this was a factor in producing the falling off of feminine interest in the game, and all that that implied in the loss of financial support. For the women of Pentre were often busy on Saturday, as on any other afternoon. For them the moving of the field from a central point in the village to right outside was almost equivalent to moving it to Castell or Tonmawr. The move made football virtually inaccessible. Many women lost interest also when the team came to be predominantly composed of outsiders. The combination of a 'foreign' team and a distant field adopted by the committee at the outset of season 1952–3 brought into the open the already existing conflict of interests between the men of the football club and the women of the supporters' club. As I have suggested, in Pentrediwaith, particularly now that most men go away to work, the full support of the women is crucial for the success of any activity. [. . .]

On a visit I paid to Pentre in late January 1954 I found that the committee had been reinforced by the father and one of the brothers of the secretary. An attempt to get the 1952–3 season's committee to come back had failed. The football club was run informally by the three committee members who remained. Gates continued to diminish and, although village interest still ran high, village support was negligible.

Disputes do not long remain unresolved within the football club. For since the common interest in keeping football going is not sufficient, the committee splits and members resign. But while disputes in committee are solved by the resignation, or a less dramatic falling-off in attendance, of dissident members, the argument continues in the village. Eventually, as had happened by the beginning of 1954, an opposition to the football club grows up. There was a large number of men who would have nothing to do with the football club, and some who went even further and worked against it. The club's posters were torn from trees and players left at short notice to play elsewhere. There was a move, to be described below, to cut off sources of financial aid from the club. A parallel opposition was built up in the women's supporters' club. On a visit to Pentre in September 1954 when the football club had ceased to operate, I learned that although the supporters still had £25 in the bank, they were refusing to let the football committee have it even to pay their outstanding debts.

It seems to me that this sort of development is characteristic in the history of Pentre institutions and, I suspect, of that of similar villages. Efforts are made to avoid conflict, but once a breach is made patent, it spreads through the village. The face-to-face nature of social contacts, and the multiplicity of ties which close residence in an 'isolated' unit brings about, makes this spread inevitable. After a period, which in the case of the football club was three years from the original difference over policy, the village becomes so divided that the particular activity cannot continue. In this case the activity perished altogether and was replaced by a carnival. [. . .]

Although conflict bedevilled the internal affairs of the football club, efforts were made to avoid it, and in this attempt strangers played their own familiar role. The English miner introduced the actual resolutions most likely to split the committee internally, or to isolate it from other villagers. When conflict did break out, it was he or I who made the conciliatory moves. Similarly, when Charley and the chairman of the parish council settled their differences it was the bank manager, an 'outsider' by class and place of birth, who was finally given the blame. The chairmen of the football club in the three seasons I have considered were all Welsh and Nonconformist, but nevertheless a little removed in outlook from the committee they led. In the first two seasons the chairmen were employers, although they worked alongside their men. In season 1953–4, the chairman was a bank clerk who, although he had played for the club and was a Welsh-speaking Chapel-goer, came from elsewhere. During this season the chair was taken in his absence by the English-speaking Co-operative Stores manager or by myself.

Although the differences of opinion which arose were on issues which were real, the individuals who clashed, Charley and Humphrey, Humphrey and Adam, Charley and Tom, were in fact motivated by loyalties and dislikes forged outside the committee or the club. In the case of the football club, conflict triumphed over cohesion, for although the football team symbolized village unity against the outside world, the organization of football was a sectional interest of the men. Amongst the men only a small group were active, although many were interested. There was insufficient external pressure to make them carry on despite their differences. [. . .]

Recreational activities which bring the village into contact and competition with other villages . . . serve, as the football club did in the years after the war until 1953, as a symbol of village prestige and unity in the face of the outside world. Their exploits are recorded in the local newspapers and noised abroad by villagers. But the internal divisions to which they give rise decrease their efficiency as symbols. The football club won only two games in the 1953–4 season. The quality of performance of the brass band and the choir also decreased as they began to crumble. This external failure in turn still further weakens the internal position of the activity. A poor performance at a football match or play or eisteddfod spoils the villager's reputation. I suspect that this hypothesis, of increasing internal and external failure as conflicts surrounding an activity grow, may be more widely applicable.[3]

We have seen that, in Pentrediwaith, activities are started with practical aims and in emulation of similar activities in neighbouring, and even distant, parts of England and Wales. Many Pentre villagers enjoy playing and watching association football, Britain's national game. Other villagers like to sing or play brass-band instruments or to listen to those who do. At different times in the past villagers attracted to these and other recreational pursuits have combined with others to take part in them. When they form associations of this kind, there are national organizations in which they can take their place and play their part. But since Pentre people feel themselves to be a community, when they combine with fellow-villagers to form a team or 'party' their association becomes more than a convenient arrangement based on the 'accident' of living together. Combining in recreational activities has social value to the villagers because it emphasizes their relationships one to another in a community. This is true of all communities. But it is especially important when the men no longer work together. In this kind of situation recreational activities provide the only system in which they can 'interact' as members of a community.[4] [. . .]

In Pentrediwaith recreational activities are not connected with prosperity or with an institutionalized structure in the village, as they are in some primitive societies.[5] They arise from the meeting of individual interests, where there is no structural arrangement of relations between these individuals, although villagers feel that the village ought to have communal activities. Hence the conflicts which intrude into the activities are between individuals in unformalized relations, and their expression does not end in a return to an ordained pattern of relations. The system is repetitive only in a limited field, and the significant divisions in the society between 'Pentre people' and 'outsiders' remain unaffected. For these last are reflections of national alignments over which Pentre villagers have no control.

In Pentrediwaith conflicts are carried over from one form of recreational activity to another, as from football to carnival. Furthermore, the new conflicts engendered in disputes over football and carnivals may extend back into everyday life and cause further divisions within the village. The degree of success with which villagers continue to co-operate in new activities is a measure of the success with which they are meeting the threat of losing their discrete village identity. [. . .]

I hope that my study emphasizes also one important point which has emerged from other studies. Despite all the cross-cutting divisions, a group such as the Swazi or the Tale people or a Zulu village has symbolic activities which are expressive of its unity. So, too, if a village in Wales is a village it undertakes activities which are village activities. All individuals are expected to join in independently of their relations with one another. If the observations of this study are borne out elsewhere, it seems that we may be able to say that if there are no such activities we have a housing-unit and not a village. Perhaps also my study of recreation in Pentrediwaith emphasizes that some form of 'ceremonial' in the sense of joint symbolic activities is necessary to maintain group loyalty in an acephalous community. This seems to me especially true when the men of the group no longer work together. [. . .]

In the past villagers worked together, played together and lived together. Their common history is a factor in their own continued cohesion. They pride themselves on being a group of kin and on being Welsh. Now only the women work together, and each successive failure of a social activity makes the next one more difficult to start. Improvements in public transport, television, radio and the cinema have already diminished the interest of the young people in the village and its affairs. Emigration in search of better economic and leisure opportunities is taking its toll. These developments decrease the number of cross-cutting ties which bind Pentre people into a community. As many of the older villagers fear, the time may come, if these developments continue, when the village ceases to be a village community and becomes merely a collection of dwellings, housing some of the industrial workers of Great Britain.

Notes

1   *The Times*, 30 September, 1843, quoted in *Report of The Royal Commission on Land in Wales and Monmouthshire*, 1893–96, p. 156.

2   The costs of running a football club even on a small scale are surprisingly high. In 1952–3 the club had a turnover of over £260. In the previous season it had one of over £200. The figures for 1953–4 are not available.

3   The rise and fall of social activities in British communities has often been commented on. See for example the works of Kempe and Whiteley listed in the Bibliography.

4   See Homans, G., *The Human Group*, for general discussion on the relations of *interaction* and *sentiment*. For particular discussion in a somewhat similar situation to Pentrediwaith, see his discussion of Hilltown in ch. xiii.

5   Gluckman, M., *Rituals of Rebellion in South East Africa*, The Frazer Lecture 1952, Manchester University Press, 1954.

Bibliography

Gluckman, Max, 'Analysis of a Social Situation in Modern Zululand', *Bantu Studies* XIV, 1940, 1 and 2; *Rituals of Rebellion in South-East Africa*, The Frazer Lecture 1952, Manchester, 1954; 'Political Institutions', in *The Institutions of Primitive Society*, Oxford, 1954.

Homans, George, *The Human Group*, London, 1951.

Kempe, J., 'A Pilot Survey of Much Marcle', *The Sociological Review* XLI, 1949.

Whiteley, Winifred, 'Littletown-in-Overspill', in Kuper, I., *Living in Towns*, London, 1953.

Brian Jackson

ON THE BOWLING GREEN

'**H**UDDERSFIELD IS THE STRONGHOLD** of Yorkshire bowls,' said the President. He was shovelling coal from the railway sidings into his wagon. He ran a one-man business, and at work wore an old sack round his waist like an apron, a dusty felt hat, a dirty grey shirt with a silk tie pulled so tight that the knot was minute. His coal-streaked suit had leather shoulder pads fitted into it. Probably ten years before he would have been formally dressed in these same clothes—suit, hat, silk tie—for a presentation ceremony on the green. At work his talk ran mostly on gambling and bowls —sometimes veering out of Yorkshire into little patches of middle class 'one does this, one does that'.

'We've had to alter a clause in our rules to say that you could have money prizes. But that was to remove abuses that were creeping in. These competitions, like the *News of the World*, they gave them vouchers. But the chap who was bowling, he'd be able to take this voucher to the shop and say "how much cash will you give me for it?" We're really amateurs here—over in Lancashire it's more of a professional game. They're betting mad—they bowl all the year round, sweep the snow off greens. They go for the bookies, you see, and you get a different sort of people going. But as far as we're concerned, the bookies aren't there. Once you get that element creeping in, you get nasty stories about bowlers not bowling their best. We've never had one proved, but we've suspected one or two. People nowadays are betting mad. They're not content with the wage they get, are they? I reckon the ordinary man earns a good wage nowadays, but they don't seem content with it; there's pools and there's Bingo. And these 'ere One Armed Bandits, well it's absolute foolishness is that. I've sat back and I've studied, now what makes a young fellow put sixpence in that thing—and being in business myself you know,

I sometimes see my money going in as well. If you understand what I mean? Money that should have been paid to me. You have to keep quiet though about it.'

The bowls played in Huddersfield is Crown Green bowls, not the Flat Green bowls played in the Midlands and South. In Crown Green, not only are the woods (bowls) biased, but the green slopes away in every direction from the crown (centre). So in trying to get the woods nearer the jack than your opponent can, you must match bias against bias. [. . .]

Huddersfield has thirty-three main bowling clubs, and many more ephemeral ones. The strongest ones are usually bowling clubs, whose whole *raison d'être* is built round the green. Next come the working men's clubs which have a green attached, then Liberal or Conservative clubs with greens, and weakest of all the clubs that spring from factories and mills, or which have tried to build themselves up in a public park. In a good summer there must be 5,000 fairly regular bowlers in Huddersfield. No other sport begins to rival it in numbers of players. In the big events Huddersfield probably enters more players than any other town. The *News of the World* Handicap will attract 350 very skilled bowlers from Huddersfield—half the total entry. The Yorkshire Merit will get 400 or so, a quarter of the entry. And there is a whole range of local competitions—knockout, handicap, merit, elimination cup, rose bowl, league. The story is that bowls is an old man's game, and certainly half that 5,000 will be aged fifty or more. But very many younger men are always to be seen on the greens, and there is a permanent scattering of women and teenagers. It would be truer to say that the game *features* old men, puts them conspicuously 'on stage'.

The clubs are very like working men's clubs—a bar, dominoes, whist drives for the Darby and Joan Club on a Monday afternoon, a concert on a Saturday evening, trips away during the summer. But the green makes a difference. It gives an outdoor focus, a stage whose montage demands its special skills and rituals. 'It takes three and a half hours to prepare this green, and during that time we walk seven miles apiece.' There is a vast amount of pegging out, fertilising, worm treading, rolling, air-hole making. From time to time, well-paid local experts are called in to bring back the quality of a green. The intensity of concern over the green is far more than that found in local cricket over the maintenance of the pitch. Only at county level does pitch culture equal the felt importance of green culture. 'This green was here twenty-five years before I was born so it'll be a hundred years old anyway. That green over there is older. This is a tricky one, but yon over there is the best one. That old one, we're gonna do it before winter comes, we're gonna get it up to scratch again.'

Crown Green bowls is the most popular sport in Huddersfield. It is almost exclusively working class; it has developed from a sport into one of the interlocking cells of community with a local 'club' life growing out from it; there is a certain perplexing intensity when people discuss it, and somehow it has a special importance to the old. [. . .]

On the last day of the formal season, came the Champion of Champions Merit. The park greens were already closed, some keen bowling clubs would play for another week or two yet, but the Champion of Champions meant the end of the game till next spring.

It was a competition between some of the winners of the better known Merit Matches in Yorkshire. There was the Working Men's Club Merit winner, the Murrfield Merit winner, the Yorkshire Merit winner, Conservative League winner and so on. Some sixteen players in all. The prize was not large, something like £20 for the winner. The chief attraction was the honour of winning the final merit.

The bowling club at Springwood was very ramshackle: two huts, in the smaller of which tea was served. Besides this, there was the large club room itself, where beer was being pulled. Entrance was two shillings. At about half past three there was a large crowd spreading round half the bowling green. Benches were arranged over this distance, and these were necessary, because most of the spectators were over the age of fifty. Quite a few of them old age pensioners. There were few younger men aged forty and below. There were few women, perhaps one to every ten men. Most of the spectators congregated on the flight of steps leading out of the club room. But by the time the players were down to the quarter finals, the spectators were grouped four deep and thicker along the club side of the green. In among the spectators were the bookmakers. There were four of these, two of them more enthusiastic than others. One man stood on a chair, another just stood quietly in the corner. As each game proceeded, they would shout to the scorers, 'What's t'game now?' And on receiving the score would rapidly work out the odds for that game. All the betting was on the final, and as the afternoon progressed the ground became littered with torn up betting slips as the various favourites went out. Much the most conspicuous bookmaker was a fat man wearing enormous pin-stripe trousers, fancy waistcoat, dark coat, and a bowler hat. He had great features, red face, glary eyes. He was a familiar figure, many of the crowd talked and joked with him throughout the afternoon. He had men about him whom he called his 'slaves'. They were also conspicuously dressed. One of them, Jim, was wearing a black Homburg, and a black coat like his boss. The other looked more American, a sharp-faced man, less conspicuously dressed in light grey suit, and trilby. His job was to stand behind the other bookmakers as they were making their book, and if possible see how they were going on. He signalled their bets to his master by the usual tick tack code. Betting was very complicated. The odds changed with every wood at some stages. Thus in five minutes in the semi-final the odds dropped from five to one, down to three to one and then to five to two. Nearly everybody seemed to make a bet at some stage or other. Many of them by astute betting managed to back both players in the finals at reasonable odds, so that they couldn't lose by the end of the afternoon. Bets were quite large, usually in paper money, a pound or two. [. . .]

The players were of widely different ages. The oldest player was seventy-six, a man called Jagger. He was not much more than five feet two high, wearing flat cap, serge pin-stripe suit, and black boots. His appearance caused much satisfied comment, 'Where are these young bowlers now, that's showing 'em up a bit, i'nt it.' Earlier in the season, at the Yorkshire Merit, people said he couldn't last out through the hot day's play, but he'd won. Now that the weather was colder, people said he wouldn't last through a cold day, and towards the evening there was much comment when Jagger was seen to be putting his coat on. Others of the players were about thirty years old. Jagger was an unspectacular player, very dour, winning the crowd's approval for his unshakability.

Each of the players tended to exhibit his personality to the crowd. A younger player for instance was 'A cocky little bugger', because he carried himself very confidently and he was given to signalling points before the final wood had come to rest, or to making confident statements about who was 'on' from a good distance. If his opponent had some luck, or even if he hadn't, he would sometimes shake his head ruefully and talk to the crowd. Or hold out his hands in despair. The crowd were half inclined to like this, but in the end they preferred the more staid play of Jagger.

The players were very active, some of the older men in particular running across the green to look at ends and then coming back before they bowled their next wood. As each round ended there was a flow into the club house to get more beer, a short intermission for drinking and then when the next round started, a flow out onto the steps again.

The Merit lasted from two o'clock in the afternoon until seven in the evening, going on into the dusk. As the game approached the finals the bookmakers offered shorter and shorter odds, until finally hardly anyone was prepared to take them. Now and again they would resort to phoney betting with each other. One bookmaker would call out the odds, the other one would offer to take him. But no money ever exchanged hands between them. The 'slaves' put money on with their boss, and ostentatiously passed pound notes across. But the crowd grew wise to this one as well. There was much dissatisfaction with the standard of bowling. One man shouted out, 'There's one bowler that would have licked them all.' And gave the name of a well-known player of a few years ago. There were mutters of approval from the back. Finally at the beginning of the final between two old age-pensioners, one man, aged sixty-five, the other man Jagger aged seventy-six, the betting ceased. Jagger won the match easily. Champion of Champions. Great applause, a presentation in the gathering dusk. Then most of the people strolled home, but a few stayed to drink in the club house. There was no check on members drinking, and no fear of the police coming. It felt like the end of a long, half-understood ceremony. The players and spectators sipping a final pint, or sensing the autumn nip as they made their way home to fireside and television. All tension had gone. [. . .]

First, bowls belong to the same plane of community as working men's clubs. In a club, the focus is the beer, and whereas the tendency in a pub (though often defeated) is to treat the establishment as a shop that sells beer, in a club the activities spread out star-wise. 'Regulars' are replaced by members; long hours go into playing dominoes or reading papers and spending nothing; there are concerts, trips, treats, that bring in children, wives, the old; there are cells of special activities—band practice, snooker team, union meetings. Bowling clubs are very similar to all this; they too are a society of members, chiefly men, who link up with other groupings—part of the network of community. But with them, the green has more importance than the bar. An interesting example is what happens when a working-class group sets up a bowls club in a municipal park. There are always difficulties between the club and the committee of the local council or its officer. The source is often the same: the officials, and the middle class councillors see the park as a public amenity. They don't much like the idea of clubs since this suggests closed membership, and they want to run the green as an object in itself. If you want to play bowls, here it is, if you don't then go somewhere else and do something else. It is a single commodity like beer in the public house. What the working-class want, and try to make of it, is rather different. They want to build around the green the familiar, interlocking cells of the community. [. . .]

Second, bowls is a sporting expression of the northern working class similar to other examples. As with Rugby League (which was formed in the George Hotel, Huddersfield) there is the awareness of a middle class or south-country sport which is not quite what they want. Rugby Union or Flat Green bowls are discussed in much the same way. Both are regarded as snooty (though working men may play bowls in the South and Welsh rugby is certainly known to be different). Both are considered to be less skilled. The northern games, adapted to working-class life, allow a mild professionalism—a matter of earning a few pounds on the side. Both allow a bit of gambling, yet at the same time, besides the drink and gambling moments, both have their moral, Methodist tone. And both are very concerned with the spectator. This doesn't make them passive rather than active sports as is sometimes argued about other games—rather they are individual or team activities within a strong communal setting. The spectator is important.

And as with Rugby League and brass bands there is a missionary feeling about the 'movement'. Rugby League is clearest here, with its annual, hopeless trip to Wembley. Brass bands travelling by coach to the Albert Hall are similar. There is no traditional missionary journey of like stature in bowls. But nearer home the spirit of pilgrimage and festival is quite as strong. With Rugby League there is a feeling that Odsal stadium, Bradford, is a very special amphitheatre, different from other grounds. With brass bands, Belle Vue, Manchester, has this place. With bowls, it's the *Talbot* and the *Waterloo* at Blackpool. [. . .]

Third, just as football—Huddersfield Town versus Leeds United—offers something like tribal conflict, with its strongest appeal to and involvement with the young and middle-aged men, so bowls is peculiarly potent for the old. Young men play it, and play it successfully. Yet they're treated as exceptions even when they are not. The meaning of bowls lies largely in its service to the old. On the green, the old men can look as vigorous as the young—it's noticeable how much they run and jump as soon as they are 'on stage'. The smooth rolling 'woods' don't require a young man's strength, and possibly there are some virtues—crossing bias with bias, knowing a green's peculiarities—that age is more likely to have. I rather doubt this though, and suspect that the premium placed on long experience is much exaggerated—another part of the old man 'myth'. The green, itself so aggressively young and fresh to look at and yet paradoxically so old and cherished, is a very special setting where an old man can, for a brief spell, be young again. Fringed by the perpetually arguing crowd, shadowed by the coming dusk, the old men briskly pursue the smooth-running woods over the green grass. One begins to see . . . how these obscured patterns of living command such loyalties—and make good sense.

Paul Corrigan

WHAT DO KIDS GET
OUT OF FOOTBALL?

[. . .]

OVER THE PAST FEW YEARS there have been claims about the increasing violence by teenagers both at dance halls and football matches. But the question arises of whether this violence *is* actually increasing or, as is more likely, there is now a different sort of experience involved.

What *is* violence at football matches and dance halls?

Question Do you watch much football?
Derek M. We chant, have a scrap with some of the lads. Perhaps have a crack at other supporters. Keep away from coppers. Watch the match too (laughs).
Question Do you get into trouble?
Derek M. Aye, but not real trouble and it's great.

Football is being offered to these boys by Sunderland F.C., or rather the right to stand and watch a football match and to shout for Sunderland. Rather than simply accept that, they take part in a complete and different set of experiences called 'going to footy'. This *includes* watching the football, and in fact is pervaded throughout by what is happening on the field in front of them,* but is a collection of experiences that are not simply watching a game of soccer. Such experiences are difficult for me to articulate, let alone

---

*In fact the only serious football riot at Roker Park occurred after they had been beaten in their second successive home match by three clear goals. This was in the year after they were relegated, and a section of the crowd did in fact smash up part of the town after the match. Thus, obviously the extra-football activities are related to the football.

the boys. To be at your team's ground in the middle of a good game of football is *more* than watching a game of soccer. To go with your mates to the Fulwell End is to take part in a collective and creative experience that starts at about half-past-one and finishes at about six o'clock. This experience may lead to violence either of a verbal (chanting) or of a physical character, but is not *necessarily* an experience characterised by violence.

Similarly in a dance hall. The music, like the football, pervades the experience but does not limit that experience to a spectator one. Taylor has written historically about the fan attempting to recapture control of his game;[1] and my research would back up this rejection of a pure spectator role in both the musical and the football experience. As was said at the beginning of this section the commercial institution offers services for money, but it also fails to limit rigidly what cannot be done by the buyer. This room for manoeuvre is the area that these boys are trying to control for themselves. Any visitor to football or dance halls over the past four years could not have failed to notice the attempts by those who run these institutions to limit that freedom to create their own non-spectator experience with the introduction of more bouncers, more stewards and, of course, more police.

The participation of these boys in the experience of a football match is a group experience with their mates. It represents a challenge to the mere spectator role of the sport and represents a possibility of the group *creation* of action. The action created – chanting, fighting, singing on the terraces, fighting, having a laugh in the dance hall – is action that represents the cultural background of the boys. There is none of the quiet appreciation of the skills of football or music that might characterise a more intellectually-inspired audience. Instead there is involvement and creation of their own kind of action. With regard to pop music this would also cut across the simplistic generational boundary drawn by the concept of 'teenage culture', since the experience of going to a dance hall would be different if one's own concern was the perception of the music, or, the feeling of the physical dance. If it's the fights and the lasses that are important, then the structure of the music cannot be the main reason for going. Similarly with football. This represents a distinctive attitude to the total experience of these spare-time activities; a way of understanding them that does not see them as a means to an end, but rather as a *total experience*.

What role, then, do commercial institutions play in spare-time activity? The young people of the working class cannot command the resources and power to build their own institutions (in terms of bricks and mortar). This can be contrasted with the student union facilities at universities which can provide an alternative to the commercial institutions of the capitalist society around the university. Consequently the working-class boys must use these organisations, all of which are run primarily for profit. Nevertheless, the question of who controls these facilities is vital for them; it is important to try to understand that control, and their reaction to it.

These differences in the type of control experienced by the boys are directly related to the type of aims that the institutions have, and to what they are trying to do 'with' or 'for' the boy. The difficulties of, say, the youth clubs are immense in that they are attempting to change the boys' attitudes and behaviour, yet do not have the compulsory powers of attendance that the schools have.

Yet this differs from the nature of the control exercised by commercial institutions. The *aims* of commercial institutions are, primarily, to make money. As far as the boys are concerned, for a certain amount of money you can buy a certain amount of freedom, since the aim of the institutions is not primarily to interfere with the behaviour or ideas of those that enter them.

Thus if we were to compare the formal control structure of a dance hall and a youth club, it would be found that both are dominated and run by non-working-class adults. Nevertheless, if you were to look specifically at the way in which the organisation attempts to interfere with boys' behaviour, it is easy to see the way in which boys experience a greater amount of freedom in the dance halls. While they are limited within the dance hall, no one is trying to get them to *think* about something that they don't feel like; they can come as often or as seldom as they like. Both sides of the *commercial* contract respect the autonomy of the other, with the single and vital proviso of all capitalist institutions that the seller can refuse the buyer if he has not got the cash to fulfil the relationship.

The increasing economic power of the young has provided individual boys with some economic power, and this enables them to gain access to these institutions. The extent of this economic power in the hands of these particular boys who have not yet left school can be grossly overestimated, since they exist for the most part on pocket-money and part-time earnings. For these boys, dance halls are expensive places, and do not necessarily enter the realm of possible realistic choices on a Saturday evening. For *those* boys the street corner is the most likely institution open: it is cheap and always accessible. Consideration of the street will figure in most of the next group of activities dealt with . . .

The nature of both of the major institutions used by boys – the dance hall and the football ground – is changing. In the very recent past these institutions have tightened up on the amount of freedom that they allow their customers. Anyone who stands behind a goal at football matches at a first division club will realise that the increase in police activity in recent years has been enormous. Football programmes and statements in the local and national press show the clubs' dislike of the bad publicity given to them by the 'small minority of fans' that have been labelled soccer hooligans. This fear of 'public' reaction has led to a tightening up in social control in football grounds culminating, at the time of writing at any rate, in a member of the Football Association calling for the banning of all under 18-year-olds from football grounds. In dance halls, recent years have seen the closing down of a number of smaller halls and the tightening of control within the two major chains, Rank and Mecca, which now try and exclude 'unruly' elements. In both institutions the amount of freedom open to the boys has been limited. This has increased the general importance of the street as an institution for youth spare-time activity.

Nevertheless, in terms of the boys' actual experience there is still an important difference between commercial and evangelical institutions.

Watching football: the TV and the ground

I've written about the boys' experience of going to a football match and tried to put it in the context of an experience outside a purely football-orientated one. Yet football itself does exist as a category of leisure activity. It must be understood, though, that most football is watched on the TV, and in reporting these activities the timing of the research as pre-Sunderland-football-revival is obviously important. During the research Sunderland were relegated and football appeared to be in a sad state on Wearside. Briefly, during the revival, I would have expected to see much more activity based upon Sunderland as a team; such revivals are short-term-based, though, unless they represent a long-term change in the fortunes of the local club, as has happened at Leeds over the last twelve years. For the most part, though, TV plays the most important part in football-watching.

Question	Do you watch much football?
John S.	Every chance I can.
Question	Do you ever go to Roker Park?
John S.	Sometimes . . . not very often.
Question	Do you and your friends talk much about football?
John S.	Aye, when we come out on Sunday morning, we start to talk about *Match of the Day* from Saturday night.

Thus watching football is not necessarily a cold Saturday afternoon on the terraces. An interest in watching football *for the game in itself* as a spectator sport is in fact better served by watching the television than by watching Sunderland at Roker Park.

Question	Do you watch much football?
Edward	Saturday and Sunday on the telly. In the week when it's on.
Question	Do you go down Roker Park?
Edward	Not much this year. It's not much, you know. When you see footy on the telly Roker Park isn't as good.
Question	Why?
Edward	Well, Leeds are just a lot better to watch than Sunderland.

Anyone who has watched football over the last couple of years will recognise that football as a game in terms of skill is indeed better to watch on telly, unless you live near a good first division side. Watching Liverpool, Leeds and Manchester United on the television every week had reduced the attraction of watching 'workmanlike' sides. Also, if you are purely interested in the skills of the game, the technology of television with its famous action replays shows the game much better.

Thus the question 'Are you interested in football?' was answered yes by 81 and no by ten. Yet an interest in football was never sufficient of itself to get people on to the terraces. There was another question, answered at a time when there had been nine or ten first-class games played at Roker that season; so six or more visits shows a fairly heavy commitment out of the possible opportunities:

How many times	Never	32
have you been	Once or twice	16
to Roker Park	Three to five times	13
this season?	Six or more	22
	No answer	10

Therefore, out of 81 very interested in soccer a large number seem never to go to Roker Park to watch football. I believe this backs up the impression about the different sorts of interest in the game that different sorts of supporters represent. 'Going to a football match' shows one sort of interest; watching footy on *Match of the Day* a very different sort. Therefore it becomes important, in trying to understand these activities, to look specifically at the structure of the activity as much as at the content.

Why, then, do boys get into trouble?

We are left, therefore, with a very different way of understanding 'getting into trouble' at football matches. The whole experience for the boys is a lot less instrumental than I at first thought: the getting into fights and so forth is also intelligible only in a different way. We must see it in relation to the *structured* leisure activities that are imposed upon the boys at youth clubs and schools. Within *these* structures activities occur for instrumental reasons. The boys reject those structures, and those organisations; when they take part in activities that they choose they create very different sorts of structures which allow them much greater possibilities of involvement. Once more, as in the educational system, it is of no use offering these boys involvement in the *content* of the activity; of itself this is rejected as a sham participation. It is essential for the boys to be allowed to create their own *structure* of activity. This is true in the fields of playing and watching sport, as well as music.

Footy and pop provide for these boys degrees of freedom from interference as a participator and a spectator. It provides them with an identity separate from those groups that are trying to mould their behaviour into more acceptable forms.

Note

1   I. Taylor, 'Soccer Consciousness', in S. Cohen (ed.), *Images of Deviance* (Harmondsworth: Penguin, 1971).

Loïc Wacquant

BODILY CAPITAL AMONG PROFESSIONAL BOXERS

[. . .]

THIS ARTICLE PURPORTS to address this gap [the lack of focus upon 'specific social worlds' and 'concrete incorporating practices' in studies of the body – editor] by way of an ethnographic inquiry into the social structuring of bodily capital and bodily labor among professional fighters in an American metropolis. It explores how practitioners of a particular bodily craft (boxing), most of whom are embedded in a social setting that puts a high premium on physical force and prowess (the contemporary black ghetto), conceive of, care for, and rationalize—in both Weber's and Freud's sense—the use of their body, as a *form of capital*. It is based on an ethnography of a boxing gym and on participant observation of the daily lifeworld of boxers conducted over a four-year period on the South Side of Chicago. It draws on three main types of data: my field notes and personal experiences as an apprentice-boxer who learned the trade *in situ*, eventually acquiring sufficient proficiency in it to enter the Chicago Golden Gloves tournament and to spar on a regular basis with professional fighters (Wacquant, 2004); in-depth interviews with fifty professional pugilists and over three dozen coaches, managers, and assorted members of the guild such as 'cutmen,' referees and matchmakers active in the Greater Chicagoland area; and specialized publications, reports from the boxing press, and the (auto)biographies of champions and renowned trainers.[1]

Bodily capital

Walk into a boxing gym and you cannot but be struck by the sight and sounds of bodies everywhere and enraptured by the strange, ballet-like spectacle they offer, gliding across the ring, colliding and clinching, feet squealing on the thick blue mat, or moving back and forth in measured steps in front of a mirror, shadow-boxing in pursuit of an invisible opponent, circling heavy bags hung from the ceiling, punching speed bags as if in imitation of a machine-gun, or rhythmically skipping rope and folding in half for endless series of sit-ups, all in unison, the washboard abdominals, chiseled torsos and cut-up quadriceps, sculptured backs, tight behinds and thighs, and the grimacing faces glistening with sweat: so many visible indices of the bodily labor that makes up the trade of the pugilist. On the walls, posters exhibiting the hardened, trim, taut physique of champions are there for everyone to admire, silent models that offer, in stereotypic poses, fists clenched and muscles flexed, a championship belt strapped across the shoulder or around the waist, living yardsticks to measure oneself by.

To say that pugilism is a body-centered universe is an understatement. As Joyce Carol Oates (1987: 5) perceptively noted, 'like a dancer, a boxer "is" his body, and is totally identified with it.' Fighters feel and know this equation well, for their organism is indeed the template and epicentre of their life, at once the site, the instrument and the object of their daily work, the medium and the outcome of their occupational exertion —'that's your asset: you know, without your body you're not gonna accomplish many things,' whispers one of my gym mates as he wraps his hands in the dressing room.[2] And their whole existence is consumed by its servicing, moulding, and purposeful manipulation. If, following Pierre Bourdieu (1986: 241), we define capital as

> accumulated labor (in its materialized form or its 'incorporated', embodied form) which, when appropriated on a private, i.e., exclusive, basis by agents or groups of agents, enables them to appropriate social energy in the form of reified or living labor,

then we may conceive boxers as holders of and even *entrepreneurs in bodily capital*[3] of a particular kind; and the boxing gym in which they spend much of their waking time as a social machinery designed to convert this 'abstract' bodily capital into *pugilistic capital*, that is, to impart to the fighter's body a set of abilities and tendencies liable to produce value in the field of professional boxing in the form of recognition, titles, and income streams. One sparring partner whom I asked why he had decided to 'turn pro' had this striking reply: 'It was just a small black kid tryin' to open his own business with his fists.'

The fighter's body is simultaneously his means of production, the raw materials he and his handlers (trainer and manager) have to work with and on, and, for a good part, the somatized product of his past training and extant mode of living. *Bodily capital and bodily labor are thus linked by a recursive relation* which makes them closely dependent on one another. The boxer uses what Marx (1977: 173) calls 'the natural forces of his body' to 'appropriate' that particular part of nature that is his own body so as to optimize the growth of these very forces. Properly managed, this body is capable of producing more value than was 'sunk' in it. But for that it is necessary for the fighter to know its intrinsic limits, to expand its sensorimotor powers, and to resocialize its physiology in accordance with the specific requirement and temporality of the game. In addition, the fighter's body is a system of signs, a symbolic quilt that he must learn to decipher in order better to enhance and protect it, but also to attack it. For what is unique about boxing is that the boxer's body is both the weapon of assault and the target to be destroyed.

First, much like fixed capital and like all living organisms, the body of fighters has inherent structural limitations, including a limited life expectancy. As famed trainer-manager and founder of Detroit's Kronk gym Emanuel Steward put it, 'the human body is like an automobile. It's got so many miles on it and that's it' (in Halpern, 1988: 278). Boxers have an acute sense of dependency on their body and of its temporal finitude:

'I see my body as (chuckle) *my life*, somethin' I gotta really *tone down*, you know, to be perfect' says a hopeful contender in the lightweight division; 'you have to take care of yer body—once you destroy yer body (sternly), you can hang it up,' adds a rising middleweight who recently moved to the city's far South Side. This explains that boxers must carefully manage the investment of their physical assets over time (Wacquant, 2004): they should stay in the amateur ranks long enough to gain experience but not so long that they wear themselves down and get 'frozen' into the amateur mould; they must constantly push themselves in training and stay in tip-top shape in case a fight is offered to them on short notice (as a last-minute substitute for another injured boxer, for instance) but beware of 'burnout' or getting hurt in the gym; they should, to the extent that they can (i.e., that they are protected by an influential manager or promoter), postpone or space out tough fights against 'serious customers'—it may take but one brutal 'beating' for a given fighter to deplete his capacity for absorbing blows and to become 'shot.' Pugilistic obsolescence is described in terms of the erosion of the body and the guild has evolved an extensive vocabulary to designate boxers who keep stepping into the ring despite the obvious deterioration of their bodily capital: a fighter who is 'washed up' is known as a 'punching bag' or, more cruelly, as 'dead meat.'[4]

From the time he first steps into a gym till the day he 'hangs up' his gloves and retires from the trade, the body of the boxer is the focus of unremitting attention. The first thing that the coach of the Woodlawn Boys Club, a highly regarded trainer of over five decades who was my mentor, pays notice to when a new recruit walks in his back-room to sign up is the physical 'hardware' he brings in with him, the brute matter he will have to chisel and develop: his height, weight (which he can visually estimate within a couple of pounds) and the volume as well as shapes of his body, square or round, straight or curved, its deportment and motility, stiff and rigid or relaxed and supple, the size of his neck and wrists, the form of his nose and eye sockets. Often I heard him lecture on how blessed Muhammad Ali was to have had the bodily assets he did, including a granite jaw, a snake-slow pulse that enabled him to summon enormous spurts of energy and to recover from punches with unusual celerity, a round face that would not swell and allowed for great peripheral vision, and the excellent skin that did not cut, unlike that of his archrival Joe Frazier whose face would turn into a messy pulp in the course of their furious clashes.

Just like the proverbial 'tale of the tape' shown before every major televised bout [see Document 1, p. 264]), the detailed evaluation of top pugilists which is a standard fare of boxing magazines always includes separate measurements and ratings of their different physical attributes, stamina, power (ability to knock opponents out), and 'chin' (capacity to withstand power punches to the head). Judgements boil down to an appreciation of strategic bodily parts such as the face, hands, arms, and feet (for their speed and swiftness). The inherited somatic endowment (notably the muscular-skeletal structure) of a fighter is of particular concern because it largely selects the style and ring strategy he must adopt by predefining the tools he will have to work with on offence and defence alike. Thin and lanky pugilists tend to become what the occupational lingo calls 'boxers,' that is, stylists who fight from a distance, using reach, speed, and technique to maintain their opponents at bay so as to pile up points or create an opening for a knock-out strike from long range. Shorter, stubby fighters with large, strong upper bodies, on the other hand, will generally be 'fighters' (also known as 'sluggers' or 'brawlers') who have to walk inside—or through—the punches of their opponents to wear them down by means of repeated body attacks and short blows to the head from up close.

Tale of the Tape
How Evander Holyfield and
Riddick Bowe measure up:

	HOLYFIELD	BOWE
Age	30	25
Weight	205	235
Height	6-2	6-5
Reach	77½	81
Chest (normal)		
	43	46
Chest (expanded)		
	45	50
Biceps	16	17
Forearm	12½	12½
Wrist	7½	8
Fist	12½	13½
Neck	19½	17½
Waist	32	36
Thigh	22	26½
Calf	13	16½
Record	28-0	31-0
Knockouts	22	27

Document 1 'Tale of the Tape': The official valuation of bodily capital before the Holyfield/Bowe heavyweight world title fight, *New York Times*, November 13, 1992

This fit between bodily capital and style is suggested in this excerpt from a gym conversation in which a noted manager talks about a tall and filiform fighter known for his quickness and reach but lacking in body strength:

Manager: Jay can fight a guy like T. [current champion] who isn't physical, he could do alright with. I don't know how well he does with a *tough* guy that's gonna come, keep a lot of pressure on him. I think he's gonna have *problems*, 'cause I don't see him gettin' strong either. You know that you're not strong: you are what you are. You can only do so many things. A short guy can't stretch himself and all of a sudden become a tall guy.

LW: (laughing) Yeah, that's what Ronnie [a fighter sparring in the ring in front of us] was saying.

Manager: An' that's the thing, Ronnie is very *short*. He's too, he's *way* too short for his weight [5′5″ for 140 pounds]. But he's *tough*. Tough, rugged, *very* tough guy. So, he somewhat *compensates* in that way. That's what he's got to do. An' Ronnie'd be in bad shape if he's gonna stand back an' try to *box* somebody. He's got to keep pressure because there's no other way for him to uh, to *fight*. There's nothin' else for him to do but be rough, tough, aggressive guy. Only way he can do it. (. . .)

LW: So really the body you have limits . . .

Manager: It determines to a great degree what you've got. The only thing you can do with things like that, you've gotta try, take a kid like that, an' teach him how to *slip* punches as such as not to get *hit* with everything comin' in. But he's got to um . . . he's basically got to be an aggressive

guy, comin' in throwin' hooks an' big punches because that's *all* he can
do. His style is going to negate him doing anything else.

LW: Do you sometimes get guys that have the build of a brawler but they
want to stand back and box?

Manager: That's right, that's right. An' it don't work. A lotta times fighters
don't fight the *style* that *their bodies say they should*. You have exceptions
to all the rules.

Style, in turn, impinges on longevity: as a rule, sluggers (or counter-punchers) have
shorter careers than boxers (or 'boxer-punchers') because of the much greater 'wear and
tear' that their body sustains in the squared circle. But anatomy is not destiny. We must
not forget that the human organism, far from being the unchangeable biological integu-
ment of the self, is an 'active, self-transforming subject' (Freund, 1988: 851). The body
is unlike most instruments of production in its degree of flexibility; it can, within given
parameters, he refurbished, retooled, and significantly restructured. Even basic physiological processes, such as our respiratory system and our blood pressure, are subject to
social influences (Buytendjik, 1974) and many of the fundamental metabolic and homeo-
static mechanisms of our organism can be purposefully modified through intensive
training (Arsac, 1992). The gym is a social factory for remaking human bodies into virtual
'fighting machines.' Says a veteran trainer from a South Side gym: 'I like creatin' a monster, jus' see what you can create . . . like the master Frankenstein: I created a monster,
I got a fighter, I created a good fighter, same difference.' [. . .]

. . . [M]ost fighters live in inner-city neighborhoods where the objective probability
of injurious death is inordinately high and violent crime a depressingly, common occurence
(Wacquant, 1998). The prevalence of public homicide in the ghetto and the fatalistic
worldview it encourages gives massive plausibility to the notion, frequently voiced by
trainers and boxers alike, that stepping into the ring is, everything considered, not much
more dangerous than crossing the street or walking down to the corner store: 'You're
takin' a chance doin' anything, Louie.' Members of the guild are also adept at citing
publicized studies showing that the 'fistic science' is a less deadly sport than many others,
including some that enjoy the favor of boxing's overwhelmingly white upper- and middle-
class detractors, forgetting that statistics about fatalities do not take into account serious
non-lethal injuries such as brain damage and vision impairment. Not to mention that
physical courage and the ability to recover from severe injuries are officially glorified by
the pugilistic field.

'You have to take care of your body so it will take care of you.' One of the ways
in which boxers can and do protect their corporeal capital is by steadfastly applying the
techniques of body-repair and care that are part of the pugilistic lore and that they learn
from trainers and more experienced gym associates. A myriad rules of thumb and tricks
of the trade, ranging from hand-wrapping methods to the rehearsal of specific defensive
moves to analgesic creams, help them minimize disrepair of the body in the gym.

Notes

1   The fifty boxers interviewed comprise almost the entire universe of professional fighters active
in the Chicago–Gary metropolitan area at the time of the survey (summer 1991), thereby
obviating problems of sampling. They include 36 blacks (two of them of West Indian descent),
eight whites, five Puerto Ricans and one Mexican. The interviews were semi-structured and

lasted an average of two hours, generating over 2,000 pages of transcripts. I have occasionally changed minor identifying characteristics such as age and weight class in order to guarantee the anonymity of the respondents. For more details on the setting and methods of this research, see Wacquant (2004: 2–11 and 2005). Words or phrases in quotes are either drawn from interviews and conversations with boxers and trainers, or expressions that are part of the 'stock of knowledge' shared by members of the pugilistic universe. Unless otherwise indicated, the emphases in the quotes are those of the locutor.

2   For a discussion of the generalized concept of capital and its various species, see also Bourdieu and Wacquant (1992: 115–120).

3   I will leave aside the complication introduced by the fact that many professional boxers are legally bound to managers who contractually enjoy exclusive rights over their ring performances. Briefly put, we may say that boxers *possess* their bodily capital while their managers *own* the right to convert it into (potential) pugilistic value. What matters for purposes of the present analysis is that it is boxers who exercise rulership over their bodies in the phenomenological sense. Also, for lack of space, this paper does not explicitly discuss the question of the relation between boxing and the production and ritual affirmation of manhood. Suffice it to say that the bodily labor of fighters is fundamentally a work of *engenderment* in the sense that it creates a new being but also a gendered being embodying and exemplifying a definite form of masculinity: plebeian, heterosexual, and heroic.

4   Some promoters specialize in the provision of 'used bodily capital,' i.e., washed-up boxers or 'opponents' who can provide valiant but riskless opposition to up-and-coming fighters who need to 'build up' their record. They are known in the business as 'flesh wholesalers' (see Brunt, 1987: 200seq. and Shapiro, 1988, for a description of the traffic in 'opponents').

References

Arsac, Laurent (1992) 'Le corps sportif, machine en action', pp. 79–91 in Claude Genzling (ed.), *Le corps surnaturé. Les sports entre science et conscience*. Paris: Editions Autrement.

Bourdieu, Pierre (1986) 'The Forms of Capital', pp. 241–258 in John G. Richardson (ed.), *Handbook of Theory and Research for the Sociology of Education*. New York: Greenwood Press.

Bourdieu, Pierre and Wacquant, Loïc (1992) *An Invitation to Reflexive Sociology*. Chicago: The University of Chicago Press; Cambridge: Polity Press.

Brunt, Steven (1987) *Mean Business: The Rise and Fall of Shawn O'Sullivan*. Hammondsworth: Penguin.

Buytendjik, F.J. (1974) *Prolegomena to an Anthropological Physiology*. Pittsburgh: Duquesne University Press.

Freund, Peter E.S. (1988) 'Bringing Society into the Body: Understanding Socialized Human Nature', *Theory and Society* 17 (6): 839–864.

Halpern, Daniel (1988) 'Distance and Embrace', pp. 275–285 in Joyce Carol Oates and Daniel Halpern (eds), *Reading the Fights*. New York: Prentice-Hall.

Marx, Karl [1867] (1977) *Capital*. Vol. 1. New York: Vintage.

Oates, Joyce Carol (1987) *On Boxing*. Garden City: Doubleday.

Shapiro, Michael (1988) 'Opponents', pp. 242–249 in Joyce Carol Oates and Daniel Halpern (eds), *Reading the Fights*. New York: Prentice-Hall.

Wacquant, Loïc, (1998) 'Inside the Zone: The Social Art of the Hustler in the Black American Ghetto', *Theory, Culture, and Society*, 15 (2), May: 1–36.*

Wacquant, Loïc (2004) *Body and Soul: Notebooks of an Apprentice Boxer*. New York: Oxford University Press.*

Wacquant, Loïc (2005) 'Carnal Connection: On Embodiment, Membership, and Apprenticeship', *Qualitative Sociology* 28 (4), Winter: 445–471*

[*These references have been updated by the contributor, 2006.]

SECTION SIX

Race and ethnic identities

INTRODUCTION

THE READINGS IN THIS SIXTH SECTION provide studies of black Caribbean sports clubs in early twentieth-century Trinidad, 1960s Bermuda and 1990s Leeds; the emergence of black sportsmen in professional sport and the persistence of stereotyping; and sport examples such as rugby, football and cricket, as experienced by British Asian and Afro-Caribbean people.

The first Reading is an account by **C.L.R. James** of how, during his childhood and youth in Trinidad, cricket clubs were status-based institutions. James's style, as seen too in the opening Reading of Section Three, is personal but also political, autobiographical and, at the same time, sociological. It is an excellent example of what C. Wright Mills called the sociological imagination at work in the blending of biography and history (*The Sociological Imagination*, Harmondsworth, Penguin, 1970). As James writes: 'These are no random reminiscences.' Suitably inspired by James, the novice sport scholar might do worse than write his/her own autobiographical account of the induction process into a sporting club or association, and ask whether such a process is a marker of ethnic or racial identity.

The second Reading is from a study by US anthropologist **Frank Manning**. Again, the club or the voluntary association is the focus. These sorts of organizations are important because they are indicators of the existence of civil society, that form of 'public life rather than private or household-based activities' which exists separate from the family or the state, and accepts the framework of the rule of law (John Scott and Gordon Marshall (eds), *A Dictionary of Sociology* (3rd edn), Oxford, Oxford University Press, 2005: 72). When reading Manning's account, think too of debates about cultural autonomy and multiculturalism. Why did Bermudan blacks form their own clubs? What is the importance of the sphere of what Manning calls 'the game' in black Bermudan culture?

Although some pioneering black footballers played in English and Scottish professional leagues in the early decades of the professional game, it was not until the 1980s that more than a few black players broke through into the professional level. An early student of black sportsmen in this British context was **Ernest Cashmore**, English sociologist, sport studies researcher and writer and cultural commentator (also under the authorial name Ellis Cashmore). What are the benefits of sport for black people, and in what way is the study of black sporting culture 'a study of failure'? Cashmore's conclusion to his study is reproduced in full in this third Reading in the section.

The sporting contest at its professional level is a free, open market. The stadium is a public space, accessible to all who can find the cost of entrance. Or is it? If that is the case, why can crowds at sporting encounters look relatively homogeneous. Why do the fans flocking to the professional football game in England – despite welcome, progressive changes in marketing and the rising profile of family groups and women fans – still seem so dominated by white males? Why, in cities with large Asian populations, are Asian fans rarely seen at the football ground? In the fourth Reading, English sport and leisure studies team **Jonathan Long, Ben Carrington** and **Karl Spracklen** turn the investigative lens upon rugby league in the north of England. Is sport identified as white cultural territory? What is 'stacking' in professional team sports? Their study guides readers to some critical basic questions concerning racist discourses in sport.

We are socialized into our sports just as we are socialized into our political views or our national culture. Without the insights of cultural study or the knowledge generated by the social sciences, it would be (and for many is) easy to see the world merely in terms of our own limited experience; to see the world in this way is to have an ethnocentric approach, an understanding of the world based upon only one's own experience and cultural assumptions. The fifth Reading, by English sport studies scholar and physical educationist **Scott Fleming**, shows how easy it is to misrepresent a culture, in this case to see all South Asians as the same, and then to perpetuate stereotypes. Think, as you work through this Reading, what stereotypes are still prevalent among sport fans, particularly concerning race and ethnic influences.

Ben Carrington's study of the Caribbean Cricket Club, in Leeds, England, was conducted in the mid-1990s, and excerpts from a 1998 version of the study provide the sixth Reading. Carrington chose an ethnographic method, drawing upon participant observation and interviews, to study the club, and offers a study – as he writes in his own abstract for the article – 'of how a black cricket club in the north of England is used by black men as both a form of resistance to white racism and a symbolic marker of the local black community'. What is the role of masculinity in this? And what does Carrington say about nostalgia and the meaning of the club to the older players?

It has been established beyond doubt that some sport practices and institutions have sought to address the problem of racism, and it is with the emergence of black sports-people that white individuals of limited cultural experience and perhaps conservative or racist tendencies have been encouraged to question their own prejudices. In Britain, for instance, there have been genuinely progressive advances made in anti-racism campaigns related to football and cricket. Nevertheless, in the seventh Reading, **Scott Fleming** and **Alan Tomlinson** catalogue persisting forms of racial prejudice and racism as expressed in English football culture, by players, club officials and spectators. The critical question to consider in the light of such examples is how far the campaigns and changes in public behaviour have changed actual beliefs?

Finally, in this section, cultural studies scholar **Pnina Werbner** examines selected aspects of the popular culture of British Pakistanis. She draws upon the sociological pedigree of the French sociologist Emile Durkheim (1858–1917), English-born anthropologist Victor Turner (1920–83), and Russian cultural theorist Mikhail Bakhtin (1895–1975) in accounting for the place of play spaces in social life. Everyday culture, she shows, expresses moral values and debates. The 'youthful domain of sport' allows young British Pakistanis to express their sense of 'disaffection from British society', and 'their love of both cricket and the home country'. Werbner's study is powerful reaffirmation of sport as a 'distinctive symbolic space'.

COMMENTARY AND FURTHER READING

Grant Jarvie has listed six popular arguments suggesting how sport has contributed to 'explanations of race relations within the sociology of sport' ('Sport, Racism and Ethnicity', in Jay Coakley and Eric Dunning's edited *Handbook of Sports Studies*, London, Sage, 2000: 334). These arguments suggest that:

*   Sport's inherent conservatism contributes to the consolidation of racism, nationalism and patriotism.
*   Some 'inherent property' of sport makes it conducive to the fostering of integration, and harmony in race relations.
*   Sport has been used in colonialist and imperialist projects (as a form of cultural politics).
*   Sport has made contributions to political struggles for black people and other ethnic groups.
*   Sporting stereotypes have contributed to fuel discrimination, as have prejudices and myths.
*   Sport provides a vehicle for 'displays of black prowess, masculinity and forms of identity'.

Reflecting on the Readings in the section, select the most relevant of these popular arguments listed by Jarvie, and ask what evidence the studies provide for the credibility of those arguments.

In 1994 Gajendra K. Verma and Douglas S. Darby published *Winners and Losers: Ethnic Minorities in Sport and Recreation* (London, The Falmer Press, 1994), based upon a two-year study carried out in Manchester, England, and based upon 1,000 respondents from seven ethnic minority groups. They reported that many Muslim women were doubly disadvantaged in their sporting aspirations, suffering the problems encountered by women from many ethnic backgrounds (see Section Seven of the Reader) but also constrained by men wielding 'the authority of religion, culture and custom' (p. 151). More generally, they found that males and females of all ethnic groups wanted to take part in more activities, 'but could not' (p. 148).

A main follow-up source to the Readings in this section is *'Race', Sport and British Society*, edited by Ben Carrington and Ian McDonald (London and New York, Routledge, 2001). Carrington and McDonald write that they have often had complaints from students about the lack of appropriate study resources when looking to research race and sport: this was the basis for the production of their text. Paul Gilroy, Professor of Social Theory at the London School of Economics (then Professor of Sociology and African Studies at Yale University) recognized the Carrington and McDonald contribution in a Foreword to their book, and also took sociology to task: 'Sociology is culpable for its failures of imagination and principle and for its persistent, symptomatic refusal to address the interconnection of nationalism, racism and popular culture' (p. xi). The Readings in the preceding section show that some social scientists and researchers were making amends, at least in part, for any such refusal. Also in the Carrington and McDonald collection, Chris Searle, in 'Pitch of Life: Re-reading C.L.R. James' *Beyond a Boundary'*, re-evaluates the importance and impact of James's book.

In his study of young British Asians' affiliations to the England national football and cricket teams, Daniel Burdsey has argued that diasporic young British identities are influenced and shaped by increasing contact with young people from other ethnic cultures, decreasing links with previous generations, a growing sense of distance from the Indian subcontinent, the influence of Western commodities and consumption, and 'a desire to construct a multilateral social identity that simultaneously emphasizes their British citizenship and their ethnicities' ('"If I ever Play Football, Dad, Can I Play for England or India?": British Asians, Sport and Diasporic National Identities', *Sociology*, Vol. 40, No. 1, 2006: 24). Such debates also take place with reference to the question of postcolonialism, and John Bale and Mike Cronin provide a lucid overview of sport and postcolonialism, including a list of seven types of postcolonial 'sportoid forms', in their introduction to their edited volume *Sport and Postcolonialism* (Oxford, Berg, 2003: 4).

C.L.R. James

THE LIGHT AND THE DARK

I LEFT SCHOOL and had my year of cricketing glory. I headed the second-class averages with over seventy per innings. I never approached the same form again, and woefully disappointed all my friends. In over ten years I was once chosen for the North against the South. That is my score and biography, the frame in which all references to my own performances are to be seen.

That year I played for a new club called Old Collegians. We were a composite of the motley racial crew who attended the colleges, with one significant exception: only one white man joined our team, and he was a Portuguese of local birth, which did not count exactly as white (unless very wealthy). We swept through the second division, but at the end of the season the team broke up. With my excellent batting record, good bowling and fielding, admittedly wide knowledge and fanatical keenness, it was clear that I would play for one of the first-class clubs. The question was: which one? This, apparently simple, plunged me into a social and moral crisis which had a profound effect on my whole future life.

The various first-class clubs represented the different social strata in the island within clearly defined bounds. Top of the list was the Queen's Park Club. It was the boss of the island's cricket relations with other islands and visiting international teams. All big matches were played on their private ground, the Queen's Park Oval. They were for the most part white and often wealthy. There were a few coloured men among them, chiefly members of the old well-established mulatto families. A black man in the Queen's Park was rare and usually anonymous: by the time he had acquired status or made enough money to be accepted he was much too old to play.

The second club (in prestige) was Shamrock, the club of the old Catholic families. It was at that time almost exclusively white. At one time there had been a political upheaval and a bloody riot in the island. As part of the pacification, the British Government appointed a local coloured lawyer as Attorney-General. His sons were members of Shamrock.

I would have been more easily elected to the M.C.C. than to either. Constabulary, the cricket detachment of the local police force, was also out. I would have had to become a policeman, I did not want to become a policeman, and, in any case, in those days people with secondary education did not become policemen. The inspectorate was reserved exclusively for whites. Even the Constabulary team, all black, was captained by a white inspector.

Also excluded for the me of those days was Stingo. They were plebeians: the butcher, the tailor, the candlestick maker, the casual labourer, with a sprinkling of unemployed. Totally black and no social status whatever. Some of their finest players had begun by bowling at the nets. Queen's Park and Shamrock were too high and Stingo was too low. I accepted this as easily in the one case as I did in the other. No problem there. Two more clubs remained and here the trouble began.

One of these clubs was Maple, the club of the brown-skinned middle class. Class did not matter so much to them as colour. They had founded themselves on the principle that they didn't want any dark people in their club. A lawyer or a doctor with a distinctly dark skin would have been blackballed, though light-skinned department-store clerks of uncertain income and still more uncertain lineage were admitted as a matter of course.

The other club was Shannon, the club of the black lower-middle class: the teacher, the law clerk, the worker in the printing office and here and there a clerk in a department store. This was the club of Ben Sealey the teacher, of Learie Constantine the law clerk and W. St. Hill the clerk in a department store. Their captain was Learie's father, an overseer on an estate. He enjoyed such immense prestige that it didn't matter what work he was doing. This did not, however, apply to his children.

None of these lines was absolute. One of the founders of the Maple Club was Kenneth Gibson, a soccer forward who in my eyes remained unexceeded in natural gifts until I saw Stanley Matthews. Kenneth had a lifelong friend, old Q.R.C., a charming boy, well connected, a splendid player—but dark. Maple on principle didn't want him. Kenneth refused to play if his friend was not accepted. So in the end the very first Maple eleven that took the field included Kenneth's outsider. Genius is wayward. In later years Kenneth had a row with Maple and left them to play for another club, Sporting Club, whose foundation members ranged themselves between the lighter members of Maple and the dark Portuguese.

The reader is here invited to make up his mind. If for him all this is 'not cricket', then he should take friendly warning and go in peace (or in wrath). These are no random reminiscences. This is the game as I have known it and this is the game I am going to write about. How could it be otherwise? A dozen years after, just before I left Trinidad, I wrote the following as part of a political study of the West Indies.

> The Negroid population of the West Indies is composed of a large percentage of actually black people and about fifteen or twenty per cent of people who are a varying combination of white and black. From the days of slavery these have always claimed superiority to the ordinary black, and a substantial majority of them still do so (though resenting as bitterly as the black assumptions of white superiority). With emancipation in 1834 the blacks themselves established a middle class. But between the brown-skinned middle class and the black there is a continual rivalry, distrust and ill-feeling, which, skilfully played upon by the European peoples, poisons the life of the community. Where so

many crosses and colours meet and mingle the shades are naturally difficult to determine and the resulting confusion is immense. There are the nearly white hanging on tooth and nail to the fringes of white society, and these, as is easy to understand, hate contact with the darker skin far more than some of the broader-minded whites. Then there are the browns, intermediates, who cannot by any stretch of imagination pass as white, but who will not go one inch towards mixing with people darker than themselves. And so on, and on, and on. Associations are formed of brown people who will not admit into their number those too much darker than themselves, and there have been heated arguments in committee as to whether such and such a person's skin was fair enough to allow him or her to be admitted without lowering the tone of the institution. Clubs have been known to accept the daughter who was fair and refuse the father who was black; the dark-skinned brother in a fair-skinned family is sometimes the subject of jeers and insults and open intimations that his presence is not required at the family social functions. Fair-skinned girls who marry dark men are often ostracized by their families and given up as lost. There have been cases of fair women who have been content to live with black men but would not marry them. Should the darker man, however, have money or position of some kind, he may aspire, and it is not too much to say that in a West Indian colony the surest sign of a man having arrived is the fact that he keeps company with people lighter in complexion than himself. Remember, finally, that the people most affected by this are people of the middle class who, lacking the hard contact with realities of the masses and unable to attain to the freedoms of a leisured class, are more than all types of people given to trivial divisions and subdivisions of social rank and precedence.

I had gone to school for years with many of the Maple players. But I was dark. Left to myself I would never have applied for membership to the Maple Club. Some of them wanted me, not all subscribed to the declaration of independence of the Founding Fathers. The Maple cricket captain, concerned only with getting good men for his team, declared that he had no patience with all that foolishness and he was ready to have James in the club; also his brother was married to my mother's sister. He approached me in a roundabout manner: 'Well, I hear you want to join us,' he said with a big smile.

Other faces also wore smiles. When I was scoring heavily W. St. Hill had made it his business to come and watch me at the nets. He had told his friends that James could bat and was a coming man. Already whenever he and I met we used to talk. Similarly with Constantine Jnr. Though St. Hill and Learie said nothing to me, Shannon wanted me to join them and let me know it. My social and political instincts, nursed on Dickens and Thackeray, were beginning to clarify themselves. As powerful a pull as any was the brilliant cricket Shannon played. Pride also, perhaps, impelled me to join them. In social life I was not bothered by my dark skin and had friends everywhere. It was the principle on which the Maple Club was founded which stuck in my throat.

Interested paragraphs began to appear in the Press that I was joining this one or the other. Finally I decided to do what even then I very rarely did—I decided to ask advice. I spoke to Mr. Roach, Clifford Roach's father, a close friend, himself a brown man, but one openly contemptuous of these colour lines. He listened gravely and told me to let him think it over, he would talk to me in a day or two. (Clifford, as tens of thousands of English people know, was as dark as I am, but his hair was not curly and both his parents were brown.)

When Mr. Roach was ready he said: 'I understand exactly how you feel about all this God-dammed nonsense. But many of the Maple boys are your friends and mine. These are the people whom you are going to meet in life. Join them; it will, be better in the end.'

Not altogether convinced, but reassured, I joined Maple and played cricket and football for them for years. I made fast friends, I became a member of the committee and vice-captain of the cricket club. The original colour exclusiveness of the Maple Club has gradually faded out, but it mattered very much then, in fact it was my first serious personal problem. For that I did not want to be a lawyer and make a lot of money and be nominated to the Legislative Council by the Governor, that I preferred to read what I wanted rather than study statics and dynamics, those were never problems to me. They involved me in conflict with others. They cost me no inner stress. This did. If Mr. Roach had told me to join Shannon I would have done so without hesitation. But the social milieu in which I had been brought up was working on me. I was teaching, I was known as a man cultivated in literature, I was giving lectures to literary societies on Wordsworth and Longfellow. Already I was writing. I moved easily in any society in which I found myself. So it was that I became one of those dark men whose 'surest sign of . . . having arrived is the fact that he keeps company with people lighter in complexion than himself'.

My decision cost me a great deal. For one thing it prevented me from ever becoming really intimate with W. St. Hill, and kept Learie Constantine and myself apart for a long time. Faced with the fundamental divisions in the island, I had gone to the right and, by cutting myself off from the popular side, delayed my political development for years. But no one could see that then, least of all me.

Frank Manning

BLACK CLUBS IN BERMUDA

Voluntary associations of various types have long been prominent features of Bermuda's social landscape. White Bermudians have formed yacht clubs, civic clubs, sports associations, charitable organizations, historical and literary societies, philatelic societies, garden clubs, kennel clubs, dramatic societies, and the like. A few of these have been the private preserve of the Forty Thieves. In other clubs, membership qualifications are based on social position, achievable through occupation, education, or economic standing. There are also a number of clubs founded by the ethnically mixed expatriate population. These include the Caledonian Society, the Cambrian Society, the Bermuda Irish Association, the American Society, the Canadian Club of Bermuda, and a few sports clubs comprised mainly of schoolteachers from England. In addition there are several clubs with a membership almost entirely Portuguese-born or of Portuguese descent.

Bermudian blacks responded to segregation by forming their own clubs, mainly for sports and recreation but more recently for the pursuit of the arts, charitable work, horticulture, and fashion. The latter kinds of clubs have attracted the middle and upper-middle classes, together with others who emulate the bourgeoisie in their life style. The sports and recreational clubs have attracted all classes, though primarily the working class.

Some of the sports and recreational clubs are licensed to serve liquor, others are not. The licensed clubs, which are fewer in number but much larger in membership, are the main concern of this book. Nevertheless, as will be clear to anyone familiar with black Bermudian clubs, much of what I say is true of the smaller, nonlicensed clubs as well. [. . .]

Some black clubs have remained sports clubs in the sense that their only major activity is the sponsorship of sporting teams. Others acquired liquor licenses or merged with licensed clubs, and have expanded their programs to include a broader range of recreational activities. Yet in the licensed clubs, sports are still a major focus of activity. In a survey

I took among 55 club members, about two-thirds of the respondents said that an interest in sports was one of their main reasons for joining the club. Nearly one-third of those who joined for other reasons said that the sporting program was presently one of the major attractions they found in club life.

The clubs assumed a greater role in sports when soccer gained popularity after World War II. Black soccer teams were started in neighborhoods throughout the island, as had been the case with cricket several decades earlier. Most of these teams joined licensed clubs or other sports clubs, and eventually took the club name. The white clubs were also assembling teams at this time, so that in soccer as well as in cricket a dual athletic system came into existence.

When legalized segregation finally ended in the 1960's, new integrated leagues were created. By then, however, most white clubs had discontinued or de-emphasized cricket and soccer, and were concentrating instead on sports not generally popular among blacks, such as yachting, rugby, field hockey, and squash. Blacks were left with virtually unchallenged dominance in cricket and soccer, the major team sports. The leagues and governing bodies that administer these sports are now staffed mainly by representatives elected from the black clubs.

Other programs and activities undertaken by the black licensed clubs have also been the outgrowth of segregation. Before 1959 blacks were barred from hotels and nightclubs, forced to sit in restricted sections of theaters, prevented through various legal and customary means from using certain public facilities, and almost totally cut off from the ceremonial events that constitute the "social" calendar in a British colonial society. The clubs were therefore one of the few places where blacks could gather in an atmosphere free of inhibitions and sheltered from racial discrimination. The clubs also provided, especially after the demise of the lodges, all-purpose centers for the black community. They sponsored public forums, made their premises available for wedding receptions and meetings held by other black organizations, and provided a variety of recreational activities, not only for their male members but for the entire community, including youth. More recently, with the rapid growth of membership and the expansion of facilities, the clubs have begun holding entertainment events on a large scale. These include dances, shows, an annual fair, evening cruises, and the like. Most clubs also sponsor tours abroad, usually to the United States, Canada, or the West Indies, but occasionally to Europe.

Perhaps one might ask why the clubs have experienced their greatest popularity since the end of legalized segregation. There are several reasons. The first is that while *de jure* segregation was gradually phased out in the 1960's, *de facto* segregation has continued in most social institutions. Employment opportunities are theoretically (and to some extent in practice) open to all, but interracial mixing is confined to the job. As one black working in an integrated office put it, "We both come down the same elevator at five o'clock. He [a white co-worker] goes right and I go left, and we don't see each other again until nine o'clock the next morning."

A second reason for the continuance and growth of the clubs is that in the few areas of society where integration has taken place, it has not involved the black working classes, who comprise most of the membership of the licensed clubs. Rather, it has been blacks from the middle and upper-middle strata who have been invited to join white organizations, placed in positions previously restricted to whites, and rewarded with white status designations. With the partial substitution of class for color as a basis of social division, the working-class black people remain confined to a black world.

A third reason stems from the modern development of black consciousness. Like other black peoples around the globe, Bermudians have become aware of currently popular ideas regarding racial identity and solidarity. These sentiments have made many blacks less desirous of joining white groups. Their reluctance is heightened by the realization that where integration has taken place in Bermuda, it has been a one-way process. Blacks have joined white organizations, but the reverse has not been true. Hence an increasingly common view among blacks is that they should support the institutions and traditions that represent the black struggle, or else these institutions will not be preserved. [. . .]

The club world is a world of play and hedontistic indulgence. Sports, games, fairs, festivals, dances, parties, shows, and celebrations are the highlights of club activity. [. . .]

Club life

Recalling his reasons for joining a club, a forty-year-old man observed:

> You couldn't participate in sports unless you belonged to a club, because they were the only places that could provide the facilities, And I think sports was really *the* part of a black man's life in Bermuda for a long period. You had no other form of outlet. . . . You could be a Christian, you could attend church, you could take part in church activities, but if you wanted some other form of outlet you just didn't have it.

His statement reveals both the centrality of sports in the clubs and the distinction between a club member and a "Christian" or church member.

Among the two-thirds of my survey respondents who said that an interest in sports was one of their major reasons for joining a club, most played cricket or soccer in organized competition during their adult lives. The high degree of participation in sports is made possible by the large number of teams. There are three divisions both in the senior soccer league and in the senior cricket league, and most of the larger clubs sponsor teams in more than one division of each league. During the year I was in Bermuda, the black clubs sponsored 19 senior soccer teams and 23 senior cricket teams. They also sponsored 15 teams in the junior soccer league.

Those who do not participate in sports are rabid fans. Club members not only attend Bermudian events but also travel abroad for sports classics such as the World Series (baseball), the World Cup (soccer), test cricket matches, championship boxing matches, the Commonwealth Games, and the quadrennial Olympic Games. Club teams making regular international tours are accompanied by a contingent of fans. No topic of conversation is easier to start or sustain in the clubs, and no subject more frequently discussed, than sports. Those who are known for having an especially detailed knowledge of sports are usually among the most highly regarded members of the club.

To be appreciated and analyzed, sports must be placed in a broader sphere of play, which includes many forms of competitive activity and chance-taking. I call this sphere "the game."

Ernest Cashmore

BLACK SPORTSMEN

At most, sport has led a few thousand Negroes out of the ghetto. But for hundreds of thousands of other Negroes it has substituted a meaningless dream.

Jack Olsen, American sports writer

I've had enough of athletics. I won't be running again, I don't think. My speed didn't improve and the coaches didn't seem interested in helping me. I haven't been down the club for a few months and I can't see me ever going back now. Anyway, I'll be able to concentrate on my job [as a carpenter] with the extra time I'll save. . . . Some mates of mine have been down to a boxing gym; I might give that a go.

Leroy Brown, ex-sprinter

Champions of failure

...THERE HAS BEEN A NAGGING TENSION [throughout my study of black sportsmen]. I have argued in favour of sport, always stressing the positive, uplifting effects and its quality as a provider of achievement orientations. On the other hand, I am forced to concede that many of the hopes stoked up by sports involvement are destined to remain unfulfilled. When all is said and done, sport is not a viable career for the majority of aspirants. But, crucially, it will continue to attract black youth and, for that reason, this work contains a warning.

For all its benefits, sport profits from failure: the failure of black kids to integrate more satisfactorily, gain qualifications more readily, find careers more easily. Social conditions militate against black youth finding in school and work areas in which to develop potentialities. With the psychologist Carl Rogers, I view all human beings as striving productively for fulfilment and development: what he calls 'actualization' (1942; 1961). In Rogers' perspective, we are set at birth to grow: we are active and forward moving and, if the conditions are permissive, we attempt to develop our potentialities to the maximum. The specifics of human growth vary from person to person. One individual may choose to become intensely involved in family life and the rearing of children, heightening his experiences in that context, whereas another may immerse himself in his occupation, improving his competence without pursuing domestic bliss. Yet, for Rogers, they may both share the same primary motive: the actualizing tendency.

Although the form of actualization differs from one individual to another, and from one population to another, there are some common features to the tendency: flexibility rather than rigidity is sought; openness rather than restrictedness; freedom from external control rather than submission to control. But the conditions must be conducive to such developments and, in sport and education, there are contradictions. Rigidity in learning may be a condition of flexibility in expression. Applying such ideas to black youth in modern Britain, it could be said that conditions are not conducive to their actualization in the spheres of education and work, so they turn to sport as the vehicle for actualization. Certainly, the fulfilment many derive from sport in terms of expression and identity is suggestive of this.

What can be done to make other areas with more tangible possibilities facilitate actualization? I have already acknowledged that many of the forces rendering vital areas bankrupt are beyond the sphere of influence. Raise employment levels, obliterate racist thought, eliminate racialist behaviour sound as naive and as futile as imperatives to change totally the capitalist system in one thrust; yet many would argue that the latter is a precondition of the former. I assume that, for the moment at least, the basic structure of society will remain intact and therefore the problems germane to this study will have to be confronted at another level – the immediate one.

There is, I feel, a growing understanding amongst Caribbean parents about the roles they must play in providing stimulating home environments for their children. I am mindful that the practical circumstances of many families often make the provision of such difficult or impossible and it may be a taxing request to make of parents who were rather poorly educated themselves in the West Indies, particularly those from Jamaica. As Christopher Bagley writes: 'One of the reasons for the underachievement of Jamaican children in English schools seems to be the relatively low level of educational achievement of their parents' (1979, p. 69). Boxer Cecil Williams, who was brought up by his illiterate grandparents, thought this problem would 'iron itself out with time'. As he says,

> There's no solution to it, now, you can't go about trying to re-educate all
> the parents. But, eventually, the next generation will understand the problems
> and pressures of school and give their kids help and assurance and the
> motivation to do well.

I endorse this view and add only the wish that some latitude be introduced into the often cruelly disciplinarian system of control in the Caribbean family. The investigations of Bagley, Bart and Wong revealed, amongst other things, that high-achieving black school children had parents 'who tended to be "non-authoritarian"' (1978). Generalizing this tendency may bring higher achievements all round. Discipline is also an issue at school. Most of the sportsmen feel that there is not enough of the right kind of discipline, the type that yields respect rather than fear or retaliation. Stories of hitting teachers back after provocation abound, a fairly typical one coming from Rupert Christie who recalled that, when 15:

> A teacher hit me across the face, so I punched him back. I could have stood him giving me the cane or something like that; I wouldn't have done anything. But hitting me in the face – I wasn't going to stand for that. He punched me back and we started fighting.

Whilst in his third year at school, javelin thrower Andrew Jarrett recounted similar episodes, one culminating thus: 'The teacher broke down and started crying in front of us. They're scared of some kids who'll stand up to them. But, if they insult you, you've got to have a go back at them.'

It seems such incidents are commonplace in the inner city schools and black kids accept them as part of the fabric of their school lives. Interestingly, however, the sportsmen generally find them unnecessary and undesirable. There is a dislike of indiscipline. Chris Egege, for example, moved from Birmingham to Bradford, where his educational performance benefited from more discipline and he reckoned: 'You can get on and learn something up here; the teachers were too soft in Birmingham.' He echoed the views of many.

An obvious factor behind this is that the sportsmen are more disposed to accept discipline either because they realize its possible rewards, having experienced the effect of rigidly supervised training in their performances, or because they may have been predisposed to accept discipline in the first instance before approaching sport at all – though I doubt it.

The expressed wish of the majority of black sportsmen, those at school and at work, is that teachers blend authority with imagination, that they set tasks the meaning and purpose of which are clear to all and reinforce the methods of achieving them, always straining to make obvious why certain methods are adopted rather than others. Sportsmen, of course, appreciate discipline and understand how coaches will subject them to almost sadistic treatments in order to produce results. 'He pulls it out of me', said Phil Brown of his coach. 'He knows I hate some aspects of my training, but he keeps making me do it. And I respond 'cause I know we've both got the same aim at the end of the day – even if it doesn't seem like it sometimes.'

Well, perhaps there are things to be learned from the relationships developed between coaches and sportsmen. Coaches 'pull it out' of their charges not because they impose their wills forcibly; sportsmen surrender themselves and obey instructions because they have trust in their mentors, a trust based on 'the same aim'. The goal is improving performance and it is shared by both. Might the attainment of skills, knowledge and the development of ability be goals shared in the classroom? Coaches do not encourage such affective goals as self-expression, fulfilment or self-analysis; they do not have to, they come through anyway. The sportsmen themselves create self-expression; they are merely provided with the fundamental equipment – fitness, strength, stamina, basic skills, etc. – by the coaches and given the avenues along which to develop them by competitive sport.

My conclusions tie in with those of Maureen Stone: 'Whilst not decrying all attempts at curriculum innovation and creativity, the need for schools to retain a commitment to the mastery of basic intellectual skills and competencies by all children has been expressed' (1981, p. 254). The view is backed by the research findings of Michael Rutter and his colleagues who found that: 'children tended to make better progress both behaviourally and academically in schools which placed an appropriate emphasis on academic matters' (1979, p. 114). Such an emphasis was found to fulfil pupils' expectations also.

Sport is an immensely fruitful area for creativity and expression, though these are not necessarily prime targets. Coaches and trainers establish the exact nature of the objective, whether it be a particular time to be broken or trophy to be won, and set about trying to reach it by pushing the sportsmen through routines which will give them the basic physical competence and mental alertness. These enable the sportsmen to be creative and express themselves. In sport, the conditions exist which are conducive to creativity: they aid growth in capability. To the uninitiated, the gym, track or training pitch may seem dominated by inflexibility, control and repression, but these are exactly the features which enable the sportsman eventually to be innovative, fluid, creative. Without undergoing the developmental rigours, he is impotent, lacking the capacity to create.

Accordingly, I am sceptical about many of the programmes of multi-racial education which stress the more expressive components of education for black youth: dialect classes, black drama, dance and music groups. These represent therapeutic devices for improving the supposedly problematic self-concept or self-esteem of black youth. Yet there is no satisfactory evidence to suggest that black kids do have inadequate self-concepts (see Kardiner and Oversey, 1951; Rosenberg and Simmons, 1971, for American studies). Because teaching personnel may have low expectations of black youth does not necessarily mean it translates into the youths themselves having devalued senses of self. As I have tried to indicate, there are many sources of identity; other people provide the all-important mirrors. Black kids do not rely on negative images from teachers, for they can seek alternative reflections, such as those they derive from other sportsmen.

If there are instructive statements to be drawn out of the study of one group of highly motivated, industrious, receptive, achieving black people, sportsmen, they are that learning and actualization are best promoted when certain conditions can be satisfied: when tangible objectives are specified and determined and when the methods for their attainment are established firmly; when such methods are directed towards the development of basic proficiency, skills and competence; when the methods are held together by discipline backed by a degree of authority; when periodic achievements are reinforced by rewards in order that the achiever feels his efforts are recognized and has palpable evidence of this; when individuals can feed off each other, sustaining each other's endeavours and helping each other improve – as sportsmen train collectively.

It follows that the more therapeutic elements of educational programmes aimed exclusively at black kids should be de-emphasized, that alleged problems of black self-esteem be forgotten, that teachers gear up their expectations of blacks in intellectual spheres and gear down those in relation to natural sports ability, orienting towards them as they would children of any colour while at the same time, recognizing what Winston McLeod called 'the special problems' experienced by black youth in home life. Black kids do drift away from others near school-leaving time or just after and perhaps some initiatives at school might be aimed at curtailing this, though it must be accepted that the critical factors behind this trend lie beyond the pale of the school. In a very pressing way, those critical factors outside the school are the ones which matter.

The study of black sportsmen is a study of success and a study of failure. A theme of this work has been that sport benefits from social adversity. My ambition has been to learn from sport in an effort to see how that adversity may be lessened. But, countering my lessons, there are seemingly immovable obstacles. How do we persuade a youth that the qualifications for which he is working have meaning in the context of proliferating unemployment? How do we convince him that the skilled or unskilled manual work for which he may be destined is not intrinsically dull and monotonous? How do we explain to him the contradiction of an educational system where the majority are fated to fall way short of the ideals set before them? How do we tell him that he will grow up in a world where the colour of a man's skin may well be the crucial feature of his entire life and determine his future? These are the questions of relevance which will inevitably undermine my conclusions.

Sport has and will continue to prosper from the massive contributions of young blacks. All black sportsmen give a great deal to sport in terms of skill, commitment, industry; all will take something, some much, much more than others. But this cannot disguise the more disquieting situations which effectively function to produce the phenomenon of the black sportsman. He is both a champion and a symbol of failure. They are time-honoured roles. From the 1770s and Bill Richmond to the 1980s and Garth Crooks, sport has been a route to fame and material comfort for thousands of blacks and will continue to be exactly that in future. For tens of thousands of others it will be illusory, only a route to nowhere. Sport conceals deep, structured inequalities and, for all the positive benefits it yields, it remains a source of hope and ambition for blacks only as long as those inequalities remain.

Bibliography

Bagley, Christopher (1979), 'A comparative perspective on the education of black children in Britain', Comparative Education, Vol. 15, No. 1 (March), pp. 63–81.

Bagley, Christopher, Bart, M. and Wong, Siu-Ying J. (1978), 'Cognition and scholastic success in West Indian 10-year-olds in London', Educational Studies, Vol. 4, pp. 7–57.

Kardiner, Abram and Oversey, Lionel (1951), The Mark of Oppression, New York, World Publishing.

Olsen, Jack (1968), The Black Athlete: a shameful story, New York, Time Life.

Rogers, Carl (1961), On Becoming a Person, Boston, Mass., Houghton Mifflin.

Rosenberg, Morris and Simmons, Roberta G. (1975), Black and White Self, Washington DC, American Sociological Association.

Rutter, Michael, Maughan, Barbara, Mortimore, Peter and Ouston, Janet (1979), Fifteen Thousand Hours, Shepton Mallet, Open Books.

Stone, Maureen (1981), The Education of the Black Child in Britain, London, Fontana.

Jonathan Long, Ben Carrington and Karl Spracklen

'ASIANS CANNOT WEAR TURBANS IN THE SCRUM'

Explorations of racist discourse within professional rugby league

[. . .]

ALTHOUGH MOST OF THE GENETIC ARGUMENTS regarding racial predisposition to success in sport were countered 20 years ago (e.g. Edwards, 1973; Phillips, 1976), their popularity persists. . . . The resilience of such rationalizations in the face of compelling argument suggests that they must appeal at a deep psychological level to many people or, alternatively, are convenient to many (sometimes including black athletes themselves). [. . .]

. . . [S]tudies have . . . shown that racist practices are evident within elite-level sport in Britain. [. . .] Maguire (1991) found evidence of 'stacking' (the disproportionate allocation of black and ethnic minorities players to particular positions and almost complete lack of representation in others because of perceived racial attributes) in both rugby union and association football. He also identified stereotyped attitudes held by managers and coaches concerning the physical and mental abilities of black players. [. . .]

Rugby league and black involvement

[In the United Kingdom] rugby league is played predominantly in parts of the industrial north of England, and is associated with the working class (Moorhouse, 1989). Contrary to the opinion of rugby union commentators, rugby league is not 'the professional code' of the game of (until recently) amateur rugby union. Besides the fact that the games are different, rugby league is predominantly amateur, with over 1400 amateur teams as opposed to the 35 clubs of the professional Rugby Football League (Moorhouse, 1995). Until the advent of the Super League, only the top three clubs in the RFL were professional full time. In this country the game's roots in the industrial parts of the north have given it a parochial, alien identity in the sporting culture of the nation, although it is arguably one of the most popular sports in Australia and the South Pacific, and the national sport of Papua New Guinea.

Like many other sports, rugby league can trace black involvement on the pitches to its early years. However, it was not until the 1950s that black players became more than just an 'exotic' footnote in history. Part of this involvement was due to black Welshmen, such as the famous Billy Boston of Wigan, following the 'trail up north' because of discrimination in Welsh rugby union. But other black players were drawn from the local communities in the north, players like Roy Francis and Cec Thompson (the first black player to represent Great Britain in 1951) who both went on to become coaches of professional clubs.

This precedent of famous black players in rugby league, and their involvement at international level, came long before black soccer players put on England shirts. Rugby league provided Great Britain sport with its first black captain, when Clive Sullivan (another Welsh exile) captained the World Cup side in 1972. In the late seventies, Hunslet led the way again with an Asian player called Gurdip Singh, the first and only Asian rugby league professional until the Butt brothers signed for Leeds. Both Singh and a black teammate, Francis Jarvis, have gone on to become coaches and organizers of amateur rugby league teams.

In recent years black players in rugby league have been given even more prominence. Rugby league's biggest two stars of the eighties and nineties have been Ellery Hanley and Martin Offiah. Hanley is acknowledged as one of the best players of all time, a captain and coach at both domestic and international level, and on the field played in the central positions of stand off and loose forward, though he started, as most black players start, on the wing. More recently, Ikram Butt became the first Asian to represent England at rugby league. Ironically, it is the very success of these sporting heroes that allows racism to exist behind the mask with protestations that there is no racism in 'our' game.

An analysis of professional players and their ethnic origin provides clear evidence that stacking is occurring in rugby league. Such trends pose many troublesome questions, particularly about access, coaching beliefs and societal assumptions about physical attributes of players who are not 'white'. Selecting two weekends of fixtures, we examined the teams recorded in the newspaper. Our first analysis was on a weekend in September during the 1994/5 Rugby Football League season. At the time, the first division contained 16 teams, four of which had no players from UK ethnic minorities playing that day. In our analysis we were interested in identifying the UK Asian and black players, so we distinguished these from players of Polynesian origin and white players from other nations. Although the figure of 8.3% UK Asian and black players gives no indication of under-representation, only one out of 240 first division players was Asian. The figure from the second division, of 7.9%, hides the fact that five out of 16 of the second division clubs had no black players, and there were no Asian players at any club. We found clear evidence of stacking towards the running positions in the game: the wing, the rest of the back line and the second row. Of the UK Asian and black players in the first division, 65% were wingers and a further 10% played elsewhere in the back line; only five were forwards. Crucially, none of the players were in the controlling positions of scrum half or stand off, and only one was in the 'dummy half' role.

On the second weekend (4 December in the 1995/6 Centenary Season) the clubs of the top division were similarly analysed. Because of the structural change in the league there were only 11 teams, ten of which played that weekend (the other team had only one UK black player in its squad). Of 170 players (13 on the field plus four substitutes, a new rule), only ten were UK Asian and black (5.3%), nine black players and a solitary Asian. Of the ten, seven were wingers, one other back and one second row forward. Apart from a utility forward substitute, every UK Asian and black player was in a running position. Rather than ameliorating, the situation seems to have worsened, though one cannot draw firm conclusions from this alone.

Meanwhile on the terraces there is still a marked absence of spectators from these communities. During our match day surveys the survey team recorded only 24 black (in the widest sense of the term) fans among total crowds of over 31,000. Even if we failed to record several times that number of black supporters, it represents a very small proportion of the spectators. This is not unlike other sports. It may be that spectating at elite sports matches is just not a part of the leisure lifestyles of people from Asian and black communities, but why should that be? Three plausible explanations suggest themselves:

- historical development – rugby league is not established as an integral part of black and ethnic minority communities where soccer and basketball are more appealing. That may be true, but there are few black spectators at those events either.
- avoiding confrontation – if people expect racist abuse they are unlikely to put themselves in circumstances where they may well attract it. Having to jostle in a crowd and risk blocking someone's view may invite abuse.
- white culture – quite simply the rugby league terraces represent alien territory.[1]
  [. . .]

The language of abuse

If people do not contest racism when they encounter it, the racist position is strengthened; repetition and acceptance allow the attitudes to be normalized and reproduced. Although 87% of supporters thought that it was never acceptable to abuse players because of the colour of their skin, only 16% of those who had heard such abuse complained directly to the people chanting and only 6% complained to stewards. Even these reactions are probably a mix of what actually happened and what was seen to be a proper response to the question. Replies were largely unaffected by the type of group the respondent was with, though those with their family were slightly more likely to complain directly to the chanters. It is interesting that what should be the easier option was taken less frequently, presumably because of the lack of immediate availability of stewards. The significance of the *Let's Kick Racism Out of Football* campaign is that it has encouraged fans to counter racism on the terraces to show that it is unacceptable and try to challenge its normalization in the culture surrounding the game.

The lack of challenge to racism may also arise from a denial of its presence, or a displacement of it to somewhere/one else. For some reason the officials were rather less aware than their supporters of chanting against black players at their grounds (33% – it was the chairmen and coaches who were least aware). On the other hand, when asked if their ethnic minority players were picked on at some clubs they visited, over half reported that happening and less than a third disagreed. Similarly, over half the club officials (52%) had witnessed racist behaviour at some clubs. Although this may be a property of probability (the more clubs you visit, the more chance you have of witnessing racist behaviour) it seems that club officials are more ready to recognize aspects of racism elsewhere than at home.

Explanations for what is seen to be unpleasant are also commonly externalized. The reason or rationalization is attributed to some characteristic of the ethnic minority in question. So, for example, the reason that Asians do not play rugby is because of some presumed physical, psychological, social or cultural attribute rather than that they may not be encouraged or made welcome in rugby. Several clubs would protest on the basis that they have tried all sorts of initiatives (even giving tickets away) to attract Asians to the game. Yet no one who has seen the eyes of the youngsters Ikram Butt works with could maintain that there is no interest.

If all the players, half the club officials and almost half the fans revealed that they had witnessed some form of racism, how is it possible for there to be so many protestations that there is no racism in the game? One of the coaches aggressively asserted that the research was a waste of time. 'I don't know what you're bothering for, there's no racism in rugby league.' Yet earlier that afternoon we had received what people thought were formal complaints (they assumed we were from the RFL) because:

> Every time _____ gets the ball this woman behind us SCREAMS, 'You f**** black twat' or 'Kill that black twat'.

And from field notes of another game his team played:

> Stood behind the posts at the western end – mix of supporters in the first half, almost all from _____ in the second. Lots of denim jackets – amused myself with the idea that they were Take That fans. Quite a lot of racist comments – too far away for me to do anything about – e.g. 'Hanley, you black bastard, I'm f**** your girlfriend'. Even [black player on their own team] not immune.

And each of the players (black and white) interviewed from that club was able to cite evidence of racism in the sport. It is perhaps unfortunate that the culture of sport does not require a coach to talk with 'his' players The denial of racism is itself a product of the normalization of racist attitudes, the inevitable outcome is its continued reproduction. [. . .]

Conclusion

Affirmation of identity is clearly central to involvement in sport. Chants of 'Yorkshire, Yorkshire' can be heard at most matches on this side of the Pennines when clubs visit from Lancashire (and vice versa). In classic hegemonic terms it is not merely a site of subjugation. There are, however, important differences associated with certain ethnic divisions and while such differences are unaddressed, it is in the nature of systems that inequalities are likely to increase. For example, it became clear from our interviews with players that, almost without exception, the white players had found their way into the sport through family networks (it truly is a family game) that included some-one who had introduced them to a rugby league club. Not a part of the same local networks, the Asians and black players had to find other routes into the game. It was partly because of this that the players were united in their call for black and ethnic minority development workers to carry rugby league to those who might otherwise be lost to the game.

It should be remembered that this study was of a largely male sporting culture. We thus recognize that, like the bulk of studies in sport, the position of women has for the most part been overlooked in our work.[2] However, the gender dimension is clearly evident in the significance attached to particular masculinities, especially with regard to sexuality and sexual prowess (Spracklen, 1996). The extent to which gender and sexuality act as the modality through which notions of masculinity and 'race' are constructed also requires further examination. The 'dressing room banter' of white players that focuses on the power of the black phallus (though not described in those terms) and the associated white male envy are clearly important. The abuse directed at Ellery Hanley (quoted above) can perhaps be understood as an attempt to challenge the myth of black male sexuality by reconstructing the notion of white masculine superiority.

One respondent suggested that some black players take the opportunity to get their own back on white people: 'You couldn't do it on the street, but you can do it on the pitch'. At a very personal level rugby league offered a way of resisting and challenging racism from 'white society'. Obviously such a 'site of resistance' is limited and we do not wish to make too many claims for this form of action. Nevertheless it does raise interesting social-psychological questions about the role of sports for Asian and black people in responding to racism in their everyday lives. It may also help us to begin to understand more fully the underlying drives behind the formation of 'all-Asian', or black sporting teams, which perhaps offer a more coherent, community-based, articulation of the problems faced by these groups.

We have shown that racial stereotypes persist among players, supporters and club officials in rugby league. It is only by examining their articulation and challenging them at every possible opportunity that progressive steps will be made to eliminate harmful stereotypes and to improve social relations more generally. Although exposing such views will not, in itself, lead to the elimination of racism from society, the central role of sport in constructing a sense of communal identity (be that gendered, racial or national) means that these issues cannot be ignored. At the symbolic level at least, the increased participation of, for example, Asian players in the 'hard white working class culture' of rugby league would make the stereotyped claims about Asian passiveness and fragility all the more difficult to maintain.

In this sense we would agree with Pieterse's (1995, p. 13) qualified endorsement of the effects of combating stereotypes when he says, 'stereotypes are but one link in the multiple chains of social hierarchy. Decoding social representations is a necessary but not sufficient condition for improving the position of stereotyped groups.'

Notes

1   One of the black players suggested it was seen as an 'old fashioned game for white men'. The image of pits and pubs and pit bulls is off-putting to southerners too, but as administrators try to change this perception of the game many of its supporters encourage it as it helps to define their identity.
2   We know from the fans' survey that women were less likely to be aware of racism, but more likely to act if they did hear racist chanting.

References

Edwards, H. (1973) *Sociology of Sport*, Dorsey, Chicago.

Holland, B. (1995) 'Kicking racism out of football': an assessment of racial harassment in and around football grounds, *New Community*, **21**(4), 567–86.

Long, J., Tongue, N., Spracklen, K. and Carrington, B. (1995) *What's the Difference: A Study of the Nature and Extent of Racism in Rugby League*, RFL/CRE/LCC/LMU, Leeds.

Maguire, J. (1991) Sport, racism and British society, in *Sport, Racism and Ethnicity* (edited by G. Jarvie) Falmer, London, pp. 94–123.

Moorhouse, G. (1989) *At The George and Other Essays*, Hodder & Stoughton, Sevenoaks.

Moorhouse, G. (1995) *A People's Game*, Hodder & Stoughton, Sevenoaks.

Pieterse, J. (1995) *White on Black: Images of Africa and Blacks in Western Popular Culture*, Yale Press, London.

Phillips, J. (1976) Toward an explanation of racial variations in top-level sports participation, *International Review of Sports Sociology*, **11**(3), 39–53.

Spracklen, K. (1996) Playing the Ball. Constructing community and masculine identity in rugby: an analysis of the two codes of league and union and the people involved. Unpublished Ph.D. thesis, Leeds Metropolitan University.

Scott Fleming

SPORT AND SOUTH
ASIAN YOUTH
The perils of 'false universalism' and stereotyping

[. . .]

'False universalism'

'FALSE UNIVERSALISM' IS THE TERM borrowed from Eisenstein that Raval (1988) has used to describe the collective treatment of South Asians without acknowledging, or even considering their heterogeneity. It typically occurs when the process of logical induction is applied inappropriately, and on the basis of limited evidence huge generalizations are made. Consequently, people are often treated stereotypically, and it will become apparent that these stereotypes are damaging and dangerous. False universalism affects the leisure lifestyles and sports participation of young South Asians on (at least) three different levels: the collective treatment of all minority groups as similar; mistaken assumptions about South Asians collectively as an homogenous group; and the failure to acknowledge the complexity of the numerous inter-connected variables that influence South Asian ethnicity.

'Sport for all' (?)

It has been recognized for some time that ethnicity is a significant variable that affects sports participation (Kew 1979, Roberts 1983); and in his chapter on 'ethnic minorities' in *Youth and Leisure*, Roberts (1983) has suggested that young people from minority groups share just one set of common experiences: racial disadvantage and harassment. But Roberts himself also acknowledges that besides this there are more differences than similarities amongst Britain's minority groups, and it is clear that racism is experienced differently by various ethnic groups (Jarvie 1991b). Racism affects the use of sports facilities by minority groups (Lashley 1991), but not surprisingly, it affects them differently.

Of late, serious consideration of the sport–ethnicity relation has acknowledged that the role and function of sport, and the meanings attached to it differ amongst and between ethnic groups (Lyons 1991). To emphasize the point, however, the experiences of the PE profession should serve as a reminder of the danger of a 'colour blind' approach to young people from minority groups, for as Williams (1989, p. 163) argues: 'Treating all children the same means treating them all like white middle class children. This will inevitably mean that all children's needs are not being equally met'. There is no doubt that this has occurred, for PE departments in schools have frequently made certain assumptions about the sporting preferences of young people from minority groups, and based whole PE curricula upon them (Townsend and Brittan 1973); but crucially, they have often failed to acknowledge the cultural differences *between* the ethnic groups for whom they catered.

As a major agency of sports provision, the Sports Council has been influential in creating opportunities and providing access for minority groups. But it is only in the last few years that a real commitment to minority groups has become apparent (Sports Council 1991a, 1991b). Previous attempts to address the issues affecting minority groups and sport were characterized by superficiality and the absence of a detailed knowledge base. By merely targeting 'ethnic minorities' (Sports Council 1982), a huge and generalized assumption was made about the collective needs of minority groups. There was little evidence upon which to base such an assumption, and as Roberts (1983, p. 149) has succinctly put it: 'We cannot assume that the minorities would wish to emulate middle-class whites' leisure habits, if granted equal opportunities'.

Allied to this, there is also the temptation to make comparisons between different ethno-cultural groups based on spurious criteria. Again the experiences of the educational institutions are instructive, for just as performance in academic examinations has been used as: 'A stick with which to beat the West Indian community' (Tomlinson 1983, p. 381), so apparent South Asian under-representation in organised sport is seen as an indicator of a 'problem' (DES 1991, Botholo et al., 1986, Rigg 1986). The reality is, of course, as Tomlinson (1986, p. 4) indicates, that: 'Blanket comparisons are . . . of dubious value because they assume that the experiences of pupils in schools and society are similar, and this is clearly not the case'. Her comments apply equally to young people involved in sport, for it is apparent that the experiences of South Asians collectively are different from those of other ethnic groups, and participation in sport is affected accordingly.

Sport and all South Asians

It is well established that South Asians are heterogeneous groups of people, and do not share a similar lifestyle and a uniform culture (Brah and Minhas 1985, Taylor and Hegarty 1985, Ballard 1990, Clarke et al., 1990). Yet the most common and potentially damaging occurrences of false universalism are those identified by Raval (1988): the tendencies to generalize about all South Asians as a single group. As Ballard (1990, p. 220) explains:

> As it becomes increasingly obvious that settlers of differing backgrounds are following varied, and often sharply contrasting, social trajectories, so it is

becoming steadily more difficult, and indeed increasingly inappropriate, to make generalizations which are valid for all 'Asians' in Britain.

Heterogeneity amongst young South Asians in Britain is reflected in sports participation and leisure activities (Livingstone 1978, Roberts 1983, Lloyd 1986, Lovell 1991, Verma et al., 1991), and is affected by numerous complex and inter-connected factors. They include, for example religion (and sects within a religion); class, mobility (social and economic) and caste; family (structure, size, relationships); place of origin (nationality, region, urban/rural); immigration (place, timing, causes); linguistic group; generation (and degree of acculturation); gender and kinship networks. In spite of all these variables, however, the sport–ethnicity relation for South Asians has often been treated in a way that fails to fully acknowledge ethno-cultural differentiation (e.g., Field and Haikin 1971, Lewis 1979, Dixey 1982, Ikulayo 1982, Sports Council 1982, Leaman 1984, Williams 1989, BAALPE 1990).[1]

Paradoxically, attempts to explain, rationalize and predict behaviour are often based on commonalities, and a typological framework that makes the world 'cognitively manageable' (Wright 1992), and this creates a real dilemma. On the one hand, it is clear that failure to consider the full complexity of South Asian ethnicity inevitably leads to false universalism; whilst on the other, embracing all the variables together is absurd reductionism. That is to say, there are so many variables that influence South Asians in Britain that when they are all accommodated at once, there is little basis for commonality. Groups become so sensitively defined, and there are so many of them, that South Asian cultures remain cognitively unmanageable. What is important therefore, is to locate the factors that are most significant for understanding the sports participation of South Asians in Britain. To this end, Hargreaves' (1986) analysis of sport in Britain provides a useful point of departure, for he asserts that three of the primary influences on sports involvement are ethnicity, class, and gender. These profoundly affect the experiences of young South Asians (Raval 1988). [. . .]

For some time now, there has been a well-established link between social class and sporting involvement (Sports Council 1979, 1982, Roberts 1981, Hargreaves 1982, 1986, Whannel 1983, Mason 1988, 1989, Holt 1989). The combined impact of ethnicity and class on young South Asians is made explicit by Roberts (1983, p. 148): 'Ethnic minority youth face the disadvantages of being working class, only more so'. [. . .]

. . . [S]outh Asians' experiences of sport and leisure are affected by gender, and as with other aspects of South Asians' lifestyle, the influence of the traditional culture of origin is considerable (Lovell 1991). Even now, sport in India is no more than: 'Almost approaching emancipation' (Callaghan 1991), and the popular culture of the sub-continent also affects the gender divisions within leisure. Werbner (1992, p. 13) observes: 'Popular culture in South Asia has its traditional spaces sited in two major domains: a feminised youthful domain I shall call popular wedding culture, and a youthful male domain of sport'. Thus it is inevitable that the role of sport within the popular culture of South Asians in Britain is experienced very differently by males and females. [. . .]

South Asians, sport and stereotypes

The process of stereotyping, as outlined by Nugent and King (1979, p. 28) is simple, and involves three stages:

(a)   the identification of a category such as policemen (sic), hippies, or blacks;
(b)   the attribution of traits to the category;
(c)   the application of the traits to anyone belonging to the category.

This process is more than mere typification, for stereotypes of minority or subordinate groups in a society are constructed by the dominant group, and are unlikely to reflect the perceptions that the members of that group have of themselves (Klein 1993). Moreover, the traits or characteristics that are ascribed are often false (Nugent and King 1979).

There have been two particularly prevalent stereotypes of young South Asians. The first has been identified by Tomlinson (1984) and Brah (1992), and is concerned with the tendency to pathologize South Asian family life. The second, also identified by Tomlinson (1986) has focused on the myth of South Asian educational achievement. One of the consequences of the latter especially, is that a third stereotype has emerged, that of the 'academic, but non-sporting' young South Asian (Lashley 1980a). Indeed the perception of young South Asians being physically less able than their peers from other ethno-cultural groups became very widespread, especially in educational discourse. Stereotypic rumours, myths and assumptions about South Asian young people became commonplace within the PE profession, and these were often couched in very negative terms. Some are generalizations about the physiological and anatomical capacities of young South Asians:

> 'Asian children have low ball skills, low coordination and are weak', 'Asian and West Indian children dislike the cold' (cited in Bayliss 1983, pp. 6–7);

> 'Asian girls have great difficulties in PE', and 'have difficulty in reproducing some simple body postures' (cited in Cherrington 1974, pp. 34, 41);

> 'Where stamina is required, Asian girls are often at a disadvantage as they are usually small and quite frail' (Lewis 1979, p. 132);

> 'Asians are too frail for contact sports' (cited in Bayliss 1989, p. 20).

Such stereotypes as these are especially insidious as they are based on the use of quasi-scientific evidence and, . . . as Tomlinson (1986) has termed it 'scientific racism'. Most worryingly, though, these findings have been uncritically presented as 'academic research', and have therefore been granted scholarly and professional credibility. In short, fallacious evidence has created a climate in which young South Asians are often perceived as likely to under-perform in PE and sport, but to achieve in the classroom (Lashley 1980a, Williams 1989). Consequently, just as young Afro-Caribbeans have been channelled into sport (Lashley 1980a, Cashmore 1982, Carrington and Wood 1983), so young South Asians have been channelled away from sporting activities.

The further implication of this general perception is the tendency to make stereotypic assumptions about the sporting aptitude and preferences of young South Asians:

> 'Asians are poor swimmers', 'Asian children dislike contact sports but excel in individual skill sports such as badminton', 'Asian children are good at hockey' (cited in Bayliss 1983, p. 6);

> 'Asians can only play hockey' (cited in Bayliss 1989, p. 20);

> 'Pakistani boys are exceptionally good at badminton at an earlier age than most other groups';

'Indian boys generally prefer non-contact games' (cited in Cherrington 1974, p. 34);

'Sikh children not liking rugby' (cited in Coventry LEA 1980, p. 28).

Thus, in addition to the channelling that has occurred, there has also been a process of 'funnelling' into certain activities, and away from others, based on little more than crude stereotypes and uninformed speculation. Indeed, there have even been attempts to explain the erroneous perceptions of the sports participation and involvement of young South Asians that have drawn upon the forces of socialization during the formative years:

'[South Asian girls are] not encouraged to play with toys, balls or ropes, but the daily household chores are stressed as important' (Lewis 1979, p. 132);

'Asian children are not encouraged to play with toys, balls, ropes, and this effects (sic) their ability to play games' (cited in Bayliss 1983, p. 6).

Consequently, the stereotypes that exist are manifest in the prevalent physiological and psychological prejudices about South Asians. Hence, as John Williams of the Sir Norman Chester Centre for Football Research at the University of Leicester indicates, the 'established wisdom' reflects widely-held stereotypic views within football:

They do tend to say things like 'Asian players are too excitable and they're too indisciplined. And maybe they don't have the character, and maybe they haven't got the build' (BBC TV 1991[b]).

The key point is that once these stereotypic notions become entrenched as part of coaching folklore and professional (mis)understanding, they are constantly re-affirmed and become self-perpetuating (Williams 1989).

Internalising stereotypes

When stereotypes become embedded in the dominant culture, they are often internalized by the very people to whom the stereotypes apply (Tsolidas 1990, Lovell 1991); or as Cashmore has put it: 'they swallow the myths themselves – and it's not surprising' (BBC TV 1990[a]). Some of the remarks that were made to me by young South Asian males and their parents indicate the extent and impact of such views (Fleming 1992a):

Rajesh: 'Hindus aren't that good at football . . . They don't know how to play football, they only know how to play cricket . . Cricket is a famous game in India. Their ancestors taught them how to play, so they still play. But they don't want to play football, they don't like it'.

Mr Patel: 'Indoor sports are the only things that we take up. I haven't seen any Asians playing football – soccer, over here; neither rugby. These are "harsh" sports, too harsh for us'.

Mr Raja: 'I think that looking at the background as an Asian, I think we prefer not too much of a physical contact, let me put it that way. Most of the Asians don't go in for rugby because it is too rough and violent for them'.

It is clear too, that the absence of sporting role models with whom young South Asians in north London could identify was an important force in shaping perceptions of appropriate sporting behaviour for young South Asians – not only at the elite level of sports competition, but also at sub-elite and recreational levels:

Jitendra: 'They only play certain types of sport. There's cricket, badminton, squash . . . Hmm, I think that's it. They're the most publicised with Asians in it. They don't play the others'.

Arun: 'I had a football book and there was no Indian playing for any team. They're probably no good'.

Rajesh: 'I went to (the sports centre) with my dad, and I looked very carefully, and I saw that there weren't any Indians there . . . They must be scared of coming there as well . . . I don't know why, but I kept looking to see any Indians there. I was wondering why there weren't any Indians. We were the only ones and I was a bit scared . . . White people don't like us, and they might do something. I was embarrassed, I couldn't find any Indians doing anything. That's what my brother is scared of, no Indians there'.

Concluding remarks

The role of sport amongst South Asian cultural groups has become the focus for greater interest by academic researchers, the PE profession, sports-providers and the media; and with more attention, there is an expanding body of knowledge around some of the key themes. The attention to cultural difference, however, reflects misplaced research priorities. For whilst a major criticism of some of the work in this area is the concern with South Asian differentness from the dominant culture in Britain, ethnocultural diversity amongst South Asian groups has been neglected. More important though, the preoccupation with cultural difference is a diversion and a distraction from *the* most fundamental issue – the pervasive impact of racism in all of its guises.

The second significant criticism of some of the work that has addressed the sport-ethnicity relation and young South Asians, is that of Eurocentrism. It is clearly inappropriate to assume that the lifestyles of minority groups with some facets characterized by continuity of traditional culture, will adopt the patterns of behaviour and way of life of the dominant groups. Sport and leisure are aspects of traditional culture in which there has been continuity that has been sustained despite migration to a very different social system (Fleming 1992b, Werbner 1992). Thus it is unreasonable to apply the criteria typically associated with the sports involvement of white, middle-class males to young South Asians. Values, perceptions and attitudes to sport are inevitably different.

Failure to acknowledge Eurocentrism also leads to invalid comparisons between different sets of minority groups. The proportional over-representation of Afro-Caribbeans in sport at all levels is contrasted with the relative under-representation of South Asians, and it is concluded that sports participation for South Asians is therefore a 'problem' to address. The critical aspect of the analysis that is overlooked is that there is an implied assumption that the role and significance of sport is the same amongst Afro-Caribbean cultural groups as it is amongst different South Asian groups. Shared experiences of social

disadvantage and racial discrimination – which may in themselves be contested as being
. . . very different in any case (Jarvie 1991b) – are not sufficient grounds upon which to
construct a comparative analysis of sporting involvement. Importantly too, the
methodological basis for assessing sporting involvement may be fundamentally flawed,
for it is assumed that sports participation can be measured with both validity and reliability;
and that experiences of what actually constitutes sport are common across all groups.
This is clearly not so.

The reality is, as Jarvie (1991a, 1991b) observes, that in spite of some of the claims
that sport provides democratization and equality, real equality of opportunity is denied
to many young people of South Asian origin. He concludes:

> We might all be equal on the starting line, but the resources (political, economic
> and cultural) that people have and the hurdles that people have to leap to get
> there are inherently unequal. Sporting relations themselves are vivid expressions
> of privilege, oppression, domination and subordination.
>
> (Jarvie 1991a, p. 2)

This is a useful point of departure as it highlights the critical relational issues of power,
class and ethnicity. But the analogy of the track race is not quite sufficient as there is an
implicit assumption that all those taking part are doing so for the same reasons. It is
abundantly clear that sport occupies different roles both between and within different
ethno-cultural groups.

Acknowledgements

I should like to acknowledge my thanks to Lesley Lawrence, Alan Tomlinson and an
anonymous referee for their constructive comments on an earlier draft of this paper. The
final product is, of course, my own responsibility.

Note

1   My own review of the literature that existed at the time (Fleming 1989) was an attempt
     to acknowledge heterogeneity – indeed it was fore fronted as a central element of
     discussion. Inevitably, however, given the sources under review, there was a tendency
     to over-generalize in the synthesis of material.

References

Ballard, R. (1990) Migration and kinship: the differential effect of marriage rules on the
     processes of punjabi migration to Britain. In C. Clarke *et al.* (Eds) *South Asians Overseas*
     Cambridge University Press, Cambridge, pp. 219–49.
Bayliss, T. (1983) Physical education in a multiethnic society, *Physical Education*, ILEA, London.
Bayliss, T. (1989) PE and racism: making changes, *Multicultural Teaching*, 7, 19–22.
BBC Television (1990a) *Inside Story – the Race Game*. London, BBC1.

BBC Television (1991b) *Birthrights – Who's Batting for Britain?*, London, BBC2.

Botholo, G., Lewis, J., Milten, J. and Shaw, P. (1986) *A Sporting Chance*, Greater London Council Sports Sub-Committee 1983–85 and Review of Brixton Leisure Centre, GLC, London.

Brah, A. (1985) Women of South Asian origin in Britain: issues and concerns. In P. Braham *et al.* (Eds) *Racism and Antiracism*, Sage, London, pp. 64–78.

Brah, A., Minhas, R. (1985) Structural racism or cultural difference: schooling for Asian girls. In G. Weiner (Ed) *Just a Bunch of Girls*, Open University Press, Milton Keynes, pp. 14–25.

British Association of Advisers and Lecturers in Physical Education (BAALPE) (1990) *Perceptions of Physical Education*, BAALPE, Dudley.

Callaghan, J. (1991) *The Control and Development of Sport in the Sub-Continent – The Challenge for India*, Paper presented at the ICHPER 34th World Congress, Limerick, Ireland.

Carrington, B. and Wood, E. (1983) Body Talk: Images of Sport in a Multi-Racial School, *Multi-racial Education*, 11, 29–38.

Cashmore, E. (1982) *Black Sportsmen*, RKP, London.

Cherrington, D. (1974) Physical education and the immigrant child. In I.R. Glaister (Ed) *Physical Education – an Integrating Force?*, NATFHE, London, pp. 33–45.

Clarke, C., Peach, C. and Vertovec, S. (1990) Introduction: themes in the study of the South Asian diaspora. In C. Clarke *et al.* (Eds) *South Asians Overseas*, Cambridge University Press, Cambridge, pp. 1–29.

Coventry Local Education Authority (1980) *Physical Education in a Multi-Cultural Society*, Elm Bank Teachers' Centre, Coventry.

Department of Education and Science (1991) *Young People in the 80s. A Survey*. HMSO, London.

Dixey, R. (1982) Asian women and sport, the Bradford experience, *British Journal of Physical Education*, 13, 108 and 113.

Field, F. and Haikin, P. (1971) *Black Britons*, Oxford University Press, London.

Fleming, S. (1989) Asian lifestyles and sports participation. In A. Tomlinson (Ed) *Youth Cultures and the Domain of Leisure*, Leisure Studies Association, Eastbourne, pp. 82–98.

Fleming, S. (1992a) *Sport and South Asian Male Youth*. Unpublished Ph.D. thesis. CNAA, Brighton Polytechnic.

Fleming, S. (1992b) Multiculturalism in the Physical Education Curriculum: The Case of South Asian Male Youth, Dance and South Asian Dance, *Multicultural Teaching*, 11, 35–8.

Hargreaves, J. (1982) Sport, culture and ideology. In J. Hargreaves (Ed) *Sport, Culture and Ideology*, Routledge & Kegan Paul, London, pp. 30–61.

Hargreaves, J. (1986) *Sport, Power and Culture*, Polity, London.

Holt, R.(1989) *Sport and the British*. Oxford University Press, Oxford.

Ikulayo, P. (1982) Physical ability and the ethnic link, *British Journal of Physical Education*, 13, 47.

Jarvie, G. (1991a) Introduction. In G. Jarvie (Ed) *Sport, Racism and Ethnicity*, Falmer, London, pp. 1–6.

Jarvie, G. (1991b) Ain't no problem here. *Sport and Recreation*, 32, 20–1.

Kew, S. (1979) *Ethnic Groups and Leisure*, Sports Council and Social Science Research Council, London.

Klein, G. (1993) *Education towards Race Equality*. Cassell, London.

Lashley, H. (1980a) The New Black Magic. *British Journal of Physical Education*, 11, 5–6.

Lashley, H. (1991) Promoting anti-racist policy and practice, *Sport and Leisure*, 32, 16–17.

Leaman, O. (1984) Physical education, dance and outdoor pursuits. In A. Craft and G. Bardell (Eds) *Curriculum Opportunities in a Multicultural Society*, Harper & Row, London, pp. 210–22.

Lewis, T. (1979) Ethnic influences of girls' PE, *British Journal of Physical Education*, 10, 132.

Livingstone, P. (1978) *The Leisure Needs of Asian boys aged 8–14 in Slough, Berkshire*, The Scout Association, London.

Lloyd, N. (1986) *Work and Leisure in the 1980s*, Sports Council, London.

Lovell, T. (1991) Sport, racism and young women. In G. Jarvie (Ed) *Sport, Racism and Ethnicity*. Falmer, London, pp. 58–73.

Lyons, A. (1991) Participation Patterns, *Sport and Recreation*, 32, 12.

Mason, T. (1988) *Sport in Britain*, Faber & Faber, London.

Mason, T. (1989) Ed *Sport in Britain – A Social History*, Cambridge University Press, Cambridge.

Nugent, N. and King, R. (1979) Ethnic minorities, scapegoating and the extreme right. In R. Miles and A. PhizackJea (Eds) *Racism and Political Action in Britain*, Routledge & Kegan Paul, London, pp. 28–49.

Raval, S. (1988) Gender, leisure and sport: A case study of young people of South Asian descent – A response, *Leisure Studies*, 8, 237–40.

Rigg, M. (1986) *Action Sport – An Evaluation*, Policy Studies Institute, London.

Roberts, K. (1981) *Leisure*, 2nd edition, Longman, Harlow.

Roberts, K. (1983) *Youth and Leisure*, George Allen & Unwin, London.

Sports Council (1979) *People in Sport*, Sports Council, London.

Sports Council (1982) *Sport in the Community . . . The Next Ten Years*, Sports Council, London.

Sports Council (1991a) *Equality in Sport – Black and Ethnic Minorities Sports Council Position and Policy Statement*, Sports Council, London.

Sports Council (1991b) *Sports Equity – Ethnic Minorities and Sport Policy Statement*, Sports Council, London.

Taylor, M.J. and Hegarty, S. (1985) *The Best of Both Worlds . . .?* NFER Publishing, Windsor.

Tomlinson, S. (1983) The educational performance of children of Asian origin, *New Community*, 10, 381–92.

Tomlinson, S. (1984) Home, school and community. In M. Craft (Ed) *Education and Cultural Pluralism*, Falmer, Lewes, pp. 143–60.

Tomlinson, S. (1986) *Ethnic Minority Achievement and Equality of Opportunity*, University of Nottingham School of Education, Nottingham.

Townsend, H.E.R. and Brittan, E.M. (1973) *Multi-Racial Education: Need and Innovation*. Schools Council Working Paper 50, Evans/Methuen Educational, London.

Tsolidas, G. (1990) Ethnic minority girls and self-esteem. In J. Kenway and S. Willis (Eds) *Hearts and Minds: Self-Esteem and the Schooling of Girls*, Falmer, Lewes, pp. 53–70.

Verma, G.K., MacDonald, A., Darby, D. and Carroll, R. (1991) *Sport and Recreation with Special Reference to Ethnic Minorities*, Manchester University, Manchester.

Werbner, P. (1992) Fun spaces: on identity and social empowerment among British Muslims. Paper presented at Institute of Social and Cultural Anthropology, Oxford University.

Whannel, G. (1983) *Blowing the Whistle*, Pluto, London.

Williams, A. (1989) Physical Education in a Multicultural Context. In A. Williams (Ed) *Issues in Physical Education for the Primary Years*, Falmer, Lewes, pp. 166–72.

Wright, C. (1992) Early Education: Multiracial Primary School Classrooms. In D. Gill *et al.* (Eds) *Racism and Education*, Sage, London, pp. 5–41.

Ben Carrington

SPORT, MASCULINITY, AND BLACK CULTURAL RESISTANCE

[. . .]

The racial signification of sport

> When you talk about race in basketball, the whole thing is simple: *a black player knows he can* go out on the court and *kick a white player's ass*. He can beat him, and he knows it. It's that simple, and it shouldn't surprise anyone. The black player feels it every time. He knows it from the inside.
>
> (Rodman, 1996, p. 129)

GIVEN THAT SPORT IS one of the few arenas where public displays of competition, domination, and control are openly played out (Birrell, 1989), it is not surprising, as bell hooks (1994) suggests, that, historically, "competition between black and white males has been highlighted in the sports arena" (p. 31).

Messner (1992), drawing on a Gramscian analysis of the hegemonic nature of sport, highlights the way in which sport provides opportunities for subordinated groups to challenge the established order. Messner argues that subaltern groups are able to "use sport as a means to resist (at least symbolically) the domination imposed upon them. Sport must thus be viewed as an institution through which domination is not only imposed, but also contested; an institution within which power is constantly at play" (p. 13). Therefore, within racially inscribed societies we can see how the sociocultural, psychological, and political meanings of public displays of sporting contestation come to take on specifically racial significance. As Kobena Mercer (1994) notes,

> As a major public arena, sport is a key site of white male ambivalence, fear and fantasy. The spectacle of black bodies triumphant in rituals of masculine

competition reinforces the fixed idea that black men are "all brawn and no brains," and yet, because the white man is beaten at his own game—football, boxing, cricket, athletics—the Other is idolized to the point of envy. . . . *The ambivalence cuts deep into the recess of the white male imaginary.*

(pp. 178–179)

Mercer's perceptive analysis highlights the implicit role of sport as central to the racial, and national, imaginary, and the wider social and (unacknowledged) psychological meanings invested in the physical and competitive struggles played out in the sports arena between Black and White men. A further, pertinent, question would be to ask what happens when sporting contests between Black men and White men actually take place? That is, to move from cultural representations to cultural practices. What is the significance for those involved, both Black and White, and how do wider racialized discourses affect the game itself?

Michael Messner's (1992) argument pertaining to the role of sport in allowing for the realization of a masculine identity for subaltern groups is relevant here. Messner suggests that "subordinated groups of men often used sport to resist racist, colonial, and class domination, and their resistance most often took the form of a claim to 'manhood'" (p. 19). It is precisely this attempt to reconstruct Black masculinity, which colonialism had configured "as feminised and emasculated" (Vergès, 1996, p. 61), that is central to Frantz Fanon's (1986) analysis of colonial racism, and further shows why it is impossible to separate, in any simple way, questions of masculinity from race. For Fanon, the claim to manhood is realized via a claim to *black* manhood because it is on the basis of the Black male's racialized identity, that is, because he is Black, that his masculine identity is denied: "All I wanted was to be a man among men" (Fanon, 1986, p. 112). Confronted with this denial, or lack of recognition, Fanon responds, "I resolved, since it was impossible for me to get away from an *inborn complex*, to assert myself as a BLACK MAN. Since the other hesitated to recognize me, there remained only one solution: to make myself known" (p. 115).

It is not surprising then that it is the traditionally highly masculinized arena of sports through which Black men often attempt to (re)assert their Black identity, that is, gender acts as the modality through which a racialized identity is realized (Gilroy, 1993, p. 85). As the quote from the enigmatic basketball player Dennis Rodman suggests, sports can therefore be seen at one level as a transgressive liminal space where Black men can attempt, quite legitimately, to (re)impose their subordinated masculine identity through the symbolic, and sometimes literal, "beating" of the other, that is, White men.[1] Therefore, what we might term the "racial signification of sport" means that sports contests are more than just significant events, in and of themselves important, but rather that they act as a key signifier for wider questions about identity within racially demarcated societies in which racial narratives about the self and society are read both into and from sporting contests that are imbued with racial meanings. [. . .]

This study focuses on the Caribbean Cricket Club (CCC), which is situated near an area of Leeds, a large city in the north of England where the majority of the city's Asian and Black residents live.[2] [. . .]

The CCC is one of the oldest Black sports clubs in Britain. It was originally formed in the late 1940s as a social and sporting club by a group of West Indian soldiers who had fought in the Second World War and had settled in the city (Wheatley, 1992;

Zulfiqar, 1993). Over the years, the club became more successful, culminating in the late 1970s when it won the league three years running and won the treble on a number of occasions. In the late 1980s, the CCC moved on to play in one of the strongest leagues in Yorkshire County, the Leeds League, where it has played for the past 10 years. It currently has three senior men's teams and three junior boy's teams. Nearly all of the senior players are Black except for three Asian players and three White players. [. . .]

. . . [T]he club's significance goes beyond merely being a cricket club and assumes a heightened social role as a Black institution within a wider White environment, providing many of the Black men with a sense of ontological security. This can operate on a number of related levels, from being a space removed, albeit not entirely, from the overt practices of White racism, as a social and cultural resource for Black people, and as an arena that allows for Black expressive behavior. These elements can be traced in the various ways in which the importance of the CCC was discussed by its members. The club was often labeled by the players and members in the interviews and discussions as a *Black space*, by which was often meant a place where Black people could be themselves (for example, in being able to tell certain jokes and speak in Caribbean patois), free from the strictures imposed by the White gaze. Thus, the club's importance transcended its sporting function.

The current chair and manager of the CCC, Ron, came to Leeds in the late 1950s and joined the CCC in the 1970s, when in his early 20s. For Ron, it was important to acknowledge the historical social role of the club within the area. When asked whether he saw the club as being more than just a sporting club, he replied,

> Oh yeah, because when it started in '47 it wasn't just a sports club, it was a focal point for those people who were black and in a vast minority, because in 1947 I don't think there were the amount of black people in Leeds that there are now. It was a focal point, it was a survival point for the people that were here. So it was more than a club then and it's still more than a club now, so it will always be that.

The use of the language of survival is interesting. It highlights the historical significance of the club in providing a safe space within a wider (hostile) environment for the earlier Caribbean migrants, which is then mapped onto the present, showing the continuities of the club and its role in the light of the persistence of racism: "It was more than a club then and it's still more than a club now, so it will always be that."

Nicholas, a 17-year-old who played for both the senior and junior sides, referred to the CCC as an important social space for Black people. As he played for another junior cricket team in another part of Yorkshire, he was able to contrast his experiences of playing for White and Black teams. Nicholas had experienced racial abuse from an opposing player while playing junior cricket for his other team, Scholes, which had increased his feelings of isolation at his predominantly White club.

> Nicholas: Some teams, if you're batting against them, and you start hitting them all over the place they always have to come out with their racist remarks to try and put you off. . . . It even happened to me this season when we played a team from Garforth, and I was hitting the opening bowler who has played for Yorkshire [Juniors]. I was hitting him for

quite a lot of fours, and then he started to go on and call me names on
the pitch . . . and then he got me out, and then, he was all "mouthy
mouthy."

BC: But how did that make you feel?

Nicholas: Well, it's the first time it's happened, it made me feel kind of
funny. I didn't know whether to answer him back or to walk away from
him.

BC: If you were playing for Caribbean do you think he would have said it?

Nicholas: If I were playing for Caribbean he wouldn't have dared say it because
if he was saying it to one person he's really saying it to the whole team
. . . but at Scholes there is only two of us there, and all the rest are
White, so it was more easier for him to say it there.

Such incidents compounded his feeling of isolation and otherness in a White setting,
and he thus felt more relaxed and secure when at the CCC. It is instructive that Nicholas's
(non)response to the racist abuse he received (in this sporting context) almost paralyzes
him in his inability to speak or move ("I didn't know whether to answer him back or
to walk away"), especially when we consider Fanon's observations on the discursive
power of racism: "overdetermined from without . . . I am *fixed*" (Fanon, 1986, p. 116).
In this sense, the CCC can be seen as providing Nicholas with an environment where
his Blackness takes on a lesser significance—"As long as the black man is among his own,
he will have no occasion, except in minor internal conflicts, to experience his being
through others" (Fanon, 1986, p. 109)—and offers, in both a symbolic and very real
sense, protection from the more overt practices of White racism.

The achievement of creating and sustaining a cricketing Black space within a White
environment was often reflected on, somewhat nostalgically, by the club's members,
particularly the older ones. There was a sense of pride among many of the players and
members that despite all the problems the club had faced, including increasing financial
pressures, the CCC was still going and now had its own ground and pavilion. Pete, one
of the older players, who had come to England from Barbados in the late 1960s, echoed
these views, while being interviewed in his car at The Oval. He said,

I tend to think there are people out there who don't want us to have this.
. . . But I hope we can carry on. I mean look at this [he gazes at the pan-
oramic view across the ground overlooking the city], this is great as far as
I'm concerned!

[. . .] [F]or a number of Black men, sport, and in particular cricket, can provide a
modality through which Black cultural resistance to racism can be achieved. Sports provide
an arena whereby Black men can lay claim to a masculine identity as a means of restoring
a unified sense of racial identity, freed, if only momentarily, from the emasculating
discourses imposed by the ideologies and practices of White racism.

However, we should be cautious not to overstate unproblematically the benefits of
such sites of resistance. For one, Black women often occupy marginal positions within
sports clubs such as the CCC (especially those that do not have women's teams), which
are perhaps more accurately described, as I have tried to make clear throughout, as Black
men's cricket clubs. Without acknowledging such limitations, the complex positioning of

Black women, in particular, within "white supremacist capitalist patriarchal societies" (hooks, 1994) gets overlooked. Thus, any claims for such cultural practices as being in some way emancipatory must be qualified. Otherwise, as Black feminists have consistently pointed out, the requirements for Black resistance become equated with the need for Black *male* emancipation. The overcoming of the crisis of Black masculinity is frequently misrecognized as the panacea for the Black community as a whole, thereby silencing the voices and needs of Black women; the politics manifest within certain (conservative) Black nationalisms being the most obvious example of this. [. . .]

Acknowledgement

The author wishes to acknowledge the invaluable assistance, theoretical guidance, and encouragement throughout the research period of Pete Bramham and Sheila Scraton. Special thanks also to Barnor Hesse for constantly pushing me to think at the limits. I would also like to thank Vilna Bashi, Caroline Allen, Max Farrar, and Alan Tomlinson for their insightful comments on a earlier draft of this much revised paper. The usual disclaimers apply.

Notes

1   Interestingly, Rodman's comments were echoed by a Black professional rugby league player when interviewed as part of a survey looking at racism within rugby league. . . . He said, "I think a lot of Black players play rugby league, in my opinion . . . as they see it as a way to get their own back, or to take their aggression out on people, *white* people. . . . You couldn't do it on the street, but you can do it on the pitch" (as cited in Long, Carrington, & Spracklen, 1996, p. 13 [also cited in Reading 44 – editor]).

It is also within this context that we can understand the comments made by the cricketer Brian Lara, currently captain of the West Indies, after his side's inexplicable loss to Kenya in the cricket World Cup in 1996. In private remarks to the Kenyan side after the game, which were eventually reported by the media and for which he later apologized, he said, "It wasn't that bad losing to you guys. You are Black. Know what I mean. Now a team like South Africa is a different matter altogether. You know, this White thing comes into the picture. We can't stand losing to them" (as cited in Marqusee, 1996, p. 136). St Pierre (1995) similarly suggests, in relation to cricket, that West Indian Test players "will tell you, privately, that a victory against England carries with it a special savour" (p. 77). Clearly, as I explore further in the rest of the article, the significance of these last two examples has as much to do with historical colonial and political relationships as it has with race.

2   The research is based on my doctoral study. In-depth semistructured interviews conducted between 1995 and 1997, and participant observation during the summer cricket seasons of 1995, 1996, and 1997, have been used to collect the data. Pseudonyms for the players and club members are used throughout. I am using the nomenclatures *Black* and *Asian* to refer to those groups who, due to the process of racialization, are visibly marked as belonging to different races. Within this context, those referred to as Black are those people of sub-Saharan African descent and those referred to as Asian are of south Asian descent.

References

Birrell, S. (1989). Racial relations theories and sport: Suggestions for a more critical analysis. *Sociology of Sport Journal*, 6, 212–227.

Fanon, F. (1986). *Black skin, White masks*. London: Pluto.

Gilroy, P. (1993). *The Black Atlantic: Modernity and double consciousness*. London: Verso.

hooks, b. (1994). *Outlaw culture: Resisting representations*, London: Routledge.

Long, J., Carrington, B., and Spracklen, K. (1996, April). *The cultural production and reproduction of racial stereotypes in sport: A case study of rugby league*. Paper presented to the British Sociological Association annual conference, Reading, UK, April.

Mercer, K. (1994). *Welcome to the jungle: New positions in Black cultural studies*. London: Routledge.

Merqusee, M. (1996) *War minus the shooting: A journey through South Asia during cricket's World Cup*. London: Heinemann.

Messner, M. (1992) *Power at play: Sports and the problem of masculinity*. Boston: Beacon.

Rodman, D. (1996). *Bad as I wanna be*. New York: Delacorte.

St Pierre, M. (1995). West Indian cricket as cultural resistance. In M. Malec (ed.), *The social roles of sport in Caribbean societies*. Luxembourg: Gordan & Breach.

Vergès, F. (1996). Chains of madness, chains of colonialism: Fanon and freedom. In A. Read (ed.), *The fact of Blackness: Frantz Fanon and visual representation*. London: Institute of Contemporary Arts.

Wheatley, R. (1992). *100 Years of Leeds League cricket*. Leeds, UK: White Line Publishing.

Zulfiqar, M. (1993). *Land of hope and glory? The presence of African, Asian and Caribbean communities in Leeds*. Leeds, UK: Roots Project.

Scott Fleming and
Alan Tomlinson

RACISM AND XENOPHOBIA
IN ENGLISH FOOTBALL

[. . .]

WE UTILISE THE DEFINITION OF RACISM developed by Cole (1996), in which social groups or collectivities are differentiated by the allegedly unchanging nature of their (biological and/or cultural) characteristics; and in which such perceived difference is a source of evaluated characteristics or stereotypes, which can distort and mislead, with "ultimately negative" effects (even if they at first appear to be positive). By xenophobia, we mean "the exaggerated hostility towards or fear of foreigners", which is, according to Klein (1993: p. 14), more psychologically than socially acquired, and is "the irrational fear or hatred of 'otherness'". [. . .]

A small survey of racism on the terraces of football grounds in England conducted by *The Guardian* at the start of the 1993 season (*The Guardian*, 1993) captured forms of the abuse that is directed towards African–Caribbean players—one 'terrace fan' hurling racist abuse at Southampton's Ken Monkou, "Someone sort the big nigger out, f***ing black twat", as heard by Randeep Ramesh. The influence of the Far Right in football grounds is through an everyday racism which is mobilised along more explicit lines, and white working-class masculinity has been vociferous in its racist invective against black players. Other rivalries—of region or locality, for instance—are transcended as the evaluated characteristics of "race" are brought to bear in a situation. In April 1994 at an English Endsleigh League match between Fulham (a West London club) and Burnley (a North-east Lancashire club in the North of England), a robust challenge by one of Burnley's black players on one of Fulham's white players incensed some spectators in the front row of seats. One of them rose to his feet, gesticulated aggressively at the Burnley player, and shrieked "Fuck off back up North, you fucking Northerner". One of his companions immediately added: "He ain't a fucking Northerner, he's black". This distortion of history and humanity has been far from unusual at English football matches, and this particular instance of it reveals the complexity as well as barbarism of some forms of cultural affiliation in football. In the labelling of the Other, the vilification of the threat of difference, the difference of region ("Northerner") is collapsed in a perception of the more fundamental "difference" of "race". [. . .]

There are . . . other widespread and more easily identifiable forms of racism in football of a more "personal" kind; that is to say, they are direct, overt and individual. A montage of typical examples is illustrative.

From players—

> Stoke City striker Mark Stein punched an opponent who racially abused him at the end of a second division promotion match, a jury heard yesterday. . . "There was simply ugly and abusive language and Stein was giving as good as he was getting." . . . Mr Stein then turned towards Mr Gannon and said: "What is the fucking score then?". Mr Gannon called Mr Stein "a short, ugly, black wanker". . .
>
> (*The Guardian*, October 27, 1993: p. 7)

From managers, coaches and administrators—

> John Bond [televised comments on Dave Bennett before 1981 FA Cup final] illustrates some traditional football attitudes towards black players: ". . . like a lot of coloured players in this country . . . you pull your hair out with them . . . they drive you mad . . . he's got so much ability and so much potential".
>
> (Redhead, 1987: p. 28)

> Ron Wylie commented to Garry Thompson, "I think you're a coward. All you people are".
>
> (Cashmore, 1982: p. 193)

> When invited to contribute to the TV documentary Great Britain United, one First Division football manager responded: "What do I think about the black bastards you mean?".
>
> (Wilson, 1991: p. 41)

> Dick Wragg, ["Chairman" of the English FA's International Committee] commenting on the issue of racist chanting at a Sheffield United v Newcastle United game: "They're so used to seeing all-white football teams, that they don't like to see darkies introduced . . . I'll tell you this, a lot of my friends don't like to see a lot of black people in the teams. But as far as I'm concerned, I tell everybody this, knowing the English players, and our own dark players, they are normally better dressed and better spoken than seventy-five per cent of the white people. The dark fellows who come into the England team, they're tremendously well-behaved, they really are."
>
> (Davies, 1991: p. 94)

From the boardroom—

> I don't think too many can read the game . . . You get an awful lot, great
> pace, great athletes, love to play with the ball in front of them . . . when it's
> behind them it's chaos.
>
> (Hill, 1991: p. viii)

> When you're getting into midwinter in England you need . . . the hard white
> man to carry the artistic black players through—Ron Noades.
>
> (Wilson, 1991: p. 41)

From spectators—

> Ian Wright: There's a team in South London, which I won't name, where I
> wouldn't take my family. The fans there throw peanuts on to the pitch.
>
> (*The Guardian*, August 13, 1993: p. 20)

Letter to the Everton fanzine *When Skies are Grey* in May 1991—

> I speak for the majority of blues when I say Everton are white and should
> remain so. Quite simply we don't want any coons, pakis, wops, dagos or
> little yellow friends pulling on the royal blue shirt . . . Everton are a club of
> great tradition and we do not want to see any banana chewing wogs at Goodison.
> Quite simply the majority say keep Everton white.
>
> (Colin English, Maghull)
> PS The police don't clamp down on racist abuse because they agree with it.

> National Front "thugs" following England's 1984 tour in Brazil, when John
> Barnes scored a marvellous individual goal: "these people (who took the same
> flight as the squad from Montevideo to Santiago, and barracked Barnes all the
> way) said the score was only 1–0, because 'Nig goals don't count'".
>
> (Davies, 1991: p. 244)

Elsewhere—

> The ex-Manchester United star [George Best] outraged dinner guests by
> describing the Brazilian ace [Pele] as "not bad for a nigger" (Rowe, 1993:
> p. 9); and more recently, during 'An Evening with George Best and Rodney
> Marsh', Best was asked about the sale of Andy Cole. His reply was, allegedly:
> "£7 million is a lot to pay for a nigger".[1]

[. . .] Xenophobia as the irrational fear of the other and as the denigration of difference
must be opposed in any open-minded and civilised society and culture. But the collapsing
of all difference would be absurd, and would be a sham. . . . How, [then,] can ethnic
and cultural differences be celebrated without perpetuating racist stereotypes or cultivating
xenophobic values? Football's role in asserting cultural distinctiveness is a reminder of
the complexities of this question. [. . .]

Sport has been a major factor in breaking down racial and religious barriers; long may it continue to pioneer this cause. Sport can bring about a situation of oneness regardless of colour. For some, it has continued to epitomise the true spirit and brotherhood of "man" (Hamilton, 1982: p. 10). But the idealised capacity of sport to promote such universalised values is counterbalanced by other tendencies. [. . .]

. . . [F]ive negative and three more positive points arise concerning the question of Euroracism, xenophobia, cultural identity and football:

- players and fans have to tolerate persisting forms of racism in the public culture of the football ground;
- racist aspects of extremist far-right politics are worryingly compatible with established elements in British football culture;
- personalised racism is widespread in the everyday discourses of football culture;
- xenophobia and racism are characteristic of governing bodies at national and international levels;
- popular culture, in forms such as the comic-book football narrative, perpetuates cultural stereotypes and xenophobic values.

On a more positive side:

- the passion of football can be celebratory of difference without being denigrating of it;
- "race"-based cultural separatism, and ethnic distinctiveness, can find valuable expression in a sport such as football;
- football is a source for the articulation of complex "race"/place dynamics, which translate into shifting expressions of identity.

In Britain racist prejudices run deep, and despite all the institutional interventions in the world the misplaced cultural pride of dominant racist groups continues to promote unacceptable types and levels of racist discourse and practice. Nick Hornby (1992) has written of his wish that fans, players and commentators would express their disgust at and opposition to racism. There is a fine balance between cultural caricaturing, offensive stereotyping and a damaging xenophobia—but there *is* the possibility of a pre-offensive non-threatening balance. A xenophobic element connected to a racist disposition—a not uncommon cocktail in British football culture—is, though, a threat to the standards of a civilised society and a culturally tolerant international community. It is for this reason the football community must be castigated—at all its levels, from the terrace fan to the world governing body—for its complacency and its naïveté in either denying the extent of racism in the game, or hoping that it will simply go away. [. . .]

Acknowledgements

Many thanks to: Dr Mike Cole for his comments on the early drafts of this paper; Dr John Sugden for his detailed analytical response to the extended second draft of the paper.

Note

1   Could it be that the fact that Best [was] an East Belfast Protestant (or "Prod") [was] significant here? To a white working-class Protestant from East Belfast to call someone a "nigger" is a fact of everyday life. We are grateful to John Sugden for suggesting this connection.

References

Cashmore, E. (1982) *Black Sportsmen*. London: Routledge.
Cole, M. (1996) "'Race' and racism", in M. Payne (ed.) *A Dictionary of Cultural and Critical Theory*. Blackwell: Oxford.
Davies, P. (1991) *All Played Out—The Full Story of Italia '90*. London: Mandarin.
The Guardian (1993) "Soccer's true colours", 16 August: pp. 2–3.
Hamilton, A. (1982) *Black Pearls of Soccer*. London: Harrap.
Hill, D. (1991) "The race game", *The Guardian Guide*, 31 August: pp. viii–ix.
Hornby, N. (1992) *Fever Pitch*. London: Victor Gollancz Ltd.
Klein, G. (1993) *Education Towards Race Education*. London: Cassell.
Redhead, S. (1987) *Sing When You're Winning: The Last Football Book*. London: Pluto Press.
Rowe, D. "Pelé slur gets Best red card", *Sunday Mirror*, 16 May: p. 9.
Wilson, P. (1991) "The black man's burden", *Observer Sport*, 22 September: p. 41.

Pnina Werbner

FUN SPACES
On identity and social empowerment among British Pakistanis

> The state of effervescence in which the assembled worshippers find themselves must be translated outwardly by exuberant movements . . . religion would not be itself if it did not give some place to the free combinations of thought and activity, to play, to art, to all that recreates the spirit. . . .
>
> (Durkheim, 1915: 381–2)

IN THE CORROBOREE, Durkheim tells us, an emotional aesthetics of play and sensuality, of song, music, movement and merry-making, goes beyond mere play, to release and revitalize the moral forces of society stripped of any quotidian 'fatigue'. The pulsating oscillation between the 'slavishness of daily work' and the exuberance of religious effervescence marks the continuous renewal of society as a moral reality beyond the individual.

Durkheim's insights provided, of course, the ground for Turner's analysis of liminality as communitas (Turner, 1974) and for Douglas's interpretation of humour as anti-rite (Douglas, 1968). Both recognize the emotional camaraderie and fellow-feeling released by humour and licensed behaviour, and the levelling of difference, structure and hierarchy these imply. Similar themes seem also to echo through Bakhtin's analysis of the medieval carnival. He too identifies the pulsating rhythm of a 'two world condition' in which the carnival spirit of fun, laughter and bodily sensuality surfaces periodically in relation to the natural cosmic cycle (Bakhtin, 1968: 6, 9). During carnival, hierarchy is suspended along with all privileges, norms and prohibitions, as people are 'reborn for new, purely human relations' (Bakhtin, 1968: 10).

Yet the Bakhtinian affirmation of grotesque realism disguises also a darker allegory – of repression, of the 'prohibition of laughter' (Pomorska, 1984: ix) even if the laughter of carnival is 'indestructible' (Pomorska, 1984: 33). Durkheimian morality is here transmuted into a semiotic struggle over the definition of morality, waged between an elitist, official, unchanging aesthetic and the unofficial parodic freedom of folk culture. The shift is to a focus on a politicized aesthetic, empowering different class segments. The present paper discloses the way in which such a morally grounded, semiotic struggle has developed among diasporic Pakistanis in Britain. [. . .]

. . . [L]ived-in 'worlds' become the grounds for real struggle in *internal* Muslim and Pakistani symbolic battles, fought over the definition of moral value and the practices embodying it. [. . .]

In Manchester, the Pakistani ethnic public sphere, as a contested arena, went through a radical transformation in the 1990s during which the authority of Pakistani male elders and their monopoly of communal public space were contested. The challenge came from Pakistani women, on the one hand, and young Pakistani men, on the other, two groups currently carving a space for themselves in the public sphere.

Very roughly, three historical phases mark this transformation. The first phase, between about 1950 and the mid-1980s, was a period of communal reconstruction and consolidation dominated by first-generation immigrant Pakistani men. It was followed by a brief period, from the mid-1980s onwards, which was one of intense political contestation between male elders, women and youth. This was also a time of male protest against *The Satanic Verses*. Since then there has been a partial capitulation of exclusive control by men, and with it the emergence of a gendered and familial Pakistani space of voluntary action which is also a space of 'fun', that is, marked by gaiety, humour, music and dance. [. . .]

South Asian popular culture

To further appreciate the struggle for the definition and control of a collective 'voice' in the public sphere, the need is to consider more general transformations arising out of the commodification of South Asian culture. Popular culture in South Asia has its traditional spaces sited in two major domains: a feminized youthful domain I shall call wedding popular culture, and a youthful male domain of sport. The first domain, that of wedding popular culture, draws its symbolic inspiration from female pre-wedding ritual celebrations, and especially the *mhendi* rite (see Werbner, 1990a), a ritual initiation of the bride and groom which licenses fun, music dancing and transvestite masquerade. [. . .]

While wedding popular culture is the space of romantic love, sport, and especially cricket, is an expression of controlled masculine aggression and competitiveness. The intense enthusiasm for cricket as spectacle in South Asia amounts to a cult glorifying the human body, not as a denied vessel to be transcended by ascetic practices, but as an active, valorized vehicle to be nurtured and cultivated in order to enhance human physical capacity *in* the world. Hence sport is the masculinized domain of popular culture. Cricket, the game of the 'Other', the former imperial oppressor, which has become a national and international sport, has become also a popular cultural expression of modern Pakistani nationalism and of friendly competition in the international arena. It is the sport of the Commonwealth, a medium of communication, along with the English language, between prior colonies. It is a subculture with its own values of *noblesse oblige*, fair play, upright conduct, sportsmanship, correct public behaviour, team spirit and so forth. The national cricket team is an emblem of the modern nation-state, Pakistan, as a 'Western' invention. Since cricket has become a part of professionalized mass media entertainment, its stars have become national heroes. The huge financial stakes involved in the international game make it more exciting, competitive and contentious than its imperial predecessor, subject today to highly controversial public disputes, screened live on satellite television, between national teams, or between team captains and umpires, and to allegations of corruption and bribery, involving hundreds of thousands of pounds. All this adds to the masculine glamour and politicization of the game.

Here, then, are two popular cultural domains which Pakistanis both at home and abroad all share and which are not specifically Islamic, although they mesh with Islamic traditions as domestic manifestations – a feminized domain of 'marriage' popular culture and a masculinized domain of male 'honour', power and aggression. Both are transgressive of Reform Islamic precepts which stress purity, bodily containment, spirituality and intellect. Both also transcend and hence transgress (from the Islamist viewpoint) the boundaries of the Muslim community or *umma*. Wedding popular culture encompasses a pan-Asian Urdu- and Hindi-speaking population, including Muslims, Hindus and Sikhs, who share common aesthetic traditions, similar wedding songs and dances, musical instrumental genres, as well as comic and satirical tropes which cut across religious and even regional linguistic boundaries. Cricket, too, transgresses the boundaries of the *umma*, creating links between nations having different religious persuasions, while at the same time it poses an alternative to the religious community in its glorification of the modern nation-state, a Western invention which promotes a very different definition of order, law and morality than does Islam. Pakistani identities thus draw on three intersecting transnational cultural spaces, *none of which coincide with the nation-state*.

Performative space and identity

As performative spaces, each cultural domain also represents a source of personal gendered and generational identity empowerment, and dramatizes a powerful aesthetic tradition through voluntary activities enacted by opposed social categories: Islam – by male elders; wedding popular culture – by women and youth; and cricket – by men, especially young men. [. . .]

Young men's empowerment as an autonomous social category focused initially on cricket. Playing cricket, as against entertaining cricket stars, is regarded as a legitimate activity, and the control of male elders in this domain is minimal. But when young men organized a public benefit dinner for the captain of the Pakistani cricket team, Imran Khan, the event was sabotaged by unidentified elders and later dubbed by the Pakistani male establishment a 'failure'. Before the event, which mobilized almost 1,000 primarily young Pakistani male textile workers and market traders, serious attempts were made to prevent its staging. The event itself was disrupted by an offensive attack on Imran Khan. The benefit dinner, which raised £5,000, was clearly regarded as a threat to elder male domination. Unlike women, however, young Pakistani men can be gradually incorporated into elders' associations as they mature. The line between 'youth' and 'elderhood' is highly ambiguous and depends on the achievement of further status attributes (wealth, professional or political standing, etc.). Young men are often recruited to meetings requiring factional shows of physical strength or voting power (Werbner, 1991). Their exclusion from leadership in the prestige public domain is thus temporary, yet it remains particularly significant in the British context. For it is in the field of sport that young British Pakistanis express their love of both cricket and the home country, along with their sense of alienation and disaffection from British society, through support of their national team.

It is at the level of Pakistani mass cultural stardom, in a space created by Imran Khan himself, that the publicly 'official' and 'unofficial' were merged in the city for the first time, so that the 'feminized' domestic sphere of popular entertainment, music and humour, and the young Pakistani male cult of masculinity received the seal of Pakistani male elder legitimacy as an expression of Pakistani nationalism. At this point, however, the organization was taken over once again by male elders who dominated, throughout. Nevertheless, the other social categories – women and youth – were not excluded, hence the new space created was defined as simultaneously *public and familial, Islamic and universal.* This was a truly creative innovation, a revolution rather than a rebellion. Yet it did not appear revolutionary. On the contrary, once created, it seemed so natural and responsive to Pakistani (middle-class) cultural sensibilities that it was as though this had always been the shape of local public action. [. . .]

Diaspora: symbolic identifications

For diasporic Pakistanis popular culture, sport and religion are vehicles for the expression of transnational identifications. In April 1992 the Pakistan international cricket team, captained by Imran Khan, won the World Cup Limited Overs Cricket Competition in Sydney. The cliffhanger between Pakistan and England revealed a hidden but obvious truth: that when it comes to sport, passions transcend territorial boundaries. While the English mourned their defeat, British Pakistanis all over the United Kingdom were celebrating their team's victory. A young Pakistani, born and bred in Britain, told his English friends: 'I'm proud to be British but when it comes down to the hard core, I'm really Pakistani.' Young Pakistanis in the city field a large number of amateur cricket teams, playing in local amateur cricket leagues. The average age of team players is about 30, and the vast majority were either born or grew up in Britain.

British Pakistanis' taken-for-granted support of their national team seemed to need no additional explanations. Pakistani friends merely shrugged their shoulders in response to my questioning. Loyalty to the Pakistani national team, they implied, was natural and instinctive, something they seemed to feel, they had imbibed with their mother's milk, or inherited along with their father's blood. As one celebrating young man told a *Guardian* reporter: 'If you cut my wrists, green blood will come out' (Chaudhary, 1995). The Pakistani flag is green. Green is the symbolic colour of Islam.

Two years previously, in a controversial speech made in the House of Commons in April 1990, on the eve of the Indian test series, Norman Tebbit, the hard-liner Tory MP, castigated British Asians and declared that they should demonstrate their loyalty by supporting England. 'If you come to live in a country and take up the passport of that country, and you see your future and your family's future in that country, it seems to me that is your country. You can't just keep harking back.'

Tebbit's remarks, greeted by a storm of protest at the time, were clearly absurd in a country which regularly fields four national teams for any sporting contest (English,

Scottish, Welsh and Irish). The equation between national loyalty and team loyalty made here is quite evidently spurious, despite attempts by the Right to impute South Asian support for the home country's team to an apparent unwillingness on their part to 'integrate'.

What Tebbit's earnest nationalism seemed to miss was that sporting contests both objectify social divisions and nationalist sentiments while simultaneously pointing to an alliance between contesters, a shared fanaticism. There is a sense of friendship and fun in the competing loyalties. Sporting contests are, it would seem, like *moka* ceremonials in Melanesia, a *substitute* for war, a domain of symbolic agonism, a token not of hatred and disloyalty but of friendly rivalry in the midst of peace.

Revealed identities

The context in which my paper is set is one in which there has been an apparent shift in Pakistani communal discourses in the public sphere: from being a 'British Pakistani' to being a 'British Muslim', from a stress on national to a stress on religious identity. This shift was linked to a growing realization by immigrants from Pakistan that their stay in Britain is permanent, and that the most pressing need is to fight local battles for religious rights (see Nielsen, 1988, 1992). Initially, on arrival in Britain, the problem seemed to be one of combating racism and gaining recognition as an ethnic minority. The publication of *The Satanic Verses* revealed, however, a deep clash between Islam and British nationalism. 'Islam' was now a term to be defended at all costs, a matter of personal and communal honour. British Pakistanis 'became', officially, in the media, and in their own eyes, 'Muslims'.

Yet publicly paraded identities, however sacred and universal, conceal *submerged yet equally deeply felt* communal identifications. If cricket reveals the sentimental depths of nationalism, of being a 'Pakistani', then having 'fun' reveals Pakistanis' deep South Asian cultural roots and identity. Outside prayer times or politics, British Pakistanis love having fun. They watch Indian movies, hero-worship Indian film stars, listen avidly to modern *bhangra* music, dance and sing, celebrate and enjoy life like all other South Asians. Thus, we saw, *Al Masoom*, the local Pakistani women's organization which had openly challenged male authority, raised money by providing amusement and fun for other Pakistani women and children, drawing on familiar South Asian genres of entertainment. The women created their own dramas in which they lampooned men, sang and danced. Their fund-raising was aggressively attacked by businessmen and community leaders, despite the women's piety and the clear sanctity of their cause.

If official religion, nationalism and economic production are the domain of male elders, then sports, entertainment and consumption are the domains of youth, women and families. The sacred which is elevated above the profane is thus elevated as a *compartmentalized* preserve of elder male honour. To challenge this ranking of values by controlling fund-raising or by hosting dignitaries is to provoke the hostility of male elders. It is only an international mass media celebrity such as Imran Khan, adored, classy and elitist, who can challenge this hierarchy successfully and reach out to a broader humanism *with* elder male approval. Yet daily life, the quotidian, which is profane, is dominated by women and youth. As diaspora Pakistanis sink roots in Britain, and as they come increasingly to resemble their English neighbours in matters of fund-raising and celebration, so too women and young men are likely to increasingly claim their share of the prestige public domain. [. . .]

The extent to which 'fun' and the spaces of fun are constitutive of identity and subjectivity – whether ethnic, gendered or generational – remains to be fully theorized, although discussions of youth subcultures and popular culture have highlighted certain dimensions of this conjuncture. By juxtaposing a variety of 'social situations', all of them equally typical and pervasive among British Muslims (who are also Pakistanis, mostly Punjabis and more-or-less Westernized) the present paper has examined not only how sited identities shift in their situational salience, but the ways in which they are differentially imaged and constituted in internal ethnic contestations for power and influence. Rather than a pure, unchanging vision of Islam, I have attempted to illuminate the ways in which British Islam is differentially objectified or denied, in a context which incorporates both South Asian and English postcolonial themes, comments on them, and plays upon them.

One thing is evident. Despite the public privileging of an Islamic identity, diaspora Pakistanis continue to valorize their national roots; their loyalty and sentimental attachments to Pakistan are as deep as ever. [. . .]

The creation by British Pakistanis of distinct symbolic spaces in which distinct practices and discourses are articulated and publicly negotiated, draws on prior experiences to create new political mythologies played out in front of contemporary British Pakistani audiences. A 'space' includes both actors and audience. In challenging the hegemonic dominance of Pakistani male elders, Pakistani women and young men, positioned differently yet sharing dual or even multiple worlds of lived-in realities, are presently transforming, it seems, the imagining of their ethnic group's shared collective identities in Britain.

Notes

This paper has benefited greatly from the comments made by participants at the conference on 'European Islam: Societies and States' in Turin, May 1992; at the International Centre for Contemporary Cultural Research's seminar series on 'Creative Social Spaces', University of Manchester; and at the Oxford University 'Ethnicity and Identity' seminar series on 'Sport and Identity'. Research was conducted in Manchester with the support of grants from the Economic and Social Research Council, UK. The paper has been elaborated and updated in the context of a current ESRC project under my directorship 'South Asian Popular Culture: Gender, Generation and Identity'. I am extremely grateful to the Council for its generous support. I would like to thank Michael Fischer and Zygmunt Bauman for their especially helpful comments.

References

Bakhtin, Mikhail (1968) *Rabelais and His World*, transl. by H. Iswolsky. Cambridge, MA: MIT Press.
Chaudhary, Vivek (1995) 'The Prince of Pakistan', *Guardian* 7 February.
Douglas, Mary (1968) 'The Social Control of Cognition: Some Factors in Joke Perception', *Man* (NS) 3: 361–76.

Durkheim, Emile (1915) *The Elementary Forms of the Religious Life*. London: George Allen & Unwin.

Nielsen, Jorgen S. (1988) 'Muslims in Britain and Local Authority Responses', pp. 53–77 in Tomas Gerholm and Yngve Georg Lithman (eds) *The New Islamic Presence in Western Europe*. London: Mansell.

Nielsen, Jorgen S. (1992) 'Islam, Muslims, and British Local and Central Government: Structural Fluidity', paper presented at the Conference on 'European Islam: Societies and States', Turin.

Pomorska, Krystyna (1984) 'Prologue', in Mikhail Bakhtin, *Rabelais and His World*. Bloomington, IN: Indiana University Press.

Turner, Victor (1974) *Dramas, Fields, and Metaphors: Symbolic Action in Human Society*. Ithaca, NY: Cornell University Press.

Werbner, Pnina (1990a) *The Migration Process: Capital, Gifts and Offerings among British Pakistanis*. Oxford: Berg Publishers.

Werbner, Pnina (1991) 'Factionalism and Violence in British Pakistani Politics', pp. 188–215, in Hastings Donnan and Pnina Werbner (eds) *Economy and Culture in Pakistan: Migrants and Cities in a Muslim Society*. London: Macmillan.

Gender and sexualities

INTRODUCTION

IT HAS ALREADY BECOME CLEAR, in previous sections of this Reader, that sport has provided a strong and enduring patriarchal framework: men have dominated sporting institutions, and women's sport has been marginalized, in both its professional and participation profiles. There are strong women's sports, and there have been progressive policy interventions. In some sports, too, such as tennis, gymnastics, and Olympic track and field sports, women's sports have made great strides. The Readings in this section offer perspectives on this general area, studies of selected practices and spaces, evaluation of interventions, an overview of constraints on women, and radical perspectives and interventions challenging heterosexual assumptions about the nature and importance of sport.

The first Reading is from **Eric Dunning**'s book *Sport Matters*. Dunning, with Kenneth G. Sheard, published one of the earliest and most influential studies of sport as a male-dominated sphere: 'The Rugby Football Club as a Type of Male-Preserve' (*International Review of Sport Sociology*, Vol. 8, No. 1, 1973: 5–24). In this Reading, he looks back at his own and others' contributions to the study of such male-dominated sporting worlds, and also contextualizes our understanding of these worlds in a wider consideration of male–female dynamics. The theoretical context is the figurational analysis of gender and gender relations, and what Dunning calls, following Norbert Elias, a concern with the balance of power between the sexes. What is his conclusion about 'gender equalization' in sport, and beyond?

The second and third Readings are based upon the fieldwork studies of English feminist anthropologists. They raise intriguing questions about the nature of public space, and the ways in which institutions of civil society serve the interests of more powerful groupings in a community. **Audrey Middleton** conducted a participant-observation study of a village of 1,500 people on the borders of West and North Yorkshire, northern England, from the broad perspective of how both sexes experienced village life. Her focus is on what she calls a 'sexual geography', the ways in which boundaries are established to mark off men's space from women's space. Reading her account, think back to some of the claims that have been made for cricket as a kind of social cement, an expression of the integrated community. Whose community?

Shirley Prendergast studied the significance of the game of 'stoolball' in Sussex. Stoolball was played, reports suggest, in Wales, Sussex and Lancashire in the later 1600s, and is said to have still been played by children in late-nineteenth-century Lancashire. Also in the late nineteenth century, it was revived in its modern eleven-a-side bat-and-ball form in Sussex (John Arlott (ed.), *The Oxford Companion to Sports and Games*, Oxford, Oxford University Press, 1976: 882–5); and in this form it is still played today (most prominently in the southern regions of England, especially Sussex), primarily by women, though sometimes it is also seen as a way of introducing young boys to cricket! Prendergast, though, goes a long way beyond the technicalities of the game to show how sport, and the physical, bodily dimensions of sport, embody social relations and cultural meanings. What was it about women playing sport in open public space that made local youths so aggressive in their responses?

In the fourth Reading, English feminist and sociologist of sport **Sheila Scraton** identifies the culture of femininity that distinguishes girls' subcultures from other subcultures, including those of sport. She shows how women athletes are perceived and presented in the media, and outlines the incompatibility between the culture of femininity and the image of physical education. Writing in the mid-1980s, Scraton was calling here for a physical education curriculum and sporting culture that would be more meaningful for young adolescent women. In Britain, since this call for a critical self-appraisal by the physical education profession, governments have claimed to have revitalized school sport, using initiatives with provider-partners, and sport colleges favoured by the post-1997 Labour government. Drawing on your own school experiences and observations, has the situation changed for adolescent girls?

If patriarchal interests remain entrenched, as they appear to in a variety of sport-cultural contexts, then critical analysis needs to be blended with institutional initiatives: critical and radical organization may be needed in order to progress – a lesson from feminism in relation to numerous cultural spheres. The fifth Reading is by Canadian sport sociologist and feminist **M. Ann Hall**. She looks at four organizations that were set up to represent women's sporting interests, in Australia, Canada, the UK and the USA. As a context for this, Hall outlines liberal and radical feminist agendas. Have these initiatives been successful in challenging 'male-defined sport'?

The male-dominated base of sporting cultures has persisted despite policy interventions, critique and radical challenges. This is not to say that there have not been real advances for women. Given that women were not allowed to run the Olympic marathon until the 1984 Los Angeles Olympic Games, there have been huge gains. But at the level of participation, there have been continuing inequalities rather than significant equalizing tendencies. It is sobering, then, to look at past patterns and to ask whether things are any different in the here-and-now. In the sixth Reading, feminist sociologist and educationalist **Rosemary Deem** combines survey findings and qualitative studies from the mid-1980s in identifying what limits women's so-called choices in sport. She argues that the only way forward is to challenge social relationships and male power in spheres beyond sport, not just in sport itself. Is this realistic? Has it happened, and if so, where and how?

The final two Readings invite the reader to see sport in ways that have been neglected or marginalized, and provide a form of radicalized interpretation of the sporting world and its cultures. Football has been seen for far too long as a dominant male practice, and, as English feminist, queer theorist and sociologist of sport **Jayne Caudwell** writes, 'with heterosexuality inscribed in the public playing areas'. Recognition of the negotiation by gay sportsmen and women of queer space for sports is a reminder of the heterosexual male dominance of football space. How might this 'political sexualization' of the sporting body affect mainstream male sporting culture – if at all?

One high-profile event that has sought to champion minority rights and at the same time offer an alternative to male dominance in sport is the 'Gay Games'. **Jennifer Hargreaves** includes a vignette of the Gay Games in her study *Heroines of Sport*, from which the final Reading is taken. The Gay Games prioritizes the display of the lesbian or gay body in an explicitly political and challenging fashion. Here, then, sport acts as a vehicle for a wider cultural politics. For Hargreaves, the profile of an event such as the Gay Games can contribute to the eradication of homophobia and discrimination. She reports some startling figures, claimed by advocacy groups – a population of 2 million gay and lesbian people in New York alone. Is there a substantive, credible basis for this claim by the New York Gay and Lesbian Visitor's Centre? If the figure is correct, is it not likely that many non-heterosexuals are already integrated into mainstream sport and culture?

COMMENTARY AND FURTHER READING

There is, in Sheila Rowbotham's famous phrase, a 'hidden history' remaining to be unearthed in the social history of women's sport. This would identify, as in the history of women's football in England, how dominant male institutions have blocked the growth of women's sports on anything like an equal footing. Two of the star players of the popular women's game that thrived during and after the First World War were Alice Woods and Lily Parr, and their story is told in Barbara Jacobs, *The Dick, Kerr's Ladies* (London, Robinson, 2004), in an account that conjures up the flavour of the industrial working-class culture of post-First World War Lancashire ('Dick, Kerr's', incidentally, was the name of the Preston-based tram manufacturing company which formed the celebrated women's works team). It was the Football Association, in 1921, which curtailed this promising boom in the women's game when it banned women's teams from playing matches at professional grounds. Study of the historical background to other women's sports would be likely to identify comparable strategies to marginalize women's sport, an historical influence that clearly still affects the prospects of women's participation today.

The most recent statistics (from the 2002/3 General Household Survey [GHS]) for the UK 16+ population have been analysed by the government's Office for National Statistics, and provide a framework for some trend analysis, given that the GHS has included questions on sport and leisure since 1973, and a consistent set of questions since 1987. Here are the top ten for men and women (participation in the four weeks before interview, with seasonality considered):

Men %		Women %	
Walking	36	Walking	34
Snooker etc.	15	Keep fit/yoga	16
Cycling	12	Swimming	15
Swimming	12	Cycling	6
Soccer	10	Snooker etc.	4
Golf	9	Weights	3
Weights	9	Running	3
Keep fit/yoga	7	Ten-pin bowling	3
Running	7	Horse-riding	2
Ten-pin bowling	4	Tennis	2

Note the absentees from the respective top tens: soccer (0.5%) and golf (1%) are not in the women's list; horse-riding and tennis are not in the men's list. (K. Fox and L. Rickards (2004) *Sport and Leisure: Results from the Sport and Leisure Module of the 2002 General Household Survey*, London, TSO.)

As several authors in the selected Readings have noted, participation data are notoriously difficult to corroborate. But these UK-based figures (available to anyone through the Office for National Statistics and Department for Culture, Media and Sport websites) show clearly that participation sport remains a relatively minority activity, for both men and women, but especially so for women. The task is to identify the factors that make this the case and also any interventions that could change this, should such change be seen to be a realistic and desirable social goal.

It is useful to focus upon particular sports, and the case of football is revealing. Why has women's football developed strongly in some contexts rather than others? Consider China, Germany, Norway and the USA: how have these nations developed such high levels of participation in the women's game? On Germany, see Gertrud Pfister, 'The Future of Football is Female!? On the Past and Present of Women's Football in Germany', in Alan Tomlinson and Christopher Young's edited collection *German Football: History, Culture, Society* (London and New York, Routledge, 2006: 93–126). Pfister quotes the cultural theorist Judith Butler, who coined the term 'gender troublemakers' to refer to people who oppose the existing gender order, and redefine and so enact gender differently. The stakes are high in some of the challenges presented by such 'gender troublemakers' to the male-dominated social and cultural order of sport.

For further readings on gender and sport, see Sheila Scraton and Becci Watson's edited volume, *Sport, Leisure Identities and Gendered Spaces* (Publication No. 67, Eastbourne, LSA (Leisure Studies Association), 2000), which includes analyses of media bias, body fashion, subcultural initiations and discussions of sexuality as well as gender.

See too Sheila Scraton and Ann Flintoff's edited collection *Gender and Sport: A Reader* (London and New York, Routledge, 2002). This includes illuminating readings on feminist theory, history, the media and the body. Scraton and Flintoff themselves, in Chapter Three, provide 'an overview of the distinctive strands of second wave feminist thought and how they have been applied within sports feminism' (p. 30). In this section of *The Sport Studies Reader*, the selected Readings show how male space has frequently dominated public culture, how gendered cultures have favoured men, and how some radicalized sporting spaces raise challenging issues of sexuality. The section has been compiled to give novice students an empirical grasp of the nature and realities of gender-influenced sport cultures. For theorizations of this, the Scraton and Flintoff Reader is an ideal follow-up.

One innovative early formulation of the critical analysis of women in sport was by Paul Willis, in *Working Papers in Cultural Studies* (No. 5, Centre for Contemporary Cultural Studies, University of Birmingham, 1974). In his article 'Women in Sport [2]' (pp. 21–36), Willis proposed that ideology constrains the representation of women and their physical and sporting possibilities. It can be challenged in what he calls 'sub-regions' (of radical interventions and the like), but it is widely reasserted, in what he calls 'the located rebirth of ideology' (p. 28). Women sportspeople are either glamorized as sex objects, or de-feminized. Consider the Readings in this section of the Reader, and ask how Willis's theory of ideology can be applied in your developing understanding of the gendered basis of sport.

On feminist theorizing, see Susan Birrell, 'Feminist Theories for Sport', in Jay Coakley and Eric Dunning's *Handbook of Sports Studies* (London, Sage, 2000: 61–76). Birrell sees our Western culture as characterized by gender privilege, and confirms 'sport as a preferred site for the reproduction of that privilege' (p. 72), with no prospect of change in these fundamental relationships. She concludes, therefore, that feminist theories will continue to make a fundamental contribution to understanding sport.

Eric Dunning

SPORT, GENDER AND CIVILIZATION

[. . .]

EXCEPT FOR PEOPLE WHO are professionally involved, sport, of course, is a leisure activity but, if my argument so far has any substance, it appears to be one which is of considerable importance in the identity formation and habitus, particularly of males (Dunning, 1986). Indeed, such is the pressure to participate in sport – from the media, in schools, from their age peers and, of course, their parents, especially their fathers – that British males, virtually independently of social class though not perhaps of religious and ethnic affiliations to the same degree, are forced to develop an internalized adjustment to it. That appears to be the case whether they conform and follow a sporting route in their leisure and perhaps their occupational lives, whether they deviate or resist and identify with the forms of 'anti-sports' subcultures which have grown up in British society (Marples, 1954: 130ff.) or whether they take a course which is intermediate between these poles.

Also worthy of note is the fact that, in many parts of British society, perhaps especially in all-male schools, 'deviant' males who, for whatever reasons, opt to follow an 'anti-sports' course are liable to be categorized as 'effeminate', perhaps even as 'homosexual', by their peers. This goes hand in hand with a parallel tendency for sportswomen to be categorized as 'lesbian' or 'butch', an antimony which, in and of itself, is suggestive of the fact that sport poses interesting problems for sociological research. That is the case independently of whether the labelled individuals 'really' are, through some degree of choice, heterosexual, homosexual or bisexual, or whether they are pushed into heterosexual or homoerotic attachments biologically, by a labelling process or by some combination of the two. That the USA experiences similar patterns has been shown by Nelson (1994). In our still heavily andrarchal world they are probably experienced in most other countries, too. Let me explore the issue further by endeavouring to ascertain whether Elias's theory of civilizing processes can be of help in teasing out some of the connections between sport and gender. [. . .]

The figurational analysis of gender and gender relations

It seems to me that there are five main ways in which the theory of civilizing processes may be of use for the exploration of problems of sport and gender. More particularly, by looking at such issues relationally and processually, it can arguably provide the beginnings of an explanation of: (1) the meaning/significance of sport for males who remain committed to variants of traditional male identities and roles; (2) the relative empowerment of females to an extent sufficient to allow them to challenge with increasing success for entry into what started out as an exclusive male preserve; (3) the corresponding changes at an ideological and value level regarding what constitute socially acceptable 'feminine' habituses and behaviour; (4) the reactions of males who feel threatened by the increasing 'encroachment' of females into this former male preserve; and (5) the motivational sources which lead growing numbers of females to want to take up sport and their reaction to men – and women – who seek more or less consciously to block their entry. In order to show how that is so, it is necessary to spell out some of the core figurational assumptions regarding gender and gender relations.

The first core figurational assumption in relation to gender is the idea that, like all other social relations, the relations between males and females are fundamentally affected by the character and overall structure of the society in which they are lived. The form of the economy, for example whether it takes one or another variant of the capitalist or socialist types, together with the society's level of economic development are clearly of significance in this regard. So is the position of the society in relation to others and the degree to which its intersocietal relations are war-like or peaceful. Generally speaking, war (including civil war and revolution) tends to favour males, peace to favour females. Arguably just as crucial, though, is whether a society has a state and, if so, the degree to which its state has managed to secure an effective monopoly of physical force and correlatively, of taxation, the major means of ruling in societies above a given level of complexity and crucial to their degrees of internal pacification. In other words, if Elias's work was on the right lines, the specific character of gender relations and gender identities in a society, together with its specific values and ideologies regarding gender and gender relations, will be in part a function of the specific trajectory of that society's civilizing process and the level reached in that connection.

The second core assumption is that, although the current level of knowledge regarding the 'nature–nurture' interface remains rudimentary, gender relations and identities are built on and around a partly determining biological substratum. One implication of this is that males and females are radically interdependent because they need each other for reproductive purposes and because any society which did not rank reproduction at least relatively highly in its value-scale, whatever mix between heterosexuality, homosexuality and bisexuality its dominant norms allowed, would soon experience severe population problems and perhaps die out. Males and females need each other sexually as individuals too, though, of course, variable numbers of each sex develop homoerotic tendencies. (As an aside, it is worth noting that the degree of tolerance accorded to 'gays', bisexuals, transsexuals and non-violent sexual 'deviants' generally can be counted as one mark of a society's level of civilization). In short, our second core assumption holds that the relations between males and females are characterized by a fundamental interdependence which derives in part from bio-psychological roots as well as from roots which are socio-cultural in character. In other words, while we do not deny the *crucial* significance of culture and learning in this regard as stressed, for example, by Gagnon and Simon (1973) and Plummer (1975), it is our view that their perspective reflects a variant of what Wrong (1961) called 'the oversocialized conception of man' (*sic!*).

The third core figurational assumption regarding gender is that, again like other human interdependencies, the interdependence of males and females is best conceptu-alized as involving at a fundamental level a 'balance of power' or 'power ratio' (Elias, 1978). The term 'balance' is not used in the static sense of 'equality' or 'equilibrium' but to signify, via the analogy with a set of scales, the fundamentally dynamic, relational and relative character of power. The fourth core assumption is that, at the heart of the dynamic balance of power between the sexes in any society lies not only the relative capacities of males and females to control economic, political and symbolic/ideological resources, but also their relative capacities to use violence and bestow sexual favours on each other or withhold them.

Connected with this constellation of core assumptions are at least two ostensible facts:

1   that although (a) there is obviously a degree of overlap between the sexes in this regard, (b) some people are born neither unambiguously male nor unambiguously female, and (c) the size differences of men and women are a function not simply of biology but also of social processes connected, for example, with the sexual division of labour and levels of economic development and therefore of the social construction of bodies (Durkheim, 1964; Shorter, 1982; Maguire, 1993a), males have tended in all known societies up to now to be bigger, physically stronger and faster than females and therefore better equipped as potential fighters.
2   menstruation, but, above all, pregnancy and the nursing of infants tend to incapacitate women, among other ways as far as fighting and participating in warfare are concerned.

Of course, modern weapons technology implies a potential for offsetting and perhaps removing altogether the in-built fighting advantages of males. Similarly, invention of the tampon has reduced the inconvenience associated with menstruation, modern birth-control techniques have reduced the proportion of their life-course spent by women in pregnancy, and bottle feeding has made it possible for men to nurse infants. In other words, the power chances derived by men from their strength and capacity for warfare and fighting – there is a long tradition which sees in this one of the principal sources of andrarchy (Sayers, 1982: 65–83; Brownmiller, 1976) – tend to vary inversely with scientific and technological development; that is, they tend to be greater in societies where levels of scientific and technological development are low and vice versa. However, it is reasonable to suppose that the level of state formation of a society, in particular the degree to which its state is capable of maintaining effective monopoly control over the use of physical force, is likely to be a significant influence within it on the developing balance of power between the sexes.[1] [. . .]

[I]n the context of relatively pacified and, in that sense, relatively 'civilized' societies, some fields of sport – along with such occupations as the military and the police – will come to represent an enclave for the legitimate expression of masculine aggression and the production and reproduction of traditional male habituses involving the use and display of physical prowess and power. It will come, that is, to represent a primary vehicle for the masculinity-validating experience. [. . .]

Female responces to male dominance

[. . .] Writing in 1988, Vulliamy offered the following as part of a description of a group of England fans in Stuttgart where they were attending the European Football Championships. They were, he said,

> assembled at the Bierfässle Bar . . . in shorts and tee shirts, calculating beer prices, scratching their testicles and singing 'Get yer tits out for the lads' whenever a young woman walked by.
>
> (*Guardian*, 13 June 1988)

In the 1980s, another standard part of the repertoire of many hooligan and fringe-hooligan groups of English soccer fans when they travelled away to support their teams involved chanting or singing the following refrain: 'Leicester (Newcastle, Liverpool, Tottenham, etc.) boys, we are here. Fuck your women and drink your beer.' This signalled a predatory intent towards local males but it also symbolized a crude objectification of females and a view of them as 'male property'. As one can imagine, large numbers of females are deterred from attending soccer by such displays. They are deterred in less obvious but no less demeaning ways as well. A prime example is provided by the fact that females are barred from entering the boardrooms of many English soccer clubs, even the female friends and relatives of directors when the latter are using the boardroom to entertain guests.

A more blatant example was provided in 1993 by a BBC TV documentary about women and football. In it, a Stockport County fan – Stockport is a town adjacent to Manchester – described his technique for dissuading a woman who had expressed a desire to watch soccer from attending more than once. Here is a paraphrase of what he said:

> If she insists on going, by all means take her but take her to the worst part of the ground, somewhere in the open where she's bound to get wet. She won't want to go again in a hurry and things will be as they should be once more. Football is a game for men.

This is remarkably similar to what a former Secretary of the FA said at a meeting in 1988. His name was Ted Croker and here, again, is a paraphrase of his words:

> Football is a game of hard, physical contact, a form of combat. It is, and must remain, a man's game. Women have no place in it except to cheer on their men, wash and iron their kit, and prepare and serve refreshments.

Massey offers an interesting comment on how many females respond to the male dominance of public space which results from andrarchal values of this kind. She writes:

On the way into town we would cross the wide shallow valley of the River
Mersey, and my memory is of dank, muddy fields spreading away into a cold,
misty distance. And all of it – all of these acres of Manchester – was divided
up into football pitches and rugby pitches. And on Saturdays . . . the whole
vast area would be covered with hundreds of . . . people, all running round
after balls, as far as the eye could see! . . . I remember all this very sharply.
And I remember, too, it striking me very clearly – even then as a puzzled,
slightly thoughtful little girl – that all this huge stretch of the Mersey flood
plain had been entirely given over to boys.
     I did not go to those playing fields – they seemed barred, another world
(though today, with more nerve and some consciousness of being a space-
invader, I do stand on the football terraces – and love it). But there were
other places to which I did go, and yet where I still felt they were not mine,
or at least that they were designed to, or had the effect of, firmly letting me
know my conventional subordination.

(Massey, 1994: 183)

In societies such as Britain, it is not only gender but class and race as well which induce
such a sense of exclusion and subordination. In other words, it is not only females
who have such feelings but many male members of subordinate, outsider groups as
well, though, of course, many female members of such groups tend to be doubly, even
trebly disadvantaged. This caveat notwithstanding, Massey's observations on some of
the continuing connections between 'sport, place and gender' are perceptive regarding
the limited degree to which gender equalization has occurred in modern Britain whether
in sport or other spheres. [. . .]

Conclusion

[. . .] Whilst large numbers of women have tended so far to accept the hegemonic
definition of sport as a predominantly male preserve, [a] shift in the balance of power
between the sexes, whilst not by any stretch of the imagination very great, has arguably
continued to occur following the initial spadework of the suffragettes. If nothing else, it
has clearly been sufficient to make it impossible for traditionally inclined males to prevent
females from entering this erstwhile male bastion in growing numbers. The barriers
erected against them have been strongest in the combat/contact sports but, in recent
years, more and more women have taken up sports such as soccer and even rugby and
boxing. Indeed, in the USA this process appears to have gone further than in Britain at
least as far as soccer is concerned. Thus the Association form of football has been rapidly
accepted as an appropriate sport for females in the USA, a process marked among other
ways by the success of the US women's team in winning the Women's World Cup in
1992. Its level of civilization relative to American football and rugby may have played a
part in its widespread acceptance by American females.
     The growing direct involvement of females in sport represents, in and of itself, an
equalizing trend. Nevertheless, this growing female participation in what started as
an exclusive male preserve has tended to involve two specific sets of penalties for sportswomen which show that modern sport and society still remain predominantly andrarchic.

On the one hand, in contrast to the confirmation of their masculinity through participation in sport by males, the femininity of sportswomen tends to be compromised in the eyes of others, especially as a result of their participation in combat/contact sports. In some cases, it tends to be compromised in their own eyes, too, a reaction which is typical of 'outsider' groups to the extent that they have internalized the 'group charisma' of those who are more established, in this case males (Elias and Scotson, 1994). A possible example is provided by what Wheatley calls the 'subcultural subversions' represented in the mimicking – with an anti-male and pro-lesbian focus – by, for example, female rugby players, of the anti-female, anti-homosexual culture associated with male Rugby Union (Wheatley 1994: 193–211).[2] On the other hand, females face numerous obstacles with respect to participation in sport which are not experienced by males. As part of the same overall equation, however, male sports are, at the same time, dependent in many ways on 'servicing' by women. Such services may, in some cases, be 'voluntarily' given. Nevertheless, to the extent that 'servicing' of this kind is based more on internalization of the group charisma of males and less freely given and fully reciprocated (i.e. by the provision of comparable services by males), it can be accurately described in neo-Marxist terms as involving the exploitation of unpaid female labour. If I am right, such exploitation, much of it at a taken-for-granted and not fully conscious level on the part of many males as well as many females, constitutes just one of the many sources of inequality in the sphere of sports involvement in the 'late barbarian' societies of today (Elias, 1991b).

Notes

1   This balance tends to vary, for example, in the life-course of individuals. Zurcher and Meadow provide a revealing example in their 'On Bullfights and Baseball' (1971: 178), when they write of the Mexican family that: 'The wife and daughters seem to develop a solidly female "mutual protection society", adopt a passively controlling "martyr" role, and wait patiently to seize control whenever the father's dominance falters.'

2   By understandably engaging in behaviour of this kind, these women arguably give legitimacy to the homophobic behaviour of their male counterparts, thereby undermining the expression of 'civilizing' tolerance towards 'gays'.

References

Brownmiller, S. (1976) *Against Our Will: Men, Women and Rape*, Harmondsworth: Penguin.
Dunning, E. (1986) 'Sport as a Male Preserve: Notes on the Social Sources of Masculine Identity and its Transformations', in N. Elias and E. Dunning (eds) *Quest for Excitement: Sport and Leisure in the Civilizing Process*, Oxford: Blackwell, pp. 267–83.
Durkheim, E. (1964) *The Division of Labour in Society*, New York: Free Press.
Elias, N. (1978) *What is Sociology?*, London: Hutchinson.
Elias, N. (1991b) *The Symbol Theory*, London: Sage.
Elias, N. and Scotson, J.L. (1994) *The Established and the Outsiders*, 2nd edn, with a new introduction by Norbert Elias, London: Sage. (First published 1965.)
Gagnon, J.H. and Simon, W. (1973) *Sexual Conduct: The Social Sources of Human Sexuality*, Chicago: Aldine.
Maguire, J. (1993a) 'Globalization, Sport Development and the Media/Sport Production Complex', *Sports Science Review* 2(l):29–47.

Marples, M. (1954) *A History of Football*, London: Collins.

Massey, D. (1994) *Space, Place and Gender*, Cambridge: Polity.

Nelson, M.B. (1994) *The Stronger Women Get, The More Men Love Football: Sexism and the American Culture of Sports*, New York: Harcourt Brace.

Plummer, K. (1975) *Sexual Stigma: An Interactionist Account*, London: Routledge.

Sayers, J. (1982) *Biological Politics*, London: Tavistock.

Shorter, E. (1982) *A History of Women's Bodies*, New York: Basic Books.

Wheatley, E.E. (1994) 'Subcultural Subversions: Comparing Discourses on Sexuality in Men's and Women's Rugby Songs', in S. Birrell and C.L. Cole (eds) *Women, Sport and Culture*, Champaign, IL: Human Kinetics.

Wrong, D.H. (1961) 'The Oversocialized Conception of Man in Modern Sociology', *American Sociological Review* 26(2): 183–93.

Zurcher, L.A. and Meadow, A. (1971) 'On Bullfights and Baseball', in E. Dunning (ed.) *The Sociology of Sport: A Selection of Readings*, London: Cass.

Audrey Middleton

MARKING BOUNDARIES
Men's space and women's space in a Yorkshire village

Although some studies of 'deprivation' have noted differences in impact on women's and men's lives, there is a tendency to assume that both sexes experience 'a village' in the same way. This chapter examines that assumption. My study by participant observation in a Yorkshire village revealed that social movement in all its aspects – travel, employment mobility, social contact and, most tellingly, use of village space – is consistently curtailed for women. Women recognise the way these boundaries are marked and maintained, and they experience village life in a very different way from men.[1] [. . .]

Sexual geography

Public space is unquestionably the domain of men; women spend their lives in the private sphere which is nevertheless controlled by men. In their homes, women are isolated from each other as they perform those conversion tasks necessary for the comfort of their families. Confined to the domestic sphere, women do not have access to the sorts of authority, prestige and cultural value that are the prerogatives of men. Given this imbalance, any woman who tries to exercise power is seen as deviant and thus subject to sanctions applied by the men. The only avenues through which women can legitimately gain prestige and a sense of value are shaped and limited by their association with the domestic world.

There is a temporal element in the organisation of social space; not only do men and women use space in different ways, they use it at different times. The daytime village is in the hands of women and children. At various times during the day, women appear on the streets taking their children to and from the playgroup and school, and purchasing goods from the local shops. They occupy the village but only temporarily and even so are in isolation from each other as women. There is no space for them to meet casually and relax in the same way that men can meet by dropping into the pub.

Some sociologists have written that the launderette and the corner shop provide the same sort of space for women that the pub provides for men. This is not the case. Women go to the launderette or the shop to perform tasks which are extensions of their domestic roles – they do not go specifically to relax with others of their kind in a casual way. The trunk road which bisects the village combined with the narrow footpaths does not make the village an attractive place in which to linger and talk, especially when there are small children to be considered. Young women, out shopping, are hampered by their responsibility for recalcitrant or whining children who want to go home, go to the lavatory or want a drink or some sweets. Not for them the relaxed casual atmosphere of the pub. And in the shop, which is said to be the women's equivalent of the pub, those who stop for a while to chat are called back to their duties by the tugging of a toddler or the knowledge that they must get back to perform certain chores before husband and family get home.

This temporal occupation of space is associated with women's roles as wives and mothers and not with their needs as women. They occupy the village hall from time to time but only for the playgroup, the Mothers' and Toddlers' Group and the Women's Institute. These activities are not available seven days a week as is the pub for men. The playgroup meets for a few hours on weekday mornings during term time, the Mothers' and Toddlers' Group meets on one afternoon a week and the WI meets about once every six weeks. Women's comings and goings are mapped out by the tasks they must perform as wives and mothers. The public space of the village belongs to the men, and women are largely confined to their homes. [. . .]

Danger zones

Although women are largely confined to the village, they by no means have access to all village space. On the contrary, the village is studded with 'danger' and 'keep out' signs for women (Poggi and Coornaert 1974). The use of physical space is typically linked to the regulation of social relations. Every society controls the spatial movement of its members; such movement is controlled to provide reasonable reassurance that territoriality will remain integrated with the stratification system. The village is no exception; it is endowed with a set of rules which represents the interests and values of the dominant sex. It is not merely a cluster of buildings and connecting pathways but a structure which expresses social relations and has a role in their reinforcement. Women have only limited entry to places of leisure; they may be tolerated in these but with restrictions. They are in fact kept on the fringes of community space. [. . .]

Wicket keeping and boundary maintenance

The cricketers are a team of men from both middle and working class backgrounds whose ages range from 14 to 60. They are without doubt the 'prima donnas' of the community: other village events are arranged around their fixture list; they give no support to other village activities and yet expect support from the community; they dominate the bar area of the sports and social club; and no other sport is allowed to take part on 'their' pitch – even in the off-season.

The cricket pitch is situated in what is becoming the new centre of the village bounded by the river, the grounds of the new school and expensive small housing developments. The clubhouse of the village Sports and Social Club was designed so that the verandah overlooks the cricket pitch and not the tennis courts which stand in its shade. And the benches which stand on the clubhouse perimeter of the pitch have their backs fixed so that, sitting on them, one has to face the cricket field rather than the tennis courts.[2]

On a fine day when the cricket team is at home, it seems as though the whole village turns out to watch. Not all come intentionally; some stop by after setting out for a stroll by the river, but the effect is support for the cricket team. The verandah and steps of the clubhouse are packed with spectators: looking from the cricket field, men sit on the right of the french windows with women on the left.[3] Other spectators sit on benches or on the grass while women push their prams around the perimeter of the field. On these occasions, no woman is allowed to set foot on the pitch.

But in the private sphere, women are hard at work producing leisure for men. Besides being responsible for maintaining the 'whites' of the team, there is a rota of women who provide teas for the cricketers. From early afternoon onwards, women may be seen arriving at the village hall, adjacent to the clubhouse, with plates of sandwiches and cakes which they carry into the kitchen. In the hall itself, they set up trestle tables onto which they load the food they have brought. When the men have been playing for a couple of hours, a woman emerges from the kitchen with a tray of drinks which she carries to the edge of the pitch where it is taken from her by a man who carries it to the 'square'. At 5 o'clock, the teams leave the field for the village hall where the women serve them the food they have prepared. And after the return of the men to the field, the women clear the tables, dismantle them, wash up and go home where eventually they will be handed the grass-stained 'whites' to prepare for the next match.

After the end of the match, the two teams return to the clubhouse for showers. The corridor in which the men's changing rooms are located is forbidden to women, even though this corridor leads from the bar to the kitchen. Women who want to enter the bar from the kitchen have to walk around the outside of the building. However, most women are not usually to be seen in the bar after the match; having provided leisure for their men, they are not welcome. Later in the evening, some wives do reappear in order to drive home husbands who have had too much to drink. I did, however, stay on in the bar on such occasions and was either re-classified as 'not there' by fellow-officers and committee members or subjected to the sort of joking which defined me as an 'object to be screwed' (Whitehead 1976).

Once a year, women are allowed onto the 'square' on the occasion of the men versus women cricket match. This takes place on a weekday evening so that it does not interfere with the fixture list, and usually lasts between two and three hours. The men field a young, inexperienced side dressed in their usual 'whites'. The women's team comprises the wives of young cricketers plus young girls from the village. They wear a 'uniform' of brief badminton skirts, tan coloured tights, men's cricket sweaters which reach almost to the hemline of their skirts, and plimsolls. They are watched from the club verandah by the established cricketers on the right and their wives on the left. The play is accompanied throughout by a barrage of obscene comments on the play of the male cricketers from their more experienced colleagues on the balcony. The women, aware of the exposure of their legs, run awkwardly to field the ball to the accompaniment of sexual banter from the male spectators.

In this match, right-handed men have to play with their left hands and left-handers with their right, but the men still have enough control of the game to ensure, with instruction from the 'elders' on the balcony, that the game comes to its ritual end of the women winning by one run. Long before that point is reached, however, the men on the balcony show their impatience and contempt for their junior colleagues by shouting at them to 'get on with it' so that they can retire to the clubhouse for an evening's drinking.

Once a year, then, women are allowed to intrude on the male space of the 'square' where they are encouraged to flaunt their femininity and where inexperienced cricketers are defined as 'women', by being beaten by them. This event is a calendrical rite of status reversal, similar to the *Nomkubulwana* ceremony of Zululand[4] where once a year "a dominant role was ascribed to the women and a subordinate role to the men" (Gluckman 1954), The Yorkshire village ritual, in which the male cricketers are deliberately made weaker and the women are made to look strong has the long-term effect of emphasising the strength and permanence of the usual order. As Turner (1974, pp. 165–166) observes:

> Cognitively, nothing underlines regularity so well as absurdity or paradox. Emotionally nothing satisfies as much as extravagant or temporarily permitted illicit behaviour. Rituals of status reversal accommodate both aspects. By making the low high and the high low, they reaffirm the hierarchical principle. By making the low mimic (often to the point of caricature) the behaviour of the high, and restraining the initiatives of the proud, they underline the reasonableness of everyday culturally predictable behaviour between the various estates of society.

After watching the men versus women's game in 1981, I decided, as secretary of the Sports and Social Club to try to make some space for women in the village to play seriously as a team. Discreet enquiries in the village elicited the information that some women were keen to play hockey. It was about this time that the cricket club refused to pay an increase in 'rent' which had been imposed on all users of the recreation land by the Sports and Social Club. I used this dispute to get support from the committee for my suggestion that hockey be played on the outfield of the cricket pitch during the winter. Support was given in the belief that the suggestion of a women's hockey team was merely a stick with which to threaten the cricket team into payment of 'rent' rather than a reality of 11 women actually wanting to play hockey. When the seriousness of the project was realised, support was withdrawn. Not, however, before I had had the matter discussed in several meetings, the minutes of which were posted out to committee members and passed from them to members of the cricket team.

Walking into the Sports and Social Club bar one evening, I was greeted with overt hostility – not even disguised as humour. Comments recorded included: 'I've no time for strangers who come into this village and try and change it'; and – most tellingly – 'if women are allowed on the cricket pitch, this village will fall apart'.

Until I left the village, the issue of a women's hockey team continued to be put on the agenda of committee meetings at which women were outnumbered 15 to 2. Consideration was given to letting a hockey team play on the old school playing field which is unusable: it is adjacent to a busy trunk road; is uneven; gets flooded at certain times of the year; and slopes down to the river. The football team had refused to use it as a practice ground, and the children's swings had recently been moved to a safer part of the village. A request for goalposts to the village charitable trust, which owns all the recreation grounds and which provided the cricket team with its roller and scoreboard, was not acknowledged. The message was clear both from the committee of the Sports and Social Club, which had withdrawn its support for a women's hockey team once the cricket team had paid its 'rent', and from the charitable trust which effectively denied women access to public ground. Women, as a women's team, would be seen as 'matter out of place' (Douglas 1970) on public land in this Yorkshire village.[5]

Women, indeed, are seen as 'out of place' in most public space in the village. They spend most of their lives in the home, enmeshed in family activities, whilst men of the village fraternise with whomever they find to talk to in public space and predominate in economic, political and cultural activities. The two sexes have distinct lives and inhabit different domains. As Frankenberg (1957) suggests in his study of [a Welsh village], there are, in effect, two villages – one of women and one of men – which rarely mingle.

Notes

1   My fieldwork was carried out between 1979 and 1982. For the first two years I lived alone.
2   Women, of course, are allowed to participate in tennis and thus pollute it so that within the Sports and Social Club it has relatively low status. For an analysis of the concepts of pollution, see Mary Douglas (1970).
3   Herz (1973) writes, "Society and the whole universe have a side which is sacred, noble and precious and another which is profane and common: a male side, strong and active, and another, female, weak and passive; or, in two words, a right side and a left side".
4   Status reversal rituals are not confined to Zululand but take place in many southern African societies.
5   My suggestion that a women's hockey team should play on the outfield of the cricket pitch was greeted with incredulity by some male sociologists when I presented a paper (Middleton 1982) on my work at a British Sociological Association's Ethnography Study Group meeting in January, 1982 (in Lancashire!).

References

Douglas, M., 1970. *Purity and Danger: An Analysis of Concepts of Pollution and Taboo.* (Harmondsworth, Penguin).
Frankenberg, R., 1957. *Village on the Border.* (London: Cohen & West).
Gluckman, M., 1954. *Rituals of Rebellion in South-East Africa.* (Manchester: Manchester University Press).
Herz, R., 1973. The pre-eminence of the right hand. Originally in French, 1909: transl. In: *Death and the Right Hand*, (ed.) R. Needham. (London: Cohen & West).
Middleton, A. 1982. An endangered species: feminist ethnography in a rural setting. Paper presented at a meeting of the British Sociological Association's Ethnography Study Group. University of Manchester, 23–24 January, 1982.
Poggi, D. and Coornaert, M. 1974. The city: off-limits to women. *Liberation*, July–August.
Turner, V.W., 1974. *The Ritual Process: Structure and Anti-structure.* (Harmondsworth: Penguin).
Whitehead, A., 1976. Sexual antagonism in Herefordshire. In: *Dependence and Exploitation in Work and Marriage*, (eds) D.L. Barker and S. Allen. (London: Longman).

Shirley Prendergast

STOOLBALL — THE PURSUIT OF VERTIGO?[1]

> There is still played in the countryside around Stantons an old Sussex game, stoolball, sometimes called 'bittle-battle', the game which tradition says was invented by milkmaids, thereby, countering Tennyson's question: 'but when did women ever yet invent?' This game is a sort of feminine version of cricket played by girls and women. The milkmaids are supposed to have fashioned their implements from milking-stools, one of which might well have served as a wicket . . .
>
> (Woodward, 1938:174)

SO WROTE MARCUS WOODWARD in 1938. In 1977 I spent one year in a rural parish where stoolball is still enthusiastically played as a women's game; in the wider area of the two counties of the Weald—Kent and Sussex—it appears to have a history, going back at least 100 years, and probably longer.[2] To my astonishment the playing of stoolball was surrounded by a whole mythology of meaning and explanation, in the minds of men particularly, that simply did not occur in the equivalent male game, cricket. When I say did not occur, I mean by this that the significance of stoolball in the minds of men had no parallel in the idea of cricket in the minds of women. There were most certainly other ideas about the meaning of village cricket, but on the whole it was enacted with little comment from the wider community, outside those involved in the game as spectators or players. Cricket was part of the natural order of things. For the moment I have to leave the broader questions concerning the existence and development of the game; in passing perhaps to point out the dearth of games played by and for women (if one compares them to, for instance, the widespread cricket and football clubs), organized at the community as well as the institutional level. [. . .]

. . . [S]ignificance lies not so much in what men and women say they do, but rather in a detailed analysis of their actual behaviour. Indeed it is in this conceptual and ideological gap between what people do, and what they say that they do, that some of the most penetrating observations of the social sciences are located. [. . .]

[Stoolball] has been played regularly by working women, in many Kent and Sussex villages, for as long as they can remember, at least 70–100 years. As played today it is an extremely fast and flexible game, adaptable to being played in the evenings, usually from late May to September. The villages in the area where I lived all had teams and played one another in a series of tournaments.[3] In the two that I knew best the team acted as a focus for many women's activities over the Summer months and into Autumn: meeting weekly for practice games and again for proper matches involved a lot of planning and organizing. The practices in particular (often attended by up to 25 women and girls), were typified by a racy atmosphere, joking gossip, shouting, and much physical display of falling, leaping and running for the ball, in which the individual performance was little taken into account: indeed, often there would be so much laughter and distraction that the next player would forget that she was 'on', and the whole game would come to a halt while it was sorted out.

Such behaviour did not pass unnoticed in the village. During the previous winter I had heard many references to the game, and to the alleged promiscuity of the women who took part, always with the connotation that in playing the game they were putting themselves on public display, and that in so doing, deserved 'all they got'. I had heard too, how the local boys played games on them, and 'mucked' around on the evenings of the stoolball practices and games.

The jokes of the boys, as I later saw for myself, started with noisy play at the other end of the field, which as they got more excited took the form of riding their cycles and motor-bikes round and round the stoolball pitch, revving and hooting and shouting remarks to one another about the player's finesse (or lack of it), their legs, and what they were going to do later at the pub. On several occasions it culminated in them actually riding up through the players during the game, this seemed to achieve their objective, to make the women take notice of them, and they left triumphantly, being shouted off the field. Other incidents such as flat tyres and remarks in the pub are also said to have taken place, but I did not see these. In the pub itself I never heard any proper discussions about stoolball as a game, whereas those about football and cricket were legion—the relative merits of the different village teams, and the quality of different players were an important part of pub talk.

The remark of an older man, a shepherd, perhaps serves to illustrate the particular combination of explicit sexual meanings of the game, as read into it by men, with its corollary, the suggestion that men could easily control this display if they so wished. 'I'd be in two minds as to send me old dog down there and get 'em all up for the tup.' . . . He was saying in effect, that the women were like the ewes that were, on the word of the farmer, brought up from the marshes and mated with the rams, in order to lamb in the Spring. He was with a group of several men, some farmworkers too, but not all, and the remark led to many more in the same vein. When I later said, to this same man, that I wanted to play stoolball, he said in a bemused tone, 'Oh no, you don't want to do that'. This response was echoed by others of a similar nature. There also were more bitter comments: to start with the council estate where most of the younger women lived was called 'Peyton Place'[4] (and in another village it was called 'Spivs Alley'). There were unsubstantiated allegations that their children were neglected, their houses pigstyes and their husbands without a 'good hot meal' in the evening. They were selfish leaving their houses, and finally it was often said that they were greedy for money. This last grievance against the women was frequently aired in the context of more general gossip, as well as stoolball, and at first this seemed to be one of those illogical connections, where the string of offences is so long that a few more were neither here nor there. It was not until the game commenced that I understood how greed and money were related to the cluster of 'significant facts' that people identified with the stoolball women. These were, firstly, that all the women of marriageable age were married (there were a few young girls as well).[5] Secondly, that all the women had children, and that all the children fell into the approximate 5–13 age range. Thirdly, was the fact that many of the women were either related, or were childhood friends, having grown up in the village together, and lastly the majority of the women worked together in the fields, although there were a few in other village jobs (the local shop).[6]

. . . [T]hese four areas of involvement to which the individual women had access, constituted a formidable network of information when they came together at stoolball. The frequent meetings of the stoolball team served as a place of very intense gossip and observation, especially in relation to women with children at school and newcomers to the village. The amount of information that could be gathered by comparing the different children's version of events at school, alone, was quite phenomenal[7] and to this must be added the network of relatives and friends, casual talk in the shops, and the comparison of notes by work mates. Some outsiders would be asked to come to stoolball, but there was also the possibility of her as a new workmate. For an outsider, getting farm work in the village, with no previous contact, was extremely difficult, as I soon discovered, for the farmers relied on their regular women to replace themselves and introduce new labour for the months of heavy work, consequently there were few floating jobs. Yet at stoolball I was offered a coveted job in the strawberry fields, and the possibility of more work later in the year. If gang work is to be both maximally lucrative and fairly pleasant (both important factors), the personality and family situation of its individual members are of central interest. The addition of a woman with a very small child or children make the going much slower, and with constant interruption. The relationship with the farmer or the foreman is also more ambiguous if children are present, for the women do not feel free to complain or bargain so easily because of, they say, constantly 'having to be thankful that he's putting up with the kids'. (Presumably also knowing that there are more women wanting work.) A prudish woman can also inhibit the flow of conversation and behaviour in the fields, which can get rather explicit at times.

The informal situation of stoolball is a chance to assess how a person will fit into the work gang. Admission to it meant in the village, the badge of being a certain kind of person, hence the puzzlement as to why I should want to play (since I could not disguise myself as a person with another kind of history and background, even if I had so wished). Apart from the knowledge about one another and about women not present, their strength was even more emphasized in that they (informally) control access to much of the available work for women, and by group action can make life extremely unpleasant for a woman who managed to bypass them and to whom they took a dislike.[8]

To summarize I would say that the connections between work and stoolball are strongly present in the material sense, in fact so much so that one often had difficulty in discovering what event or conversation took place where. At a deeper level their connection is more subtle. For instance, both work and stoolball provide the spectacle of women being physically active, and, what is perhaps even more significant, being active outside of the home and its legitimate social spaces outside—the garden, the street, the village shop. This adds tremendously to its aura of being provocative. As many writers have shown a woman's 'proper' work takes place inside, as does her 'proper' sphere of interest and leisure, the children and home-making in the rather more creative sense. The idea of legitimate and illegitimate spaces and the sexual division of labour, is a powerful organizing factor in farming life too, following lines of demarcation in symbolic as well as physical terms. The existence of a gang of women, working in the open fields, far from the farmyard, still seems to disturb some farmers and farmworkers, and to generate a level of myth and comment corresponding closely to that described in relation to stoolball. [. . .]

. . . [T]he game was seen by the village youths and the men at the pub as a manifestation of the strength of women when they act as a group, rather than their 'ideal' state of division and isolation in the home. Their response, too can be seen as 'situations in which "joking abuse" is used by men to control the behaviour of women' (Peters 1972: 179). [. . .]

. . . [T]he major channel of aggression was the suggestion that the women were behaving improperly, and displaying their sexuality, the medium of control via the crude image of latent force inherent in man's control over nature. (Notice how these ideas become combined in the way that the youths harassed the players by 'rounding them up', e.g. by physically encircling the field, the game and the women, which is at the same time a symbol of their desire to control and contain, and also the way in which a farmer gathers up stock. Indeed there is a whole vocabulary related to this very topic, for instance, the saying . . . 'run 'em round again', which is often said about a group of girls or women in the street or at a dance, and which is derived from the cattle market call to have the animals returned to the ring, so that they can be displayed to the bidders once more, the hidden meaning of which is that they are poor quality and so haven't been sold the first time.) [. . .]

Notes

1   Callois says that there are four basic characteristics to 'play': Ago—competition; Alea—chance; Mimicry—pretence; Iluix—vertigo.
     '. . . the fourth fundamental tendency, is an answer to one's need to feel the body's stability, and equilibrium momentarily destroyed, to escape the tyranny of perception, and to overcome awareness'. 1969, p. 55.
     I have misused Callois' description of vertigo here since he uses it to describe the sensations achieved on fairground equipment, skiing, mountaineering etc., but I could not resist applying it to the rather violent and breathless way that women throw themselves around at stoolball.
2   I did fieldwork over the period of 1 year in three Sussex parishes. I have yet to finish collecting data and have only just begun to think and write about that which I have. I was supported during my fieldwork by an SSRC grant as part of my (as yet unfinished), Ph.D.
3   There were three kinds of occasions: Sunday tournaments; weekday matches usually in the evenings; weekday evening practices.
4   Peyton Place was a television soap opera of the 1960s in which scandalous marital happenings were the staple viewing.

5　It is not entirely relevant here, but there is strong evidence to suggest that the game makes a social space where girls, between the ages of 12–15 (who actually play the game, rather than watch, like the other children, from the edge of the field), learn some of the salient facts about being a village woman, and other, even more salient facts of life (for there are very explicit references to sex, and to marital violence and discord), before they virtually vanish from the scene and begin to court outside of the village.

6　Womens' jobs were always in the 'natural division of labour', e.g.: to do with cooking, cleaning or children.

7　I know that my own daughter was cross-questioned regularly on details of my activities and background.

8　When a vicar's wife decided to have a spell in the fields, she was left to work alone, they did not help her with the ropes of the work and ate their lunch to giggles and silences. She left after 4 days.

References

Callois, R. 1969. The structure and classification of games. In: Loy, J. and Kenyon, G. eds. *Sport, Culture and Society*. Collier Macmillan, London.

Peters, E.L. 1972. The Control of Moral Ambiguities. In: Gluckmann, M. ed. *The Allocation of Responsibility*. Manchester University Press, Manchester.

Woodward, M. 1938. *The Mistress of Stantons Farm*. Heath Cranton, London.

Sheila Scraton

'BOYS MUSCLE IN WHERE ANGELS FEAR TO TREAD'

Girls' sub-cultures and physical activities

[. . .]

YOUNG WOMEN'S SUB-CULTURES . . . do not correspond to male sub-cultures in any simplistic way and an understanding of gender-, class-, race- and age constraints is important. Indeed the term 'sub-culture' takes on 'masculine' connotations. It is more useful perhaps to consider young women's 'cultures' which are structurally separate and distinct from those of male youth. McRobbie (1978a) identifies 'romance' and the 'culture of femininity' as central to the daily lives of adolescent young women. Her research highlights the importance for young women of talking and planning around fashions, make-up and boyfriends. The culture revolves around the intense task of 'getting a man' but always within the constraints of 'keeping a good reputation' (Cowie and Lees 1981) which is by no means easy or unambiguous. Young women are well aware of the inevitable future, influenced by political, economic and ideological constraints, in which a heterosexual relationship leading to marriage, home and family is the expected outcome. Within this 'culture of femininity' there are obvious class and race differences. Just as 'masculinity' cannot be viewed as a static, universal concept so 'femininity' demonstrates marked variation across class and ethnicity. [. . .]

The way forward

The 'culture of femininity' is based on the social construction of women's roles and behaviour. The ideology of biology emphasises women as passive and submissive and presents them in appearance, dress and style in terms of their sexuality. This influences not only women's work opportunities but also their use of leisure, and their domestic and family commitments. These images of women cut across class, race and age although at each of the levels (work, leisure, family, sexuality) there are differences depending on women's individual location in society. The media reinforce this imagery even when dealing with women involved in sporting activities (Graydon 1983). Women athletes are presented *positively* as conforming to the desired image: Zola Budd – 'the waif'; Donna Hartley – 'the golden girl'; Joyce Smith – 'mother of two', or alternately *negatively* as having overstepped the boundaries of femininity: Martina Navratilova – 'the machine'; Jarmila Kratchvilova – 'the man'.

School PE fails to provide 'meaningful experiences' for many young adolescent women because it appears at odds with the culture of femininity. Their resistances which are complex and not always consistent, relate to what they perceive as on offer from PE:

a)   the development of muscle
b)   sweat
c)   communal showers/changing facilities
d)   'childish', asexual PE kit
e)   low status activities.

It is acceptable for the 'tomboy' in junior or lower secondary school to participate in and enjoy these activities but not so acceptable to adult femininity.

As shown, therefore, PE remains trapped within possibilities which will 'appeal' to young women but will consequently reinforce the culture of femininity. This is intensified by the training and ideological constraints of women PE teachers. Even so-called 'progressive' moves, for example, mixed PE, provide only superficial challenges to the ideologies of femininity. Any suggestion of substantive change to give young women positive experiences in PE tends to be met with scepticism because it is assumed that young women are so steeped in the deterministic *Jackie* mentality [see McRobbie, 1978b] that they will reject more positive physical values of assertiveness, strength, control, etc. There is not necessarily real substance to this argument. Adult women's experiences are not *totally* determined and the past decade and a half has seen a substantial shift through the development of new directions in the reconstruction of women's sexuality and consciousness. These include the development of self-help groups in medical care/mental health, the emergence of well-women's clinics and other all-women projects geared to giving women more control over their own health, bodies, etc. Women's groups have developed, resisting male violence with rape crisis centres, women's refuges, etc. Education has seen the introduction of 'NOW' courses, 'outreach' projects, women's writing groups, etc., where women are encouraged to gain confidence and assertiveness in intellectual situations. Women's physical control over their own bodies can be seen further in the development of self-defence/assertiveness training[1] and women's fitness programmes which are geared to developing health, strength and physical well-being rather than the traditional construction of 'womanhood' around appearance, body physique, etc. These latter developments indicate a qualitative shift in definitions of 'the physical'. Women in these programmes are reclaiming the right to physical development and appearance on *their own terms* rather than on the terms laid down in the traditions of 'feminine culture' which are learned and reinforced in youth. As Lenskyj (1982) describes from her own experience, that after years of upbringing women are:

alienated from our bodies not knowing the extent of our physical strength and endurance and not daring to find out. Those of us who have dared have found a new avenue for self-realisation as women and as feminists – joyful at the discovery that our bodies are strong and resilient, capable of hard work and hard play.

It is with these developments in adult women's projects that women's PE should be concerned rather than a concentration on equal access to male-based sports, e.g. women into soccer, etc. For these are part of the same institutional relations of patriarchy (i.e. cults of masculinity) which produce young women's sub-cultures and define/constrict young women's opportunities. By contrast, women's PE needs to develop a new programme geared to assertiveness, confidence, health, fitness and the capacity to challenge patriarchal definitions of submissiveness, passivity, dependence, etc. This is by no means an easy task but nonetheless a direction in which we must, at least, begin to move.

The unifying feature of all the adult women's projects mentioned, is the emphasis on collective support.[2] PE is in the perfect situation to offer young women opportunities for collective support through co-operative and enjoyable physical activity. Whilst the relationship between teacher and student will retain an age-related power structure, young women can be encouraged to work together through such activities as dance, outdoor pursuits, self-defence, etc. Indeed Willis (1982) suggests:

> A sport could be presented as a form of activity which emphasizes human similarity and not dissimilarity, a form of activity which expresses values which are indeed immeasurable, a form of activity which is concerned with individual well-being and satisfaction rather than with comparison.

Many young men thrive on their collective 'rugby club' experiences. Young women, too, need the space for collective physical experience whilst rejecting and challenging the competitive, 'macho' values of the male sporting ethos. Adolescence is a time to develop group and collective experiences rather than the channelling of young women into individually based activities which deny the opportunities to develop group confidence and identity.

Young women also need the space to develop confidence, interests, etc. This is especially true in mixed schools for the evidence clearly indicates that in all social situations men dominate space – physically, verbally, etc. (See Spender 1982; Young 1980.) In co-educational schools the primary female-only space is in the toilets, cloakrooms and changing rooms. These are the areas where young women 'hang out', where they spend time together away from 'the lads' and the teachers (Griffin et al. 1982). It would be a positive contribution if women PE teachers could recognise the need of young women to have their own space in which to chat, plan or simply 'have a laugh'. This is clearly problematic given school organisation and the enforcement of school rules and regulations. However, it would be a positive move to open up changing rooms and facilities during breaks, lunchtime and after school and encourage young women to use the space available for their 'leisure' whether it be netball, table tennis *or* chatting with a friend. Too often young women are allowed into the PE wing only if they are taking part in organised, formal PE activities. It would be an encouraging move to give young women more control over their extra curricular PE activities and to provide the space for meeting and chatting together.

Just as adult women are beginning to reclaim the right to control and develop their own bodies for intrinsic satisfaction rather than sexual exploitation, so PE must emphasise these values for young adolescent women. They must be encouraged to enjoy physical movement; to develop strength and muscular potential; to work together to discover body awareness and confidence. It will be only when young women collectively become confident and assertive with control both physically and mentally over their own bodies that they will move towards redefining their position. PE has an important contribution to make towards the denial of ideologies of 'femininity'. For this to occur it requires a critical self-appraisal and a more sensitive understanding of young women's position in our schooling system and in wider society.

Acknowledgments

Many thanks to Pat Craddock, Rosemary Deem and Phil Scraton for their help, support and critical comments. Also personal thanks to Sally Channon.

Notes

1   For a discussion of the redefining of women's strength and power and the development of self-defence techniques see Quinn, K. (1983).
2   See Dixey and Talbot (1982) *Women, Leisure and Bingo*, Trinity and All Saints College, pp. 78–9 for a discussion on the importance of contact and support for women during their leisure.

References

Cowie, C. and Lees, S. (1981), 'Slags or drags', *Feminist Review*, 9, Autumn.
Graydon, J. (1983), 'But it's more than a game. It's an institution: "feminist perspectives on sport"', *Feminist Review*, 13, Spring.
Griffin, C. *et al.* (1982), 'Women and leisure' in Hargreaves, J. (ed.) (1982), *Sport, Culture and Ideology*, Routledge & Kegan Paul, London.
Lenskyj, H. (1982), 'I am strong' in *The Women's News Magazine*, University of Toronto, March/April. Women's Studies Group, Centre for Contemporary Cultural Studies, University of Birmingham.
McRobbie, A. (1978a), 'Working class girls and the culture of femininity' in *Women Take Issue: Aspects of Women's Subordination*, Hutchinson, London.
McRobbie, A. (1978b), *Jackie: An Ideology of Adolescent Femininity*, Stencilled paper. Centre for Contemporary Cultural Studies.
Quinn, K. (1983), *Stand Your Ground*, Orbis, London.
Spender, D. (1982), *Invisible Women: The Schooling Scandal*, Writers and Readers Co-operative, London.
Willis, P. (1982), 'Women in sport in ideology', in Hargreaves, J. (ed.), *Sport, Culture and Ideology*, Routledge & Kegan Paul, London.
Young, I.M. (1980), 'Throwing like a girl: a phenomenology of feminine body comportment, mobility and spatiality', *Human Studies*, Vol. 3, 1980.

M. Ann Hall

FEMINIST ACTIVISM IN SPORT
A comparative study of women's sport advocacy organizations

I N 1974 THE AMERICAN professional tennis player Billie Jean King took the prize money she had won as the year's best female athlete and donated it to start the Women's Sports Foundation. King and other top athletes including Donna de Varona, Micki King Hogue, and Wyomia Tyus met and sketched out their ideas of what a foundation advocating women's sports might hope to achieve. Then they set up a board of trustees including other well known athletes like Chris Evert, Kathrine Switzer, Sheila Young, Joan Joyce, Jane Blalock, and established a work space in the California office of King Enterprises (Halpert, 1989). The Women's Sports Foundation was the first of the advocacy organizations established explicitly to achieve a better deal for girls and women in sport.[1] Today, there are several organizations in various countries around the world with similar goals most of which were formed because of the initiative in the United States. Some of these organizations are modelled on the Women's Sports Foundation, and indeed have taken the same name, but most have evolved quite differently given the unique features of the sport systems in these countries.

The purpose of this chapter is to document, analyze and explain the differences in history, structure and function of organizations in different countries whose purpose is to advocate on behalf of sportswomen. Four in-depth case studies systematically examine organizations in the United States, Australia, Canada, and the United Kingdom which have emerged between 1974 and 1991: (a) the Women's Sports Foundation in the United States (WSF); (b) the Canadian Association for the Advancement of Women in Sport and Physical Activity (CAAWS); (c) the Women's Sports Foundation in the United Kingdom (UK WSF); and (d) Womensport Australia.[2] Another goal of this study is to examine the extent to which these organizations see themselves as feminist, and as part of the larger women's movement within their country. In other words, to what extent are these organizations "pro-woman" in the sense of improving women's collective status, opportunities, power and self-esteem, as well as being political and socially transformational (Martin, 1990)? [. . .]

Of the four organizations being compared here, CAAWS has certainly been studied the most either through student theses or academic papers (cf. Forbes, 1993; Lenskyj, 1991a, 1991b; Scott-Pawson, 1991; Theberge, 1983). [. . .]

Feminist ideology and values: liberal to the core

Feminist organizations either officially or unofficially endorse an ideology which can be classified according to type: liberal, radical, socialist, Marxist, lesbian, or other (Martin, 1990). Despite the cross-cultural differences, the organizations discussed here are officially liberal in the sense that their focus is on ensuring girls' and women's right to equal access to the sport and recreation opportunities that have long been available to boys and men. . . . [D]iscussing the organizations with respect to why they have followed a liberal path, I want to explore briefly the liberal versus radical feminist agendas in sport activism.

Liberal versus radical feminist agendas in sport

Over the past decade there has been a subtle shift in the discourse of human rights in many Western societies from "equality" to "equity." This has occurred in most areas of organizational life including sport. Equality generally meant "equality of opportunity" and women (along with other disadvantaged groups) were identified as target groups. In sport, equal opportunity programs were designed to increase women's overall participation by opening up opportunities for them to enjoy equal access. The shift to equity signals a more comprehensive view where the focus is no longer exclusively on women (or any other group) but on a system, in this case sport, which needs to change to accommodate them.[3] As long time Canadian sport activist Bruce Kidd puts it: "Equality focuses on creating the same starting line for everyone; equity has the goal of providing everyone with the same finish line" (CAAWS, 1993, p. 4). Another way to state this is: "An athletics program is gender equitable when the men's program would be pleased to accept as its own the overall participation, opportunities and resources currently allocated to the women's program and vice versa" (*Athletics Administration*, April 1993, p. 22). For many sport organizations this would be seen as a "radical" departure from the past.

Whether the focus is on equality or equity, the fundamental philosophy underlying both is best described as liberal reformism. Sport feminists have worked hard especially over the last decade to ensure that more sports are now more accessible to more women than ever before. They have fought for, and sometimes won, "easier access and better facilities for women in sports, improved funding and rewards, equal rights with men under the law, top quality coaching on par with men, and an equivalent voice with men in decision-making" (Hargreaves, 1994: p. 27).

While liberal approaches to sport equity often seek to provide girls and women with the same opportunities and resources as boys and men, and remove the barriers and constraints to their participation, they do not always see as problematic the fundamental nature of male-defined sport with its emphasis on hierarchy, competitiveness and aggression. Liberal feminism in sport also tends to treat women as an homogenous category, not recognizing that there are enormous differences among us in background, class, race, ethnicity, age, disability and sexual preference which lead to very different expectations and experiences of sport.

A more radical feminist approach would adopt an unequivocal women-centred perspective which recognizes and celebrates differences among women, and at the same time seriously questions male-dominated and male-defined sport. It also recognizes the centrality of issues around sexuality in women's experiences of oppression. Women involved in sport advocacy work often fail to take up issues raised by their more radical feminist counterparts outside sport, such as sexual harassment and abuse, male violence against women, lesbian visibility, and the politics of difference. In practice, radical feminists have, as Helen Lenskyj, suggests "worked towards establishing autonomous clubs and leagues that are completely outside state-controlled amateur sport systems" (Lenskyj, 1991a: p. 132). These include the many women-only clubs and leagues, some openly lesbian or lesbian-positive, which are free to modify the rules and organize their play along explicitly feminist principles of participation, recreation, fun, and friendship. Examples in Canada include the Notso Amazon Softball League in Toronto and an outdoor group in Edmonton called Women of Outdoor Pleasure. Jennifer Hargreaves, a British sport sociologist, describes a netball club called Queens of the Castle which is situated in an inner-urban area of London with a predominantly working-class and black membership. Defying the strait-laced, schoolgirl image of British netball, the Queens of the Castle have created their own sport culture by encouraging non-conformist and flamboyant playing clothes, the open discussion and negotiation of all values and practices, a truly caring ethos and support network, and opposition to all forms of racial harassment. They have become successful at attracting young, urban, working-class women to a sport not noted for its egalitarianism (Hargreaves, 1994, pp. 250–51). [. . .]

Feminist organizing and sexual politics

Even though these organizations are expressly liberal feminist, there are still struggles within them around differing ideological positions. The difference has primarily been between those who proclaim a liberal approach versus those who seek a more radical feminist agenda, and for the most part, the struggle has been around sexual politics. As was pointed out earlier, women involved in sport advocacy work have often been reluctant to take up issues like sexual harassment and abuse, raised by their more radical feminist counterparts outside sport.

Sexual politics and lesbian visibility have been viewed very differently in each of the four organizations considered here. They have been virtually ignored and suppressed when necessary in the WSF despite the fact that its founder Billie Jean King has acknowledged her bisexuality and seems comfortable with gay rights (King, 1982: pp. 26–28), and tennis player Martina Navratilova, who is openly lesbian and increasingly active in gay and lesbian politics, is a member of the WSF Board of Trustees. For example, at the 1983 New Agenda Conference, co-sponsored by the Women's Sport Foundation and the US Olympic Committee, and funded by a host of corporate sponsors, organizers agreed to table a resolution that dealt openly with lesbianism when these same corporate sponsors threatened to withdraw their funding if the word "lesbian" appeared in official conference documents (Cahn, 1994: pp. 267–68; Krebs, 1984). My interviews indicate that sexuality issues have been deliberately "kept under the rug" until the late 1980s, but in the past few years the WSF is quietly undertaking a number of initiatives. For example, they now have a non-discrimination statement which includes sexual orientation:

> The Women's Sports Foundation seeks to encourage diversity and equal opportunity in sports and therefore does not discriminate in any of its programs or activities on the basis of race, age, religion, color, national origin, sex, handicapping condition or sexual orientation.

They took a firm stance in 1993 against the homophobic Amendment 2 (no protected status based on homosexual, lesbian or bisexual orientation) in Colorado when they dropped the city of Denver from the potential candidates to house the WSF offices. They have also incorporated homophobia discussion panels at some of their annual conferences, and they have held homophobia workshops for their staff. Finally, they are fully supportive of an independent film-maker who is currently making a documentary film about homophobia in women's sport. In sum, their approach is certainly not pro-active; it is quiet, educative, and liberal.

CAAWS, on the other hand, has at various times in its history been embroiled in sexual politics, and the debates have been both public and well documented (see Lawrence-Harper, 1991, 1993; Lenskyj, 1991a, 1991b). Throughout its existence, CAAWS has made a serious effort to be both anti-homophobic and lesbian-positive. [. . .]

There has [though] been relative silence on the issue for the past few years, and to some extent the state has played a role in enforcing this silence with the 1987 directive from the Secretary of State Women's Program (which at the time was a major source of funding for CAAWS) that it would no longer fund proposals and groups whose primary purpose was "to promote a view on sexual orientation."

The UK WSF is yet a different story of sexual politics. An early membership brochure dating from the late 1980s included statements from members, one of which read: "Lots of people think all sportswomen are lesbians. Well, some of us are. So what?" It is easy to conclude that this reflected a deliberate effort on the part of the UK WSF to be openly lesbian-positive and anti-homophobic when in fact this issue met with continued debate and resistance within the organization. Information obtained through interviews suggests that originally the UK WSF was seen as "an organization for dykes" although in reality the early membership was split on the advisability of making the organization unequivocally lesbian-positive. Those who were against such a move believed that sexuality was a private and not an organizational issue, whereas those who were pushing such a step were well versed in radical feminist politics.

Several events dramatically changed the organization. The first was that in 1990 the WSF UK was officially recognized by the British Sports Council and was eligible for government funding. Coupled with the 1988 Local Government Act which introduced Clause 28 prohibiting the promotion of homosexuality using public money, this meant that it was extremely difficult for groups like the WSF to declare openly that it supported lesbianism. Debate took place within the organization, but clearly those who argued that it was inappropriate and highly damaging for the WSF to be associated with lesbianism won the day. Then in 1992, the Tambrands corporation contributed $100,000 to sponsor the Tampax/WSF Sports Awards for Girls and Young Women the goal of which was to celebrate young women's (age 11–19) achievements in sport as well as reduce the drop-out rate of teenagers from sport. Motivated by the fear of losing funding from the Sports Council, and certainly their corporate sponsor, all public discussions about lesbian visibility have ceased, and the issue has been depoliticized. The latest membership brochure does not have a single reference to lesbian visibility.

Womensport Australia, to my knowledge, has not begun to deal with these issues at least not publicly. However, an incident occurred in early 1994 which has provoked considerable debate and controversy. A leading player with the Australian national cricket team alleged that she was dropped from the team because of sexual politics, which the governing sport body strongly denied.[4] As a heterosexual, she claimed that selections to the team were made on the basis of sexuality, not ability. She also attempted to file a complaint with the state anti-discrimination board which could not deal with her allegations under present legislation. The ensuing uproar has, as one account suggested, "given everyone an excuse to explore the sexual behaviour of women cricketers and, to a wider degree, that of women in other sports" (Wilson, 1994). The controversy has been devastating to women's cricket in Australia, and to some degree women's sport in general. Women athletes, whether they are straight or gay, have no way of effectively countering the innuendo unless they publicly declare their sexuality. The negative public reaction, especially in the media, also points out why Australian women's sport organizations have been very reticent to deal openly with lesbianism and homophobia as well as the dangers of not doing so. Like most women's sport communities, it is polarized around these difficult issues, and Womensport Australia will need to negotiate its role in the continuing debates very carefully. [. . .]

Conclusion: politicizing women's sport (and women in sport)

Sportswomen have generally been resistant to taking an overtly political stance on women's issues and on issues of discrimination. As Jennifer Hargreaves suggests, the politicization of women's sports is unusual because sportswomen tend to see sports in an insular way and often claim there is no connection between participation and politics (Hargreaves, 1994, p. 254). Nor have the politics and practice of feminism been recognized as particularly important nor relevant. By politics we both mean the struggle to define and control women's sport: its meanings and values, the structures required, and the debates over policy. Feminist practice in sport, when it does occur, varies between liberal reformism to a more controversial radicalism thus producing the inevitable tensions between the two approaches. Where governments have made women's sport a priority, their programs and policies have been overwhelmingly liberal but with a welcome shift from a focus on equality to equity over the past decade. When women's sport advocacy groups, such as the organizations studied here, become more dependent for funding on either the state or the private sector, they focus more on a liberal gender equity framework for change and are less willing, often resistant, to engage in radical cultural politics. This effectively depoliticizes the issues surrounding women in sport (homophobia is a good example), and makes it difficult for those interested in pursuing more radically defined issues and change to be effective. Male-defined sport can be, and often is, challenged and resisted but primarily at the local level far removed from state-controlled amateur sport systems.

There is a very long road ahead before any form of radical cultural politics is recognized as being both viable and necessary to future change in women's sport. . . . [The] international conference on women's sport organized by the British Sports Council and supported by the International Olympic Committee [attracted] some 300 delegates from over 85 countries [May 1994] representing governmental and non-governmental organizations, national Olympic Committees, international and national sport federations, and educational and research institutions. The conference specifically addressed the issue of "how to accelerate the process of change that would redress the imbalances women face in their participation and involvement in sport," and it approved a declaration with the overriding aim "to develop a sporting culture that enables and values full involvement of women in every aspect of sport" (The Brighton Declaration on Women and Sport, 1994). Thematic workshops addressed the continuing problems that plague women's sport: the lack of women in sports administration, development of women coaches, and gender bias in physical education and research. Issue seminars focused on the usual topics: equal opportunity legislation, integration versus separation, cross-cultural differences, challenging sexism, marketing strategies, working in a male environment, and admittedly a few more controversial topics such as women's sport in Muslim cultures, sexual harassment, homophobia, and integrating women athletes with disabilities. Skills seminars provided information on mentoring, networking, advocacy and lobbying, community sports leadership, dealing with the media, and gender awareness training. Delegates agreed to establish and develop an International Women in Sport Strategy which they hope will be endorsed and supported by governmental and non-governmental organizations involved in sport development on all continents, and enable model programmes and successful developments to be shared among nations and sporting federations. There was general agreement that strong, international women and sport networks are needed for mutual support, for exchanging knowledge, skills and "good practice," and for sharing resources.

A new organization, Womensport International, was also announced at the conference. It aspires to be an umbrella group which will seek positive change for girls and women in sport and physical activity by facilitating global networking and communication. Given the fact that the founders of Womensport International wish the organization to be global in scope and outlook, and to connect a vast array of differing cultures, it is no wonder that notions of politicization and radical cultural struggle are absent from its vision. However, it must take on board this more radical perspective or become just like every other women's sport advocacy association, some of which have made significant gains in bringing more girls and women into sport, but sport itself remains as male-dominated and as male-defined as always. This is not necessarily meaningful progress.

Acknowledgements

I am grateful to the University of Alberta for research monies for this project through its Support for the Advancement of Scholarship Fund. My colleague Trevor Slack, and graduate students Brenda Grace and Janis Lawrence-Harper assisted with the collection of data and information. I also wish to thank the many women in each organization who patiently and willingly took the time to answer my questions and to provide supporting documentation.

Notes

1   There are some who would question the veracity of this statement given the women's
     sport governing bodies in the United States such as the National Section on Women's
     Athletics (NSWA) of the American Physical Education Association which was formed
     in 1932. In 1957 it became the Division for Girls' and Women's Sport (DGWS) of
     the American Alliance for Health, Physical Education and Recreation. There was also
     the Association for Intercollegiate Athletics for Women (AIAW) which began in 1972
     as a division of AAHPER and in 1979 became an autonomous governing body for
     women's intercollegiate sport until it ceased to exist in 1984 since women's programs
     are now controlled by the former men's organization, the NCAA. Also, established
     prior to many of these organizations is the International Association of Physical Education
     and Sports for Girls and Women. Founded in 1952 primarily through the efforts of
     the American physical educator Dorothy Ainsworth, the IAPESGW continues to be
     recognized throughout the world as an organization that brings together women of
     many different countries working in the field of physical education and sport. However,
     I argue that all of these organizations were founded prior to the modern women's
     movement, in most cases were sport governing bodies, and have never defined
     themselves as feminist in any way.
2   There are of course other national women's sport advocacy organizations. For example,
     the Women's Sports Foundation Japan was founded in 1981. I have been able to obtain
     some materials from this group such as newsletters and newspaper articles, all of which
     are in Japanese, and although I have had them translated, they provide only a minimal
     amount of information pertaining to the organization itself. There is also the Women's
     Sport and Fitness Foundation of Malaysia about which I know very little. At an
     international women and sport conference in England in May 1994, a new organization,
     the Association for African Women in Sport, was formed. There are also several well
     established "women's committees" which are affiliated with national sports bodies, and
     which function very much as women's sport advocacy groups. For example, the Women's
     Committee of the Norwegian Confederation of Sports (founded in 1985) has published
     two informative booklets in English which outline the history, objectives, and work of
     the committee (Norwegian Confederation of Sports, 1990, 1994). There is also a
     similar group in Germany, called the Federal Committee for Women in Sport, which
     is one of seven committees in the German Sports Confederation. Finally, there is the
     Women and Sport Working Group of the European Sports Council (see Fasting, 1993).
3   For a more thorough discussion of these issues, see Hargreaves (1994): pp. 237–42;
     and the Sports Council (1993).
4   I am grateful to Jim McKay, a sport sociologist in Australia, for sending me numerous
     newspaper accounts of this controversy.

References

Brighton Declaration on Women and Sport (1994) Women, Sport and the Challenge of
     Change International Conference, Brighton, England, May 5–8.
Cahn, S. (1994) *Coming on strong: Gender and sexuality in twentieth-century women's sport*. New
     York: The Free Press.
Canadian Association for the Advancement of Women and Sport and Physical Activity (CAAWS)
     (1993) *Towards gender equity for women in sport: A handbook for national sport organizations*.
     Gloucester, ON: CAAWS.

Fasting, K. (1993) *Women and sport: Monitoring progress towards equality: A European survey*. Oslo: Women's Committee, Norwegian Confederation of Sports.

Forbes, S.L. (1993) *Government and interest group relations: An Analysis of the Canadian Association for the Advancement of Women and Sport*. Unpublished master's thesis. Wilfred Laurier University, Waterloo, Ontario.

Halpert, F.E. (1989) "Fifteen years of the Women's Sports Foundation," *Headway* (Fall): pp. 6–9.

Hargreaves, J. (1994) *Sporting females: Critical issues in the history and sociology of women sport*. London and New York: Routledge.

King, B.J. (1982) *Billie Jean* (with Frank Deford). New York: The Viking Press.

Krebs, P. (1984) "At the starting blocks: Women athletes' new agenda," *Off Our Backs*, Vol. 14, No. 1: pp. 1–4.

Lawrence-Harper, J. (1991) *The herstory of the Canadian Association for the Advancement of Women and Sport*. Report prepared for CAAWS, November.

Lawrence-Harper, J. (1993) *Change in a feminist organization: The Canadian Association for the Advancement of Women and Sport and Physical Activity 1981–1991*. Unpublished Master's thesis. University of Alberta, Edmonton, Alberta.

Lenskyj, H. (1991a) "Good sports: Feminists organizing on sport issues in the 1970s and 1980s," *Resources for Feminist Research/Documentation sur la recherche feministe*, 20(3/4), pp. 130–135.

Lenskyj, H. (1991b) "Combatting homophobia in sport and physical education," *Sociology of Sport Journal*, Vol. 8, No. 1: pp. 61–69.

Martin, P.Y. (1990) "Rethinking feminist organizations," *Gender and Society*, Vol. 4, No. 2: pp. 182–206.

Norwegian Confederation of Sports (1990) *Women in sport*. Women's Committee Program 1985–90.

Norwegian Confederation of Sports (1994) *Developing equity for women in the Norwegian Conferation of Sports*. Women's Committee.

Scott-Pawson, S. (1991) *The Canadian Association for the Advancement of Women and Sport (1981–1991): An organizational case analysis of a feminist organization*. Unpublished master's thesis. Queen's University, Kingston, Ontario.

Sports Council (1993) *Women and sport: Policy and frameworks for action*. London: The Sports Council.

Theberge, N. (1983) "Feminism and sport: Linking the two through a new organization," *Canadian Woman Studies/les cahiers de la femme*, Vol. 4, No. 3: pp. 79–81.

Wilson, C. (1994) "Cricket's battle of the sexes," *Sunday Age*, Melbourne, Victoria (January 23): p. 13.

Rosemary Deem

WOMEN AND SPORT

[. . .]

SPORT . . . **APPEARS NO DIFFERENT** to any other form of leisure. But sport is different from other kinds of leisure in at least four ways. Firstly, it has a national and international significance which most other forms of leisure do not have, because of the media coverage and the amount of sport played. Secondly, sport, unlike most forms of leisure, is actually specifically taught in schools, and is in fact one of the most gender-segregated areas of the curriculum (Leaman 1984, Scraton 1986). Thirdly, there is an ongoing debate about the importance of connections between sport and physical fitness and health. Fourthly, sport is often associated with competitiveness and aggression as well as with masculinity. Sport is in fact not marginal to the lives of some women, but the kinds of sport women participate in are on the whole different from those in which men participate, women are often excluded from male-dominated sports even if they want to participate, and many women switch off from sport in their early teens whilst still at school (Scraton 1985, 1986). Those few who do continue are likely to reduce or cease involvement in sport when they have children or get married. [. . .]

1   In which sports do women participate?

The national surveys suggest that the most popular sports amongst adult women are walking, swimming, keep-fit and darts (*Social Trends* 1985, quoting the 1983 General Household Survey). Whereas amongst men, walking also emerges as the most popular, other activities which are popular include billiards and snooker, swimming, darts, football, golf and squash, although for both sexes the percentages of people of all ages participating in sport does not exceed 17 per cent of the population for women and 19 per cent for men. Nevertheless this very general evidence suggests that women tend to opt for non competitive sports and those which can easily accommodate other family members, whilst men prefer competitive sports (walking and swimming excluded) and those which typically occur in all male environments. It is also fair to say that participant sport is not a majority interest for either sex in the U.K. For males and females the participation rates are highest amongst the 16–19 age group, but the decline in participation after that age is much less marked for men than for women.

When we come to look at the evidence from studies specifically concerned with women we find a not too dissimilar picture. In the Milton Keynes sample A, the most favoured sports were walking, swimming, yoga and keep-fit, badminton and squash. But this sample was intentionally biased towards those women for whom a significant part of their leisure takes place out of the home, which explains the appearance of two sports which require both equipment and facilities as well as some knowledge of the skills involved. In response to questions about leisure activities which have been given up, Sample A women instanced sport in general, along with dancing and swimming at the top of the list and not only amongst the older age-groups. A typical response is summed up by the following comment:

> I used to be a keen swimmer and also played hockey for a local team when I was in my early twenties. That all stopped when I started courting – my boyfriend wanted me to spend my time with him. I did think I'd start swimming again – in fact I did go when I was pregnant – but then afterwards it wasn't the same – I did take the eldest to Mums and tods swimming but it was her that did the swimming not me – when you've been really good at something you can't be satisfied by doing it half-heartedly – a couple of lengths was all I could manage, so I decided it wasn't worth it. The main exercise I get now is running after the kids and the occasional walk on a Sunday – and to tell you the truth I get so tired I couldn't face anything more strenuous – I can't imagine how I used to play hockey at all!' (woman in early thirties, two children under seven, husband an engineer).

Even where sport has been liked and enjoyed, lack of support from the rest of the household and the responsibilities imposed by children often sound the death knell. The woman just quoted nevertheless had a husband who still played football regularly and whose only period without active sports involvement had been six weeks three years ago when he broke his leg!

If sport was never attractive in the first place, few reasons are needed to stop all physical activity except that strictly necessitated by the daily routine, although often the point at which children enter their teens may be one at which a keep-fit class or something similar is taken up. In the Milton Keynes sample B less than one-third of the 168 women involved took part in any sport other than walking and most of that walking fell well below the 'At least two miles' criterion used by the General Household Survey. Amongst the thirty percent who did do some form of sport, swimming, yoga and keep-fit were the most likely choices. Swimming is often chosen because it does fit in with children's own leisure interests, and as the woman I just quoted points out, when children are small the amount of swimming that an accompanying adult can do is minimal. For many women in the two Milton Keynes studies I carried out, sport was either something done by their male partners on Sundays or weekday evenings, or it was something you infrequently watched on TV (usually when there was no alternative viewing). A group of women from a local organization had this to say about sport; 'It's what men do isn't it . . . it was bad enough at school having to play all those ghastly games and run around in a silly games skirt freezing to death but when there's a choice . . .'.

However it is important not be misled by this notion of 'choice'. Yes, many women do 'choose' not to do sport. They also, as we have already seen, may 'choose' not to have much leisure. In both instances the choice is a forced one and is closely related to structures of male power over women as well as to prevailing ideologies about masculinity and feminity. One reason why women do not choose sport is because it is closely associated with masculinity, male aggression, status and power; it is not seen as something for women. Even those women for whom sport has an appeal may not actually keep up their participation rate as they move into their thirties and forties. Here the significant factor is likely to be their heavy burden of domestic labour and childcare (despite in most cases having an adult male around) plus lack of independent money and transport. When women do participate it is often in a sport which reinforces traditional ideas about femininity – yoga, keep fit, swimming – and which are hence compatible with stereotypes of beauty, grace and female attractiveness. What is much less rarely acceptable is women doing sports which involve physical contact, getting dirty or sweating profusely, or having to wear unfashionable clothes. A P.E. teacher interviewed by Scraton (1986), asked her views about girls playing soccer said 'I have yet to see an elegant woman footballer. Maybe I'm just prejudiced but they just look horrible.' Another P.E. teacher said 'I don't think soccer is a girls' sport – physical contact and all that rolling in the mud' (Scraton 1986, p. 20). As Hargreaves (1985) notes, 'In sport, 'masculine' identity incorporates images of strength, aggression, muscularity and activity, but it implies, at the same time, an opposite, 'feminine' identity, associated with relative weakness, gentleness and grace . . . It seems to follow logically that men are 'naturally' better suited to sport' (Hargreaves 1985, pp. 26–27).

In the Sheffield study only 23 per cent of the 707 sample of women surveyed played some kind of sport, and once again swimming was very popular (Green, Hebron and Woodward 1985b). Other choices for women who did enjoy sport included badminton, tennis, running and squash. But participation was least amongst older women, working class women and those with low incomes – very similar to the Milton Keynes findings that it is mostly middle class women in their twenties to forties with some money of their own, or childless single young women, for whom sport is most attractive. [. . .]

Once women have left full-time education their involvement in sport begins a downhill descent from which it never recovers. Young women are often preoccupied with fashion, music and boyfriends. Whilst for a few, sport may continue in this phase, as Leonard's (1980) research on engaged couples in Wales demonstrates, once serious relationships are established many of the woman's interests tend to decline, although her male partner is much more likely to continue his, including sport. [. . .] Many of the same factors which restrict women's leisure are responsible for women not taking a more active role in sport. Although facilities may be available in the shape of sports centres and so on, they are often expensive, have no childcare provision (or only in the daytime, not at weekends or evenings) are difficult to get to by public transport and are often perceived as unwelcoming to the novice or inexperienced. Sport requires time, something that as we have already seen, many women do not have much of; when they reach an age when their home commitments and work obligations are lessening, declining physical powers and or ill-health are likely to mean that sport is not something which is turned to. Because sport is seen largely as a male preserve, and is controlled by men, women lack the kind of servicing and support which many male sports players receive from their female partners. This is particularly true of working class women whose housework, childcare and paid jobs are likely to leave them exhausted and wanting to spend any free time they have in a passive rather than an active way (Westwood, 1984). In my Milton Keynes interviews a woman in her early thirties with two children, one ten, the other twelve, said of her attempts to go jogging:

> Well first of all I tried going early in the mornings but then everyone complained I was making them late by enjoying myself rather than getting on with breakfast. Then I thought I'd go at lunchtime – but the girls at work laughed at me and anyway I have to shop most days – so finally I decided I'd try the evenings – after we'd eaten I'd wait an hour or so and then go – that was OK in the summer but of course now its [sic] dark I don't feel safe – also Ron (husband) doesn't much like me running anyway – he says I'm getting leg muscles and that feminine women don't get all sweaty.

Even though this woman was unusually determined it still wasn't really possible. For many others sport wasn't even considered:

> Sport? I'd never have the energy – it takes me all I've got to do the house, look after the kids and go to work – the only thing I like to do in the evenings is sleep or watch a video (woman in late twenties, three children, job as an office worker, Milton Keynes interviews).

[. . .] Women's lack of interest in sport is as much due to the stranglehold which men have over sport (its image, its management and participation) as to poor facilities, as the Women's Sports Foundation (founded in 1984) has been at pains to point out. But patriarchal power relations with regard to sport do not stop with sport itself; they extend to the ways in which men perceive women either as housewives and mothers or sex-objects, and to the manner in which men develop strategies to control women's behaviour and sexuality. Thus the only way in which significantly more women are likely to come to see sport as something which is both enjoyable and in which they have a right to participate is to actually change the nature of the social relationships and male power which surround sport itself. Sports goods and clothing for women also reinforce gender stereotypes – pink shoes, 'pretty' bicycles.

Bibliography

Green, E., Hebron, S. and Woodward, D. (1985b). 'Leisure and Gender; women's opportunities, perceptions and constraints', unpublished report to ESRC/Sports Council Steering Group, January.
Hargreaves, J. (1985). 'Their own worst enemies', *Sport and Leisure*, July/August, pp. 20–8.
Leaman, O. (1984). *Sit on the Sidelines and Watch the Boys Play: Sex Differentiation in Physical Education*. Longman/Schools Council.

Leonard, D. (1980). *Sex and Generation*. Tavistock.

Scraton, S. (1985). 'Boys muscle in where angels fear to tread; the relationship between physical education and young women's subcultures', paper given to Leisure Studies Association Conference, Ilkley, 12–14 April.

Scraton, S. (1986). 'Images of femininity and the teaching of girls' physical education', in Evans, J. (ed.). *Physical Education; Sport and Schooling: Studies in the Sociology of Physical Education*. The Falmer Press.

Social Trends 1985 (1985). OPCS, HMSO.

Westwood, S. (1984). *All Day, Every Day*. Pluto.

Jayne Caudwell

SEX AND POLITICS
Sites of resistance in women's football

[. . .]

Contemporary 'queer' sites – dykescapes and empowerment

CLEARLY FOOTBALL HAS a historical and cultural past bound up with male domination. The identity of players has been assumed to be male and heterosexual, with heterosexuality inscribed in the public playing areas. Lesbians playing football not only challenge the male ownership of the 'football fields', but also question the normalised construction of heterosexual space. Recent research indicates that lesbians and gays are adopting strategies to *destabilize, subvert* and *resist* the construction of heterosexual space. For example, work in *Mapping desire: geographies of sexuality* (Bell and Valentine, 1995) and 'Queers in space' (Ingram, Bouthillette and Retter, 1997) offers analysis of the ways in which this is being achieved by a multitude of groups. This evidence suggests that there is some (re)negotiation of public space whereby lesbians and gays are constructing what is being called 'queer' space.

The term 'queer' has been appropriated by both lesbian and gay groups to symbolise a political strategy which embraces the otherness and pluralism of sexual styles. Queer has been used by activists, in this country, since the late 1980s, early 1990s (ACT UP (Aids Coalition to Unleash Power] established in 1989; and OutRage, established in 1990) to assert and promote an 'in your face' attitude to lesbian and gay sexuality. However, some lesbian groups and some feminist groups are opposed to queer politics since it can be argued that the movement reflects the interests of white gay males. For example, those critical of queer politics warn that the generic term queer will inevitably come to mean men, as both homosexual and gay have done previously (Jeffreys, 1993), and Anna Marie Smith (1992) believes the potential for lesbian invisibility within queer politics is significant and reflects prevailing sexism. I share these beliefs and, although I value both politics and strategy which make marginalised sexualities visible, I prefer to use the term *dykescapes* rather than queer space when referring to lesbian space.

According to Carrie Moyer (1997), her experience of the American activist organisation Queer Nation was that it rarely focused on lesbian issues and, as a result, she helped set up DAM – Dyke Action Machine. DAM represents a working group concerned with providing "lesbians on the street with the pleasure of seeing their own images in professional, well designed public art" (p. 440). One example, taken from images created by Carrie Moyer, is a poster for a faux film. The 'Straight to hell' poster was plastered all over Manhattan for Stonewall 25 in 1994. The text reads: "She came out, so they kicked her out. Now she's out for blood". The film being advertised is a spoof lesbian revenge film, the iconography and language are the same as those used for pop-culture films such as those of Steve Segal or Arnold Schwarzenegger. The design and exposure of the poster aims to "articulate and represent a lesbian reality that dominating visual images ignore, deny, and repress" (p. 443). Clearly, public advertising space is being used to destabilize and subvert the unspoken norms of heterosexuality, and the poster campaign offers what can be referred to as a 'micro dykescape'. The approach DAM adopts provides an example of how sites can be used for empowerment and resistance. Sally Munt (1995) refers to this kind of strategy as a 'politics of dislocation', whereby socially constructed norms are displaced or put out of joint.

Despite work by DAM and other lesbian activist groups, the 'in your face' attitude is not always so easy to endorse, as Gill Valentine (1996) points out:

> Heterosexual looks of disapproval, whispers and stares are use[d] to spread discomfort and make lesbians feel out of place in everyday space. These in turn pressurize many women into policing their own desires and hence reinforce the appearance that 'normal' space is straight space. (p. 149)

Valentine continues by arguing that "the heterosexing of space is a performative act naturalised through repetition and regulation" (p. 146). Her work conducted with Lynda Johnson (1995) illustrates that the processes involved in the production of 'normal', 'proper' space extend to domestic environments. In an article entitled 'Wherever I lay my girlfriend that's my home' they explore the performance and surveillance of lesbian identity. The research describes how both time and space strategies are employed by lesbians to separate a lesbian identity from a daughter identity in the parental home. Like other realms, lesbians involved in sport and active leisure are compelled to contend with the conspicuous 'heterosexing' of the spaces they use. Within the male dominated, conservative world of sport the construction of dykescapes involves great risk and many lesbians adopt strategies which reflect coercion and result in a silencing of their lesbian identity.

Research by Susan Cahn (1994) suggests that lesbians in sport follow a code of 'play it, don't say it' since this will "ensure their own survival in a hostile culture while protecting one of the few social spaces that offer some degree of comfort and freedom" (p. 187). Similarly Gill Clarke (1997) offers analysis of the diverse and complex ways lesbians in physical education negotiate and manage various identities. Strategies used seem to lie on a continuum ranging from concealment to risk taking. Pat Griffin (1992, cited in Clarke, 1997) identifies techniques such as passing, covering, being implicitly out and explicitly out, as ways lesbian teachers negotiate the public display of their sexuality. Clearly, in an attempt to avoid confrontation, many lesbians in sport exercise self vigilance; they censor their own dress, behaviour and desire.

Passing, covering and being implicitly out must be understood within a historical, social, political and cultural framework. Just one example which begins to illuminate this point can be taken from the interwar period when lesbianism was increasingly being defined by the then established field of sexology. In 1935 the *Daily Herald* reported on an educational conference and the work of Dr. Williams, who stated:

> You cannot confine the desire and aptitude for combat to cricket and football. They inevitably appear in the whole character, and what was originally a gentle, feminine girl becomes harsh and bellicose in all relations to life. The women who have responsibility for teaching these girls are, many of the themselves embittered, sexless or homosexual hoydens who try to mould the girls into their own patterns. And far too often they succeed.
>
> (cited in Oram, 1993: p. 105)

Ideas and beliefs established by sexology carry a legacy which greatly influences contemporary sport's discourse on women's participation. Despite the prevailing heterosexism, however, it is possible to find a limited number of examples of 'sportsdykes'; those prepared to resist, subvert, dislocate and destabilize heterosexuality.

Women footballers have always received innuendos and direct comments concerning their sexuality, for example "a bunch of dykes running around a football field: women trying to be men" (cited in Williams and Woodhouse, 1991: p. 98). Comments like these have often been deliberately directed as an insult, and for some women the derogatory nature of such remarks [has] been received as an insult: a put down. However, lesbian players prepared to risk being 'out' are in fact reclaiming and reappropriating labels such as 'dyke'. Within the women's Greater London football league there are now five self identified 'out' lesbian teams (Watson, 1997). Hackney and Phoenix have been particularly active in their campaign to be visible: "Hackney Women's Football Club has blown the whistle on the whole game by coming out en masse" (Davis, 1991: p. 34). These 'out' players overtly make use of signifiers of lesbian identity such as dress and style. They also openly appropriate symbols of lesbian identity with the labris and triangle as part of the club logo, and the 'freedom' rainbow colours as part of the summer tournament playing kit. This process of stylization represents a performative act and is evidence of players who are prepared to celebrate explicitly their lesbian lifestyle and their marginalised sexuality. Clearly the team, as a site of empowerment, demonstrates "the difference space makes" (Valentine, 1993: p. 111), and offers a further example of a micro dykescape.

The players who are 'out' and part of teams which adopt the 'in your face' tactic, represent transgression, since they trespass both 'man-made' and heterosexual landscapes. Teams such as Hackney provide evidence that lesbians who have entered the 'football fields' on their own terms are, to varying degrees, renegotiating and reconstructing this space: "Lesbian desires and manners of being can restructure space" (Probyn, 1995, cited in Valentine, 1996: p. 150). [. . .]

Acknowledgements

I'd like to thank Gail Newsham for kindly giving her permission to use slides from photographs appearing in her book *In a league of their own* (republished 1998 by Scarlet Press) and Jean Seymour for her generous permission to use a reproduction of her 1946 photograph. These visual images appeared in the presentation of this paper at the LSA conference at Roehampton Institute London; 9–11 September, 1997, Finally, I'd like to thank my supervisor Judy White for providing support, encouragement and advice during the inarticulate stages I have experienced while writing this paper and ongoing pieces.

References

Bell, D. and Valentine, G. (1995) *Mapping desire. Geographies of sexualities*. London: Routledge.

Cahn, S. (1994) *Coming on strong. Gender and sexuality in twentieth century women's sport*. London: Harvard University Press.

Clarke, G. (1997) 'Playing a part: The lives of lesbian physical education teachers', in G. Clarke and B. Humberstone (eds) *Researching women and sport*. London: Macmillan, pp. 36–50.

Davis, M. (1991) 'Innings and outings', *The Guardian* 12 Dec., p. 34.

Ingram, G.B., Bouthillette, A.M. and Retter, Y. (eds.) (1997) *Queers in space. Communities/public places/sites of resistance*. Seattle: Bay Press.

Jeffreys, S. (1993) *The lesbian heresy. A feminist perspective on the lesbian sexual revolution*. London: Women's Press.

Johnson, C. and Valentine, G. (1995) 'Wherever I lay my girlfriend that's my home: The performance and surveillance of lesbian identities in domestic environments', in D. Bell and G. Valentine (eds) *Mapping desires. Geographies of sexualities*. London: Routledge, pp. 99–113.

Moyer, C. (1997) 'Do you love the dyke in your face?', in G.B. Ingram, A.M. Bouthillette and Y. Retter (eds) *Queers in space. Communities/public places/sites of resistance*. Seattle: Bay Press, pp. 439–446.

Munt, S. (1995) 'The lesbian flaneur', in D. Bell and G. Valentine (eds) *Mapping desires. Geographies of sexualities*. London: Routledge, 114–125.

Oram, A. (1993) 'Embittered, sexless or homosexual: Attacks on spinster teachers 1918–39', in Lesbian History Group *Not a passing phase. Reclaiming lesbians in history 1840–1985*. London: Women's Press, pp. 99–118.

Smith, A.M. (1992) 'Resisting the erasure of lesbian sexuality. A challenge for queer activism', in K. Plummer (ed.) *Modern homosexualities – fragments of lesbian and gay experience*. London: Routledge, pp. 200–213.

Valentine, G. (1993) 'Desperately seeking Susan: A geography of lesbian friendships', *Area* Vol. 25, No. 2: pp. 109–116.

——— (1996) '(Re)negotiating the "heterosexual street"', in N. Duncan (ed) *Body Space*. London: Routledge, pp. 146–156.

Watson, K. (1997) 'Football's coming homo!', *Diva* June/July, pp. 27.

Williams, J. and Woodhouse, J. (1991) 'Can play, will play? Women and football in Britain', in Williams, J. and Wagg, S. (eds) *British football and social change. Getting into Europe*. London: Leicester University Press, pp. 85–108.

Jennifer Hargreaves

MEN AND WOMEN AND
THE GAY GAMES

[. . .]

THE GAY GAMES HAS GONE A LONG WAY towards breaking down conventional gender divisions and facilitating the co-existence of lesbians and gay men. Nevertheless, as Gloria Stein (1998: 561) points out, 'co-sexual' homosexual culture does not compensate for

> Real, persistent structural differences in style, ideology, and access to resources among men and women. This recurring problem suggest[s] that while the new queer politics represent[s] the assertion of sexual difference which could not be assimilated into feminism, neither could gender be completely subsumed under sexuality. Despite their apparent commonalities, lesbians and gay men [are] often divided along the same lines as heterosexual women and men.

Although at the Gay Games the narrow heterosexual distinctions between masculinity and femininity are invalidated, there has been a history of male domination – both in participation and in administration – similar to the male domination of mainstream sport. Women have been increasingly assertive over the years and the Gay Games 1998 organizers worked for equal representation of female and male participants and recognition of the diversity in lesbian culture. Publicity material for Amsterdam 1998 declared that the Games were 'by, for, and about both women and men.' And to achieve this a programme 'exclusively for women has been put together in addition to the sports and cultural program that is open to everyone.' In Amsterdam, there was more equal gender representation that in previous Games. It was roughly estimated that 44 per cent of the participants were female.

The bias towards men that exists in many sports varies from country to country. In the United States, there is in general a much greater focus on equal opportunities between men and women than in other countries in the West, and in some teams – for example, Team Philadelphia – there is a very strict adherence to a philosophy of gender equality. In Australia, as well, there is close attention paid to equal representation of women and men. Outside the West there are much smaller numbers of lesbians involved in the Gay Games than gay men, and for that reason a women's outreach programme is being put in place both to examine the multiple reasons why this may be so and to provide funding to increase women's participation.

With some exceptions, men have held the key positions of authority and power – the Federation of Gay Games in particular has been very male-dominated. At the beginning of the year 2000, there were 50 directors of the Federation of Gay Games, only 12 of whom were women. Rosemary Mitchell, Tom Waddell's wife, is one of the exceptional strong female personalities who has shared decision-making power with men and has been respected by them.[1] Paula Pressley, a lesbian activist, was executive director of the 1994 New York Gay Games, and the co-president of Gay Games IV was also a woman – Jay Hill. In October 1999, Sue Emerson from England became the fourth female co-president of the Federation of Gay Games and the first non-American to hold this office. Her appointment signified a shift in the exclusively North American control of the Gay Games.

But inequalities and differences are not just at the levels of participation and administration between men and women. There are ideological and cultural distinctions as well, which separate lesbians from gay men and create divisions among Gay Games lesbians. For example, the exaggerated displays of body and sexuality . . . are perceived to derive mostly from gay men, and opposition to them comes from lesbians and other gay men who want to protect the original spirit of the Gay Games. The specific incentive to address lesbian issues at the Gay Games reflects the wider discourse of sexual politics and lesbian identity. It is a struggle linked to the fashionable, rather male-oriented 'queer' movement in sport. Among some lesbians at the Gay Games there is a preference for the use of the term 'dyke' instead of 'queer', and Gay Games 'sportsdykes' want to distance themselves from narcissistic and vulgar images.[2] One of the athletes explained:

> Sex and sleaze is not how lesbians want to be perceived in the gay world. Many lesbians dissociate themselves from the idea. They are *normal* people who care about their towns, are interested in the environment, and are involved in community politics and so on. . . . And many lesbians who come here are passionate about sport and that's the most important reason for coming – to be able to take part in sport without the usual obstacles and homophobic attitudes. . . . This portrayal [sex and sleaze] might have been down to the fact that the symbol of Amsterdam is sex – very much aimed at the male market. Amsterdam put out the wrong message (although the organization of the Games and how it was run was fantastic). . . . I found the official programme offensive with its images of naked bodies and sex. This is a total myth of what gay people are about. Hopefully Australia have heard this is not the image gay people want to project, and will take note.

This articulation reflects the tension between lesbians who prioritize sport as the reason for going to the Gay Games and lesbians who prioritize sexuality. That the Gay Games are fun, non-divisive, fundamentally non-discriminatory, and accommodating of sportsmen and women of all abilities and backgrounds – in line with Tom Waddell's original vision – is considered by some to be the most important feature of the Gay Games. There is concern that the success of the Games as an athletic festival will be masked if lesbians and gay men indulge in a sexual carnival that attracts stereotyping and places sport in the background.

In spite of the struggles over values and identities, the Gay Games have become a principal heroic symbol of lesbian and gay celebration, a ritual enactment of group identity, representing community, belonging and the translation of 'me' into 'us'. Whereas lesbians are almost invisible in dominant sports culture, in the Gay Games they are thrust into the limelight, and by their sheer numbers make an impact on popular consciousness. Taking part in the Gay Games is a politics of visibility which can become a source of individual and collective power (Fraser 1999: 114). Munt (1998: 23) suggests that the diversity of a lesbian community 'transposes the multiformed single subjectivity into a multicultural community, in its idealization of difference. . . . The lesbian community is then presented as the embodiment of the multivalenced heroic agent.' Each lesbian, Munt argues, 'becomes an heroic fragment of the greater struggle'.

Lesbians at the Gay Games temporarily make their sexuality visible and political, in stark contrast to the often general repression and invisibility of sexuality in Western culture. Such an act of visibility is an open challenge to compulsory heterosexuality and is part of a wider movement which is challenging the sexual and cultural norms of Western societies. Altman (1998: 310) claims that 'To join a gay group is an act of affirmation that is often cathartic in its effect. Whatever the possibilities for individual liberation without full social liberation . . . the act of involvement with gay liberation brings with it a new perception of the world that is remarkably radicalizing.' At the Gay Games, lesbians and gays from around the world can be open about their sexuality and need not disguise any aspect of their lifestyle – an experience which, it is claimed, 'is usually unequalled in one's lifetime' (*Unity '94*). But, for many lesbians and gay men, attendance at the Gay Games is an act of courage – for example, for elite athletes from the West who risk being 'outed' in mainstream sport if their presence at the Gay Games is discovered. It was hoped that top international athletes would come out at the 1998 Gay Games in Amsterdam, but this did not happen. One of the organizers explained that

> Elite athletes are still nervous about negative exposure if they come out, and worried that they will lose sponsorship if they do. You can be the sleaziest top international person if you're heterosexual and still get all your endorsements. That's OK. That's allowed. But it's not allowed to be gay. . . . It affects huge numbers of sportswomen who are lesbians. . . . One woman on the English discus team wanted to participate in the Gay Games, then pulled out at last minute, scared to be recognised.

The fear of recognition is even greater for women from countries where homosexuality is illegal; for them, attendance at the Gay Games is associated with risk and danger. The number of women who come to the Games from such countries is minute and their identities are concealed. Those who choose to take part in the Gay Games calculate that the risks are outweighed by the sense of normality and freedom experienced in this special context, which is welcoming, 'safe' and provides collective support. The Gay Games provides for them a haven, a place for confirmation of sexuality and identity, and a setting for the renewal of personal and group politics. [. . .]

The gay rights group Stonewall claims that one in ten women in Western cities (fewer in the country) is a lesbian. Based on Kinsey's research on sexuality, gays are also estimated to be 10 per cent of the population, with higher percentages in some major cities and areas. The 1990 US census estimates that Washington DC's gay population is about 19 per cent of the total (*Advocate* 30 November 1993), and Judy Goldstein from the New York Gay and Lesbian Visitor's Centre estimates the city's gay population to be nearly 25 per cent. Even at 10 per cent, New York's gay and lesbian population would number roughly 800,000 people – larger than the population of many of America's largest cities, including San Francisco. But lesbians and gay men are not visible in representative numbers in mainstream sport and culture, and there is still a tendency for them to remain closeted and ghettoized, clustered in gay urban subcultures. In sport throughout the world, at all levels, there is a relatively tiny number of 'out' lesbians and gay men and, although these estimated figures of numbers of lesbians and gay men in the general population are impossible to confirm, they indicate the huge move that has to be made in order to integrate non-heterosexuals into mainstream sport and culture and to eradicate homophobia and discrimination based on sexual difference. [. . .]

Many lesbian sportswomen live constantly with the tension created between their gayness and their desire for integration, which could be eased if they were courageous enough to come out in mainstream sport in greater numbers, and if more heterosexual sportswomen were prepared to stand up and speak out against heterosexism and homophobia.

Notes

1   Although Rosemary Mitchell is a lesbian and Tom Waddell was a gay man, because they both wanted a child they decided to marry and to share the parenting.
2   Sportsdykes have been influenced by the activities of DAM (Dyke Action Machine), which was set up in reaction to the failure of 'Queer Nation' (an American activist organization) to address lesbian issues adequately (Caudwell 2000: 156).

Bibliography

Altman, D. (1998) 'The End of the Homosexual?', in Nardi, P. and B. Schneider (eds) *Social Perspectives in Lesbian and Gay Studies*, London: Routledge, pp. 306–11.
Butler, J. (1990) (1993) *Bodies That Matter*, London: Routledge.
Caudwell, J. (2000) 'Sex and Politics: Sites and Resistance in Women's Football', in Aitchison, C. and F. Jordan (eds) *Gender, Space and Identity*, Brighton: LSA Publication 63: 151–61. [See also Reading 55 in this volume.]
Fraser, M. (1999) 'Classing Queer: Politics in Competition', in Bell, V. (ed.) 'Performativity and Belonging', *Theory, Culture and Society* 16(2): 107–31.
Munt, S. (1998) *Heroic Desire*, London: Cassell.
Stein, A. (1998) 'Sisters and Queens: The Centering of Lesbian Feminism', in Nardi, P. and B. Schneider (eds) *Social Perspectives in Lesbian and Gay Studies*, London: Routledge, pp. 553–88.

Subcultures

INTRODUCTION

T HE TERM 'SUBCULTURE' REFERS TO the collective meanings and values expressed by a group or groups within a society, usually when such meanings and values are recognizable and identifiable in distinct forms of behaviour, style or language. Sport cultures (and other forms of leisure) are conducive to the formation and expression of subcultures and their associated values, not least because of the perception that sport is a significant source for the expression of personal and cultural identity. Subcultures are, of course, strongly linked with other social influence, as Readings in previous sections on race, class and gender show. The sport subcultures that feature in this section are climbing (mountaineering), boxing, football fandom (its hooliganism variant), windsurfing, lesbian physical education, skateboarding and bodybuilding.

English sociologist of sport **Peter Donnelly**, long based in Canada, provides the first Reading. He makes the critical distinction between subcultures of achievement and subcultures that are ascribed, the latter referring to what are essentially inherited values, and have much more set cultural characteristics and boundaries. Donnelly develops appropriate ways of conceptualizing sport cultures as achieved subcultures. In the excerpts chosen for this Reading, the focus is upon the characteristics of such achieved subcultures, and in particular the levels of membership identifiable in the subculture. Anyone with any experience of sport and its subcultures can use this Reading as a model for illuminating, in a systematic way, the subcultural profile of that sport.

In Section Five, the work of Wacquant was featured, showing the ways in which subcultures emerge in particular class locations. In the full article from which the Reading is taken, Wacquant acknowledged the pioneering work of **John Sugden** on boxing subcultures. Sugden spent two years studying the Memorial Boxing Club in an inner-city neighbourhood in the north-east USA, in the late 1970s. Any credible subcultural study must show a sensitivity to the detail of the subcultural setting, and this Reading focuses upon Sugden's description of the boxing club and its physical environment as the basis of his study of the occupational culture of the black boxer. How does this evocative description of the cultural setting of the sport contribute to Sugden's conclusion on the 'exploitation of many . . . who will not succeed'?

The third and fourth Readings are early and influential contributions to the debate on the nature and significance of football hooliganism in England, as manifest at professional football games. The Oxford University group of social psychologists, **Peter Marsh, Elizabeth Rosser** and **Rom Harré** provide an analysis of 'life on the terraces', based upon non-participant observational study of the Oxford United football supporters. Video evidence was gathered about where fans stood in identifiable groupings: five groups were identified and the notion of career is considered in relation to the 'linear hierarchy' of the fans, and – though this is not detailed in the Reading itself – the aggressive behaviour of some of these fan groupings is accounted for as a form of ritualized aggression. Critical responses to the Oxford group have included that from the (University of) Leicester group, and **Eric Dunning, Patrick Murphy** and **John Williams** draw upon alternative sociological sources in seeking to account for the football hooligan phenomenon of the 1970s and 1980s. They see the Oxford group's research as an unconvincing 'theoretical mélange', that misleadingly underestimates the violence characteristic of the football hooligan subculture. Nevertheless, Dunning *et al.* recognize some strengths in the Oxford group's work, and when reading these opposing perspectives it is important to look out for commonalities of findings, and for evidence and data that possibly transcend the theoretical disputes and incompatibilities.

If sport has been in many respects a male preserve it is hardly surprising that subcultural studies have been dominated by studies of men and of masculinity and its values as expressed in sport. In the fifth Reading, based on the fieldwork undertaken by English subcultural and lifestyle sports specialist **Belinda Wheaton**, she and **Alan Tomlinson** consider – as they put it in their abstract – how a newer sport form promising the possibility of new and multiple identities expresses tensions between a dominant masculinity familiar in traditional sport forms and physical culture, and the potentially empowering dimensions of the activity for women. Has windsurfing subverted in any way the established gender order?

Subcultures are not always visible in public culture: they may be so unacceptable to the mainstream that they must operate behind the scenes of public life. Some subcultures, too, might 'stand in direct opposition to the dominant culture of the society in which they are located, rejecting its most important vales and norms and endorsing their opposites' (John Scott and Gordon Marshall, *A Dictionary of Sociology*, Oxford, Oxford University Press, 2005: 119). Such subcultures have been described as 'contra-cultures', or counter-cultures. English physical educationist and qualitative scholar **Gill Clarke**, in the sixth Reading, does not offer a traditional subcultural study (look at her sample and research method): but her findings suggest that lesbian sportswomen and physical education professionals are forced into a kind of corner, subtly coerced into a barely visible contra-cultural and marginalized space. What are the implications of this for what Clarke calls the 'heterosexual order'?

The penultimate Reading is by US sociologist of sport **Becky Beal**. In subcultural studies, there has been much debate about the impact of subcultures. Do they simply run alongside the mainstream or dominant culture? Or do they offer alternative possibilities for identity formation and cultural expression? Can they challenge the assumptions of the dominant culture? How does the mainstream respond to subcultural challenges – by way of appropriation, a kind of combination of takeover and acceptance/legitimation? Many such questions lead the subcultures researcher to the question of resistance, and Beal's study of skateboarding in north-eastern Colorado in the late 1980s details how such resistance is expressed in the practices and values of the subculture.

The final Reading raises complex questions of sexuality as well as resistance. US anthropologist **Alan M. Klein** spent seven years between 1979 and 1986 studying the bodybuilding subculture at four prime locations on the West Coast of the US. In reporting the study, based on ethnographic field notes, participant observation, interviews and surveys, he 'decided on the creation of a single fictitious gym' (p. 281), a fascinating technique with obvious challenges to the writer. Klein's analysis shows the complexities of a culture, its inner nature and public image, and relates the values and practices of the subculture to prevalent cultural myths about masculinity, sexuality and the body. In this, Klein employs the valuable perspectives of Erving Goffmann (1922–82). Taking these ideas and approaches about what is shown as the public face of a culture, but seeing what is actually practised, consider sketching an outline of a subculture with which you are familiar.

COMMENTARY AND FURTHER READING

Sport has proved a rich source for subcultural studies and a fruitful focus for the application of qualitative techniques to the study of sport culture. Some dangers must be avoided in such work, and these include reading too much into the practice or activity under scrutiny, and over-emphasizing the difference between groups. The latter danger can lead to a kind of romanticization of the subcultural project. A huge influence on the study of subcultures, both in Britain and beyond, was the work of Birmingham University's Centre for Contemporary Cultural Studies (CCCS), which in 1975 published a double issue (Vols 7 and 8) of its *Working Papers in Cultural Studies* series, entitled *Resistance through Rituals*. In this volume a long overview essay on subcultures, cultures and class showed that the study of subcultures could be integrated with an analysis of class: and, as shown by Angela McRobbie in her discussion of girls and subcultures, subcultural study should not be delimited to the experience of male-dominated formations. The influence of the CCCS contribution and the major studies that were produced by contributors to that volume has been immense, and any further serious study of subcultures should recognize that enduring contribution. The Readings by Sugden and Scraton in particular, in this section of the Reader, acknowledge the CCCS contribution.

A complementary way of analysing subcultures is found in the interesting work of US sociologist Robert A. Stebbins, who applied his concept of 'serious leisure', an arresting oxymoron, to amateur cultural performers for whom their leisure commitment was the main source of personal aspiration and fulfilment in life (see *Amateurs, Professionals and Serious Leisure*, Montreal, McGill/Queen's University Press, 1992). Watch the local cricket match where Sunday cricket still flourishes; the netball leagues in municipal facilities on a Saturday morning in suburban Australia; the dejected faces of the supporters at a World Cup match that their team is losing – the subcultural affiliation in such cases is a serious business indeed.

On lifestyle sports, see Belinda Wheaton's edited collection *Understanding Lifestyle Sports: Consumption, Identity and Difference* (London and New York, Routledge, 2004). This includes analyses and discussions of skateboarders' identities and of risk in adventure sports, surfing, climbing and rock-climbing, windsurfing, adventure racing and frisbee, using case studies showing the increasing prominence of lifestyle sports in a range of cross-cultural contexts.

Some argue that subcultural theory has had its day. Debates rage on whether, in an age of postmodern popular culture and postmodern sport, the concept of subculture is too descriptive, too limited. In looking at football fan subcultures, for instance, Steve Redhead has written of post-fandom in a period of 'accelerated culture mediatization' (*Post-Fandom and the Millennial Blues: The Transformation of Soccer Culture*, London and New York, Routledge, 1997: 1). For other examples of how new media have transformed the subcultural terrain see Part Eight, on 'Mediated and virtual subcultures' in Ken Gelder and Sarah Thornton's edited collection *The Subcultures Reader* (London and New York, Routledge, 1997). Though most of their examples in that section focus upon popular music, the themes they raise are widely applicable to the sport-cultural sphere. The Gelder/Thornton collection also provides access to valuable classic contributions to general subcultural study. Whatever the nuances in the debates about the concept and its scope, subcultural approaches are likely to continue to provide richly informing studies of the sporting world, and accounts of the ways in which sport cultures connect to the wider social world.

Peter Donnelly

TOWARD A DEFINITION OF SPORT SUBCULTURES

[. . .]

Subcultures are cultural units sharing much in common with the larger parent cultures, but also possessing identifiable cultural elements of their own. For example, one may conceive in a general sense of American culture, Canadian culture, or even Western culture, but within and between these larger cultures are numerous subcultural units. Subcultures, which may be based on either ascribed or achieved characteristics, are much more amenable to study than total cultures.

For the purposes of sport sociology, those subcultures based on achieved characteristics are of most interest. [. . .]

Characteristics of an achieved subculture

Achieved subcultures are defined by the following characteristics:

1   *Identifiable groups:* Subcultures are identifiable groups within a culture or across cultures.
2   *Composition:* Subcultures are collectivities of small groups and individuals.
3   *Cultural characteristics:* Their members employ similar artifacts and symbols, engage in similar types of behavior, and adhere to a set of norms and values specific to the subculture.
4   *Distinctive nature:* These cultural elements have a distinctive nature and are somewhat different from those of the culture(s) in which they exist.
5   *Life style and resources:* Achieved subcultures represent a major element in the life style and allocation of resources of their members.

6   *Scope and potential:* Achieved subcultures are formed around beliefs and behaviors that have scope and potential.
7   *Fulfillment of individual needs:* Subcultures are actively created and maintained by their members as long as they meet the needs of their members.
8   *Interaction and communication:* Subcultures are created and maintained by face-to-face interaction and other forms of communication between their members.

[. . .]

Life style and resources

A subculture may be pictured as a series of concentric circles, each representing one of five levels of membership. The model is based on the relationship between subculture and life style, and on the premise that total membership in a subculture may be seen as the dominant aspect of an individual's life style. Two additional variables are also relevant— commitment and information.

At the Primary level of membership, the core of the concentric circles, are found the principal members of a subculture. These are the individuals for whom the subculture is *the* dominant aspect of their life style; the individuals for whom the subculture represents a major commitment in terms of time, energy, money, friendships, information and other resources; and the individuals who are in possession of the most information regarding the meanings and ways of the subculture. Information is the basic currency of subcultures and core members are those individuals who create and modify the characteristics of a subculture. As such, they are often the best known members of the subculture.

Boundaries between the various levels of membership are usually diffuse, and at the Secondary level of membership are also found members for whom the subculture is the dominant aspect of their life style. Secondary or "auxiliary" level membership includes individuals who aspire to the Primary level, individuals who are fading from the Primary level, and a number of relatively static members. Auxiliary members commit a significant proportion of their resources to membership in the subculture, and are in possession of a great deal of the information that is peculiar to the subculture, but they rarely innovate, modify or create any aspect of the subculture.

At the Third level of membership are found what may be termed "associate members" for whom the subculture is an important but not dominant aspect of their life style. They commit a certain proportion of their resources to membership and possess enough of the subcultural information to be clearly recognized as members. But they adapt more slowly to new language, dress, techniques or other aspects of the meanings and ways of the subculture than Primary and Secondary level members because their information is more limited. And, as with the Secondary and Fourth levels of membership, the Third level will contain members who are moving toward or away from the core as well as static members.

Fourth level members may be termed 'marginal members' since the subculture represents a relatively minor aspect of their life style. Membership at this level will largely be made up of novices who are just beginning to learn the meanings and ways of the subculture, and retiring members whose knowledge of the meanings and ways is out-of-date. There is a low level of commitment and only partial recognition of Fourth level members as members by those belonging to the first three levels of membership.

Finally, at the Fifth level, are those individuals for whom the subculture cannot be considered as an aspect of their life style. They may be occasional participants with some knowledge of the subcultural meanings. [. . .]

The subculture of climbers

The subculture of climbers meets all of the criteria for being considered as a legitimate (achieved) subculture. Climbers are an identifiable sub-group of a number of national cultures who, at the first four levels of membership, identify strongly with their subculture. Members are able to identify each other by means of observation or the "credentialing" process (Donnelly, 1978) and maintain a level of subcultural integrity by employing these processes to distinguish members from non-members or "pseudo-members." The processes are also employed to determine mutual status within the subculture because, unlike the more institutionalized sports, climbing does not have a structured status system.

While members of the subculture learn accurately to identify other members during their period of socialization into the subculture, identification of climbers by non-climbers is likely to be much less precise. They are frequently deceived by novices and pseudo-climbers (i.e., non-climbers posing as climbers) because they are not in possession of the requisite information necessary to interpret cues. Novice climbers often rely on these miscues in their willingness to carry equipment, and particularly the rope, for more experienced climbers. They are aware that non-climbers are likely to identify them as the more experienced climber or the leader because they have the equipment, and they wish to be identified as such. But despite such mistakes in identification, it is important that non-climbers believe that the subculture exists, and that they are able to identify the members.

Formation of the subculture

The subculture of climbers originated in the Alps during the first half of the nineteenth century. At that time it was possible for scientists and tourists to hire local guides to take them to the summits of certain mountains. While climbing remained in the province of science and tourism, no subculture was possible since it is unlikely that a subculture would be based on scientific experiments requiring altitude or on a unique tourist experience. Similarly, to give a modern example, tourists who have visited the top of the Empire State Building are unlikely to form a subculture. The subculture began to emerge as a change in attitude occurred—as some of the scientists and tourists began to enjoy the experience of climbing, began to repeat the experience purely for pleasure, and began to make a commitment to the activity. The preconditions for subculture development were established, but because the individuals involved were uncertain of public reaction to any suggestion that they were climbing purely for pleasure, they maintained the guise of science and tourism for a time.

Eventually the need occurred for individuals who were climbing for pleasure to begin to interact. Differential interaction resulted from a need to share experiences and information with a wider circle of individuals than those immediately involved in a specific climb, and to share them with individuals of a similar background (i.e., other

British upper and upper-middle class individuals, as opposed to the guides who were peasants from Alpine villages). Differential interaction occurs in two different ways. The first is recruitment—socializing friends and acquaintances into climbing in order to share the experience with individuals with whom one enjoys interacting. The second is to make contact with other climbers beyond one's immediate circle of friends in order to share information and experiences, and to meet new climbing partners. Differential interaction also provided mutual affirmation and support for what was, at the time, a radically new and different type of behavior.

The need to interact in order to share experiences and information and to provide mutual affirmation, encouragement and support, provides the key to subculture formation. If the need to interact did not exist (as among tourists who have visited the top of the Empire State Building), no subculture would be formed because subcultures are actively created and maintained by their members as long as they meet the needs of their members. There appear to be three distinct phases of subculture development which McDougall (1979) has termed "informal affiliations," "incipient institutions," and "advanced institutional development." During the early stage of development subcultures expand only by direct recruitment of new members. This stage lasts while informal means of communication (word of mouth and letter) are feasible.

Once a critical mass is attained, the point at which informal means of communication cease to be efficient, the subculture will move into the second stage of development. While smaller groups continue to interact and recruit on a face-to-face basis, communication in the form of books, articles, newsletters and journals appears to link the various groups and keep them informed. In addition, the publications begin to reach a wider audience, thereby creating new recruits who seek contact with a member of the subculture.[1] A third stage of development occurs when the means of recruitment, socialization, and advancement within the subculture become formalized or institutionalized. The subculture of climbers has largely resisted this third stage, preferring the informality and individuality of the second stage. But there are signs that the subculture is moving into the third stage of development.

In order for the cycle of subculture development to occur the activity must be perceived to have scope and potential. While the object of climbing was to attain the summits of the major peaks in the Alps, its scope and potential was limited and it could have faded out as a fad or a craze once those summits were all attained. A change in emphasis after 1865 (when the Matterhorn—the last major summit in the Alps—was climbed) led to the development of the 'search for difficulty' and ensured the future of the subculture. The search for difficulty involved climbing major peaks in other important mountain ranges, seeking alternative routes to the summits of major peaks in the Alps, climbing minor peaks in the Alps, and developing rock climbing and snow and ice climbing in minor mountain areas as practice for the summer season in the Alps. The change was aided by the fairly strong subcultural foundations that had been laid in that the participants were not prepared to let the activity die out, and the search for difficulty vastly increased the scope and potential of climbing. Despite the fact that each generation of climbers until the present one has felt that it has achieved the ultimate in what was possible (thereby marking the end of the subculture because of the lack of future scope and potential), each subsequent generation has proved them wrong.

Characteristics of the subculture

The cultural characteristics of a subculture develop at two levels. At the Primary level are the beliefs and behavior directly associated with the subculture. In activity-based subcultures such as the subculture of climbers, the behavior exists before the development of the subculture, but once the subculture begins to form, the act of climbing and the knowledge associated with climbing become the unique possession of the subculture. The acts of recruitment and socializing new members into the subculture lead to a certain amount of standardization in teaching climbing skills and the knowledge necessary in order to climb safely. These become the primary level of cultural characteristics.

Ancillary knowledge and behavior not directly concerned with the act of climbing develop as a secondary level of cultural characteristics. A number of the secondary characteristics eventually become primary characteristics. For example, the development of new techniques, equipment and ethics (informal rules of climbing) initially appears at the secondary level. Individuals, usually at the core of the subculture, begin to experiment with new equipment, techniques and limitations on climbing. If these are considered to be advantageous or necessary to the development of climbing they become accepted by the whole subculture and thus become primary characteristics. Present-day novices are taught different techniques from their predecessors and learn a different code of ethics.

Secondary level characteristics that are not directly associated with the act of climbing, include the following: dress and language specific to the subculture (these characteristics tend to undergo frequent changes); status concerns—the development of stratification within the subculture and associated with the grading (difficulty) of climbs, the recording of ascents, lore concerning the difficulty of certain climbs and the ability of certain climbers, and the development of subcultural heroes; other concerns, including environmental and ethical concerns, access problems, the response to accidents and fatalities, and concern over external controls and growing institutionalization; and the social characteristics associated with non-climbing behavior. The latter category includes not only knowledge of social meeting places such as equipment stores, camp sites and bars, but also the ability to interact correctly with other climbers. The code of interaction involves not bragging, and downplaying one's achievements, not asking outright how good another climber is, not overtly displaying the fact that one is a climber (e.g., sitting in a bar with a climbing rope slung across one's shoulders can gain one a reputation as a 'poseur'), and by deferring to better climbers in route selection.

The combination of primary and secondary characteristics constitutes the normative domain of a subculture, and the exclusivity of a subculture is related to the distance of cultural norms from the subcultural norm. The normative behavior of, for example, tennis players may be extremely close to the cultural norm. Tennis is readily accessible, within the normative experience of a great many people, and widely understood because of widespread media coverage. Exclusivity exists only near the core of the subculture of tennis players among the highly skilled professionals and top class amateurs. The normative behavior of climbers appears to be more removed from the cultural norm. Climbing is not readily accessible (although it is becoming more so), not within the adult normative experience of many people (although many will have enjoyed scrambling on rocks and small cliffs as children), and not readily understood because of the lack of media coverage (another aspect that is beginning to change rapidly). Therefore, the subculture of climbers may be considered to be more exclusive than the subculture of tennis players, and many other more conventional sport subcultures, and the exclusivity has greater pay-offs in terms of identity.

The subculture of climbers is unique among sport subcultures. It may be considered as the first of the high risk sport subcultures, but it has resisted the conventional pattern of development and institutionalization. Climbing is a sport without rules. There are no ruling bodies and no officials to govern behavior within the sport. However, there are self-imposed limitations on climbers that take the form of a socially constructed and socially sanctioned code of ethics. The ethics developed because modern equipment and techniques have made the ascent of any mountain or cliff possible by almost any route. Ethics are created in order to maintain the sporting element in climbing and to ensure the possibility of failure. They set limitations on the type of equipment and techniques that may be employed on different types of climbs.

Climbing may now be considered to have reached the borderline between the second and third stages of subcultural development, and resistance to the third stage is apparent. Even the subculture of hang gliders, which shares many characteristics with the subculture of climbers as another high risk activity, has reached the third stage of development although it has been in existence for less than fifteen years. There is certification and formal assessment of skill levels, and there are ruling bodies and formal competitive meets. The lack of overt, rule-based, competition and disregard of negative publicity has been characteristic of climbers in non-Communist countries who have had neither the need nor the desire to institutionalize their activity. If one observation supercedes [sic] all others it is that climbers enjoy the mystique and the informality associated with climbing. It is an unconventional activity that appeals to individuals who wish to avoid the badges, certificates, rankings, rules and formality associated with other more conventional activities.

Note

1   Modern media, particularly television, also create new recruits.

References

Donnelly, P., "On Determining Another's Skill." Paper presented at the Annual Meeting of the Canadian Sociology and Anthropology Association, London, Ontario, May, 1978.
McDougall, A.A., *The Subculture of Hang Gliders: Social Organizations of a High Risk Sport.* Unpublished Master's thesis, University of Western Ontario, 1979.

John Sugden

THE EXPLOITATION OF DISADVANTAGE
The occupational sub-culture of the boxer

[. . .]

The setting

HIDDEN IN THE SHADOWS of the sky-scraping office blocks which dominate Insurance City's profile, there is a loosely connected ring of low-income housing estates, an area of ghetto-overspill, into which the poorest of the city's poor families have been drawn. Amongst them is the Burnt Oak housing project, a decaying, barrack-like settlement which typifies modern American urban poverty. Burnt Oak is a pocket of human subsistence, populated by blacks and hispanics and kept from the view of respectable middle America. Unemployment is high, with up to two-thirds of the adult population not involved in regular work. There are many single-parent families and the local economy tends to boom and slump with the cycle of welfare payments and food stamps. People with better jobs or better prospects simply do not come to, and certainly do not linger long in, the likes of Burnt Oak.

In the heart of the area stands an oblong block-house, somewhat larger than any of the warren of dwellings which surround it. This is the Burnt Oak Community Centre and, like its neighboring buildings, it is heavily daubed with multi-colored graffiti and in a poor state of repair. Most of the windows are either bricked or boarded up and the rest are screened with heavy, wire-mesh grills. Large sections of cement and plaster on the outer walls have crumbled away, leaving the building with a mottled and camouflaged appearance. This is not the place for community singing, amateur dramatics, bridge or other forms of family recreation and the city's housing development executive has given up trying to impose a formal timetable of rational community use.

In the daytime, when the heavy steel door which guards the entrance to the hall remains barred, local youngsters use the exterior of the building for a variety of improvised sporting activities. The broad and flat rear of the centre looks on to an open square, making an ideal backdrop for a variety of ball games. The meshed window grills, together with the drain pipes, make the north face of the building a tricky climb and the concrete canopy which overhangs the main door is an excellent highboard from which to execute acrobatic leaps into the tangle of shrubs and bushes below. If this becomes too exhausting, there are always the folk murals to add to and, as the daylight begins to fade, the sheltered doorway becomes a favorite gathering area for talking, horse play, listening to music and shouting comments to anyone who happens by.

In the early evening, a troubled caretaker pushes and curses his way through the crowded porch and unlocks the steel door. The inside of the community centre is little better than its exterior. With broken doors and window frames, flaking paintwork and crumbling plaster, the whole place is badly in need of renovation. A large hall, complete with stage and gallery, dominates the centre. Originally intended for public meetings and other forms of community entertainment, the seating has been removed to make way for the spontaneous local drama acted out in the chaotic game of basketball, which is the main event of each evening. There is no obvious structure to the game: no referees; no official teams; no formal scoring system; no out of bounds; no stoppages for fouls; and no time keeping. It appears to be every man for himself as players join and leave the game as they please and attack baskets at either end of the hall. A pass is rare and most of the time the ball is carried end to end through dazzling displays of dribbling, to arrive in or near the basket after an acrobatic lay-up or shot from an improbable angle and distance.

The atmosphere is thick and scented with a mix of cigarette smoke, reefer, alcohol and the more pungent odour of the poorly maintained washrooms. Around the edges of the game, on the stage and in the hallways, young men and women hang out, half watching the play, teasing and joking with each other and calling out to the players as they go hurtling by.

The conversations are necessarily loud, shouted above the pandemonium of the basketball game and competing with a confusion of rhythm, blasting out from the large portable tape recorders spread throughout the company. In a parallel social world, gangs of younger boys and girls dash in and out of the rubble-strewn rooms which open into the main hall, demonstrating their own spontaneous athleticism as they weave in and out of the basketball game, shrieking at one another and adding their own shrill commentary to the general discord.

The boxing club

Beneath the unrestrained youth culture surrounding the basketball game there is a more formally organised drama taking place. Each evening, in a basement room directly below the main hall, the members of the MBC (Memorial Boxing Club) gather to share in a different sort of ritual. Anybody wishing to enter the club has first, as we have seen, to thread a path through the throngs gathered in the entrance to the community centre, and turn across the crowded lobby before descending a short flight of stairs into the darkness below. At the foot of the stairs there is a reinforced wooden and steel door which is barred from within and it takes a sustained drumming to coincide with a lull in the activity taking place inside, before the bolts are drawn and the visitor is invited into a different world.

The club consists of a single, rectangular room, no larger than 30 feet by 35 feet. Immediately in front of the door, like a muted belfry, hang three large, worn, sail-cloth punch bags: heavy, heavier and heaviest. Flush to the near-side wall and sited ominously next to a set of scales, stands a small, electrically powered turkish bath. It is hard to imagine the need for such a device since the ceiling of the gymnasium is slung with the central heating pipes for the rooms above. Owing to a defective thermostat, they carry a volume of boiling water twenty-four hours a day, throughout the seasons, ensuring that the whole room heats up like one big sweat box. When it rains, a steady flow of sluggish grey water drains in from the streets above and gradually evaporates in the unnatural heat of the basement, exaggerating the sweated body heat of the boxers and making the atmosphere in the gym fetid and steamy.

One half of the club is dominated by an undersized boxing ring with loosely hanging ropes and a worn canvas, long since rendered threadbare by ten years of dancing feet and falling bodies. Surrounding the ring are a series of rough wooden benches; on these and on the hooks above are draped a mixture of sports gear, street clothes and the general bric-à-brac of the boxer's trade: gleaming red and black boxing gloves; high-waisted shorts; flashy robes; protective headgear and defensive equipment for the waistline and groin; a selection of mouth-guards; multicoloured boxing vests; jump ropes; hand wraps and several pairs of boxing boots. Every inch of wall space is covered with a colorful array of photographs, posters, magazine features and yellowing newsprint, blending to herald the past and present achievements of the club's own heroes and the feats of boxing's legendary champions.

The most important figure in the club, its manager and patron, J. 'Mack' Murphy, leans on a broom in the centre of the gymnasium, taking a break from a vigorous spell of sweeping which has left the bottoms of his $350 business suit speckled with mud and dust. In opposite corners of the ring, two dark-skinned youths wearing gloves and protective headgear move slowly from tiptoe to tiptoe, loosening and flexing their muscles and gulping in precious draughts of the warm and clammy air. One or two others lean across the ropes to give advice, tie a loose glove, offer a drink and generally act as seconds. Throughout the rest of the room, skinny boys, athletically-developed teenagers and powerfully-built young men sit on the benches or rest against the walls, likewise breathing heavily in competition for the scarce oxygen.

Apart from the fidgeting of the youths in the ring, the scene is relaxed and sedentary until the red second hand of the large clock on the wall sweeps around to twelve and, in the baritone voice and brisk manner of a Boston bar tender, Mack bellows, 'Time!'. The gymnasium [erupts] into life. The boxers in the ring gingerly leave their respective corners to begin an ever-diminishing circular dance around the faded canvas. As they draw close, there is a sudden change of tempo and direction as one or other of them darts inside and both fighters momentarily become engulfed in a blur of jabs, hooks, crosses and upper-cuts, before breaking away to recommence orbiting soft-shoe. The sporadic slaps and thuds of leather against flesh and muscle blend into the steadier beat of more measured energy and aggression being unleashed outside of the ring: muffled combinations as they are hammered into the heavy bags; the metronome rhythm of jump-ropes slapping off the concrete floor and the jarring rat-tat-tat-tat of the speed bag. Meanwhile, several young fighters manage to exhaust themselves without equipment, boxing shadows or stabbing and snorting at their own image reflected in a full length mirror which dominates one wall. In the remaining space, other club members balance on mildewed matting and execute an exhausting series of callisthenics: sit-ups; push-ups; sit-ups; squat-thrusts; sit-ups; toe-touching and inevitably back to the stomach hardening sit-ups.

Even the manager takes some aggressive sweeps with his broom, guiding a dark trickle of dust mixed with the evening rain water towards a small drain in the middle of the floor. At the same time he provides his audience, real or imaginary, with a loud and abrasive running commentary, shouting advice and insults to the fighers in the ring and encouragement and abuse to the characters working throughout the gymnasium. The whole performance builds to a frenzied physical climax and deafening crescendo as the second hand sweeps towards twelve for the third time and, without looking up, Mack interrupts his own diatribe once more to call, 'Time', bringing the scene to a gasping halt.

The athletes in the ring, the young men boxing their own shadows, the powerful men hammering the heavy bags, the manager in the $350 business suit and the physical structure of the basement gymnasium are at the core of an occupational subculture: a social process which connects the impoverished streets of Burnt Oak and the leisure practices of its inhabitants at the MBC to the multi million dollar atmosphere of the sports entertainment industry and Madison Square Garden. The roots of this process and the bedrock of the sub-culture are to be found in the everyday practices of boys and young men growing up in and around the streets of Burnt Oak. [. . .]

Being tough

While learning how to cope physically with a cycle of confrontation and challenge, the young men of Burnt Oak pick up a streetwise repertoire of attitudes and sentiments: a stoic, male code of honor and courage: a simmering 'machismo', requiring coolheadedness and resilience in the face of danger. These values, activated by a streak of machiavellian opportunism, invest social encounters with an atmosphere of ruthless self preservation and a sense of timing whereby 'to get in first' becomes the rule of thumb. As one fighter remarked, in order to get through the day in the ghetto, a youth has to be 'tough-tough', that is to be cool and calculating and able to stand up for himself. When translated into the ring, toughness and coolness blend to provide the foundations of 'a fighting heart', a quality much valued in a business built around the spectacle of giving and taking punishment.

The sports creed

The push of inner-city youth culture in the development of a boxing sub-culture is augmented by the sport's traditional affinity with the urban poor. As Edwards (1981) argues, sport in general takes on an enlarged significance in the ghetto. An overarching ideology, or sports creed, penetrates areas like Burnt Oak, stressing the all-American virtues of sport and its capacity to serve as an escalator to wealth and status for those who are effectively barred from other avenues of social mobility. Because only a tiny minority of the multitudes who try can ever make a decent living from professional sport, Edwards views this promise as false and damaging to the general development of black communities in America. This view is endorsed by Brown (1978) who views the massive commitment to sport by minorities as an indication of oppression and a buttress to racism, rather than a sign of integration or equality.

From the perspective of a young man growing up in a pocket of urban poverty such as Burnt Oak, the image of the black or [h]ispanic professional sport super-star is undoubtedly a powerful one. Other careers and educational opportunities tend not to be available. Even if they were, in a largely unsupervised adolescent world, given a choice between training to be a professional athlete or preparing for a career in the law or teaching, the vast majority of teenagers would opt for sport. Also, because the farm system of professional boxing is not tied up with survival in the education system, unlike American football, basketball and, to a certain extent, baseball, it is held in special regard by the children of the inner cities who traditionally underachieve at school. [. . .]

Conclusion

The centre stage of the basement gym is a boxing ring. The ring is in fact square and this is symbolic of the paradox around which the boxing sub-culture is constructed. The main, but largely unspoken, objectives of the club revolve around the production and training of professional fighters. For the most part, this is achieved through a framework of junior and amateur boxing. The exploitation of disadvantage which takes place is made to appear laudable by locating the boxing club within a pocket of urban poverty: a declared ideology of moral and social devleopment legitimates the club's targeting on the male youth of the urban poor, offering itself as a deterrent against juvenile delinquency and a series of related social ills. However, the states of mind and physical skills displayed by male youth in Burnt Oak, which the boxing club purports to deter, are precisely those attributes required by the professional boxing stable as its raw material. In this way, Mack, the manager, is in the same position as the preacher who is dependent upon the devil for the size of his congregation.

Once involved in the club, recruits share a process through which their streetwise qualities are honed and controlled in the service of professional boxing. Their volatile aggression and physical assertiveness, their courage and pride, their 'tough-toughness' are given new rhythms and disciplined around the timing of the professional ring. Their identities gradually become centred on the role of boxer and, as they mature through adolescence and become aware of a world beyond Burnt Oak, it is the light of the professional ring which is construed to offer them hope in the shadow of urban poverty.

Thus, through the intervention of Mack into the social life of Burnt Oak, the circle is squared. Through his agency, self improvement and character development are tied to an individual's progress through the various hurdles of a boxer's career. Going all the way to the top is appraised as a sign of moral transubstantiation, as well as commercial and occupational success. For a few, at least for a while, the squaring of the circle offers a genuine chance for self-fulfilment. But, to make one contender it takes the exploitation of many others who will not succeed. The boxing sub-culture takes them as boys off the streets and shows them a glimpse of the big time: a vision which can only reinforce a sense of failure when they find themselves without their gloves, without an education and without jobs, back amidst the poverty of Burnt Oak.

References

Brown, R. (1978), '"The Jock Trap": How the black athlete gets caught', in Straub, W. (ed.), *Sport Psychology*, Ithaca Movement, pp. 171–84.
Edwards, H. (1981), *The Sociology of Sport*, Homewood, Illinois, Dorsey Press.

Peter Marsh, Elisabeth Rosser and Rom Harré

LIFE ON THE TERRACES

[. . .]

INITIAL RESEARCH WORK at Oxford United's ground consisted mainly of making a large number of video-recordings of fans in the London Road End. These were made discreetly with the aid of a telephoto lens and with the full co-operation of the club. Early analysis of these tapes revealed a grouping pattern in the London Road End which remained quite static over a considerable period of time. Later reports from the fans themselves revealed that they were very aware of such groupings and were able to attribute a number of salient behavioural and social characteristics to them. The main groupings are shown in Figure 59.1.

Group A comprised boys mainly between the ages of 12 and 17. The mean age of a sample of thirty-four boys in this group who were to contribute greatly to the later stages of the research was 15.1 years. The most distinctive aspect of this group was the pattern of dress – the 'Aggro Outfit'. . . . The presence of flags, banners and emblems of allegiance was also very marked. When the newspapers and television hold forth about football hooligans it is usually to members of groups like this that they are referring. Not only are they the most identifiable group in terms of their appearance, but also in terms of the high level of activity among the group which is apparent even to the casual observer. They make the most noise – singing, chanting and shouting imprecations against the opposition fans – they run the most and they can represent a rather awesome spectacle to their rivals. For this reason we refer to this group as the *Rowdies*, rather than the media appellation of hooligans, for as we shall see, the label 'hooligan' carries special meaning within the soccer micro-culture.

Group C, in contrast to the Rowdies group, consisted of rather older boys and young men up to the age of about 25. The mean age of a sample of fourteen was 18.7. The style of dress within this group was unremarkable and differed little from that worn by

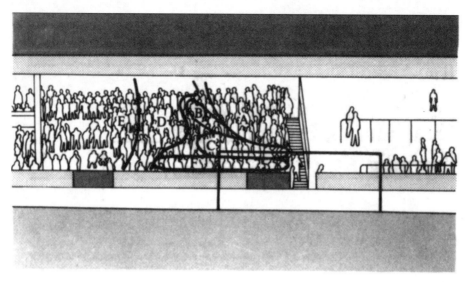

Figure 59.1

people of this age group in most social contexts. Nor were any banners or flags visible. In fact, members of this group would not be identifiable as football fans at all outside of the ground. Younger fans referred to this group as the 'Town Boys' and were clearly deferential to them.

Group B, lying between the Rowdies and the Town Boys on the right-hand side of the London Road Terrace, was a much less distinct group which varied in composition from game to game. One consistent characteristic, however, was the presence of a disproportionately high number of boys with a record of arrests, probation and care orders. Out of a total of seventeen boys from this group interviewed over a period of one year, no fewer than ten had been in trouble with the police for offences not connected with activities at football matches. This compares with an overall average of about 8 per cent for the London Road End as a whole.

Apart from this characteristic, the group seemed to have features of both the Rowdies and the Town Boys groups. The average age was about 16.5 and some of the more distinctive dress elements were present. The activity level, however, was much lower than that of the Rowdies and some of the fans in this group were only infrequent attenders at football matches.

Groups D and E were much less homogeneous than any of the others and effectively marked the edges of the active arena in the London Road End with which we are concerned. In the main, they both consisted of boys and young men who were rather more reluctant to join in the ritual chanting and singing and were even less keen to get mixed up in the aggro. The only difference between the groups was that those in E were generally a little older and a few females were also to be found there. Both groups contained a number of fans who were scathingly referred to as 'part-time' supporters by those in the Rowdies and the Town Boys groups. Among such part-timers were a few public-school boys playing at being football fans but failing really to understand what it was all about. The left-hand boundaries of these groups was totally undefined.

In group F were to be found young children (average age about 10) who sat, when they were not moved off by the police, on the wall in the front of the terrace, overlooking the dry moat. Their major occupation consisted of watching the antics of those at the back in the Rowdies group. Because of the age and inexperience of these boys, we refer to this group as the 'Novices'. Other fans simply call them little kids, but they are to be distinguished from other 'little kids' in other areas of the ground.

The pattern of grouping described here is probably unique to Oxford United's ground, but analogues of such groups appear to be present at all league club grounds – with the possible exception of some of the very small Fourth Division grounds. What is most striking about such groupings is that they provide for *careers* on the football terraces. The Novices, Rowdies and Town Boys provide a fairly linear hierarchy. Fans may aspire to progress through this hierarchy, and within each group certain role positions are open. The role positions enable demonstrations of character and worth, leading to the attainment of status, to take place within an ordered and rule-governed framework. 'Becoming somebody' on the terraces is a highly structured affair, and an understanding of this structure is the first step in rendering the apparently anomic behaviour at football matches intelligible.

Careers

In using the by no means original sociological concept of 'careers' we do not wish to imply that action of the part of soccer fans is somehow *determined* by a restricting set of institutional restraints. We would certainly want to use the term 'careers' in a rather different way from some criminologists who speak of 'delinquent careers' in which young deviants are inescapably forced along the path of community school, borstal and prison. Rather we see careers in a much less mechanistic way – as available structures in a youth culture for the establishment of self. At this point we are seeking only to explain the social frameworks which render certain actions intelligible, and we do not wish to imply causal links between social frames and social action. The extent to which fans will carve out careers for themselves on the terraces will, to a large extent, reflect their commitment to the soccer culture and to their immediate peer group. The greater the commitment, the more a fan has at stake. But, as we shall see, the richness of the soccer social world provides for commitments to be expressed in many different ways.

We have suggested that the Novices–Rowdies–Town Boys groups provide a distinct hierarchical framework for careers. Such a framework has more than a passing similarity with the career structure observed by Howard Parker in his study of young delinquents in Liverpool. Although his groups, 'Tiddlers', 'Ritz', and 'Boys', reflected increasing involvement in delinquent activities, they served the same function of enabling young people to achieve the sort of reputations and images denied them in mainstream society. On the football terrace, however, the other groups mentioned serve as side channels to the main career framework. They provide for the less committed who still wish to enjoy some of the fruits of the soccer culture. Groups D and E can certainly be seen to have this function. A fan who was totally uncommitted to the culture, who simply wanted to watch the match, would probably choose not to go into the London Road End at all but rather to one of the quieter side terraces. Group B, on the other hand, seems a little anomalous. To some extent we see members of this group as 'failures' in the career development process. They occupy fringe positions to both the Rowdies and Town Boys but have status in neither. Their high delinquency level also puts them at a further distance. But more will be said of this 'delinquent fringe' later.

In charting the progress of fans' careers, two types of data have been used. The first, and the easiest to collect, consisted of biographical material obtained from samples of fans in each of the groups, with special attention given to the Rowdies and Town Boys. The second type of data was obtained from close observation of the changes in the compositions of the groups and in the holders of clearly defined role positions within the groups. Both types of data, however, are problematic in that the whole structure within which careers are established changes over time. Physical locations of groups, for example, are very much influenced by changes in official club policies regarding the positioning of barriers and turnstiles. At one time, the Club went as far as refusing to allow juveniles a reduced entrance price for the London Road terrace but allowed them half price for other areas. The intention was clearly to deter younger fans from getting into what were viewed as 'trouble spots' and, at the same time, to improve the total gate money a little. (Oxford United is a very impecunious football club.) For a time fans were split. Many remained in the London Road End, but others established a new piece of territory at the other end of the ground where it was cheaper.

Other changes in structure developed more slowly, but although the pattern *looked* different over a period of a few years, analogues of the basic groups seem to have been present ever since the phenomenon of the contemporary football fan arose in the middle to late 1960s. There has always been the equivalent of the Novices group, for example, allowing entrance to the soccer microculture for any boy willing to learn the rules of being a fan. Similarly, the Rowdies have always made their presence felt – as any 'old-timer' will eagerly tell you. At one time the Rowdies were mainly Skinheads for whom the terraces were but one of a number of arenas for collective action. Those most dedicated to soccer culture became known as 'Terrace Terrors', but their successors are currently moving away from the baggy trouser and braces image that they fostered. Rowdies today often have quite elaborately coiffeured hairstyles – contrasting markedly with the heavy Dr Marten footwear which they still retain. Finally, Rowdies have always had the more manly and mature equivalent of the Town Boys to join once they had proved their worth and their masculinity.

In interpreting data, then, the gradual changes in the social framework at Oxford United have been taken into account. Note has also been taken of where particular groups have positioned themselves at various times in their evolution, and of the differences in style which have characterized such groups over time.

Two distinct aspects of the career process are to be distinguished. The first of these, the between-group *graduation* process, is concerned with movement from one group to another and with the fact that membership of a particular group affords a certain status in relation to members of other groups. The second, the within-group *development* process, is concerned with the establishment of certain well-defined status positions within each group and with the acquisition of the appropriate social knowledge to equip a member to 'carry off' the performances required by such roles. [. . .]

It would be a mistake to claim too much for the career structure or to suggest that the graduation process is a rigid one. There were many fans who drifted in and out of the groups without making any sequential progress at all and the groups to the left of the terrace always provided for an escape from the soccer 'rat race'. One should also remember that for a period of about three or four months in the summer the terraces are closed completely. Positions and statuses are held in abeyance until the following season until they can be redefined and re-established. It would also be a mistake to suggest that the rhetoric of careers is present as such in the everyday conceptual system of fans. In fact it is not – it is a gloss which we have imposed on the accounts and stories they have provided. But this does not mean that any undue 'stretching' of the data has taken place. On the contrary, some of the best evidence for the presence of a linear graduation process has come from the biographical material given by samples of fans in the three major groups.

In collecting biographical material fans were asked to give accounts of the ways in which they had come to their present position in the terraces and to indicate on a sketch plan of the London Road End, past, and projected future locations. They were also asked to describe the major characteristics of the groups in which they had found themselves at each point in their time on the terraces. Such material was collected in a variety of ways, ranging from formal tape-recorded interviews to casual discussions in and around the football ground.

Information from the Novices showed quite clearly that they all saw themselves as working towards a position at the back of the terrace. When asked why they would make such a move, most replied that

'It's more fun up there.'
'My mates are up there.'
'It's where everyone goes.'

Such a move, however, would rarely be made during the course of a particular season. Instead, the Novice would wait until the start of a new season and, having managed to buy some appropriate clothes, would then 'appear' at the back of the terrace. Observations of the composition of the groups over three seasons confirmed that this was what happened. Many of the Novices also expressed an ambition of 'getting in' with a particular group of individuals in the Rowdies group. From their lowly status they were still able to perceive who was who in the Rowdies hierarchy and which sub-units were worth making a try for. Many, of course, had brothers or older friends in the Rowdies group and had already had some experience of 'hanging around' with them in other social arenas away from the terraces.

Novices who had been in the London Road End for at least a good part of one season displayed quite a detailed acquisition of social knowledge which was appropriate to correct conduct in the Rowdies. Most seemed to know what one should do there in a variety of situations in order to be an accepted member. Those lacking this knowledge tended not to succeed in the first graduation step and usually were to be seen a year or so later in either group D or E.

All of the sample of Rowdies were able to plot very accurately where they had stood on the terraces over the last few years, who they had been with, and where they expected to be in the future. There was a steady shift over time from the edges of the group to positions near the central barrier and towards the front of the group. Most talked about an increasing feeling of security within the group. David, for example, had this to say about the three years he had been in the group:

'When I used to come here first of all I didn't know everybody like now. I knew some of the kids from school but not most of the City kids [he lived in Witney]. But that's the thing about football. Because you're all United fans you become part of something that's big. Its the atmosphere that does it – its electric. Other kids get to know who you are and what you're made of. If you show them you're not scared to really get in there you make a lot of friends. They know me now in the London Road and that's great. They know me and Paul and Steve 'cos we've been around here in this bit of the London Road for three seasons now and they know that we wouldn't let them down.'

With regard to their futures, most of the Rowdies felt that they would 'pack it all in' when they left school or when they were 17 or 18. By 'packing it in' they meant that they would stop wearing the uniform and 'tearing around' so much. Some felt that they had mellowed already and that they weren't so active as they had been before. A few said that they would like to be a 'Towny' or at least be able to command similar respect. None, however, felt that it was possible to 'join' the Town Boys in any simple sense. There was a feeling that the Town Boys were an arrogant elite and to actually get in with them you would probably have to do a lot of serious drinking in the Marlborough Arms. Living outside of Oxford would also be a serious handicap.

The origins of some of the Town Boys have already been mentioned. From the biographical material it was sometimes difficult to chart progress accurately because the groups from which they had graduated were no longer in existence. Many, for example, talked about the gangs they had once been involved in but these gangs, if they remained at all, were not, as one Town Boy said, 'a shadow of what they used to be'.

We have been suggesting that career structures can serve well in the explanation of social behaviour which might otherwise appear to have little rationality. The activities of a fan become intelligible if we can interpret them as being instrumental in establishing him in a particular role, or if such activities can be shown to be acceptable demonstrations of character and worth among his peers. This is not in any way to imply any moral or ethical stance on our part. The task is not one of excusing behaviour or of attributing condemnation to it – only one of rendering it explicable in terms of a revealed social order. We may not like what fans do and we may view aggro leaders and their like as unhappy reminders of a violent society in which we live. Similarly we may see the nutter as a pathetic figure who has to resort to self-humiliation in order to establish an identity for himself. But at the same time, we must pay careful attention to what such young people are actually *doing* rather than to the easy caricatures of them which some seem to prefer. Whilst we may feel that it is unfortunate that such career structures exist at all we might do well to examine our own mechanisms for getting ahead. In doing so, we might, to our discomfort, recognize that football fans are playing a very similar game to the rest of us in society.

Bibliography

Parker, H. (1974), *View from the Boys* (Newton Abbot, David & Charles).

Eric Dunning, Patrick Murphy and John Williams

ORDERED SEGMENTATION AND FOOTBALL HOOLIGAN VIOLENCE

O VER THE PAST DECADE much has been written on 'football hooliganism' and undoubtedly some advances have been made in our understanding of the phenomenon. However, a central aspect of football hooliganism which remains to be satisfactorily explained is the precise nature of hooligan confrontations. To date, the most prominent attempt to explain this dimension of the phenomenon is that of Peter Marsh and his colleagues at Oxford.[1] In contrast to popular and media perception which depicts such confrontations as anarchic and violent, the Oxford group point to their ordered and ritual character. They argue that, in the normal course of events, these ostensibly violent clashes do not involve serious violence or lead to serious injury. For our part, we remain unpersuaded of the empirical validity of this claim. It is our view that its inadequacy can be traced to the theoretical and methodological shortcomings which characterise the approach adopted by the Oxford group.

The theoretical perspective of Marsh *et al.* appears to emanate from an uneasy amalgam between a weak sociobiological hypothesis and a form of action-theory influenced by both phenomenological idealism and Saussurean structural linguistics. Such a theoretical melange has at least two negative consequences for their research. Firstly, it prevents them from penetrating to the social structural core within which occurs the generation of the norms and values expressed in football hooligan confrontations. Secondly, it impedes their appreciation of the fact that popular, media and official concern about football hooligan violence derives from the application of different social standards; standards which are dominant in society at large. Adherence to these prevailing standards tends to lead to an exaggeration of the violence involved in football hooliganism. In contradistinction the approach of March *et al.*, in our view, leads to an underestimation of the violence involved. [. . .]

. . . [F]ootball hooligan confrontations are occasions when norms expressive of a violent or aggressive masculine style are displayed. These norms are socially generated outside football, more particularly in structural contexts that approximate to the social configurations which the American sociologist Gerald D. Suttles, drawing on parallels discussed in the anthropological literature, has described by the term 'ordered segmentation'.[2] [. . .]

Central to the analysis offered by Marsh and his colleagues is a dichotomy between 'real violence' and 'rital aggressive action'. The former consists of "physical violence directed in an aggressive way towards another human being": the latter is 'symbolic' or 'metonymic', that is, it involves the display, but not the use, of weapons, and action sequences that are 'aborted' but which would if carried through, lead to injury or death. [. . .]

. . . [A]ccording to Marsh et al. the ritual encounters of football hooligans are self-regulating systems and they suggest that this in itself is a necessary condition for the maintenance of their ritual character. [. . .]

The Oxford group's reliance on an ethological model blinds them to the fact that, as far as human beings are concerned, it is wrong to conceptualize 'ritual violence' and 'serious violence' as mutually exclusive alternatives. While they correctly see that the arousal and control of human aggression are principally culturally determined and, hence, based primarily on social learning, they apparently fail to grasp the enormous range and complexity of forms of violent behaviour made possible by that fact. Thus, there are several intervening types and grades of violence between genocide and harmless aggressive rituals and, just because football hooligan confrontations are not as seriously violent as the former does not automatically mean that, in all cases, they are as innocuous as the latter. [. . .]

Although Marsh and his colleagues failed to undertake a systematic examination of the social background of hooligan fans, some of the interview data they obtained are sociologically revealing in this regard. For example, one of the Oxford United supporters reported in their study said of the neighbourhood from which he comes:

> If you live up on the Leys (a local housing estate) then you have to fight or else people piss you about and think you're a bit soft or something. At the football I try to keep out of it. If fans from Millwall or Villa or somewhere like that come down – causing trouble and that, then I'll have a go. I mean you can't let them come here and think they can do what they want. So I'm in there, making them run – that's what you're trying to do – and make them feel small. So you're round outside after the game and down the road after them. But I don't go round thumping people all the time. You don't have to. People know who you are.[3]

This suggests, firstly, that football hooligan confrontations are occasions when norms of masculinity that lay stress on physical toughness and ability to fight are expressed, and, secondly, that such norms are not simply specific to the football context. In fact, the norms associated with a 'violent masculine style' have been reported in a number of studies as typical of the socio-economically lowest sections of the working-class. The authors of a Sports Council/Social Science Research Council report even introduce Wolfgang and Feracutti's concept of the 'subculture of violence' in this connection, suggesting that "the core members of fan groups are drawn from communities where these values still hold", and that they are "re-affirmed and given a new location in football hooliganism".[4] Whilst we would strongly contend that football hooliganism is not solely a contemporary phenomenon, the position of the joint report as regards the core members of hooligan groups is broadly consistent with our own observations. It remains, however, to discuss three main points. First, how such masculinity norms compare with those that are dominant in society at large. Second, how they are socially generated. And, third, what it is that makes football an attractive locale for their expression. It is to these issues that we shall now address ourselves.

The norms expressed in the violent masculine style characteristic of the socio-economically lowest sections of the working-class appear to differ from those that are currently dominant in most social groups: firstly, in the degree of stress that is laid by the former on physical toughness, ability to fight, courage and group loyalty, and secondly in the fact that such attributes are not counterbalanced by an emphasis on scholastic attainment, achievement in the field of formal sport, or by a 'softer', more egalitarian attitude towards women. In addition, groups approximating gangs and fighting between such groups appear to be near universal characteristics of lower working-class life. In our view, this point is crucial, since the existence of a type of social configuration which persistently generates the formation of gangs and gang rivalry must loom large in any explanation of the sociogenesis of a violent masculine style. That is because fighting will be more common in social configurations of that sort and because, under such conditions, aggressiveness, ability to fight and gang loyalty are likely to be key determinants of masculine social status. Indeed, the formation of gangs and the existence of an emphasis on a violent masculine style appear, almost universally, to be interdependent, mutually reinforcing characteristics of lower working-class communities. The point is to explain why.

A useful clue in this connection is provided by Suttles' concept of 'ordered segmentation'. This is used to describe "the overall pattern (of an area) . . . where age, sex, ethnic and territorial units are fitted together . . . to create a larger structure". Suttles coins the term 'ordered segmentation' to describe this pattern in order to indicate two related features: "the orderly relationship between groups and the sequential order in which groups combine in instances of conflict and opposition". Cohen and Robins paint an essentially similar picture in their study of relationships on a North London working-class estate.[5] According to Suttles, the dominant unit of such a community is the single sex peer group or street corner gang. Such groups, he argues, seem "to develop quite logically out of a heavy emphasis on age grading, avoidance between the sexes, territorial unity and ethnic solidarity". However, he documents the regular occurrence of intra-ethnic conflict between such groups and acknowledges elsewhere that ethnic differentiation and solidarity are contingent rather than necessary factors in their formation. That is, age grading, sexual segregation and territorial unity appear to be the crucial *internal* structural determinants. [. . .]

. . . [A]dolescent gangs and a violent masculine style are correlatively generated by specific structural characteristics of lower working-class communities. It remains, however, to explain why football should form an attractive setting for gang fighting and the display of a violent masculine style. We should like to hypothesise that a combination of at least four attributes of the Association game serve to make its grounds into social enclaves that from a hooligan standpoint are virtually ideal. These are its traditional working-class associations, the fact that norms of masculinity are central to the game itself, its inherently oppositional character, and the fact that its teams represent social units that form easy foci of working-class identification. Let us expand briefly upon these themes.

The game of Association Football dates from the foundation of the Football Association in 1863. It was, at first, an exclusive activity of the upper and middle-classes but, starting in the 1870's, it began to spread down the social scale. As this happened, the game attracted a growing spectator following that consisted mainly of males but included a not insignificant female component. Two important consequences followed from this process: the game started to be commercialised and professionalised, and, at the same time, to become a source of growing 'public' (principally upper and middle-class) concern. This concern stemmed partly from the fact that commercialisation and the payment of players ran counter to the dominant amateur ethos, and partly from the occurrence of crowd disoderliness in various forms. Thus, as Hutchinson has written: "(R)iots, unruly behaviour, violence assault and vandalism appear to have been a well-established but not necessarily dominant pattern of crowd behaviour at football matches, at least from the 1870's."[6] Between them, professionalisation and the occurrence of crowd disorder deterred many spectators from the upper and middle-classes and many female spectators from attending matches, thus accelerating the process of proletarianisation and growing male predominance which began in the 1870's. Thus, from about the 1890's, although the game as such and the professional clubs remained controlled by personnel from sections of the upper and middle-classes, and although members of these classes continued to watch from the stands, the soccer terraces became essentially working-class male preserves.

Working-class men were – are – attracted to the game partly because it injected an element of spectacle and excitement into their otherwise routinised lives, and partly because norms of masculinity are intrinsic to it in the sense that soccer is basically a 'play-fight' in which masculine reputations are won or lost. Its inherently oppositional character, furthermore, means that it lends itself readily to group identification and the enhancement of in-group solidarity in opposition to a series of easily identifiable out-groups, the opposing team and its supporters. Its teams, moreover, are named representatives of the towns and cities where the industrial working-classes live.

The working-class associations of the game, the fact that it is a play-fight in which norms of masculinity are central, its inherently oppositional character and the fact that its teams represent social units that are easy foci of working-class identification, all serve to enhance the appeal of soccer to the male members of communities characterised by ordered segmentation. To the extent that some fans are drawn from communities of this type, football hooliganism in the form of fighting between rival gangs seems a more than likely result. That is, it brings regularly into their town and onto the terraces they regard as their preserve, the members of rival, equivalent social segments. For such groups, this territorial invasion is a challenge to fight which is magnified by the open display of insignia of identification with a rival collectivity, by the vocal support given to the rival team, and by the vocal denigration of the home team and its supporters. In fact, explicit challenges to fight are made both in the songs and chants of hooligan groups, and when their members encounter one another face-to-face.

Such groups appear to be interested in fighting one another as much as or more than they are in watching football. They seem to need the concrete excitement of a 'real' fight in order to enjoy themselves at football matches. Similarly, they seem to need to establish direct dominance over their rivals by fighting them and putting them to flight.

And when the visiting team brings only a small number of supporters from communities that are segmentally ordered, local divisions which have been temporarily submerged in the face of a common enemy may resurface to form the social basis of intra-fan group fighting.

As Hutchinson's study shows, such a pattern appears to have been associated with the game since its proletarianisation began in the 1870's. From about the late 1950's however, increasing affluence meant that younger fans were less restricted to their immediate localities. In growing numbers they were enabled, by the improved, cheap transport system and their capacity to pay, to travel regularly all over the country in support of their teams, thus spreading the incidence of violence and vandalism at matches. At the same time, their activities began to be reported regularly and in a sensationalised manner by television and the national press, a fact which probably contributed to the factual escalation of football hooligan violence which began around that time. That is, one of the effects of media coverage was to provide models for youths who wanted to 'get in on the action', and have their local reputations enhanced by an appearance in the press or on T.V. This kind of coverage also gave the phenomenon a pronounced national dimension, spreading the violent reputations of the most notorious fan groups across the country. If our hypothesis is correct, such coverage would have constituted an irresistible source of challenge to other young males from lower working-class communities characterised by ordered segmentation. Youths from such communities will traditionally have been the core groups engaging in fan disorder, and the main source of recruitment for the escalation which began in the 1960's. However, our hypothesis does not imply that all youths who engage in football hooligan violence come from segmentally structured communities, merely that such youths are the most *centrally* and *persistently* involved.

Notes

1   Peter Marsh, Elizabeth Rosser and Rom Harré, *The Rules of Disorder*, Routledge & Kegan Paul, London, 1978.
2   Gerald D. Suttles, *The Social Order of the Slum*, University of Chicago Press, Chicago, 1968; and *The Social Construction of Communities*, University of Chicago Press, Chicago, 1972.
3   *The Rules of Disorder*, p. 69.
4   Social Science Research Council/Sports Council, *Public Disorder and Sporting Events*, 1978, p. 40.
5   David Robins and Philip Cohen, *Knuckle Sandwich: Growing Up in the Working-Class City*, Penguin, Harmondsworth, 1978.
6   John Hutchinson, 'Some Aspects of Football Crowds Before 1914', paper delivered at the Society for the Study of Labour History Conference on "The Working-Class and Leisure", 1975. Hutchinson's paper is the thirteenth in the collection, which is available in the University of Sussex's Library and Brighton Reference Library.

Belinda Wheaton and Alan Tomlinson

THE CHANGING GENDER ORDER IN SPORT?
The case of windsurfing subcultures

[. . .]

The windsurfing subculture

WINDSURFING IS A SPORT WITH a short history, having only been in existence since the late 1960s. In common with many other new or postmodern sports (see Wheaton & Tomlinson, 1995) that have emerged over the past 20 years—such as snowboarding, skateboarding, in-line skating, and mountain biking—windsurfing portrays a public image that emphasizes individuality, freedom, hedonism, and an anticompetition ethos. These characteristics differentiate windsurfing from more traditional, rule-bound, competitive, and "masculinized" sport cultures, themselves marked by combative competition, aggression, courage, and toughness. As Whannel highlights: "To be good at sport is to be strong, virile and macho" (Whannel, 1983, pp. 28–29; cited in Tomlinson, 1997, p. 138); sport is central to being a "real man." Thus, although traditional competitive institutionalized sport in Britain has been a central site for the creation and reaffirmation of masculine identities and the exclusion/control of women, are gender relations in alternative sports cultures like windsurfing renegotiated or even reconstructed? Does windsurfing afford women (and "other" men) opportunities to construct identities and control their own lives through the embodied experience of sport? As Hargreaves (1994) has highlighted, there is a need for empirical studies of sport that examine the lived realities of men's and women's sporting experience, particularly how changing values are linked to evolving masculinities and femininities in sport. In the spirit of Hargreaves' challenge, in this article we draw upon ethnographic work on leisure sub-cultures, conducted during 1994–1996, which focused on a windsurfing community on the south coast of England. The day-to-day experiences of the women within the wind-surfing subculture are our primary focus.

The ethnography demonstrates that women's involvement in the subculture is heterogeneous and contradictory. The meaning of femininity and "being a woman" differs between groups of women in the subculture. For some of the women, windsurfing participation is an empowering experience and an important site for the creation and negotiation of a cultural identity that is detached from their roles as mothers and from their partners. For others, their lack of involvement and passivity conforms to traditional gender roles. [. . .]

Traditional gender roles: windsurfing widows

Discussing the sexist nature of surfing subcultures in Australia, Fiske (1989) and Pearson (1982) comment on the gender order, where females are nonsurfers, passive, their role that of "passengers, spectators" (Fiske, 1989, p. 60). Many women's marginal role in the windsurfing subculture conformed to traditional inactive feminine roles. The windsurfers' own argot for the girlfriends or wives who spend days at the beach and are involved in the lifestyle but never or hardly ever sail, is windsurfing widows. As Scraton asserts: "Sport is seen primarily as a male pursuit bound up with masculine values. Young women spectate, support and admire: they do not expect to participate" (1987, p. 176). Many windsurfing widows of all ages did not participate in the sport, yet their leisure revolved around supporting their male partners: accompanying their partners to the beach, watching them, and supplying them with food and drink. For example,

> One smartly dressed woman in her 40s was carrying her husband's mast across the car park, which I remember thinking was an odd sight. She looked so out of place on the beach wearing "city" clothes with a windsurfing mast resting on her shoulder. I said to her "it looks like you drew the short straw—he goes windsurfing and you are carrying his kit." She replied, "as long as I don't have to get wet, I am happy."
>
> (Field notes, December 1994)

The category of windsurfing widows encompassed a variety of women, including marginal windsurfers, girlfriends, groupies,[1] and girlies. Girlies were predominantly younger windsurfing widows, including less committed female windsurfers, who negotiated an identity in the mixed sex environment by emphasizing their heterosexual femininity, particularly through their clothing and feminized appearance; Connell (1987) calls this "emphasised femininity" (see also Flintoff, 1997).

Women windsurfers: "real women"

> Most women aren't that involved, because most women don't like the idea of getting cold. (Michael, male intermediate windsurfer)

Women windsurfers were expected to be, and mostly were, less proficient than the majority of the men. Contributing to this was the accepted convention that women were assessed by male standards of sporting prowess and commitment. Michael's statement (above) reflects a prevalent attitude, based on cultural stereotypes of femininity, that women dislike discomfort and are more interested in visual appearance than sport. Thus, women were less committed windsurfers than men (commitment was a key subcultural value). However, this stereotype of femininity, which predominates in explaining women windsurfers' behavior, does not acknowledge the diversity of experience and action, among both women and men, as highlighted by Stephanie, a core [in terms of subcultural membership] woman:

> I think you know there is that thing about "oh women won't windsurf because they don't like breaking their nails, or it's cold" and things like that. And a lot of women are like that. But I expect there's a good few men who only sail when it's warm as well. (Stephanie)

Despite the lack of expectation that women windsurfers would participate at the elite level, women could and did gain status in the subculture as active participants— albeit in distinctively gendered statuses. Yet paradoxically, as the observations of the female field-worker studying a male dominated subculture confirmed, the acceptance of women depended on their gaining status as windsurfers, not as women. One might assume that it would be hard for a female field-worker to gain full access to such a male-dominated sports culture. However, in many ways the field-worker's subcultural role was as "one of the lads." Due to her status in the subculture, based on windsurfing proficiency and commitment to the sport, she was able to participate in most sporting and social activities, including those of the core men. She had almost full access to the men's activities and conversations, including the time that their own partners were not welcome in the group.

Men's narratives also illustrate that women were respected as active sports women, and to a far greater extent than in other, more traditional sport cultures:

> Men's rugby despises women's rugby—it is seen as a joke. [But] yes, there is an awful lot of respect for the women who sail. . . . I have the greatest respect for Jane and Becky, as they are faster than I am. (Stephen, male racer)

Moreover, the women who were committed active sports participants and focused on their windsurfing gained more respect than the beach bunnies or girlies:

> The ones that are too feminine, or concentrate on being feminine have less rapport than those that get stuck in, and do the same things as men. So beach bunnies, nonsailors, definitely have less respect. (Scott)

Likewise, committed women windsurfers argued that the men differentiated them from the girlies and windsurfing widows:

> BW: Are we [windsurfing women] seen as a separate type of women by the men?
> Emma: Yes, . . . I definitely see that all the time. There are the women who windsurf who are actually thought of as a different breed by the men who windsurf, than the windsurfing widows, "the girlies." And the

> guys make comments about it . . . from more complimentary comments, like "you are the real women on the beach," to something more derogatory like "you are a man woman." We are thought of as different.

As Emma acknowledged, despite her status as a sport participant, her role as a woman windsurfer provoked a degree of ambiguity in the response of some men, highlighted by the term *man woman*. Feminists have argued that women who excel in sports that signify traditional male physicality are deemed masculine or at least not real women (Gilroy, 1989; Hargreaves, 1986).

Most men in the windsurfing culture, though, did not have that view, and real women themselves did not experience a sense of conflict between being a windsurfer and a woman.[2] Core women ardently denied that windsurfing was a masculine sphere or that they as women were excluded. As Caroline, an elite French woman windsurfer, contended, windsurfing was an environment where women could engage in a demanding physical activity and express their femininity:

> I think if there is a sport that is made for women, then surfing and windsurfing is it, it is a sport that gives a chance to the femininity to give an expression, and because it is in a natural surrounding, you don't need to be strong . . . you only need to be strong if you do crazy loops, but not for planning, using the harness, gybing. If you have feeling you don't need to be strong, you just need to adapt your equipment. (Caroline)

[. . .]

The centrality of leisure: privileging personal pleasure

> For women who have historically been defined by their ability to nurture others, a commitment to nurture themselves, through windsurfing, or any other means, is a radical departure from what is expected of them. (Woodward, 1996, p. 6)

Studies that have demonstrated women's lack of involvement in active (and public) leisure have illustrated how ideologies of femininity contribute to women putting their domestic responsibilities and families before themselves (see, e.g., Deem, 1987). Although in this research, family commitments did curtail many women's involvement, the committed women in this research prioritized active leisure (as well as their professional careers) over traditional nurturing roles, without experience of guilt.

A culture of commitment

> I don't want babies because I want more time, more money. I think they are a bit of a luxury if you are a windsurfer. You know I don't want to give up windsurfing to have them. (Stephanie)

For the core members who formed the focus of this ethnographic study, windsurfing was a "culture of commitment" (Tomlinson, 1993; Wheaton & Tomlinson, 1995). Windsurfing was central in their lives: It organized their leisure time, their work time, their choice of career, and where they lived. Committed windsurfers, like surfers, defined windsurfing as a lifestyle and tended to identify with the values and culture of the defined role of windsurfer (see Farmer, 1992).

> It's a lifestyle thing. I'm willing to spend my whole year and set up my life so that when that day happens I'm ready and I can go. (Mike Waltz, professional windsurfer)
>
> ("Southend-on-Sea," 1993, p. 70))

The core women windsurfers were dedicated, committed windsurfers, and in several cases more so than their male partners. As with dedicated men, their lifestyles were adapted to accommodate windsurfing. For example, Stephanie was an advanced windsurfer, more than 40 years old. She had been forced into part-time employment, but observed that despite her low income it gave her time and flexibility to windsurf. On several occasions, Stephanie confided in the researcher that her decision not to have children had been influenced by her desire to be able to keep windsurfing:

> I'm sailing whenever I can. . . . I never had kids because I thought it would interfere with my windsurfing too much. . . . In fact, I thought I was pregnant recently, which was one hell of a shock. . . . I don't think that it's possible to have kids and keep sailing seriously. Everyone I know that has had kids has ended up giving up the sailing, or at least it has made it very difficult. (Stephanie)

Many of the dedicated women windsurfers interviewed did not have children. They perceived that motherhood would severely limit their windsurfing. Due to the weather-dependent nature of windsurfing, it places great demands on the participants' time. Committed participants needed flexibility in their lives. Thus, it was the lack of flexibility that being a mother entailed that was deemed problematic. As Emma explained

> I'm sure it [windsurfing] has had a bearing on not wanting kids, well now— actually I can't see myself wanting kids . . . the flexibility, the need for flexibility in your life, that is a very strong need for me in my life. (Emma: core windsurfer, late 20s)

Multiple gender identities: real women's identity in leisure

The women whose experiences are the basis of the analysis provided in this article were advanced and expert recreational windsurfers, but they were not professionals: For them, windsurfing was no more than a "serious leisure activity" (Stebbins, 1992). Yet, their commitment to windsurfing was a disincentive to motherhood, a refusal—for the moment at least—of what has been perceived by some feminists as "the most ubiquitous element of the gender axis" (Bordo, 1990, p. 146). For many of these windsurfing women, their sense of gender identification was distinct from domesticity or their role of mother. As Bradley (1996) argues,

> There are many ways of being a woman . . . awareness of gender may involve traditional ways of displaying femininity, through domestic or caring roles, motherhood, or assertion of sexuality. Given that gender experience is so differently felt by women of different ethnic groups, age, religions, nationalities or sexual orientations, it is evident that there are multiple versions of womanhood. . . . Gender identities, then are multiple.
>
> (Bradley, 1996, p. 106)

Moreover, contrary to the windsurfing widows who felt they were identified as appendages—their partner's nonsignificant other—the committed women, such as Stephanie, claimed that windsurfing offered a sense of identity, or self, that was detached from other people, particularly any identification as a girlfriend or wife:

> Stephanie: It's having an identity as a person who is empowered to do their own thing, really or, you know, a professional identity is important, I think, too. I don't like the idea of being just someone's wife, or mother, or whatever. . . . It's given me a sense of identity, that is detached from other people.
> BW: Do you think windsurfing is quite important for you within that identity, of being who you want to be?
> Stephanie: It certainly has been—I am more relaxed about it now—I am not fussed in a way. I just like to do it—you know because it makes me feel good.
> BW: You used the word empowering—do you think that it is empowering?
> Stephanie: Yes—yes definitely, definitely—if I didn't windsurf I'd have to find some other thing that would do it for me. . . . So—yes it is empowering in a way. It's so kind of stamped into me as a person, that I don't even think of it as an identity thing, but it definitely is.

For real women, windsurfing gave them a sense of independence. As Sarah, a core woman, stated, "You should meet my friend Mary. She learnt to windsurf without a man. Actually, she is like me, she used it as a therapy to get away from men and relationships" (field notes, July 1995). Similarly, a recurring theme in the narratives of elite women windsurfers, interviewed in *Wahine* magazine, is how windsurfing was empowering, articulated by the women as the freedom, confidence, independence, and sense of self procured through the activity:

> It's a freedom thing. . . . you go out there and do what you want and express yourself in the way you want. . . . There is nobody to answer back to: it's just me and the water and the wind.
>
> (Jessica Crisp, *Wahine*, 1996, p. 14)

These women's dialogues emphasize that, as in the case of the women in this study, windsurfing was part of their feminine identity—their sense of self as a woman. Men, whether partners, husbands, or friends, did not play a part in their dialogues. The women stressed, above all, their independence:

I became more independent and proud of myself . . . being out there has helped me to open up and believe in myself. Windsurfing has been a sort of therapy.

(Angela Cochran, *Wahine*, 1996, p. 15)

To summarize, for core women, windsurfing participation was an important site for the creation and negotiation of a cultural identity, one that was detached from their roles as mothers and from their male partners. [. . .]

Acknowledgments

The fieldwork was conducted for Belinda Wheaton's doctoral study (Wheaton, 1997a). We are grateful to the U.K.'s Economic and Social Research Council, which awarded the research studentship on which the doctoral study was based (ESRC Postgraduate Grant Number ROO 429334379).

Notes

1   Groupies are young women who had limited interest in the windsurfing activity but actively participated in the social activities that accompanied the lifestyle.
2   Interviewees highlighted that the image of the sport—in the media and other cultural products, an image signifying sexual difference and that windsurfing was a macho activity—affects outsiders' perception of the sport.

References

Birkenfeld, K., & Moore, K. (1996). Windsurfing champions talk story. *Wahine*, 2, pp. 14–19.

Bordo, S. (1990). Reading the slender body. In M. Jacobus, E. Keller, & S. Shuttleworth (Eds.), *Body/Politics: Women and the discourses of science* (pp. 83–112). London: Routledge.

Bradley, H. (1996). *Fractured identities: Changing patterns of inequality*. Cambridge, MA: Polity.

Connell, R. (1987) *Gender and power*. Cambridge, UK: Polity.

Deem, R. (1987). The politics of women's leisure. In J. Horne, D. Jary, & A. Tomlinson (Eds.), *Sport, leisure and social relations* (Sociological Review Monograph 33, pp. 210–228). London: Routledge.

Farmer, R. (1992). Surfing: Motivations, values and culture. *Journal of Sports Behaviour, 15*(3), 241–257.

Fiske, J. (1989). *Reading the popular*. London: Unwin Hyman.

Flintoff, A. (1997). Learning and teaching in PE: A lesson in gender. In A. Tomlinson (Ed.), *Gender, sport and leisure: Continuities and challenges* (pp. 49–62). Aachen, Germany: Meyer & Meyer.

Gilroy, S. (1989). The EmBody-ment of power: Gender and physical activity. *Leisure Studies, 8*(2), 163–171.

Hargreaves, J. (1986). Where's the virtue? Where's the grace? A discussion of the social production of gender relations through sport. *Theory, Culture & Society, 3*(1), 109–121.

Hargreaves, J. (1994). *Sporting females: Critical issues in the history and sociology of women's sports*, London: Routledge.

Pearson, K. (1982). Conflict, stereotypes and masculinity in Australian and New Zealand surfing. *Australian and New Zealand Journal of Sociology, 18*(2), 117–135.

Scraton, S. (1987). "Boys muscle in where angels fear to tread": Girls' sub-cultures and physical activities. In J. Home, D. Jary, & A. Tomlinson (Eds.), *Sport, leisure and social relations* (Sociological Review Monograph 33, pp. 160–187). London: Routledge.

Southend on Sea, Essex (1993, December). *Boards,* 101, 70.

Stebbins, R. (1992). *Amateurs, professionals and serious leisure*. Montreal, Canada: McGill/Queen's University Press.

Tomlinson, A. (1993). Culture of commitment in leisure: Notes towards the understanding of a serious legacy. *World Leisure and Recreation, 35*(1), 6–9.

Tomlinson, A. (1997). Ideologies of physicality, masculinity and femininity: Comments on *Roy of the Rovers* and the women's fitness boom. In A. Tomlinson (Ed.), *Gender, sport and leisure: Continuities and challenges* (pp. 135–72). Aachen, Germany: Meyer & Meyer.

Whannel, G. (1983). *Blowing the whistle: The politics of sport*. London: Pluto Press.

Wheaton, B., & Tomlinson, A. (1995). *Consumer culture, gender identity and lifestyle in post-modern sports: Windsurfing subcultures*. Paper delivered at Shouts From the Street: Culture, Creativity and Change, the First Annual Conference for Popular Culture. Manchester, UK: Manchester Institute for Popular Culture, Manchester Metropolitan University.

Woodward, V. (1996) *Gybe round the buoys! – Femininity, feminism and windsurfing women.* Unpublished draft paper, March 1996.

Gill Clarke

OUTLAWS IN SPORT AND EDUCATION?

Exploring the sporting and education experiences of lesbian physical education teachers

[. . .]

Lesbian teachers

THE STORIES AND SCENARIOS that are portrayed in this paper emanate from research into the lives and lifestyles of lesbian physical education teachers. The vignettes are derived from questionnaires and in-depth interviews/conversations with 14 white able bodied women. The questionnaire was distributed in the summer of 1995 and focused on their sporting pastimes, and the interviews were conducted between 1993 and 1995, focusing on: lesbian identity, activities of teaching, interaction with pupils and relationships with colleagues. These areas for discussion grew out of my experiences as a 'good' lesbian teacher [that is, I think I passed fairly convincingly as (pseudo) hetero-sexual] and out of my reading of Pat Griffin's (1992) and Madiha Didi Khayatt's (1992) research into the lives of lesbian teachers in North America. The women in this research are aged between 23 and 47 and their teaching experience varies from just over one year to over 25 years. At the same time of the interviews they taught in a variety of schools from: mixed Comprehensives, Roman Catholic, Church of England to Independent schools. In order to preserve their anonymity, all the women were from the outset given a pseudonym; they were also informed in writing of the procedures that would be adopted to maintain this confidentiality and how the information was to be subsequently used. This was essential as none of the teachers were totally out about their sexuality in school. I make no claim here that these women are necessarily representative, indeed I believe there is no generic lesbian 'woman', nor am I arguing for any false universalism of their experiences.

Harassment and anti-lesbian comments

This research has provided considerable evidence of anti-lesbianism within sporting activities; many of the women had had direct experience of verbal abuse. For example, Barbara recalled how a supporter had shouted "lezz" when she'd scored a goal, Caroline described how other netballers had mocked the county coach who was a closet lesbian. Deb remembered how she had umpired a mixed tournament and drunken men had made anti-lesbian comments along the side line. Ethel recounted how on several occasions when training or preparing for a game when people had walked past the pitch they had made comments such as: "look at the lezzies, there must be a few lesbians out there". However, she also said that she had never experienced anti-lesbian comments on the pitch. Harriet revealed that the captain of the men's hockey 1st XI said that the majority of the men's teams didn't attend social functions because of the high proportion of lesbians in the women's teams who attend the social functions and are not discrete [sic] in displaying their sexual preferences. Lucy recollected that homophobic comments had been made when she was younger, but nothing had been directed at her personally, but she remembered being made aware that lesbian activity was not approved of by her peers at that time. Naomi had also heard homophobic comments, though again they had not been directed at her personally; at social events she had been aware of negative comments and jokes being made about lesbians.

What do these scenarios tell us about lesbian women in sport? I would contend that although these are the experiences of only a small group of lesbian women, they are not necessarily atypical. The sporting arena has historically been the prerogative of men and the training ground for the development of hegemonic masculinity, it was an area women entered at their peril. For the Victorians, a woman was a frail character, whose femininity and reproductive role was to be protected: sport was seen as potentially deleterious to her health and child bearing functions. This legacy has been a long time passing—as the history, for instance, of the Modern Olympics bears witness: women continue to compete in lesser numbers and in fewer events than men. For those women who dared to enter this male domain, their performances were subject to the scrutiny of the male gaze, which in many cases trivialised their performances and also suggested that where they performed well then they must be some sort of freak of nature, indeed possibly a man! What I am trying to do in this historical snapshot is to illustrate that women in sport have not had an easy time, and this has been particularly so in those sports that have traditionally not been seen as stereotypically feminine. Thus whilst it may be socially acceptable for a woman to be a successful gymnast/ice skater, it may be less acceptable for her to be a successful rugby/football player. The former carry an acceptable (heterosexual) feminine image whereas the latter do not: that is, the image is not feminine, therefore it must be masculine, and hence women engaged in such sport must be masculine and therefore lesbian. As Messner and Sabo (1994, p. 110) comment:

> Lesbianism is thus recast by heterosexist culture as an emulation of masculinity.
> In contrast male homosexuality is considered a negation of masculinity.

It is perhaps no wonder that many women would feel uncomfortable playing in sports in an environment where their sexuality is likely to be questioned. Therefore, it is not surprising that many women within sport seek to distance themselves from any possible suggestion of or association with lesbianism through the making and confirming of their femininity and their (hetero)sexuality overtly visible. Thus we often see evidence of what has been described as hyperfemininity (see Felshin, 1974 and Lenskyj, 1994)—that is, the wearing of make-up, jewellery and other adornments to proclaim a so called 'normal sexuality'. This is not confined to the way that the athlete presents herself: it is also replicated by the way that the media portray women in sport; very often it is not their performance that is commented on but the fact that they are a mother, wife and so on. Reference is also frequently made to what they are wearing and to their appearance. As sport is now big global business, the media moguls and sponsors are increasingly all powerful in determining what constitutes an acceptable, marketable image and product. It is clear from the female sporting superstars who have made it that heterosexuality and hyperfemininity are the order of the day. When Martina Navratilova came out as a lesbian she lost millions of dollars in sponsorship and endorsements. By this stage of her career arguably she could afford to, but how many others could? Most then choose to keep their lesbianism carefully hidden for fear of their careers being destroyed.

The world of sport as has been illustrated in this paper is not a welcoming one for lesbian participants. What is also disturbing is that within this sporting world we have largely failed to discuss and address the difficulties that lesbian women face within this arena. There have been some notable exceptions to this claim (see for example the work of Griffin and Lenskyj). But whilst we remain silent, I would argue that we continue to perpetuate and reinforce myths, stereotypes and fears about lesbian women in sport. Through these practices we deny them the right to participate openly and fully in sport. This right to participate should be a basic human right and not something reserved for the heterosexual majority.

It is apparent that at all levels of sporting participation, lesbian women feel the need to remain invisible if they are to survive. This has also meant that when they were aware of homophobia or anti-lesbianism they did not always feel able to challenge it. Harriet indicated how she was:

> . . . resigned to being put down, and am not always surprised or deeply hurt by it when I hear it now—if you hear it often enough you begin to believe it and accept it.

It's OK as long as we don't draw attention to ourselves

This final section seeks to analyse the lesbian sporting experience. What is evident from the vignettes portrayed here is that sport for these lesbian women seems in general to be another arena where they still cannot be themselves. Or perhaps they can be, but at a price—so as long as they don't draw attention to themselves, and know how to be a 'good' lesbian in sport they are 'tolerated'. But as we saw previously, the moment they reveal their sexual preferences they are not welcome. Harriet described how 'a member of our women's first eleven wished to transfer to the other major club in [the town] but they have discussed her transfer and have denied it, on the grounds of her sexuality'. Clearly, this woman would seem not to be a 'good' lesbian. Others too have found their sporting progress curtailed when they failed to display heterosexual credentials. As Lenskyj (1992, p. 28) states:

. . . there is ample evidence that the women in sport and physical education who are lesbian have to survive in a most inhospitable climate because of the pervasiveness of homophobia, which often takes the form of discriminatory hiring and firing practices.

Indeed, Gert Hekma's (1994) research into the discrimination that Dutch lesbian women and gay men experience in organised sports in Holland was pointedly titled: '*Als ze maar niet provoceren*' ('If they don't provoke'), a comment that was made by two sports clubs who said that they had no problems with gays and lesbians as long as they did not provoke. This would appear to mean that it's OK to be a lesbian woman or a gay man in sport, but don't make it obvious, don't do anything that will give your (homo) sexuality away. It is clear from this small scale research that these women make every attempt not to make their sexuality obvious: for instance, only two of the 14 women interviewed were totally out in their sports; the remainder were either out to only a small group of friends or to none of their team mates. For those who were out to a certain extent, this was not necessarily a positive experience. Harriet revealed that her team mates at hockey found out more by mistake than design and that she wished they didn't know. She made it clear that she has no intention of telling those with whom she plays other sports. Further to this, she commented:

> When some of my married, heterosexual friends at hockey found out about me, they quickly changed their way of relating to me and talking to me. I felt let down obviously and, but I also felt 'dirty', like I really was doing something wrong.

This feeling 'dirty' reveals still further the power of the lesbian label to intimidate women regardless of their sexuality. However, it should not be thought from these examples that lesbian women are powerless—rather, by virtue of living a lesbian existence they are challenging compulsory heterosexuality. And for some women, the lesbian label is a powerful source of unity and pride. Lenskyj (1994, p. 365) reveals how:

> Lesbian sporting leagues organized on feminist principles provide one example of the potential for sport to be reclaimed . . . (and) to include the celebration of female physicality and sexuality.

Though Lenskyj is referring to sporting leagues in North America, it should be noted that there are a number of lesbian sporting teams [in England], for example: 'Dynamo dykes' (volleyball), 'South London Studs' (football), 'The London Amazons' (softball) and 'London Hiking Dykes' (a lesbian walking group). What is indicated, though, by Harriet is that lesbianism is something to be feared and avoided in case of contamination. Again in the light of such views, it is no wonder that many women may fear even entry to the sports field. I find these fears and phobias in some ways paradoxical, and in many ways confusing. If LeVay's (see Vines, 1992, p. 2) claims are accepted—that homosexuals are *born*, not *made*, since sexual orientation is established in the womb as a result of the action of hormones on the brain of the developing foetus—how then can anybody become 'contaminated'? They've either already 'got' it (that is lesbianism), or they haven't! What

I also find interesting, yet troubling, is the scrutiny with which we interrogate lesbianism, yet in the main heterosexuality has largely escaped this. (A notable exception is the work by Sue Wilkinson and Celia Kitzinger.) In reflecting on Harriet's words, what is perhaps most disturbing is how she is led to feel, that it is something wrong and dirty that she is engaged in. In the light of her feelings and the actions of homophobic heterosexuals it is no wonder that the suicide rate for young lesbians and gays is higher than for other groups. Are lesbian women really so dangerous? Certainly there seems to be a belief that we are, that we threaten the cultural norms of heterosexuality and patriarchal power, and that other women need to be protected from us. Where, might we ask, is the evidence that supports these views?

The impact of the events described above is abundantly clear; to be out is a personal risk, the costs of which many understandably are not prepared to face. These concerns, I would argue, serve to keep most sporting lesbians invisible and silent and preserves the privileging of the hegemonic heterosexual order.

It should be noted, though, that this is not the case for all lesbian women: some have found the space within sport to occupy the ground that they wish—as Yvonne Zipter (1988) clearly describes in 'Diamond's are a dyke's best friend'. And more latterly this is illustrated by Susan Fox Rogers (1994) in 'Sportsdykes: stories from on and off the field'. Both books celebrate and explore the lesbian sports experience. Zipter writes about dykes in softball, '. . . assessing its [softball] place and function in our community nation-wide, why most of us love it (but some of us don't), its origins, foibles, and pitfalls' (Zipter, 1988: p. 14). Rogers, on the other hand, has edited a rather eclectic collection of articles which range 'From serious investigative journalism to works of lyrical fiction, the life of the "girl jock" is vividly revealed . . .' (Rogers, 1994: Front book jacket).

Before closing, I want to return to some of the findings of Hekma's (1994) research since they are relevant to my own findings. Perhaps most telling was his conclusion that discrimination against lesbians and gay men occurs regularly in organised sport. Though the women interviewed for this research had not all been subject to homophobic comments and so on, the majority thought that it was common in sport. Hekma found that the most common form of abuse took that of verbal comments. This too was evidenced by the women in this study, and took the form of remarks made by spectators or passers by. Some of the women were also subjected to anti-lesbian comments from their team-mates rather than the opposition. By way of contrast, some of the women had had no experience of homophobia—but I would suggest that this may be associated with the fact that they are so deeply hidden in the closet, that nobody knows they are there.

In conclusion, it can be seen how—for this group of women—a lesbian existence is perceived as somewhat perilous. The conservative world of education and in particular physical education makes for a precarious existence for lesbian teachers. To survive requires that these teachers are able to at least 'pass' as heterosexual and to cover their lesbian tracks. The sporting world for these women is not so dissimilar to that of education. The homophobia and heterosexism faced by these women has led them in the main to continue to conceal their lesbian idenitity. What is manifest from both these worlds is the power of the lesbian label to force women into narrowly prescribed gender roles; it is a power that few feel able to confront and challenge. Until we remove the power and stigma of the lesbian label, little is likely to change.

References

Felshin, J. (1974) 'The dialectic of woman and sport', in E.W. Gerber, J. Felshin, P. Berlin and W. Wyrick (eds) *The American woman in sport*. USA: Addison-Wesley Publishing Company, pp. 179–279.

Griffin, P. (1992) 'From hiding out to coming out: Empowering lesbian and gay educators', in K.M. Harbeck (ed.) *Coming out of the classroom closet: gay and lesbian students, teachers, and curricula*. New York: Harrington Park Press.

Hekma, G. (1994) *Als ze maar niet provoceren. Discriminatie van homoseksuele mannen en lesbische vrouwen in de georganiseerde sport*. Amsterdam: Het Spinhuis.

Khayatt, M.D. (1992) *Lesbian teachers: An invisible presence*. USA: State University of New York Press.

Kitzinger, C. (1987) *The social construction of lesbianism*. London: Sage Publications.

Lenskyj, H. (1992) 'Unsafe at home base: Women's experiences of sexual harassment in university sport and physical education', *Women in Sport and Physical Activity Journal*, Vol. 1, No. 1, Spring: pp. 19–33.

—— (1994) 'Sexuality and femininity in sport contexts: Issues and alternatives', *Journal of Sport and Social Issues*, November, Vol. 18, No. 4: pp. 357–376.

Messner, M. and Sabo, D. (1994) *Sex, violence and power in sports: rethinking masculinity*. USA: The Crossing Press.

Rogers, S.F. (ed.) (1994) *Sportsdykes: Stories from on and off the field*. New York: St Martin's Press.

Vines, G. (1992) 'Obscure origins of desire', *New Scientist*, 28 November, No. 3: pp. 2–8.

Wilkinson, S. and Kitzinger, C. (eds) (1993) *Heterosexuality: A feminism and psychology reader*. London: Sage Publications Ltd.

Zipter, Y. (1988) *Diamonds are a dyke's best friend*. USA: Firebrand Books.

Becky Beal

DISQUALIFYING THE OFFICIAL

An exploration of social resistance through
the subculture of skateboarding

[. . .]

OBSERVATION, PARTICIPANT–OBSERVATION, AND semi-structured in-depth interviews were used to investigate the subculture of skateboarding in northeastern Colorado. In June 1989, I began observing skateboarders in Jamestown and Welton, Colorado, at popular skateboard spots (e.g., parking lots, university pedestrian walkways), skateboard shops, and a locally sponsored skateboard exhibition.[1] The first subjects were friends' children and employees at skateboard shops. I introduced myself to others while they were skateboarding on the streets and asked if I could talk with them. They call themselves "skaters," and the act of skateboarding they call "skating." I met one of the female skaters (a rarity) through mutual membership in a local feminist group. I used snowball sampling, so these initial contacts led to many others. Over a 2-year period (1990–1992), I talked with 41 skaters, two skateboard shop owners, and several parents and siblings.

Of the 41 skateboarders, 24 were interviewed more than once, and 6 of those became my best informants since we formed a closer relationship that fostered more trust. This relationship consisted of continual feedback by which they checked the reliability of the information I was gathering and I, in turn, could continually refine and ask more pertinent questions. In addition, I spent over 100 hours observing skateboarders, many of whom I did not interview (they were observed in public spaces). Only 4 of the 41 participants were female. In addition, all were Anglo except for two Hispanic males. The average age of those participating was 16, but ages ranged from 10 to 25 years. The participants had skateboarded for an average of 4 years, but the range of their participation was from 1 to 15 years. My most consistent contacts were from two friendship groups of skaters. The group from Jamestown was younger (ages 10–16 years) and included two Hispanic males; the second group was from Welton, was older (ages 15–25 years), and included a female.

Once the study was complete, the analysis of their subculture was presented to approximately one third of the participants. Their comments served to reaffirm and fine-tune my conclusions. They especially wanted me to note their heterogeneity: Although they shared many norms and values, they did not share all values, and, therefore, just because they were all skateboarders did not mean that they were all good friends or were as homogenous as they are often portrayed in the media.

It is necessary to elaborate on the above comment because there was not a ubiquitous skateboard subculture. In fact, a variety of subgroups skateboarded. The skateboarders demonstrated a continuum of hegemonic to counterhegemonic behavior ranging from those who embraced the corporate bureaucratic form of the activity to those who resisted it. This study focused on those who resisted, but even within that group resistance was demonstrated through a variety of styles.

Skaters described those involved in corporate bureaucratic skating as "rats," individuals who bought the commercially produced paraphernalia and plastered all their belongings with corporate logos. But, more distinctively, they were defined as kids who aspired to skate professionally. These skaters frequently sought sponsorship, which was pursued, for example, by creating videotapes of their skating and sending them to different corporations. In addition, these skaters entered competitions with the intent of seeking the needed recognition for sponsorship.

Another group of skaters resisted the professionalization of their physical activity. They defined skateboarding as a way of living and rejected any notions that the activity should be used a way of making a living. As a consequence, their relationship with commercially produced products was carefully negotiated. For example, they bought commercially produced skateboards (many tried to make their own but claimed they were not as good) but decorated their boards with their own symbols, which, in a few cases, included poetry. They no longer bought the "right" clothes or commercially produced stickers; instead they were more innovative with their clothing and often created their own stickers, leaving samples displayed where they skated. The styles of expression varied greatly, and the skaters classified each by an association with a type of music or style of skating. Some of these included "hippies," "punks," "skinheads," "fratboys," "old timers" (e.g., those who did slalom skating as opposed to "trick" skating).

Although the skaters recognized and labeled their internal differences, they also acknowledged their own subcultural status. The following letter to a newspaper editor from a teenage skater illustrates this self-definition:

> Skaters have a completely different culture from the norms of the world's society. We dress differently, we have our own language, use our own slang, and live by our own rules. People feel threatened by foreign attitudes. Everyone has his own views on different types of society and their own stereotypes. . . . Please stop viewing us [as] a totally negative race of people. The few people who have come up and watched us skate and spoken to us know that we are nice, educated, and intelligent.
>
> (Maeda, 1991, p. 17)

This study concentrates on those who opposed the professionalization of their activity. [. . .]

Daily practices of resistance

Scott (1990) argues that most resistances occur on a subtle and daily basis, what he refers to as "hidden transcripts." These hidden resistances occur in a language that only the subculture can understand, and it is within subordinate subcultures that a logic of resistance is created. This subtle, covert, and daily resistance is what Scott calls "infrapolitics," because it is the grounding on which overt political movements stand. As Scott states, "Each of the forms of disguised resistance, of infrapolitics, is the silent partner of a loud form of public resistance. Thus, piecemeal squatting is the infrapolitical equivalent of an open land invasion: both are aimed at resisting the appropriation of land" (1990, p. 199). The overt resistance to the [Colorado Skateboard Association] CSA-sponsored contest exemplifies the skaters' behaviors and the values of their typical daily interactions; it illuminates the infrapolitics of the subculture of skateboarding. One parallel that can be drawn between the amateur contest and the skateboarders' daily practices is the opposition to elite competition.

De-emphasizing elite competition

Especially significant for the subculture of skateboarders was creating a physical activity in which most people could participate, and to encourage participation they de-emphasized the role of competition. In fact, the skaters were very outspoken against competition when used as a means to an elite and exclusive status. All the skaters were asked to describe the characteristics of a skater, and I phrased the question as, "What makes a skater cool or uncool?" Overwhelmingly, they responded that an uncool skater was competitive and exclusive, while a cool skater was supportive and did not show off. Charles blatantly stated, "Skaters who are assholes are people who brag or skate to compete." Within the subculture there were status differences, but they were not established through competition with others. There were two criteria for high status: One must be highly skilled and creative, and one must not use those skills to belittle others. Although there was skill differentiation, it was not used to promote exclusivity from others because status is gained primarily by promoting cooperation and inclusion. Brian, a young teenager from Welton, commented on his attitude:

> Well, we don't, we're not like competitive, like saying, "I can ollie [a specific skater stunt] higher than you so get away from me," and stuff like that. We're like, we just want to do a few things people are doing, and skaters help out skaters . . . and if I were to ask a good skater like some people I skate with, like Brad Jones, he's the best skater I know in Welton. If I asked him, he would like give me tips and stuff, you know, on how to do it, and that's just how we do it, we want to show other people how to skate.

My 2 years of observing skaters' interactions confirms these statements. Skaters were very supportive of each other. It was common to see skaters who on their first meeting encouraged each other, gave tips, and laughed at their own mistakes. When I frequented the various privately owned skateboard parks, I often saw the more skilled skaters help the newcomers, especially in the skill of dropping into a half-pipe ramp. A half-pipe is a ramp that literally looks like piping cut in half lengthwise. The basic technique is to roll back and forth in the half-pipe. The next step is to "drop in" to the half-pipe. To drop in is to start skating from the top edge of the ramp. The skater situates the board so that only the two back wheels are touching the edge of the ramp while most of the board is extended in the air and toward the middle of the ramp. The skater places most of his or her weight on the back wheels, and then to drop in, the skater rolls the back wheels over the edge and drops the nose of the board into ramp, which starts the rolling motion down the side of the ramp. Dropping in is nerve-racking, and, therefore, emotional support along with technical tips is very helpful.

The support given by skaters is in marked contrast to what is common in more traditional sports being played by young people. For example, one day I passed a public tennis court where two preadolescent boys were playing tennis. They were yelling at each other about how good they were and announcing how they were going to "kick" the other one's "ass." Unlike the skaters, they did not show each other tips on playing, support the good shots of the other, or laugh at each other. The significant aspect of this observation was the response I received when describing this incident to a group of skaters in Welton. One of the skaters, Doug, commented, "That's because we don't skate against somebody we skate with them."

The implications of competition for friendships and self-esteem were concerns addressed by many skaters. They felt that the lack of competition enhanced opportunities for friendship and self-esteem, while sport that emphasized competition was a difficult place to make friendships and foster self-esteem. For example, Eric stated, "In skating you're only responsible for you. If you mess up, you won't mess up the whole team, [you're] not going to lose friends over messing up in skating. . . . If you're the worst one on the baseball team others give you shit [and that] makes you feel bad. In skating if you are bad, no one makes you feel bad about that."

The vast majority of skaters explicitly differentiated skateboarding from mainstream competitive sport. Pamela, a 19-year-old skater, made this comparison:

> Soccer is a lot of pressure . . . you have to be as good if not better than everybody else, you have to be, otherwise you don't get to play at all. Skating you can't do that. You just have to push yourself harder and harder. Swimming is just sort of there, you get timed, now for me you go against the clock. Now when you skate you don't go against anything, you just skate. That's what it is.

In addition, skaters often mocked the mainstream emphasis on competition and winning. For example, Jeff and Philip shared with me an inside joke about dancing that they used to ridicule the pervasiveness of competition and the win-at-all-costs attitude. Philip, Jeff's younger brother, plays in a local rock-and-roll band, and the type of music they play usually involves a "pit," which is a dance space where dancing is rough and there is plenty of physical contact. Philip: "And this guy walks by and he's wearing a Yankees hat and a Jordan T-shirt, a typical jock looking guy, and he walks by and he leans over to his friend and he goes, 'Man, is there going to be a pit here, if there is, dude, I'm going to win.'" Both Philip and Jeff laughed, and Jeff commented, "The object is not to win." The general de-emphasis on competition indicates that the meaning of skating is based on other standards, and for skaters I talked with, these were values that promoted the participants' control of the activity.

Participant control

Another parallel that can be drawn between the skateboarders' behavior at the amateur contest and their daily practices was the resistance to an elite or authoritarian-controlled sport, because in both situations the participants controlled their activity. The popular practice of skateboarding does not use rules, referees, coaches, or organized contests. As Paul claimed, "[You] don't need uniforms, and no coach to tell you what to do and how to do it." Kathleen, an 18-year-old skater, added, "No referees, no penalties, no set plays. You can do it anywhere and there is not a lot of training." This lack of formal structure led to a very flexible environment where the participants not only controlled their own activity but engaged in creative endeavors. Often, the skaters created and named their own games and tricks. The two brothers, Jeff and Philip, discussed this flexible and creative emphasis. Philip: "Skateboarding is young and there are so many new tricks people are doing, it's not like baseball where all the rules have been set down." Jeff: "Well, there are no rules to skating." Philip: "When was the last time someone invented something in baseball."

Most of the skating I observed was not bound by rules; rather, it tested the physical limits and imagination of the participants. Generally, a skating session involved practicing certain techniques, finding fun places to skate, and trying to do new tricks on the new obstacles found. When skaters created more organized forms of games, they were the ones who made the rules. Different groups of skaters created different games, but all incorporated some form of risk-taking challenges. Variations of follow-the-leader were common. Generally, a skater led a line of others through various tricks and obstacles; when the leader made a mistake (couldn't "land" a trick), then he or she went to the back of the line and the next person was the new leader.

The lack of elite control was reflected in the lack of elite standards; as Craig commented, "There is no such thing as a perfect '10' for a trick." Skaters challenged themselves at whatever level of skill they had. Effort and participation were essential to skating, not achieving some elite defined objective. These values and the ability to control their physical activity often led to feelings of empowerment. Many skaters expressed this simply by stating that they loved to learn new tricks and enjoyed seeing themselves improve. Grace, a 21-year-old skater, drew the connection more explicitly by discussing how she did not want skating to become a sport because she did not want practices, coaches, and specific tricks to learn: "For who's to say what trick is better? I like to do stuff that feels cool, that gives me butterflies in my stomach."

The participants' desire to control their activity was reflected in their statements about having more flexibility to be creative or to be expressive through skateboarding. For example, James, a college freshman, wrote this in an English paper: "Skating to me is all about having a good time. This is easy to do while skating since to me skating is relaxing. Skating is all based on being creative with the mind. This starts with the mind, then goes to the tricks I do." Doug claimed,

> A lot of them [skaters] are really involved with artistic endeavors, are very artistic. You can see the parallel; it's kind of a freedom of expression that skating is. How do you express yourself playing football, playing basketball? When you're skating it's, basically skating reflects your mood at the time and how you're skating, what you are doing, you know, it's definitely, you know, a way to express yourself.

Although it can be argued that one can express oneself through organized sport, what Doug argued for was the degree of flexibility in that expression. In a separate interview, Mark explicitly addressed this by claiming that different styles of skating are accepted, whereas he felt one would be kicked off the football team for having a different style. Grace's statement about her frustration over the commercialization of skating epitomizes these concerns: "[Skateboarding] is a symbol of freedom that can't be cut up and processed and sold, [one] can't do that with freedom."

The opposition of skateboarders to the CSA-sponsored contest is an overt and explicit example of the daily and more subtle resistance to the values and norms associated with corporate bureaucracies and corporate bureaucratic sport. Skateboarders resisted the values and norms of elite competition, and authority as expert, by encouraging cooperation and creating a participant-controlled activity.

Note

1   The names of cities and participants have been changed to help ensure the anonymity of the participants.

References

Maeda, K. (1991, October). Rights for skateboarders [Letter to the editor]. *Windsor Beacon*, p. 17.
Scott, J. (1990). *Domination and the arts of resistance: Hidden transcripts*. New Haven, CT: Yale University Press.

Acknowledgments

I would like to thank George Sage and Peter Donnelly for their insightful suggestions. I would also like to acknowledge James Beal and the anonymous reviewers for their helpful comments. I appreciate the support of the Department of Physical Education in Northern Illinois University during the writing of this manuscript.

Author note

At the time of publication, the National Skateboard Association was defunct.

Alan M. Klein

PUMPING IRONY
Crisis and contradiction in bodybuilding

[. . .]

THIS, AND SUBSEQUENT CHAPTERS, examine bodybuilding subculture as being resistant at the same instant it is being contained. The concept of "frontstage and backstage" behaviors that play essential roles in symbolic interaction is helpful in this regard.[1] John Fiske[2] also makes much of this function of subculture and style in his various studies, but whereas much of sociological analysis tends to see subculture as either normative or deviant, the present study sees it as straddling the fence. On the one hand, many of the contradictory claims and practices in bodybuilding subculture make more sense once we put them into this historical setting, which sees the practices and stylistic meanings it creates as slightly out-of-sync responses to earlier issues (both individual and social). On the other hand, the subculture tries desperately to take advantage of current possibilities for legitimation. [. . .]

"Resolve," determination (as in, "he'll die trying"), and discipline (as in the training and work that this and other individuals put into their programs) are all "testimony" to the self-reliant man or woman. A variation of the "rugged individualist" is pervasive in bodybuilding subculture. Structurally, the sport lends itself nicely to it by being an individualized sport that does not require performance (rather, just the perception of having performed; i.e., posing on a platform). A subculture and sport that revolve around such a structure tend to select for individuals who reflect it. The preceding chapter pointed out the degree of individualism found among men as they narrated their tendencies toward social isolation:

> I began developing a strong sense of individuality quite early. I was always turned off by team sports. I just didn't like being part of a team and the back-slapping and groupie sweating and all that. I would rather spend my time in my basement pumping iron.

No less a personage than Arnold Schwarzenegger has expressed the same sentiments:

> . . . by the time I was thirteen team sports no longer satisfied me. I was already off on an individual trip. I disliked it when we won a game and I didn't get personal recognition. The only time I felt rewarded was when I was singled out as being best. I decided to try some individual sports.[3]

[. . .]

Enhancing heterosexuality versus hustling

Heterosexuality is formally enshrined in the pages of bodybuilding magazines and other institutional proceedings. Each issue abounds with attractive color photos (in both articles and ads) of men and women together, staged to appear as if they are enjoying each other. The articles in *Muscle and Fitness* cover such topics as: "What Body Parts Women Love to Look At," "Are You Sexy and Satisfied?" and "Are Hard Bodies Sexier?" In the early 1980s, the cover of *Muscle and Fitness* changed from the obligatory male in full muscle pose to the male "adorned" with a female. These women are shown as adjuncts to the male, who is still the center of the cover. Although there are women bodybuilders who should grace the covers because of their size and symmetry, it is always a man who is centrally featured on the cover. The male is shown slightly tensed, with well-oiled body (to show muscularity), whereas the woman, always less muscular, is posed to fit around him. By the late 1980s, other bodybuilding magazines began to follow suit. The idea behind this is threefold: the ideologues of the sport want more cultural acceptance, they want to attract a broader audience for their products, and the idea behind much of a man's search for being more attractive to women and generally feeling better about himself is locked up in building a better body. Joe Weider stated his position straightforwardly in one interview: "Ya know? In every age, the women, they always go for the guy with muscles, the bodybuilder. They [the women] never go for the studious guy."

Bodybuilding has always accepted this position. Dating back to the nineteenth century strong man and physique contests,[4] men's view has centered on virility and strength as characteristics most cherished by women. The Charles Atlas ads that ran in men's magazines and children's comic books underscored this premise. The Atlas ad scenario (in cartoon form) begins with a thin young man out to impress the woman of his dreams. While at the ocean, they run into an imposing beach bully who insults the skinny would-be suitor and "kicks sand in his face." The latter has virtually become a cliché in our society, synonymous with being emasculated. Miraculously, the young woman is impressed with the bully's display, or so we are led to believe. An ad in his comic book leaps out at our unlikely hero. It promises metamorphosis, a new, secure, and permanent grip on his masculinity: a big body. Weeks later he avenges himself on the bully by outsizing him and meting out physical punishment. In the course of this ludicrous scenario, the woman is again impressed and content to become the prize in a minidrama between two males.

For all this heterosexual posturing, bodybuilding has long existed under a cloud of suspicion. Be it the inordinate vanity on the part of men (a quasi violation of blue-collar mores), the preoccupation with scantily clad, hairless-bodied men prancing about on stage, or an awareness that for all that size (form) there is little function behind body-building, many outsiders see bodybuilders as sexually suspect. The views of vanity, male quasi nudity, and nontraditional activities, usually carried out with other men, may all be legitimate in bodybuilding subculture, but until recently, mainstream society tended to associate this with its clichéd sense of homosexuality.

I will only mention the institution of hustling here because it directly contradicts the convention of bodybuilding as enhanced heterosexuality. Hustling, the selling of sex or sexuality by bodybuilders to gay men, is fairly common on the West Coast. Estimates provided to me by members of the core communities at four West Coast gyms with a preponderance of competitors ranged from 30 percent to 80 percent. I will only briefly outline hustling. [. . .]

The institution of hustling is complexly instituted and ambivalently perceived by people within the subculture of bodybuilding. Selling sex to a gay male is, at most times, distinguished from being gay. As one nonhustler put it, "You gotta do what you gotta do to get by in this [bodybuilding] world." However, being accused of hustling carries with it the connotation that one "might be" gay. The stigma is as much the result of the sex act . . . as of the fact that gay men are able to purchase the bodybuilder. In a typical statement by a member of Olympic Gym, hustling is equated with being gay:

> We have always had gays in the gym . . . when I first went to Olympic Gym, it was then that I learned from Bob, who was hustling, that all the pros were. And that really opened my eyes. But now, there is such a heavy gay concentration in the gym.

Hustling is also understood to be an economic survival strategy in a subculture where competitors are hard-pressed to find the time and money to train. For many of the young men who go to the West Coast and expect to be instantly successful at bodybuilding, the initial indifference they encounter can be jolting. Few come prepared emotionally or with enough money to pay the dues demanded by the sport or lifestyle of competitive bodybuilding. In short order, bodybuilding novices find themselves strapped financially and bereft of emotional support to continue their quest for a title. Getting a "regular" job would cut into the demanding training schedule that, at times, includes twice daily workouts, yet many simply hold down such jobs. Others, more determined to circumvent the job-workout dilemma, find hustling a means to an end. The entrance into the world of hustling is mostly a transitional phase of one's career. Since it is seen as an economic strategy, once the bodybuilder begins to earn money from the sport he is likely to leave hustling.

The period of time spent in hustling brings pressures to bear on the hustler. First, he must deal with the construction of a set of patterned behaviors that are at odds with what he has been socialized to believe is the norm; i.e., he must be able to commit homosexual acts. The stress that such a dichotomy engenders is significant. Second, the hustler must behave carefully within the subculture of bodybuilding to deflect suspicion of his activity, all the while using segments of the bodybuilding community to carry out the hustling activities. Although institutionally fostered and widely practiced, hustling can, at times, create major crises for its practitioners. This happens because of the breakdown of compartmentalization that is necessary to maintain.

Conclusion

Thus, hustling contradicts enhanced heterosexuality, and, like health and individual body-building successes, constitutes a set of cultural fictions. Nevertheless, it is important to understand the nature and function of their presence. On one level the discrepancies discussed here constitute a cultural lag that exists between the public's current perception of bodybuilding and the view that bodybuilding ideologues think they have in the public's eye. Decades of neglect and/or denigration by the currents of popular culture and sport have made the bodybuilding community somewhat insular. The tendency for the bodybuilding community has been to pursue respectability via traditional notions of culture. According to this, respect comes from perceiving bodybuilding as a repository of wholesomeness (e.g., health, vigor, heterosexuality, conventions of virility and femininity illustrative of American values of hard work and clean living). Bodybuilding ideologues such as the Weider brothers would be inclined to think of bodybuilding as projecting such an image. However, the more claustrophobic elements of bodybuilding point to an insular world where success is limited and jealously guarded. The new economic opportunities now available have not yet registered in all sectors of the subculture; hence the discrepancy may reflect the gap between the emerging cultural mainstream view of bodybuilding with the historical one (in which normative transgressions were necessary). Even though more economic opportunities exist, most competitors still need to make use of hustling to get by. The increased money in the sport represents legitimacy to the moguls and so they seek to conceal the presence of hustling even more.

Another view of the discrepancy between ideal and real culture patterns may have to do with what Goffman[5] and others[6] have called "frontstage" versus "backstage" behavior. This view sees no lag between what was necessary in the past and the current norms, but rather, that ideal-real discrepancies are structurally normal, pertaining to the requirements of different segments of the population. The performance of funeral directors in their dealings with bereaved family members is designed to reflect back to them notions that they, as grieving people, need to have (i.e., that their loved one is "asleep" in a "peaceful" and dignified state). These are cultural as well as individual needs that are being "dramaturgically" met.[7] Backstage, there is a very different set of behaviors, behaviors that would in fact be seen (by the bereaved) as a violation of that cultural fiction. Funeral workers need a personal and social distance from the "objects" of their attention as well, and they fashion it by violating the frontstage decorum. There is an additional layer to this discrepant behavior that is cultural. Cultural (normative) expectations are being mirrored back to the audience in such performances.[8] We need to view these contradictions as the presentation of normative myths back to a population that requires periodic assurances of the continued presence of these cultural myths, even if they are in fact only partially realistic. Bodybuilding is particularly appropriate as one subculture (there are many) that is more than willing to perform this function. Like the child that never quite received the unconditional love of a parent, bodybuilding has, in part, leapt to the defense of these fictions to fulfill its craving for cultural affection that it never got.

Much of the discrepancy we have noted for bodybuilding can be interpreted along these lines as well. The desirability of propping up culturally normative fictions (for example, individualism, upward mobility and work, heterosexuality and muscularity, and health as self-mastery) are ways of gaining acceptability, as well as economic success.

To accomplish this successfully, an ideal projection of these attributes is demanded. The violation of these fictions reflects the more multi-layered reality of human society, which includes complexity and opposition, rather than one-dimensionality. Hence, the complex interaction of self-reliance and social dependence is altered to reflect our societal predisposition toward individualism. The healthy nature of normal bodybuilding is betrayed in trying to oversell the idea of health and a robust body, since ours is a society forever trying to outdo itself. Finally, the appeal of the human male form to other men is denied in an effort to short-circuit the homophobia that exists more widely in this country than any other.[9] In subsequent chapters these issues will be more completely dealt with, but suffice it to say that our cultural demands are in large part responsible for twisting behaviors in certain ways; and in bodybuilding, this cultural demand has found an insecure subculture emotionally starved for cultural acceptance that is willing to provide overblown representations of these cultural myths.

Notes

1   Erving Goffman, *Behavior in Public Places* (Garden City, NY: Doubleday Books, 1959).
2   John Fiske, *Reading the Popular* (Boston, MA: Unwin Hyman, 1989).
3   Arnold Schwarzenegger and Kent Hall, *Arnold: The Education of a Bodybuilder* (New York: Simon and Schuster, 1977), 14.
4   Harvey Green, *Fit for America: Fitness, Sport and American Society* (New York: Pantheon, 1986).
5   Erving Goffman, *The Presentation of Self in Everyday Life* (New York: Doubleday, 1959).
6   For instance, Ronny Turner and Charles Edgley, "Death as Theatre: A Dramaturgical Analysis," *Sociology and Social Research: An International Quarterly* 60(4) (1989): 377–91.
7   Ibid.
8   See the work of Victor Turner, e.g., *The Anthropology of Performance* (New York: PAJ Publications, 1988).
9   Arlo Karlen, *Sexuality and Homosexuality* (New York: W.W. Norton, 1972); Walter Williams, *The Spirit in the Flesh* (Boston, MA: Beacon Press, 1990).

Consumption and spectacle

INTRODUCTION

W E CAN PLAY SPORT and we can watch sport (live or via the media). Sport can provide a source for sociable human interactions, for idle gossip, for serious political purposes. Obviously the *meanings* of sport vary. It does not mean the same thing at the recreational level, where pleasure and well-being are the motivations of the Sunday afternoon cyclist, as it does at the top competitive level where a combination of sun-drenched French mountains and lethal cocktails of performance-enhancing drugs can have fatal consequences for the ambitious Tour de France competitor. The links between these levels are not always easily identifiable, but it is beyond doubt that sport has a hold on many as a form of consumption (both doing and watching); and that the power of sport as a high-profile cultural event (mega-event or spectacle) has been increasingly acknowledged in the global media and international tourist market. In this final section of the Reader the selections have been chosen in order to show the importance of these themes. Several of the Readings are theoretically demanding – the first three are from the works of French scholars working in particular theoretical traditions – and in this sense they act as signposts to a more advanced level of study of sport's social significance and cultural meanings.

The first Reading is from the inestimably influential study *Distinction: A Social Critique of the Judgement of Taste*, London, Routledge & Kegan Paul, 1986), by **Pierre Bourdieu**, and comprises excerpts from his chapter on 'the habitus and the space of lifestyles'. *Habitus* is a critical concept here. It has been claimed that the concept was first used in 1939 by Norbert Elias (John Scott and Gordon Marshall, *A Dictionary of Sociology*, Oxford, Oxford University Press, 2005: 260), and that French anthropologist Marcel Mauss first used the term in 1935 (see J.J. MacAloon, 'A Preparatory Note to

Pierre Bourdieu's "Program for a Sociology of Sport"', *Sociology of Sport Journal*, Vol. 5, No. 2: 150). Whatever its lineage, the term has been applied widely in sport studies, most often as derived from Bourdieu. Grant Jarvie writes: 'Habitus as a specific notion refers to the acquired patterns of thought, behaviour and taste which are said to constitute the link between social structures and social practices' (*Sport, Culture and Society: An Introduction*, London and New York, Routledge, 2006: 222), and uses the concept in his discussion of the sporting body and its social context. It is such a widely used term that it is worth quoting Bourdieu himself, from a footnote in *Distinction*, where he refers to habitus as a system of dispositions:

> It expresses first the *result of an organizing action*, with a meaning close to that of words such as structure; it also designates a way of being, a habitual state (especially of the body) and, in particular, a *predisposition, tendency, propensity or inclination*.
>
> (p. 562, footnote 2)

Bourdieu is dense reading at times, but worth the effort as he provides flashes of illumination on habitus and sporting lifestyles (so widely bound up with class habitus), and the way in which sport is a form of bounded consumer choice. How does what Bourdieu calls the 'leanings of their habitus' affect consumers' so-called choices in the marketplace of sporting practices?

Spectacle is a term with much currency in everyday parlance. Sport commentators in the media use the term as a shorthand, or even a lazy substitute for fuller description or analysis: 'the race was quite some spectacle'; 'the sterile teams robbed the crowd of the spectacle'. In such usage the nature of the spectacle goes largely unquestioned. The word itself stems from Latin and French roots, terms for 'looking', and has given us the word for the cultural or sport-based onlooker, the spectator. Questions relating to sporting spectacle should therefore ask what it is that draws people to look, what it is that holds their attention. What are the motives of those who stage the spectacle? In sport studies the term has been used too often without these questions in mind, often drawing upon French theorist and revolutionary writer **Guy Debord**'s polemical study *The Society of the Spectacle*. Debord (1931–94), in this second Reading, links the spectacle to the commodity. He gives no specific examples of the spectacle, let alone sporting cases. But look at what he says about the 'economy's triumph as an independent power' – what sporting examples might be better understood with an application of Debord's thinking? What limitations can you see in the Debord argument?

French social theorist **Jean Baudrillard** has been described by Richard Giulianotti as 'probably the most provocative and controversial social theorist of the last twenty years' ('The Fate of Hyperreality: Jean Baudrillard and the Sociology of Sport', in Richard Giulianotti's edited collection *Sport and Modern Social Theorists*, Basingstoke, Palgrave Macmillan, 2004: 225). Though famous for his proposition that in the age of media and virtual technology football could soon take place in empty stadiums, Baudrillard also wrote more generally on the nature of consumer society. This second Reading invites the reader to think of leisure and associated sports and bodily practices as forms of display. Reading this selection from the early Baudrillard, consider whether there are any limits on the reach of consumerism.

The fourth and fifth Readings are from the work of US-based writers. Media and communications scholar **Herbert I. Schiller** (1919–2000) takes sport as an example of his more general theory that corporate interests are dictating more and more the nature of public culture and social life, and what he calls 'public expression'. If this sounds like an exaggeration, look more closely at the staging of some large-scale sporting events and the profile of the corporate sponsors. **Christopher Lasch** (1932–94), historian, social critic and cultural commentator, argues that sport has been degraded, in an age of business and entertainment. What is it, in Lasch's view, that sport has lost? What is his notion of the spectacle of sport?

One way in which the spectacle of sport is consumed is through the bestowal of rewards upon the sport performer, not just as admired athlete and competitor, but as celebrity and superstar, a kind of cultural icon of the age. This is a process that got under way long before the global profile of a Michael Jordan or the worldwide marketing of a David Beckham. In the sixth Reading **Leo Lowenthal** (1990–1993), the German-born US-based scholar and last surviving member of the Frankfurt School of critical theorists, traces, in the first known study of its kind, the shift from idols of production to what he calls idols of consumption. What is it about sport that makes it so prominent a part of this emerging culture of celebration of popular figures?

The seventh Reading is by the late US-born scientist and radical critic **Paul Hoch**. The subtitle to the book from which this Reading is taken, 'A prison of measured time', says everything about his analytical perspective. What is sport's contribution to society, from this perspective? Hoch has faced much criticism for his left-wing revolutionary analysis of sport, condemning sport, in Marxist terms, as the opiate of the masses, or a form of false consciousness. Christopher Lasch catalogues Hoch's radical clichés, noting that Hoch's book provides such clichés 'in richest profusion and expresses them in the purest revolutionary jargon' (*The Culture of Narcissism*: 263). But is there not something clear-cut about Hoch's analysis of how sport is produced and consumed; and was there something prescient, too, about his commentary on drugs and sport performance?

The final Reading in the section takes a particular case – ice hockey in its commercial form in Canada – and discusses the political and economic forces that have transformed the game. Canadian academics **Richard Gruneau** and **David Whitson** bring together the themes of consumption and spectacle when they show 'how much additional consumer activity can be generated around . . . sporting entertainments', and discuss the implications of this for local community and tourist markets. What is the nature, and what are the effects, of the 'global consumerism' that Gruneau and Whitson argue is central to the transformation of the game?

COMMENTARY AND FURTHER READING

As stated in the introduction to this final section of Readings, the themes of consumption and spectacle are presented in relatively theoretical, and what might seem at times rather abstract, terms. To think through the arguments and the analyses, where possible follow up the actual sources. Look in depth at the extended arguments of the authors themselves, and look out for more examples and empirical illustrations that support or question their arguments.

For more material on mega-events, see Maurice Roche, *Mega-Events and Modernity: Olympics and Expos in the Growth of Global Culture* (London and New York, Routledge, 2000); *Sports – Mega-events*, a special issue of *International Review for the Sociology of Sport*, Vol. 35, No. 3, 2000; and Alan Tomlinson and Christopher Young's edited collection, *National Identity and Global Sports Events: Culture, Politics, and Spectacle in the Olympics and the Football World Cup* (Albany, State University of New York Press, 2006).

There is a rich range of material about the Olympics, on the basis of which arguments can be developed concerning the nature of the mega-event or the sporting spectacle. This material includes the following edited collections: Kay Schaffer and Sidonie Smith, *The Olympics at the Millennium: Power, Politics and the Games* (New Brunswick, Rutgers University Press, 2000); John Bale and Mette Krogh Christensen, *Post-Olympism? Questioning Sport in the Twenty-First Century* (Oxford, Berg, 2004); and Kevin Young and Kevin B. Wamsley, *Global Olympics: Historical and Sociological Studies of the Modern Games* (London, Elsevier, 2005).

A critical response to Debord on spectacle can be found in Alan Tomlinson, 'Theorising Spectacle: Beyond Debord', in Alan Tomlinson and John Sugden's edited book *Power Games: A Critical Sociology of Sport* (London and New York, Routledge, 2002). Steve Redhead's 'Media Culture and the World Cup: The Last World Cup' is a consideration of selected aspects of the work of Jean Baudrillard and a discussion of their application to the study of events such as the 1994 World Cup in the USA (see the final chapter in Alan Tomlinson and John Sugden, eds, *Hosts and Champions: Soccer Cultures, National Identities and the USA World Cup*, Aldershot, Ashgate, 1994).

On consumption and sport, see John Horne, *Sport in Consumer Culture* (London and New York, Routledge, 2005); and, with a focus on fans and supporters, Gary Crawford, *Consuming Sport: Fans, Sport and Culture* (London and New York, Routledge, 2004). On the place of advertising in sport consumption, see the collection edited by Steven Jackson and David L. Andrews, *Sport, Culture and Advertising: Identities, Commodities and the Politics of Representation* (London and New York, Routledge, 2004).

Pierre Bourdieu

THE UNIVERSES OF STYLISTIC POSSIBLES

THUS, THE SPACES DEFINED BY PREFERENCES in food, clothing or cosmetics are organized according to the same fundamental structure, that of the social space determined by volume and composition of capital. Fully to construct the space of life-styles within which cultural practices are defined, one would first have to establish, for each class and class fraction, that is, for each of the configurations of capital, the generative formula of the habitus which retranslates the necessities and facilities characteristic of that class of (relatively) homogeneous conditions of existence into a particular life-style. One would then have to determine how the dispositions of the habitus are specified, for each of the major areas of practice, by implementing one of the stylistic possibles offered by each field (the field of sport, or music, or food, decoration, politics, language etc.). By superimposing these homologous spaces one would obtain a rigorous representation of the space of life-styles, making it possible to characterize each of the distinctive features (e.g., wearing a cap or playing the piano) in the two respects in which it is objectively defined, that is, on the one hand by reference to the set of features constituting the area in question (e.g., the system of hairstyles), and on the other hand by reference to the set of features constituting a particular life-style (e.g., the working-class lifestyle), within which its social significance is determined.

For example, the universe of sporting activities and entertainments presents itself to each new entrant as a set of ready-made choices, objectively instituted possibles, traditions, rules, values, equipment, symbols, which receive their social significance from the system they constitute and which derive a proportion of their properties, at each moment, from history.

The distributional properties which are conferred on the different practices when they are evaluated by agents possessing a practical knowledge of their distribution among agents who are themselves distributed into ranked classes, or, in other words, of the probability, for the different classes, of practising them, do indeed owe much to past

A sport such as rugby presents an initial ambiguity. In England, at least, it is still played in the elite 'public schools', whereas in France it has become the characteristic sport of the working and middle classes of the regions south of the Loire (while preserving some 'academic' bastions such as the Racing Club or the Paris Université Club). This ambiguity can only be understood if one bears in mind the history of the process which, as in the 'elite schools' of nineteenth-century England, leads to the transmutation of popular games into elite sports, associated with an aristocratic ethic and world view ('fair play', 'will to win' etc.), entailing a radical change in meaning and function entirely analogous to what happens to popular dances when they enter the complex forms of 'serious' music and the less well-known history of the process of popularization, akin to the diffusion of classical or 'folk' music on LPs, which, in a second phase, transforms elite sport into mass sport, a spectacle as much as a practice.

patterns of distribution, because of the effects of hysteresis. The 'aristocratic' image of sports like tennis, riding or golf can persist beyond a—relative—transformation of the material conditions of access, whereas *pétanque* (a form of bowls), doubly stigmatized by its popular and southern origins and connections, has a distributional significance very similar to that of Ricard or other strong drinks and all the cheap, strong foods which are supposed to give strength.

But distributional properties are not the only ones conferred on goods by the agents' perception of them. Because agents apprehend objects through the schemes of perception and appreciation of their habitus, it would be naive to suppose that all practitioners of the same sport (or any other practice) confer the same meaning on their practice or even, strictly speaking, that they are practising the same practice. It can easily be shown that the different classes do not agree on the profits expected from sport, be they specific physical profits, such as effects on the external body, like slimness, elegance or visible muscles, and on the internal body, like health or relaxation; or extrinsic profits, such as the social relationships a sport may facilitate, or possible economic and social advantages. And, though there are cases in which the dominant function of the practice is reasonably clearly designated, one is practically never entitled to assume that the different classes expect the same thing from the same practice. For example, gymnastics may be asked—this is the popular demand, satisfied by body-building—to produce a strong body, bearing the external signs of its strength, or a healthy body—this is the bourgeois demand, satisfied by 'keep-fit' exercises or 'slimnastics'—or, with the 'new gymnastics', a 'liberated' body—this is the demand characteristic of women in the new fractions of the bourgeoisie and petite bourgeoisie.[1] Only a methodical analysis of the variations in the function and meaning conferred on the different sporting activities will enable one to escape from abstract, formal 'typologies' based (it is the law of the genre) on universalizing the researcher's personal experience; and to construct the table of the sociologically pertinent features in terms of which the agents (consciously or unconsciously) choose their sports. [. . .]

. . . [J]ust as a history of the sporting practices of the dominant class would no doubt shed light on the evolution of its ethical dispositions, the bourgeois conception of the human ideal and in particular the form of reconciliation between the bodily virtues and the supposedly more feminine intellectual virtues, so too an analysis of the distribution at a given moment of sporting activities among the fractions of the dominant class would bring to light some of the most hidden principles of the opposition between these fractions, such as the deep-rooted, unconscious conception of the relationship between the sexual division of labour and the division of the work of domination. This is perhaps truer than ever now that the gentle, invisible education by exercise and diet which is appropriate to the new morality of health is tending to take the place of the explicitly ethical pedagogy of the past in shaping bodies and minds. Because the different principles of division which structure the dominant class are never entirely independent—such as the oppositions between the economically richest and the culturally richest, between inheritors and parvenus, old and young (or seniors and juniors)—the practices of the different fractions tend to be distributed, from the dominant fractions to the dominated fractions, in accordance with a series of oppositions which are themselves partially reducible to each other: the opposition between the most expensive and smartest sports (golf, sailing, riding, tennis) or the most expensive and smartest ways of doing them (private clubs) and the cheapest sports (rambling, hiking, jogging, cycling, mountaineering) or the cheapest ways of doing the smart sports (e.g., tennis on municipal courts or in holiday camps); the opposition between the 'manly' sports, which may demand a high energy input (hunting, fishing, the 'contact' sports, clay-pigeon shooting), and the 'introverted' sports, emphasizing self-exploration and self-expression (yoga, dancing, 'physical expression') or the 'cybernetic' sports (flying, sailing), requiring a high cultural input and a relatively low energy input.

Thus, the differences which separate the teachers, the professionals and the employers [who formed the sample for this study] are, as it were, summed up in the three activities which, though relatively rare—about 10 percent—even in the fractions they distinguish, appear as the distinctive feature of each of them, because they are much more frequent there, at equivalent ages, than in the others . . . The aristocratic asceticism of the teachers finds an exemplary expression in mountaineering, which, even more than rambling, with its reserved paths (one thinks of Heidegger) or cycle-touring, with its Romanesque churches, offers for minimum economic costs the maximum distinction, distance, height, spiritual elevation, through the sense of simultaneously mastering one's own body and a nature inaccessible to the many.[2] The health-oriented hedonism of doctors and modern executives who have the material and cultural means of access to the most prestigious activities, far from vulgar crowds, is expressed in yachting, open-sea swimming, cross-country skiing or underwater fishing; whereas the employers expect the same gains in distinction from golf, with it[s] aristocratic etiquette, its English vocabulary and its great exclusive spaces, together with extrinsic profits, such as the accumulation of social capital.[3]

Since age is obviously a very important variable here, it is not surprising that differences in social age, not only between the biologically younger and older in identical social positions, but also, at identical biological ages, between the dominant and the dominated fractions, or the new and the established fractions, are retranslated into the opposition between the traditional sports and all the new forms of the classic sports (pony trekking, cross-country skiing, and so on), or all the new sports, often imported from America by members of the new bourgeoisie and petite bourgeoisie, in particular by all the people working in fashion—designers, photographers, models, advertising agents, journalists—who invent and market a new form of poor-man's elitism, close to the teachers' version but more ostentatiously unconventional.

The true nature of this counter-culture, which in fact reactivates all the traditions of the typically cultivated cults of the natural, the pure and the authentic, is more clearly revealed in the equipment which one of the new property-rooms of the advanced life-style—the FNAC ('executive retail' shops), Beaubourg, *Le Nouvel Observateur*, holiday clubs etc.—offers the serious trekker: parkas, plus-fours, *authentic* Jacquard sweaters in *real* Shetland wool, *genuine* pullovers in *pure natural* wool, Canadian trappers' jackets, English fishermen's pullovers, U.S. Army raincoats, Swedish lumberjack shirts, fatigue pants, U.S. work shoes, rangers, Indian moccasins in supple leather, Irish work caps, Norwegian woollen caps, bush hats—not forgetting the whistles, altimeters, pedometers, trail guides, Nikons and other essential gadgets without which there can be no natural return to nature. And how could one fail to recognize the dynamics of the dream of social weightlessness as the basis of all the new sporting activities—foot-trekking, pony-trekking, cycle-trekking, motorbike trekking, boat-trekking, canoeing, archery, windsurfing, cross-country skiing, sailing, hang-gliding, microlights etc.—whose common feature is that they all demand a high investment of cultural capital in the activity itself, in preparing, maintaining and using the equipment, and especially, perhaps, in verbalizing the experiences, and which bear something of the same relation to the luxury sports of the professionals and executives as symbolic possession to material possession of the work of art?

In the opposition between the classical sports and the Californian sports, two contrasting relations to the social world are expressed, as clearly as they are in literary or theatrical tastes. On the one hand, there is respect for forms and for forms of respect, manifested in concern for propriety and ritual and in unashamed flaunting of wealth and luxury, and on the other, symbolic subversion of the rituals of bourgeois order by ostentatious poverty, which makes a virtue of necessity, casualness towards forms and impatience with constraints, which is first marked in clothing or cosmetics since casual clothes and long hair—like the minibus or camping-car, or folk and rock, in other fields— are challenges to the standard attributes of bourgeois rituals, classically styled clothes, luxury cars, boulevard theatre and opera. And this opposition between two relations to the social world is perfectly reflected in the two relations to the natural world, on the one hand the taste for natural, wild nature, on the other, organized, signposted, cultivated nature.

Thus, the system of the sporting activities and entertainments that offer themselves at a given moment for the potential 'consumers' to choose from is predisposed to express all the differences sociologically pertinent at that moment: oppositions between the sexes, between the classes and between class fractions. The agents only have to follow the leanings of their habitus in order to take over, unwittingly, the intention immanent in the corresponding practices, to find an activity which is entirely 'them' and, with it, kindred spirits. The same is true in all areas of practice: each consumer is confronted by a particular state of the supply side, that is, with objectified possibilities (goods, services, patterns of action etc.) the appropriation of which is one of the stakes in the struggles between the classes, and which, because of their probable association with certain classes or class fractions, are automatically classified and classifying, rank-ordered and rank-ordering. The observed state of the distribution of goods and practices is thus defined in the meeting between the possibilities offered at a given moment by the different fields of production (past and present) and the socially differentiated dispositions which— associated with the capital (of determinate volume and composition) of which, depending on the trajectory, they are more or less completely the product and in which they find their means of realization—define the interest in these possibilities, that is, the propensity to acquire them and (through acquisition) to convert them into distinctive signs. [. . .]

It follows that it is only by increasing the number of empirical analyses of the relations between relatively autonomous fields of production of a particular class of products and the market of consumers which they assemble, and which sometimes function as fields (without ceasing to be determined by their position in the field of the social classes), that one can really escape from the abstraction of economic theories, which only recognize a consumer reduced to his purchasing power (itself reduced to his income) and a product characterized, equally abstractly, by a technical function presumed to be equal for all; only in this way is it possible to establish a genuine scientific theory of the economy of practices.

Notes

1   See J. Defrance, 'Esquisse d'une histoire sociale de la gymnastique (1760–1870)', *Actes*, 6 (December 1976), 22–47.
2   Another distinctive feature, which sums up the opposition between two relations to the body and to social interactions: two-thirds (59.8 percent) of the teachers say they never dance, whereas dancing is very common in the professions (only 18 percent, the lowest proportion in the whole population, say they never dance).
3   More than half the members of the Saint-Nom-la-Bretèche golf club are bankers, industrialists, commercial entrepreneurs or company directors, 26 percent are managing directors, executives or engineers and 16 percent are members of the professions.

Guy Debord

THE COMMODITY AS SPECTACLE

[. . .]

42   THE SPECTACLE CORRESPONDS to the historical moment at which the commodity completes its colonization of social life. It is not just that the relationship to commodities is now plain to see – commodities are now *all* that there is to see; the world we see is the world of the commodity. The growth of the dictatorship of modern economic production is both extensive and intensive in character. In the least industrialized regions its presence is already felt in the form of imperialist domination by those areas that lead the world in productivity. In these advanced sectors themselves, social space is continually being blanketed by stratum after stratum of commodities. With the advent of the so-called second industrial revolution, alienated consumption is added to alienated production as an inescapable duty of the masses. The *entirety of labor sold* is transformed overall into the *total commodity*. A cycle is thus set in train that must be maintained at all costs: the total commodity must be returned in fragmentary form to a fragmentary individual completely cut off from the concerted action of the forces of production. To this end the already specialized science of domination is further broken down into specialties such as sociology, applied psychology, cybernetics, semiology and so on, which oversee the self-regulation of every phase of the process.

43   WHEREAS AT THE PRIMITIVE stage of capitalist accumulation "political economy treats the *proletarian* as a mere *worker*" who must receive only the minimum necessary to guarantee his labor-power, and never considers him "in his leisure, in his human-ity," these ideas of the ruling class are revised just as soon as so great an abundance of commodities begins to be produced that a surplus "collaboration" is required of the workers. All of a sudden the workers in question discover that they are no longer invariably subject to the total contempt so clearly built into every aspect of the organization

and management of production; instead they find that every day, once work is over, they are treated like grown-ups, with a great show of solicitude and politeness, in their new role as consumers. The *humanity of the commodity* finally attends to the workers' "leisure and humanity" for the simple reason that political economy *as such* now can – and must – bring these spheres under its sway. Thus it is that the totality of human existence falls under the regime of the "perfected denial of man."

44   THE SPECTACLE IS a permanent opium war waged to make it impossible to distinguish goods from commodities, or true satisfaction from a survival that increases according to its own logic. Consumable survival *must* increase, in fact, because it continues to enshrine deprivation. The reason there is nothing *beyond* augmented survival, and no end to its growth, is that survival itself belongs to the realm of dispossession: it may gild poverty, but it cannot transcend it.

45   AUTOMATION, WHICH IS at once the most advanced sector of modern industry and the epitome of its practice, confronts the world of the commodity with a contradiction that it must somehow resolve: the same technical infrastructure that is capable of abolishing labor must at the same time preserve labor as a commodity – and indeed as the sole generator of commodities. If automation, or for that matter any mechanisms, even less radical ones, that can increase productivity, are to be prevented from reducing socially necessary labor-time to an unacceptably low level, new forms of employment have to be created. A happy solution presents itself in the growth of the tertiary or service sector in response to the immense strain on the supply lines of the army responsible for distributing and hyping the commodities of the moment. The coincidence is neat: on the one hand, the system is faced with the necessity of reintegrating newly redundant labor; on the other, the very factitiousness of the needs associated with the commodities on offer calls out a whole battery of reserve forces.

46   EXCHANGE VALUE COULD only have arisen as the proxy of use value, but the victory it eventually won with its own weapons created the preconditions for its establishment as an autonomous power. By activating all human use value and monopolizing that value's fulfillment, exchange value eventually gained the upper hand. The process of exchange became indistinguishable from any conceivable utility, thereby placing use value at its mercy. Starting out as the condottiere of use value, exchange value ended up waging a war that was entirely its own.

47   THE FALLING RATE of use value, which is a constant of the capitalist economy, gives rise to a new form of privation within the realm of augmented survival; this is not to say that this realm is emancipated from the old poverty: on the contrary, it requires the vast majority to take part as wage workers in the unending pursuit of its ends – a requirement to which, as everyone knows, one must either submit or die. It is the reality of this situation – the fact that, even in its most impoverished form (food, shelter), use value has no existence outside the illusory riches of augmented survival – that is the real basis for the general acceptance of illusion in the consumption of modern commodities. The real consumer thus becomes a consumer of illusion. The commodity is this illusion, which is in fact real, and the spectacle is its most general form.

48   USE VALUE WAS formerly implicit in exchange value. In terms of the spectacle's topsy-turvy logic, however, it has to be explicit – for the very reason that its own effective existence has been eroded by the overdevelopment of the commodity economy, and that a counterfeit life calls for a pseudo-justification.

49   THE SPECTACLE IS ANOTHER facet of money, which is the abstract general equivalent of all commodities. But whereas money in its familiar form has dominated society as the representation of universal equivalence, that is, of the exchangeability of diverse goods whose uses are not otherwise compatible, the spectacle in its full development is money's modern aspect; in the spectacle the totality of the commodity world is visible in one piece, as the general equivalent of whatever society as a whole can be and do. The spectacle is money for *contemplation only*, for here the totality of use has already been bartered for the totality of abstract representation. The spectacle is not just the servant of *pseudo-use* – it is already, in itself, the pseudo-use of life.

50   WITH THE ACHIEVEMENT of a purely economic abundance, the concentrated result of social labor becomes visible, subjecting all reality to an appearance that is in effect that labor's product. Capital is no longer the invisible center determining the mode of production. As it accumulates, capital spreads out to the periphery, where it assumes the form of tangible objects. Society in its length and breadth becomes capital's faithful portrait.

51   THE ECONOMY'S TRIUMPH as an independent power inevitably also spells its doom, for it has unleashed forces that must eventually destroy the *economic necessity* that was the unchanging basis of earlier societies. Replacing that necessity by the necessity of boundless economic development can only mean replacing the satisfaction of primary human needs, now met in the most summary manner, by a ceaseless manufacture of pseudo-needs, all of which come down in the end to just one – namely, the pseudo-need for the reign of an autonomous economy to continue. Such an economy irrevocably breaks all ties with authentic needs to the precise degree that it emerges from a *social unconscious* that was dependent on it without knowing it. "Whatever is conscious wears out. Whatever is unconscious remains unalterable. Once freed, however, surely this too must fall into ruins?" (Freud).

52   BY THE TIME society discovers that it is contingent on the economy, the economy has in point of fact become contingent on society. Having grown as a subterranean force until it could emerge sovereign, the economy proceeds to lose its power. Where economic id was, there ego shall be. The *subject* can only arise out of society – that is, out of the struggle that society embodies. The possibility of a subject's existing depends on the outcome of the class struggle which turns out to be the product and the producer of history's economic foundation.

53   CONSCIOUSNESS OF DESIRE and the desire for consciousness together and indissolubly constitute that project which in its negative form has as its goal the abolition of classes and the direct possession by the workers of every aspect of their activity. The opposite of this project is the society of the spectacle, where the commodity contemplates itself in a world of its own making.

Jean Baudrillard

THE DRAMA OF LEISURE
OR THE IMPOSSIBILITY OF
WASTING ONE'S TIME

[. . .]

TIME RETAINS A PARTICULAR MYTHIC VALUE for its equalizing of human conditions, a value which has been taken up again strongly and thematized in our own day in the concept of leisure time. The old adage that 'all men are equal before time and death', which once encapsulated in its entirety the demand for social justice, today lives on in the carefully tended myth that all are equal in leisure.

> Going harpoon fishing together and sharing the Samos wine created a deep sense of fellow-feeling. On the boat back, they realized that they knew each other only by their Christian names and, wishing to exchange addresses, discovered to their amazement that they worked in the same factory, the one as technical director, the other as nightwatchman.

This delightful little fable, which sums up the entire ideology of the Club Méditerranée, involves several metaphysical postulates:

1   Leisure is the realm of freedom.
2   Every man is, by nature, in substance free and equal to others: he has only to be put back in a state of 'nature' to recover this substantial liberty, equality and fraternity. Thus, the Greek islands and the underwater depths are heirs to the ideals of the French Revolution.
3   Time is an a priori, transcendent dimension, which pre-exists its contents. It is there waiting for you. If it is alienated and subjugated in work, then 'you don't have time.' When you are away from work or unconstrained, 'you have time.' As an absolute, inalienable dimension, like air or water, in leisure it once again becomes everyone's private property.

This last point is the key one: it hints at the fact that time might well be only the product of a certain culture and, more precisely, of a certain mode of production. In that case, it is *necessarily* subject to the same status as all the goods produced or available within the framework of that system of production: that of property, private or public, that of appropriation, that of the **object**, possessed and alienable, alienated or free, and, like all objects produced by that systematic mode, partaking of the reified abstraction of exchange-value. [. . .]

The demand underlying leisure is, therefore, an insolubly contradictory and truly desperate one. Its fervid hope for freedom attests to the power of the system of constraints which is nowhere so total, precisely, as at the level of time. 'When I speak of time, it is already gone,' said Apollinaire. Of leisure we may say that 'When you "have" time, it is no longer free.' And the contradiction here is not one of terms, but of substance. This is the *tragic* paradox of consumption. Everyone wants to put – believes he has put – his desire into every object possessed, consumed, and into every minute of free time, but from every object appropriated, from every satisfaction achieved, and from every 'available' minute, the desire is already absent, necessarily absent. All that remains is *consommé* of desire. [. . .]

Thus, everywhere, in spite of the fiction of freedom in leisure, 'free' time is logically impossible: there can only be constrained time. The time of consumption is that of production. It is so to the extent that it is only ever an 'escapist' parenthesis in the cycle of production. But, once again, this functional complementarity (variously shared out in the different social classes) is not its essential determination. Leisure is constrained in so far as, behind its apparent gratuitousness, it faithfully reproduces all the mental and practical constraints which are those of productive time and subjugated [*asservi*] daily life.

It is not characterized by creative activities: creating, artistically or otherwise, is never a *leisure* activity. Leisure is generally characterized by regressive activities of a type pre-dating modern forms of work (pottering, handicrafts, collecting, fishing). The guiding model for free time is the only one experienced up to that point: the model of childhood. But there is confusion here between the childhood experience of freedom in play and the nostalgia for a stage of social development prior to the division of labour. In each of these cases, because the totality and spontaneity leisure seeks to restore come into being in a social time marked essentially by the modern division of labour, they take the objective form of escape and *irresponsibility*. Now, this irresponsibility in leisure is homologous with, and structurally complementary to, irresponsibility in work. 'Freedom' on the one hand, constraint on the other: the structure is, in fact, the same.

It is the very fact of the functional division between the two great modalities of time which constitutes a system and makes *leisure the very ideology of alienated labour*. The dichotomy establishes the same lacks and the same contradictions on both sides. So, everywhere, we find in leisure and holidays the same eager moral and idealistic pursuit of accomplishment as in the sphere of work, the same **ethics of pressured performance**. No more than consumption, to which it belongs entirely, is leisure a praxis of satisfaction. Or, at least, we may say that it is so only in appearance. In fact, the obsession with getting a tan, that bewildered whirl in which tourists 'do' Italy, Spain and all the art galleries, the gymnastics and nudity which are *de rigueur* under an obligatory sun and, most important of all, the smiles and unfailing *joie de vivre* all attest to the fact that the holiday-maker conforms in every detail to the principles of duty, sacrifice, and asceticism. [. . .]

Leisure, which is still very unequally distributed, remains, in our democratic societies, a factor of cultural distinction and selection. We may, however, envisage this trend reversing itself (at least we may imagine this): in Aldous Huxley's *Brave New World*, the Alphas are the only ones who work, the mass of the others being condemned to hedonism and leisure. We may admit that, with the progress of leisure, and the generalized 'promotion' of free time, there will be a reversal of this privilege and the great thing will be to set aside less and less time for *obligatory consumption*. If, as is probable, though it is the opposite of what are ideally their goals, leisure activities, as they develop, increasingly sink into competitiveness and the disciplinary ethic, then we may suppose that work (a certain type of work) will become the place and time in which to recover from one's leisure. And work can even now be a mark of distinction and privilege once again, as is the case with the affected 'servitude' of top executives and managing directors who feel they have to work 15 hours a day.

So we come to the paradoxical end-point where it is work itself that is *consumed*. To the extent that work is *preferred* to free time, that it meets a 'neurotic' demand, and that the excess of it is a mark of prestige, we are in the field of the consumption of work. But we know that anything can become a consumer object. [. . .]

In an integrated and total system like ours, there cannot be any free availability of time. And leisure is not the availability of time, it is its **display**. Its fundamental determination is the *constraint that it be different from working time*. It is not, therefore, autonomous: it is defined by the absence of working time. That difference, since it constitutes the deep value of leisure, is everywhere connoted and marked with redundancy, over-exhibited. In all its signs, all its attitudes, all its practices, and in all the discourses in which it is spoken of, leisure thrives on this exhibition and over-exhibition of itself as such, this continual ostentation, this **marking**, this **display**. Everything may be taken away from it, everything stripped from it but this. It is this which defines it.

Herbert I. Schiller

THE TRANSNATIONALIZATION
OF CORPORATE EXPRESSION

[. . .]

Other displays in the corporate exhibition hall: sports

THE TRANSNATIONAL CORPORATE ORDER'S USE of commercialized and privatized media to increase sales, create consumers, and transmit a mindset supportive of the system is especially evident in the sphere of organized sports. As with many marketing practices, the commercialization of sport is an American speciality, rapidly being extended to the rest of the world. The Superbowl serves as the model. In this professional football extravaganza, promoted beforehand for months in all the media, the marketing message reaches half the American population, an estimated 125,000,000 viewers, The payoff of the carefully constructed frenzy preceding the game is the cost of a 30-second commercial during the game—$625,000 to $675,000 in 1987. For this amount, beer, automobile, insurance, and cosmetic companies get their product seen by half the country's population. It is, in the words of one sports writer, "the great corporate event."[1]

It is reported that "more than 3,400 U.S. companies (in 1987) will spend $1.35 billion to sponsor sporting events. . . . They'll spend another $500 million hiring athletes as (product) endorsers. . . . Along with ads and promotions directly tied to sponsorship, the amount may top $3.5 billion, or more than double the $1.4 billion in revenues the networks receive from selling ads during sports shows."[2]

Meanwhile, a new twist has been added in the current era of "total" marketing. Advertisers now may sponsor the sporting event itself rather than just buying a chunk of airtime during the show. The internationalization of this practice is already substantial. Transnational corporations committed at least $300 million to support the 1988 Olympic Games in Calgary and Seoul. Though the Olympics are still short of full corporate appropriation, the giant sums already involved suggest total envelopment may not be far off. Even now, the Olympics are regarded by corporate sponsors, "as a marketing tool throughout the world."[3] In 1994, the World Cup soccer tournament, one of world's premier sporting events, will be held in the United States, though soccer is not a major sport in America. To secure the tournament, the U.S. bid "enlisted help from eight American-based corporations, most of them multinational companies and three of them—Anheuser Busch, Gillette and Coca-Cola, sponsors of the 1990 tournament [in Italy]."[4]

In privatized broadcasting systems, corporate-sponsored sports are a large and growing source of revenue, bearing many similarities to the corporate-sponsored art exhibit or, more grandiose still, the corporate-sponsored museum. An American sports promotion company, for example, has created among its many commercialized sports packages for sale to corporate clients twenty European gold tournaments.[5]

Grand Prix automobile racing also is getting corporate attention. "Executives of the (Data General Corporation) say (its) involvement in racing helps to open the doors for salesmen overseas and enhances its reputation as a high-tech problem solver."[6] Philip Morris has used the Grand Prix since 1972, and R.J. Reynolds, another major cigarette company, joined the crowd of sponsors in 1987.

With the capture of sports for corporate promotions, the audience is targeted in its most vulnerable condition, relaxed yet fully receptive to the physical action and the inserted sales pitch. It is the ideal ambiance for the penetration of consciousness by a wide variety of ideological messages. [. . .]

A world secure for global advertising?

The Global Media Commission of the International Advertising Association anticipates the future with enthusiasm and optimism. This may be customary with marketing folk. Is there a basis for this confidence? As the ad people see it, ". . . television, that most efficient and spectacularly effective of all mass media, will soon be available to serve as global marketing's instrument of consumer access."[7] It will be transmitted by satellite and delivered to cable systems, bringing advertising and programming to audiences whether their governments like it or not, compelling national systems to accept commercialization to survive. And so, " . . . the state monopolies [the favorite negative language employed by the experts of the transnationals] will be able to survive only by competing. The number of channels will multiply. Private television will grow. Advertising time will expand and flourish in both private and public broadcasting systems."[8] Transnational corporate culture will be triumphant. There is, the admen believe, "an inexorable momentum."[9]

It is difficult to disagree. The global push of transnational capital in the information-cultural sphere has been remarkably successful to date. No activity, national or international, is exempt from the corporate sponsor—not even, apparently, the worldwide programs of the United Nations. This is the message delivered by a highly placed UN official in the World Congress on Public Relations in Melbourne, Australia, in April 1988. The UN's under-secretary for public information told the congress:

A critical component in my new approach is to explore corporate and institutional sponsorship. Recently we have started to work with corporations in putting the UN message across to the people of the world . . . We have realized that both [PR] agencies and their clients would benefit substantially in corporate image terms in their association with us and the work that we do. . . . a particularly attractive opportunity for sponsorship is the 40th anniversary of the *United Nations Declaration of Human Rights in 1988* . . . the opportunities for joint promotion are as wide as the United Nations global network around the world.[10]

With this invitation, corporate sponsorship could be magnificently expanded from Grand Prix and Olympics events to the United Nations itself. Imagine the commercials showing the U.S. fleet in the Persian Gulf as a UN event sponsored by Exxon. When asked why there should be subsidized national theater in England funded from the state treasury, Peter Hall, the British director, observed that a national theater had to be considered the last defense against U.S. commercial-television programming.[11]

But it is not only U.S. television programming that carries the virus of transnational corporate culture. Politics, sports, tourism, language, and business data flows transmit it and reinforce it as well. One event gives a sense of the process at work. It was a rock-band concert in Tijuana, just across the border from San Diego, California. The newspaper account of this concert attended by 27,000 people, a small turnout for such an event, noted: "While staged in Mexico, the concert scene could have been transplanted from the United States." Mexican national sovereignty was disregarded. "Some souvenir booths carried signs saying 'No Acceptamos Pesos'—we don't accept pesos." The reporter from Los Angeles reasonably concluded: "The theme of cross-cultural cooperation apparently did not extend to accepting the Mexican national currency on Mexican soil."[12]

Notes

1   Ira Berkow, "The Superbowl Strut," *New York Times*, Feb. 1, 1988.
2   "Nothing Sells Like Sports," *Business Week* (Aug. 31, 1987).
3   "Will Corporate Sponsors Get Burned by the Torch?" *Business Week* (Feb. 1, 1988).
4   Michael Janofsky, "U.S. Soccer Officials Say World Cup Would Revive Game," *New York Times*, July 4, 1988.
5   "Nothing Sells Like Sports," *Business Week* (Aug. 31, 1987).
6   John Holusha, "A New Fast Lane for Business," *New York Times*, June 19, 1987.
7   "Global Marketing," p. 18.
8   "Global Marketing," p. 24.
9   Ibid.
10 Terese P. Sevigny, UN Under-Secretary General for Public Information, address to the Eleventh Public Relations World Congress, Melbourne, Australia, April 28, 1988.
11 *New York Times*, Feb. 16, 1986.
12 Patrick McDonnell, "MexFest Bash: Rock Rolls Crowd Across the Border," *Los Angeles Times*, July 1, 1987.

Christopher Lasch

THE DEGRADATION
OF SPORT

The spirit of play versus the rage for national uplift

AMONG THE ACTIVITIES THROUGH WHICH men seek release from everyday life, games offer in many ways the purest form of escape. Like sex, drugs, and drink, they obliterate awareness of everyday reality, but they do this not by dimming awareness but by raising it to a new intensity of concentration. Moreover, they have no side effects, hangovers, or emotional complications. Games simultaneously satisfy the need for free fantasy and the search for gratuitous difficulty; they combine childlike exuberance with deliberately created complications. By establishing conditions of equality among the players, according to Roger Caillois,[1] games attempt to substitute ideal conditions for "the normal confusion of everyday life." They re-create the freedom, the remembered perfection of childhood, and mark it off from ordinary life with artificial boundaries, within which the only constraints are the rules to which the players freely submit. Games enlist skill and intelligence, the utmost concentration of purpose, on behalf of activities utterly useless, which make no contribution to the struggle of man against nature, to the wealth or comfort of the community, or to its physical survival.

The uselessness of games makes them offensive to social reformers, improvers of public morals, or functionalist critics of society like Veblen, who saw in the futility of upper-class sports anachronistic survivals of militarism and prowess. Yet the "futility" of play, and nothing else, explains its appeal—its artificiality, the arbitrary obstacles it sets up for no other purpose than to challenge the players to surmount them, the absence of any utilitarian or uplifting object. Games quickly lose their charm when forced into the service of education, character development, or social improvement.

Today the official view of the beneficial, wholesome effects of sport, which has replaced the various utilitarian ideologies of the past, stresses their contribution to health, fitness, and hence to the national well-being, considered as the sum of the nation's "human resources." The "socialist" version of this ideology hardly differs from the capitalist version promulgated, for example, by John F. Kennedy[2] in his tiresome pronouncements on physical fitness. Attempting to justify the creation of his President's Council on Youth Fitness (headed by the Oklahoma football coach, Bud Wilkinson), Kennedy cited the consistent decline of strength and fitness as measured by standard tests. "Our growing softness, our increasing lack of physical fitness, is a menace to our security." This attack on "softness" goes hand in hand with a condemnation of spectatorship.

Socialist pronouncements sound depressingly similar. The Cuban government announced in 1967 that sport should be considered part of the "inseparable element of education, culture, health, defense, happiness and the development of people and a new society." In 1925, the central committee of the Soviet Communist party declared that sport should be consciously used "as a means of rallying the broad masses of workers and peasants around the various Party Soviet and Trade Union organizations through which the masses of workers and peasants are to be drawn into social and political activity." Fortunately, people of all nations intuitively tend to resist such exhortations. They know that games remain gloriously pointless and that watching an exciting athletic contest, moreover, can be emotionally almost as exhausting as participation itself—hardly the "passive" experience it is made out to be by the guardians of public health and virtue. [. . .]

The attainment of certain skills unavoidably gives rise to an urge to show them off. At a higher level of mastery, the performer no longer wishes merely to display his virtuosity—for the true connoisseur can easily distinguish between the performer who plays to the crowd and the superior artist who matches himself against the full rigor of his art itself—but to ratify a supremely difficult accomplishment; to give pleasure; to forge a bond between himself and his audience, which consists in their shared appreciation of a ritual executed flawlessly, with deep feeling and a sense of style and proportion.[3]

In all games, particularly in athletic contests, display and representation constitute a central element—a reminder of the former connections between play, ritual, and drama. The players not only compete; they enact a familiar ceremony that reaffirms common values. Ceremony requires witnesses: enthusiastic spectators conversant with the rules of the performance and its underlying meaning. Far from destroying the value of sports, the attendance of spectators makes them complete. [. . .]

As spectators become less knowledgeable about the games they watch, they become sensation-minded and bloodthirsty. The rise of violence in ice hockey, far beyond the point where it plays any functional part in the game, coincided with the expansion of professional hockey into cities without any traditional attachment to the sport—cities in which weather conditions, indeed, had always precluded any such tradition of local play. But the significance of such changes is not that sports ought to be organized, as a number of recent critics imagine, solely for the edification of the players and that corruption sets in when sports begin to be played to spectators for a profit. No one denies the desirability of participation in sports—not because it builds strong bodies but because it brings joy and delight. It is by watching those who have mastered a sport, however, that we derive standards against which to measure ourselves. By entering imaginatively into their world, we experience in heightened form the pain of defeat and the triumph of persistence in the face of adversity. An athletic performance, like other performances, calls up a rich train of associations and fantasies, shaping unconscious perceptions of life. Spectatorship is no more "passive" than daydreaming, provided the performance is of such quality that it elicits an emotional response. [. . .]

The trivialization of athletics

What corrupts an athletic performance, as it does any other performance, is not professionalism or competition but a breakdown of the conventions surrounding the game. It is at this point that ritual, drama, and sports all degenerate into spectacle. [. . .]

After the exciting match between Vilas and Connors,[4] in the 1977 finals of the U.S. Open at Forest Hills, an unruly crowd spilled onto the court immediately after the last point and thus broke the hours of tension that should have been broken by the traditional handshake between the players themselves—incidentally allowing Connors to escape from the stadium without acknowledging his rival's victory or taking part in the closing ceremonies. Repeated transgressions of this kind undermine the illusion games create. To break the rules is to break the spell. The merging of players and spectators, here as in the theater, prevents the suspension of disbelief and thus destroys the representational value of organized athletics. [. . .]

George Allen's dictum—"winning isn't the most important thing, it's the only thing"— represents a last-ditch defense of team spirit in the face of its deterioration. Such pronouncements, usually cited as evidence of an exaggerated stress on competition, may help to keep it within bounds. The intrusion of the market into every corner of the sporting scene, however, re-creates all the antagonisms characteristic of late capitalist society. With the free-agent draft, the escalation of athletic salaries, and the instantaneous stardom conferred by the media on athletic success, competition among rival organizations has degenerated into a free-for-all. It is no wonder that criticism of competition has emerged as the principal theme in the rising criticism of sport. [. . .]

Only the recognition that sports have come to serve as a form of entertainment justifies the salaries paid to star athletes and their prominence in the media. As Howard Cosell has candidly acknowledged,[5] sports can no longer be sold to the public as "just sports or as religion. . . . Sports aren't life and death. They're entertainment." Even as the television audience demands the presentation of sports as a form of spectacle, however, the widespread resentment of star athletes among followers of sport—a resentment directed against the inflated salaries negotiated by their agents and against their willingness to become hucksters, promoters, and celebrities—indicates the persistence of a need to believe that sport represents something more than entertainment, something that, though neither life nor death in itself, retains some lingering capacity to dramatize and clarify those experiences.

Sports and the entertainment industry

The secularization of sport, which began as soon as athletics were pressed into the cause of patriotism and character building, became complete only when sport became an object of mass consumption. The first stage in this process was the establishment of big-time athletics in the university and their spread from the Ivy League to the large public and private schools, thence downward into the high schools. The bureaucratization of the business career, which placed unprecedented emphasis on competition and the will to win, stimulated the growth of sports in another way. It made the acquisition of educational credentials essential to a business or professional career and thus created in large numbers a new kind of student, utterly indifferent to higher learning but forced to undergo it for purely economic reasons. Large-scale athletic programs helped colleges to attract such students, in competitive bidding for enrollments, and to entertain them once they enrolled. In the closing years of the nineteenth century, according to Donald Meyer, the development of an "alumni culture"[6] centering on clubs, fraternities, alumni offices, money drives, homecoming ceremonies, and football, grew out of the colleges' need not only to raise money in large amounts but to attract "a clientele for whom the classroom had no real meaning but who were by no means ready to send their sons out into the world at age eighteen." At Notre Dame, as Frederick Rudolph has pointed out, "intercollegiate athletics . . . were consciously developed in the 1890s as an agency of student recruitment." As early as 1878, President McCosh of Princeton wrote to an alumnus in Kentucky: "You will confer a great favor on us if you will get . . . the college noticed in the Louisville papers. . . . We must persevere in our efforts to get students from your region. . . . Mr. Brand Ballard has won us great reputation as captain of the football team which has beaten both Harvard and Yale."

In order to accommodate the growing hordes of spectators, the colleges and universities, sometimes aided by local business interests, built lavish athletic facilities—enormous field houses, football stadiums in the pretentious imperial style of the early twentieth century. Growing investment in sports led in turn to a growing need to maintain a winning record: a new concern with system, efficiency, and the elimination of risk, Camp's[7] innovations at Yale emphasized drill, discipline, teamwork. As in industry, the attempt to coordinate the movements of many men created a demand for "scientific management" and for the expansion of managerial personnel. In many sports, trainers, coaches, doctors, and public relations experts soon outnumbered the players. The accumulation of elaborate statistical records arose from management's attempt to reduce winning to a routine, to measure efficient performance. The athletic contest itself, surrounded by a vast apparatus of information and promotion, now appeared almost incidental to the expensive preparation required to stage it.

The rise of a new kind of journalism—the yellow journalism pioneered by Hearst and Pulitzer, which sold sensations instead of reporting news—helped to professionalize amateur athletics, to assimilate sport to promotion, and to make professional athletics into a major industry. Until the twenties, professional sports, where they existed at all, attracted little of the public attention lavished on college football. Even baseball, the oldest and most highly organized of professional sports, suffered from faintly unsavory associations—its appeal to the working class and the sporting crowd, its rural origins. When a Yale alumnus complained to Walter Camp about the overemphasis on football, he could think of no better way of dramatizing the danger than to cite the example of baseball: "The language and scenes which are too often witnessed [in football games] are such as to degrade the college student and bring him down to a par with or even lower than the average professional baseball player."

The World Series scandal of 1919 confirmed baseball's bad reputation, but it also set in motion the reforms of Kenesaw Mountain Landis, the new commissioner brought in by the owners to clean up the game and give it a better public image. Landis's régime, the success of the eminently respectable and efficient New York Yankees, and the idolization of Babe Ruth soon made professional baseball "America's number-one pastime." Ruth became the first modern athlete to be sold to the public as much for his color, personality, and crowd appeal as for his remarkable abilities. His press agent, Christy Walsh, developer of a syndicate of ghost writers who sold books and articles under the names of sports heroes, arranged barnstorming tours, endorsements, and movie roles and thus helped to make the "Sultan of Swat" a national celebrity.

In the quarter-century following World War II, entrepreneurs extended the techniques of mass promotion first perfected in the marketing of college football and professional baseball to other professional sports, notably hockey, basketball, and football. Television did for these games what mass journalism and radio had done for baseball, elevating them to new heights of popularity and at the same time reducing them to entertainment. [. . .]

In a society dominated by the production and consumption of images, no part of life can long remain immune from the invasion of spectacle. Nor can this invasion be blamed on the spirit of debunking. It arises, in a paradoxical fashion, precisely out of the attempt to set up a separate sphere of leisure uncontaminated by the world of work and politics. Play has always by its very nature, set itself off from workaday life; yet it retains an organic connection with the life of the community, by virtue of its capacity to dramatize reality and to offer a convincing representation of the community's values. The ancient connections between games, ritual, and public festivity suggest that although games take place within arbitrary boundaries, they are nevertheless rooted in shared traditions to which they give objective expression. Games and athletic contests offer a dramatic commentary on reality rather than an escape from it—a heightened reenactment of communal traditions, not a repudiation of them. It is only when games and sports come to be valued purely as a form of escape that they lose the capacity to provide this escape.

The appearance in history of an escapist conception of "leisure" coincides with the organization of leisure as an extension of commodity production. The same forces that have organized the factory and the office have organized leisure as well, reducing it to an appendage of industry. Accordingly sport has come to be dominated not so much by an undue emphasis on winning as by the desperate urge to avoid defeat. Coaches, not quarterbacks, call the plays, and the managerial apparatus makes every effort to eliminate the risk and uncertainty that contribute so centrally to the ritual and dramatic success of any contest. When sports can no longer be played with appropriate abandon, they lose the capacity to raise the spirits of players and spectators, to transport them into a higher realm of existence. Prudence, caution, and calculation, so prominent in everyday life but so inimical to the spirit of games, come to shape sports as they shape everything else. [. . .]

. . . [T]he emergence of the spectacle as the dominant form of cultural expression . . . ends with the demystification of sport, the assimilation of sport to show business.

Notes

1   Roger Caillois, "The Structure and Classification of Games," in John W. Loy, Jr., and Gerald S. Kenyon, *Sport, Culture, and Society* (New York: Macmillan, 1969), p. 49.

2   John F. Kennedy, "The Soft American" (1960), reprinted in John T. Talamini and Charles H. Page, *Sport and Society: An Anthology* (Boston: Little, Brown, 1973), p. 369;

Philip Goodhart and Christopher Chataway, *War without Weapons* (London: W.H. Allen, 1968), pp. 80, 84.

3 This does not mean that virtuosity is the principal component of sport. In implying a comparison, here and elsewhere, between athletic and musical performances, I wish to make just the opposite point. A performer who seeks merely to dazzle the audience with feats of technical brilliance plays to the lowest level of understanding, forgoing the risks that come from intense emotional engagement with the material itself. In the most satisfying kind of performance, the performer becomes unconscious of the audience and loses himself in his part. In sport, the moment that matters is what a former basketball player describes as the moment "when all those folks in the stands don't count." The player in question, now a scholar, left big-time sport when he discovered he was expected to have no life outside it, but he retains more insight into the nature of games than Dave Meggyesy, Chip Oliver, and other ex-athletes. Rejecting the simple-minded radicalism according to which "commercialization" has corrupted sports, he says: "Money [in professional sports] has nothing to do with capitalism, owners, or professionalism. It's the moment in some games where it doesn't matter who's watching, all that counts is that instant where how you play determines which team wins and which team loses."

If virtuosity were the essence of sport, we could dispense with basketball and content ourselves with displays of dunking and dribbling. But to say that real artistry consists not of dazzling technique but of teamwork, timing, a sense of the moment, an understanding of the medium, and the capacity to lose oneself in play does not of course mean that games would have the same significance if no one watched them. It means simply that the superior performance has the quality of being unobserved.

4 On the Vilas–Connors match, I am indebted for these suggestions to Herbert Benham.

5 Casell was quoted in Michael Novak, *The Joy of Sports* (New York: Basic Books, 1976), p. 273.

6 On alumni culture, see Donald Meyer, "Early Football" (unpublished paper); Frederick Rudolph, *The American College and University* (New York: Vintage, 1962), p. 385.

7 On Walter Camp, see Meyer, "Early Football."

Leo Lowenthal

THE TRIUMPH OF
MASS IDOLS*

THE FOLLOWING STUDY IS CONCERNED with the content analysis of biographies. This literary topic had inundated the book market for the three decades previous to the writing of this article in 1943, and had for some time been a regular feature of popular magazines. Surprisingly enough, not very much attention had been paid to this phenomenon, none whatever to biographies appearing in magazines, and little to those published in book form.[1] [. . .]

The popular biography was one of the most conspicuous newcomers in the realm of print since the introduction of the short story. [. . .] Even if it were only a passing literary fad, one would still have to explain why this fashion has had such longevity and is more and more becoming a regular feature in the most diversified media of publications. [. . .]

We might say that a large proportion of the heroes in samples [in the first three decades of the twentieth century] are idols of production, that they stem from the productive life, from industry, business, and natural sciences. There is not a single hero from the world of sports and the few artists and entertainers either do not belong to the sphere of cheap or mass entertainment or represent a serious attitude toward their art as in the case of Chaplin. [. . .] The first quarter of the century cherishes biography in terms of an open-minded liberal society which really wants to know something about its own leading figures on the decisive social, commercial, and cultural fronts. Even in the late twenties, when jazz composers and the sports people are admitted to the inner circle of biographical heroes, their biographies are written almost exclusively to supplement the reader's knowledge of the technical requirements and accomplishments of their respective fields.[2] These people, then, are treated as an embellishment of the national scene, not yet as something that in itself represents a special phenomenon which demands almost undivided attention.

We should like to quote from two stories which seem to be characteristic of this past epoch. In a sketch of Theodore Roosevelt, the following comment is made in connection with the assassination of McKinley:

> We, who give such chances of success to all that it is possible for a young man to go as a laborer into the steel business and before he has reached his mature prime become, through his own industry and talent, the president of a vast steel association—we, who make this possible as no country has ever made it possible, have been stabbed in the back by anarchy.[3]

This unbroken confidence in the opportunities open to every individual serves as the *leitmotiv* of the biographies. To a very great extent they are to be looked upon as examples of success which can be imitated. These life stories are really intended to be educational models. They are written—at least ideologically—for someone who the next day may try to emulate the man whom he has just envied.

A biography seems to be the means by which an average person is able to reconcile his interest in the important trends of history and in the personal lives of other people. [. . .]

Consumption—today

When we turn to our present-day sample we face an assortment of people which is both qualitatively and quantitatively removed from the standards of the past.

Only two decades ago people from the realm of entertainment played a very negligible role in the biographical material. They form now, numerically, the first group. While we have not found a single figure from the world of sports in our earlier samples given above, we find them now close to the top of favorite selections. The proportion of people from political life and from business and professions, both representing the "serious side," has declined from 74 to 45 per cent of the total.

Let us examine the group of people representing non-political aspects of life. Sixty-nine are from the world of entertainment and sport; twenty-five from that which we called before the "serious side." Almost half of the twenty-five belong to some kind of communications professions: there are ten newspapermen and radio commentators. Of the remaining fifteen business and professional people, there are a pair of munitions traders, Athanasiades and Juan March; Dr. Brinkley, a quack doctor; and Mr. Angas, judged by many as a dubious financial expert; Pittsburgh Phil, a horse race gambler in the "grand style"; Mrs. D'Arcy Grant, a woman sailor, and Jo Carstairs, the owner of an island resort; the Varian brothers, inventors of gadgets, and Mr. Taylor, an inventor of foolproof sports devices; Howard Johnson, a roadside restaurant genius; Jinx Falkenburg, at that time a professional model; and finally, Dr. Peabody, a retired rector of a swanky society prep school.

The "serious" people are not so serious after all. In fact there are only nine who might be looked upon as rather important or characteristic figures of the industrial, commercial, or professional activities, and six of these are newspapermen or radio commentators.

We called the heroes of the past "idols of production": we feel entitled to call the present-day magazine heroes "idols of consumption." Indeed, almost every one of them is directly, or indirectly, related to the sphere of leisure time: either he does not belong to vocations which serve society's basic needs (e.g., the heroes of the world of entertainment and sport), or he amounts, more or less, to a caricature of a socially productive agent. If we add to the group of the sixty-nine people from the entertainment and sports world the ten newspaper and radio men, the professional model, the inventor of sports devices, the quack doctor, the horse race gambler, the inventors of gadgets, the owner of the island resort, and the restaurant chain owner, we see eighty-seven of all ninety-four non-political heroes directly active in the consumers' world. [. . .]

By substituting such a classification according to spheres of activity for the cruder one according to professions, we are now prepared to present the vocational stratifications of our heroes in a new form. It is shown in Table 70.1 for the *SEP* and *Collier's* of 1940–1941.

Table 70.1 The heroes and their spheres

	Number of stories	Per cent
Sphere of production	3	2
Sphere of consumption	91	73
Entertainers and sports figures	69	55
Newspaper and radio figures	10	8
Agents of consumers' goods	5	4
Topics of light fiction	7	6
Sphere of politics	31	25
Total	125	100

If a student in some very distant future should use popular magazines of 1941 as a source of information as to what figures the American public looked to in the first stages of the greatest crisis since the birth of the Union: he would come to a grotesque result. While the industrial and professional endeavors are geared to a maximum of speed and efficiency, the idols of the masses are not, as they were in the past, the leading names in the battle of production, but the headliners of the movies, the ball parks, and the night clubs. While we found that around 1900 and even around 1920 the vocational distribution of magazine heroes was a rather accurate reflection of the nation's living trends, we observe that today the hero-selection corresponds to needs quite different from those of genuine information. They seem to lead to a dream world of the masses who no longer are capable or willing to conceive of biographies primarily as a means of orientation and education. They receive information not about the agents and methods of social production but about the agents and methods of social and individual consumption. During the leisure in which they read, they read almost exclusively about people who are directly, or indirectly, providing for the reader's leisure time. The vocational set-up of the dramatis personae is organized as if the social production process were either completely exterminated or tacitly understood, and needed no further interpretation. Instead, the leisure time period seems to be the new social riddle on which extensive reading and studying has to be done.

The human incorporation of all the social agencies taking care of society as a unity of consumers represents a literary type which is turned out as a standardized article, marketed by a tremendous business, and consumed by another mass institution, the nation's magazine reading public. Thus biography lives as a mass element among the other elements of mass literature. [. . .]

The mythology of success in the biographies consists of two elements, hardship and breaks. The troubles and difficulties with which the road to success is paved are discussed in the form of stereotypes. Over and over again we hear that the going is rough and hard. The baseball umpire goes "the long, rough road up to that night of triumph"; the lightweight champion "came up the hard way"; a Senator knew in his youth the "long hours of hard work"; and the ballet director "worked hard." In identical words we hear that the baseball manager and the great film star "came up the hard way." The "hard way" it was for Dorothy Thompson and for Billy Rose. We are reminded of official military communiques, reporting a defeat or stalemate in a matter-of-fact tone, rather than descriptions of life processes.

The same applies to the reverse side of hardship: to the so-called breaks. All our stories refer to successes and it is fair enough that somehow we must be informed when and how the failures stopped. Here the tendency to commute life data into facts to be accepted rather than understood becomes intensified. Usually, the beginning of the peak is merely stated as an event: A high civil servant was "fortunate in her first assignment"; a cartoonist merely gets a "telegram offering him a job on the paper" which later leads to his fame; a columnist "bursts into certain popularity"; an actor "got a break"; another "got the job and it turned out well"; for a middleweight champion "the turning point of his career had arrived." If any explanation is offered at all, we are told that the turn occurred in some freakish way: the night club singer gets started by "a king's whim"; Clark Gable's appointment as a timekeeper with a telephone company appears as the turning point in his career; a baseball player goes on a fishing trip, loses his old job and thereby gets another one which leads to his success.

These episodes of repetition and freakishness seem to demonstrate that there is no longer a social pattern for the way up. Success has become an accidental and irrational event. The dangers of competition were tied up with the idea of definite chances and there was a sound balance between ambition and possibilities. Appropriately enough, our heroes are almost without ambition, a tacit admission that those dangers of the past have been replaced by the cruelties of the present. It is cruel, indeed, that the ridiculous game of chance should open the doors to success for a handful, while all the others who were not present when it happened are failures. The "facts" of a career are a reflection of the lack of spontaneity. Behind the amusing, fortuitous episode lurks a terrible truth.

The spectacle of success, hardships, and accidents is attended in the biographies by an assortment of numbers and figures which purport to bestow glamour and exactness to the narration. The ideal language of modern biographies seems to belong to the scientific mentality which sees its ideal in the transformation from quality into quantity. Life's riddle is solved if caught in a numeric constellation. The majority of figures refer to income, to which may be added relatively few data on capital. Other figures pertain to the spectators of a ball game, to the budget of a city, or to the votes of an election.

Hardships and breaks are standard articles for the reader. They are just a better brand of what everyone uses. The outstanding has become the proved specimen of the average.

By impressing on the reading masses the idols of our civilization, any criticism or even reasoning about the validity of such standards is suppressed. As a social scientist the biographer represents a pitiless, almost sadistic trend in science, for he demonstrates the recurring nature of such phenomena as hardships and breaks, but he does not attempt to reveal the laws of such recurrence. For him knowledge is not the source of power but merely the key to adjustment. [. . .]

Superlatives

Our analysis would not be complete without some discussion of our stories' language which has several characteristic features. The most obvious one is the superlative.[4] Once we are made aware of this stylistic device, it cannot be overlooked. The heroes themselves, their accomplishments and experiences, their friends and acquaintances, are characterized as unique beings and events. The superlative gives a good conscience to the biographer— by applying a rhetorical gadget, he achieves the transformation of the average into the extraordinary. [. . .]

As if the biographer had to convince himself and his public that he is really selling an excellent human specimen, he sometimes is not satisfied with the ratio of one superlative per sentence but has to pack a lot of them into a single passage. Pittsburgh Phil is "the most famous and the most feared horse player in America." The German Labor Front is "the best led, most enlightened and most powerful labor organization in Europe." The producer, Lorentz, "demands the best writing, the best music and the best technical equipment available." The baseball manager, Clark Griffith, "was the most colorful star on the most colorful team in baseball." Tilden is ". . . the greatest tennis player in the world and the greatest guy in the world."

This wholesale distribution of highest ratings defeats its own purpose. Everything is presented as something unique, unheard of, outstanding. Thus nothing is unique, unheard of, outstanding. Totality of the superlative means totality of the mediocre. It levels the presentation of human life to the presentation of merchandise. The most vivacious girl corresponds to the best tooth paste, the highest endurance in sportsmanship corresponds to the most efficient vitamins; the unique performance of the politician corresponds to the unsurpassed efficiency of the automobile. There is a pre-established harmony between the objects of mass production in the advertising columns and the objects of biography in the editorial comment. The language of promotion has replaced the language of evaluation. Only the price tag is missing.

The superlative pushes the reader between two extremes. He is graciously attempting to become conversant with people who are paragons of human accomplishment. He may be proud that to a great extent these wonderful people do nothing but entertain him. He has, at least in his leisure time, the best crowd at his fingertips. But there is no road left to him for an identification with the great, or for an attempt to emulate their success. Thus the superlative, like the story of success itself, brings out the absence of those educational features and other optimistic implications which were characteristic of biographies during the era of liberalism. What on first sight seems to be the rather harmless atmosphere of entertainment and consumption is, on closer examination, revealed as a reign of psychic terror, where the masses have to realize the pettiness and insignificance of their everyday life. The already weakened consciousness of being an individual is struck another heavy blow by the pseudo-individualizing forces of the superlative. Advertisement and terror, invitation to entertainment, and summons to humility form their unity in the world of superlatives. The biographer performs the functions of a side show barker for living attractions and of a preacher of human insignificance. [. . .]

The important role of familiarity in all phenomena of mass culture cannot be sufficiently emphasized. People derive a great deal of satisfaction from the continual repetition of familiar patterns. There are but a very limited number of plots and problems which are repeated over and over again in successful movies and short stories; even the so-called exciting moments in sports events are to a great extent very much alike. Everyone knows that he will hear more or less the same type of story and the same type of music as soon as he turns on the radio. But there has never been any rebellion against this fact; there has never been a psychologist who could have said that boredom characterized the faces of the masses when they participate in the routine pleasures. [. . .]

The reader who obviously cherishes the duplication of being entertained with the life stories of his entertainers must have an irrepressible urge to get something in his mind which he can really hold fast and fully understand. It has been said of reading interests that: "In general, so long as the things of fundamental importance are not presenting one with problems, one scarcely attends to them in any way."[5] This remark has an ironical connotation for our biographies, for it can hardly be said that "things of importance" are not presenting us with problems today. Yet they are scarcely attended to unless we would admit that our heroes' parents, their likes and dislikes in eating and playing and, in the majority of cases, even their professions were important data during the initial stages of the second World War. But the distance between what an average individual may do and the forces and powers that determine his life and death has become so unbridgeable that identification with normalcy, even with Philistine boredom becomes a readily grasped empire of refuge and escape. It is some comfort for the little man who has become expelled from the Horatio Alger dream, who despairs of penetrating the thicket of grand strategy in politics and business, to see his heroes as a lot of guys who like or dislike highballs, cigarettes, tomato juice, golf, and social gatherings—just like himself. He knows how to converse in the sphere of consumption and here he can make no mistakes. By narrowing his focus of attention, he can experience the gratification of being confirmed in his own pleasures and discomforts by participating in the pleasures and discomforts of the great. The large confusing issues in the political and economic realm and the antagonisms and controversies in the social realm—all these are submerged in the experience of being at one with the lofty and great in the sphere of consumption.

Notes

*The first published version of this chapter appeared as "Biographies in Popular Magazines" in *Radio Research: 1942–1943*, edited by Paul F. Lazarsfeld and Frank Stanton (New York: Duell, Sloan and Pearce, 1944). Copyright by Paul F. Lazarsfeld and Frank Stanton, reprinted by permission of Professor Lazarsfeld.

1   Cf. Edward H. O'Neill, *A History of American Biography* (Philadelphia: University of Pennsylvania Press, 1935). His remarks on pp. 179ff. on the period since 1919 as the "most prolific one in American history for biographical writing," are quoted by Helen

McGill Hughes, *News and the Human Interest Story* (Chicago: University of Chicago Press, 1940), p. 285f, copyright 1940 by the University of Chicago. The book by William S. Gray and Ruth Munroe, *The Reading Interests and Habits of Adults* (New York: The Macmillan Company, 1930), which analyzes readers' figures for books and magazines, does not even introduce the category of biographies in its tables on the contents of magazines, and applies it only once for books in a sample analysis of readers in Hyde Park, Chicago. The only comment the authors have to offer is: "There is some tendency to prefer biographies and poetry, especially in moderate doses to other types of reading except fiction" (p. 154). Finally, I want to quote as a witness in this case of scientific negligence, Donald A. Stouffer, *The Art of Biography in Eighteenth Century England* (Princeton, N.J.: Princeton University Press, 1941), who in his excellent and very thorough study says: "Biography as a branch of literature has been too long neglected" (p. 3).

2   See, for instance, the *SEP* [*Saturday Evening Post*], September 19, 1925, where the auto-racer, Barney Oldfield, tells a reporter details of his racing experiences and of the mechanics of racing and automobiles; September 26, 1925, in which the vaudeville actress, Elsie Janis, comments on her imitation acts and also gives details of her techniques. The same holds true for the biography of the band leader, Sousa, in the *SEP*, October 31, 1925, and of the radio announcer, Graham McNamee, May 1, 1926; after a few remarks about his own life and career, McNamee goes on to discuss the technical aspects of radio and his experiences in radio with famous people.

3   *The Saturday Evening Post*, October 12, 1901.

4   A study by this writer on popular German biographies in book form shows that they also are characterized by the use of superlatives. These books by Emil Ludwig, Stefan Zweig, and others are on a different intellectual level, yet it seems probable that similar sociological implications hold for them as for magazine biographies. See, Leo Lowenthal, "Die biographische Mode" in *Sociologica*, Frankfurt a.M.: Europäische Verlagsanstalt, 1955, pp. 363–86.

5   Franklin Bobbitt, "Major Fields of Human Concern," quoted in Gray and Munroe, op. cit., p. 47.

Paul Hoch
[with Bob Kellarman]

OWNING AND SELLING
THE SPECTACLE

[. . .]

FROM THE VIEWPOINT OF THE OWNERS, the small elite of top jocks
does yeoman service. Not only do they help socialize the working class to the elitism
that is so essential in keeping them divided one from the other, but they are also the
perfect pseudo elite for the workers to identify with—a beefsteak pseudo elite of brawn
not brain, myth without power, and one completely under the thumb of the real bosses.
So we learn our phony elitism.

Is the competitiveness taught by the sports establishment any less phony? We've already
seen how the competitiveness is supposed to be directed only at the other workers, not
at the management. The origin of all the competitiveness for starting places on varsity
and pro teams is that same elitist split between players and fans. It is not necessary. The
money now spent on varsity teams and intercollegiate sports, for example, *could* be spent
on intramural sports aimed at making everyone a player. If everyone was out playing
they would have much less time to be fans. And if they had fulfilling, creative jobs, they
wouldn't need to look for the pseudo satisfactions of being fans.

The competitiveness between opposing teams is also part of a pseudo world. What
difference does it really make who wins and who loses in sports? Jake Gaudaur,
Commissioner of the Canadian Football League, once perceptively remarked, "It matters
not whether you win or you lose, just as long as the fans aren't sure in advance which
it's going to be." (The *Financial Post*, November 28, 1970.) He perhaps should have added
—"and just as long as the fans think that it's important." The question has been fairly
thoroughly analyzed by my close friend Bob Kellermann:

> One can say that the relationship between producers (players) is really *not*
> one of competition between teams but rather they co-operate to produce a

product (commodity) just as in other capitalist enterprises. However, here, unlike elsewhere, the product itself is the "spectacle-of-competition." Evidence that players consciously or unconsciously come to know this lies in the fact that there is a strong tendency to "fix" the game, i.e., produce the "appearance" of competition while at the same time actually co-operating. [Leonard Shecter gives scores of examples of this in his book *The Jocks*.] The "spectacle of competition" is, after all, only a spectacle, and its social function is served as long as the consumers (fans) believe there is competition. This is obvious in wrestling matches, where only particularly ignorant people believe in the appearance. The reality of fixed matches remains hidden to them. Similarly in horse-racing. (Only here almost all the bettors assume the thing is fixed, and try to figure out the pattern of fixes.)

Perhaps the best proof of how the spectacle-of-competition is more important than whether there is real competition was the recent computer world championship of boxing. Here there was no fight at all, only the coming together of images, ghosts. Yet millions actually believed in the reality of the Marciano-Ali competition (and probably sat in their seats cheering).

The "winning" of the spectacle of competition is in fact the *least* important part of this social process, for it is the spectacle itself which is socially significant. Here we see that the reality is the exact opposite of the appearance, which in men's consciousness is expressed in the belief that winning is the only thing that counts. But obviously this winning is only important within the extremely narrow confines of the "rules of the game," which in these contests are, after all, only the rules of a *game* (an illusion). The reality is that there *must be both* a winner and a *loser* in order for the spectacle-of-competition to have any meaning. So that in *social* terms the losers are just as essential to the spectacle as the winners.

This becomes much clearer when one sees the spectacle of competition through the eyes of those who *own* and *sell* this product and who employ the workers (players) who produce it. What they want to see is a "good show." Who wins or loses is almost irrelevant, since the profits depend on the appearance of "good competition," not on who wins the game. This is obvious when one man owns both teams. (We've already seen that James Norris not long ago owned three teams in the National Hockey League.) But it is just as true when there are different owners who run one league together. After all, everyone knows that the owner of a losing team benefits from the appearance of a winning team at *his* arena where he collects the profits. And in the event that one team is too weak (i.e., cannot provide a marketable commodity when combined with another team in the spectacle) the other teams' owners will try to strengthen the losing team, which is a loser for *all* the owners in terms of profits. The strengthening of losers in order to ensure the spectacle-of-competition, which ensures profits, is institutionalized in the *draft*, a process whereby the weakest teams—their competitive weakness on the field is almost certainly to be reflected at the box office—are allowed first choice of the new players. (Moreover, in the Canadian Football League, for example, the owners actually have a gate equalization pot, whereby those "losers" who attract fewest fans are paid receipts from the "winners.")

The real competition, which is not just appearance is (i) the competition between producers to make the same team, (ii) the competition between owners of opposing leagues [although even here there is very strong evidence that although owners in opposing leagues compete for rookies, they usually have a "truce" on veterans]. In the latter case we see the problem which capitalism inevitably faces—saturation of markets. There are only so many commodities (spectacles-of-competition) which a particular market of consumers (fans) can absorb. This can result in owners of these spectacles competing to sell their products since not all will be able to dispose of them. Thus, when the AFL first started, the NFL owners opposed it bitterly because they saw it as a threat to their profits, though they tried to disguise their real interest by alluding to the quality of football, etc. The AFL, being new in the market, had to break the "brand loyalty" of the NFL consumers and therefore sold their tickets (product) at a lower price. Of course they also tried to tap new customers by going to different cities if possible. But TV makes the market almost nationwide so competition was inevitable.

Of course once their product caught on they raised their prices, and the consumers who benefited from this short [untypical in the stage of monopoly capitalism] bout of competition were once again facing monopoly rip-off prices. This brief bit of competition also helped the producers (i.e., players). While it lasted the AFL capitalists were forced to pay higher salaries in order to sign rookies to produce the same quality spectacle-of-competition and prevent them from going to the NFL. So there was a price war for a short period in which some producers and consumers were the beneficiaries.

If the NFL had had the power to keep the AFL out of business, and thereby protect their right to exploit the market as a monopolist, they would have done so. But the AFL was able to make it a battle. Therefore, like all good capitalists, the owners of both leagues realized that their competition was only benefiting the consumers and the producers, and unlike the spectacles they sell, they decided they would *both* be winners. Thus, in contrast to the ideology they perpetrate, in true monopolist fashion they decided to merge. This way they could agree to share the market, raise their prices together and ensure the continued rip-off of the consumers (fans). They could also stop the situation which put the producers (players) in a stronger bargaining position. When the two leagues were competing the players could in theory play one off against the other and get slightly better salaries. But once the leagues merged the players were again faced with only one possible employer, since they would now all be subject to the same draft and same monopoly.

It is important to see that in their behavior as capitalists in the monopoly stage of capitalism, these owners *avoid* competition with each other at all costs while, at the same time, they sell a product whose main ideological function is to perpetrate the belief in competition.

It might be added that whenever the players suggest that the reserve or option clauses that bind them to indentured servitude for one owner be discarded, the owners bashfully retreat behind the veil of their pretended competition and claim that this would mean that the richest team would sign all the best players. At the stage of monopoly capitalism, this is simply nonsense. If there was any danger of this happening, the owners would simply collude to stop it. They could, for example, pass a statute preventing any given team from signing more than a certain number of players from other teams each year. Because General Motors is richer than Chrysler does not mean that they sign all the best engineers. They are all in the game together.

Organized team sport is really becoming the passive robot production of the assembly line, and increasingly of the now proletarianized white collar jobs as well. In Veblen's day, opiates like sports, betting, and religion may have been enough to provide the drugged workers for drugged production. In our own time, as the legitimacy of the system has eroded further, as the gap between "democratic" mythology and authoritarian reality becomes more and more painful, the functioning of the system from one moment to another requires *real drugs*. And it requires them in great quantities. [. . .]

Jack Scott (1971, pp. 148, 150) says that when he was covering the 1968 Olympics, the discussions among the U.S. track and field men were not about whether it was right or healthy to take drugs, but which drugs were most effective and which could you get away with. At the 1960 Olympics, Danish cyclist Knud Jensen collapsed and *died* after his race. It was established that he had taken Ronicol, a blood-vessel dilating drug. Scott says, "It is widely recognized in track and field circles that it is next to impossible to get to the top in most weight events and the decathlon without the use of these drugs since most of the top athletes are using them." For example, anabolic steroids have been used to put twenty, thirty, even sixty pounds of added plastic muscle on a jock's frame. (These drugs were developed, after all, to fatten up prize cattle!) But in many cases they have the embarrassing side effect of shrinking the testes. So the tendency seems to be toward the production of *plastic Supermen with no balls*. In the case of pep pills, what starts out as an added edge to help jocks win championships, produce more, becomes in the end a necessity just to get them to function at all.

There is nothing unique about this in America. One medical study I saw estimated that the average American consumes about a dozen pills per day. In many districts tranquilizers are even being given to tiny school children, to keep them nicely quiet and functioning. We are rapidly reaching the point where the whole society is patched together with drugs and could not function without them. In fact, that point may already have been passed. It's not surprising that the sports world finds itself in the same bag. But the NCAA and the NFL issuing solemn warnings against drugs on their telecasts each week is like the mafia issuing warnings against crime. The system and its victims cannot function without drugs, and pretty soon they will not be able to function with them.

Reference

Scott, Jack, *The Athletic Revolution*. New York: The Free Press, 1971.

Richard Gruneau and David Whitson

HOCKEY AND THE NEW POLITICS OF ACCUMULATION

COMMERCIAL HOCKEY IN CANADA has been transformed, albeit unevenly, by the entertainment industry's growth away from live audiences as the principal source of revenue to television and other sources of auxiliary income as key components of commercial viability. This tendency is not exclusive to hockey. On the contrary, every major North American professional sport has become dependent upon revenues from sources beyond the live gate. The escalating pressures to increase money spent on team and league promotion and to sustain multimillion-dollar salaries and expensive playing facilities have led to an aggressive pursuit of subsidiary revenues. The money comes primarily from larger television audiences that can be sold to advertisers, but it also comes from cross-ownership (such as Labatt's ownership interests in the Blue Jays and TSN), corporate sponsorship, and merchandising. Since the mid-1970s, technological innovations in mass communication and pressures to liberalize international trade have created new opportunities to pursue these subsidiary revenues and audiences throughout North America and around the world. The result is that North American professional sports today are beginning to position themselves in an increasingly global sports entertainment market. It is a market where Canadians now have more access to more U.S. sports than ever before, while Canadian and U.S. fans alike are also more exposed to European sporting events and personalities.

Paralleling these developments has been a loosely related set of international dynamics involving urban growth and decline. We now live in a world that has produced heightened competition between cities for major-league franchises and international sporting events, and a near-global economy in which capital has secured unprecedented mobility across political boundaries. In hockey several Canadian cities have found their hard-won major-league status to be somewhat precarious. For example, in Quebec and Winnipeg, local leaders have recently gone to considerable lengths to keep the Nordiques and the Jets in town. In Edmonton in early 1993, the Oilers' owner Peter Pocklington was threatening to take the team to Hamilton unless he got a new arena or access to all revenues generated by the publicly funded Northlands Coliseum. The point is that it is simply through the negotiation of the financial interests of team owners (that is, in maximizing the profitability of their franchises) and the co-ordination of these interests with the growth strategies of local political and business elites that new arenas are built or not, and that teams come to and threaten to leave cities like Edmonton, Winnipeg, or Quebec.

Indeed, the pursuit of major-league franchises and "world class" events today is now best understood as part of a larger project in which corporate and civic elites struggle to establish and maintain their cities' status in a transnational economic and cultural hierarchy of cities. In this project, economic growth is the ultimate objective, but major-league franchises and international events are also widely understood as badges of a city's stature, a symbolic sign of "arrival" from which other forms of growth will (presumably) follow. But, surely, we need to ask whose interests are best served by a city's pursuit of "world class" status? What is at stake in the struggle to define what being world class really means? Who is positively and negatively affected by the pursuit of world class status, particularly in the area of commercial sporting entertainment?

Capital accumulation and franchise placement in the hockey business

To explore these questions we need to review the current dynamics of capital accumulation (in other words, the dynamics of making money), both in sports entertainment and in urban development, and consider how they intersect. In the first case, we've already argued that the availability of professional sport, as well as of other kinds of professional entertainment, quickly became one of the characteristic features of modern urban life. It was part of what made, and still makes, cities exciting and attractive places with "lots to do." To enhance the profitability and stability of local professional teams, urban elites have frequently offered public subsidies to sports entrepreneurs, typically in the form of free civic land for an arena or stadium, construction of necessary facilities with public funds, zoning concessions, and often negligible rents for using public facilities. If such subsidies have needed any justification – and they usually don't because of the popularity of local pro teams – the justifications offered have typically been of the boosterist sort, emphasizing the business and enhanced reputation that a professional team can bring to the city.

Over the past two decades professional sporting entertainments came to be seen not only in terms of how much money they bring in directly from ticket sales, but also in terms of how much additional consumer activity can be generated around them (for instance, through advertising, tourism, and merchandising). These criteria were to have decisive effects both with respect to which sports were able to produce successful subsidiary consumer activity and with respect to the increasing importance of star athletes who could draw crowds. The saleability of star quality underwrote the development of a system of publicity in which the presence of stars and then superstars came to be increasingly hyped. Along with this came a process of valorization (that is, making valuable) and revaluation of urban lands. The construction of arenas and ballparks became an integral part of "property development" in which land became commodified and land values came to be determined by exchange values (that is, how much the land could be sold for) rather than use values.

Of course, the two types of value aren't unconnected, but once land is designated as commercial its value becomes a function of how much money can be made from and around it. The great sports palaces of early twentieth-century North America – the Forum, Maple Leaf Gardens, Madison Square Gardens, the Olympia – were, along with movie theatres and concert halls, part of the creation of modern downtowns in which the presence of "world famous" entertainments, shopping, and restaurants all drew people into the city core. Each contributed potential business to the other, and together they helped constitute the spatial and commercial patterns of city life. They also supported huge increases in the value of downtown real estate, increases often based as much, if not more, on the values attributed to shopping and leisure rather than to office buildings and factories. [. . .]

While a franchise and the capital invested in it are mobile, a local community is not. Fans of the Oilers or the Nordiques will be able to cheer for their old favourites if they are sold to San Diego or Phoenix or relocated to a larger Canadian market like Hamilton-Niagara, just as fans of the old Brooklyn Dodgers could follow their team's fortunes in Los Angeles. They will be disabused, though, of any illusions they might have harboured that their team "belonged" to them. Teams move in search of larger markets and greater profitability, and they trade actively on the discourse of community in their new location, urging the locals to get behind what is now "their" team. In professional sport the word "franchise" is increasingly revealed as having the same meaning as in the travel or fast-food industries: the right to offer a nationally recognized product, in this case NHL hockey, in a protected market area. We can see clearly, also, the interest of the franchisor, in this case the league as a cartel, in placing franchises in markets most likely to enhance its general revenue potential. [. . .]

As civic governments have competed for new kinds of investment beyond older industrial investments, they've become more self-consciously "entrepreneurial." These "entrepreneurial cities" now compete to be financial centres, administrative centres, and (most important for our purposes) cultural and entertainment centres.[1]

Several factors contribute to the enhanced importance of culture and entertainment. First, there is simply the enormous economic importance of the "culture industries" today, and beyond this there is the extent to which famous entertainment events and entertainers have become the stuff of daily media fare and hence effective vehicles for getting a city into the news. When civic boosters claim that a sports event or a major-league team will put their city "on the map," they are banking on this aspect of media appeal. Second, an analysis of the redevelopment strategies of a series of older downtowns indicates that projects oriented around high value-added culture and consumption – upmarket shopping and restaurant complexes, as well as concert halls and professional sports facilities – have been important in bringing the affluent middle classes back down-town.[2] Finally, there is the phenomenal growth of tourism in the new urban economy. In North America this urban strategy has also been very much directed at attracting conventions. The boom in hotel construction and convention centres of the 1960s through the 1980s – a key factor in the revalorization of downtown property – created a need for a variety of attractions to draw conventioneers and tourists. Sports stadiums, convention centres, festivals, and upscale retail developments all received public subsidies in a strategy for urban revitalization based around leisure and tourism. [. . .]

For Canadian cities on the periphery of the recognized international circuits of cultural production and attention, the attraction of sporting and cultural events has typically meant significant infusions of money from senior levels of government. Indeed, the pursuit of federal and provincial funding for facilities suitable for major-league franchises has often been a subtext in civic bids for international games and events. In the case of Montreal three levels of government were willing to spend public money on Olympic "monuments." The Olympic Stadium was also intended to be a "world class" home for the Expos and, some hoped, for an NFL franchise too. In Edmonton and Calgary the bids for the 1978 Commonwealth Games and 1988 Winter Olympics provided opportunities to get funding from senior levels of government for facilities that would become appropriate venues for the Eskimos and the Flames. In both cities there were also significant commitments of civic lands and civic funding, and they were justified to the public on this basis. [. . .]

    . . . [L]arge numbers of people enjoy professional sport *as consumers*. Even if fans only consume them through the media, teams become part of a city's collective life. The cycles of predictions and postmortems, the trade talk, and the excitement generated around the annual playoff and pennant races all contribute to a continuing "buzz" of sports talk that many people follow avidly and others enjoy as background noise. Television clearly has the lead role here, but the newspaper coverage, the radio stations that carry the games, the talk shows, and the marketing of caps, sweaters, and other team souvenirs all play their part in building and sustaining the community of fans who are the constituency of professional sport. Each of these contributes to the sense of excitement and interest that is generated and amplified in city life as professional sports teams like the Montreal Canadiens and the Toronto Blue Jays pursue successful seasons. [. . .]

    . . . [C]ivic boosters have long sought to create popular identification with the idea of *growth itself* and to suggest that a status attaches to the city as a result of the presence of major-league teams, "world class" events, and giant facilities. In the postwar era this approach has included among other things, NHL teams, professional baseball franchises, domed stadiums, ballet/opera houses, world's fairs, and Olympic Games. The imagery circulated around such teams, events, and civic monuments has typically had a twofold purpose. Although these projects are clearly intended to impress visitors from elsewhere, they have also sought to reconstruct the self-image and aspirations of the home population: from a focus on "normalcy" to a more ambitious and competitive mentality with national and international reference points rather than local. In this sense, major-league teams and "world class" events and monuments have always served large cities as symbols for a public discourse about ambition, growth, and civic greatness. [. . .]

    . . . [C]ommercialization and professionalization have reconstructed traditional understandings of the representativeness of sports teams. This reconstruction has taken place along lines that commercial sport could trade on, lines suited to modern capitalism and urban development. We've noted how the search for new and larger audiences meant that professional hockey left western Canada for a long time; and indeed it didn't return until the competition for players from the WHA led the NHL to incorporate demonstrably popular operations in Winnipeg, Edmonton, and Quebec. . . . [T]he increasing internationalization of the sports entertainment industry has also meant vigorous competition for audiences, involving many new sports, or at least sports not previously promoted to Canadian audiences. As a result of *Wide World of Sport* and *Sportsweekend* and the advent of specialty sports channels on cable TV, more and more Canadians are becoming consumers and fans of PGA golf, WCT tennis, NBA and NCAA basketball, and NFL football. This consumerism is part of a global trend in which Europeans, Japanese, and Australians are also becoming audiences for the same sporting events. Sports marketers frequently suggest that this is a welcome indicator that all of us are becoming more sophisticated in our sporting tastes. [. . .]

. . . [S]ports fans today are increasingly addressed as free-floating consumers rather than as customers with assumed loyalties. Neither individual teams nor whole sports can afford to take "brand loyalties" or even national loyalties for granted, because there are other teams and other sports trying to win over the audiences, which is all part of the more competitive struggle for *product preference*. It is precisely this expansion of consumer choice that modern sports promoters and, indeed, modern capitalism itself, love to celebrate. In the view of marketing guru Theodore Levitt, as well as transnational advertising and public relations firms such as Saatchi & Saatchi, the wave of the future is precisely the development of global markets and, along with them, "world standard" products. The international marketplace is portrayed in this discourse as a modernizing and liberating force that brings more and better choices to everyone than the protectionist politics of nations and of regions would allow. Indeed, the new rhetoric of consumer sovereignty suggests that as people gain better access to global information, they will develop global needs and demand global products, ultimately becoming global citizens.[3] We are all encouraged to think that our lives are made richer in the process. Beyond this, as we suggested at the end of the previous chapter, all of us are encouraged to think of our cities along the model of shopping centres. The best cities are the ones that offer the "world famous" shops and entertainments – whose fame is itself a product of international marketing.

There remain, however, at least two reservations that need to be entered against this celebration of the apparent global marketplace. The first of these builds on a concern about the limitations of consumer identities. What is ultimately being promoted by Saatchi & Saatchi, and by global marketing generally, is a personal sense of "membership" in a global consumer culture, a sense of membership realized primarily through personal consumption patterns and product preferences. Within this global marketing discourse there is an implicit hierarchy of identities. It is implied that one will feel the greatest sense of membership by consuming global brand-name product-lines and "world class" entertainments and by visiting or, better yet, living in "world class" places. The problem with this discourse is that the taste for world class entertainment is essentially the taste for big-budget, high-cost entertainment that effectively excludes a great many people in even the most exciting cities, except insofar as they can follow this entertainment through the media.

What global marketers like to celebrate as a growing convergence of lifestyle interests and tastes around the world can be more accurately represented as an actively cultivated convergence of lifestyle and consumer behaviours among affluent groups in the "developed" world. Indeed, the cultivation of transnational audiences for major-league sports is not much different, in this respect, from the international promotion of golf and ski resorts, or indeed croissants and sushi bars.[4] All of these items constitute real and pleasurable expansions of consumer choice for people who can afford them; and all of them have become familiar and widely appreciated options in the lifestyles and identities of our increasingly cosmopolitan business and professional elites. What is less widely appreciated is "the imposed loss of identity, the almost 'no person' status of those not able to make meaningful market choices or even present themselves as potential buyers."[5] This is not often remarked upon, precisely because in the discourse of consumer sovereignty, the *buying* public is the only public that counts.

The second reservation relates to what the increasing internationalization of consumer opportunities means for standardization of major cities (and many minor ones too), as well as the standardization of sporting and cultural "interests" around the developed world. Although many cities have sought to construct themselves as "world class" centres of culture and consumption and have invested hundreds of millions of dollars trying to construct a distinctive "place identity" that would position them favourably in the competition for tourism and convention business, the distinctiveness and successes of these glitzy developments are often short-lived. Each domed stadium, each architecturally novel hotel or cultural centre, each harbour development is quickly reproduced elsewhere, in what David Harvey calls "serial monotony"; and the effect is that the leisure and consumption districts of major cities around the world – the parts of these cities where money is spent – have lost much of their distinctive national characters.[6] In addition, overinvestment in large-scale shopping malls, harbour developments, and cultural facilities in cities tends to make the values embedded in urban space highly vulnerable to devaluation. This type of land devaluation hit urban centres around the world especially hard at the end of the 1980s, pushing many of even the most innovative developers into bankruptcy.

The language of global consumerism has vigorously celebrated as "progress" the spread of global products, global images and entertainment forms, and global superstars; and in doing so it has traded very skilfully on the idealism of an older kind of internationalist discourse. In that idealistic discourse, cultural exchanges and travel and even pictures and stories of other places were all supposed to make us interested in other people, to help us transcend stereotypes about "the other" and encourage cross-cultural understanding. A cosmopolitan was someone who was knowledgeable about other cultures and interested in engaging with those cultures on their own terms. That internationalist project and cosmopolitan identity represent something fundamentally different from the ideas of global culture in the current conjuncture. This newer sense of global culture is part of a business-led agenda. It idealizes an expensive international culture in which differences are smoothed over and standardized, in which North Americans, Europeans, and Japanese follow the same sports in similar "world class" facilities. The meaning of "world class" relates simply to the standard of facility these upmarket entertainments require and the standard of production that their upmarket audiences are accustomed to. The agenda of "global culture" has nothing to do with cross-cultural understanding and everything to do with the larger profits to be gained by expansion into new and affluent markets. Indeed, as cultural products become directed at international markets rather than at national or regional markets, many of the traditional connections between cultural practices and national identities threaten to be lost in the process – with the connections between hockey and Canadian "national" identity as a prime example.

Notes

1   This discussion draws on David Harvey, "Flexible Accumulation Through Urbanization: Reflections on 'Post-Modernism' in the American City," *Antipode*, 19,3 (1987).

2   Harvey, "Flexible Accumulation Through Urbanization"; and B. Frieden and F. Sagalyn, *Downtown Inc.: How America Rebuilds its Cities* (Cambridge, Mass.: MIT Press, 1989).

3   See Theodore Levitt, *The Marketing Imagination* (London: Collier Macmillan, 1983). Our discussion of Levitt is indebted to Kevin Robbins, 'Tradition and Translation: National Culture in its Global Context," in John Corner and Sylvia Harvey, eds., *Enterprise and Heritage: Crosscurrents of National Culture* (London: Routledge, 1991).

4   Our discussion here draws on Ulf Hannerz, "Cosmopolitans and Locals in World Culture," *Theory Culture and Society*, 7 (1990); Robbins, "Tradition and Translation"; and Brian Stoddart, "Wide World of Golf: A Research Note on the Interdependence of Sport, Culture and Economy," *Sociology of Sport Journal*, 7,4 (1990).

5   John Corner and Sylvia Harvey, "Introduction: Great Britain Limited," in Corner and Harvey, *Enterprise and Heritage*.

6   Harvey, "Flexible Accumulation Through Urbanization"; and David Harvey, *The Condition of Postmodernity: An Enquiry into the Origins of Cultural Change* (Cambridge, Mass.: Basil Blackwell, 1990).

Afterword

■ Alan Tomlinson

AS STATED IN THE GENERAL INTRODUCTION to this Reader, other teachers and scholars would make different selections from the ones included here. The sections chosen, though, are fundamental themes for any sociocultural study of sport, and offer the students a foundation for further study. Other editors may have organized things differently, but before going on to issues such as globalization, identity, space and the body, this editor has judged that the student should become familiar with some of the classic interpretive debates in sport studies, and some of the accessible and illuminating studies of the different dimensions of sport that show *why* themes such as globalization, identity, the body and space are appropriate ones to study in more depth after a foundation in the area.

For the geographical study of sport, see John Bale, *Sports Geography* (2nd edn, Routledge, 2003). Bale states the concerns of sports geography as the exploration of: sports activity on the earth, and the changing spatial distribution of sport over time; the sports landscape's changing character over time, and the connections between sport participants and their environment; and how prescriptions for spatial and environmental change are made (p. 5). The scope and reach of such geographical work is wide. Bale sees such explorations as ranging from a sports stadium and its surroundings to the scale of the 'world itself' (p. 5). Locality and place, and space and culture are clearly evidenced as vital aspects in many of the sections in this Reader, and that marks the geographical dimension as an important dimension of the sociocultural study of sport. John Bale's *Sports Geography* and other related works by him are an ideal starting point for pursuing this direction of study. Bale emphasizes the globalization of sport as one of the main foci of the geographical approach.

Grant Jarvie dedicates an early chapter of *Sport, Culture and Society: An Introduction* (Routledge, 2006) to the theme of globalization. A number of Readings in the Reader have established the escalating scale of sport, and its global expansion based upon economic forces and the explosion of media forms. These are useful materials with which to think about the historical process of globalization. Jarvie comments that 'the term globalization itself has been poorly defined, often meaning different things to different people' (p. 93), and this is one of the reasons why it is good to develop an understanding of historical processes, an awareness of sociocultural influences, and a sense of aspects of the international expansion of sport, before embarking on an analysis of the globalization process. Jarvie's book also includes a chapter on the body, and this Reader has included numerous Readings that highlight the importance of the body and of thinking critically about the cultural meanings of the body. The Jarvie text is recommended for those seeking an accessible synthesis and overview of sport, the body and society. Again, this editor has seen the burgeoning sphere of the critical analysis of the body as a more advanced stage of study for the sport studies student. Stimulating essays also relevant to this focus can be found in Henning Eichberg, *Body Cultures: Essays on Sport, Space and Identity* (John Bale and Chris Philo (eds), Routledge, 2000).

Finally, economics is another discipline that is relevant in a multi-disciplinary model of sport studies. It can be quite a specialist area of study, but the key themes of ownership and governance as they affect the sport of professional football and the general business of sport are clearly laid out and discussed in Stephen Morrow's *The People's Game? Football, Finance and Society* (Palgrave Macmillan, 2003).

The multi-disciplinary study of sport calls for an open-minded approach to how sport is studied, to what methods and techniques of analysis are adopted when undertaking scholarly study and research. The way in which the Readings have been presented should make clear how sport studies scholars have gone about their work: in the footnotes and bibliographies retained in the Readings and excerpts, there are models for how the sociocultural study of sport should be done, and reported and referenced. Accessible and useful in its sport-related applications, Ian Jones and Chris Gratton's *Research Methods for Sports Studies* (Routledge, 2003) offers useful discussions and overviews on methodological issues, debates and techniques. The keen and ambitious student of sport cultures and sport in society should, though, be as equipped as any other sociocultural scholar or social scientist to acquire an appropriate grasp of methodological issues and fieldwork skills. For this, no British text betters Alan Bryman's *Social Research Methods* (Oxford University Press, 2001). The challenge of a multi-disciplinary sociocultural study of sport is an exciting and demanding one. This introductory Reader has drawn on diverse disciplines and a multiplicity of analytical and interpretive research approaches. To capture the nuances and cultural specificities of sport as both participation and performance, at its various levels, the selection has an open-minded approach to research methods, though favouring qualitative methods in certain areas. There is much yet to do in the field; and it is hoped that, whatever debate might take place about the appropriateness of particular editorial selections, *The Sport Studies Reader* has inducted the novice student and embryonic scholar into this most fascinating and increasingly important area of study.

Index

Page references in **bold** indicate Readings. Also, unless a country is specifically stated, entries are of a general nature or relate to the United Kingdom.

United States 119, 124, 137, 138–9, 194, 213–14, 326, 357, 363, 437–8, 451, 454; American football 140, 214, 225–6, 450; baseball 140, 438–9; bodybuilding 412–16; boxing 261–6, 375–9; fitness publishing 202–8; leisure class 223–7; skateboarding 406–11; women's organizations 343, 345–6, 349n1
university sport, US 437–8
Upton Park football team 101n14
urban development, Canada 452–7
use value 427–8
USSR *see* Soviet Union

Valentine, Gill 357
valley ball (girls' game) 82–3
Veblen, Thorstein 219, **223–7**
Verma, Gajendra K. 269
Victorian era: amateurs/professionals, football 96–102; athleticism/rational recreation 62, 73–5, 84–90, 91; class and leisure 91–5; girls' schools 78–9, 80–3; moral reform 61–3; traditional sports' survival 66–70
violence: barbarism, American football 226; dance halls 256–8, 260; 'violent masculine style' 388–91; *see also* football hooliganism
virtuosity 440n3

Wacquant, Loïc 221, **261–6**
Wales 141, 242–9
Weber, Max 26–7
wedding culture, South Asians 310–11
Werbner, Pnina 269, **309–15**
West Indies, cricket 113–17, 271–4
Whannel, Garry 166, **185–91**
Wheaton, Belinda 366, **392–9**
Whitson, David 153, 419, **452–8**
Williams, Cecil 279
Williams, Dr. 358
Williams, John 293, 366, **387–91**
Williams, Raymond 36, 168
Willis, Bob 181
Willis, Paul 321, 341
Willmott, P. 235
Wilson, John 110, **136–41**
Windham, William 60, 64n15, 91
windsurfing 392–8

Winter Olympic Games 126, 126–8, 129n16
Wolfenden Committee (1958) 197
women 121, 204, 232–3, 340–1, 413; exclusion from sport 301–2, 325–7; femininity 339–42, 353, 393, 394–5, 402; Pakistani culture 310–12, 313–14; participation in sport 351–4; sport advocacy organizations 343–9; and stoolball 334–8; *see also* gender; girls; lesbians
Womensport Australia 347
Womensport International 348
Women's Sports Foundation, US/UK (WSF/UK WSF) 345–7
Woodard, Nathaniel 72
Woodward, Marcus 334
work 31, 426–7, 430–1; sport as reflection of 16–17, 20–2; and stoolball 336–7
'Workers Playtime', BBC documentary 131–2
working classes 233–4, 235, 240; bowls, Huddersfield 235, 251–5; masculine identities, 1900s 103–7; 1700s/1800s 60–1, 62–3, 63–4, 64n15, 67–8, 172; Victorian era 86, 87, 88, 89n10, 92; youth culture 256–60, 388–91; *see also* social class
'world class' facilities, North America 453, 454–5, 456, 457
World Cup, football 125, 433
world sport *see* international sport
Worrell, Frank 115, 116
wrestling, US 194
WSF (Women's Sports Foundation), US 345–7

xenophobia: football 304–8

Yorkshire: Caribbean Cricket Club, Leeds 299–302; Crown Green bowls, Huddersfield 235, 251–5; gender divisions, village life 329–33
Young, M. 235
youth culture: black underachievement 278–82; football hooliganism 256–8, 260, 325, 381–6, 387–91; girls' subcultures 339–42; Memorial Boxing Club, US 375–9; skateboarding, US 406–11; South Asian stereotyping 289–95

Zipter, Yvonne 404